The Intimate Sex Lives
of Famous People

The Intimate Sex Lives of Famous People

by Irving Wallace, Amy Wallace,
David Wallechinsky and Sylvia Wallace

Associate Editor: Elizebethe Kempthorne

Senior Staff Researchers: Helen Ginsburg, Loreen Leo, Anita Taylor, Linda Schallan, Torene Svitil, Claudia Peirce

Assistant Staff Researchers: Diane Brown Shepard, Kristine H. Johnson, Karen Pedersen, Sue Ann Power

Editorial Aides: Linda Laucella, Lee Clayton, Joanne Maloney, Patricia Begalla

Photograph Editor: Danny Biederman

Foreign Researchers: Dr. Primo Povolato (Italy), Dr. L. Alonso Tejada (Spain)

Copy Editor: Wayne Lawson

When "The Eds." is used, it means the material has been contributed by the authors and staff of *The Intimate Sex Lives of Famous People*.

A.E.	Ann Elwood	M.S.	Michael Sheeter
A.K.	Aaron Kass	M.W.	Mark Wheeler
A.L.G.	Alan L. Gansberg	N.C.S.	Nancy C. Sorel
A.P.	Adam Parfrey	P.A.R.	Patricia A. Ryan
A.S.M.	Anthony S. Maulucci	R.G.P.	Roberta G. Peters
A.W.	Amy Wallace	R.J.F.	Rodger J. Fadness
B.B.	Barbara Bedway	R.J.R.	R. John Rapsys
B.C.	Barnaby Conrad	R.K.R.	R. Kent Rasmussen
B.J.	Burr Jerger	R.M.	Robert McGarvey
C.D.	Carol Dunlap	R.S.F.	Robert S. Fenster
C.H.S.	Charles H. Salzberg	G.A.M.	Greg A. Mitchell
C.L.W.	Craig L. Wittler	I.W.	Irving Wallace
C.O.	Carol Orsag	J.A.M.	Joshua A. Martin
D.M.L.	Deci M. Lowry	J.E.	John Eastman
D.R.	Dan Riley	J.H.	Jannika Hurwitt
D.W.	David Wallechinsky	J.M.	Josef Marc
E.K.	Elizebethe Kempthorne	J.M.B.E.	John M. B. Edwards
E.Z.	Ernest Zebrowski	J.M.M.	John M. Moran
F.C.	Flora Chavez	R.W.S.	Roy W. Sorrels
J.L.	Jason Louv	S.B.	Skip Baumgarten
J.Z.	John Zebrowski	S.L.W.	Sandra L. Weiss
K.P.	Karen Pedersen	S.W.	Sylvia Wallace
L.A.B.	Laurie A. Brannen	T.C.	Tim Conaway
L.K.S.	Laurie K. Strand	V.S.	Vicki Scott
L.L.	Loreen Leo	W.A.D.	William A. DeGregorio
L.S.	Linda Schallan	W.A.H.	William A. Henkin
M.B.T.	Marguerite B. Thompson	W.K.	Walter Kempthorne
M.J.T.	Michael J. Toohey	W.L.	William Lawren

The way in which people make love may tell us more about them than any searching analysis could.

—Maurice Nadeau, editor of *Les Lettres Nouvelles*

Contents

The New, Expanded *Intimate Sex Lives of Famous People*

When the first edition of this book was released back in 1981, with long-suppressed information about political, scientific, literary and musical leaders, it was not the sort of thing that normally saw distribution on the front tables of major booksellers. Sure, there was *The Joy of Sex* and myriad racy how-to tomes, but rarely did this newfound sexual freedom impinge on the official biographies of well-known and distinguished men and women in world history.

It really seemed shocking to read about the intimacies of buttoned-up world leaders, one kink after the other. According to the authors, the search for facts was difficult and challenging. They read biographies, over 1,500 of them, including many in foreign languages that they had translated just for the purpose. They pored over rare pamphlets, correspondence, periodicals and newspapers on microfilm; they also leafed through legal transcripts and medical reports. They talked with lovers, confidants and associates of numerous people within the book.

The authors of this book were in fact a famous publishing family on their own. Father Irving Wallace (March 19, 1916–June 29, 1990) was a bestselling author of dozens of novels, non-fiction books and screenplays; son David Wallechinsky co-wrote the influential *What Really Happened to the Class of '65?*, expert collections on the winter and summer Olympics, and the book *Tyrants* that adds to his yearly feature on the "World's Worst Dictators" for *Parade* Magazine. Wife and mother Sylvia Wallace (who passed away in 2006) wrote the bestselling novels *The Fountains* and *Empress*. Daughter Amy Wallace also wrote, among many other books, *Sorcerer's Apprentice*, the fascinating memoir of her life with the invisible guru, Carlos Castaneda.

The Wallaces put together such bestselling books as the multi-volume *The Book of Lists*, *The People's Almanac*, and *The Book of Predictions*. *The Intimate Sex Lives of Famous People* (originally published by Delacorte Press) was one of the most fascinating works by this enterprising, daring and industrious family.

More than 25 years later, Amy Wallace and David Wallechinsky return to *Sex Lives* adding new profiles on Kurt Cobain, Wilt Chamberlain, Nico, Ayn Rand, Aleister Crowley, Jim Morrison, Anna Nicole Smith, Malcolm X, Michael Hutchence, Tupac Shakur and Carlos Castaneda. David and Amy have also added a handy cross-referenced list of Sexual Characteristics held by the many people of influence within the book.

Perhaps the best thing about *The Intimate Sex Lives of Famous People* is its rectitude, respect and (yes) fairness. If only the tabloid gossip-mongers had such sophistication. Yes, you can have your cake and eat her too.

— Adam Parfrey
Feral House

I

Sex Symbols

Star of the Folies

JOSEPHINE BAKER (June 3, 1906–Apr. 12, 1975)

HER FAME: In the 1920s and 1930s, dancer-singer Josephine Baker became the first black female entertainer to star in the Folies Bergère as well as the first American black woman to achieve international renown. Dancing the Charleston, wearing only a blue and red ring of feathers around her hips, she took Paris by storm.

HER PERSON: Her mother, Carrie Smith, told Josephine that her father was a Spaniard whose family would not allow him to marry a black woman. As an infant, Josephine was sent to live with her grandmother. She had an affinity for music and on Saturdays joined in neighborhood jam sessions. By the time Josephine returned to her mother, Carrie had married a man named Baker and had given birth to three more children. They lived in a one-room shack in the poorest section of St. Louis, Mo.

As the oldest child, Josephine was sent out to do domestic work for white families. She never forgot the cruelties that were inflicted on her, but she also remembered the kindness of one family, the Masons, who took her to the theater for the first time and encouraged her to build her own makeshift theater in their basement. When Josephine confided to Mrs. Mason that Mr. Mason had come into her room at night and stood beside her bed breathing heavily, she was sent back to her family.

While job hunting, 13-year-old Baker walked into the Booker T. Washington Theater and applied for work. That evening she left St. Louis employed as singer Bessie Smith's maid. On Bessie Smith's advice, Baker became a chorine at New York's Cotton Club.

In 1925 Baker went to Paris as part of *La Revue Nègre*. Asked to dance at the prestigious Folies Bergère, Baker prepared for opening night by holding bowls of cracked ice against her bosom to make her breasts firm and pointed. In her initial appearance onstage, she impressed the audience with her satin-like hair and her costume, which consisted of a belt of bananas and nothing else. Her wildly darting image was reflected a thousand times as she danced before a background of mirrors. Improvising, Baker sang and closed her act by leaping into a banana tree, spreading its leaves, crossing her eyes, and waving to the audience, which was applauding thunderously. To the French, this was the epitome of "le jazz hot." Overnight, Josephine Baker became a sensation and the reigning queen of the Folies.

With the advent of WWII, Baker became a member of the French Resistance, delivering to the Allies the original copy of an Italian-German codebook. Baker's marriage to a Jewish businessman, Jean Leon, brought her to the attention of the Gestapo. They decided to liquidate her. According to the plan, Hermann Göring invited her to dinner. Her fish course contained cyanide. Forewarned, Baker excused herself from the table as soon as the fish was served, saying she had to go to the powder room. There she intended to drop herself down the laundry chute into the arms of Resistance members below. Before she could leave the table, however, Göring—gun in hand—ordered her to eat the fish. She ate it, complained of dizziness, stumbled to the powder room, and lowered herself into the laundry chute. Resistance members broke her fall and rushed her to an underground clinic, where her stomach was quickly pumped. After lingering between life and death for a month, she slowly recovered. Word was put out that she had died in Morocco. The poisoning episode caused her to lose all her hair (she wore wigs from then on). Her courage won her the Croix de Guerre, the Rosette of the Resistance, and the Legion of Honor. In the decades following the war, Baker returned to the stage. Also, to prove universal brotherhood was possible, she adopted 11 children of different races and religions from places as diverse as Korea, Algeria, and Israel.

SEX LIFE: Baker's serious affairs began when she moved to Paris at the age of 19. She fell in love with a fair-haired, handsome Frenchman named Marcel, who set her up in a luxurious apartment on the Champs Élysées which she called her "marble palace." Marcel appeared every evening and brought live gifts with him—white mice, a parrot, a miniature monkey. At last Baker asked him when they would be married. He said marriage was impossible because she was black and a public dancer. The next day she walked out on her palace and her menagerie.

Baker's first distinguished admirer was a Moroccan she called "the Sheik of Araby." He sent her a tame panther wearing a diamond necklace, and took both Baker and the panther to dinner. However, she decided that having sex with him was impossible. He was short and chubby, and she was tall. "The problem," she said, "was that when I was young I used to like to do it standing up, and if I had ever done it with him, he would have been jabbing me in the knees."

In 1929 Crown Prince Adolf (future King Gustavus VI) of Sweden, entranced by Baker, visited her dressing room and invited her to his country. Although Baker knew the prince was married, she sent him a one-word telegram later that night: "When?" The following morning she had his reply: "Tonight." That evening Baker boarded the prince's private railroad car with its gold interior and Aubusson carpets. In her sleeping quarters was a swan-shaped bed covered with satin sheets to highlight the shapely contours of her dusky body. After she had settled into bed, the Prince arrived. When she complained of being cold, he warmed her heart by fastening a three-strand diamond bracelet on her arm. While grateful, she told him that her other arm was still cold. He roared with laughter and gave her another bracelet. Undressing, he pulled down the sheets and joined her, kissing her softly. They maneuvered their bodies together and allowed the undulating movements of the railroad car to set the tempo of their lovemaking. "He was a real fox," Baker said afterward. "He was my cream and I was his coffee, and when you poured us together, it was something!"

They spent a warm winter month together in his isolated summer palace, making love when indoors and playing like children in the snow outdoors. The last night of their idyll he draped a floor-length sable coat around her, took her in his arms, and they danced a silent waltz. They never met again.

At a cabaret, Josephine Baker was introduced to Count "Pepito" Abatino, an Italian administrator. They danced a tango, which led to a night of lovemaking. Before long Abatino had become her lover and manager. They never married, but Baker always presented him as her husband. He was a jealous lover as well as a tough manager, sometimes locking her in her room to force her to work on dance routines. The affair lasted 10 years and ended in New York when Baker decided she wanted to be free of his domination.

On Nov. 30, 1937, Baker married French industrialist Jean Leon. He wanted children and a home in the country. Together they leased Les Milandes, a château that became her dream house. When Baker became pregnant but miscarried, she lost not only the baby but Leon as well. The judge who dissolved their marriage in 1939 said, "They were two strangers who never really met."

It was five years before Baker fell in love again. In 1933 she had met Jo Bouillon, a French orchestra leader, when he came backstage at the Folies to ask her for an autographed picture. They met again in October of 1944 when she asked Bouillon to donate his services to the cause of Free France. They began seeing each other. On June 3, 1947, they were married. During their marriage Baker purchased the château she had once leased, Les Milandes, and had it renovated into a resort. She incurred huge debts, placing tremendous pressure on the relationship with her husband. Her marriage to Bouillon lasted 13 years.

In her last years Josephine Baker gave more and more time to her adopted children and to her growing struggle against racism, especially in the U.S., where many of her bookings had been canceled. Ironically, it was following a triumphant tour of the U.S. that Baker died of a heart attack in Paris at the age of 68.

—F.C.

The Girl Who Had It

CLARA BOW (Aug. 6, 1905–Sept. 27, 1965)

HER FAME: As F. Scott Fitzgerald embodied the Roaring Twenties in literature, she embodied it on film, having 48 films to her credit by the age of 25. In 1927 she was receiving 40,000 fan letters a week.

HER PERSON: Clara's was the classic Hollywood story—up from obscurity at age 19 to become the reigning sex goddess of her time, collecting the obligatory emotional scars all along the way. Father Robert was often either unemployed or footloose; Mother Sarah was bitter. She'd stick Clara in the closet of their Brooklyn tenement while she turned tricks for food and rent money. Once, when she learned that Clara and her father were submitting a picture of Clara for a magazine beauty contest, she crept into Clara's bedroom with a knife, vowing that her daughter wouldn't live to be one of those whores who primps before cameras for the pleasure of men. Luckily Clara escaped into the bathroom that night, with her life and her career. She won the contest and an initial stab at Hollywood, which eventually led to her signing with Paramount.

She became one of the studio's biggest stars, earning $7,500 a week. And thanks to the insomnia which resulted from her mother's late-night threat on her life, she was able to live in a manner that embellished her on-screen image. She'd speed up and down Sunset Boulevard in an open convertible accompanied by a couple of chows who matched her hennaed hair. She'd run up fabulous gambling tabs in Las Vegas. And she was perfectly scandalous in her personal affairs. In 1931 those affairs brought her down when she sued Daisy DeVoe, her private secretary, for embezzling $16,000 from her. During the trial, the judge would not permit Daisy to discuss Clara Bow's sexual escapades, so Daisy sold her exposé to Bernarr Macfadden's New York *Evening Graphic* (incidentally, the authors of this book scoured the U.S. for a copy of the exposé issue, but no copy was available anywhere). Daisy was found guilty and sent to jail for a year. Word got out about Clara's private life and damaged her career.

SEX LIFE: In her heyday Clara reputedly made love to Gilbert Roland, Victor Fleming, Gary Cooper, John Gilbert, Eddie Cantor, Bela Lugosi, and the entire University of Southern California football team.

She met Roland, Paramount's Latin lover, during their filming of *The Plastic Age*. He was the first man she ever cared about, she said, but it wasn't enough for the temperamental Roland, who went into fits of jealousy at Clara's continued interest in other men. When he proposed marriage as a remedy for his insecurity, she dismissed the proposal, saying that no man would ever own her.

Thus she set the pattern for most of her relationships with men. She'd love them, but never enough to satisfy their egos. Director Victor Fleming was 20 years older than Clara and had vast prior experience with women, but neither fact helped him cope with her, especially when he learned that after they'd finish having sex together, she'd climb into her roadster and head off for a session with another, usually younger man.

Most notable amongst those younger men was Gary Cooper, who had a bit part in *It* and was dubbed the "It" boy for his involvement with Clara, the quintessential "It" girl. In later years Coop tried to dismiss his relationship with Clara as just so much publicity, but Clara told delicious stories of his bathing her and her dogs in the morning and making love to her all night.

There was the "Thundering Herd," the University of Southern California's football team, which Clara entertained on a regular basis at her Beverly Hills home. Those with a vested interest in the Trojan sports program have always maintained that the post-game get-togethers at Clara's place were nothing more than good, clean fun, but neighbors and "friends" told tales of nude football games on the front lawn and all-night orgies. The legend grew that Clara introduced the team concept to lovemaking by taking on more than a single player at a time. Whatever the truth to the stories, a sign was eventually posted in the Trojan locker room making Clara Bow off limits.

Clara took a brief fancy to East Coast football in the person of Robert Savage, a millionaire's son who played for Yale. Unlike most of Clara's other lovers, who merely went off and brooded when they found out that they weren't number one in her program and number one in her heart, Savage tried to kill himself by slashing his wrists and letting the blood flow onto an autographed picture of Clara. Clara exclaimed, "Jesus Christ, he's got to be kidding. Men don't slash their wrists, they use a gun!"

Harry Richman, top-salaried Broadway singing star in the 1930s, did not become a Hollywood immortal like some of Clara's other lovers, although he tried to do so by flaunting their relationship. He boasted that she was the only woman who could ever keep up with him sexually. She gave him a $2,000 ring. He gave her a child (which she had aborted), put detectives on her tail when he was out of town, and even followed her himself to see where she went after their nights together. Needless to say, they did not live happily ever after.

She might have achieved that blissful state with William Earl Pearson, a Texas doctor who performed an emergency appendectomy on her during the filming of *Dangerous Curves*. She loved him enough to try monogamy for a while (gifting him with a $4,000 watch), but when he returned to his wife in Texas, Clara was left with nothing but an alienation-of-affections suit that had been filed against her, which was settled out of court.

There had been actors, ballplayers, stunt men, airmen, and guys off the street, but finally there was Rex Bell, a cowboy actor and staunch Republican who twice became lieutenant governor of Nevada during the 1950s. Clara married Bell in 1931 and he saw her through the Daisy DeVoe trial, a failed comeback in the early 1930s, and a series of emotional breakdowns. Because of her unstable emotional condition, she lived apart from Bell and their two sons, seeking help in various sanitariums. In 1961, the 59-year-old Bell died of a heart attack. Clara succumbed four years later while watching television with a nurse-companion in her Los Angeles home.

HER WORDS: "Most men want me on their terms. The trouble with men is that they all want to make you over into something else. It burns me up. Especially since it's me as I am that they fall for. The more I see of men, the more I like dogs."

—*D.R.*

Clubfooted Libertine

LORD BYRON (Jan. 22, 1788–Apr. 19, 1824)

HIS FAME: Considered one of the great 19th-century poets, George Gordon, Lord Byron, was the incarnate symbol of romanticism. In his works he created the "Byronic hero," a mysterious and lonely young man defiantly hiding some unspeakable sin committed in his past. Byron's autobiographical masterpiece, *Don Juan*—left unfinished upon the poet's death—won universal acclaim for its combination of lyrical storytelling and satirical realism.

Byron at age 26

HIS PERSON: A British lord by age 10, young Byron was influenced adversely by an unstable mother and a foot so crippled that he once begged a doctor to amputate it. Nevertheless, he became an excellent distance swimmer, easily lasting for 5 mi. or more. This exercise did not end his constant battle against obesity, and at 17 he entered Cambridge University carrying 212 lb. although he was only 5 ft. 8 in. tall. To maintain his weight at a reasonable level in adult life, Byron fasted frequently while taking drugs to reduce, and kept to a fairly steady diet of hard biscuits plus a little rice, washed down by soda water or diluted wine. An occasional gorging on meat and potatoes when he could no longer resist the temptation triggered an immediate digestive upset and added rolls of fat about his middle. Byron hoped that his lifelong Spartan regimen would also "cool his passions," but it didn't. In 1809 he sailed with John Cam Hobhouse for a two-year "grand tour" of Europe. Upon his return, Byron published *Childe Harold's Pilgrimage*, a fictionalized narrative of the trip done in Spenserian stanzas, and the poem brought instant fame. He followed the success quickly with a series of Greco-Turkish tales (*The Bride of Abydos*, *The Corsair*, *The Siege of Corinth*, and others) that enhanced his reputation further. Driven from England by public reaction to his sex life, Byron made his way to Italy. He continued to write brilliantly, producing *Manfred* (1817) and *Beppo* (1818) along with *Don Juan* (1819–1824). Intrigued by Balkan politics, Byron slipped into Greece to fight against its Turkish masters but perished from malaria at Missolonghi before achieving battlefield honors. His death fulfilled a fortune-teller's prophecy, made to his mother in 1801, that he would die in his 37th year.

SEX LIFE: Byron was sexually initiated at age nine by the family nurse, May Gray. The devout, Bible-quoting Scottish girl seized every chance for three years to creep into the child's bed and "play tricks with his person." Arousing the boy physically by every variation she could think of, May also allowed him to watch while she made love with her uninhibited lovers. Thus primed, Byron—eager for continued stimulation—moved with ease into sexual activities during four years at Harrow, one of England's prestigious boarding schools. There he preferred the company of young boys: the Earl of Clare, the Duke of Dorset, among many others. Although he may have been bisexual, the thought of having sex with adult males repelled him. One such proposition from 23-year-old Lord Grey de Ruthyn, tendered while Byron was visiting on holiday from Harrow, sent the future poet fleeing in terror. In 1805, entering Trinity College (Cambridge), Byron fell in love with choirboy John Edleston, who gave him a heart-shaped carnelian to seal their friendship. Byron combined three years of intermittent studies with an orgiastic existence in London, staging bacchanalian revelries that nearly killed him. Living on laudanum (a tincture of opium), he cavorted nightly with prostitutes while maintaining at least two mistresses, one of whom he dressed in boy's clothing and passed off as a cousin. The deception ended when "the young gentleman miscarried in a certain family hotel in Bond Street, to the indescribable horror of the chambermaids."

Leaving England for the Continental tour in 1809, Byron spent almost two years traveling through Greece, Albania, and Asia Minor. In Turkey he was fascinated that the major physical difference seemed to be "that we have foreskins and they none," and that "in England the vices in fashion are whoring and drinking, in Turkey, sodomy and smoking. We prefer a girl and a bottle, they a pipe and pathic."

The publication of *Childe Harold* in March, 1812, brought Byron into contact with Lady Caroline Lamb, the uninhibited 27-year-old wife of William Lamb, who later became Lord Melbourne, prime minister of England. Meeting Byron, she confided in her journal that he was "mad, bad, and dangerous to know." Her slender, boyish figure met Byron's standards and they were soon lovers. A notorious exhibitionist and outspoken eccentric, "Caro"—as Byron fondly called her—proved a unique sex partner. In August, a startled Byron opened an envelope to find a thatch of Caro's curly black pubic hair and a long note. "I cut the hair too close," she wrote, "and it bled. Do you not the same." She asked for a like gift, admonishing him to be careful when handling the scissors. Amused, Byron complied but soon tired of her constant presence and erratic behavior. With the help of his good friend Lady Melbourne (who was also Caro's mother-in-law) he broke off the affair in December. Caro burned Byron in effigy, vowed revenge, and bided her time. Fleeing from Caro's fury, he moved in with Jane Elizabeth Scott, the 40-year-old wife of Edward Harley, the Earl of Oxford. Happily making love to Lady Jane until the following June, Byron was the latest in a series of lovers she had enjoyed during her marriage. (The Oxford children were known as the "Harleian Miscellany" because of their uncertain paternity.)

In July, 1813, Byron broke the ultimate sexual taboo—incest—by seducing his married half sister, Augusta Leigh. Reared separately, the two children born to Capt. John "Mad Jack" Byron rediscovered each other with an intense passion. Nine months and two weeks later, Augusta gave birth to a daughter, Medora, and a proud Byron left little doubt as to the father. Referring to the belief held in the Middle Ages that incestuous intercourse produced monsters, he wrote Lady Melbourne that "it is not an ape, and if it is, that must be my fault." To silence the malicious gossip that his open affection for Augusta had created, Byron married Annabella Milbanke, a prim and scholarly heiress who believed she could reform him. Their one-year marriage was a total disaster. Byron became almost psychotic, verbally taunting her for months with embellished stories of his past orgies. He suffered continual nightmares, awakening at the slightest body contact with Annabella, screaming, "Don't touch me!" or crying out, "Good God, I am surely in hell!" in his dim awareness of the red damask curtains around the huge four-poster and the flickering tapers he kept burning in the bedroom. Since Byron felt "a woman should never be seen eating or drinking," Annabella took her meals alone. In December, after the birth of their daughter, Augusta Ada, a fearful Lady Byron fled and sued for a legal separation. The ensuing scandal feasted upon rumors about Byron's sexual perversions: e.g., he'd made love to the aging Lady Melbourne at *her* request; he'd sodomized his terrified wife in the final month of her pregnancy; he'd attempted to rape Lady Oxford's 13-year-old daughter. The sensational charges, which were viciously helped along by a vengeful Lady Caroline bent on Byron's ruin, ostracized him so completely that he was forced to leave England for good on Apr. 25, 1816, his reputation in shreds. But in his final month, Byron "put it about" (his adopted term for copulating) one last time, with Claire Clairmont, the plain 17-year-old stepdaughter of free-love advocate William Godwin. Attracted by Byron's notoriety, Claire brazenly propositioned him in a series of provocative letters. Drawn by her persistent suggestions that he use her body at his earliest convenience, Byron finally gave in a week before departure. Their brief coupling produced Allegra, born the following January.

Once an expatriate in Venice, Byron resumed his sexual excesses in earnest. He found rooms near St. Mark's Square and immediately took his landlord's wife, dark-eyed Marianna Segati, as his next mistress. Almost simultaneously, he acquired a second partner, the Junoesque (5 ft. 10 in.) baker's wife Margarita Cogni. The fiery amazon's explosive jealousy forced Byron to schedule his other assignations very carefully. Although very religious—she crossed herself every time prayer bells rang, even when making love with Byron—Margarita would have stabbed any rival caught in her lover's bed. In 1818 Byron broke with Marianna and rented the Palazzo Mocenigo. The palace doubled as a personal brothel for Byron, populated by a harem of mistresses and streetwalkers. For a time his gentle "tigress," Margarita—secure in her role as the poet's primary mistress—served as housekeeper, but her temper tantrums proved too much for Byron to accept. When Byron asked her to leave, she threatened him with a knife and stabbed his hand. She then threw herself into the canal. Finally convinced that Byron no longer wanted her, she returned to her husband.

Byron once estimated that almost half of his annual expenses had gone for purchased sex, parceled out to at least 200 women. "Perhaps more," he wrote, "for I have not lately kept the count." The orgies were not without additional cost. Byron was plagued by gonorrhea, the "curse of Venus" having been passed along by his ladies.

In April, 1819, tiring of endless promiscuity and growing fat, Byron met Teresa Guiccioli, a 19-year-old countess trapped in a marriage of convenience. He became her *cavalier servente*, fulfilling the role of official public escort as allowed by Italian custom for such marriages. Privately, the two fell genuinely in love. Byron cut down sharply on his sexual prowling, writing friends that he had "not had a whore this half year," and had confined himself "to the strictest adultery." At Count Guiccioli's invitation, Byron moved in under the same roof, thereby simplifying the affair. Eventually, however, Guiccioli tired of the arrangement, and after an emotional confrontation Teresa was granted a separation. Ironically, the four-year affair domesticated Byron almost completely, and he wistfully pictured himself as a living example of conjugal happiness. Teresa and Byron lived together until July, 1823, when he left for Greece.

—W.K.

The Lover's Love

GIOVANNI JACOPO CASANOVA (Apr. 2, 1725–June 4, 1798)

HIS FAME: His name has come down in history as a synonym for a great lover. He was also a gambler, writer, and practitioner of the occult, as well as an escape artist and inveterate traveler, who lived and loved by his wits.

HIS LIFE: "I was not born a nobleman— I achieved nobility," declared Casanova, who was sensitive about his antecedents. His mother was a promiscuous young Venetian actress, Zanetta Farussi, who married a dancer named Casanova; his father, he believed, was Michele Grimani of the patrician theatrical family. (His brother Francesco is said to have been fathered by the Prince of Wales, the future George II, while Zanetta Casanova was on tour in England.) He was raised by his grandmother, boarding out as a student at the University of Padua, from which he received a doctorate in law at the age of 17. After being expelled from a seminary for alleged homosexual activity, Casanova eventually made his way into the Venetian army.

At 21, having acquired a knowledge of the healing arts and the occult, Casanova nursed back to health an aging Venetian aristocrat named Matteo Bragadin, who adopted him in gratitude. Incarcerated in Venice's Leads Prison for various peccadilloes—many of them sexual in nature—Casanova escaped to spend the next 18 years wandering all over Europe. He was a compulsive gambler who served briefly as organizer of the French state lottery; a litterateur who translated the *Iliad* and wrote many books, including a prophetic novel in five volumes. He visited Voltaire in Switzerland, fought a duel with a Polish count, interviewed Russia's Catherine the Great (about calendar reform), and affected the title of Chevalier de Seingalt.

Returning to Venice in 1774, Casanova served the Inquisition as a spy and bureaucrat for seven years, until he was exiled for writing a satire on the Venetian ruling classes. He ended his life as librarian to Count von Waldstein in a castle in Dux, Bohemia.

HIS PERSON: Tall, dark, and powerfully built, with the witty manner of a Harlequin or a Figaro, Casanova possessed the ability to insinuate himself into every picaresque possibility. His sexual conquests were legion. "There was not a woman in the world who could resist constant attentions," he claimed. A Machiavelli of sexual intrigue, he would court, cajole, scheme, insult, and threaten until he got his way; rebuffed, his ardor would only increase. Continence caused illness, he thought, whereas indulgence resulted in at least 11 bouts with venereal disease. (Perhaps on this account, but also because he was sympathetic to the woman's risk of pregnancy, he was familiar with the use of a "protective covering" as well as a contraceptive diaphragm made of half a lemon, the citric acid acting as a spermicide.) A vigorous sexual athlete, he refers casually to "running my sixth race," and more. In his prime he was capable of having sex anywhere, with anyone, and in any position, with particular reference to the positions described by 16th-century satirist Aretino.

Unlike a Don Juan with a constant need to prove his virility, according to Dr. Robert B. Greenblatt Casanova was a connoisseur of sex who "enjoyed the sexual encounter as much for the pleasure it afforded him as for the satisfaction obtained in the seductive process itself, and in the mystique of the adventure."

Gourmand as well as connoisseur, Casanova celebrated women with all his senses. "The odor of those I loved was always fragrant to my nostrils," he wrote. And of course he had a highly developed sense of taste. One of his specialties was the oyster orgy, which involved passing the savory aphrodisiacs from mouth to mouth, retrieving them with his lips should they happen to fall between "alabaster spheres."

Above all, Casanova was an incurable romantic who constantly fell in love. "Without love this great business is a vile thing," he believed. He was forever rescuing damsels in distress, then extricating himself with difficulty. He considered marriage "the tomb of love," preferring instead the "inexpressible charm of stolen pleasures." He described these pleasures in exquisite and occasionally fictional detail in the 12-volume *Histoire de ma vie* ("History of My Life").

HIS LOVERS IN PARIS: Sexual awakening came when Casanova was 11 or so at the hands of Bettina Gozzi, his landlord's sister, who, while washing him, touched his thighs suggestively. His first complete sexual experience, six or seven years later, involved not one but two budding young nymphets, Nanetta and Marta Savorgnan. Conspiring to introduce himself into their bed, he lulled them into a deceptive sense of security by feigning sleep. Gradually he uncurled first one girl, then the other, slowly moving toward his ultimate object. After washing together, the three aroused themselves to such a state of sexual intoxication that they spent the remainder of the night "in ever varied skirmishes."

"With a female friend," Casanova discovered, "the weakness of the one brings about the fall of the other." The pattern later repeated itself with Helena and Hedwig, cousins in Geneva. Having pierced their maidenheads and bathed them (an activity that always delighted him), Casanova found his ardor renewed by their curious hands, which aroused him to fill "their cup of happiness for several hours, changing from one to the other five or six times before I... reached the paroxysm of consummation." Even then, one of the girls was delighted on kissing his "pistol," as Casanova occasionally referred to his member, to prompt yet another eruption.

HOMOSEXUALITY: In his youth Casanova became obsessed with what he mistakenly believed to be a castrato, one of the young boys playing women's roles on the Italian stage. "Bellino" turned out to be Teresa, a 16-year-old girl with whom he initiated an affair. Later, unwilling to forgo any new sexual experiences, he indulged in more than one homosexual encounter. Bragadin, Casanova's adoptive father, may have been a pederast. And in Russia Casanova exchanged "tokens of the tenderest friendship, and swore eternal love" with the beautiful, androgynous Lieutenant Lunin.

LESBIANS AND VOYEURS: "C.C." (Casanova usually concealed the identity of his lovers) was a 15-year-old who, relieved of her virginity by Casanova, was locked up by her father in the convent at Murano. While visiting her there Casanova caught the eye of Mother "M.M.," a beautiful young nun with a very catholic libido, who proposed an assignation at her lover's casino. Their first coupling was staged for the voyeuristic pleasure of M.M.'s lover, Abbé François de Bernis, France's ambassador to Venice, who was observing them from a hidden chamber. On another occasion, C.C. was persuaded to join M.M. and Casanova. M.M. and C.C. began by exploring "the mysteries of Sappho." Then "all three of us," Casanova wrote, "intoxicated by desire ... and transported by continual furies, played havoc with everything visible and palpable ... freely devouring whatever we saw and finding that we had all become of the same sex in all the trios which we performed."

Another nun, also referred to as M.M., later seduced a 12-year-old boarder at a French convent for Casanova's pleasure. By demonstrating the manual technique of verifying virginity, Casanova aroused the child to perform fellatio. She "sucked the quintessence of my soul and my heart," Casanova related in his memoirs. The entire encounter took place through the grating which separated the nuns from the visitors.

INCEST: "I have never been able to understand how a father could tenderly love his charming daughter without having slept with her at least once," wrote Casanova, having discovered the pleasures of incest. He had fallen in love with Leonilda, the mistress of a homosexually inclined duke, only to find that she was his daughter by Lucrezia, with whom he had enjoyed copulating marathons 17 years earlier. Leonilda personally observed her parents' reenactment of her conception, undressing ("saying that as her father I was entitled to see all my handiwork"), and even taking part somewhat in their lovemaking. The relationship between father and daughter was consummated, nine years later, when Leonilda was married to an impotent old marquis and Casanova fathered her son.

SEX FOR FUN AND PROFIT: Casanova had a sense of humor about sex, as evidenced by his affair with "Mlle. X.C.V." (Giustiniana Wynne). Since the lady was already pregnant, his motives were initially honorable—to help her obtain an abortion. All else having failed, he tried a cure from cabalistic literature: the "aroph of Paracelsus," a concoction which was to be applied to the mouth of the uterus, by means of an object 6 to 7 in. in length, when the subject was in a state of sexual arousal. Casanova was convulsed with laughter when the moment arrived, but soon recovered enough to achieve repeated penetration if not the abortion.

Casanova's most elaborate episode of sexual charlatanry involved the widowed Marquise d'Urfé, a rich eccentric whose consuming passion was to be reborn as a male child. He proposed first to impregnate personally an "angelic virgin" with a son, into whom the marquise would breathe her soul. But the "virgin" proved to be more of a trollop, and Casanova was forced to consider the necessity of procreating with the elderly marquise. This would of course require aid and inspiration from a "divine spirit" in the person of Marcoline, actually a lesbian nymphomaniac. Marcoline arrived dressed all in green, with a note in invisible ink introducing her as a water sprite, adept at certain ceremonial ablutions. The marquise failed to bear the desired male child, but she was good for about two years' worth of pocket money.

LOVERS (CONTINUED) Casanova's other conquests included the mayoress of Cologne; a nun, a lock of whose pubic hair he kept for remembrance; a black woman, out of curiosity; an actress with two humps on her back and an erotically irregular vulva. Eager to explore all the combinations and permutations of sexual pleasure, he assembled more than one harem of nubile young seamstresses. Most of his women were of the demimonde or lower classes, with a few exceptions. Casanova's most rewarding affair, according to biographer John Masters, was with a well-bred, well-educated Frenchwoman named Henriette, his equal in adventure and hedonism. They spent three months together before she returned to her home. Years later, Casanova found himself in the same hotel room in Geneva, on the window of which she had scratched with a diamond her fateful farewell message: "*Tu oublieras aussi Henriette*" ("You will also forget Henriette").

Exhausted by his prodigious endeavors, Casanova's sexual potency began to flag before he reached 40. In London in 1763 he resorted to advertising for a companion, was driven to distraction by an unwilling beauty, and was drained of his cash by five mercenary Hanoverian sisters. He began to revisit the same cities, repeating his old conquests. Back in Venice there was an uneducated seamstress, Francesca Buschini, who remained faithful for years. Otherwise, he was forced to frequent the women who could be had by anyone, for a price.

And during the 13 years as a librarian in Bohemia, there were probably no women at all. There were only the pleasures of eating ("since he could no longer be a god in the gardens," a contemporary wrote, "he had become a wolf at the table"), of writing, and of reading, which prompted an aphorism on his favorite subject: "Woman is like a book which, be it good or bad, must begin to please with its title page." Needless to say, even though he was impotent during his final years, Casanova was "always curious to read new ones."

HIS THOUGHTS: "My vices have never burdened anyone but myself, except the cases in which I have seduced; but seduction was never characteristic of me, for I have never seduced except unconsciously, being seduced myself."

—*C.D.*

Blond Bombshell

JEAN HARLOW (Mar. 3, 1911–June 7, 1937)

HER FAME: The reigning sex queen of the 1930s, Jean Harlow played comedic movie roles in which she was the platinum-blond floozy with a heart of gold, a "combination good kid and slut." Among her best-known films are *Hell's Angels*, *Dinner at Eight*, *Public Enemy*, *Bombshell*, and *Red Dust*.

HER PERSON: Jean was born Harlean Carpenter in Kansas City, Mo. Her mother divorced her dentist husband and two years later married Marino Bello, an Italian-American of uncertain profession with shady gangster connections. Marino and "Mama Jean," as she was called, managed Jean's career and

Wedding photo of Jean Harlow, Paul Bern and friends

leeched large sums of money from her. The family moved to Hollywood when Jean was a teenager, and her first important part was in *Hell's Angels*, a fabulously expensive Howard Hughes production. Hughes coined the term "platinum blond" for Harlow (her almost white hair was to become her greatest trademark) and had his costumer design the lowest-cut evening gown ever photographed for the screen. Jean, wearing very little to begin with, caused a sensation when she uttered the immortal line "Do you mind if I slip into something more comfortable?" The next step was to superstardom, although Mama Jean, Marino, and Jean's friends still called her by her childhood nickname: "the Baby."

SEX AND LOVE LIFE: Stories about her amorous life range from one extreme to another: that Harlow was sex-crazed and promiscuous; that Harlow hated sex; that Harlow was a normal, healthy girl who just had bad luck with men. Probably a little of each is true.

One thing her biographers do agree on is that she had her first sexual experience at 16. Partly in order to escape from a girls' boarding school in Illinois, she eloped with 21-year-old Charles McGrew, the son of a wealthy investment broker. She lied about her age and succeeded in getting married, but the newlyweds' families separated the young bride and groom almost immediately. They probably never saw each other again, and a divorce was obtained in 1929. Jean remembered her first act of love as "messy" and not very satisfying.

She had no other lovers until she married her second husband, Paul Bern, in 1932. This was a highly unusual and much-gossiped-about courtship. Bern was a small, mustachioed, almost weasely-looking man twice her age—an odd choice for a woman who had her pick of the great Hollywood leading men. Most likely she was seeking a father figure and enjoyed the fact that Bern appeared to be interested in her mind rather than her body. He was suave, intellectual, and gentlemanly. He was also Irving Thalberg's assistant at MGM, and was called Hollywood's "little father confessor" because he loved to listen to other people's problems. Before he married Jean, he had had an unusual arrangement with another girl. He had set the girl up in a Hollywood flat and visited her every afternoon. The girl would disrobe and lie naked on the bed while he read poetry to her. Then they would have tea and he would leave.

But the mystery of the Harlow-Bern liaison has still not been solved. The most famous story of the fateful wedding night and following weeks is this: After a happy wedding, the couple went to their home to consummate the union. Several hours later Jean's agent, Arthur Landau, received a tearful phone call from his distraught client. He picked her up outside the house, and she revealed that a drunken Bern had beaten her with a cane, leaving long, ugly welts all over her snowy body. He had also bitten her thighs so savagely that they bled. Jean spent the remainder of her wedding night with the Landaus. Entering the house the next morning, Landau found Bern nude and weeping. He said to Landau, "Every man I know gets an erection just by talking about her. Arthur, didn't I have the right to think Jean could help me at least that much?" Apparently Bern had the penis and testicles of an infant boy and was completely impotent. (A variation on the story was told by Jean's maid, who quoted Bern as saying, "The Baby's still a virgin.")

Whatever happened was not good, but they kept up appearances for the sake of Jean's career. Finally, one night two months after the wedding Bern gained entry into Jean's usually locked bedroom. He strode in wearing an enormous dildo, with huge testicles and a bulb which shot water out of the end of the artificial penis. Jean burst into hysterical laughter, and Bern pranced around the room sporting the giant phallus until the two of them removed it and flushed it down the toilet.

The next evening, probably while Jean was out (the sequence of events is fuzzy), the butler discovered Bern's naked body sprawled before a full-length mirror. It was drenched in his wife's favorite perfume, Mitsouko. Bern had shot himself in the head with a .38 caliber pistol. The note he left gave the press a field day. It read: "Dearest Dear, Unfortunately this is the only way to make good the frightful wrong I have done you, and to wipe out my abject humiliation. I love you. Paul. You understand that last night was only a comedy."

Three days later the body of a blond was found in the Sacramento River. The suicide was Dorothy Milette, who had claimed to be Bern's common-law wife before Jean had married him.

A distraught Jean turned to promiscuity—as self-punishment, to find out what sex was all about, and because she suddenly wanted to have a baby. She cut her hair very short (studio heads were furious when they found out), wore a black wig and sunglasses, and began to pick up men, starting with a salesman with whom she spent two nights in a sleazy hotel in San Bernardino. She met one of her pickups in front of a San Francisco movie theater showing *Red Dust*, her latest film with Clark Gable. The man told her she resembled Jean Harlow and ought to go to Hollywood to try out for the job of stand-in or double. But Harlow could be choosy; when Louis B. Mayer, the head of MGM studio, propositioned her, dangling a fur coat as bait, she turned him down. In any case, her attempts to get pregnant failed, and she eventually found out she was sterile.

The last of Jean's "three marriages of inconvenience," as she called them, was to Hal Rosson, a talented and successful cameraman. Rosson resembled Paul Bern and was 16 years older than Jean. The couple happily eloped in 1933, but the marriage lasted only eight months. No one knows why exactly, though it is speculated that Mama Jean and Marino's interference led to the breakup. The complaints Jean filed for the divorce proceedings were ridiculous; for example, she charged that he was ruining her career by reading in bed until late at night, thus making her sleepy on the set.

Jean's final affair was with actor William Powell, probably her one true love. Like Bern he was intelligent and sauve, and he too resembled Bern physically. Powell was 43 to Jean's 24, and on the third anniversary of their first date he brought Jean a cake with a card saying, "To my three-year-old from her Daddy." They were probably engaged at the time of Jean's sudden collapse at the age of

26. She quickly died of uremic poisoning because Mama Jean was a Christian Scientist and would not allow her to have medical help until it was too late.

It is believed that at her funeral Powell was the one who placed in her hand a single gardenia, her favorite flower, along with a note that read, "Good night, my dearest darling," and that the empty plot next to Jean and her mother's graves is reserved for him.

QUIRKS: Harlow was the first actress in Hollywood to appear regularly in films without a bra; in fact, she rarely wore any underwear. Years before when a high school teacher reprimanded her for this, the 15-year-old replied, "I can't breathe when I'm wearing a brassiere." She also rubbed her nipples with ice to make them stand out for the camera, and dyed her pubic hair platinum to match the hair on her head.

HER THOUGHTS: "My God, must I always wear a low-cut dress to be important?"

—A.W.

The Eye of the Day

MATA HARI (Aug. 7, 1876–Oct. 15, 1917)

HER FAME: An exotic dancer famous for her sensational nude performances, Mata Hari was the toast of Europe in the early years of the 20th century. In 1917 she was executed by a French firing squad for acting as a German spy during WWI. Though her name now connotes a treacherous and fascinating female spy, it has never been proved that she was in fact a double agent.

HER PERSON: Eighteen-year-old Gertrude Margareta Zelle, her convent schooling over, answered an Amsterdam newspaper ad supposedly placed by an army officer seeking a wife. Actually it was a joke set up by one of the officer's friends. Nonetheless, the officer, balding 39-year-old Rudolph MacLeod, ended up marrying Margareta.

Mata Hari in costume for her Javanese dance

For the next two years they lived in Holland, where she bore their son, Norman. When MacLeod was reassigned to the Dutch East Indies, he took his family with him. There Margareta had another child, Jeanne; flirted with young officers and planters (arousing MacLeod's jealousy); and watched Javanese temple dancers, who inspired her future career. MacLeod drank, was unfaithful, and beat her. At least once he threatened her with a loaded gun. One story, probably legendary, states that their son was poisoned by a native soldier incensed over MacLeod's seduction of his girl friend, the boy's nurse. Margareta later claimed that she strangled the poisoner—with her bare hands, of course.

The MacLeods returned to Holland and separated, and by 1904 Margareta was in Paris, without husband or child. "I thought that all women who ran away from their husbands went to Paris," she said.

At her debut as a dancer, she met Émile Étienne Guimet, the owner of an Oriental art museum, where she soon gave an electrifying performance of Oriental dances, dressed in jeweled bra and see-through draperies in a setting of palms, bronze statues, and garlanded columns. Theater critic Édouard Lepage described her appearance in the hyperbole typical of the times: "supple like the unrolled serpent which is hypnotized by the snake charmer's flute. Her flexible body at times becomes one with the undulating flames, to stiffen suddenly in the middle of her contortions ... with a brutal gesture, Mata Hari rips off her jewels ... throws away the ornaments that cover her breasts. And, naked, her body seems to lengthen way up into the shadows! ... she beats the air with her shattered arms, whips the imperturbable night with her long heavy hair." (Some sources say that she never danced completely nude, but always concealed her breasts, which had been bitten and thus permanently disfigured by MacLeod.)

By then, she had become Mata Hari (Malay for "eye of the day," the sun), complete with story—that she was the child of a 14-year-old Indian temple dancer who had died giving birth; raised by temple priests who taught her dances sacred to the Hindu god Siva; danced nude for the first time at the age of 13 before the altar of a Hindu temple. She looked the part—tall, dark, strong-featured, with velvety eyes. Her career skyrocketed and she became a sensation in most of the major capitals of Europe. And she was a scandal; the directress of one of her performances went so far as to force her to wear a piece of red flannel, diaper-fashion, at her crotch.

The spy plot, true or not, began on the day WWI was declared and she rode through the streets of Berlin with a police official. It was all high drama: the bottles of invisible ink given her by the Germans (she threw them into a canal, she said); her German code number, H 21; her seduction of high German officials (for money, love, or secrets?); her agreement to spy for the French for the million francs she needed to impress the father of the love of her life, Vadime de Massloff, a Russian captain; her grandiose plans for manipulating noblemen through jealousy, greed, and lust; the French spies tailing her in Madrid, one disguised as an old man on a bicycle, and so on.

She was arrested by the French in February, 1917. Some say she greeted the arresting officers naked on a couch in her hotel room. This is no more true than the rumor that she took milk baths while Parisian children starved or that she danced nude in her cell at Saint-Lazare Prison.

The file on her was 6 in. thick, but the evidence was inconclusive. A tube of "secret ink" in her possession turned out to be oxycyanide of mercury, which she injected into herself after making love as a birth-control method. Her aged lover Maître Clunet defended her at her trial, and another lover, Jules Cambon of the Ministry of Foreign Affairs, testified in her behalf. A third lover, old and amiable General Messimy, sent a letter written by his wife which asked that the general be excused from testifying since he didn't know the defendant. At that, Mata Hari laughed, "Ah! He never knew me! Oh, well. He has a nerve!" The jury laughed with her, but humor did not save her from her awful sentence—death by a firing squad.

The nun who came to fetch her on the day of her execution chastised her for showing too much leg while putting on her stockings in front of the prison doctor. She was dressed to the teeth. On the way out of prison, she was asked whether she was pregnant (according to French law, a pregnant woman could not be executed). This question arose, some say, from a last-ditch attempt by Clunet to save her by claiming to be the father of her unborn child.

She was shot at the polygon of Vincennes, at her own request without a blindfold. It is not true that she pulled open her coat to reveal her naked body, so astounding the firing squad that not one man could squeeze a trigger. Nor did a playboy aviator boyfriend strafe the field. Nor did another lover—inspired by the plot of the opera *Tosca*—bribe the firing squad to use blanks, put her in a ventilated coffin, and bury her in a shallow grave so that he could spirit her away. The truth? No one claimed her body, so it was contributed to a medical school for dissection. Was she guilty? That's still a question.

LOVE AND SEX LIFE: Though she accepted money for sex, she was so infatuated by "the uniform" that she often slept with soldiers for nothing. She may have hated most men, in spite of the fact that she exploited their sexual urges in order to support herself.

Judging by her letters signed "your loving little wife," she was intimate with MacLeod before their marriage. Her long string of later lovers included innumerable military men of several nationalities; the crown prince of Germany; the head of a dirigible company; the president of the Dutch council; and two boys, 17 and 18 respectively, when she was close to 40. Her price, when sex was a business deal, was $7,500 a night, or so she claimed. Upon occasion Mata Hari turned a candidate down—an American munitions salesman with bad table manners, for example.

Her first important lover was Lt. Alfred Kiepert, a rich, married landowner in the German Hussars, who set her up in an apartment in 1906. About a year later they parted, and she returned to Paris with the story she had been on a hunting trip in Egypt and India. In 1914 they were back together again. A newspaper snidely reported: "When Mata Hari, the beautiful dancer, said good-bye to the rich estate owner Kiepert, who lives just outside Berlin, she took along a few hundred thousand as a farewell present. Whether the shine of the money has worn off or whether it is love that brought her back to her former friend, during the last few days they could be seen, apparently happy and closely intimate, in a private dining room of a fashionable restaurant in town."

In 1910 she lived in the French region of Touraine as the mistress of Xavier Rousseau, a stockbroker. He spent weekends with her at their hideaway, the Château de la Dorée, where once she rode a horse up and down the outer staircase. After they split up, he became a champagne salesman. His wife claimed that Mata Hari had ruined him.

After Rousseau came Édouard Willen van der Capellen—rich, married, and a colonel in the Dutch Hussars. But her passion reached full flower with her Russian captain, Vadime de Massloff, whom she visited in 1916 in Vittel, a French resort in the military zone. He was recuperating from a wound; she may have been spying. When she was arrested, several photographs of De Massloff were found in her hotel room. Written on the back of one was: "Vittel, 1916. In memory of some of the most beautiful days of my life, spent with my Vadime, whom I love above everything." When jailed, she wrote a pathetic letter to an interrogator begging for news of De Massloff. Yet De Massloff claimed their relationship had been a minor affair.

HER THOUGHTS: "I never could dance well. People came to see me because I was the first who dared to show myself naked to the public." To an interrogator, while she was jailed: "I love officers. I have loved them all my life. I prefer to be the mistress of a poor officer than a rich banker. It is my greatest pleasure to sleep with them without having to think of money. And moreover I like to make comparisons between the various nationalities…. I have said yes to them with all my heart. They left thoroughly satisfied, without ever having mentioned the war, and neither did I ask them anything that was indiscreet. I've only kept on seeing De Massloff because I adore him."

—*A.E.*

The Prince of Playboys

PRINCE ALY KHAN (June 13, 1911–May 12, 1960)

HIS FAME: Aly Khan was once heir apparent to Aga Khan III of India, but his international pursuit of fast cars, horses, and beautiful women cost him the post of imam—spiritual leader to over 20 million Muslims of the Ismaili sect—which had been held by his father.

HIS PERSON: Born in Italy and reared in Europe, Prince Aly Suleiman Khan inherited a fortune and learned early how to enjoy it. In 1929, after the death of his mother, Aly threw himself into high-society London, where he had been sent to study law. The short and swarthy teenager stood out among the pale gentry, and his exotic looks, boundless energy, and skill at racing cars and horses won him fame and the adoration of that year's debutantes. He went on to compete in European auto races and hunt on African safaris, all the while managing his horse-breeding

Aly Khan with Rita Hayworth

farms and villas in Ireland, France, Switzerland, and Venezuela. The Allies found his daring and his fluency in English, French, and Arabic invaluable during WWII, awarding him the Croix de Guerre and the U.S. Bronze Star for his work in intelligence. Though some consider his most outstanding conquest to be Rita Hayworth, whom he married in 1949, he earned great respect as Pakistan's delegate to the U.N., where he served from 1958 until his death in a car accident two years later.

LOVE LIFE: Two skills from race-car driving and army service stood him well in his career as a lover: speed and logistics. With houses all over the world, he had only to capture a woman's attention and he could woo her wherever he wished. His blitzkrieg involved the "eyes-across-the-crowded-room" approach: staring intently at the chosen prey until he had her attention. Then he wangled an introduction, following it up with dozens of roses, constant phone calls, and attention to his victim's every whim and desire. The international celebrity hostess Elsa Maxwell wrote that Aly made a woman "feel no other person exists for him. He talks to her with breathless excitement…. He dances with her slowly and rapturously, as though it is the last time he will ever hold her in his arms…. When he tells a woman he loves her, he sincerely means it at the moment. The trouble is that a moment passes so quickly." Even a married woman could carry on an affair rather discreetly with the prince, who always traveled with a crowd of people and kept everyone guessing who, among the current crew, was the chosen one. A bewildered member of Parliament, Mr. Loel Guinness, told a divorce court in 1936 that he had left a happily married woman, his beautiful blond wife, Joan, with such a retinue, and returned from a business trip to find she wanted a divorce to marry Aly Khan. Joan was Aly's first wife and she gave him two sons, Karim (who became the fourth imam when Aly's father died in 1957) and Amyn.

Though Aly continued to stalk other women, he didn't bother to ask Joan for a divorce until he met Rita Hayworth in 1948. The sultry actress was vacationing on the Riviera. As competition Aly had Hollywood's leading men as well as the shah of Iran, also vacationing there and planning seductions of his own. Aly won, gallantly helping Rita forget her inattentive husband, Orson Welles, by whisking her off to Paris, London, and Madrid. For Rita, seeking privacy and respite from a grueling Hollywood schedule, marriage to Aly was a bitter disappointment. He felt alone with anything less than a mob, she said. She took their daughter, Yasmin, back to America with her, becoming the first woman to walk out on Aly Khan. They divorced in 1953 and Aly renewed old interests, shuttling between countries on visits, so involved he often did not leave his hotel suite. His father once became incensed when a delegation of Ismailis, in London on a visit from India, were kept waiting in the lobby for over an hour while Aly entertained a young woman upstairs. Aly's reputation had grown to such an extent that one friend claimed: "You were déclassé, démodé, nothing, you hardly counted, if you'd not been to bed with Aly."

Though Aly changed women as often as he changed cars and horses, his romances were so intense that few women complained. Juliette Greco admired his perfect timing. Kim Novak found other people seemed only "half-alive" compared to Aly. Even actress Gene Tierney—at first so unimpressed she thought to herself on meeting him, "That's all I need, some Oriental superstud"—became smitten and hoped at one time he would marry her. But none of his romances had quite such historical import as his dalliance with Lady Thelma Furness, who was the Prince of Wales' loving companion until she fell for Aly. Angered, Edward VIII turned to the American divorcée Wallis Simpson, for whom he eventually gave up the throne of England.

QUIRKS: Aly's claim that "I think only of a woman's pleasure when I'm in love" came out of a unique education given him by an Arab doctor in Cairo, where his father sent him as a boy for instruction in the sex technique called *Imsák*. A woman described it this way: "No matter how many women Aly went with, he seldom reached climax himself. He could make love by the hour, but he went the whole way himself not oftener than twice a week. He liked the effect it had on women. He liked to get them out of control while he stayed in control—the master of the situation."

HIS THOUGHTS: "They called me a bloody nigger and I paid them out by winning all their women."

—B.B.

Marilyn

MARILYN MONROE (June 1, 1926–Aug. 5, 1962)

HER FAME: She was the reigning sex symbol of the staid 1950s, the all-American dumb blond with a campy, exaggerated come-on. Fragile and insecure in her personal life, she sought security in sex, trading up from Hollywood producers to an ill-fated president of the U.S.

In 1949, Marilyn posed for this famous calendar shot

HER PERSON: She began life as Norma Jean Mortenson, the daughter of Gladys Monroe Baker Mortenson, a hardworking but emotionally unstable Hollywood film cutter, and Gladys' second husband, Edward Mortenson, a man of Norwegian extraction and uncertain employment, who disappeared shortly before she was born.

Norma Jean had a deprived, Depression-poor childhood. She boarded with one family until she was seven, joined her mother until Gladys was institutionalized for paranoid schizophrenia, and spent the next three years in an orphanage and foster homes. Grace Goddard, her mother's best friend, took care of her from the age of 11 until her marriage at 16.

Escaping into an imaginary world filled with Saturday matinee images, Norma Jean fantasized about a father who looked like Clark Gable and about glamorous seduction scenes involving tropical islands, yachts, palaces. She also had a recurring dream in which she took her clothes off in church and the shocked congregation silently admired her naked splendor.

Marriage to Jim Dougherty, a blue-collar savior, protective and possessive, soon proved disappointing. Contradicting the lurid tales she would later tell of having been raped and sexually abused, even impregnated as a foster child, Dougherty would report that his Norma Jean was a virgin. In any case, she became bored with playing house and was relieved when her husband went overseas in 1944. While working in a war plant, she was discovered by a photographer. Norma Jean loved to pose, and the camera (her only true lover, some would say) revealed a beautiful young woman, eager to please and be noticed, voluptuous yet vulnerable, a combination of allure and innocence.

Obsessed by the dream of stardom, she divorced her husband, became a popular model (photographer André de Dienes fell in love with her and proposed), and in 1946 presented herself at 20th Century-Fox. She demonstrated remarkable "flesh impact" in a silent screen test, on the basis of which the studio signed her, lightened her hair, and changed her name to Marilyn Monroe.

SEX ON THE CASTING COUCH: Marilyn emanated a strong sexual aura, by all accounts. She thought about sex all the time, considering it with every man she met, but would describe herself as selectively promiscuous, submitting only to men she liked, the main requirement being that they be "nice." Her preference was usually for older men, kindly, warm father figures.

Hollywood in the late 1940s was an "overcrowded brothel," in Marilyn's words, and she needed all the help she could get to move up from third-string blonde at Fox. Her first patron was veteran producer Joe Schenck, then nearly 70. Schenck wined and dined the starlet and invited her regularly to his home and office, where he would fondle her breasts and talk about the old days while she performed fellatio.

Schenck introduced Marilyn to Harry Cohn, the tyrant of Columbia Pictures, but she was fired after her first film, allegedly for rejecting Cohn's imperious sexual demands. Comedian Milton Berle, who succeeded where Cohn failed, claimed, "She wasn't out to please me because I might be able to help her … [but] because she liked me." At the time, she was also in love with Fred Karger, her vocal coach, who enjoyed her sexual favors but did not reciprocate her feelings.

An intimate glimpse of Marilyn's sexuality in this period is afforded by Anton LaVey, then an 18-year-old accompanist at a strip joint where the 22-year-old actress worked briefly after being fired from Columbia. LaVey, who had a two-week affair with Marilyn in motels (or, when they were broke, in her car), describes her as sexually passive, a tease who enjoyed the ogling admiration of men but not their more pressing attentions.

Marilyn's biographers are inclined to agree. Fred Guiles wrote that she was "too self-absorbed to respond to men most of the time," while Norman Mailer concluded that she was "pleasant in bed, but receptive rather than innovative."

And Marilyn was still pathetically insecure. "I don't know if I do it right," she murmured after making it with actor Marlon Brando. Or she would jump into bed, nude, pleading, "Don't do anything but just hold me."

Succeeding Schenck as Marilyn's patron was Johnny Hyde, a top Hollywood agent. Hyde was short, well barbered, and at 53 suffered from a serious heart ailment. He was infatuated with Marilyn and wanted to marry her, but she refused. He gave her a sense of security and a new wardrobe and paid for plastic surgery on her nose and chin. Most important, Hyde used his influence to line up Marilyn's best early roles, both as kept women, in *Asphalt Jungle* (1950) and *All About Eve* (1950). Marilyn didn't enjoy sex with Hyde but would fake ecstasy in order not to offend him.

When Marilyn signed her first big contract, she is said to have exclaimed,

"That's the last cock I'll have to suck." In fact, she was already setting her sights higher. Kidding around with onetime roommate Shelley Winters, she made a list of the men she'd like to sleep with. The names included an eminent man Marilyn would marry, another she would seduce, and Albert Einstein. Shelley Winters would later come across a photo of the genius inscribed to Marilyn, "With respect and love and thanks."

LOVERS AS HUSBANDS: Joe DiMaggio was Marilyn's first real-life hero-lover, a Galahad of an all-time great baseball star. Just retired at 37, he was in prime physical shape, a fitting complement to the blond bombshell who would become a superstar with the release of *Gentlemen Prefer Blondes* and *How to Marry a Millionaire* in 1953. Unfortunately, however, DiMaggio didn't want his wife to be a superstar after their 1954 marriage. The strong, silent type, proud, possessive, and old-fashioned, and detested Hollywood. He disliked Marilyn's drama coach and mentor, Natasha Lytess, who retaliated by suggesting that Marilyn got along better with women. In a desperate effort to save their marriage, DiMaggio conspired with his friend Frank Sinatra to catch Marilyn with "the other woman"—presumably to force her into dropping her divorce suit. But Lytess' allegation was never proved.

Trying to break away from her studio-imposed stereotype of the sexy blond, Marilyn left Hollywood for the East Coast, where she thought she had finally found a man interested in more than her body. Playwright Arthur Miller, whom she had first met in 1950 ("He sat and held my toe and we just looked into each other's eyes"), was as respected in radical intellectual circles as DiMaggio was in baseball circles. They were married in 1956.

Lena Pepitone, her maid, described Marilyn's daily life in New York between acting classes and sessions with a psychiatrist. While Miller worked in his study, the actress would lie alone in her bedroom, sipping champagne and talking for long hours on the telephone, or listening to "Frankie" records and admiring her naked image in the mirrors. (She also preened before a full-length picture of DiMaggio in the closet.) Totally uninhibited, Marilyn belched and farted constantly. She rarely bathed, although she did take the trouble to bleach her pubic hair ("I want to feel blond all over") which gave her infections, and she owned no underwear. She ate in bed, wiping her hands on the sheets, which had to be changed frequently, particularly when she had her period.

At first the Millers embarrassed friends with their physical possessiveness. After one night of lovemaking, Marilyn would not let her maid change the sheets, saying, "I want to lie on these all day." Then Marilyn suffered two miscarriages, despite corrective surgery, followed by increasing depression. Her later films were completed under great strain (and mounting cost to the producers, for Marilyn, was chronically late or absent). Unable to sleep, she became a heavy barbiturate user, narcotizing herself into oblivion. More than once Miller rescued her from accidental overdosing. After collaborating on *The Misfits* (1960), the Millers were divorced—prophetically, on the day that

John F. Kennedy became president.

LOVERS AND OTHER STRANGERS: Now approaching 35, alone and desperately worried about aging, Marilyn was hungry for reassurance. She had engaged in a highly publicized affair with Yves Montand, her co-star in *Let's Make Love* (1960), who disappointed her terribly by ending the affair, not wanting to leave his wife, Simone Signoret. There were meetings in seedy hotels with Danish journalist Hans Jørgen Lembourn, whose hands made her sleep, she said. She went bar-hopping, according to her maid, entertained her handsome chauffeur, and became intimate friends with her masseur, Ralph Roberts. DiMaggio occasionally stayed overnight, but they still disagreed about Marilyn's career. Another old friend and sometime lover was Frank Sinatra, whose sexual demands and protective dominance so excited and pleased her that she indulged in fantasies of marriage. Then Sinatra introduced her to the Kennedys.

She was enjoying secret assignations with the President at his brother-in-law Peter Lawford's Santa Monica beach house, at the Beverly Hills Hotel in California, and on the presidential jet. She bought a house and moved back to Los Angeles, she told friends, because "it sure beats hanging around [hotel rooms] for God Himself Jack Kennedy to show up." Kennedy's performance was "very democratic" and "very penetrating," she giggled. "I think I make his back feel better," she joked to her masseur.

John Kennedy liked to pat and squeeze her, Marilyn said, but was embarrassed on putting his hand up her dress under the table at a dinner party to discover she wore no underwear. He also began to be annoyed by her lateness and her constant telephone calls, and he was fearful of publicity. Marilyn was becoming too hot to handle by the time JFK's 45th-birthday fund-raiser was held at Madison Square Garden that May. Marilyn stole the show singing "Happy Birthday."

By June, cushioning the blow of rejection, the President had handed her over to his brother Bobby. Bobby and Marilyn consummated their relationship in a car outside Lawford's house, it was rumored, and Marilyn began fantasizing marriage again. When her trust proved to be devastatingly misplaced, and RFK changed his phone number to escape her calls, she talked idly about calling a press conference to blow the whistle on him.

Suicide? Or murder? Marilyn's moods during that last summer of 1962 swung from gaiety to despair, the latter relieved by pills and daily psychiatric sessions. She had been fired from her last picture for absenteeism and was despondent over her inability to hold a man—"to fulfill anyone's total needs," she wrote in a letter, never mailed, to DiMaggio. Her life had been so disordered, with so many rehearsals for death, that it came as a shock but not a total surprise when she was found dead of an overdose early one Sunday morning.

The love goddess died for lack of love.

—*C.D.*

"Toujours Prêt"

PORFIRIO RUBIROSA (1909–July 6, 1965)

HIS FAME: Ostensibly he was a diplomat in the service of the Dominican Republic, representing his country with no recorded distinction in Germany, Argentina, France, Belgium, and Cuba. In actuality he was the last and greatest of that exhausted breed, the quintessential international playboy-lover.

LOVE LIFE: They called him *"Toujours Prêt"* ("Always Ready"), and throughout his amorous career, which embraced five headline-making marriages and countless scandalous affairs, no woman ever disputed the whispered nickname; nor has anyone ever stepped forward with a better explanation for the romantic triumphs of Porfirio Rubirosa. As he once announced, "I consider a day in which I make love only once as virtually wasted." He came from a middle-class family in the Dominican Republic, had a brief education in Paris where his father worked in the Dominican legation, and returned to his homeland to join the army. In manhood, he was short, dark, flat-nosed, and bow-legged from riding polo horses. He was shrewd rather than bright, aggressively attentive to women, and he spoke English with a French accent.

His first wife was 17-year-old Flor de Oro ("Flower of Gold") Trujillo, daughter of the notorious dictator Generalissimo Rafael Trujillo. Although the generalissimo felt little enthusiasm for his 22-year-old son-in-law, he declared a bank holiday on his daughter's wedding day. He then dispatched the young couple to his legation in Berlin, thus launching *"Toujours Prêt"* on his unremarkable career of diplomacy and his remarkable career of lovemaking. Five years later, when Flor and Rubi were living in Paris, Flor announced that she was tired of her husband and wanted her freedom. Rubi stepped aside gracefully, by then a wealthier man than he'd been as a bridegroom. The divorce did not disturb his father-in-law, who soon promoted Rubirosa within the Dominican legation, declaring: "He is an excellent diplomat because women like him and because he is a liar." Rubirosa played the field until he and the lovely French actress Danielle Darrieux fell in love. When the Germans took over Paris, Rubirosa was arrested and interned. Compromising her future, Darrieux agreed to entertain the Nazis in exchange for Rubirosa's release. In 1942 Rubirosa and Darrieux were married, vowing they would remain together only as long as their mutual passion survived. When Danielle's mother moved in with them, Rubi's passion subsided and the union sputtered and died.

In 1947 Rubirosa hit his stride. He became the husband of tobacco heiress Doris Duke, then the richest woman in the world. Doris provided the wedding ring and Rubi provided the cigarettes which he smoked throughout the ceremony. Thirteen months later the marriage ended and Rubi walked away from the wreckage praising Doris for her "extremely generous" settlement. An even greater coup awaited him. In 1953 he married the second-richest woman in the world, dime-store heiress Barbara Hutton, veteran of four previous mismatings (one to Cary Grant, who did not want or take any of her money). News photos show the bride looking slightly spacey. It was Rubirosa who kept his head. Seventy-three days later, when love had fled, Rubi and Barbara called the whole thing off. Rubirosa is thought to have emerged from the Hutton fling with a settlement of between $1 million and $5 million. Weaving throughout his marital diversions were several affairs and two divorce suits in which irate husbands named Rubirosa as corespondent.

And then there was his notorious on-again, off-again romance with actress Zsa Zsa Gabor. Since neither party ever retreated from publicity, their tender love story was conducted with all the secrecy and delicacy of WWII. It was highlighted by an event involving Zsa Zsa's then husband, actor George Sanders. Wanting out of what he called his "ridiculous marriage," encouraged by reports of Zsa Zsa's faithlessness, Sanders chose Christmas Eve to visit the house in which his wife was then bedding down with Rubirosa. He threw a gift-wrapped brick through the bedroom window, then calmly climbed a balcony, followed the brick with his person and two detectives, and proclaimed, "Merry Christmas, my dear!" Rubirosa, it is reported, fled to safety in the bathroom.

At 44 Rubirosa reappraised his life and his financial position and declared, "Never again will I marry for money." He took his last bride, 19-year-old French starlet Odile Rodin, in 1957. The pair were still happily wed when Rubirosa, exhilarated by a spectacular win on the polo field, dropped Odile at their apartment and alone continued off into the night to celebrate. After a few drinks at a nightclub near the Champs Élysées, he climbed back into his Ferrari and started home through the Bois de Boulogne. In an accident eerily similar to the one which five years earlier had claimed the life of his good friend Prince Aly Khan, Rubi crashed into a tree. He died en route to the hospital. At least 250 celebrated friends attended his funeral.

—S. W.

I'm a Sad Clown

ANNA NICOLE SMITH (Nov. 28, 1967–Feb. 8, 2007)

HER FAME: Anna Nicole Smith made her fame as the 1993 *Playboy* Playmate of the Year, then went on to become something of a one-woman carnival sideshow for the next decade and a half, a luminary of the golden age of public confessional and reality television. Her highly publicized marriage to dying octogenarian billionaire J. Howard Marshall and the subsequent U.S. Supreme Court battle over his money, as well as her fluctuating weight, was public fodder, and led to her appear in her own reality show.

HER PERSON: Born Vickie Lynn Hogan in Houston, Texas, Anna Nicole's father abandoned the family shortly after her birth. She was raised by various family members, and after failing ninth grade, she dropped out of school. She was soon working as a waitress at Jim's Krispy Fried Chicken in Texas. At seventeen she married the sixteen-year-old cook, Billy Wayne Smith. Her son Daniel Wayne Smith was born the next year; the couple was separated shortly after. To support herself and Daniel, Anna Nicole worked at Wal-Mart, Red Lobster, and as an exotic dancer. It was while dancing at a strip club that she met oil billionaire J. Howard Marshall, 63 years her senior. After auditioning for *Playboy*, she was chosen by Hugh Hefner to appear on the cover of the March 1992 issue, under the name Vickie Smith. Many, including Anna Nicole, attributed her immediate popularity to her resemblance to Marilyn Monroe. Anna Nicole was one of many women who reinforced the trend for massive surgical breast enhancement. Anna Nicole finally settled on the name Anna Nicole Smith by the time of her election as the 1993 Playmate of the Year. She then married Marshall, who died 13 months later, initiating a bitter legal battle between Anna Nicole and Marshall's disowned son James Howard Marshall III (technically Smith's stepson) for the oil magnate's $1.6 billion estate. She returned to widespread fame as the public face of the TrimSpa diet method (before going on a diet, the grossly overweight Smith had been asked by Conan O'Brien what her "playmate diet" was, to which she immediately replied "fried chicken"), as well as with her own reality TV show, *The Anna Nicole Smith Show*, which largely put her and her close relations on display like prescription-drugged zoo animals.

It was announced on June 1, 2006 that she was pregnant again and the apparent father was her lawyer Howard K. Stern. Her daughter Dannielynn Hope Marshall Stern was born in September 2006. Her first child, 20-year-old Daniel Smith, died shortly after the new birth, while visiting his mother and Dannielynn in the hospital; an autopsy showed that he had died of a lethal combination of Zoloft, Lexapro and methadone, likely obtained from his mother. Smith herself was found comatose a few short months later in a Hollywood, Florida hotel room and pronounced DOA at the emergency room of an apparently lethal combination of sleeping pills and large numbers of other prescription drugs in her system, many of them prescribed to Howard K. Stern.

LOVE AND SEX LIFE: Anna Nicole's life is significant not for the sexual debauch but for the depths of misery and isolation she felt about her behavior. A bizarre psychosexual symbol, Smith was paid lucratively to be the object of 13-year-olds' masturbatory fantasies, and paid even more to be the kept woman of an ancient billionaire—the phrase "gold-digger" was frequently volleyed in the media. Despite Anna Nicole's profuse claims of love, the couple never lived together. During and after her second pregnancy, a string of men came forward claiming paternity after affairs with Smith, including Zsa Zsa Gabor's husband Frédéric Prinz von Anhalt, former bodyguard Alexander Denk, and ex-boyfriend Mark "Hollywood" Hatten. It was also rumored that she had used Marshall's frozen sperm to conceive the child. DNA tests after Smith's death confirmed that another ex-boyfriend, entertainment photojournalist Larry Birkhead, was the actual father.

In the year before her death, Anna Nicole told *Entertainment Tonight* that she had been physically and sexually abused as a child, and raped by multiple male family members, which her mother—who also beat her until she left home—knew about but did nothing to stop. Much of her adult behavior is textbook for survivors of sexual abuse. Diaries from the early nineties released after Smith's death—and subsequently sold on eBay for over $500,000 to a German businessman—opened an insightful window into her private life: she wrote often of her great love for Marshall as well as her disdain for sex—"I hate for men to want sex all the time... I hate sex."

In her controversial exploitative book *Blonde Ambition*, television host Rita Cosby suggests that Anna Nicole most enjoyed lesbian liaisons and obsessively watched a videotape of attorney Howard K. Stern having oral sex with Larry Birkhead. In turn, Stern filed a $60 million lawsuit against Cosby and her book's claims.

HER THOUGHTS: In a video released after her death, Howard K. Stern follows a drugged and pregnant Anna Nicole—who is inexplicably wearing full clown make-up around the house—goading her with the camera, until, cornered, she wails "Iiii'm a saaad cloooown."

—*J.L.*

The Italian Sheik

RUDOLPH VALENTINO (May 6, 1895–Aug. 23, 1926)

HIS FAME: Valentino made the woman in the silent-picture audience fantasize that he would take her in his arms, force his lips on hers, and tempt her beyond her power to resist. He was the embodiment of love in its most primal form in such films as *The Sheik* (1921), *Blood and Sand* (1922), and *The Son of the Sheik* (1926).

HIS PERSON: Rodolfo Guglielmi di Valentina D'Antonguolla, from the small town of Castellaneta, Italy, was a wayward boy and a daydreamer. He applied himself just long enough to get through an agricultural school, after which he took a holiday in France and squandered his family's hard-earned money in night spots and restaurants. He had to borrow funds to get home. His mother was horrified by the change in him; he now associated with show girls and "loose" women. Rather than run the risk of disgrace, his parents shipped him off to the U.S. He arrived in New York City as Rodolfo Guglielmi, age 18, friendless and unable to speak the language.

Rodolfo first sought work as a gardener and was employed on a millionaire's estate until he wrecked his boss' motorcycle. He went hungry for a time and was locked out of his hotel room for nonpayment of rent. But he learned English quickly and, with his suave European charms, he procured jobs as a dancing partner for unescorted ladies at cabarets and hotels. Women clamored to dance with the flirtatious young man, and soon he was offered professional dance spots. He tangoed with headliner Joan Sawyer until he appeared as a witness against her in a divorce trial in which Joan was named as a corespondent. After that, he once again had difficulty finding work. In September, 1916, he was arrested, along with a Mrs. Georgia Thym, in a vice and white slavery investigation. "Many persons of means, principally 'social climbers,'" said *The New York Times*, "had been blackmailed after discreet visits to [Mrs. Thym's] house." Why Rodolfo was there was never clarified, but he was jailed for a few days as a "material witness." The charges against him were apparently dropped, but rather than face the possibility of deportation he left New York.

After joining a musical comedy show that folded in Utah, he made his way to San Francisco, where he sold bonds for a while. When that business went under, he took a job as a dancer with an Al Jolson troupe that was moving to Los Angeles. There he tried desperately to break into films. From 1917 to 1921 he played bit parts as a "foreign type" or a "villain" until scriptwriter June Mathis spotted him and helped him land the role of Julio in *The Four Horsemen of the Apocalypse*. Between 1921 and his death from peritonitis at age 31, the man known as Rudolph Valentino acted in 14 completed films. He was perhaps best loved for his role in *The Sheik*, in which he portrayed passion personified.

LOVE LIFE: Valentino had a sexual-fantasy film image which no mortal could sustain in real life. But women found the tall, lean young man always polite and impeccably, though sometimes gaudily, dressed. When he arrived in Hollywood, Valentino fell prey to the charms of Jean Acker, an aspiring young actress. They were kindred spirits, both looking for that big break. Their marriage in 1919 was spur-of-the-moment, and as soon as the ceremony was over, Jean knew she had made a "big mistake." Before Valentino could scoop up his bride for the traditional ride across the threshold, she dashed inside ahead of him and bolted the door. Valentino spent his wedding night alone, and the marriage was never consummated. Friends suspected that Jean had been in love with someone else, and she admitted that she had married the struggling actor out of pity. Rather than set up house with her husband, she moved in with her intimate friend Grace Darmond. (Just prior to Jean's marriage, the two women had had an argument that split up their friendship; afterward Grace protected Jean from Valentino's attempts to see his wife.) Ironically, Jean sued Valentino for divorce on grounds of desertion. The actor counter-sued, and after admitting in court that he and his wife had never had sex, he won an interlocutory decree of divorce which became final at the end of a year, in March, 1923.

But late in 1920, while at work on *Uncharted Seas*, Valentino met Natacha Rambova (her real name was Winifred Shaughnessy), stepdaughter of cosmetics tycoon Richard Hudnut, the woman who became the moving force in his life. As a strong-willed, ambitious teenager, she had run away from home to join Kosloff's Russian ballet company. When Valentino met her, she was working on another set with Russian actress—and purported lesbian—Alla Nazimova as a costume and set designer. In Natacha, Rudy found his greatest love; she made him "touch ecstasy," he once said. They were married before his divorce became final. The groom was promptly arrested on charges of bigamy and jailed for several hours until bond could be posted. Valentino was once again forced to admit in court that his marriage hadn't been consummated, and the charges were dropped. Though he and Natacha lived apart until they could legally remarry, she became a part of his life and his career. He trusted her judgment and bowed to her decisions. Especially after his great success in *The Sheik*, she envisioned him as another Douglas Fairbanks, appearing in epic films rather than in the "small, trifling, cheap, commercial pictures" Paramount gave him. For almost two years—late 1922 to early 1924—he made no movies because of contract disputes in which he protested, at her instigation, the parts he was getting and the studio's treatment of Natacha.

Rudy and Natacha legalized their union in March, 1923, and the newly-weds earned a living by dancing for the Mineralava Company, promoting beauty clay. To further supplement their income, the Valentinos wrote a book of poetry called *Day Dreams*. The contract problems ended when an independent filmmaker agreed to shoot Valentino's films and let Natacha act as consultant. She became involved in every facet of his pictures, provoking the press to say that she wore the pants in the Valentino family. They snickered at the platinum slave bracelet she gave him. Her mistake, she said later, was to go overboard in incorporating "beauty" into his films. It was beauty that hurt his career; in the films in which Natacha "meddled," Valentino seemed effeminate. In *Monsieur Beaucaire* he wore powdered wigs and a heart-shaped beauty spot on his face. The publicity became vicious: *Photoplay* ran an article stating that "All men hate Valentino," and the Chicago *Tribune* ran an editorial called "Pink Powder Puffs," which blamed Valentino for the fact that a powder-vending machine had been installed in the men's room of a Chicago ballroom. Finally, the independent filmmaker refused to work with the Valentinos and scrapped a film they had already begun. United Artists approached Valentino with a lucrative contract, but the company banned Natacha from its sets. Valentino tried to assuage her feelings by backing her in her own endeavor, a movie called *What Price Beauty?* It failed miserably, and critics thought they detected lesbian-fantasy scenes in it. Once she no longer shared his career, Natacha wanted no part of Rudy's bed. Valentino insisted that what he really wanted was a homemaker, not a business partner. He told the press, "Mrs. Valentino cannot have a career and be my wife at the same time." They were divorced in 1925.

The "Great Lover" was a bachelor again. Detectives herded him home if he got too friendly with strange women, because the studio didn't want more bad publicity if Valentino should turn in a less-than-successful amorous performance. But no one could keep him away from Pola Negri. He met the actress through Marion Davies, the mistress of publisher William Randolph Hearst. As Pola wrote in her autobiography, "Valentino's true sexuality reached out and captured me." She was fascinated, she said, by "the way in which he used his body," and he took her in "a perfect act of love." Valentino preferred sex first and intimate conversation afterward. She found him a very accomplished lover, able to size up a woman and judge exactly the right approach which would maneuver her into bed. One time he decided that strewing rose petals on Pola's bed would do the trick, and it did. Pola hoped to marry him, though as a form of New Year's resolution in 1926 he bet that he would still be a bachelor by 1930. No one knows whether he would have won. After a brief illness, he died in 1926. Thousands of men and women crushed each other to view the body; some women who never knew him committed suicide, and for years a "Lady in Black" visited his grave on the anniversary of his death.

HIS THOUGHTS: "To generalize on women is dangerous. To specialize on them is infinitely worse."

—*W.A.D. and V.S.*

II

Acting It Up

The Great Profile

JOHN BARRYMORE (Feb. 15, 1882–May 29, 1942)

HIS FAME: The son of Maurice Barrymore and the brother of Ethel and Lionel Barrymore, Jack was a member of the most distinguished family of actors to appear on the American stage. Although he conquered the legitimate theater with his good looks, he in turn was conquered by a riotous life of dissipation in Hollywood. His career was a duel between his awesome talents and his inexorable drive toward self-destruction.

HIS PERSON: Inherently lazy and an alcoholic from the age of 14, Jack chose the stage as the easiest way of making a living. He had been fired from a job as a caricaturist on a New York newspaper because of his heavy drinking, so he joined an acting troupe on its way to Australia. Before departing, he managed to sleep through the great San Francisco earthquake of 1906. Soldiers pressed him into clearing rubble, causing his uncle to remark, "It took a calamity of nature to get him out of bed and the U.S. Army to make him go to work."

He returned to America a polished light comedian and shortly was the toast of Broadway. The young matinee idol was kept busy trying to support his profligate lifestyle, and even though he despised the repetition involved in stage acting, his characterizations of Richard III and Hamlet are still regarded as classics. He made 15 films before following his drinking buddies Ben Hecht, Gene Fowler, and W. C. Fields from New York to Hollywood. At his peak in pictures, he was earning a minimum of $76,250 per film and was nationally acclaimed as "the Great Lover." However, he hated his pretty-boy image and never missed an opportunity to act in grotesque makeup, relishing roles like Svengali, Mr. Hyde, and Captain Ahab.

Barrymore was a notoriously cruel wit. At the funeral of a friend, he was about to depart with the other mourners when he saw a doddering old man lingering behind, staring down into the grave. Barrymore sidled up to the old fellow, leaned over, and whispered, "I guess it hardly pays to go home." When he met columnist

Louella Parsons at a social function, he commented in a voice loud enough to be heard by the entire roomful of people: "She's a quaint old udder, isn't she?" He described another woman as looking "exactly like a dental filling."

Barrymore was equally well known for his nearly superhuman drinking, which aged him rapidly. In 1935, in an attempt to dry out, he took his daughter Diana on a cruise on his yacht. All liquor was removed from the boat before it sailed. Yet Barrymore was drunk during the entire voyage, for he found a means of siphoning off alcohol from the yacht's engine-cooling system.

By the end of his life the once great actor was reduced to a pitiful series of self-mocking roles that reflected his tarnished reputation—that of a lecherous old drunkard. A friend summed up Barrymore's life by observing, "Nobody can run downhill as fast as a Thoroughbred." He lived voraciously up to the moment of his death from extreme old age at 60.

SEX LIFE: At age 15, Jack lost his virginity to his stepmother, who seduced him. After that he was to make love to countless women, but he could never really trust any of them. His first romantic scandal solidified this feeling. He had been sleeping with 16-year-old show girl Evelyn Nesbit, the girl friend of society architect Stanford White. Evelyn's parents discovered the affair and hastily married her off to Harry K. Thaw, a psychotic millionaire. Thaw publicly murdered White out of jealousy, and Barrymore was forced to hide out for months until the case blew over.

In 1910 Jack married a debutante named Katherine Harris. Blond, shapely, cultured, and intelligent, Katherine married the actor against her parents' wishes, yet she was the envy of her peers. However, Jack's accelerating career, coupled with his impromptu drinking binges, brought their marriage to an end in 1917. On the rebound, he met and married Blanche Thomas, who led suffragette marches and wrote poetry under the pen name Michael Strange. The couple startled New Yorkers of the day with their unisex attire—matching outfits of black velvet. His time with Michael Strange was marked with slugfests and sonnets and the birth of a daughter, Diana. When he divorced the poet in 1928, he renounced all rights to their infant daughter and headed west.

In Hollywood his lust seemed insatiable. Although most starlets succumbed to his charm, he struck out with a young Southern actress named Tallulah Bankhead. One afternoon he invited her to his backstage dressing room and, as Tallulah recalled, started making "little animal noises" as he led her to his casting couch. She refused to have sex with him and escaped intact. He was far more successful with 17-year-old Mary Astor, who would appear in his suite on Sundays, accompanied by her mother. After sending the mother outside onto the veranda to enjoy the sun, he would take Mary into his bedroom.

Soon the golden-haired bit player Dolores Costello caught his eye, and he chose her as his leading lady in *The Sea Beast*. When Michael Strange saw the love scenes in the film, she said bitterly, "That's not acting. He's in love with the girl." She was right. Barrymore dropped Michael flat for Dolores and conceded, "I'm just a son of a bitch." He made Dolores his protégée and married her, but he was insecure in the relationship. In a rage of jealousy, he snatched her away from a party when he saw her dancing with David O. Selznick, took her home, and lectured her until daybreak. He accused her of plotting an affair with Selznick and insisted that all married women were constantly unfaithful. On another occasion he physically ejected her obstetrician from the house, claiming she was infatuated with the man. Maybe she was; after divorcing Jack, she married the doctor.

In later years Barrymore was drawn to exotic prostitutes. When he took a trip to India in search of a guru, he wound up in a Calcutta whorehouse, which he described as a "pelvic palace." He was delighted by the "gentle music that went directly to the scrotum and cuddled there," and he stayed on for a month. "And so I never met my saint," he explained. "I met only dancing girls and singing girls, all of them devout students of the *Kamasutra*, which teaches that there are 39 different postures for the worship of Dingledangle—the god of love." His sojourn in Calcutta was followed by a visit to a brothel in Madras, where he enjoyed himself so much that he rented the establishment exclusively for himself for an entire week.

His last wife, Elaine Barrie, married the wreckage of the once great actor in 1936. She met him when she was a sophomore at Hunter College and spent the next year chasing him across the country. The day before their wedding he told his cronies, "Gentlemen, you are talking to a man who is about to go over Niagara Falls in a barrel." On their wedding night he was insanely jealous because she was such a good lover. He demanded to know exactly how, when, and where she had learned her skills. Later he said of Elaine: "That little filly made a racehorse out of me again." Elaine made a banned film called *How to Undress in Front of Your Husband*, starring "Mrs. John Barrymore." Then, aware that he was nearly washed up in films, Elaine took her husband on the road in a play called *Dear Children*. People flocked to see the great Barrymore, a sick old man, humiliate himself. He vomited onstage and often relieved his bladder in public—once in a hotel lobby sandbox and another time in a socialite's private elevator.

Aware that he was dying, he faced the end with his own brand of gallantry. When a priest entered his hospital room with an extremely ugly nurse and asked, "Anything to confess, my son?" Barrymore replied, "Yes, father. I confess having carnal thoughts." Astonished, the priest asked, "About whom?" Barrymore pointed at the ugly nurse. "About her," he said.

The night Barrymore died, his longtime friend Gene Fowler and his son Will held vigil by his body at Pierce's Funeral Home. The only person who came to pay him homage was an old prostitute, who knelt in silent prayer and then disappeared into the dark.

John Barrymore had earned over $3 million in his day. When his estate was auctioned off after he died, he was still $75,000 in debt.

HIS THOUGHTS: "It's a slander to say my troubles come from chasing women. They begin when I catch them."

—*M.S. and the Eds.*

The Tramp

CHARLIE CHAPLIN (Apr. 16, 1889–Dec. 25, 1977)

HIS FAME: The king of silent screen comedies, Charles Spencer Chaplin made 80 films and gained international fame with his portrayal of a pathetic yet humorous little tramp in such cinema classics as *The Kid* (1920), *The Gold Rush* (1925), *City Lights* (1931), and *Modern Times* (1936). He was knighted in 1975 for his achievements.

HIS PERSON: Chaplin learned to sing and dance at an early age by watching his mother, Hannah, perform in the music halls of his native London. His alcoholic father, Charles, left the family shortly after Charlie's birth, and because Hannah was often confined to mental institutions, Chaplin spent his childhood—when not on the street—in a series of orphanages and

Chaplin cavorting during his later years in Switzerland

workhouses. As an adolescent, he earned a living by working as a lather boy in a barbershop, as a janitor in music halls, and as a bit-part vaudeville performer.

Chaplin's film career began in December, 1913, after he had come to the U.S. on tour with the Fred Karno Company, a British vaudeville troupe. He was spotted on stage by producer Mack Sennett, who signed him to Keystone Films to appear in one-reelers for $150 a week.

The funny man's salary increased with his popularity; in one year he earned $1 million for eight films. He had made 69 films by the end of 1920, but his output million as he began to control the screenwriting, directing, and producing of his pictures. A moody perfectionist, he often shot as much as 50 times the amount of footage necessary. *The Great Dictator*, released during WWII, caused some politicians and journalists to believe that Chaplin was a leftist, because in it he made an impassioned plea for the launching of a second front in Europe in order to aid the Russians. His *Monsieur Verdoux* (1947), which was vehemently attacked by censors and conservatives for its view of contemporary society, was picketed, banned in Memphis, and withdrawn from many theaters. Chaplin left the U.S. in 1952, purportedly to take an extended vacation, but apparently aware that his reentry would be challenged. It was, and he gave up his reentry visa and took up residence in Switzerland, declaring himself a "citizen of the world." He returned to the U.S. (a country he always professed to love) only once, in 1972, to receive an honorary Academy Award. He won another Oscar in 1973 for his 1952 score of *Limelight.*

SEX LIFE: Though a "workaholic," Chaplin made time for sex "between pictures" or, as he crudely put it, in "that hour when [I am] bored." When he did make the time, his preference was for young girls; the result was four marriages (three to women 18 years of age or younger), 11 children, and a long list of mistresses.

Calling himself the "Eighth Wonder of the World" and proud of his Hollywood reputation for having an oversized appendage, Chaplin relished nothing more than the prospect of deflowering a budding virgin. "The most beautiful form of human life," he once averred, "is the very young girl just starting to bloom." His first pubescent protégée was 14-year-old Mildred Harris, whom Chaplin took under his wing in 1916. He promised her a career in pictures, but Mildred was soon pregnant with Chaplin's child. Although he believed marriage would interfere with his work, there was no escaping the pressure of Mildred's furious mother, and the two were wed on Oct. 23, 1918. Mildred's pregnancy turned out to be a false alarm. Although he grew fond of her, Chaplin said Mildred's mind was "cluttered with pink-ribboned foolishness." About a year after their marriage, she gave birth to a severely deformed son, who lived only three days. When the child died, so did the marriage. They were divorced in 1920.

Chaplin loved hiring star-struck starlets to double as his leading ladies both on the screen and in his bed. Such was the case with Lita Grey, who first grabbed Chaplin's attention in 1914 when she was only six years old. By the time she turned 12, Lita was prancing around Chaplin's studio under the lovelorn, watchful eye of her domineering director. For the next three years he groomed her for her first romantic fling, and finally, in 1923, during the filming of *The Gold Rush*, he attempted to molest her in his hotel room. "He kissed my mouth and neck and his fingers darted over my alarmed body," Lita wrote in her autobiography. "His body writhed furiously against mine, and suddenly some of my fright gave way to revulsion." But over the next few months he coddled her and charmed her. They were often seen together in the company of Thelma Morgan Converse (later known as Lady Furness), whom Chaplin used as a "chaperone" so that he could date Lita without arousing the suspicions of her mother. Eventually, on the tile floor of his steam bath, he took Lita's virginity.

Chaplin was well aware of his sex appeal. Once when Lita remarked that he could probably have any one of a hundred girls in two minutes, Chaplin quickly corrected her. "A hundred," he said. "No, a thousand. But I want to be naughty with you, not with them." Despite a steady diet of sex, months passed before Lita experienced her first orgasm. Her constant pleas with Charlie to use contraceptives went unheeded; he felt rubbers were "aesthetically hideous." It was no surprise, then, when Lita became pregnant in 1924. She was 16 years old, he was 35.

Chaplin shuddered when he heard the news, and suggested she have an abortion. Lita refused. Then Chaplin offered her $20,000 if she would marry some other man. Again Lita refused.

Threatened with a paternity suit and a charge of statutory rape, Chaplin agreed to marriage. On the ride from Mexico to Los Angeles after their Nov. 24, 1924, wedding, Chaplin suggested to his pregnant wife that she commit suicide by throwing herself off the train. Yet, despite his hostility, Chaplin managed to separate sex from affection, claiming he could make love to Lita even though he detested her.

Two years and two children later, Lita filed for divorce. Her 42-page legal complaint was made public and was sold on the streets for a quarter a copy. It exposed such shocking and intimate details of their marriage as: Chaplin had no fewer than five mistresses during their two-year marriage; he threatened her with a loaded revolver more than once; he wanted to engage in a *ménage à trois* and expressed a desire to make love to her in front of an audience; and he frequently belittled her because she refused to perform fellatio on him (she said it was perverted; he insisted "all married people do it").

Chaplin's third marriage is masked in mystery. He met actress Paulette Goddard when she was 20. Some journalists claim he married the starlet in April, 1934, while at sea on his yacht, *Panacea*. Supposedly he paid the skipper to tear the telltale page from the ship's logbook. While many skeptics insist the couple never married, Chaplin gave 1936 as the year of their marriage. Though Paulette played stepmother to Chaplin's sons—Charles, Jr., and Syd—for a time, wedded bliss was once again undermined by the demands of filmmaking.

In 1941 Chaplin met 22-year-old Joan Barry when she came to his studio for a screen test. This time it was Chaplin who was pursued, at first quite willingly. But he tried to call a halt to the affair when she began coming to his home at any hour, bathing in the sprinklers, breaking windows, and threatening suicide. When she finally decided she didn't want to be an actress after all, he gladly gave her the fare back to New York. But in May of 1943 she returned to Los Angeles, broke into his home, and as a consequence spent 30 days in jail. At the time of her arrest, she was three months pregnant. In the meantime, Chaplin met Oona O'Neill, the 17-year-old daughter of famed playwright Eugene O'Neill. While Chaplin's sons engaged in a friendly rivalry for Oona's affections, their father easily outdistanced them. In June, 1943, she became his fourth and final wife.

Chaplin's marriage did not prevent Joan Barry from slapping him with a paternity suit. And, because Chaplin had given her money which she used for traveling back and forth across state lines, the federal government indicted him on morals charges. After Miss Barry's child was born in October, 1943, a blood test proved that Chaplin was not the father. During the trial the prosecuting attorney referred to Chaplin as "a runt of a Svengali" and a "lecherous hound." While on the stand, the 55-year-old actor was questioned about his virility and was forced to admit that he was still sexually quite potent. In April, 1944, Chaplin was acquitted; nonetheless, he was ordered to pay child support.

Persecuted by the U.S. press and politicians as a "debaucher" and a "leftist," he and Oona settled down in Vevey, Switzerland, to a life of domestic happiness and serenity. "If I had known Oona or a girl like her long ago, I would never have had any problems with women. All my life I have been waiting for her without even realizing it," he said. By the time he passed away, Chaplin had fathered eight more children—the last one when he was in his early 70s.

SEX PARTNERS: Chaplin prided himself on making love to prominent women. Among his conquests were Clare Sheridan, cousin of Winston Churchill; actresses Mabel Normand, Edna Purviance, Pola Negri, and Marion Davies, the starlet who carried on a long-lasting affair with William Randolph Hearst; and Peggy Hopkins Joyce, a Ziegfeld Girl who became one of the wealthiest women in the world by marrying five millionaires. She and Chaplin were sometimes seen swimming nude off the island of Catalina.

QUIRKS: This human sex-machine, who, as a prelude to sex, recited erotic passages from *Fanny Hill* and *Lady Chatterley's Lover*, was good for as many as six "bouts" in succession with scarcely five minutes' rest in between.

Chaplin also practiced voyeurism. He erected a high-power telescope in his house that gave him a bird's-eye view of John Barrymore's bedroom.

HIS THOUGHTS: "No art can be learned at once. And lovemaking is a sublime art that needs practice if it's to be true and significant."

—*A.K. and V.S.*

Coop

GARY COOPER (May 7, 1901–May 13, 1961)

HIS FAME: He won the Oscar for best actor in 1941 for *Sergeant York* and another in 1952 for *High Noon*. He was nominated for the award three more times and in 1961 received an honorary Oscar "for his many memorable screen performances" in 95 pictures.

HIS PERSON: Despite his screen persona as an American Everyman, he was hardly unworldly. He was educated in England, safaried in Africa, and conquered women everywhere. Despite his art school background he failed to sell any of his political cartoons, but his

Patricia Neal and Cooper in The Fountainhead

horseback riding experience, gained on the family ranch in Montana, did land him a job as a movie stunt man in the early twenties. However he soon grew tired of falling off horses (sometimes as both cowboy and Indian in the same picture), and hired agent Nan Collins to help him get feature roles. She changed his name from Frank to Gary after her hometown in Indiana, and he soon obtained his first starring role, in *The Winning of Barbara Worth* in 1926. Paramount signed him to a contract, and an unprecedented popularity followed. It wavered but few times. In 1944 his fans reacted negatively to his only political venture—a scathing anti-Roosevelt broadcast during the Dewey campaign. And in 1957 the critics castigated him for playing the lover of 18-year-old Audrey Hepburn in *Love in the Afternoon*. He was 56 at the time and immediately went out for a face-lift. In 1959, two years before his death from spinal cancer, he converted to Roman Catholicism.

LOVE LIFE: "Yup" and "Nope" weren't his only trademarks. When asked why she was leaving New York for Hollywood, Tallulah Bankhead said for the money and "to fuck that divine Gary Cooper." Making love to Gary Cooper became as popular a pursuit among Hollywood's leading ladies as getting their prints enshrined in front of Grauman's Chinese Theatre. Director Howard Hawks commented on Cooper's technique: "If I ever saw him with a good-looking girl and he was kind of dragging his feet over the ground and being very shy and looking down, I'd say, 'Oh-oh, the snake's gonna strike again.' He found that the little bashful boy approach was very successful."

Helen Hayes said she would have left her husband for Coop if he'd only given the word during their filming of *A Farewell to Arms*. When John Gilbert found out that his own Marlene Dietrich was in love with Cooper, he went off the wagon and drank steadily until his death—the day after Cooper was named her co-star in *Desire*. Ingrid Bergman's husband accused her of having an affair with Cooper. Said Bergman, "Every woman who knew him fell in love with Gary." But a love affair with Cooper? Bergman flatly denied it.

Coop's wife Rocky, née Veronica Balfe, was a New York debutante and would-be actress whom Coop wed in New York in 1933, saying he was "delighted to be rescued from his career as a playboy." The couple omitted the word *obey* from their wedding ceremony and allowed each other plenty of space thereafter, once even arriving at a ski resort separately, rooming separately, skiing briefly together, and then departing separately.

SEX PARTNERS: The first lover of note in Coop's life was Clara Bow, the star of *It*, in which he played a small part in 1927. Clara rated her lovers, and gave Coop rave reviews on his magnificent endowments, boasting to Hedda Hopper that he was "hung like a horse and could go all night." They liked to make love outdoors, on beaches or in walnut groves. Clara told friends that Gary was so kind that he let her take her dog in the tub whenever he gave her a bath. The rumor had it that Cooper proposed marriage to Clara, which soured her feelings toward the relationship. In the end, Cooper blanched at being called the

"It" boy to her "It" girl, and would dismiss their romance as a creation of the studio publicity department.

There was no denying his relationship with actress Lupe Velez, "the Mexican Spitfire." She was the girl friend of singer Russ Columbo when she and Coop first met for *Wolf Song* in 1929. Twenty-four hours later she and Coop were in bed together. A friend told biographer Hector Arce of his embarrassment on being trapped in a naked Cooper's dressing room while Coop and Lupe tantalized each other over the phone with talk of the forthcoming night's activities and Coop developed an unabashed erection. The affair was often characterized by screaming, violent fights, which scarred Cooper physically and emotionally. Pressure from his mother and the studio finally broke up the relationship, leaving Coop with a nervous breakdown and only 148 lbs. on his 6-ft. frame.

During a "long walk" through Europe to clear his head, he met Contessa Dorothy di Frasso, an American who had married into Roman nobility. She helped Coop become a sophisticate and returned to Hollywood with him, where she became famous for throwing lavish parties and haunting movie sets on which he was filming. The younger, beautiful Veronica Balfe soon eclipsed her in Coop's affections, and the contessa faded off to Palm Springs and an affair with gangster Buggsy Siegel.

Patricia Neal was 23 when Coop met her during the filming of *The Fountainhead* in 1949. They fell in love, and he sought a legal separation from Rocky in 1950. He took Miss Neal to Havana in hopes of having the relationship blessed by his friend Ernest Hemingway, but neither Papa nor anyone else was willing to sanction the breakup of his 17-year marriage. As for Rocky, her Catholicism wouldn't permit her to consider divorce and her pedigree wouldn't permit her to wallow in self-pity. She continued to live her life to the fullest, and before the separation became final in May, 1951, Cooper and Miss Neal had parted—she for an analyst and he for two more trivial liaisons before a reconciliation with Rocky and their daughter Maria.

—*D.R.*

The Four-Year Itch

JOAN CRAWFORD (Mar. 23, 1904–May 10, 1977)

HER FAME: During her 40-year career as an actress, she appeared in over 80 films and was one of the screen's longest-reigning stars. An emotional performance in *Mildred Pierce* earned her the 1945 Academy Award for best actress. Besides appearing in such memorable movies as *The Women*, *Strange Cargo*, *Humoresque*, and *Whatever Happened to Baby Jane?*, she served on the board of directors of the Pepsi-Cola Company.

HER PERSON: Crawford was permanently embittered by her battered, poverty-stricken childhood. Her real name was Lucille LeSueur, and she was born in San Antonio, Tex. When Lucille's father deserted the family, her mother found her jobs in Kansas City boarding schools. In one, the 12-year-old girl suffered severe beatings whenever she failed to perform her duties. Pudgy, buxom, and rather bland, she traveled to New York in 1924 and took to the stage as a dancer.

Described by F. Scott Fitzgerald as "the best example of the flapper," Lucille was dancing on Broadway when MGM discovered her there and signed her to a five-year contract. On New Year's Day in 1925 she moved to Los Angeles. Through a combination of stringent dieting and extensive dental surgery, she created a new image and was transformed into "Joan Crawford," a screen name coined for her in a fan magazine contest sponsored by MGM.

By the end of 1927, the 5-ft. 4-in. starlet had become a flamboyant off-screen personality. She changed her hair color weekly, danced in revealing short skirts, and cavorted about town with a male harem of handsome escorts.

During her tumultuous Hollywood career, she was alternately labeled "First Queen of the Movies" and "Box-Office Poison." Survival as a star was her paramount aim; everything else—husbands, lovers, and children—was secondary. She seemed to love her fans more than her family and kept in close touch with 1,500 of them right up to May 10, 1977, the day she succumbed to stomach cancer. Although she died alone, these loyal fans mourned her passing.

LOVE LIFE: Joan was married four times, and each of her marriages lasted four years. Every time she changed husbands, she also changed the name of her Brentwood estate and installed all new toilet seats.

Her first groom was Douglas Fairbanks, Jr., the charming scion of the royal Fairbanks family of Hollywood. Popularly referred to as "the Prince and Cinderella," the couple was wed in June, 1929, despite strong opposition from Joan's new in-laws. The senior Fairbanks and his then wife Mary Pickford boycotted the wedding, claiming that 25-year-old Joan was too old for 20-year-old Doug Junior.

The marriage, which for two years was ideal, ended in a shambles. Joan and "Dodo," as she called her husband, dreamed of having children. But the feisty Miss Pickford supposedly warned, "If you ever dare to make me a grandmother, I'll kill you." The marriage died shortly after Joan had a miscarriage, which she later admitted was really an abortion.

Prior to her 1933 divorce, Joan plunged into a love affair with actor Clark Gable. He too was married, but Joan enjoyed his company enough to carry on a series of love affairs with him until his death in 1960. Although she called Gable "a magnetic man with more sheer male magic than anyone in the world," she later confessed that he was an unsatisfactory lovemaker in spite of his screen image as a virile leading man. In fact, she was often faced with ploys which he devised to discourage sexual encounters between them.

Realizing that marriage to Gable was unlikely, Joan showered her affections on actor Franchot Tone, a wealthy, cultured easterner. And although she had claimed she'd never again marry, the 31-year-old Joan and 30-year-old Tone were wed on Oct. 11, 1935. This marriage was on shaky ground from the start, but Joan believed it might be saved if they had children. After suffering two miscarriages, she was informed that she could not bear children. When she caught Tone in bed with another actress, she decided that she had no further need for him anyway, and she divorced him in 1939.

While her relationship with Tone was disintegrating, she had a brief affair with Spencer Tracy. But his interest in her was fleeting. During a rehearsal, Joan betrayed her nervousness and flubbed her lines. Tracy lashed out at her: "For crissake, Joan, can't you read the lines? I thought you were supposed to be a pro." The wounded Crawford fled in tears, and the affair was over.

Now Joan centered her efforts on adopting a child. Despite her status as a single parent, in 1939 she began adoption proceedings for a baby girl, whom she named Joan Crawford, Jr. Months later Joan changed the child's name to Christina. But having a child around did not fill the void. Lonely and starving for love, the 38-year-old actress married handsome, muscular, 6-ft. 1-in. supporting actor Phillip Terry in 1942. She'd known him for only six weeks, and by her own admission she never loved Terry, who was three years her junior. Their marriage became so mechanical that the daily schedule Joan drew up for herself, and issued to staff members, always included a specific time allotted for sex—usually an hour and a half in the late afternoon earmarked as "time with Phillip." During this period she adopted a second child—a boy—and named him Phillip Terry, Jr. Following her 1946 divorce from Terry, she renamed the boy Christopher Crawford.

With another failed marriage behind her, Joan made her children the focal point of her frustration. Stories of her abusive treatment of them were well known to horrified journalists, but anyone who dared to put them in print could count on his or her career being smashed by MGM's publicity department. The rumors didn't even prevent her from adopting infants Cathy and Cynthia in 1947. Joan always referred to the girls as being twins even though they came from different families, were born a month apart, and in no way looked alike.

Joan's behavior became increasingly eccentric and unpredictable. She started drinking heavily and often greeted her dates wearing little more than lingerie. She went out with numerous men, including young actors like Rock Hudson and George Nader, and was named as the "other woman" in two divorce suits. Although her emotional life was a mess, she continued to keep her body in excellent condition. Before filming *Torch Song*, the 52-year-old actress showed up at director Charles Walters' home wearing nothing but a housecoat. Flinging it open, she told him, "I think you should see what you have to work with." Walters was impressed.

Joan's final marriage took place in May, 1955. Her fourth husband, Alfred Steele, was the dynamic, square-faced president of Pepsi-Cola. Until he died of a heart attack in 1959, they circled the globe together promoting Pepsi. Despite her happiness in the role of corporate wife, Joan's feelings for Steele often have been called into question. Six months after they had married, Joan described her 54-year-old bespectacled husband as being too fat and hard of hearing. Yet it appears that, for the first time, she actually felt loved. Toward the end of her life she confided to interviewer Roy Newquist in *Conversations with Joan Crawford*: "A pillow is a lousy substitute for someone who really cares. And when it comes right down to it, aside from Alfred and the twins, I don't think I came across anyone who really cared."

QUIRKS: After achieving stardom, Crawford refused to go in front of the movie cameras during her menstrual period, complaining that she didn't photograph well then. There was a time, however, when she was willing to go to any extreme to appear on the screen. During her peak in popularity, stories began surfacing that years before, while still known as Lucille LeSueur, Joan Crawford had made a series of stag movies bearing such exploitative titles as *Velvet Lips* and *The Casting Couch*. Joan allegedly spent $100,000 buying up every copy of these films in order to destroy them. She learned later that one collector still harbored some prints, and shortly thereafter a mysterious fire swept through this collector's home, burning to a crisp not only the sex flicks but the sleeping collector. Years after, rumor had it that a complete set of Crawford's stag films had turned up in the private collection of a Prague munitions king.

—A.K.

Little Boy Lost

JAMES DEAN (Feb. 8, 1931–Sept. 30, 1955)

HIS FAME: Few movie actors, in life or death, have been worshiped the way James Dean was after he died at the age of 24, having had major roles in only three films. These were *East of Eden*, *Rebel Without a Cause*, and *Giant*. Humphrey Bogart said of him: "Dean died at just the right time. He left behind a legend. If he had lived, he'd never have been able to live up to his publicity." Andy Warhol called him "the damaged but beautiful soul of our time." And an entire generation of teenagers saw themselves in Dean as they'd seen themselves in no other star. One publicist summed it up when he said, "I thought Dean was a legend, but I was wrong … He's a religion."

HIS PERSON: Dean's happy, healthy childhood in Fairmont, Ind., and in Los Angeles, was cruelly marred when his mother died of cancer. He was nine years old, and his father sent him back to Indiana, where he was raised on a farm by his kindly aunt and uncle. Despite his blond, boyish good looks, the sex-symbol-to-be was small and nearsighted and spoke haltingly. Growing up, he embarked on an acting career, bouncing back and forth between New York and Hollywood. Dean's personality was so intense that he made an unforgettable impression on almost everyone he met—and often for the worst. He seesawed wildly from clowning and joking to morbid, sullen depressions. Jimmy threw his powerful energy into one activity after another. He studied dance, played the bongos, learned to sculpt, wrote poetry, dabbled in art, read constantly, and won trophies racing sports cars. When he turned this energy on his greatest passion, acting, the results were remarkable.

But it was Dean's death that was truly, as the saying goes, larger than life. On Sept. 30, 1955, he was driving his $7,000 silver, aluminum-bodied Porsche 550 Spyder to a race in Salinas, Calif. At 5:45 P.M. he died in a collision with a car driven by Donald Turnupseed. The end of Dean's life was the beginning of a rabid death cult. It was bigger than Valentino's and bigger than Marilyn Monroe's. Teenagers paid 50¢ to sit behind the wheel of the crushed Spyder. They bought chewing gum wrappers supposedly peeled from gum chewed by Dean. In the three years following his death, his studio received more mail addressed to him than to any living star—hundreds of thousands of fans writing to him as if he were still alive. A magazine offering Dean's words "from the other side" sold 500,000 copies. Dean's death mask was displayed at Princeton University along with Beethoven's.

SEX LIFE: The great debate over James Dean's sex life centers on whether he was gay, straight, or bisexual. Actually, though he dabbled in sex with both females and males, he was somewhat ambivalent sexually. One friend went so far as to say that he didn't think Dean enjoyed sex, that he only wanted to be mothered. Another said that he was basically asexual in his needs and drives, that acting and car racing came first.

The crushing loss of his mother seems to have infused him with a kind of little-boy quality that both women and men found very attractive. His favorite seduction technique, which he claimed never failed him, was to curl up with his head in a woman's lap and let her cuddle him. "All women want to mother you. Give them a chance to and before you know it you're home free." He discovered by the time he was 21 that he scored most successfully with older women. Sometimes he would date a girl for sex alone, and just as often he would date a girl repeatedly without ever making advances. As with every other aspect of his life, he was capable of yo-yo emotions and behavior. When he was courting a girl, he would take her on a hair-raising motorcycle ride as a kind of initiation rite. He often went on such rides with his very close friend Eartha Kitt, who called him "Jamie."

Naturally, as the god of a death cult that fed on hysterical teenage worship, he inspired some weird rumors about his sex practices. The rumor that he was a masochist who enjoyed being burned with cigarette butts, and thus was dubbed "the Human Ashtray," is completely false. Also, the fabled pornographic photos of a young man—allegedly Jimmy—sitting nude in a tree with a huge erection show no evidence of really being Dean.

The rumors of his bisexuality do have a basis, although they are often greatly exaggerated. He probably did a bit of hustling in his early Hollywood days, when he was practically starving, calling his gay dates "free meal tickets." For a time he was "kept" by Rogers Brackett, a Hollywood ex-producer, but this was probably the only real affair he had with a man. Mostly what he did with men he did dispassionately—for the experience, for the money, or for the connections, until he found out the connections never came through. He told a friend, "I've had my cock sucked by five of the big names in Hollywood, and I think it's pretty funny because I wanted more than anything to get some *little* part, something to *do*, and they'd invite me for fancy dinners...." When asked if he was gay, he replied, "Well, I'm certainly not going through life with one hand tied behind my back."

SEX PARTNERS: His first major love affair was with Elizabeth "Dizzy" Sheridan, with whom he lived happily for a while in New York. Their relationship was a close and private one, and Dizzy remembers Jimmy as "gentle." Eventually they drifted apart, and he began what was to be a long-term love affair with the thin, high-strung young actress Barbara Glenn, whom he affectionately referred to as "my neurotic little shit." After he moved to California, Barbara finally told him she was marrying someone else. He took the news badly.

The great love of Dean's life was the petite, demure Italian actress Pier Angeli. The main impediment to their union was Pier's mother, who disapproved because of Jimmy's tough punk image, and because he wasn't a Catholic. To please Pier, Jimmy got regular haircuts, wore suits occasionally, and even talked of becoming a Catholic. Pier and Jimmy considered marriage and quarreled about it. When an interviewer asked him whether "wedding bells would be heard," he replied, "You mean with Miss Pizza? Look, I'm just too neurotic." Dean finally did ask her to marry him in New York, where he was going for a TV show. Pier said it would break her mother's heart if they eloped. So she stayed behind, and while Dean was gone she announced her engagement to singer Vic Damone. It broke Jimmy's heart.

Dean told a friend that he had beaten Pier up a few nights before her wedding, and there is a persistent story that he sat outside the church on his motorcycle during the ceremony, gunning his motor. Some time later Pier visited Jimmy to tell him she was going to have a baby. He cried after she left, and two days later he was dead.

Pier Angeli's marriage to Damone was a failure, as was her second marriage, and her life ended after a drug overdose. She never got over Jimmy Dean's magic, likening the two of them to Romeo and Juliet and saying he was the only man she had ever loved. She said in an interview, "I never loved either of my husbands the way I loved Jimmy," and admitted that when she lay in bed next to them she wished they were Dean.

Dean's last important romance was with 19-year-old Ursula Andress, who had just been imported to America from Switzerland and was being billed as "the female Marlon Brando." At first she said, "He nice but only boy." As their relationship developed, Dean discovered that she was one of the few girls who wouldn't put up with his shenanigans. Dean even studied German "so Ursula and I can fight better." When she finally got fed up with his moods and left him, he was shocked.

HIS THOUGHTS: "My mother died on me when I was nine years old. What does she expect me to do? Do it all by myself?"

—A. W.

The Juggler

W. C. FIELDS (Jan. 29, 1880–Dec. 25, 1946)

HIS FAME: William Claude Dukenfield was the product of English working-class parents who lived in Philadelphia, a city he always spoke of with disgust. He left home at the age of 11 to pursue a career as a vaudeville juggler, adopting the stage name W. C. Fields. In 1915 he settled in New York and worked in various Broadway reviews, notably the *Ziegfeld Follies*. He moved to Hollywood to break into the movies, and people soon flocked to their local theaters to see the man with the bulbous nose, cigar, and top hat be tormented by children and dogs in films such as *Tillie and Gus* (1933), *The Bank Dick* (1940), and *Never Give a Sucker an Even Break* (1941).

LOVE LIFE: Much of Fields' boyhood was spent in poverty, and as an adult he was constantly fearful of being broke. As a result, his girl friends found him a tight man with a dollar.

In 1900 Fields married Hattie Hughes, his vaudeville assistant, who bore him a son named Claude. Although Fields faithfully supported his wife and child for 40 years, he called them "vultures" who were always after his money, and he very rarely saw them. A typical Fields letter to Hattie in 1933 began, "I am in receipt of your complaint No. 68427." Fields and Hattie never obtained a legal divorce.

For seven years during the 1920s, Fields shared an apartment with Ziegfeld show girl Bessie Poole, who also bore him a son. Although Fields never publicly acknowledged the child, he sent Bessie a check every month. Friends said of Fields that he changed mistresses every seven years, but the truth is that few of his loves lasted that long. His stinginess, his drinking, and his unwarranted suspicion were more than most women could take. In Hollywood, Fields began the practice of hiring detectives to follow his girl friends. One of them, a New York show girl, fell in love with her detective and married him.

In 1932, when Fields was 54 years old, he was introduced to 24-year-old Carlotta Monti, a dark-haired, olive-skinned beauty of Italian-Mexican-Spanish descent. He doffed his stovepipe hat, bowed low, and said, "It is a pleasure, my dusky beauty." On their first date Monti asked him if he had ever been married. "I was married once," Fields replied. "In San Francisco. I haven't seen her for many years. The great earthquake and fire of 1906 destroyed the marriage certificate. There's no legal proof. Which proves that earthquakes aren't all bad."

In her book, *W.C. Fields and Me*, Carlotta describes their love life: "Beginning with the first intimate night together when we consummated our love … it was ecstasy…. Woody [her pet name for Fields] seemed starved for real love and affection, and I gave it to him in large quantities…. He was as much a perfectionist in his lovemaking as he was in his juggling. He never dropped a cigar box accidentally, and by the same token, he never fumbled during a golden moment." However, alcohol eventually disrupted his sex drive completely.

Carlotta put up with Fields' eccentricities for the last 13 years of his life. He would sometimes leave piles of money around the house to test her. Wise to him, she would add $5 to the pile to confuse him. When it came her turn to be followed by a detective, she responded by leading the man on long meandering drives around the California countryside, knowing that Fields would be charged by the mile. As soon as he got his first bill from the detective agency, Fields ended the surveillance.

When Fields died in 1946, his final words were, "Goddamn the whole friggin' world and everyone in it but you, Carlotta."

HIS THOUGHTS: "Women are like elephants to me: I like to look at them, but I wouldn't want to own one."

—M.J.T. and D.W.

In Like Flynn

ERROL FLYNN (June 20, 1909–Oct. 14, 1959)

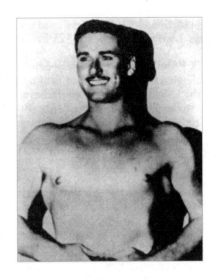

HIS FAME: One of the greatest swashbucklers in motion picture history, Errol Flynn was among Hollywood's top money-making stars in the late 1930s and early 1940s, appearing in such films as *Captain Blood, The Charge of the Light Brigade,* and The *Adventures of Robin Hood.*

HIS PERSON: In his prime Flynn stood 6 ft. 2 in., and his astonishingly handsome looks rivaled those of any idol of the silver screen. Born in Hobart, Tasmania, of Irish-American parentage, Flynn was a chronic runaway as a youth. He left home for good after finishing secondary school and spent the next few years traveling the South Seas. In the early 1930s he was leading a tour expedition of New Guinea when he met film producer Charles A. Chauvel. Soon after, Chauvel cast him as Fletcher Christian in the semidocumentary *In the Wake of the Bounty.* Bitten by the acting bug, Flynn landed a contract with Warner Bros. and spent the next 15 years playing action-adventure heroes in sea tales, costume epics, and war pictures.

In the 1950s Flynn moved first to Europe and then to Jamaica, meanwhile making a series of unsuccessful movies. He aged quickly—no doubt owing to high living, alcohol, and narcotics—and died of a heart attack at 50.

SEX LIFE: Errol Flynn boasted that he had spent between 12,000 and 14,000 nights making love. If he never actually reached that figure, it wasn't for lack of trying. Although he had three wives—actresses Lili Damita and Patrice Wymore, and Nora Eddington—Flynn did not practice fidelity during any of these unions and preferred to live apart from his wives and four children, once claiming, "The only real wives I have ever had have been my sailing ships."

Biographers have surmised that his emotional indifference to women was due to his relationship with his own mother, Marelle Young Flynn, who instilled in her son the idea that both sex and his genitals were dirty. Flynn was also obsessed with a fear of castration, having once been attacked by a knife-wielding Indian rickshaw driver. The blade, which barely missed Flynn's organs, left a deep scar in his groin.

Despite his constant sexual urges, Flynn rarely bragged about his endurance as a lover, but did claim to practice Oriental sexual techniques learned during a stay in Hong Kong. He was concerned about being able to perform whenever called upon, and was known to apply a pinch of cocaine to the tip of his penis as an aphrodisiac. His enjoyment of sex was heightened by watching other couples make love at the same time, and he also got a tremendous kick out of exhibiting himself—with a full erection—to his "straight" male friends. Flynn even installed a one-way mirror in his home so that he could observe his houseguests making love. He often indulged his taste for kinky sex in Mexico, where one could see men and women copulate on stage or have intercourse with animals. Flynn made no apologies for his self-proclaimed "wicked ways" and even urged his son, Sean, to follow in his footsteps, once sending the lad $25 for "condoms and/or flowers."

SEX PARTNERS: Certainly, Errol Flynn had a penchant for teenage girls. Nora Eddington was barely 18 and pregnant when they married, and at the time of his death he was planning to marry Beverly Aadland, then 17. When not working at the studio, Flynn would often drive with his good friend David Niven to Hollywood High School, where he would linger on the sidewalk and lament that the beautiful young girls he saw were "jailbait" or "San Quentin Quail."

In fact, Flynn's reputation as a lover stemmed partly from his being charged with statutory rape. In 1942 he was accused of having had intercourse with Betty Hansen, 17, and with Peggy LaRue Satterlee, 16. According to Hansen, a waitress with aspirations of becoming a studio employee, she had attended a tennis party at the house of one of Flynn's friends. She admitted to having flirted with Flynn, but feeling ill, she had gone upstairs to lie down. Flynn followed her and, meeting with no resistance on her part, took off her clothes except for her shoes and socks. Then, she explained, he "put his private parts in my private parts." Satterlee, who claimed Flynn had forced her to have intercourse twice on his schooner *Sirocco*, said that the actor had not made any effort to bare her feet either.

After a much-celebrated trial, Flynn was acquitted amid suspicions that the charges were not based on fact but reflected the desire of certain corrupt city officials to extort large bribes from the studio bosses. Also, the defense was able to establish that pending charges against the two girls—Hansen for oral intercourse and Satterlee for an illegal abortion—had been dropped after they agreed to testify against Flynn. Neither of these activities had involved Flynn.

Flynn emerged from the trial characterized as a "charming rogue," his popularity enhanced, and during the latter part of WWII, servicemen began to use the expression "in like Flynn" to denote a successful night with a woman. Flynn reportedly grew to despise both this expression—which implied he was a fun-loving rapist—and the snickers that greeted him when he walked into a room, but he still had not learned his lesson. Years later he was charged with raping a little-known attractive young French girl. Again he was acquitted, but the publicity intensified his self-destruction, which by this time included a dependence on vodka and an addiction to morphine.

Some 20 years after his death, in 1980, Flynn was once again in the news. Author Charles Higham published a biography, *Errol Flynn: The Untold Story*, which claimed that the swashbuckling actor had aided the Nazi and Japanese causes during WWII. Further, Higham claimed that Flynn had been bisexual, and had participated in homosexual affairs with actor Tyrone Power and writer Truman Capote. Two of Flynn's daughters, Deirdre and Rory, angered by the allegations in what they labeled "a dirty book," determined to prove the author's so-called facts were falsehoods. To clear their father's name, they considered filing suit against Higham.

HIS THOUGHTS: "There is only one aphrodisiac—the special woman you love to touch and see and smell and crush."

—*A.L.G. and the Eds.*

"Pa"

CLARK GABLE (Feb. 1, 1901–Nov. 16, 1960)

HIS FAME: Clark Gable reigned as "King of Hollywood" for more than 30 years, starring in 61 films between 1930 and 1960. Often cast as the ultimate macho male, Gable became one of the screen's greatest sex symbols. His portrayal of a newspaper man in *It Happened One Night* won him an Academy Award, but he gained his most lasting fame playing the role of Rhett Butler in *Gone with the Wind*.

Carole Lombard and Gable

HIS PERSON: Gable was raised by a strong-minded but indulgent stepmother without much interference from his itinerant oil-driller father. Never a scholar, Gable dropped out of high school in his junior year, and after putting in some time at a tire factory in his home state of Ohio and in the Oklahoma oil fields, he decided to pursue his dream of becoming an actor. Ignoring his father, who said that "acting was for sissies," Gable worked his way across the country as a roustabout in a traveling tent show. Ending up in Portland, Ore., he joined a small Portland theater group in which he received his first real dramatic training. More interested in the theater than in the movies, Gable nevertheless went to Hollywood and began working as an extra on movie sets.

Although studio executives were slow to realize Gable's potential, women quickly recognized his sexual magnetism. When MGM caught on, the studio fixed his decaying, crooked teeth and began grooming him as an "outdoorsy, he-man" type. Gable remained modest even after his rise to stardom and would make a point of striding through screaming hordes of fans to sign autographs, saying that if it weren't for them, he wouldn't have a job. An impeccable dresser who carried his 6-ft. 1-in. frame with grace, Gable was obsessed with cleanliness. He took several showers a day and shaved not only his armpits but his chest as well. Somewhat of a loner, he preferred the company of extras and studio technicians—men with whom he could drink and fish and hunt—to that of his movie-star peers. He refused to let his fame go to his head and mumbled after winning the Oscar, "I'm still going to wear the same size hat."

SEX LIFE: That women loved Gable and he loved them back is made evident by the dozens—perhaps hundreds—of affairs he carried on throughout his career. Some said he had a fixation for older women, and pointed to his first two marriages as proof. But those marriages seem to have been more a matter of convenience than of passion. Gable's first wife, Josephine Dillon, who was his acting coach and 17 years older than him, later claimed that she and Gable had no physical relationship, that theirs was a marriage "in name only." Gable next married a wealthy 46-year-old Houston divorcée, Ria Langham, who encouraged and mothered him considerably at the beginning of his career. Gable himself admitted to a preference for older women and once remarked, "The older woman has seen more, heard more, and knows more than the demure young girl ... I'll take the older woman every time."

Still, Gable wasn't firmly trapped in an older-woman syndrome. During one of his first leading-man roles he jumped into a red-hot affair with his co-star, Joan Crawford, who was 27 at the time. Crawford was to credit Gable later with "animal" attractiveness, which she attributed to the fact that "he had balls." She added that she didn't believe that any woman who worked with Gable "did not feel twinges of sexual urge beyond belief." Although Crawford and Gable were to remain friends for many years, they stoically cooled their romance on studio orders since they were both married to other people at the time.

Then he met Carole Lombard, the Hollywood screwball actress who was to become the greatest love of his life. Gable, who tended to be quiet and reserved, was instantly attracted to the petite, blond actress' zaniness and ribald humor. The two adopted the incongruous nicknames of "Ma" and "Pa" for each other and became inseparable. Lombard loved to pull pranks on Gable such as leaving a gift-wrapped knitted "cock-warmer" in his dressing room with a note: "Don't let it get cold. Bring it home hot for me." Irreverent about his sexy image, she told him that she'd arranged to have him make his "cockprint" as well as his footprints and handprints in front of Grauman's Chinese Theatre. Lombard was once heard to remark, "I adore Clark, but he's a lousy lay."

Lombard gamely trekked alongside Gable on his fishing and hunting expeditions, sleeping in the open and once even making love in a duck blind. When

Gable's divorce from Ria became final, the two eloped to Kingman, Ariz. After their marriage, Lombard tamed down considerably in order to fit in with Gable's sedate ways, causing a friend to comment that she was a different person from the one who had once flippantly remarked during a press conference that Gable wasn't circumcised. The only thing that marred the happiness of "Hollywood's favorite couple" was their failure to have children. "They were forever checking sperm," a friend said, and "tried every position known to humans," according to another. "They would have done it hanging out a window if somebody said you got pregnant that way." But no matter how much Gable loved Lombard, he would never be a one-woman man, and Lombard would periodically explode when rumors grew too hot about Gable's latest escapade with his current leading lady.

Gable was devastated by Lombard's death in a plane crash just three years after they were married. "Ma's gone," he said brokenly to a group of friends when her body was finally recovered. He was to spend the rest of his life searching for another Lombard. After going through an endless parade of women, ranging from a Palm Beach socialite to the daughter of a fishing resort owner, he recklessly plunged into a marriage with Lady Sylvia Ashley. The match ended quickly, and Gable later was to say he was drunk when he married her. At the age of 54, Gable was wed a fifth and final time to a former actress 10 years his junior, who was as close to a facsimile of Lombard as he was apt to find. Fair-haired, tiny, lovely Kay Spreckels was willing to fit herself into the mold set by Lombard, and she and Gable led a peaceful, quiet life on their ranch until he died of a heart attack after making *The Misfits*. They had one son, John, who was born five months after Gable's death.

SEX PARTNERS: Gable was promiscuous and often indiscriminate about whom he went to bed with. Screenwriter Anita Loos noted that Clark had "that old early American male idea that you must take on any girl that comes your way." Although the King could snap his fingers and get almost any woman he wanted, at times he preferred to go to bed with high-priced call girls. Asked why, when he could get it for free, Gable replied, "Because I can pay her to go away. The others stay around, want a big romance, movie lovemaking. I do not want to be the world's greatest lover." He also did not confine himself to attractive women. When an army buddy with whom he was stationed in Europe during WWII asked Gable why he was going out with a certain "dog," Gable said, "Well, she's there." Gable had one long-term love affair—it lasted over a decade—with a diminutive, plain-looking Hollywood female writer that was a secret to all but a few of his intimates. He slept with this woman regularly, and she once remarked to her closest friend, "Whenever Clark got on top of me and entered me, and started going, it never amounted to much and was never very good. But then I would open my eyes and realize this was *the* Clark Gable— Gable himself—and only then would I truly feel excited."

Gable also took advantage of a ready supply of leading ladies, making love to them both on and off the screen. Once, when looking at an MGM publicity photo of all the studio's female stars, Gable exclaimed admiringly, "What a wonderful display of beautiful women, and I've had every one of them!" Gable's name was linked romantically with nearly all his co-stars, from Grace Kelly to Ava Gardner to Jean Harlow, whether there was substance to the rumors or not. The King not only played the role of quintessential male, he was one. More than one actress was to remark, "I think every woman he ever met was in love with him." Marilyn Monroe said she "got goose bumps all over" when he accidentally touched her breast. Or as Joan Blondell put it, "He affected all females, unless they were dead."

—*L.K.S.*

Captain Bligh In Love

CHARLES LAUGHTON (July 1, 1899–Dec. 15, 1962)

HIS FAME: Laughton was respected as one of the most powerful and versatile character actors in both British and American films and in the theater. He won an Academy Award in 1933 for his performance in *The Private Life of Henry VIII.*

HIS PERSON: "I have got a face like an elephant's behind," said Laughton, and his large girth and less than handsome appearance made his desire to go on the stage seem strange to his hotel-keeping British parents. After serving in WWI, during which he was a front-line soldier and was gassed, he returned home

Laughton and Elsa Lanchester

to take up his apprenticeship in the respectable family business. Finally, at age 26, he convinced his parents to subsidize his training at the Royal Academy of Dramatic Art in London. Before long he was a well-known and much-sought-after character actor. He is best remembered by American audiences for his major film roles—King Henry VIII, Captain Bligh in *Mutiny on the Bounty* (1935), and Sir Wilfrid Robarts in *Witness for the Prosecution* (1957), all of which won him Oscar nominations. Laughton died in Los Angeles in 1962 of bone cancer.

SEX LIFE: Laughton made love with only one woman in his entire lifetime—actress Elsa Lanchester, his wife of 33 years—and with countless and mostly nameless young men. He met Lanchester at a rehearsal in 1927. Her initial response to him was not romantic: "He was plump, well, fat really, and pale." But they hit it off, they could talk, they amused each other, and they shared an interest in art and flowers. They fell in love, a love that would be sorely tested over the years, and were married in 1929.

The first two years of their marriage were happy ones, and apparently nothing happened to give the young bride a hint that her husband was homosexual. Then, as the result of a very ugly row with a boy-prostitute who insisted that he hadn't been paid, Laughton was forced to admit to his wife that he had long been a practicing homosexual, mostly with young hired companions. Upon hearing Laughton's confession, Elsa was dazed. She could only say, "It's perfectly all right. It doesn't matter. I understand." But it did matter. For the next week Elsa was stricken with deafness. As she told biographer Charles Higham: "I suppose I shut my ears off. I have since realized, or was told, that it was probably a sort of reaction to some news I really didn't want to hear." Finally, she was able to discuss the incident with Laughton. "Later on, I asked Charles what had happened. And he told me he was with this fellow on our sofa. The only thing I could say was, 'Fine. OK. But let's get rid of the sofa.'" After that, she would not consider having children. Although Elsa claimed that she simply was not fond of children, Laughton believed that she could not stand the idea of bearing a child whose father was a homosexual.

Yet their marriage continued, even though their sex life dwindled rapidly to nothing. They remained in love and continued to live together as close companions. Sexually, they both satisfied themselves with outside partners. Elsa had occasional affairs with other men over the years, and Laughton resumed his search for young males—the younger and, in most cases, the more anonymous, the better.

Laughton went through a short period of therapy to try to alter his sexual tastes, but soon gave it up. Although he would be sporadically troubled by guilt and fears of scandal (in those years homosexuality was against the law), the pattern was set. His wife kept her distance from most of his handsome young men, but in a few cases she got to know them quite well. "When he was with one in particular," she once said, "I used to go to the market every day and get two peach pies for them. I didn't mind. I don't mind a bit of peach pie myself."

Over the years there were apparently only two men who held Laughton's interest. One of them was a lean, handsome young actor whom Laughton met while in his 40s. He was involved with the young man off and on for over 20 years. When Laughton died, the young actor was a pallbearer. When in his 60s, Laughton found his other male love, a tall, good-looking member of the show-business community. The two traveled widely together until the end of Laughton's life.

—*R. W.S.*

The Divine Sarah

SARAH BERNHARDT (Oct. 22 or 23, 1844–Mar. 26, 1923)

HER FAME: One of the best-loved actresses of the modern theater, Sarah Bernhardt gained international acclaim with her performances in Victor Hugo's *Ruy Blas*, Racine's *Phèdre*, and the younger Dumas' *La Dame aux Camélias*. Her acting was characterized by an emotional intensity and inner fire which inspired poets and critics alike to sing her praises. Fellow actress Ellen Terry described her as "a miracle."

Bernhardt at age 35

HER PERSON: The daughter of a beautiful, unmarried milliner turned courtesan, Sarah was ignored by her mother. A sickly child, she suffered from tuberculosis and was not expected to live to adulthood. At 16 she hoped to become a nun. However, her mother's current lover, the Duc de Morny, half brother of Napoleon III, decided that Sarah should be trained as an actress. He used his influence to enroll her first in the Conservatoire, the French government's acting school, and two years later in the prestigious Comédie Française. She was forced to leave the Comédie in 1863 after she slapped another actress in a fit of anger.

Emotionally unpredictable, extremely thin, with a head of unruly, fair, curly hair, the distinctive young woman scored her first major triumph at the Odéon Theater in *Kean*, a play by Dumas *père*. Success followed success for the "nicely polished skeleton," and in 1880 she formed her own company and toured the world with her productions. Despite her increasing fame, Sarah continued to be plagued with stage fright. Her nervous agitation, combined with the emotional demands of her performance, would often cause her to faint after the last curtain call. Nor was she ever free of her tubercular problem, and she frequently was afflicted with spells during which she coughed up blood. Although her body was frail, her force of will was inexhaustible. She required little sleep and was said to have the energy of 10 people. Even after her leg was amputated in 1915, she kept to her demanding schedule until shortly before her death at age 78 in her Paris home.

LOVE LIFE: Reputed to have had over 1,000 affairs, the "Divine Sarah" herself proclaimed, "I have been one of the great lovers of my century." (Originally her mother had considered grooming Sarah as a courtesan, but the brash and independent girl was not temperamentally suited for that "lucrative form of slavery.") Her initial affair, at age 18, was with the Count de Kératry, but the first man who truly won her heart was Henri, Prince de Ligne. By Henri, the 20-year-old Sarah had a son, Maurice, whom many considered the real love of her life. While still in her 20s she became the toast of the Continent, and her devoted admirers included Gustave Doré, Victor Hugo, Edmond Rostand, Oscar Wilde, and Émile Zola. She was always attracted to men of talent, and she fully expected them to pay tribute to her in their art.

Although Sarah flung herself into her affairs with curiosity and passion, she rarely abandoned herself to them. Perhaps her childhood environment partly accounted for her caution. She once recalled, "My mother's house was always full of men, and the more I saw of them, the less I liked them." Nonetheless, the actress who moved in "a halo of glory" had a magnetic effect on both men and women, and she was adored by royalty.

In a pamphlet entitled "The Loves of Sarah Bernhardt," the farfetched allegation was made that she had seduced all the European heads of state, including the pope himself. There is evidence that she did indeed have "special relationships" with the Prince of Wales (later Edward VII) and Prince Napoleon, nephew of Napoleon I, to whom she had been introduced by George Sand. As for the other leaders of Europe, although she may not have occupied their beds, it is clear that she won their hearts. Emperor Franz Josef of Austria, King Alfonso of Spain, and King Umberto of Italy showered her with gifts; King Christian IX of Denmark lent her his yacht; and the Archduke Frederick allowed her to use his château.

In the theater, her emotional sparks gained intensity by the fact that her leading men usually became her lovers, the affairs often lasting only as long as the show ran. Once captivated by the Bernhardt charm, however, her conquests stayed on as friends. As she grew older, she continued the practice of having affairs with her leading men. At age 66, while on tour in the U.S., Sarah established a four-year liaison with Dutch-born Lou Tellegen, an untalented blond Hercules at least 35 years her junior. In his autobiography, *Women Have Been Kind*, he acknowledged that the time he had spent as her leading man had been "the most glorious four years of my life."

Her only marriage, in 1882, was to the outrageously handsome but dissolute Aristides Jacques Damala, a Greek diplomat-playboy-actor 11 years her junior. Described as a cross between Casanova and the Marquis de Sade, he flaunted his infidelities and seemed to take particular pleasure in humiliating Sarah in public. They separated within a year, but during the last months of his life she served as his devoted nurse. He died in 1889, ravaged by addictions to morphine and cocaine.

QUIRKS: Among Sarah Bernhardt's many eccentricities was her well-publicized satin-lined rosewood coffin. Given the doctors' verdict that she did not have long to live, the teenage Sarah entreated her mother to buy her this coffin so that she would not be consigned to "an ugly bier." She sometimes slept in it, and she had herself photographed in it more than once. In her book *The Memoirs of Sarah Barnum*, a thinly disguised, obscene "biography" of Sarah Bernhardt, actress Marie Colombier claimed Sarah "demanded that her intimate friends should keep her company in the narrow box. Some of them hesitated, because this funereal furniture killed their desires."

HER THOUGHTS: Shortly before WWI, author Octave Mirbeau asked Sarah Bernhardt when she intended to give up love. She responded, "When I draw my last breath. I hope to live as I have always lived. The strength of my energy and vitality lies entirely in their subservience to my destiny as a woman."

—The Eds.

Love's Victim

ELEONORA DUSE (Oct. 3, 1859–Apr. 21, 1924)

HER FAME: In a career rivaled only by that of the legendary Sarah Bernhardt, Duse established herself as one of the greatest, most versatile, most powerful actresses in the history of the theater.

HER PERSON: Duse's story is a classic tale of rags to riches, of anonymity to world renown. She was born in a small hotel in Vigevano, Italy, the child of poor, itinerant theatrical parents. During the course of the next half century the tiny, dynamic woman, with her dark hair and enormous eyes, electrified audiences in Europe and America in a wide variety of roles. She was highly acclaimed for her performance in the

title role of Zola's *Thérèse Raquin* and for her portrayals of Ophelia and Electra. She was also praised for her interpretations of the difficult roles provided by Ibsen, including Nora in *A Doll's House*. Of her uncanny power, the famous critic James Huneker said: "Duse's art borders on the clairvoyant ... her silences are terrifying." Unlike other great actresses of her time, she played older roles as she herself aged. "No wigs," she said, "they must accept me with my white hair." She even refused to wear makeup.

Disillusioned with her acting career and troubled by fragile health, Duse retired from the theater in 1909, but when WWI broke out she gave unstintingly of her energy and money to help wounded soldiers and their families. Her fortune depleted, she returned to the theater in 1921. In 1923 she appeared at the Metropolitan Opera House to launch a triumphant tour of the U.S. While in Pittsburgh, Pa., she caught a severe chill and died there in 1924.

Flavio Andò, "beautiful but dumb"

LOVE LIFE: Duse suffered the loss of both parents when she was a teenager. When Eleonora's mother died, a cruel fellow actress suggested that the young girl sell herself to obtain money for a mourning dress. Indeed, for a young actress alone and unprotected in the rough-and-tumble world of the 19th-century Italian theater, it must have been very difficult to preserve her virginity. But preserve it she did, although she was a passionate young woman. When she was ready to be initiated into the joys of sensuality, she sought a clever, experienced man of taste, a man who could teach her not only about sex but about art, literature, and music. Martino Cafiero, a well-known writer considerably older than Duse, was, she decided, the right man. Their relationship set a pattern that would last her whole lifetime. A passionate affair—not only of the heart and the senses but of the mind as well—would begin happily, inevitably run its course, and almost always end in heartbreak and disaster, only to be followed by another such affair.

Duse never lacked fascinating men to pay court to her dramatic sensuality. "Her power of attraction," said the actor-producer Aurélien Marie Lugné-Poë, "was unimaginable, for the very reason, perhaps, that it was satanic."

SEX PARTNERS: Martino Cafiero was the first in a long, carefully selected parade of witty, handsome, exciting lovers. Their affair ended after their son died and Cafiero deserted her. Duse then married her leading man, Tebaldo Checchi, a considerate, thoughtful, consoling man who provided a welcome stability in this first (but certainly not last) period of heartbreak in Duse's life.

She loved Checchi in her way—he was the only man she ever married and was the father of her daughter—but she was soon attracted to another actor, the strikingly beautiful, romantic Flavio Andò. Her affair with him broke up her marriage, but she quickly tired even of the dashing Andò. "He was beautiful but dumb," was her verdict.

Her next noteworthy affair, which many believe provided the most pro-found emotional experience of her life, was with Arrigo Boito. He was a composer and a novelist, a man of wide-ranging taste and sensitivity who opened Duse's mind to new levels of metaphysical and sensual beauty. Even after their affair ended, she continued to love him. When he died in 1918, she couldn't sleep or eat for days.

In 1895 the poetic genius Gabriele D'Annunzio stormed backstage in Rome, threw himself at her feet, kissed the hem of her dress, and cried out, "*O grande amatrice!*" ["O great love!"] (Years earlier, as a teenager, he had fright-ened her when he approached her with the proposal that they become lovers.) D'Annunzio was the quintessence of the romantic lover that her whole life seemed to cry out for. It was rumored that D'Annunzio would leap naked onto his sorrel stallion, race from their villa to the sea, and plunge into the surf. Duse would wait for him on the shore, ready to wrap a magnificent purple mantle about her hero. It was also said that they drank strange brews from the skull of a virgin in the light of the full moon. He had, one contemporary said, "the cold, steely gaze of a man who knows his goal, and will reach it regardless of cost, perhaps also of suffering." However, as usual, it was Duse who was to suf-fer. Her apparent pursuit of misery reinforced one critic's description of her as "the actress for all unhappy women."

D'Annunzio was an artistic vampire who sucked the life's blood from those close to him in order to provide material for his art. In 1900 he exploited his passionate affair with Duse in a novel called *The Flame of Life*. His description of a handsome, romantic younger man's affair with a fading older woman caused a public scandal and broke Duse's heart. Years after their affair had ended they met, and D'Annunzio, ever the flatterer, took her hand in his, gazed into her eyes, and murmured, "Not even you can imagine how much I loved you." Duse replied, "And now not even you can imagine how much I have forgotten you!"

After her disastrous affair with D'Annunzio, the middle-aged Duse found temporary solace with a 23-year-old lesbian who wrote one play for her and promised more. When they visited author Mabel Dodge Luhan in her Italian villa, Duse and her protégée (known only as Signorina R.) created such a com-motion in their bedroom that Mabel's husband was forced to move from the adjoining room in order to obtain a decent night's sleep. The young playwright was bursting with ideas for new vehicles for Duse, but she explained to Mabel that she required a "release" in order to accomplish her creative work. Mabel shunned her sexual advances and later learned that the girl had gone insane after she and Duse had left for London.

HER ADVICE: To women who sought advice on love, Duse preached inde-pendence. "Work; don't ask support from any man but only love; then your life will have the meaning you are looking for."

—*R. W.S.*

The Jersey Lily

LILLIE LANGTRY, née Emilie Charlotte Le Breton
(Oct. 13, 1853–Feb. 12, 1929)

HER FAME: The most celebrated "professional beauty" of Queen Victoria's London, Lillie was a pinup girl, an artist's model, an actress, and the mistress of princes and millionaires. Her beauty and wit were praised by Oscar Wilde, Mark Twain, and George Bernard Shaw, among others. Gilbert and Sullivan put her to lyrics and music: "Oh, never, never, never since we joined the human race / Saw we so exquisitely fair a face."

HER PERSON: Lillie was born on the British Isle of Jersey, the daughter of a clergyman. As a child she was something of a tomboy, but by the time she was 16 her father had been obliged to repulse several suitors. To console the girl, he allowed her a trip to London. Dazzled by city life, she vowed to live there one day. Her escape from Jersey came in the form of Edward Langtry, a moderately well-to-do yachtsman whom she married when she was 21. Edward provided her with a passport into London society.

The statuesque Lillie was 5 ft. 8 in. and had masses of red-gold hair. She had a flawless complexion and at the height of her fame appeared in advertisements for Pears soap. One of the first celebrities to endorse a commercial product, Lillie was paid £132, a sum equal to her weight. Her figure, regularly compared to that of a goddess, was maintained through jogging.

Lillie posed for the most famous artists of her day, among them James Whistler, John Millais, and Edward Burne-Jones. Her image—reproduced on postcards—was displayed on the walls of army barracks, student dormitories, and ships' cabins, thus beginning the pinup picture vogue. When she was 24, all manner of men desired her. The famous 78-year-old French author Victor Hugo once toasted her, "Madam, I can celebrate your beauty in only one way—by wishing I were three years younger."

She made her theatrical debut in 1881, and although her acting talents were uneven, she nevertheless became the toast of both England and America, playing opposite such leading men as Lionel Atwill and the young Alfred Lunt. In Texas, the infamous Judge Roy Bean renamed his saloon the Jersey Lily and moved it to the town of Langtry. After the judge's death, Lillie was bequeathed his revolver, which had reputedly been used several times to defend her honor.

In 1897, while Lillie was enjoying international acclaim, her hapless husband died broke in an insane asylum. Two years later she married Hugo de Bathe, who succeeded to a baronetcy in 1907, making Lillie Lady de Bathe. Using £55,000 of her own money, she remodeled a derelict London playhouse, the Imperial Theatre, and spent the next two decades amusing herself with acting, baccarat, and occasional visits to her friend Queen Mary. When she was 64 and a grand-mother, most of her admirers had fallen away. On a visit to New York, she was seen visiting public dance halls where she paid gigolos 50¢ to dance with her. Yet, some vestige of her beauty remained. Oscar Wilde had predicted she would "be a beauty still at 85," and she was certainly a beauty still upon her death at 74. Hugo de Bathe was useful to her as an official escort after her retirement to Monaco in 1918, but for the most part he occupied himself with chorus girls and debutantes in Nice. Lillie died, wealthy and alone, in Monaco in 1929.

SEX LIFE: Lillie enjoyed sex, but not nearly so much as she enjoyed her own glamour and notoriety. Sex was the serious business of her life, her ladder to the top. She believed that scandal was the best form of publicity and provided ample fodder for Victorian gossips.

In Lillie's heyday, London's most ambitious hostesses entered her name as a matter of course on any guest list that included her obese lover, Albert Edward, Prince of Wales (later to become King Edward VII). She was also romantically linked with Yankee millionaire Freddie Gebhard and George Alexander Baird, one of the wealthiest men in England. The mercenary Lillie parlayed these rela-tionships into a fortune in diamonds, townhouses, a racing stable, and plenty of ready cash.

For the most part, Lillie's men tended to be rich, ineffectual, and easily dominated. "Men are born to be slaves," she once remarked. Edward Langtry was a sexual dud and a drunkard, and when his fortune dwindled he was of no use to her at all. Freddie Gebhard catered to her every whim, while tolerating her peccadilloes with doglike loyalty. George Baird delighted in beating Lillie, but every time he did so she made him pay her £5,000. She could also be haughty with her lovers. Crown Prince Rudolf of Austria-Hungary once gave her an emerald ring. Angered by an argument with him, she yanked off the ring and threw it into the fireplace. The crown prince fell to his knees, desperate to retrieve the emerald from the burning coals. Disgusted, Lillie told her friends, "I couldn't love him after that."

Lillie's dominant nature and open disregard for Victorian morality enthralled Prince Albert. They would meet regularly at the homes of friends, ostensibly for tea, and were given adjoining accommodations during weekend retreats. The intimate details of their affair were kept discreetly hidden, although the fact that they were lovers was no great secret. When Albert once complained, "I've spent enough on you to buy a battleship," Lillie snapped back, "And you've spent enough in me to float one!" Edward Langtry, meanwhile, was bribed into silence. Lillie remained Albert's mistress until she playfully dropped a piece of ice down his back at a party. The prince was not amused and abruptly ended the affair.

On the rebound, Lillie consoled herself with yet another prince, Louis Alexander of Battenberg, Albert's nephew. Louis, an officer in the Royal Navy, was perhaps the only man Lillie ever really loved and the father of her only child, a daughter named Jeanne-Marie.

To Lillie's credit, she was never a hypocrite about her many affairs and could even be amused by bawdy items such as this one from a scandal sheet of the time: "We heard that Mrs. Langtry has lost her parrot.... That the lady possessed such a bird we were unaware, but we knew she had a cockatoo."

HER THOUGHTS: "We women begin the world with such limited prospects, and we surprise ourselves sometimes."

—*M.S.*

Unlucky In Love

LILLIAN RUSSELL (Dec. 4, 1861–June 6, 1922)

HER FAME: In the era just before radio and motion pictures, when the great medium of entertainment was the stage, Lillian Russell was the ranking American star. Celebrated for her great beauty, her clear soprano voice, and her flamboyant lifestyle, she specialized in light operatic and musical comedy roles.

HER PERSON: Helen Louise Leonard's parents were advanced thinkers for their day. Her father was a midwestern publisher of agnostic tracts, her mother an ardent suffragette. At 17, accompanied by her mother, Helen left Clinton, Ia., for New York to study voice with Dr. Leopold Damrosch. Too impatient to endure the long years of training for a career in grand opera, she made her debut as a teenage chorine in Gilbert and Sullivan's *H.M.S. Pinafore*. A golden blonde with cornflower-blue eyes, a peaches-and-cream complexion, and an exaggerated hourglass figure, she soon came to the attention of impresario Tony Pastor, who promoted her to overnight stardom as "Lillian Russell, the English

Ballad Singer." Russell went on to sing the role of D'Jemma in *The Great Mogul: or, the Snake Charmer*, to star in Jacques Offenbach's *The Grand Duchess*, and to appear in the vaudeville and burlesque vehicles *Whoop-dee-doo* and *Hokey Pokey*. But such was her stature that, whatever the role, her arrival onstage was greeted by a "rush of pure awe." She reigned as the toast of Broadway for some 30 years.

LOVE LIFE: Russell, who was said to possess the enchantment of a Dresden shepherdess and the radiance of Venus emerging from her bath, exuded a sexual magnetism comparable to that of Marilyn Monroe. She was surrounded by wealthy and titled suitors who showered her with flowers, furs, jewels ($100,000 worth from one anonymous admirer alone)—even cold cash. But like the latter-day sex goddess, Russell also had a streak of vulnerability, which involved her in a succession of disastrous marriages.

Russell married at 18. Her husband was Harry Braham, the musical conductor of her first show, and she bore him a child, who died while in the care of a nursemaid. (The parents were busy at the theater at the time.) The Brahams' marriage never recovered from this loss. Seduced again by music, she eloped a few years later with Edward Solomon, a composer and conductor who neglected to tell his bride that he was already legally married, and also failed to provide for Russell and their daughter. Husband number three was Giovanni Perugini (real name: Jack Chatterton), a caricature of the handsome tenor, vain, fatuous, and, as it happened, gay. Theirs was derisively called "a marriage of convenience—his," for Perugini was so absorbed in the advancement of his career that he left Russell a "kissless bride." ("I love you too much to defile you," he claimed.) Russell, who passed her wedding night playing poker, was not amused, particularly when her husband began verbally abusing her in public. She left Perugini after two months of marriage when he tried to throw her out of a seventh-story window. "When the woman is the breadwinner, the superior in both intelligence and disposition," Russell complained, "she should at least be respected and not nagged at and worried...." But Perugini had his side too. In his defense, he told a newspaper reporter: "Do you realize the enormity of this woman's offense—her crime? Do you know what she did to me? Why, sir, she took all the pillows; she used my rouge; she misplaced my manicure set; she used my special handkerchief perfume for her bath; ... Once she threatened to spank me, and she did, with a hairbrush, too. You can't expect a fellow to take a spanking with equanimity, can you?"

Her fourth and final husband was Alexander P. Moore, a politically ambitious Pennsylvania newspaper publisher, who offered her stability and respectability if not grand passion.

Russell was painted in the press of the Gay Nineties as a scarlet woman, a modern Jezebel. It was rumored that she smoked cigarettes (which ladies simply did not do), conducted orgies on the tiger-skin rugs in her New York townhouse, and went out with a circus strong man. Actually, she was involved in a long-standing affair with Jesse Lewisohn, heir to a copper fortune and a fellow poker player. Together they made up a frequent foursome with "Diamond Jim" Brady, the corpulent salesman of steel railway cars, and Edna McCauley, a woman whom Brady passed off as his niece for 12 years. Unhappily for Russell, however, this was to be another star-crossed love affair. Lewisohn eloped with McCauley, leaving Russell to console herself with Brady.

In fact, theirs was a unique friendship. It centered on their huge appetites. One appetite they shared was a taste for high living. Brady overindulged himself in everything except alcohol. It was his habit to give away everything he owned once a year and then to replace it all in a flurry of buying. He customarily wore up to $250,000 worth of precious gems. Their second shared appetite was for the pleasures of the table. Russell was by now a well-upholstered 165 lb., and Brady was a king-size 250 lb. Russell was the only woman he had ever met who could keep up with him at the table; the two of them often got together just to gorge themselves on several trays of well-buttered sweet corn. (Brady often single-handedly depleted the entire pantry at Charles Rector's restaurant on Broadway. After his death, his stomach was found to be six times normal size.) Brady proposed marriage to Russell several times, once by spilling a million dollars into her lap. She declined with thanks, fearing it would wreck a beautiful friendship, but she often took him along on her dates with other men.

In her 50s Russell retreated from the stage to a second career as a syndicated columnist, offering advice on health, beauty, and love. She also lent her celebrity to the cause of women's suffrage. When, as the greatest sex symbol of her day, whose profile was practically a national institution, she marched the length of New York's Fifth Avenue in the great suffrage parade of 1915, it was one of her proudest performances.

—C.D. and M.S.

III

Painting The Town

Painter In Paradise

PAUL GAUGUIN (June 7, 1848–May 8, 1903)

HIS FAME: Generally regarded as the best Postimpressionist painter to come out of France, Gauguin gained fame and honor, albeit posthumously, for brilliantly colored, highly subjective works of art depicting unspoiled Polynesian life. His paintings include *Daydream, Two Tahitian Women*, and the sprawling canvas *Where Do We Come From? What Are We? Where Are We Going?*

Gauguin in 1888

HIS PERSON: Born in Paris, three-fourths French and one-fourth Peruvian Creole, young Paul was taken to live in Lima, Peru, in 1851 when Napoleon III staged a coup d'état in France. Nudity was commonplace in South America, and these early experiences affected him strongly. All his life he felt most comfortable among naked women. Paul returned to France with his mother in 1855, and at age 17 he decided to explore the world as a sailor. Six years later he quit the sea for the more respectable but no less uncertain life of a stockbroker. The French Bourse enriched him for a time, but when the Paris exchange crashed in 1883, he decided to chuck it all and concentrate full-time on his hobby—painting. The decision ruined his marriage, doomed him to a life of penury, and gave the world some of its most treasured art. Gauguin's vivid, primitive canvases represented a departure from traditional art. Instead of reproducing an image with photographic fidelity, he chose to project his mind's eye and turned to primitive cultures for inspiration. He made little money at it.

Gauguin befriended other painters of the period, among them Pissarro, Cézanne, and Van Gogh, and joined in the Impressionist exhibitions of the 1880s. For 10 weeks toward the end of 1888 he lived and worked with Van Gogh in "the yellow house" in Arles, France. Their incompatibility drove Gauguin to Paris. Increasingly alienated from his wife as well as from Western civilization, Gauguin managed to sell 30 paintings in 1891 and booked passage to Tahiti. Except for a brief return to Europe in 1893, he spent the rest of his life in the South Seas, painting and sculpting. He died bitter and broke, on Hiva Oa in the Marquesas Islands.

SEX LIFE: From his early days as a teenage seaman to his last months as a dying syphilitic on the Marquesas, Gauguin had an extremely active sex life, even though a large, bumpy nose dominated his angular face and he could hardly be called handsome. With his marriage in 1873 to Mette Sophie Gad, a tall, blond Danish governess, he settled into what promised to be a life of respectability and comfort. Then one day in 1883 Gauguin came home from the stock exchange and announced, "I've handed in my resignation. From now on I shall paint every day." Mette, stunned and outraged, hoped that this was just some phase Gauguin was going through. His in-laws in Copenhagen, Denmark, where the couple lived for a time, ridiculed his aspirations. The resultant strain and lack of money caused the Gauguins to separate. Still, even after leaving for Tahiti he clung to the hope that his wife and five children would one day join him there. They never did.

In Tahiti in 1891, Gauguin found artistic inspiration and all the breasts he could fondle. At first he reveled in the local custom of welcoming a different native woman into his hut each night, but he soon learned that such promiscuity hindered his work. He longed for his own *vahine* ("woman"). He set out to find one, and at a neighboring village he was offered the hand of a nubile native, barely into her teens, named Tehura. Gauguin was instantly attracted to her. Assured that she was entering the union willingly and that she was free from disease, Gauguin took her to his hut. After a week's trial marriage she agreed to remain permanently. With Tehura by his side, frequently as his model, the artist turned out much work. Inspired one night by her fear of the *tupapau*, or evil spirit, he created *The Spirit of the Dead Is Watching*.

In 1893 he sailed for France, leaving a pregnant Tehura behind. In Paris he renewed his relationship with a former mistress, a simple, withdrawn seamstress named Juliette Huet. He also began an affair with a 13-year-old waif known as Anna the Javanese, who was half Indian, half Malay. Anna turned out to be disastrous for him. She kept him from his work, and, when they went to Brittany, her unpopularity among townspeople was immediately evident. One afternoon she stuck out her tongue and thumbed her nose at a group of children who were making fun of her outlandish clothes. The incident touched off a melee that ended with Gauguin's being kicked unconscious by a gang of 15 fishermen. Gauguin had barely recuperated when Anna deserted him after carefully stripping his studio of all valuables except his paintings.

When Gauguin returned to Tahiti in 1895, he expected to resume housekeeping with Tehura. But she had meanwhile married an islander. Although she did visit the painter for about a week as a sort of hut-warming present, she was frightened by his syphilitic sores and went back to her husband. Gauguin had lost his mate, but many others filled the void. "My bed has been invaded every night by young hussies running wild," he complained at one point. "Yesterday I had three." Looking for a "serious woman for the house," he briefly settled down with a pretty 14-year-old named Pahura, but she was not as stimulating as Tehura. Still, he did a nude of her, *Arii Vahine* ("The Noblewoman"), which he considered "the best I have ever painted."

In 1901 he moved to a 1 1/4-acre lot on one of the Marquesas, where he built a hut that he decorated with pornographic photos. In a bed into whose wooden frame Gauguin had carved an erotic scene, he slept with virtually any native woman willing to overlook the open sores festering on his legs. Whenever a new girl entered his hut, he would explore her body underneath her dress and say to her, "I must paint you." Although his syphilis grew progressively worse, it was a heart attack that eventually killed him in 1903.

Gauguin's son by Pahura, named Émile, boasted of his illustrious parentage and always hoped to become a painter of some note himself, but he died in poverty at the age of 80, in January of 1980.

HIS THOUGHTS: "In Europe intercourse between men and women is a result of love. In Oceania love is a result of intercourse. Which is right? The man or woman who gives his body is said to commit a small sin. That is debatable.... The real sin is committed by the man or woman who sells his body."

"Women want to be free. That's their right. And it is certainly not men who stand in their way. The day a woman's honor is no longer located below the navel, she will be free. And perhaps healthier, too."

—*W.A.D.*

The Dejected Dutchman

VINCENT VAN GOGH (Mar. 30, 1853–July 29, 1890)

HIS FAME: Among Dutch painters, Van Gogh, a Postimpressionist, is generally considered second only to Rembrandt. His masterpieces include *The Potato Eaters* and *L'Arlésienne*.

HIS PERSON: Born in Zundert, the Netherlands, Van Gogh was the son of a clergyman. At 16 he was apprenticed to art dealers Goupil and Co., working first in the firm's office in The Hague and later at its branches in London and Paris. After wandering from job to job, he eventually turned to religion. In 1879 Van Gogh ministered to the poor in Le Borinage, a Belgian coal-mining region, until a conflict with church authorities led to his dismissal. In great despair, he found solace in painting. From 1880 until his suicide 10 years later he turned out hundreds of watercolors, oils, and sketches. Regrettably he lived to see only

Van Gogh at 19

one painting—*The Red Vine*—sold. He lived on an allowance from his deeply devoted brother Theo. Perhaps Vincent's beautiful ideas were too unorthodox for his time. For example, he once had a fight with his art instructor at the Antwerp Academy of Art over the proper way to draw a woman. Asked to draw the Venus de Milo, Vincent endowed her with large hips, enraging his teacher, who slashed at the drawing. "God damn you!" yelled Vincent. "A woman must have hips and buttocks and a pelvis in which she can hold a child!"

In 1886 he moved to Paris, where he fell in with such artists as Toulouse-Lautrec and Paul Gauguin. Toward the end of 1888 he and Gauguin lived and worked together in Arles, in the south of France. Although the pair produced prodigious amounts of work, they were temperamentally incompatible, and their love-hate relationship provoked many feuds. During one quarrel, Gauguin refused to eat at the same table with Van Gogh, citing hygienic reasons and their differing outlooks on life. After another heated argument, Van Gogh, jealous of Gauguin's success with the Arles prostitutes, cut off part of his own left ear. The incident had definite sexual overtones: Van Gogh put the ear in an envelope and took it to a prostitute who preferred him to Gauguin. When the lady opened the envelope containing the bloody ear, she fainted.

Van Gogh suffered recurrent fits of madness, voluntarily spent a year in an asylum, and ultimately committed suicide by shooting himself in the stomach while hiding behind a manure heap in a farmyard. He was 37. His genius was not fully recognized until more than a decade after his death.

LOVE LIFE: It is quite possible that if Van Gogh had been more successful in love, he would have lived longer—but he might never have picked up a brush. The failure to find lasting female companionship throughout his life contributed to his breakdown and suicide.

One of Van Gogh's early bouts of depression followed his rejection in 1874 by Ursula Loyer, his landlady's daughter. After concealing his feelings for months while working for the Goupil Gallery in London, he suddenly exploded, blurting out his love to a shocked and repelled young lady. He repeated this performance with a second girl, his recently widowed cousin, Kee Stricker Vos, who was visiting the Van Gogh home in Etten. Again he hid his feelings until they erupted in an urgent proposal of marriage. "No! Never, never!" Kee replied and promptly returned to her parents in Amsterdam. This time Van Gogh did not give up so easily. Using borrowed money, he gave chase to Amsterdam, where he barged in on the Strickers during dinner. When he was announced, Kee ran out before he could talk to her. The Strickers tried to be polite, but Van Gogh would not leave until he saw his love. On his third visit, he plunged his hand into the flame of an oil lamp, vowing to keep it there until Kee appeared. Now more determined than ever to keep this apparent madman away from their daughter, the Strickers bluntly told Van Gogh that his suit was pointless.

By this time Van Gogh was sexually frustrated. "I must have a woman or I shall freeze and turn to stone," he once complained. Taking to the streets, he discovered that he liked prostitutes, because they were "sisters and friends" to him, outcasts like himself, and would not reject him. Van Gogh preferred faded, slightly older prostitutes whom he could nurture. He soon found the ideal candidate in a pregnant prostitute named Clasina Maria Hoornik, whom he called Sien ("His own"). She and her five-year-old daughter moved in with him, and she soon bore Van Gogh a son, Willem, whom he adored. Much to the shame of his family, Vincent lived with Sien for more than a year and considered marrying her. In return, Sien posed for him (she is the crouched nude figure in the "Sorrow" lithographs) and gave the artist a case of gonorrhea that put him into a hospital bed for more than three weeks. He did not resent this, however, feeling that the rigors of her childbearing were a far greater burden. But the idyll passed, as he saw Sien's true colors. She was slovenly, bitchy, and usually drunk. From then on, he no longer referred to her by name, but called her "the woman with whom I live," or just "the woman." When she eventually returned to the streets, Van Gogh lost his "family" and left The Hague.

In 1884 Van Gogh had a relationship such as he had never known before. This time a woman was chasing him. She was Margot Begemann, his next-door neighbor in Nuenen, a dowdy, sexually repressed 41-year-old spinster. She thought the artist was her last opportunity for marriage. Van Gogh compared her to a Cremona violin mangled by inept craftsmen. Yet, whether from pity or genuine affection or both, Van Gogh agreed to marry her. When her parents forbade the union, Margot responded by swallowing strychnine, which Vincent, in the nick of time, forced her to throw up. The marriage never took place.

In 1887 Van Gogh confided to his sister that he was going through a string of meaningless affairs "from which I emerge as a rule damaged and shamed and little else." He frequented Parisian brothels with friends like Toulouse-Lautrec, had an affair with a female café owner and another reportedly with a 19-year-old boy. He contracted venereal disease from time to time and complained of increasing impotence.

HIS THEORIES ON ART AND SEX: In a letter to a friend, Van Gogh expounded on the sexual and artistic merits of famous painters and writers.

Degas, he said, "does not like women, for he knows that if he loved them and fucked them he … would become insipid as a painter. He looks on while the human animals, stronger than himself, get excited and fuck…."

"Rubens! Ah, that one! he was a handsome man and a good fucker."

Delacroix: "He did not fuck much, and only had easy love affairs, so as not to curtail the time devoted to his work."

And so on about Courbet, Cézanne, and even Balzac.

Van Gogh summed up his comments pithily when he wrote: "Painting and fucking are not compatible; it weakens the brain…. If we want to be really potent males in our work, we must sometimes resign ourselves to not fucking much."

HIS THOUGHTS: "The world seems more cheerful if, when we wake up in the morning, we find we are no longer alone and that there is another human being beside us in the half-dark. That's more cheerful than shelves of edifying books and the whitewashed walls of a church…."

—*W.A.D., E.K., and A.W.*

The Deaf Lover

FRANCISCO DE GOYA (Mar. 30, 1746–Apr. 16, 1828)

HIS FAME: The leading Spanish artist of his day, Goya was both prolific and versatile. His work, much of it executed with a realism that bordered on caricature, ranged from official portraits of the Spanish court to gory scenes of war and torture, to religious themes, to *Los Caprichos*, a collection of more than 80 etchings satirizing Spanish society, including demonic depictions of witches; helpless human beings attacked by strange, vile creatures; and other phantasms of Goya's vivid imagination.

Goya's Self-Portrait, *1783*

HIS PERSON: Raised largely in Saragossa, Goya set out early to become an artist. His career was one of steady progress—designer of royal tapestries, member of the prestigious Academy of San Fernando in Madrid, court painter to both Charles III and Charles IV—until a near-fatal illness struck in 1792 when he was 46. He lay for a time paralyzed and nearly blind and complained of dizzy spells and funny noises in his head. Physicians diagnosed that he had syphilis. He recovered in about a year but was thereafter stone-deaf.

In 1795 he was chosen to succeed his brother-in-law Francisco Bayeu as painting director at the Academy of San Fernando, but because of his deafness he proved ineffective in the post and accepted instead the title of honorary director. Despite the political upheaval during and after the French occupation of Spain (1808-1814), Goya managed to survive as court painter. Even his sensual "Maja" paintings somehow escaped the wrath of the Inquisition, though formal charges of obscenity were lodged against him. But a crackdown on liberals in 1824 so threatened his security and peace of mind that he took refuge in Bordeaux, France, where he lived and worked in self-imposed exile.

SEX LIFE: While young, Goya sowed acres of wild oats, and once while studying art in Rome he raided a convent to kidnap an upper-class Italian girl boarding there. This led to a duel, which Goya won, and to a love affair with the Italian girl. In 1773, settled in Madrid, Goya called on a friend he had met during his travels, Francisco Bayeu, who was the official court painter for King Charles IV and Queen Maria Louisa. Francisco introduced Goya to his sister Josefa, an attractive russet blonde who was disarmingly simple and honest. Entranced by

Goya's Naked Maja

Josefa, Goya set out to seduce her. He succeeded. She was four months pregnant when Goya was forced to marry her on July 25, 1775. Five months later their first child, a son named Eusebio, was born. The boy did not survive his childhood. In all, Josefa gave birth to five—possibly six—children, but only one, a son named Xavier, lived to maturity. The marriage proved profitable to Goya in another way. His brother-in-law, after all, had court connections, and Bayeu was able to get Goya a steady job in the royal tapestry factory. Once Goya had entrée to the aristocratic ladies of Madrid, Josefa faded into the background of his life. Goya was moved to paint only one portrait of her.

The most desirable of the aristocratic women was the headstrong, spirited, promiscuous, 20-year-old Duchess of Alba, who had been wedded to the moody Marquis of Villafranca when she was 13. Goya lusted for her from the first day he saw her. He had reason to. Her beauty was breathtaking. A contemporary said of her: "The Duchess of Alba does not have a single hair on her head which would not kindle the flame of desire. There is not a more beautiful thing in the world.... When she walks in the street everybody watches her from the windows, and even the children stop playing in order to look at her."

Goya met the duchess casually at a social gathering. Then, one day in the summer of 1795, she called on him at his studio. She wanted him to paint her face, that is, she wanted a makeup job. Goya wrote his close friend Zapater that she "sneaked into my studio for this purpose and got away with it; needless to say, this gives me more pleasure than painting on canvas; I am supposed to do her full portrait."

After that he began to see the Duchess of Alba often. He wanted to possess her, and she wanted him. At last, in the words of the period, she granted him "her final favors." Ecstatic over his conquest, Goya confided in a letter to Zapater, *"I finally know what life means."*

When the Duchess of Alba's ailing husband died in 1796, she withdrew to her estate in Sanlucar de Barrameda in Andalusia to mourn the occasion properly. She took Goya along. They stayed together for several months. He devoted himself to painting and having sexual intercourse with her regularly. She posed for him both dressed and undressed. Goya painted her respectably clothed in black, but wearing rings on the index and middle fingers of her right hand; one ring was inscribed "Goya," the other "Alba." Moreover, she was shown pointing down to a phrase scratched in the sand that read, "*Solo Goya*" ("Only Goya"). Other representations of the duchess in Sanlucar were more revealing. There were hundreds of sketches, many of them showing her in total nudity. "One of them," wrote a contemporary, "shows the lady's beautiful nakedness from the back, with her buttocks, waist, and hips exposed." The duchess allowed Goya to save the drawings. On one of these he wrote, "It is madness to keep this, but each according to his own taste."

Returning to Madrid, the duchess temporarily abandoned Goya to have a love affair with an older man, Lt. Gen. Don Antonio Cornel. Embittered, Goya painted three pictures of the duchess that depicted her flightiness—one showing her with a double face. But by 1799 she was back in Goya's arms once more and posing for the two paintings that were to become the artist's most popular works, *The Naked Maja* and *The Clothed Maja*. The clothed version was to be hung in front of the naked one for propriety. Goya's nude of her was the first such oil to be depicted, in the words of André Malraux, as "erotic without being voluptuous." These two paintings the duchess kept for herself. They were later inherited by Manuel de Godoy, the queen of Spain's lover.

The Duchess of Alba died suddenly in July of 1802. She remembered her love for Goya in her will by bequeathing the sum of 3,500 reales annually to Goya's son Xavier. Ten years later Goya's wife, Josefa, died. The painter's son had married a wealthy trader's daughter by then and had his own residence. Goya was left quite alone.

He moved out of Madrid to a place by the side of the Manzanares River. There he met a lively and liberal-minded young woman named Leocadia Zorrilla de Weis. She was still married to a businessman, Isidro Weis, but soon her husband petitioned for a separation from his wife on the grounds of her "misbehavior and infidelity." Undoubtedly Goya, at 68, was making love to Leocadia. In 1814 she gave birth to a girl, whom she named Rosarito. Goya doted on the little girl and encouraged and trained her to paint, hoping in vain that Rosarito harbored real talent.

In 1824, fearful of the excesses of a new government in Spain, Goya, accompanied by Leocadia and little Rosarito, fled to France and settled down in a small house with a garden in Bordeaux. Hot-tempered Leocadia often argued with Goya, but generally she amused him and looked after him. Goya spent his time taking walks, painting a little, napping a lot. He died at the age of 82.

—*W.A.D. and I.W.*

Model Lover

AMEDEO MODIGLIANI (July 12, 1884–Jan. 24, 1920)

HIS FAME: One of this century's great original artists, Modigliani is famous for the 25 stone sculptures, approximately 350 paintings, and numerous drawings he produced during his short life. Most of his works are of women; many are nudes. Among the best-known are *Seated Nude, Little Girl in Blue*, and *Jeanne Hébuterne*.

Modigliani at 33

HIS PERSON: The youngest child of a Jewish merchant family, Modigliani was born in Leghorn, Italy, just as a business crash forced his father into bankruptcy. A quirk in Italian law eased the family's pain: A bankrupt could keep a bed in which a woman had recently given or was about to give birth. At the moment of Modigliani's birth, officials were seizing the household goods, but the family took full advantage of the law and heaped the maternal bed with personal possessions and valuables. That incident, in which good fortune was salvaged from a dire predicament, is perhaps symbolic of Modigliani's life.

In 1895 and 1898 he contracted typhus. Forced to quit school, he turned to painting, which, except for a four-year period devoted to sculpting, he never left.

Moving to Paris in 1906, Modigliani was swept up in the bohemian milieu of that city's artists (Picasso among them). A prodigious drinker, Modigliani often stumbled through the streets drunk—and sometimes naked. His fights with other men over women were legion. He consumed enormous amounts of cocaine and hashish. In 1917 his one-man show consisting almost entirely of female nudes was closed by the police, who judged his paintings indecent. It was the only exhibition of his paintings during his lifetime. Through it all, Modigliani continued to paint until tubercular meningitis took his life. His fame while he was alive was restricted to the Parisian art community, but by 1922 he had become internationally acclaimed.

SEX LIFE: Modigliani loved women. Hundreds, maybe even thousands, were made love to by this elegantly handsome painter. While still a schoolboy, he noticed how girls were smitten by his good looks. Legend places his loss of virginity at 15 or 16 years of age, when, it is said, he made love to a maid employed by his family.

Although he occasionally visited brothels, his favored sex partners were his models. During his career he had hundreds of models. Most sat for him in the nude, and before the painting sessions closed, they had usually made love with him. His preferred subjects (and lovers) were simple women, such as the peasant girls who took in laundry for a living. Flattered by the attentions of this attractive artist, these humble women eagerly gave themselves to him.

SEX PARTNERS: Despite his many sex partners, Modigliani loved only two women. The first was Beatrice Hastings, an aristocratic British poet five years his senior. They met in 1914, made love the first night, and became inseparable. They drank, danced, and fought. Modigliani beat her frequently. When enraged—usually because she had paid attention to another man—he would literally drag her down the street by her hair. She inspired him, however, and in the bloom of their love he entered his most prolific period of painting, with Beatrice often sitting as his model. Nonetheless, this affair, because of its intensity in all likelihood, did not last. Beatrice fled from him in 1916. They never saw each other again.

Modigliani mourned this loss, but not for long. In 1917 he met Jeanne Hébuterne, a 19-year-old art student from a French Catholic family. A tiny, pale girl, Jeanne and Modigliani set up house on the Côte d'Azur within months of their first meeting, despite her parents' opposition to the Italian Jew. It was her lot not only to model for Modigliani, but to see him through his final, failing years, as his health, ever fragile, worsened owing to debauchery. In November, 1918, their love produced a baby girl, and in July, 1919, Modigliani vowed to marry Jeanne "as soon as the papers arrive." Why they never married remains a mystery, since they were devoted to each other and remained together until Modigliani's death six months after his oath. As the painter lay dying in Paris, he supposedly suggested that Jeanne join him in death "so that I can have my favorite model in paradise and with her enjoy eternal happiness." Jeanne was in a state of despair on the day of Modigliani's funeral. Pregnant with a second child, she jumped out of a fifth-floor window to her death.

HIS THOUGHTS: "If a woman poses for you, she gives herself to you."

—*R.M.*

The Rich Bohemian

PABLO PICASSO (Oct. 25, 1881–Apr. 8, 1973)

HIS FAME: He was without doubt the most original, forceful, and influential personality in the visual arts in the first three quarters of this century.

HIS PERSON: Born in Málaga, Spain, son of José Ruiz Blasco, an art teacher and sometime painter, Picasso had little formal education and not much more training in art, being clearly superior to his teachers. Legend has it that when Picasso's father realized the scope of his son's artistic genius, he gave him his own brushes and colors and did not paint again. In his late teens Picasso joyfully discovered the bohemian life in Barcelona; he continued his exuberant lifestyle on visits to Paris, where he was immediately inspired by the streets of Montmartre and the works of Toulouse-Lautrec, Van Gogh, and Cézanne. He was from the beginning an extraordinarily prolific painter. From the age of 20, in accordance with Spanish custom, he signed his works with his mother's maiden name—Picasso.

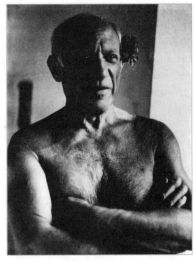

Picasso at age 66

In 1904 he quit Barcelona and moved to Paris. There he and Georges Braque, working together, founded the Cubist movement. "When I want to paint a cup," Picasso said, "I will show you that it is round, but it may be that the general rhythm and construction of the picture will oblige me to show that roundness as a square."

The outbreak of the Spanish Civil War in 1936 ended his political apathy; he became a passionate Loyalist, and the destruction of a small Basque town by Hitler's bombers inspired what many consider to be his masterpiece, the huge canvas *Guernica*. Throughout both world wars he remained in France.

Picasso's energy was relentless. Habitually a late riser, he saw his friends in the afternoon and then worked far into the night. Although he was only about 5 ft. 4 in. tall, the intensity of his black eyes and his often explosive presence gave the impression of a much larger man. He settled comfortably into fame, earning millions each year from his prodigious output—an estimated 14,000 canvases, 100,000 prints and engravings, and 34,000 book illustrations. A multitude of objects—mementos, paintings, antiques, African sculptures, junk, old clothes—were carefully retained as he moved through various houses, studios, wives, and lovers. When Picasso died at 91 in his hillside villa at Mougins, France, he left an estate valued at $1.1 billion.

SEX LIFE: Beauty and relative youth were the only qualities he consistently desired in women. Usually before and always after a sexual relationship began, his wives and mistresses became his models, though at times not recognizably so.

Fernande Olivier was the partner of Picasso's early bohemian life in Paris. She was a green-eyed, auburn-haired, provocatively voluptuous young woman whom he met one day at the common water tap of the run-down Montmartre tenement in which they both lived. She was four months his senior, which prompted him, then all of 23, to speak of her to his friends as "very beautiful—but old." She later described him as having "a sort of magnetism which I could not resist," but then resisting, or any other kind of overt action, was not Fernande's style. She liked posing, preferably in a reclining position, and she did not much mind when lack of money to buy shoes prevented her from leaving the flat for two months. Picasso provided, if at times meagerly, for their most urgent needs, and for entertainment there was always lovemaking. Picasso adored Fernande and was obsessively jealous of her. "Picasso forced me to live like a recluse," she said later.

Periodically, Picasso's restless nature required a change both in models and in sources of inspiration. Marcelle Humbert, whom he called Eva, perhaps as an assurance to her that she was now his first woman, was as small and delicate as Fernande had been robust. Because their romance paralleled Picasso's Cubist period, no portraits of her exist, but she is immortalized in the words *ma jolie* ("my pretty one"), which appear variously inscribed in several of his paintings, and two works bear the words *J'aime Éva* ("I love Éva"). She died in 1915 of tuberculosis.

In 1917 Picasso was persuaded to go to Rome with Jean Cocteau and the Ballets Russes. There he designed the curtain for Sergei Diaghilev's new ballet, *Parade*. Walking at night with the dancers along moonlit Roman streets, he singled out Olga Koklova, the diminutive daughter of a colonel. Her "good family" background and upper-class tastes appealed to him at that time as solid and lasting values. His bohemian life had died with Éva; he was becoming rich and famous. Something essentially Spanish and bourgeois in his nature told him that it was now time to settle down and start a family. He took Olga with him to Spain, introduced her to his friends and relatives, painted her in a Spanish mantilla, and married her not only in the obligatory civil ceremony but in the Russian Orthodox service as well. Then he installed her in a luxuriously decorated Parisian flat with—as if in premonition of failure—twin beds.

Picasso's first son, Paulo, was the product of that marriage—a marriage that was already coming apart when his first daughter, Maïa, was born in 1935 to his mistress and model, the large and lovely, blond and blue-eyed Marie-Thérèse Walter. Picasso was delighted. Olga had grown increasingly demanding and neurotic, and Picasso had, consciously or unconsciously, taken his revenge by painting a series of female monsters with shriveled breasts and exaggerated sexual organs. His conjugal unhappiness and sexual deprivation produced deformed female figures in his art, but once the warmhearted, gentle Marie-Thérèse appeared, a refuge offering uncritical devotion and sexual fulfillment, the sunken breasts became round and firm, the mouths smiled, and the figures, although still distorted, exuded a kind of sensual joy.

After Maïa was born, his affair with her mother became complicated by parental responsibility. Picasso's ever-roving eye was then caught by the dark eyes and serious expression of Dora Maar, whom he saw for the first time seated at a nearby table at the Deux Magots, a café on the Left Bank. A photographer and a painter herself, Dora Maar could not only converse intelligently on the creative process, she could also do it in Spanish. Picasso was charmed. Soon Dora Maar was making regular visits to the Paris studio, and paintings of a woman with flowing blue-black hair began to appear. Dora Maar offered Picasso intellectual as well as sexual companionship; unfortunately, she also matched his ferocious temperament and depressions with her own. The series of paintings of women weeping are all of Dora Maar.

In his 60s but with no apparent diminution of sexual energy—"his sexual gluttony was becoming obsessive," wrote one friend—Picasso acquired a young painter, Françoise Gilot, as his new mistress. Although she was, at the time, the sole occupant of his bed, Françoise soon discovered that Olga, Marie-Thérèse, and Dora Maar all still played their roles in his life. Summers in the south of France were enlivened by the presence of Olga, who literally dogged their footsteps on the street and at the beach, raining verbal abuse on the couple. In Paris, Thursdays and Sundays were set aside for visits with Marie-Thérèse and Maïa, and during vacations daily letters arrived outlining in loving detail for Papa Picasso the events and concerns, particularly financial, of their lives. Picasso continually insisted that Françoise accompany him when he called on or had a luncheon engagement with the now scornful and bitter Dora Maar. Forcing the women of his life to relate to each other, however violently, was for Picasso one of the more amusing aspects of longevity.

Some 40 years younger than Picasso, Françoise Gilot's relationship with him was more complicated than that of her predecessors. Whenever she became dissatisfied with her role, Picasso prescribed maternity as a cure. Their son, Claude, and daughter, Paloma, were the result. Living with Picasso was *hard*—too hard, as it turned out; after seven years Françoise took the children and left. Picasso was furious. "There's nothing so similar to one poodle as another poodle, and that goes for women, too," he said. Françoise later married the renowned Dr. Jonas Salk.

Picasso's final relationship of any duration was with a young divorcée, Jacqueline Roque, who moved in after Françoise had left. She organized his affairs and devoted herself to his well-being. When Olga died in 1955, Picasso was at last free to remarry; he and Jacqueline were wed in 1961. Jacqueline was less voluptuous than Fernande, less delicate than Éva, less graceful than Olga, less sweet than Marie-Thérèse, less intelligent than Dora Maar, less talented than Françoise. But her own expectations may have been less, too. She was in any case loyal, capable, willing, and beautiful. All of his women had been beautiful, and at different times and with varying degrees of passion Picasso had loved them all. But there had always been something of anger and hatred, too. Picasso authority Pierre Cabanne pointed out: "Sex stimulation was the basic motive force of his lyrical flights; desire, with him, was violence, dismemberment, tumult, indignation, excess." A reference in the *Diaries of Anaïs Nin*, Cabanne felt, gave a clue to Picasso's attitude toward women: "Alice Paalen, the wife of the Surrealist painter Wolfgang Paalen, who was Picasso's mistress, is quoted as saying that one of his joys was to deny women their climaxes. As Éluard wrote in transcribing a graphological analysis of him in 1942: 'Loves intensely and kills the thing he loves.'"

HIS THOUGHTS: "Nature and art, being two different things, cannot be the same thing…. Academic training in beauty is a sham. When we love a woman, we don't start measuring her legs."

"For me, there are only two kinds of women—goddesses and doormats."

—*N.C.S.*

The Promiscuous Behemoth

DIEGO RIVERA (Dec. 8, 1886–Nov. 25, 1957)

HIS FAME: Mexican artist Diego Rivera won international fame as a muralist during his long and productive career. His brightly colored, primitive murals, covering immense areas—one was 17,000 sq. ft.—often dealt with politically leftist subjects reflecting Rivera's Communist beliefs.

HIS PERSON: The son of a mine owner and a schoolteacher, Diego Rivera began drawing at the age of three. After he had ruined several walls with his scribbling, his father gave him his own studio with blackboard walls and a limitless supply of colored chalk. At the age of 13 he entered the San

Rivera and Frida Kahlo

Carlos Academy of Fine Arts to study painting, but he was expelled three years later for involvement in a political riot.

In 1907 he went to Spain to study. After traveling throughout Europe, he ended up in Paris in 1909, where he lived on and off for the next 12 years. In 1921 he returned as a mature artist to North America, where he did murals throughout Mexico and the U.S. During his career, the subject matter of his paintings frequently caused controversy. Commissioned to paint a mural for New York City's RCA Building in Rockefeller Center, Rivera included in his *Man at the Crossroads* a portrait of Lenin. A newspaper headline at the time announced, "Rivera Paints Scenes of Communist Activity and John D. Jr. Foots Bill." In the end, the mural was chipped away from the stone wall. Furious at the destruction of his work, Rivera later repainted it on a wall in the Palace of Fine Arts in Mexico City.

A childlike, violently emotional man, Rivera projected a gruesome, machismo image. He went so far as to claim that as a student he had bought cadavers and experimented with cannibalism. Supposedly, he most liked cooked female breasts and "brains in vinaigrette."

At the age of 70 he died of heart failure in bed at his home in Mexico City.

SEX LIFE: After he was caught cutting open a live mouse to find out where baby mice came from, Rivera was given a practical course in sex education, complete with anatomical texts, by his father. According to Rivera, he used this knowledge several years later at the age of nine, when he allegedly had intercourse for the first time. His autobiography reveals that his first partner was an 18-year-old American schoolteacher, who "prepared me for the arms of my second mistress, a generous Negroid girl, wife of an engineer on the Mexican Central Railroad."

It is known that, by the time Rivera arrived in Europe at the age of 21, he was highly experienced in sex as the result of numerous liaisons with actresses and prostitutes. In Europe he was pursued by countless women, who wanted to sleep with this Mexican macho who was an artistic genius even though he weighed 300 lb. and had a face like a frog's. Rivera, who easily succumbed to the advances of any woman, whether beautiful or ugly, was described by one lover as having huge Buddha breasts, hair all over his 6-ft. body, and a penis proportionate in size to the rest of his massive frame.

One of his early European loves was Maria Blanchard, a small French-Spanish hunchbacked painter who introduced Rivera to his first common-law wife, Angelina Beloff. Leaving Maria, Rivera moved in with Angelina, a Russian émigré artist. During their 10-year relationship, Angelina, who was six years older than Rivera, served as a mother figure for the emotionally erratic artist. Even though they lived together, Rivera never curbed his affairs with other women. In 1917, when Angelina became pregnant, Rivera responded by moving in with a Russian painter, Marievna Vorobiev. Deeply in love with Rivera, Marievna later recalled that his first presents to her had been two Siamese cats and a condom. Their lovemaking—in which he often bound her hands and feet—was so violent that Marievna's uterus became slightly displaced. Nevertheless, Marievna was soon pregnant, and Rivera moved back in with Angelina.

Finally, in 1921, Rivera headed for Mexico, promising both women that he would send for them later. He never did. Instead he fell in love with the wildly beautiful and violent Guadalupe Marín, who became his second common-law wife. Their relationship, which produced two daughters, was filled with arguments, physical violence, jealousy, and passionate sex. When confronted with one of his sexual escapades, Lupe slashed several of Rivera's paintings and then attacked his Cuban lover. Lupe left him once after she walked in on a sex session Rivera was having with her younger sister. At the end of seven years, this turbulent affair had burned itself out.

A short time later Rivera was officially married for the first time. The 43-year-old Rivera's new wife was Frida Kahlo, a 19-year-old Mexican Jewish girl, who grew into a well-respected and important artist in her own right. During their courtship and throughout their marriage, Rivera continued his affairs with other women. Initially Frida accepted his extramarital escapades as "proper to genius," but when he slept with her best friend, Frida went to New York, where she retaliated by having a multitude of love affairs. In 1939 the Riveras were divorced, but in 1940 they remarried. Frida agreed to the remarriage under two conditions: that she would support herself through her art, and that she and Diego would no longer have sexual intercourse. They seem to have adjusted to one another's promiscuity and even enjoyed talking about their various bedroom adventures.

Frida died in 1954, and Rivera remarried the following year. His new wife was a friend of 10 years, Emma Hurtado.

MEDICAL REPORT: According to Rivera's autobiography, his last years were sexless and his second marriage was unconsummated because he had cancer of the penis. Supposedly, his doctors repeatedly told him his penis had to be amputated, but Rivera refused to submit to such an operation.

HIS THOUGHTS: "If I loved a woman, the more I loved her, the more I wanted to hurt her."

—R.J.F.

The Coffeepot

HENRI DE TOULOUSE-LAUTREC (Nov. 24, 1864–Sept. 9, 1901)

HIS FAME: Toulouse-Lautrec's naturalistic style had a great influence on Postimpressionist French art. Considered a minor talent while alive, Lautrec achieved international renown after his death. Indeed, our image today of

Paris in the Gay Nineties is very much a result of Toulouse-Lautrec's paintings of prostitutes, bohemians, and, especially, the performers and audiences of the Moulin Rouge and other Parisian night spots.

Toulouse-Lautrec at age 26

HIS PERSON: The only surviving child of an eccentric count and his shy and patient wife, Toulouse-Lautrec suffered two falls as an adolescent which broke both his thighbones. He was left crippled for life, and his growth was frozen at 5 ft. 1 in. This greatly disappointed his father, who had been counting on a strong and healthy son to join him when he went hunting and debauching. Ugly, deformed, and quite a bit shorter than his peers, Toulouse-Lautrec nonetheless had personal charisma and a quick wit, which made him a much-sought-after companion in the counterculture of Paris in the late 1880s and throughout the 1890s. He became a well-known figure on the streets of Montmartre, dressed in baggy trousers, an overlong overcoat, and a bowler hat, and sporting a beard, a bamboo cane, and pince-nez.

Despite his blue-blooded origins, Toulouse-Lautrec felt most at home with society's outcasts and devoted extended periods of his life to living in brothels and hanging out in lesbian bars. Alcoholism, syphilis, and general abuse of his health led to his death in his mother's arms two and a half months before his 37th birthday.

SEX LIFE: Although he didn't reach too far from head to toe, Toulouse-Lautrec had unusually well developed sexual organs, even for a man of normal size. His genitals were so out of proportion to the rest of his body that he compared himself to a "coffeepot with a big spout."

Coming from an aristocratic family, Toulouse-Lautrec was introduced to brothels early. Because he was misshapen and somewhat grotesque-looking, marriage with a woman of his own class was considered unthinkable. He moved to the Montmartre district of Paris when he was 19 and divided his time between painting and observing the extremes of Paris nightlife. He began having sexual affairs with some of his models, in particular Marie Charlet, a teenaged adventuress who spread the word about the painter's sexual prowess.

In 1885 Toulouse-Lautrec became involved with model Suzanne Valadon, the mother of artist Maurice Utrillo and an artist in her own right. For three years they carried on a stormy affair, which ended abruptly when he learned that Valadon's threats of suicide, which he had taken seriously, were in fact sheer playacting. After the breakup with Valadon, Toulouse-Lautrec painted six studies of Rosa la Rouge, a red-haired prostitute from whom he contracted syphilis.

In 1891 Toulouse-Lautrec prepared his first poster for the Moulin Rouge nightclub, and his fame began. Following a breakup with another lover, Berthe La Sourde, he began frequenting brothels with great regularity and by 1894 had taken up residence in a high-class house of prostitution in the Rue des Moulins. He lived in this brothel and others on and off for the rest of his life. This unusual living arrangement provided Toulouse-Lautrec with the opportunity to indulge completely his sexual appetite, while simultaneously allowing him to observe and paint unposed nude and seminude women. "The professional model is always like a stuffed owl," he said. "These girls are alive."

He lived with the prostitutes day in and day out. He played cards with them, laughed with them, and surprised them in their beds. He shared their meals and brought in pâtés and fine wines to brighten up the menu. He kept track of each woman's birthday and brought them all presents. On their days off, he would invite these women of the night to his studio and take them to a restaurant or to the circus or a theater.

When he began to tire of brothels, Toulouse-Lautrec moved on to lesbian bars, particularly La Souris and Le Hanneton, near the Place Pigalle. Here, also surrounded by women, he again became a popular figure who could be turned to for advice.

In 1897 he fell in love with a young relative named Aline, who had just left a convent. For a while he cleaned up his act, forswearing cocktails (which he had helped popularize), talking of entering a clinic for alcoholics, and drinking only port. But when Aline's father forbade Toulouse-Lautrec to see his daughter, the artist plunged deeper than ever into the Paris underworld, eventually being sent to a mental asylum with delirium tremens. Within months of his release he was drinking heavily again. Struck down with paralysis on Aug. 20, 1901, he died three weeks later.

QUIRKS: An extreme sensualist, Toulouse-Lautrec periodically zeroed in on different parts of the female body. It was said that he could caress a woman's hand for an hour. Red hair drove him to ecstasy. His friend Thadée Natanson described how Toulouse-Lautrec would "purr with delight as he plunged his face into a woman's bosom, wrapping her two enormous breasts around him like a comforter made of human flesh." He would also "clutch a pair of women's stockings that had fallen to the ground, roll them into a ball, and inhale their scent with his eyes closed."

At one point Toulouse-Lautrec became obsessed with the actress and dancer Marcelle Lender. Night after night, more than 20 times, he reserved the same seat in the orchestra stalls so that he could watch her dance the bolero. When asked why he kept returning, he replied, "I simply come to see

Lender's back. Take a good look at it; you've never seen anything so magnificent." Apparently he was impressed with her nose as well. According to Natanson, Toulouse-Lautrec loved the sight of finely chiseled nostrils since, owing to his size, they were the first things he saw when he looked up at a woman's face.

HIS THOUGHTS: "Love is when the desire to be desired takes you so badly that you feel you could die of it."

"A woman's body, a splendid woman's body … is not for making love…. It's too beautiful, eh? For making love anything goes … anything … anything at all, eh?"

—D.W.

IV

The Quill is Compelling

Chéri

COLETTE (Jan. 28, 1873–Aug. 3, 1954)

HIS FAME: One of the most celebrated French authors of the early 20th century, Sidonie Gabrielle Claudine Colette wrote 73 books—fiction, nonfiction, and a mixture of the two—about the sorrows and delights of love. In her life, as in her art, she gave a new dimension to two of France's most enduring sexual archetypes, the schoolgirl seductress and the aging coquette.

HER PERSON: Colette grew up in the country, the adored youngest child of a fiercely possessive mother and a vaguely literary retired army captain. She was a singular child, a tomboy who went by her family surname and communed intimately with the flowers and animals in her own private enchanted garden. At 20, an ingenuous provincial with braided hair falling below her knees, she married Henry Gauthier-Villars, a 35-year-old writer and friend of the family. "Willy," as he was known, added his young bride to his collection of mistresses, ghostwriters, and pornographic postcards in decadent *fin-de-siècle* Paris.

At Willy's urging, Colette began to fill notebooks with vicariously erotic stories about the adventures of a young girl. The four Claudine novels, published from 1900 to 1903, enjoyed a great vogue, giving rise to a whole line of "Claudine" products and to a cult of the precocious schoolgirl, innocent yet alluring, a sort of androgynous Lolita.

Rebelling against her literary bondage to Willy, who signed his name to his wife's first six books, Colette began publishing voluptuous nature stories, using the name Colette Willy until 1906, and then simply Colette. (She could describe a vegetable as if it were a love object, it was said.) She took up the study of mime, divorcing Willy in 1906 to tour in mildly erotic mime melodramas. She also contributed articles (published in 1970 in book form as *Tales of a Thousand and One Mornings*) to *Le Matin*, a leading French newspaper. The editor, Henry de Jouvenel, fathered her only child (a girl) and became her second husband, in that order. This marriage also ended in divorce, but while it lasted Colette achieved her greatest fame with *Chéri* (1920), the sexual tragedy of a young gigolo and an aging coquette, followed by *The Ripening Seed* (1923), a classic tale of adolescent sexual initiation.

Married yet again in 1935, to journalist Maurice Goudeket, Colette enjoyed both fame and an active old age, raising the coquette to the rank of patriotic heroine with the publication of *Gigi* (1945) when she was 72.

LOVE LIFE: Colette's first husband, Willy, was constantly unfaithful to her. Once she followed him to an assignation and found him fornicating with one Lotte Kinceler, a foul-mouthed, hunchbacked dwarf. Sometimes, according to one biographer, Willy "brought his other coquettes to Colette's apartment, where they would finger her things and speak smut." Willy tried to promote a liaison between his young wife, who described herself as "sexually impartial," and one of his mistresses. At the time, Colette was more comfortable with her husband's male young homosexual secretaries. But as she became disillusioned with Willy, who with his bulbous eyes and drooping cheeks reminded her of Queen Victoria, she took refuge in her somewhat exhibitionistic career in mime and music-hall dancing. She also found comfort in the company of an aristo-cratic lesbian, "Missy," the former Marquise de Belboeuf and a descendant of Napoleon, with whom she lived for six years after leaving Willy.

Full-bodied and feline in her 30s, with sloe eyes and a mop of curly hair, Colette appeared in the mime theater seductively draped like an odalisque. One play required her to bare her breasts, which created "a luscious thrill of sensa-tion" in the audience. Sensation turned to scandal when, miming a ballet in which "a mummy awakes from eternal sleep, undoes its bandages, and, near nude, dances its ancient loves," she ardently embraced her "prince," who was in fact Missy, the choreographer of the ballet.

Colette and Missy de Belboeuf, who looked and dressed like a man in daily life, enjoyed what was then known as "a loving friendship." Colette, who also appeared in tuxedo at the famous sapphic banquets of the day and wore an ankle bracelet engraved "I belong to Missy," described her friend's love as maternal and possessive. She wrote of Missy: "You will give me sensual pleasure, leaning over me, your eyes full of maternal anxiety, searching through your passionate friend for the child you never had." Colette had numerous lesbian loves, one of the most colorful being Natalie Barney, an American expatriate in Paris known for her Friday salons and her affairs with other women. On one occasion, Colette sent Barney a message reading, "Natalie, my husband kisses your hands, and I the rest."

After entering the world of journalism, Colette began a whirlwind affair with the aggressive, virile Henry de Jouvenel. (Fond of pet names, she called him "Sidi the Pasha.") The affair ended in marriage when Colette, nearly 40, became preg-nant. Jealousy blooms "like a dark carnation," she wrote in reference to her husband's chronic infidelity. De Jouvenel complained, for his part, about his wife's preoccupation with "love, adultery, and half-incestuous relationships." The latter was rumored when Colette took off on a Swiss winter vacation with her 19-year-old stepson, Bertrand de Jouvenel, after her separation from his father.

It was only during the autumn of her womanhood, as Colette called it, that she was able to reconcile her fierce need for independence with both a desire for possession and a penchant for handsome young men. Colette was 52 when she met Maurice Goudeket, then 35, who later became her third husband. Whether writing in bed, surrounded by cats and cushions, or basking in the warm sunshine of Saint-Tropez, she enjoyed with Goudeket a loving companionship which renewed her creative energy and enabled her to remain vigorously active well into old age.

HER PHILOSOPHY: "The seduction emanating from a person of uncertain or dissimulated sex is powerful," wrote Colette, who refused to distinguish between normal and abnormal sexuality.

—C.D.

The Romantic Feminist

GEORGE SAND (July 1, 1804–June 8, 1876)

HER FAME: This French feminist author of more than 90 novels—among them *Lélia* and *The Devil's Pool*—was notorious for dressing in men's clothes, smoking cigars, taking on frail but brilliant young lovers, and voicing scandalous opinions.

HER PERSON: Amandine Aurore Lucie Dupin was raised by her grandmother on the family's country estate at Nohant, 150 mi. south of Paris. Her two years of formal education at a convent ended when, after a stint as leader of the *diables* ("bad girls"), she turned pious and talked of becoming a nun, whereupon her Deist grandmother yanked her out of school. At the age of 17, Aurore inherited Nohant. After an unsuccessful marriage, which produced two children, she ran off to Paris and began her writing career, taking George Sand as her pen name. When her first novel, *Indiana*, was published in the spring of 1832, it was a smashing success. Thereafter novels—most of them successful, several still considered masterpieces—flowed from her pen. A champion of woman's rights, she billed herself as "the Spartacus of women's slavery." However, her heroines, often caught in marital traps, nearly always win their freedom through fortuitous turns of fate (e.g., a husband's accidental death). According to one critic, "In George Sand, when a lady wants to change her lover, God is there to facilitate the transfer." Unfortunately, in real life, Sand usually had to make the transfer herself.

LOVE AND SEX LIFE: Interpreters of George Sand have called her fickle and heartless, have labeled her as bisexual or lesbian; have hinted at incest (in view of her enormous love for her son, Maurice) and at a covert maternal instinct that encouraged her to take younger lovers.

The cigar-smoking woman whose sexuality has aroused such interest was once described by Charles Dickens as resembling "the queen's monthly nurse." She was short and swarthy, with heavy features and dark eyes. Her manner was brusque. In her intellect and passion for living lay her sensual appeal.

Her first sexual encounter was probably with neighbor Stéphane de Grandsagne when she was 16 or 17. Grandsagne may have fathered her daughter, Solange, born in 1828. At 18 she married 27-year-old Casimir Dudevant, who proved to be a drunken boor and beat her from time to time. Although she left him—and their children—in 1831, they were not legally separated until 1836.

It was in Paris, where sexual liberation was in the air, that her love life really began. Her first Paris lover, Jules Sandeau, with whom she briefly collaborated on a book, was typical of the men who attracted her—younger than she by seven years, frail, blond, and artistic. Long after their affair ended, Sandeau, still bitter, described her as a "graveyard." Bad endings were to become typical of her love affairs.

Sand needed to be in love to enjoy sex. A short experiment in nonromantic copulation with writer Prosper Mérimée was a disaster. Though some of her lovers accused her of frigidity, it seems that in truth she was like many women—passionate when aroused by romance, indifferent when she was not. She spoke of biting, beating, and kissing Sandeau; and of Michel de Bourges, a married lover whom she adored in spite of his bald ugliness, she confessed he caused her to "tremble with desire."

When rejected, she suffered—even groveled. As her stormy relationship with the poet-playwright Alfred de Musset drew to a close, she wrote: "I was hoping you would come and waited for your call from 11 o'clock in the morning until midnight. What a day! Every ring of the doorbell made me jump! I have such a headache. I wish I were dead." She cut off her hair and sent it to him.

With Polish composer Frédéric Chopin—tubercular, aristocratic, an opium smoker, and six years younger than she—Sand ran the gamut. In 1838, at the beginning of their relationship, she compared his attitude toward sex to that of an old woman and wailed, "Can there ever be love without a single kiss, and kisses without sensual pleasure?" Long before the end of their nine years together, he complained that *she* wouldn't sleep with *him*.

Among her other lovers were engraver Alexandre Damien Manceau, who lived with her in calm serenity from the time he was 32 (she was 45) until he died 15 years later, and painter Charles Marchal, 39 to her 60, whom she called her "fat baby."

Gossip linked her with others. Gustave Planche, a literary critic with careless personal-hygiene habits, fought a duel to defend her literary honor against another critic who had attacked her novel *Lélia* (the shots misfired, the sales of *Lélia* shot up); it is not clear whether she ever had sex with him. Nor is it clear whether she had sex with women, notably with actress Marie Dorval, to whom she wrote letters that would today be considered erotic but were commonplace among women friends at the time. Example: "In the theater or in your bed, I simply must come and kiss you, my lady, or I shall do something crazy!"

And some passionate friendships were nonsexual—those with Charles Augustin Sainte-Beuve, Franz Liszt, Alexandre Dumas *père*, and Gustave Flaubert.

HER THOUGHTS: "I had no feeling of guilt because I have always felt my infidelities were caused by fate, by a search for an ideal which impelled me to abandon the imperfect in favor of what appeared to be nearer perfection. I have known many kinds of love. I loved like an artist, a woman, a sister, a mother, a nun, a poet. Some loves died the day they were born without ever being revealed to the person who had inspired them. Some made a martyr of me and drove me to despair.... Some kept me shut away for years in a sort of excessive sublimation. Every time I was perfectly sincere."

—A.E.

Salonkeeper

GERTRUDE STEIN (Feb. 3, 1874–July 27, 1946)

HER FAME: Gertrude Stein was an American writer whose avant-garde writing style and odd, masculine appearance helped establish her as an eccentric in the minds of the American public. Her permanent home in Paris, which she shared with her lover, Alice B. Toklas, served as the gathering place for expatriate writers and artists during the years between WWI and WWII.

HER PERSON: Born in Allegheny, Pa., to fairly well-to-do and restless parents, Stein spent her early years living with her family in Vienna and Paris before returning to settle in Oakland, Calif., of which she said, "The thing about Oakland is that when you get there, there's no there there." Critics believe that her early association with three different languages later influenced her writings, allowing her to use words as sounds, detached from their general meanings.

Her weak-spirited mother died of cancer when Stein was 14, leaving her tyrannical father to browbeat his daughter into the study of medicine. He died three years later, but he was a strong influence on her feelings toward men. Later she would write, "Fathers are depressing."

At Radcliffe College she studied psychology under William James, whose theory of pragmatism (understanding immediate events without applying past experiences to them) would later influence her writings. She entered Johns Hopkins Medical School for graduate study, only to flunk out four years later, when she became distracted by her first lesbian love affair and her subsequent inner struggle to accept her own sexuality, which was thoroughly at odds with the standard mores of the time.

She moved to Paris, living off the money that was willed to her by her parents. There she shared a home with her brother Leo, an art critic. The two began collecting Cubist paintings, which were new and daring at that time. Painters like Picasso, Matisse, and Braque became their close friends and began visiting regularly. During this period she wrote three books: *Q.E.D.*, written in 1903 but not published until 1950, a cathartic account of her struggle with lesbianism; *Three Lives*, published in 1909 and well received by the public; and *The Making of Americans*, written between 1903 and 1911 but not published until 1925. Leo moved out after a fight with his sister, and Alice B. Toklas moved in, becoming Stein's adviser, protector, and lover for the next 38 years.

As her literary reputation grew, so did the number of writers and artists who came to visit, people like F. Scott Fitzgerald, Sherwood Anderson, and Ernest Hemingway. With her short-cropped masculine haircut, thick girth, and loud laugh, Stein seemed an unlikely candidate for the powerful artistic figure she became, one who could make or break reputations by even the most innocuous of comments. Her most popular book was her autobiography, called *The Autobiography of Alice B. Toklas*, published in 1933. Stein died in 1946, leaving her estate to Toklas, who kept possession of her art collection until 1961, when it was appropriated by the Stein family and sold at auction for $6 million.

LOVE LIFE: Gertrude Stein had problems accepting her lesbian tendencies in her first affair with fellow student May Bookstaver. May's passionate nature led her to other affairs, leaving Stein to agonize over her own sexuality since it was so opposed to her middle-class upbringing. It wasn't until later, when she met and "married" Alice B. Toklas, that she came to accept her feelings for women: "Slowly it has come to me that any way of being a loving one is interesting and not unpleasant to me."

Stein was living in Paris, presiding over a salon populated by Pablo Picasso and other painters of future renown, when Alice B. Toklas came into her life in the autumn of 1907. Toklas had been raised in San Francisco, was well educated, and was on a visit to Europe. She was invited by Stein to see her collection of art and soon dropped by. Toklas was shy and lean, Stein was heavyset (soon to exceed 200 lb.). Mabel Dodge Luhan remembered them both at the outset, saying of the 30-year-old Toklas: "She was slight and dark, with beautiful gray eyes hung with black lashes—and she had a drooping, Jewish nose, and her eyelids drooped, and the corners of her red mouth and the lobes of her ears drooped under the black folded Hebraic hair, weighed down as they were, with long heavy Oriental earrings." And of the 33-year-old Stein she wrote: "Gertrude Stein was prodigious. Pounds and pounds and pounds piled up on her skeleton—not the billowing kind, but massive, heavy fat. She wore some covering of corduroy or velvet and her crinkly hair was brushed back and twisted up high behind her jolly, intelligent face."

It was love at first sight for both of them. Alice Toklas visited again and again, and finally Stein invited her to move in. Toklas proofread one of Stein's books, then typed 1,000 manuscript pages of another. Eventually, according to Mabel Dodge Luhan, Toklas became Stein's "hand-maiden … always serving someone … perfect for doing errands … so self-obliterating that no one considered her very much beyond thinking her a silent, picturesque object in the background." But Stein's brother, Leo, thought Toklas was more, and told Mabel Dodge Luhan, who wrote of Leo's complaints: "He had always had a special disgust at seeing how the weaker can enslave the stronger as was happening in their case. Alice was making herself indispensable.... And Gertrude was growing helpless and foolish from it and less and less inclined to do anything herself, Leo said; he had seen trees strangled by vines in the same way."

But the relationship was more, and their love was mutual. Stein proposed to Toklas. "Care for me," she urged. "I care for you in every possible way.... Pet me tenderly and save me from alarm.... When all is said one is wedded to the bed." Alice Toklas accepted, and so began an almost husband-wife relationship, with Stein the provider and Toklas minding the house and the bills and in general keeping Stein's life running smoothly.

Stein maintained close relationships with men as well, although they were nonsexual in nature. She was close to Ernest Hemingway, despite the fact that she disliked his overly macho outlook. She once chastised him for his prejudice against lesbians: "You know nothing about any of this really, Hemingway. You've met known criminals and sick people and vicious people. The main thing is that the act male homosexuals commit is ugly and repugnant and afterwards they are disgusted with themselves. They drink and take drugs, to palliate this, but they are disgusted with the act and they are always changing partners and cannot be really happy. In women it is the opposite. They do nothing that they are disgusted by and nothing that is repulsive and afterwards they are happy and they can lead happy lives together." Hemingway, for his part, said of Stein, "I always wanted to fuck her and she knew it."

As she grew older, Stein made her disgust with heterosexuality more evident: "If there are men and women, it is rather horrible...." Her life with Toklas was a contented one, and, except for the fact of their lesbianism, almost conventional. Both were faithful and loving to one another, calling each other pet names in private: Toklas was "Pussy," Stein "Lovely." But the relationship was not without passion, as related by Stein in a 1917 piece, "Lifting Belly," a long rhapsody of lesbian love. In the following poem to Alice, "Caesars" and "cow" are symbols of sexual pleasure.

> *Kiss my lips. She did.*
> *Kiss my lips again she did.*
> *Kiss my lips over and over and over again she did....*
> *I'll let you kiss me sticky....*
> *I say lifting belly and then I say lifting belly and Caesars.*
> *I say lifting belly gently and Caesars gently. I say*
> *lifting belly again and Caesars again.... I say lifting*
> *belly Caesars and cow come out. I say lifting belly*
> *and Caesars and cow come out.*
> *Can you read my print?*
> *Alice answers yes.*

In 1946, suffering from cancer, Stein insisted upon surgery. About to be wheeled into the operating room, Stein turned her head to Alice Toklas and said, "What is the answer?" Toklas did not reply. Stein nodded and said, "In that case, what is the question?" These were her last words to her beloved. Gertrude Stein died that night under anesthesia. She died convinced she was a genius, one of three geniuses she had known, the other two being Pablo Picasso and Alfred North Whitehead. At one time she had suggested another, saying, "Einstein was the creative philosophic mind of the century, and I have been the creative literary mind of the century."

Alice Toklas lived on without her for another 21 years, heartsick and lonely. At 89 Alice said simply to a friend, "I miss her; I still miss her very much."
—*M.W. and the Eds.*

The Abstract Lover

VIRGINIA WOOLF (Jan. 25, 1882–Mar. 28, 1941)

HER FAME: One of the major writers of the 20th century, Woolf is known, along with Proust and Joyce, as a pioneer of modern fiction. She was also the focal point of a gathering of English avant-garde intellectuals who met as the Bloomsbury group from 1905 to 1920.

HER PERSON: Born of beauty (her mother, Julia Duckworth, was famous for it) and brains (Sir Leslie Stephen was one of England's leading literary figures), Virginia inherited both. Tall and thin, she was both elegant and fragile, with deep-set eyes and a classic, ethereal kind of beauty. Writing was her passion in childhood, and it remained the reigning passion of her life. Virginia had a quality of other-worldliness which alienated her from people. The problem was compounded by periodic bouts of insanity—when she would hear voices and hallucinate—which forced her to retreat from society for months on end. She had four major breakdowns and was on the verge of one each time she completed a novel. At age 25 she began meeting with her brothers' Cambridge friends (the circle later known as Bloomsbury), where she became famous for her wit and fascinating flights of imagination. Though Virginia had

Woolf, age 21

many suitors, she did not marry until she was 30. The following year she completed her first novel and had her most severe breakdown, which lasted almost two years. After the breakdown she remained relatively stable for a while and quite productive, writing at least one book every two years. A well-respected writer from the beginning, she became a best-selling novelist in her 40s. At the height of WWII, having just completed another novel, Virginia felt herself going mad once more. Unable to face another breakdown, she filled her pockets with stones and drowned herself in the River Ouse. She was 59.

LOVE LIFE: Two half brothers, Gerald and George Duckworth, provided Virginia's unfortunate introduction to sexuality. When she was six, Gerald, then in his 20s, stood her on a ledge and explored her genitals with his hand, an incident she never forgot. During her adolescence George would come into her room at night, fling himself down on her bed, and kiss, fondle, and caress her. Virginia, a young Victorian, endured his habits in mortified silence until she was 22.

Not surprisingly, though Virginia flirted with men, she fell in love with women. At 16 the object of her affection was Madge Vaughan, a beautiful, dark, romantic woman who shared Virginia's literary tastes. They had an intimate friendship, but Madge soon married. At 20 Virginia began a passionate correspondence with 37-year-old Violet Dickinson, an old friend of the family. Her letters to Violet sound like those to a lover in a physical sense, addressed to "My Violet" or "My Woman," signed "Yr. Lover." They are full of endearments, demands, and longings, and such sentiments as "When you wake in the night, I suppose you feel my arms around you." Oddly enough, however, the actual sexual element was missing, as it was from most of Virginia's relationships. Her 10-year intimacy with Violet remained a purely emotional affair. Lytton Strachey, called "the arch-bugger of Bloomsbury" by Virginia's nephew Quentin Bell, proposed to Virginia in 1909. She was well aware of his homosexual preference but accepted him anyway, perhaps because of his wit and reputation as a formidable intellect. However, he retracted the proposal the next day. "I was in terror lest she would kiss me," he said. Their friendship was salvaged, and it was Strachey who suggested to political activist and writer Leonard Woolf that he court Virginia.

At 30 Virginia married Woolf, who was part of Bloomsbury, only to discover that she was frigid. "I find the climax immensely exaggerated," she said. Sexual relations ceased shortly after the honeymoon, though they remained in many ways happily married for 28 years. Virginia loved Leonard more than anyone, unless it was her sister, Vanessa, whose womanliness she also envied. (Of herself, she once said that she was "not one thing or another, not a man or a woman.") After her marriage she settled into a life of asexuality and writing. At first Virginia yearned for the motherhood and passion so beautifully embodied by Vanessa, but later she made up her mind on both of those issues: "I slightly distrust or suspect the maternal passion. I don't like profound instincts—not in human relationships." Indeed, her adolescent attitudes toward sex and passion remained with her for the rest of her life: "This vague and dream-like world [of writing], without love, or heart, or passion, or sex, is the world I really care about, and find really interesting."

Still, there were always affairs. When Virginia was 40, the 30-year-old lesbian Vita Sackville-West fell in love with her, and the feeling was soon mutual. Vita was a beautiful writer whose aristocratic lineage went back 400 years. Her affair with Virginia lasted five years, and they slept together about a dozen times. This was Virginia's only physical homosexual affair. It was also her longest-lasting sexual relationship. Remarkably, the sexual aspect of their affair was not cause for shock, guilt, or any particular elation. Nor did Leonard mind, since their marriage was not threatened. As Vita wrote a friend concerning Virginia's sexuality: "She is not the sort of person one thinks of in that way. There is something incongruous and almost indecent in the idea." And as Virginia wrote Vita: "It's a great thing being a eunuch as I am."

Whatever sexuality Virginia possessed was channeled into her writing. During her affair and subsequent close friendship with Vita, she produced her best novels—*Mrs. Dalloway, To the Lighthouse, Orlando* (a fictionalized biography of Vita, which Vita's husband, Harold Nicolson, called "the longest and most charming love letter in history"), and *The Waves.* After their affair slacked off, composer Ethyl Smith fell violently in love with Virginia, but the pursuit was largely unsuccessful. Virginia wrote two more novels before committing suicide. In her suicide note to Leonard, she said, "I don't think two people could have been happier than we have been."

HER THOUGHTS: "It is fatal to be a man or woman pure and simple; one must be woman-manly, or man-womanly."

—*J.H.*

Born Free

MARY WOLLSTONECRAFT (Apr. 27, 1759–Sept. 10, 1797)

HER FAME: This British author was an advocate of woman's rights in an era when women were kept, as she said, "in silken fetters." She wrote novels, children's stories, and, among other "miscellaneous" works, *A Vindication of the Rights of Women*, which has been a continuing inspiration to feminists of the 19th and 20th centuries.

HER PERSON: "The first of a new genus," she called herself, and she was. She supported herself as a writer, belonged to an influential intellectual circle in London, lived openly with two men, and, also openly, bore a child out of wedlock—all at a time when a respectable woman was supposed to marry and hold her tongue.

During her lifetime she assumed responsibility for what she called the Wollstonecraft "standing dish of family cares." As a child she had stood between her parents to protect her mother from the blows of an alcoholic husband (he once hung a dog in a drunken rage), and Mary had slept outside her parents' door at night when it was likely that violence might erupt and she would be needed. She also nursed her mother during her last illness and rescued her sister Eliza from an unhappy marriage.

At 15 she had vowed "never ... to endure a life of dependence." To earn a living, she spent two years as a companion to a wealthy woman, ran a day school, and was governess for the daughters of an Irish lord. Meanwhile, wearing her green eyeshade and spectacles, she was writing, and in 1787 her first book was issued by Joseph Johnson, a London publisher, who became her good friend and introduced her to Tom Paine, Joseph Priestley, William Blake, and other famous men. Her *Vindication of the Rights of Men* (1790) made her reputation; her *Vindication of the Rights of Women* (1792) brought her notoriety. The views she espoused—e.g., social and sexual equality with men, full educational rights for women—shocked many, including Horace Walpole, who dubbed her a "hyena in petticoats."

A hyena she wasn't; her manner was charming, her voice soft. Though she considered anger to be her worst fault, self-pity probably was. She was fervent, proud, and prone to melancholy and depression. Twice she attempted suicide, and at least once considered herself on the brink of madness. Tallish, with a good body, she had fair skin, long eyelashes, auburn hair, and almond-shaped hazel eyes.

She lived in France for two years, during the time of the Reign of Terror, and was a member of the Girondin circle (the Girondins lost their power while she was there) and the lover of the American Gilbert Imlay. Back in London, she ended up living with, and then marrying, William Godwin. Mary died from complications following childbirth. When Fanny, Mary's daughter by Imlay, killed herself at 22, she was wearing her mother's corset, monogrammed "M.W." Mary's daughter by Godwin, named for her mother, was to become Mary Shelley, the author of *Frankenstein*. Before eloping, young Mary and her lover, Percy Bysshe Shelley, paid final tribute to Mary Wollstonecraft by joining hands over her grave.

LOVE LIFE: Early in her life Mary had passionate, though probably nonsexual, relationships with women. She was essentially modest, shocked by the "jokes and hoyden tricks young women indulged themselves in," and she felt that "women are in general too familiar with each other." However, she wrote possessive, loving, jealous letters to Jane Arden, a childhood friend, and her relationship with Fanny Blood, whom she met when she was 16 and Fanny was 18, was "a friendship so fervent, as for years to have constituted the ruling passion of her mind," according to William Godwin. Mary and Fanny lived in the home of Fanny's parents and ran a school together. Fanny was in love with Hugh Skeys. He finally married her in 1785 and took her to Lisbon, where she died during childbirth. Her death threw Mary into a long depression.

Mary tended to like young romantic men and middle-aged geniuses like painter Henry Fuseli, a member of Joseph Johnson's circle, who was short, melodramatic, married, and bisexual. It is unlikely that Mary slept with Fuseli, though she was obsessed with him. She didn't entirely approve of his character. "I hate to see that reptile vanity sliming over the noble qualities of your heart," she once wrote him. When she asked his wife, Sophia, if she might live with them as "an inmate of the family," Sophia threw her out. Meanwhile Mary turned down a number of marriage proposals and coined the phrase "legalized prostitution" as a synonym for marriage.

Gilbert Imlay, first of the two major loves of her life, was an American frontiers-man and writer, somewhat shady, tall and lean, with a "steady, bold step." It was probably in a Left Bank hotel room that Mary first had sexual intercourse, at the age of 33 or 34. "I don't want to be loved like a goddess, but I wish to be necessary to you," she told Imlay. When he was off on business, she wrote him love letters rhapsodizing on his glistening eyes and the "suffusion that creeps over your relaxing features." In May, 1794, Fanny was born, and their passion faded after that. Mary followed Imlay back to London, where he was having an affair with an actress. Mary proposed a *ménage à trois*, but the other woman would have none of it. Twice Mary tried suicide, once by jumping into the Thames from Putney Bridge in the rain. "I would encounter a thousand deaths, rather than a night like the last," her suicide note to Imlay read. "May you never know by experience what you have made me endure." She was rescued by boatmen.

On Apr. 14, 1796, she boldly paid a call on William Godwin, the moral radical philosopher, whom she had met at an intellectual gathering five years before. (At that first meeting he had disliked her for talking too much, saying Thomas Paine couldn't even get a word in.) A genius with a head too large for his body, Godwin was known for his integrity and kind heart. It was a case of "friendship melting into love," he later said. That summer they became lovers, though after their first night together, she felt that he had acted "injudiciously," and decided to return to her role as a "Solitary Walker." He convinced her to continue the affair. It was domestic and joyous; they sent notes to each other constantly. In November she wrote, "I have seldom seen so much live fire running about my features as this morning when recollections—very dear, called forth the blush of pleasure, as I adjusted my hair." That month she missed her period. (She probably knew of no method of birth control other than Godwin's "chance-medley system," a kind of rhythm method he may have introduced her to.)

Against their basic principles (neither was religious), they were quietly married in church on Mar. 29, 1797. They did not live together. Mary wanted her husband "riveted in my heart" but not "always at my elbow," yet she was jealous when a Miss Pinkerton flirted with him.

Their child, Mary, was born Aug. 30 with the help of a midwife. (Mary gave the job to a midwife rather than a male doctor as a form of feminist protest.) However, the placenta wasn't expelled and a male physician was called in. He tore the placenta in pieces from her uterus with his hands, a procedure that caused her great agony and probably gave her puerperal fever. Puppies were brought in to suck off her excess milk, because she was too ill to breast-feed her child. When she was given opium for pain, she said, "Oh, Godwin, I am in heaven," and he, who had been tenderly nursing her, replied, "You mean, my dear, that your physical symptoms are somewhat easier." She died Sept. 10.

HER THOUGHTS: "I think there is not a subject that admits so little of reasoning as love."

"The heart is very treacherous, and if we do not guard against its first emotions, we shall not afterward be able to prevent its sighing for impossibilities."

"A master and mistress of a family ought not to continue to love each other with passion ... to indulge those emotions which disturb the order of society ... a neglected wife is, in general, the best mother."

—A.E.

V

The Pen is Prominent

Caffeinated Casanova

HONORÉ DE BALZAC (May 20, 1799–Aug. 18, 1850)

HIS FAME: French master of the realistic novel, Balzac was a genius fueled by coffee, lust, and ambition. He wrote some 97 works, including two dozen volumes of *La Comédie Humaine* ("The Human Comedy").

Balzac liked this 1848 picture for its "truthfulness"

HIS PERSON: Balzac endured a miserable childhood in Tours with an indifferent mother. She sent him off to boarding school and soon gave birth to a "love child" whom she openly preferred to him. After completing law studies at the Sorbonne and working three years as a law clerk, Balzac locked himself in an attic in 1819 and started his writing career. It would be another 10 years before he established his reputation with *Les Chouans*. In the interim, he was a hack writer, launched a short-lived printing concern, and speculated in a Sardinian silver-mining operation which drove him beyond the brink of debt. Throughout his life he remained imprudent about money.

Inspired by a desire to be the Napoleon of novelists—near his desk was a marble bust of the late emperor—Balzac began his typical workday at midnight. Dressed in a monastic white robe, he would write, wearing out a quantity of goose-quill pens and pausing only to drink several dozen cups of coffee in the next 16 hours. One could not write, he believed, without quantities of black coffee. Between books he would reach other extremes, eating orgiastically and engaging in simultaneous love affairs as he charted a course through high society.

His reputation as a novelist who "understood" women grew, and so did the number of his female admirers. Portraits do not reveal him to be especially attractive; he stood 5 ft. 2 in. and was grossly overweight. His dark hair dripped pomade and he wore even the best clothes badly. He had dirty fingernails and picked his nose in public. For his charm to shine through, however, he had only to speak; all of his conversation sparkled with vitality and wit. A lover of worthless and often useless antiques, he collected canes with handles of gold, silver, and turquoise. Inside one handle, he claimed, was the nude portrait of a "secret mistress."

Balzac's literary genius captured the essence of bourgeois life. He converted simple "romance" into a record of human experience. On his deathbed, he is said to have cried, "Send for Bianchon!"—a doctor he created in *La Comédie*

Humaine. To the end, Balzac was different; of all the great writers to have died of drinking, he was probably the only one for whom the fatal brew was coffee.

SEX LIFE: "A woman is a well-served table," Balzac observed, "which one sees with different eyes before and after the meal." By all accounts Balzac devoured his lovers as voraciously as he enjoyed a good dinner. Young girls bored him. He preferred mature women and launched virtually every affair by saying, "I never had a mother. I never knew a mother's love."

Despite his bizarre appearance, he had no trouble finding willing women and he was a virtuoso at juggling his numerous affairs. (It is surprising that he had time for such dalliances, given his immense literary output.) A number of the 12,000 letters he received from female admirers contained explicit propositions, many of which he accepted. He struck a responsive chord in these readers with his sympathetic delineations of unappreciated matrons. Biographer Noel Gerson refers to Balzac's virile and experimental bedroom manner. Apparently he had been instructed by many courtesans over the years. "He slept with aristocrats, courtesans and trollops indiscriminately," wrote Gerson, "displaying in his love life the same dazzling diversification that appeared in his writing. His yearning for romance, like all of his other appetites, was insatiable." Considering his indifference to fidelity, it is noteworthy that he also had at least two very tender and enduring affairs of the heart.

SEX PARTNERS: Balzac boasted of his chastity during his early days of writing, but at 23 he was introduced to sexual passion by Laure de Berny, a 45-year-old grandmother. Madame de Berny was prototypical of the lonely older woman with an inner fire so frequently depicted in his work. Their relationship lasted 15 years.

In the beginning of this affair, Balzac also found time to carry on with a wealthy widow, the blond Duchesse d'Abrantès. He met her in 1825, when she was 40, and set his sights on making love to this woman who had slept with Prince Metternich. Another of her charms was her fortune—always an irresistible feature in a woman—and she paid some of his mounting debts. The two reigning passions of his life—women and fame—were in part fueled by a desire for the money they could provide. He became increasingly promiscuous with age and always maintained the energy required for his demanding double life as lover and artist.

In 1832, however, he suffered rejection at the hands of the Marquise de Castries, one of the most beautiful aristocrats in France. She was perhaps the first woman of note who simply could not overcome the revulsion she felt at his appearance. Balzac got his revenge by ridiculing her in his novel *La Duchesse de Langeais*. The episode left him feeling vulnerable and depressed; he was 33, and his debts were mounting. Madame de Berny was aged and he felt the need for a protectress more than ever. Then he received an intriguing letter from the Ukraine signed "The Stranger." Balzac replied and discovered the writer, Evelina Hanska, was married to a baron. The following year Balzac and Evelina secretly met in Switzerland; they found each other plumper than they had hoped, but no matter.

They fell in love. For years they conducted a passionate correspondence. Evelina promised to marry him when her elderly husband died. Occasionally they would meet in various European cities for lovemaking that was, as he described it, "honey and fire." Balzac did not deny himself the attentions of other women, however, and throughout this time he dallied with 24-year-old Marie Louise du Fresnay, who bore him a child. She passed the infant off as her husband's. He also had a two-month affair with the most "divinely beautiful" woman he had ever seen, the notoriously promiscuous Lady Ellenborough. Another affair—with Frances Sarah Lovell, the reputedly "highly sexed" wife of Count Guidoboni-Visconti—lasted five years. She affectionately called him "Bally," paid many of his debts, and bore him a child. Throughout all of this philandering Balzac kept up his association with various prostitutes, sometimes two at a time. In 1841 Evelina Hanska's husband died, and Balzac, troubled by his coffee-assaulted stomach, was finally willing to settle down. But Evelina, who was now pregnant with Balzac's child, refused to marry him. The child was stillborn. Balzac moved in with another mistress, Louise Breugnol, and his health began to fail. When he was near death, Evelina took pity on him and, 17 years after they first met, they were wed. Balzac would die five months later, with his wife asleep in the next room.

HIS ADVICE: "It is easier to be a lover than a husband, for the same reason that it is more difficult to show a ready wit all day long than to say a good thing occasionally."

—*G.A.M.*

Never–Neverland

J. M. BARRIE (May 9, 1860–June 19, 1937)

HIS FAME: Known today only as the creator of the beloved Peter Pan, "the boy who would not grow up," J. M. Barrie was a literary giant in his lifetime. He wrote a number of best-selling novels and a steady stream of plays that wee performed to packed houses.

HIS PERSON: Wrote James Matthew Barrie, "To be born is to be wrecked on an island." Perhaps this is an apt description for one whose long life was peppered with the tragic deaths of those he loved. The first occurred when Barrie was six, growing up in the little Scottish village of

Kirriemuir. His father was a handloom weaver, and he and his wife, Margaret Ogilvy (it was a Scottish custom for a married woman to keep her maiden name), had 10 children. Margaret's favorite, David, was 13 when he died after an ice-skating accident. His death plunged her into a black depression. Little Jamie Barrie did all he could to cheer his mother; he tried to be so much like his brother "that even my mother should not see the difference." Once he even put on the dead boy's clothes and imitated his whistle, hoping to fool his mother with his disguise.

As Barrie grew up, his dream of becoming a writer solidified, and by age 25 he was a London journalist. Success came quickly as he turned to novels and plays, churning out a prodigious amount of work. Soon London was at Barrie's feet, worshiping the shy little playwright (he was barely over 5 ft. tall) who had become an immensely wealthy and famous man.

In addition to his work, Barrie amused himself with his cricket team, the Allahakbarries ("Allah akbar" is Arabic for "Heaven help us"), which was made up of noted writers and artists such as A. Conan Doyle and P. G. Wodehouse. Barrie's primary pleasure, however, was in his numerous friendships with children. Despite these diversions, his personal life was usually troubled. His mother died, one of his sisters died, and another sister's fiancé died after falling off the horse Barrie had given him as a wedding present.

These tragedies contributed to Barrie's lifelong reserve. Only children always felt comfortable with the tiny man with the deep, rumbling Scottish voice. His behavior often intimidated adults, for he would lapse into silences that went unbroken for hours and he swung regularly from dark depression to charming gaiety. One of Barrie's better traits was his unstinting generosity. He gave abundantly to friends and strangers in need, often doing so anonymously.

Barrie died at the age of 77, finally worn down by emotional duress and by the physical ailments that had long troubled him—a constant cough (he was forever puffing on his pipe), colds, headaches, and insomnia. His last words were "I can't sleep."

LOVE LIFE: Barrie had one of the most profound cases of mother fixation ever recorded. When he was 36, he wrote a book called *Margaret Ogilvy*, a sentimental memoir of his mother. The book was so personal and adoring that one critic called it "a positive act of indecency."

In addition to being completely wrapped up in his mother, Barrie was woefully self-conscious about his height, and this strongly affected his attitude toward the opposite sex. When he was 18, he made these notes in his notebook (in which he often wrote in the third person):

> *He is very young-looking—trial of his life that he is always thought a boy.*
> *Greatest horror—dream I am married—wake up shrieking.*
> *Grow up & have to give up marbles—awful thought.*

Barrie wrote of being crushed that women found him "quite harmless," and summed up his misery in this outpouring:

Six feet three inches … If I had really grown to this it would have made a great difference in my life. I would not have bothered turning out reels of printed matter. My one aim would have been to become a favorite of the ladies which between you and me has always been my sorrowful ambition. The things I could have said to them if my legs had been longer. Read that with a bitter cry.

Barrie frequently got crushes on actresses, but he did little in the way of pursuing them. In 1892 he was looking for a second leading lady for his new play, *Walker, London*. He wanted a woman who was "young, quite charming … and able to flirt." He gave the part to 29-year-old Mary Ansell, who met all the requirements.

Mary and Barrie began to see a great deal of each other. There are two versions of what ensued. In one, Barrie, after keeping Mary anxiously waiting, finally proposed. He then fell seriously ill with pneumonia—a matter of national concern—and Mary rushed to his side and nursed him back to health. In the other version, she refused to marry him many times. When he fell ill, she went to him at his mother's behest, and they were married on what was expected to be his deathbed. The wedding took place on July 9, 1894.

What followed on the fateful honeymoon is a matter of speculation. It has been much rumored that Barrie was completely impotent—he was jokingly labeled "the boy who couldn't go up"—but no one knows for sure. One biographer states that Mary told her friends that the marriage was never consummated. In Andrew Birkin's excellent biography, *J. M. Barrie and the Lost Boys*, Mary is said to have confided to a friend that she and her husband had "normal marital relations" in the early days of their marriage. John Middleton Murry, a friend of Mary's, wrote in a journal that Barrie was guilty of "unmentionable sex behavior towards Mary."

Wherever the truth lies, it does not point to sexual harmony between the Barries. Nevertheless, the couple settled down to married life, and Mary turned her frustrated maternal instincts toward Porthos, their big brown-and-white St. Bernard, who was the model for Nana in *Peter Pan*. While Mary tried to amuse herself with clothes and house-hunting, Barrie plunged himself into his work, which he never discussed with his wife. He remained silent for hours in her company and, in fact, rarely spent any time with her.

What hours they did pass together were spent walking Porthos in London's Kensington Gardens. On one such stroll, Barrie met two handsome, charming little boys wearing red berets, out walking with their nurse. They were four-year-old George Davies and his three-year-old brother Jack. They were the sons of Arthur Llewelyn Davies, a good-looking, struggling young barrister, and his wife, Sylvia, a marvelous, enchanting woman, sister of actor Gerald du Maurier and daughter of author George du Maurier. Sylvia had another boy, Peter, and would soon add two more to her brood, Michael and Nico.

Thus began the truly great love affair in J. M. Barrie's life. Barrie "adopted" the Davieses. He visited them daily, bought them presents, flirted sweetly with Sylvia (whom he worshiped), and entertained the boys with the stories of fairies and pirate adventures that were to become *Peter Pan*. Years later Barrie told the boys, "I made Peter by rubbing the five of you violently together, as savages with two sticks produce a flame." Barrie's "adoption" disgruntled Arthur Davies, but he remained a gentleman. What could he do? Barrie, as he had written of himself, was "quite harmless," and the boys loved "Uncle Jim." What Mary Barrie felt about all this can be imagined. To add to the irony, Barrie was working on a novel, *Tommy and Grizel*, and switched from Mary to Sylvia as his model for Grizel.

In 1907 tragedy struck. Arthur died of a terrible disease of the jaw, having been previously disfigured by facial operations. Barrie was at his side throughout the ordeal, and at the courageous Sylvia's side as well. It was understood that Barrie would assume financial responsibility for the family.

Two years later, as Barrie sat working at his desk in his summer cottage, a second blow fell. The gardener informed him that Mary Barrie (now in her 40s) was having an affair with Gilbert Cannan, a 24-year-old barrister and writer and a friend of the Barries. A stupefied Barrie confronted his wife, who denied nothing and asked for a divorce. In a letter to her friend H. G. Wells, she wrote, "He seems to have developed the most ardent passion for me now that he has lost me; that frightens me." In 1909 the couple filed for divorce; it was granted the following year. Barrie was shattered. In an attempt to keep publicity from further upsetting the miserable playwright, a petition was prepared asking the press to treat the matter discreetly. It was signed by Henry James, H. G. Wells, and Arthur Wing Pinero, among others.

Barrie found his only solace in his work and in the Davies family. But one year later, in 1910, Sylvia died. The 50-year-old Barrie legally adopted the five boys. George and Peter were then at Eton, Jack was in the navy, and Michael and Nico were 10 and 6, respectively. All the boys felt well loved by "Uncle Jim," though George and Michael were the favorites. Michael, particularly, had much in common with Barrie; he was sensitive, poetic, and brilliant. In 1914 George went to war in France; in March, 1915, he was killed.

Barrie's grief was terrible. But an even greater grief was waiting. In May, 1921, Michael died. He drowned with a friend in a pool at Oxford. Because he could not swim and was terrified of water, his death was thought by many to be a suicide. It was the greatest and the cruelest blow Barrie had ever received. He never fully recovered. A year after Michael's death, Barrie wrote to Michael's Oxford tutor, "What happened was in a way the end of me."

The question has often been asked: Was Barrie homosexually in love with the boys? It is a difficult question to answer, for J. M. Barrie was not a simple man. In many ways his love for the boys was an odd mixture of a father's, a mother's, and a lover's. Nico, the last Davies boy alive, does not feel it was a sexual love. He once said, "Of all the men I have ever known, Barrie was the wittiest, and the best company. He was also the least interested in sex. He was a darling man. He was an innocent; which is why he could write *Peter Pan*."

HIS THOUGHTS: From *Tommy and Grizel*: "He was a boy only. She knew that, despite all he had gone through, he was still a boy. And boys cannot love. Oh, is it not cruel to ask a boy to love?"

"What is genius? It is the power to be a boy again at will."

"Nothing that happens after we are 12 matters very much."

—*A. W.*

Lecherous Bozzy

JAMES BOSWELL (Oct. 29, 1740–May 19, 1795)

HIS FAME: James Boswell had long been known for his *Life of Samuel Johnson*, but the discovery of Boswell's papers in the 1920s made him the "best-self-documented man in all history." Entering the pages of Boswell's private journals, the armchair voyeur is propelled into the ribald life of 18th-century London, where the all-too-human Boswell, with a wink, leads his reader into the most licentious and fleshly of pleasures.

Boswell at age 25

HIS PERSON: Boswell's mother was a Calvinist, his father a stern Whig. He grew up in Scotland on the family estate, abnormally afraid of sin and hellfire. Throughout his life, he suffered from episodic depression. At 16 he was laid low by a "terrible Hypochondria" and became a Methodist vegetarian, which, like a later fling with Catholicism, did not last.

After graduating from the University of Edinburgh at 18, he hoped to become a military man, but his father insisted he study law. Boswell capitulated and began his practice in Edinburgh in 1766. Meanwhile, he pursued a literary career and spent as much time in London as he could. It was in London, in 1763, that he met the ponderous and morally wise Dr. Johnson—then 53 years old while Boswell was only 22—in the back room of a bookstore.

Boswell hunted throughout Europe for a dowried wife, recording the yearly income of various women in his journal along with their other attributes. But in 1769 he married his penniless first cousin, Margaret Montgomerie, when he suddenly realized he loved her while he was on his way to court an Irish heiress. Margaret was a buxom, witty, patient woman with beautiful eyes. Her life with Boswell was stormy. He would debauch and reform, debauch and reform. Grand gestures, hedged with prudence, were typical of him, and he would promise "from henceforth I shall be a perfect man; at least I hope so." In 1789 his wife died of tuberculosis, leaving him to raise five children, who adored him in spite of his failings. His last decade was spent in public disgrace and private remorse because of his dissolute lifestyle.

SEX LIFE: The story of Boswell's sex life is littered with a multiplicity of characters—innumerable whores, several mistresses, uncountable partners in casual sex, and many rich ladies unsuccessfully pursued with marriage in mind. Even in the context of his time he was a male chauvinist, with a great need for women and a great need to consider the opposite sex inferior.

The urge to copulate came over him strongly in times of heightened emotion. In church he lay "plans for having a woman" while having "the most sincere feelings of religion"; after seeing a notice of his mother's death in a newspaper, he assuaged his shock in a Paris brothel. He was likely to hunt for prostitutes after drinking, and often had more than one in a night. One evening, he got soused toasting a woman he was courting, then spent the rest of the night with a "whore worthy of Boswell if Boswell must have a whore."

His treatment of whores was often abominable. When a prostitute in a park complained loudly that the sixpence he had offered her was not enough for her services, Boswell told the crowd that had gathered that he was an officer on half pay and could afford no more. He then forced himself on her and "abused her in blackguard style," his euphemism for rape.

Intercourse was best for him if it was done hurriedly, while standing up, and in public places—in parks and dark spots, once on a bridge accompanied by the sound of the water gurgling below. Though often filled with remorse, he also bragged of dipping "my machine into the Canal" and performing "most manfully." He claimed that "licentious love" made him "humane, polite, generous" (generous, that is, with compliments—but not financial rewards—to prostitutes who performed well).

After his marriage he was faithful to Margaret for nearly three years, but she was often "adverse to hymeneal rites," so he told her he "must have a concubine," and she agreed. He called his practice of having many women "Asiatic multiplicity" and kept it up until the end of his life.

SEX PARTNERS: In his preteen years his partners were trees, which he assaulted by masturbating against their trunks, something he thought of as a "small sin." But by age 13 he so feared the "larger sin" of fornication that he briefly considered self-castration. He put that thought behind him when he discovered that women were attracted to him. Though short and somewhat fleshy, he was handsome, with black hair and eyes and a complex, alert expression.

It was a prostitute, Sally Forrester, who introduced him to the "melting and transporting rites of love." She was only one in a long line of whores, many of whom infected and reinfected him with gonorrhea from the age of 19 on. His short-term affairs included those with the highborn, like Girolama Piccolomini, whom he met in Siena in 1765. Though she was crazy about him, he courted another while pursuing her; he would send a valet out with a letter for Girolama in one pocket and a letter for his second *signorina* in another pocket. Even though their affair didn't last long, she wrote to him after he returned to England. And in addition there were a pregnant soldier's wife who came to his rooms in Berlin selling chocolate (with her it was "in a minute—over"); Annie Cunninghame, his wife's orphaned, teenaged niece, from whom he "snatched a little romping pleasure"; Thérèse le Vasseur, Jean

Jacques Rousseau's mistress, as he was escorting her to meet Rousseau in England; and Peggy Doig, a servant girl, who bore him a son who died in infancy.

In 1762 he planned on a "winter's safe copulation" with Mrs. Anne Lewis, his first "real" mistress. They consummated their love at the Black Lion Inn, where he performed with vigor—five climaxes in one night—at a total cost, he boasted, of only 18 shillings for bed and food. It was no bargain, as he discovered six days later. "Too, too plain was Signor Gonorrhea." In a fury, he wrote her demanding repayment of a small loan, and the affair was over. His affair with a Mrs. Dodds, a lady "admirably formed for amorous dalliance" who was "quite a rompish girl," though "ill-bred," lasted longer. She had a daughter by him, who died soon after birth.

The upshot of his relationships was not *always* seduction. Off and on, for six years, he pursued Zélide (Isabella van Tuyll), a Dutch aristocrat and writer. "She is much my superior. One does not like that." She refused his conditional marriage proposals (he demanded the right to approve whatever she wrote). They insulted each other with exquisite hostility; he suggested she turn to embroidery rather than speculate about metaphysics, and she called him "a fatuous fool" with "the arrogant rigidity of an old Cato."

Rigidity was something Boswell seldom worried about, but with Margaret, his "valuable spouse," he suffered at least one bout of impotence. He recorded only five such incidents in his entire diary. Margaret hated these logs in which he chronicled his sexual escapades by means of a Greek-letter code, which, unfortunately for her, she could decipher.

MEDICAL REPORT: In Boswell's *Clap and Other Essays*, using Boswell's detailed journals, Dr. William B. Ober has compiled a comprehensive medical chart of Boswell's 19 bouts of urethritis due to gonorrhea, from his first infection at age 19 to his last at age 50. Though Boswell often used "armour" (condoms made of dried animal intestines), his sexual drives were such that he constantly took chances. By the time he was 22, when he suffered his third infection, he recognized the symptoms and described them as "an unaccountable alarm of unexpected evil; a little heat in the members of my body sacred to Cupid, very like a symptom of that distemper with which Venus, when cross, takes it into her head to plague her votaries." He also suffered from prostatitis (inflammation of the prostate gland), epididymitis (inflammation of the testicles), and crab lice. And he suffered through the treatments as well—irrigation of the urinary tract with medicines, bloodletting, cauterization of the sores, and even something called Kennedy's Lisbon Diet Drink (a concoction of sarsaparilla, sassafras, licorice, and guaiac wood). Boswell died at age 54 of complications arising from his gonorrhea.

—A.E.

Sexual Savant

SIR RICHARD BURTON (Mar. 19, 1821–Oct. 20, 1890)

HIS FAME: Explorer, linguist, and anthropologist, Sir Richard Burton had a thirst for adventure and a disregard for sexual convention which made him one of the most famous and controversial figures in Victorian England.

Burton in 1861

HIS PERSON: Burton was born in Devonshire, the son of a handsome Irishman and a homely English girl. The elder Burton's lack of success kept the family on the move throughout Richard's childhood. Growing up in France and Italy with a great deal of freedom, Richard and his brother Edward educated themselves on the streets, where Richard early showed both a great talent for languages—"one of them pornography," it was later said—and a taste for seamy adventures. Sent to Oxford in 1840, he was expelled two years later, at which time he became an ensign in the Bombay Infantry. He was so fascinated by exotic India that he stayed for eight years. During this time he learned at least nine more languages, immersing himself in Muslim and Hindu culture and living like a native. Recalled because his investigation of homosexual brothels resulted in an outcry against him, he proceeded to write four books on India while living in France with his mother and sister. In 1853 he traveled to the Middle East, disguising himself as a Muslim so that he could secretly enter Mecca. In 1857-1859 he explored Central Africa with John Speke, and the two men became the first Europeans to discover Lake Tanganyika. Burton then traveled across the U.S. by stagecoach to Salt Lake City, where he observed the Mormon colony with great interest. He married Isabel Arundell in 1861 and spent the next four years as consul on the West African island of Fernando Po. By 1865 he was off to Brazil, which he hated. He escaped Brazil when he was appointed consul in Damascus. As a result of his own political indiscretions and Isabel's misplaced missionary zeal, he was dismissed from this post in 1871, and he left his beloved Middle East for Trieste. There he lived comfortably until his death, having gained financial success with his translation of *The Arabian Nights*. To the end of his life, Burton held that nothing could be called obscene because tastes and taboos differed throughout the world. Burton liked to tell a story about a group of Englishmen who went to visit a Muslim sultan in the desert. As the Englishmen watched, the sultan's wife tumbled off her camel. As she did so, her dress slipped up and her private parts were revealed to all. "Was the sultan embarrassed?" asked Burton. "Oh, quite the opposite; he was pleased, because his wife had kept her face covered during her accident."

SEX LIFE: Although Burton was a virtual encyclopedia of sexual knowledge, there is little evidence that he applied this expertise to his personal life. "I'm no hot amorist," he once admitted. Despite his posturing and his satanic appearance, his life was full of overtones of homosexuality, impotence, and castration complexes. As a young man he seems to have enjoyed a riotous sex life—orgies with the prostitutes of Naples, a "roystering and rackety life" among the women of Bombay, and even an attempt to kidnap and seduce a nun. (However, he complained that his Hindu *bubu* ("mistress"), who was skilled at prolonging the act of love, "cannot be satisfied ... with less than 20 minutes.") On the other hand, when Sir Charles Napier sent him to investigate a homosexual brothel in Karachi, Burton's report was so detailed and graphic as to smack of participation.

It was in his relationship with his wife that Burton's sexual vagueness was most apparent. Isabel, a beautiful girl from a titled family, set her sights on the explorer at the time of their first meeting, when his "gypsy" eyes "completely magnetized" her. It took five years of courtship—during which time Burton made protracted trips to observe sexual customs in East Africa and Mormon Utah—before the couple became engaged. Believing celibacy to be "an unmitigated evil" and polygamy the "instinctive law of nature," Burton admitted to a fascination with Brigham Young's Mormons which caused Isabel great discomfort. Nonetheless, she finally snared him, later saying, "I wish I were a man: if I were I would be Richard Burton. But as I am a woman, I would be Richard Burton's wife."

Although before her marriage Isabel had promised herself to "keep up the honeymoon romance, whether at home or in the desert," the newlyweds' bliss was shortlived. Apparently sublimating his sexual drive in his constant quest for adventure, Burton seems never to have generated much passion for his wife. He preferred to view her as a "brother," saying, "I am a spoilt twin and she is the missing fragment." What little lust he felt after his marriage was shared not with Isabel but with cronies such as Richard Monckton Milnes, an eccentric who had a world-famous library replete with the best collection of erotica in England. Always particularly intrigued by flagellation and sexual mutilation, Burton found ready material in Milnes' library.

Regardless of her frustrations as his wife, Isabel admired Burton fiercely, participating vicariously in his adventures and in his fame. Yet at the same time it was important to her to tame the man who claimed to have committed "every sin in the Decalogue." Ultimately, she was successful in binding to her the outer man, who seldom left his wife's side in their later years, but she was never able to subdue Burton's spirit.

SEX PARTNERS: After his initiation at the hands of the prostitutes of Naples, Burton's first real affair was with an unnamed Hindu woman he kept as a *bubu*. Soon afterward he met a beautiful Persian girl in a caravan near Karachi, and the memory of this girl "with features carved in marble like a Greek's" remained with him for the rest of his life. After his return from India in 1849, he fell in love with his cousin Elizabeth Stisted, but her parents would not allow a marriage. At the time he met Isabel he was carrying on "a very serious flirtation" with another cousin, Louisa. Although he was somewhat tight-lipped about his involvements with native women, he did write that the Wagogo women of East Africa were "well-disposed towards strangers of fair complexion, apparently with the permission of their husbands."

BURTON'S *NIGHTS*: One of Isabel's greatest unrealized desires was to convert her husband to Catholicism. She fooled herself into believing that he was a secret Catholic, but he in fact remained unattached to any religious faith. Unlike her, he was obsessed with man, not God, and his ceaseless study resulted in more than 50 volumes of observations on native life. By far the most famous of these works is his 16-volume translation of *The Arabian Nights*. In voluminous footnotes he presented much of the vast amount of material he had collected over the years on such subjects as childbirth, circumcision, defloration, hermaphroditism, castration, birth control, and aphrodisiacs (including recipes for hashish).

Although some reviewers considered *The Arabian Nights* a marvel of psychological insight presented in an incomparable literary style, others called it "garbage of the brothels." Singled out for special indignation was the collection's "Terminal Essay," in which Burton dealt with sex education for women and devoted over 18,000 words to a study of homosexuality. A "household edition" of *The Arabian Nights*—throughout which Isabel had judiciously substituted "assistant wife" for "concubine"—sold dismally, but the unexpurgated work netted Burton 10,000 guineas, the first appreciable sum he had ever received for any of his writings. He reflected, "Now that I know the tastes of England, we need never be without money."

The tastes of England were not Isabel's tastes, and Burton's pornographic works were a constant source of anguish to her. After *The Arabian Nights*, he embarked upon yet another scandalous project, which he called "the crown of my life": the translation of *The Scented Garden*, a 16th-century Arabian sex manual. Burton confided to a friend, "It will be a marvellous repertory of Eastern wisdom; how Eunuchs are made, and are married; what they do in marriage; female circumcision, the Fellahs copulating with crocodiles, etc." It was about to be completed on the day of his death.

As executor of his estate, Isabel was in an agony of indecision about *The Scented Garden*. Her inner turmoil was brought to an end when Richard suddenly appeared to her in a vision and clearly instructed her to burn the book. Thus, although she had been offered 6,000 guineas for it, she burned the manuscript page by page, saying that to have accepted the offer would have been equivalent to selling her soul for 30 pieces of silver. More important than the destruction of *The Scented Garden* was the tossing into the fire of Burton's diaries, which spanned 40 years. Neither her friends nor posterity could forgive her.

QUIRKS: When Burton was living in India, he once set up house for some 40 monkeys in order to study their "language." The "prettiest" of the apes Burton called his "wife," adorning her with pearls and seating her by his side at the table.

MEDICAL REPORT: Dr. F. Grenfell Baker, Burton's private physician, reported that Burton told him that his testicles had been severely damaged in an unspecified "accident" in East Africa, and that he had been sterile thereafter.

—W.L.

Thank Heaven For Little Girls

LEWIS CARROLL (Jan. 27, 1832–Jan. 14, 1898)

HIS FAME: Writing under the name of Lewis Carroll, mathematician Charles Lutwidge Dodgson authored the two best-known children's stories in the world: *Alice's Adventures in Wonderland* and *Through the Looking Glass.*

HIS PERSON: The eldest son in a family of 11 children—7 of them girls—he showed early interest in the three subjects that would dominate his career: mathematics, writing, and divinity. He entered Christ Church College at Oxford at the age of 18 and stayed there for the rest of his life, teaching mathematics and logic and serving as a deacon.

He maintained his health and youthful appearance well into his 60s. He was a shy person who stammered, although his stammer disappeared in the presence of children. He preferred the company of little girls and greatly enjoyed taking them on outings, during which he entertained them with fantastic stories. It was on one such excursion, on July 4, 1862, that Dodgson, inspired by 10-year-old Alice Liddell, created the tale that became known as *Alice's Adventures in Wonderland.* Published three years later, it brought its author more fame than was considered proper for an Oxford don.

LOVES AND QUIRKS: Lewis Carroll's sex life was one big quirk, and that quirk was little girls. Although he undoubtedly died a virgin, he had over 100 girl friends. He didn't care for little boys: "To me they are not an attractive race of beings." To one correspondent he wrote, "I am fond of children (except boys)."

At first he recruited his companions from the children of his friends, but later he expanded his horizons and discovered new child friends on the train, at the beach, or while out walking. He became a connoisseur of little girls, preferring them to be upper-class, fair of face and figure, intelligent, and energetic. He got along well with all girls up to the age of 10, although he thought 12-year-olds were the most attractive physically. Puberty ruined everything, and 9 out of 10 of his child friends disappeared from his life by age 16. Gertrude Chataway, one of the few who remained close to Carroll into adulthood, explained it thus: "Many girls when grown up do not like to be treated as if they were still 10 years old. Personally I found that habit of his very refreshing."

Carroll was an early amateur photographer, and naturally his best subjects were little girls. He often posed them in costumes, but his favorite costume was none at all. Apparently this hobby of photographing naked, prepubescent girls (though always with their mothers' permission) led to some nasty gossip, because in 1880 he suddenly gave up photography.

In the late 1880s he took to inviting girls to stay with him at his summer quarters in Eastbourne, and he loosened his age restrictions a bit. In a letter to Gertrude Chataway, when he was 59, Carroll wrote, "Five years ago ... I ventured to invite a little girl of 10, who was lent me without the least demur. The next year I had one of 12 staying here for a week. The next year I invited one of 14, quite expecting a refusal.... To my surprise, and delight, her mother simply wrote 'Irene may come to you for a week, or a fortnight....' After taking her back, I boldly invited an elder sister of hers, aged 18. She came quite readily. I've had another 18-year-old since, and feel quite reckless now, as to ages."

It has been speculated that Lewis Carroll proposed marriage to Alice Liddell, but there is no proof of this, although Alice's mother did angrily destroy all the letters Carroll had written to her daughter. It has also been suggested that he had an affair with the actress Ellen Terry, whom he first admired on the stage when she was 8 and he was 24. They did become lifelong friends, but in her autobiography she dismissed talk of a romantic involvement with the comment, "He was as fond of me as he could be of anyone over the age of 10."

HIS THOUGHTS: Carroll was very concerned about the proper age to kiss a girl. He wrote to one mother: "Are they [your daughters] kissable? ... With girls under 14, I don't think it necessary to ask the question: but I guess Margery to be *over* 14, and, in such cases, with new friends, I usually ask the mother's leave."

In another letter he wrote: "Would you kindly tell me if I may reckon *your* girls as invitable ... to tea, or dinner *singly*. I know of cases where they are invitable in *sets* only ... and such friendships I don't think worth going on with. I don't think anyone knows what girl-nature is, who has only seen them in the presence of their mothers or sisters."

HIS ADVICE: "If you limit your actions in life to things that *nobody* can possibly find fault with, you will not do much."

—*D. W.*

The Sorcerer

CARLOS CASTANEDA (Dec. 25, 1925–Apr. 27, 1998)

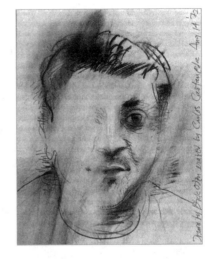

HIS FAME: One of the most prominent, most problematic and, perhaps, most profound figures of the consciousness expansion movement of the 1960s and '70s, Carlos Castaneda is famous for a series of books describing his training as a shaman under the probably fictional Yaqui sorcerer don Juan Matus. His bestselling works landed him on the cover of *Time* magazine, and inspired a generation in the use of psychoactive plants and the quest for altered and heightened awareness.

HIS PERSON: Much of Castaneda's life is shrouded in mystery and outright obfuscation—following instructions given to him by "don Juan," and which he prescribed to his students as well. Castaneda invested considerable effort in erasing the details of his life as an exercise in overcoming the personal ego, making lying about his past into a spiritual exercise, and teaching his disciples to do the same. What is verifiable, often in contradiction to what Castaneda claimed about himself, is that he was born in Cajamarca, Peru, in 1925, the son of a jeweler, and immigrated to the United States in the 1950s. He was educated at UCLA (he garnered his Ph.D. in 1970), during which time he was known by faculty and students alike as something of a pathological liar. It was also during this time that he wrote his first three books, describing his apprenticeship under the sorcerer don Juan—a Yaqui Indian that Castaneda allegedly met while doing anthropological field work along the United States-Mexico border. "Don Juan" subsequently took Castaneda on as an apprentice brujo, beginning by "blasting" Castaneda's hard-headed Western rationalism with psychoactive plants like peyote and jimson weed. Over the coming years, don Juan would mentor Castaneda in further magical disciplines—"dreaming," "stalking," ways to shift the "assemblage point" of consciousness and other aspects of the warrior's path. Don Juan, Castaneda and, later, Castaneda's many admirers and students had a paranoid view of a "predatory universe," haunted by creatures he dubbed "Flyers," energetic parasites who vampirically feed on the awareness of the masses, making us into "cattle" and increasing the creatures' power. Castaneda's work with "don Juan" not only fulfilled the requirements of his Ph.D. but also garnered him international celebrity and many prominent admirers, including William S. Burroughs, Federico Fellini, John Lennon, Jim Morrison, Joyce Carol Oates and Octavio Paz. While the anthropological world immediately called the existence of don Juan into question, the literary and art worlds (not to mention Castaneda's adoring public) responded with a resolute "who cares?"

SEX LIFE: Whether or not Castaneda's magical worldview holds any veracity, what is clear is that he used his celebrity and mystique to surround himself with flocks of adoring female disciples for decades, the inner circle of which was subject to the full gamut of cult tactics. Carlos was 5'2", and described himself as "short, brown and ugly," though photographs show an attractive man. Thus, feeling inferior as a young boy, Castaneda listened to what he claimed was his grandfather's sage advice: "You can't fuck *all* the women in world, but you can try!" Castaneda claimed in public to be appalled by this, yet it was a rule he lived by in private. Long-term Castaneda companion and his supposed sorceric equal Carol Tiggs estimated that Castaneda may have been the greatest seducer in history, and that "Wilt [Chamberlain] had nothing on him!" In 1960 he married Margaret Runyon. He had gotten a vasectomy, but wanted a child, and arranged with a friend of the couple to impregnate his wife. Jeremy Castaneda was born, doted over in his early years by his father, and as he grew up, was cruelly rejected, ultimately being cut out of Castaneda's will.

While Castaneda's public image was that of a sincere spiritual seeker and, later, a man of sorceric power and knowledge, in private Castaneda was a power-mad, paranoiac cult leader more than willing to justify any demands or cruelty imposed on his flock of female students by claiming it was for the good of their own development, regularly changing his magical rationales for his actions to suit his whim of the moment. Despite deception, cruelty and abuse, his truly magnetic personality kept his followers devoted to him for decades, all the way up to his death in 1998. Many of his inner circle, for whom he alternately filled the role of guru, lover and abusive father figure, committed suicide or went missing following his death. Despite his public claims of celibacy (which, conveniently, Castaneda's male followers and seminar attendees followed diligently, leaving more for Carlos), Castaneda was dead-set on the establishment of his own sexual empire. Women brought into Castaneda's orbit were often romanced and laden with spiritual flattery, given jewelry and other "magical" objects—given roles to play in Castaneda's world, pitted against one another, told of their special magical status or otherwise subjected to the tried-and-true technique of New Age flattery. They were also encouraged to pimp for him, as an exercise in overcoming their "human" (a.k.a. bad) jealousy. The few male members of the inner circle had rare sex with the three most advanced "witches," and any romance between group members was strictly forbidden. Amy Wallace, whose memoir of her involvement with Castaneda, *Sorcerer's Apprentice, My Life With Carlos Castaneda*, recorded Castaneda's seduction of her in detail, including his sex-magical claims that his sperm would alter her brain cells and make her a "witch," a.k.a. a sorcerer. Despite her admiration for

Castaneda's teachings and their passionate love/hate relationship, Wallace believes Carlos was spearheading a cult. Castaneda's lovers were allowed two roles—those of wife and daughter—and they were interchangeable, a situation made all the more disturbing by Carlos' frequent boasts that his "daughter," a teenage waitress he had picked up and given a high position in the groups' hierarchy, had "seduced" him at the age of seven. Women were subjected to rigorous sexual deconditioning techniques—chief among them the practice of *recapitulation*, a nigh-endless task in which disciples would make a list of every person they had ever slept with, followed by every person they had ever met—in their entire life—and then meditate on breathing away the psychic toxins left by these interactions. Castaneda terrorized his female followers with tales of energetic parasites—which he called "worms"—left in their wombs by ex-lovers. Short of receiving Carlos' sperm, women were recommended to accompany their meditations with seven years of celibacy. Presumably this would kill the worms, and they would never have sex again. Children, he believed, left a devastating "hole" in a woman's energy body, making it practically impossible for her to become a sorcerer. He strongly encouraged the outright severing of relations with children and parents, siblings and friends to reclaim lost energy. The inner circle was under orders to do so—to reclaim lost energy. In one book Castaneda recounts a tale of don Juan convincing him to eat his own child (the waitress) which he does, after which it is revealed that it was only beef jerky, a test of his obedience.

Carlos lived in a Spanish-style compound in Westwood, Los Angeles, with two close companions, his "witches." He had a separate entrance, and snuck his lovers in to bathe their genitals in a magical potion of rosemary which grew in his garden, supposedly given to him by don Juan. Washing the genitals with this liquid was believed to further detox and purify the womb from poisonous human sperm. He believed almost all humans are incapable of experiencing sexual pleasure.

Castaneda's predatory universe, in which he said "fear was his guide," justified his by-any-means-necessary approach to breaking into freedom. In that, he was not far from the taboo-busting behavior of Hindu tantrics, or the "crazy wisdom" of Tibetan Buddhist teachers like Chögyam Trungpa. Like many spiritual figures, however, Castaneda had convinced himself that he was a "nagual," a kind of god—and he and his circle were the only people in the world who had access to true sorceric knowledge. In his mythos, they would burn together, spontaneously combusting, their bodies reforming on another plane, where they would begin their eternal travels in Infinity. Mere human death was seen as a shameful failing.

Carlos died of complications from adult-onset diabetes and pancreatic cancer, and remaining cult members attempted to keep his death a secret. His body was cremated, and five of the top-ranking witches disappeared to commit group suicide, being unable to live without him. So far, only one body has been recovered, and a Missing Persons search is in progress. Remaining cult members have denied that the missing women planned a suicide pact.

HIS THOUGHTS: "Man is being exterminated. There's nothing of our own in our minds—we have flyers' (the parasitic creatures) minds. pendulum-like, back-and-forth They make us morose, depressive; they fill us with kinky sexual thoughts—all masturbation comes from the flyers. And we don't even like our own genitals! That's the flyers, too. They make us frigid... And luhh-hvvvveee... that's the worst thing of all, *human love*. It's a flyer trick, looking for 'love,' but we just replace one head with another, changing all the time! That's not *love*."

—J.L.

The Satyr

GABRIELE D'ANNUNZIO (Mar. 12, 1863–Mar. 1, 1938)

HIS FAME: A controversial poet and politician during the Fascist era, D'Annunzio laced his works so heavily with vivid descriptions of sex and death that author Henry James labeled them "vulgar." The eccentric writer, who was also Italy's greatest WWI flying ace, will perhaps be best remembered as one of the founders of realism in Italian fiction. His works include *The Innocent, The Flame of Life*, and *The Child of Pleasure*.

HIS PERSON: By the time he graduated from the Cicognini College in Prato, D'Annunzio, son of the wealthy mayor of Pescara, had published his first volume of poetry and earned a scandalous reputation as a Don Juan. Women found the handsome, muscular, 5-ft. 6-in. poet irresistible, and he engaged in hundreds of affairs during his lifetime, often using them as story lines for his novels.

In 1883 he settled down long enough to marry Maria Gallese, daughter of the Duke di Gallese. Despite the fact that D'Annunzio continued his illicit affairs, Maria bore him three sons in the next four years. D'Annunzio spent their income frivolously—on clothes, servants, and other women—until his lavish lifestyle forced him into bankruptcy. In 1910 he fled to France to escape creditors.

When WWI erupted, D'Annunzio returned to Italy. In 1915 he enlisted as an aviator and was commander of the air squad at Venice; he gained recognition after flying a number of dangerous missions. His heroics cost him his left eye when it was struck by an enemy bullet. Undaunted, he led a troop of 12,000 "Arditi" into the city of Fiume in 1919, conquered it, and ruled the Italian town as a dictator for over a year. In reward for his vociferous support of Mussolini's Fascist government, D'Annunzio was named Prince of Monte Nevoso in 1924.

Surrounded by 100 servants and separated from his family, D'Annunzio lived out his final years at his elegant estate on Lake Garda. Obsessed with making his death as memorable as his life, he claimed he'd like to be shot from a cannon or die by having his body dissolved in acid. Undramatically, he died of a cerebral hemorrhage, while sitting at his desk, 11 days before his 75th birthday.

LOVE LIFE: D'Annunzio, who considered himself a "high priest of erotica," was a sexual maniac whose life and writings were guided by women. By age seven he had fallen in love for the first time. At 12 he was turned in to school officials for trying to guide the hands of a nun who was fitting his uniform toward his "private parts." When he turned 16, D'Annunzio had his first woman, a Florentine prostitute, after pawning a watch to pay her fee.

His reputation as a womanizer did not prevent his marriage to Maria Hardouin di Gallese. Her father, the Duke di Gallese, despised D'Annunzio, but Maria ignored her father's threats of boycotting the wedding and severing all family ties. The 20-year-old author married his 19-year-old bride in a sad, somber ceremony on July 28, 1883. No one knew the willowy blond-haired Maria was already three months pregnant.

Repulsed by his wife's pregnant body, D'Annunzio took to sleeping with other women, but he still treated Maria to an "intoxicating night" from time to time. He left her in 1887, and before Maria died she had earned the title "*madone des tantes*" ("madonna of the aunties") for having charmed a number of male homosexuals.

Though he viewed women as enemies, was rarely compassionate, had eyes which Sarah Bernhardt described as "little blobs of shit," and was bald by age 23, women dreamed of making love to him. Ladies were willing to risk their wealth, marriages, and reputations to sleep with him, although D'Annunzio was well known as "a fickle lover whose passions were swift and changing."

D'Annunzio's tastes knew no boundaries. He was susceptible to the beauty of young boys and engaged in an affair with a lesbian mistress, whom he taught "the parting of the legs." Even in his old age, the author's sexual prowess did not wane. He paid people to visit neighboring villages and bring him women "whose novelty would stimulate his fancy." He boasted of having enjoyed 1,000 female conquests in his lifetime.

SEX PARTNERS: Many of his affairs ended tragically. His romance with the religious, moralistic Countess Mancini created such a severe guilt complex in the countess that she went mad and was institutionalized in an asylum. Likewise, his relationship with Marchesa Alessandra di Rudini Carlotti, daughter of an Italian prime minister, ended in ruin. A "sinner of love" who desired to repent for her frenzied lovemaking, the marchesa abandoned her children, became a nun, and died as the mother superior of a convent in Savoy.

D'Annunzio was instantly awestruck by Barbara Leoni's goddesslike beauty when they met at a concert in 1887. They shared a passionately intense love and met at secret hideaways as often as they could. She confessed to him, "You have had a virgin in me." He kept one of Barbara's hairs in a locket, and throughout their five-year affair, while making love, D'Annunzio would cover her body with rose petals. As she lay nude in bed sound asleep, he would sit alongside her jotting down details of their lovemaking bouts and noting the contours of her body for future use in *The Innocent*.

In 1891 D'Annunzio kindled an affair with 30-year-old Countess Maria Anguissola Gravina Cruyllas di Ramacca, wife of a Neapolitan nobleman. The statuesque woman was driven mad by jealousy and squandered a fortune in a futile attempt to retain D'Annunzio's love. They were charged with, and found guilty of, committing adultery and sentenced to five months in prison. Their sentences, however, were later suspended, and D'Annunzio went on to father two out-of-wedlock children by the countess during the course of their affair. When their son, Dante Gabriele, was born, the countess threatened to kill the baby unless D'Annunzio remained faithful. He refused to do so, however, showering his affections instead on the actress Eleonora Duse.

D'Annunzio's affair with Duse, a woman four and a half years his senior, was the zenith of his romantic career. For "La Duse," who also had had many lovers, D'Annunzio proved the consuming passion of her life. Starting in 1895 they lived together, on and off, for nine years. She not only demanded little of him, but gave him her money, inspiration, companionship, and advice. In return, he wrote plays in which Duse performed.

During the good days, they drank strange brews together from a virgin's skull, and on one birthday she sent him a dozen telegrams, one every hour. But in 1900 Duse was stunned by the publication of a novel written by D'Annunzio which detailed their affair intimately. According to *The Flame of Life*, D'Annunzio had tired of his 42-year-old lover because her body had grown old and her breasts (to D'Annunzio a woman's most important asset) had begun to droop. They parted company in 1904, and after Duse died D'Annunzio claimed he could communicate with her spirit by biting into a pomegranate while standing in front of a statue of the Buddha.

HIS THOUGHTS: "We always believe that our first love is the last, and that our last love is the first."

—*A.K.*

The Unhappy Husband

CHARLES DICKENS (Feb. 7, 1812–June 9, 1870)

HIS FAME: Generally considered to be the greatest English novelist of all time, Dickens authored such classics as *Pickwick Papers, Oliver Twist, A Christmas Carol, David Copperfield, A Tale of Two Cities*, and *Great Expectations*.

HIS PERSON: One of his grandfathers was a domestic servant and the other was an embezzler. His father, a clerk, made a good living, but was an extravagant spender and ended up in debtors' prison in 1824. Twelve-year-old Charles was forced to drop out of school and work in a factory. After working for some years as a newspaper reporter, Dickens began his first comic serial, *Pickwick Papers*, in 1836. Within a matter of months he had become the most popular writer in England. Over the next 30 years he produced a stream of enormously successful stories, which brought him popularity among rich and poor alike.

Dickens giving a reading

Dickens was a source of endless energy. A witty conversationalist, he was always the center of attention. In later life he discovered that it was more enjoyable, as well as more profitable, to give public readings of his works than it was to write new ones. Dickens was a fantastic performer, and his audiences invariably left the theater in a state of emotional exhaustion. The intensity that he brought to these performances, which numbered over 470, is thought to have contributed to his early death at age 58.

LOVE LIFE: What we know of Charles Dickens' love life is colored by the fact that while letters written *by* him (over 10,000, in fact) are well preserved, letters written *to* him are almost nonexistent. Acutely aware of his reputation as a symbol of wholesome family life, Dickens once a year made a bonfire and burned private letters which he had received.

When he was 17, he fell deeply in love with Maria Beadnell, a flirtatious 18-year-old who wore her dark hair in ringlets. Maria toyed with him capriciously until, after four years of agony, Dickens—his pride badly wounded—finally gave up the courtship. His experience of rejection was so strong that he learned to suppress his emotions, and many years later he wrote that he was still "chary of showing my affections, even to my children, except when they are very young."

Not surprisingly, when Dickens chose a woman to be his wife, he approached the relationship in a different manner. Catherine Hogarth (or Kate, as she was known) was quiet and slow-moving, and Dickens made it clear from the beginning that he expected her to bear children and do what she was told. Ten children later, Kate was much fatter and less discerning than when she had married Dickens, and submitted totally to his will. As the years went by, Dickens not only lost his affection for his wife, but came to resent and detest her. He engaged in numerous flirtations and infatuations, usually with teenage girls, whom he found to be the essence of innocent perfection.

In fact, the most important woman in Charles Dickens' love life was not his wife, Kate, but her younger sister, Mary, who was also Kate's best friend. When Charles and Kate married in 1836, 16-year-old Mary came to live with them. The three got along remarkably well. Mary was not as pretty as Kate but she had a greater appreciation of literature, and Dickens enjoyed her companionship. Then one Saturday night in May, 1837, tragedy struck. Kate, Mary, and Charles had returned from the theater and bidden one another good night when Charles heard a strangled cry from Mary's bedroom. Mary had been stricken by a heart attack. The next day she died peacefully in Dickens' arms at the age of 17. He removed a ring from her finger, put it on his own, and wore it for the rest of his life.

For months he dreamed about Mary every night. He saved her clothes, wished to be buried in her grave, and—a very rare occurrence—was unable to write for two months.

No woman, neither his wife nor any of the young women to whom he was attracted, was able to compare in Dickens' mind and heart with Mary Hogarth. It was impossible to compete with the memory of someone who was frozen in time as a virginal, uncorrupted teenager.

However, if anyone had the potential to excite similar feelings in Dickens and to relieve him of the boredom of his marriage, it was his first love, Maria Beadnell, whose handwriting he recognized on a letter in his daily mail in February, 1855. Over 20 years after the unfortunate termination of their youthful romance, she wrote to him. She was now Maria Winter, married with two daughters. Although she wrote that she was "toothless, fat, old and ugly," Dickens' heart went immediately back to 1830. Once again he wrote her passionate and suggestive letters and arranged for them to meet—alone.

When the rendezvous finally took place, Dickens' wild and uninhibited fantasies plummeted back to the real world suddenly and with great force. Maria had become fat and silly and bore a greater resemblance to his wife than to the Maria Beadnell of his youth. As soon as he saw her, Dickens began the long and irritating process of terminating their relationship.

Although Dickens spent much time in the company of women, it is probable that he had only one sexual affair. Two years after the Maria Winter debacle, the 45-year-old Dickens met Ellen Ternan, an actress who was 18 years old—the same age as his eldest daughter. Ellen was bright and intelligent, and Kate became jealous of the time her husband spent with young "Nelly," as Ellen was known. Less than a year later, a shocked public read Dickens' announcement of his separation from his wife of 22 years.

Ironically, the separation announcement set off rumors that Dickens was having an affair, not with Ellen Ternan, but with another of Kate's sisters, Georgina Hogarth. Georgina had moved into the Dickens household in 1842, when she was 15 years old, and over the years she had supplanted her sister as head of the household, even taking over the responsibility of raising the children. It could be that Georgina and Dickens did make love at some point, but there is no evidence to support this possibility. Not only was Georgina not jealous of Ellen Ternan, but she had a genuine fondness for her.

During the last years of his life, Dickens spent much of his free time with Ellen and her family and supported them financially. It has been said that Dickens and Ellen had a child who died in infancy, but this is unproven. He did mention Ellen first in his will.

Dickens may have achieved some romantic satisfaction with Ellen Ternan, but the lifelong feeling of incompleteness which he experienced is best expressed in a letter which he wrote to a friend: "Why is it, that as with poor David [Copperfield], a sense comes always crushing on me, now, when I fall into low spirits, as of one happiness I have missed in life, and one friend and companion I have never made?"

QUIRKS: While he was living with Kate, Dickens would occasionally divert his frustrations and nervous energies into mock passions. For example, he pretended to be hopelessly in love with the youthful Queen Victoria, and he greatly annoyed his wife by parading about the house singing:

> My heart is at Windsor,
> My heart is not here,
> My heart is at Windsor,
> A-following my dear.

When the queen married, Dickens told his friends that he was considering suicide. He continued this charade long after it ceased to be funny, and rumors spread that the great author had gone mad.

HIS ADVICE: From *Pickwick Papers*: "Wen you're a married man, Samivel, you'll understand a good many things as you don't understand now; but vether it's worth while goin' through so much to learn so little, as the charity-boy said ven he got to the end of the alphabet, is a matter o' taste."

—*D. W.*

The Late Bloomer

FËDOR DOSTOEVSKI (Nov. 11, 1821–Feb. 9, 1881)

HIS FAME: Obsessed with human suffering and man's capacity for evil, Dostoevski became famous for writing novels which addressed these themes— most notably *Crime and Punishment, The Idiot, The Possessed,* and *The Brothers Karamazov.* He is one of the most widely read 19th-century authors today and is recognized as having had a profound influence on world literature.

HIS PERSON: Short, frail, and awkward, Dostoevski had such a strong tendency toward nervousness that his face and lips twitched in social situations. Nervous attacks in his teens developed into epilepsy in his 20s, and during one attack he damaged his right eye, causing it to become permanently distended and giving his eyes an asymmetrical appearance. In every way a passionate man, when Dostoevski became excited about something, he worked himself up into a frenzy, gesticulated wildly, and, some say, even foamed at the mouth.

Personal events intensified Dostoevski's preoccupation with sorrow and crime. When he was 13 his mother died of consumption, and five years later his drunken, miserly, and lecherous father was killed by his serfs in an act of retribution. Soon afterward Dostoevski abandoned his career as a military engineer to become a writer, and at 25 his first novel, *Poor Folk,* was well received. Yet a few years later he was charged with revolutionary conspiracy for his involvement with a socialist circle and placed before a firing squad. The death sentence was commuted at the last minute, and he was exiled to Siberia instead. It was 10 years before he was able to return to St. Petersburg (now Leningrad) and resume writing, and another seven years before he began producing his major works. Despite fragile health and a life fraught with tragedy, failed love affairs, and poverty, Dostoevski lived to be 59 and died a happily married man, having achieved relative creative and financial stability and a recognition commensurate with his work.

SEX LIFE AND PARTNERS: Called "the Russian Marquis de Sade" by his contemporary Turgenev, Dostoevski did not have a major affair until he was 34, and did not find any semblance of sexual fulfillment until his mid-40s. His lack of romantic involvement in his 20s was probably due to a lack of both self-confidence and opportunity; it is thought that he did sleep with prostitutes. After being transferred from hard labor to soldiering in Siberia, his sex life became more active. He dallied with several attractive young ladies before becoming involved with the pretty, soon-to-be-widowed Marya Isayeva, whom he later married. Dostoevski was as attracted by Marya's suffering (she was consumptive and her husband had been an alcoholic) as by her feminine virtues. He had a major epileptic fit on their honeymoon, which set the tone of their romantic life together. They were very unhappy (he once said that the more they suffered, the more he loved her), and neither received any sexual satisfaction from the union. Marya died seven years later, and Dostoevski continued an affair he had begun with Apollinariya Suslova. The proud, red-haired, fiery "Polina" was an emancipated woman, 20 years his junior, with a formidable intellect and personality, but after their first year together she kept Dostoevski at arm's length, teasing and torturing him for several years before ending the affair. (Later it became evident that she was sadomasochistic and sexually cold.) The highly sexed Dostoevski began finding release in gambling, and his passion reached such a frenzy while traveling with Polina that he would pawn their valuables and beg his relatives for money. His gambling mania did not abate until the happiness he experienced in his second marriage encouraged him to stop.

After Polina, Dostoevski was determined to marry a woman with whom he could establish some sort of domestic order and attempt to normalize, or at least stabilize, his sexual energies. Following two unhappy relationships, fortune finally smiled on the long-suffering lover. Dostoevski was 45 when he married his 20-year-old stenographer, Anna Snitkina, who idolized him and wrote that she was "prepared to spend the rest of my life on my knees to him." Young and inexperienced, Anna found nothing strange in the extreme passion, and sometimes violence, of her husband's lovemaking, during which he could reach a blind frenzy similar to that he experienced in his epileptic fits, and after which he sometimes lay as rigid as a dead man. His erotic fantasies were highly diverse and sometimes involved the simulation or actual act of corporal punishment. Unfortunately, Anna obliterated the truly salacious details of Dostoevski's letters to her. However, by the time of their marriage his penchant for violent and unusual forms of lovemaking was well known. The letters do show that Dostoevski enjoyed vast amounts of sexual pleasure with Anna, that a feverish physical longing would overcome him after not seeing her for a short while, and that he continually had nightmares over the possibility that she was unfaithful. (She never was.) His passion was intensified by the awareness that his young, attractive wife found him sexually satisfying as well, and he often pleaded with her to speak more frankly on the subject. Dostoevski's love and lust for Anna actually grew more intense during their 14 years of marriage, and at 57 he was able to say that "[my] ecstasy and rapture are inexhaustible."

QUIRKS: Dostoevski was a foot fetishist. There is often mention, in his letters to Anna, of his longing for her feet: "I go down on my knees before you and I kiss your dear feet a countless number of times. I imagine this every minute and

I enjoy it." Anna had been a little diffident about the matter, and hence he insisted: "I bear witness that I long to kiss every toe on your foot and you will see I shall achieve my purpose."

He was also obsessed with young girls. There was a rumor that Dostoevski had actually had sex with a little girl (presumably a child prostitute) when her governess brought the child to him in his bath. Certain friends claimed he even bragged about it, but this was never substantiated. It is true, however, that in both his conversation and his novels the sexual fantasy of an older man who corrupts a young girl appears constantly; it was evidently much on his mind.

—*J.H.*

The Exuberant Satyr

ALEXANDRE DUMAS (July 24, 1802–Dec. 5, 1870)

HIS FAME: The most prolific author of the French Romantic school, Dumas wrote or collaborated on 91 plays and hundreds of volumes of fiction, travel, cookery, and biography. He is best remembered for *The Three Musketeers*, *The Count of Monte Cristo*, and *The Man in the Iron Mask*.

HIS PERSON: Dumas' paternal grandparents were a French nobleman and a black woman from Santo Domingo. His father, a general during the French Revolution, died when Alexandre was three years old, and from him he inherited vitality, fearlessness, and great physical

Dumas and Adah Isaacs Menken

strength. Dumas' African ancestry was evident in his coarse hair and Creole accent, and a salon habitué who was crude enough to comment on the writer's heritage received the reply: "My father was a mulatto, my grandmother was a Negress, and my great-grandparents were monkeys. My pedigree begins where yours ends."

Young Dumas received a scanty education from a priest in his home village of Villers-Cotterêts near Soissons. At age 20, thanks to his beautiful handwriting, he was employed in Paris as a clerk for the Duc d'Orléans, later King Louis Philippe. Dumas set up housekeeping with Catherine Labay, a dressmaker eight years his senior, who bore him a son in 1824. Alexandre Dumas *fils* was destined to become an author like his father.

In 1829 the elder Dumas scored his first great dramatic success with the play

Henri III et sa cour, and by 1831, when the drama *Antony* was staged, he was the darling of Paris and a Byronic hero in his own right. A lifelong pattern of mistresses, extravagance, and superhuman work habits began to crystallize. Dumas was earning huge sums, but he spent all he received and then some. His estate, Monte Cristo, was a carnival of starving artists, predatory actresses, playmates of the moment, and unclassified parasites.

Dumas was a first-rate cook, an excellent hunter, and with age became a devoted father. He liked to boast that he had sired 500 illegitimate children, but the figure was somewhere closer to the three he acknowledged.

SEX LIFE: Dumas was a tireless satyr from the time he lost his virginity at 17 until his death at 68. His women described him as being like a "force of nature." Incapable of fidelity himself, he never demanded it of others, not even his wife. Once he caught her with his friend Roger de Beauvoir in her bedroom. It was a cold night, and Dumas, although piqued, invited de Beauvoir to share their bed. At dawn Dumas looked across the sleeping form of his wife and caught de Beauvoir's worried glance. "Shall two old friends quarrel about a woman, even when she's a lawful wife?" Dumas asked and shook de Beauvoir's hand.

In his later years Dumas amused himself by presenting his many young lovers with ribald epigrams and obscene poems that he had written. When a lady was offended, he pointed out that "all that comes from Daddy Dumas will fetch a good price someday."

A female visitor once surprised Dumas while he was "at leisure." She barged in on the author to find his obese body stuffed into crimson tights, while three naked girls were festooned around his chair. To Dumas' vast amusement, the woman turned and fled. However, the maestro found the infrequent visits of his disapproving son anything but a laughing matter, and he would run around the house frantically hiding women in closets whenever the younger Dumas was announced. Dumas *fils* would tell friends that his father was a "grown-up child I had when I was very young."

As time went on, father and son reached an understanding. How close they eventually became is illustrated by a conversation overheard by a group of mutual friends. "You know, Father," said Dumas *fils*, "it's a great bore, you always giving me your old mistresses to sleep with and your new boots to break in!" "What are you complaining about?" his father replied. "You should look on it as an honor. It proves you have a thick prick and a narrow foot."

SEX PARTNERS: Dumas did not believe in the sanctity of wedlock, and his one official marriage was the result of blackmail. Ida Ferrier, a small, rotund actress with whom the author was having an affair, had an accomplice buy up all of Dumas' unpaid IOUs and gave him the choice of either marriage or debtors' prison. The Viscount of Chateaubriand, who acted as a witness at their wedding, is said to have stared at the sagging bosom of the bride and remarked to a guest, "You see, my friend, everything I bless collapses." The marriage itself collapsed about four years later, when Ida ran off with an Italian nobleman.

Dumas favored actresses, and at one point three of his lovers found themselves in the awkward position of acting together in a Dumas play. The author bore up well under the resultant friction. However, Fanny Gordosa, a dark, passionate Italian, was more trying. Her first husband had become so overwhelmed by her enormous sexual appetite that he had forced her to wear wet towels around her middle in an effort to cool her off. Dumas unwrapped the lady, but her habit of receiving visitors while perched on a chamber pot and chasing his other women out of the house he found intolerable. He finally sent Fanny away, pretending that he suspected her of "playing duets" with her music teachers.

Dumas toured Garibaldi's Italy in the company of Émilie Cordier, whom he called "the Admiral." By day he kept her dressed up as a sailor lad, thereby fooling nobody. The ruse proved impractical when Émilie became pregnant, and the "Admiral" finally presented Dumas with a daughter, Micaella, whom he loved dearly. Much to his sorrow, Émilie refused to let Dumas acknowledge the child legally, and thus Micaella was deprived of her rightful share of her father's royalties when she came of age.

The author had a brief affair with dancer Lola Montez, whose lurid stage performances shocked women, delighted men, and made her the reigning sex symbol of her day. She spent only one or two nights with Dumas, but she performed on those occasions with unparalleled panache.

Even when Dumas was in his 60s, he remained a favorite subject of gossip. His final fling came with Adah Isaacs Menken, a Jewish girl from New Orleans, whom the world knew as "the Naked Lady." Adah's most famous stage role called for her to be bound to the back of a galloping horse, clad only in a sheer leotard. The spectacle impressed both bondage fetishists and morality crusaders, who called her show "a libel upon women, whose sex is hereby depraved and whose chastity is corrupted." Needless to say, she was everything Dumas asked for in a woman.

Adah was something of a literary groupie, an aspiring poet who boasted of her friendships with Bret Harte, Mark Twain, and other authors. She cajoled Dumas into having his picture taken with her. The resultant photo, which shows vampish Adah draped all over the aging Papa Dumas, circulated throughout Paris and went a long way toward destroying his waning prestige. It was his last great scandal. He died soon after, unrepentant, but depressed by his fears that his literary works were of no value.

MEDICAL REPORT: It has been rumored that Dumas died of the effects of advanced syphilis, contracted around the time of his affair with Lola Montez. Like many high-living men of his century, the author regarded the disease as an unfortunate adjunct to having a good time, a minor ailment that usually disappeared. According to one of his friends, Dumas "continued his irregular mode of life until the very moment that disease paralyzed both his brain and his limbs."

FROM HIS OWN LIPS: "I need several mistresses. If I had only one, she'd be dead inside eight days."

—*M.S.*

The Farmer

WILLIAM FAULKNER (Sept. 25, 1897–July 6, 1962)

HIS FAME: Though he often referred to himself as a farmer, William Faulkner was one of the greatest American writers of the 20th century. His novels, which include *The Sound and the Fury, Light in August, The Hamlet*, and *As I Lay Dying*, won him great critical acclaim, as well as the Nobel Prize for literature in 1949.

HIS PERSON: William Faulkner (he added the *u* himself) was born in New Albany, Miss., not far from Oxford, which was to become the model for his fictional town of Jefferson, in the fictional county of Yoknapatawpha—the setting for most of his novels and stories.

Faulkner's mistress' favorite photo

His ancestors were wealthy and powerful Southerners, ruined by the Civil War. His father, Murry, who owned a livery stable and hardware store—both of which failed—became business manager of the state university. Faulkner—shy, slow-moving, and soft-spoken—was the eldest of four brothers. He dropped out of high school after two years and worked in a bank. When WWI broke out, he tried to enlist in the army, but was rejected because he was only 5 ft. 5 in. tall and underweight. He joined the Royal Air Force in Canada, and though the war ended before he could see action, his experiences left him with a lifelong love of airplanes. He returned home and took several odd jobs to earn enough for "paper, tobacco, food, and a little whiskey," while he read voraciously and began to write. In 1925 he moved to New Orleans and met Sherwood Anderson, who recommended Faulkner's first novel, *Soldiers' Pay*, to his own publisher.

The hard-drinking, nattily attired (he leaned toward tweeds), pipe-smoking Faulkner made little money from his fiction and was forced to go to Hollywood, where sporadically, for more than a decade, he wrote for the screen while he continued writing novels and short stories. "I write when the spirit moves me," he said, "and the spirit moves me every day." By 1946 his books were out of print, but upon publication of *The Portable Faulkner* his star rose rapidly. In spite of the fact that he despised ceremonies, he interrupted a drinking spree and came out of his alcoholic stupor long enough to accept a Nobel Prize in 1949. He won the Pulitzer Prize for *The Fable* in 1954 and traveled abroad extensively for the State Dept. in later years. In May of 1962 he returned to Oxford, the town he had made famous in his novels. He died there a few months later of a coronary thrombosis, with his wife and family by his side.

SEX LIFE: As a teenager, Faulkner's first love was the daughter of a neighbor, Estelle Oldham, but she married another man and moved to China, leaving Faulkner's world in pieces. He was usually attracted to small, childlike women. His next love, Helen Baird, fitted this description, and he dedicated his novel *Mosquitoes* to her. Eventually she spurned him and married someone else. Eleven years after Estelle departed for China, she returned as a divorced woman, and Faulkner began courting her again. They were married in 1929. Their first child, Alabama, died soon after birth. They had a second daughter and named her Jill. The Faulkner marriage was a rocky one. Whether out of predilection or despair, both drank heavily. However, neither moved toward divorce.

While in Hollywood Faulkner met Meta Carpenter, secretary to director Howard Hawks, for whom Faulkner was also working. Meta was 10 years his junior, very attractive, petite, and a fellow Southerner. Faulkner pursued her ardently until they became lovers. He was, according to her, a very passionate lover. "In the art of love, Bill, the restrained, remote man by day, was seized with a consuming sexual urgency.... Sexual gratification made him voluble and outgoing. He told bawdy stories and kissed the blushes that inflamed my skin." Faulkner reportedly told Meta, "I've always been afraid of going out of control, I get so carried away." He was a romantic (he once covered their bed with gardenia and jasmine petals), and he often presented her with erotic drawings and poems like the following:

Meta
Bill
Meta
who soft keeps for him his love's
long girl's body sweet to fuck.
Bill.

In a letter he wrote, "For Meta, my heart, my jasmine garden, my April and May cunt; my white one, my blonde morning, winged, my sweetly dividing, my honeycloyed, my sweet-assed gal. Bill." In 1937 Meta married someone else, but she kept in touch with Faulkner for the next 16 years. In 1950 Faulkner met Joan Williams, a 21-year-old writer. They became lovers, but the difference in their ages proved too great and they broke up in 1953.

HIS THOUGHTS: From a 1925 letter to his mother: "After having observed Americans in Europe I believe more than ever that sex with us has become a national disease. The way we get it into our politics and religion, where it does not belong any more than digestion belongs there. All our paintings, our novels, our music, is concerned with it, sort of leering and winking and rubbing hands on it. But Latin people keep it where it belongs, in a secondary place. Their painting and music and literature has nothing to do with sex. Far more healthy than our way."

From a letter to Joan Williams: "One of the nicest conveniences a woman can have, is someone she can pick up when she needs or wants him; then when she doesn't, she can drop him and know that he will still be right there when she does need or want him again. Only she should remember this. Sometimes when she drops him, he might break. Sometimes, when she reaches down for him, he might not be there."

—C.H.S.

Paradise Lost

F. SCOTT FITZGERALD (Sept. 24, 1896–Dec. 21, 1940)

HIS FAME: As the young author who christened the 1920s "the Jazz Age," Fitzgerald enjoyed early success as spokesman for a rebellious generation. However, his popularity had waned by the end of the decade, and when he died at age 44, not one of his books was in print. Ironically, his novels *The Great Gatsby* and *Tender Is the Night* are today regarded as classics of American literature.

HIS PERSON: While still a boy in St. Paul, Minn., Francis Scott Key Fitzgerald was more comfortable in the company of girls than with his own sex. He made a sincere effort to play football in school, but he preferred Mr. Van Arnum's dancing class, where a gentleman danced with a handkerchief in his right hand so he would not soil the back of the girls' dresses. Scott's father, who was by no means coarse, once said he would give $5 just to hear his son swear.

In contrast to his contemporary Ernest Hemingway, Scott was put off by blood, sweat, grime, and the seamy side of life. His stories and novels dealt mainly with the very rich, whose intrigues and decadence fascinated the middle-class, Irish Catholic Fitzgerald. He once remarked to Hemingway, "The very rich are different from you and me." To which Papa replied, "Yes, they have more money." Scott's first novel, *This Side of Paradise*, was about flaming youth at Princeton University, a hotbed of liquor and indiscriminate kissing. The book was quite scandalous for 1920, and as a result it sold well. At the age of 23 Fitzgerald was a best-selling author with all the money, fame, and opportunities that go with that distinction. He married Zelda Sayre, the daughter of an Alabama Supreme Court justice, and with her began a party that would last 10 years and span two continents. Scott never again duplicated his initial literary success. Although his subsequent novels were well received by critics, they did not sell. *Gatsby* earned him about $1,200, a third of what *The Saturday Evening Post* paid him for hack-written short stories. So Scott stayed busy writing short stories, at first to support his and Zelda's extravagant lifestyle, and later on to pay for Zelda's care after her nervous breakdowns. In 1937, deeply in debt to hospitals and friends, Scott went to Hollywood to write screenplays for MGM. The pay was substantial, but Fitzgerald often found himself at odds with the Hollywood establishment and eventually lost his contract with the studio. He was at work on a novel about the film industry, *The Last Tycoon*, when he died of a heart attack at age 44. Eight years later Zelda burned to death in an asylum fire.

SEX PARTNERS: As an army lieutenant stationed in the South, Scott met Zelda Sayre at a Montgomery Country Club dance. The strikingly beautiful blond 17-year-old was surrounded by a pack of hopeful young men, but Scott would not be outdone. "I was immediately smitten and cut in on her. She was the most beautiful girl I had ever seen in my life. And from the first moment I simply had to have her." Scott later said Zelda had been "sexually reckless" during their courtship. He had wanted to postpone sex until their wedding night, but Zelda delighted in flouting conventions, and they became lovers a year before their marriage. Scott's Catholic upbringing made him reluctant to use any form of birth control, yet he never appeared to share Zelda's guilt about the three abortions she had during their marriage. Their union produced only one child, a girl they called Scottie.

Both Scott and Zelda were extremely jealous, and one rarely went anywhere without the other. Once Isadora Duncan flirted openly with Scott, and Zelda flung herself down a flight of stairs in protest. When Zelda found herself attracted to a handsome French aviator named Édouard Jozan, Scott went so far as to lock her in their villa for a month to keep her away from his rival. The affair was probably quite innocent, and it is doubtful whether Zelda and Jozan ever slept together. Still, Scott was tormented for years by the episode.

Scott contended that he was unfaithful to Zelda only after she had been committed. In the summer of 1935, while Zelda was hospitalized, Scott lived at a resort hotel in Asheville, N.C. There he blatantly carried on with a married woman named Rosemary, who was vacationing in the South with her sister. It was also in Asheville that he met the prostitute Lottie, who recalled an evening when Scott made the mistake of spouting white-supremacist rhetoric in her presence. "I asked if he'd ever gone to bed with a colored girl. He gave me the damnedest look, like I'd accused him of sleeping with his sister. Before he could answer, I told him that he had. Yes, not once or twice, but a dozen times.... When he got over that shock, he walked away like I had leprosy and told me to put on my clothes."

Scott's companion for the last three years of his life was Sheilah Graham, a young, attractive, English-born columnist living in Hollywood. She shocked Scott at the outset of their affair by admitting she had had eight lovers before him. As Graham described it in her book, *The Real F. Scott Fitzgerald*, it was probably Scott's first healthy, uncomplicated relationship. "In all our time together, I don't remember seeing him naked. But I was just as shy about my own body. However, this modesty did not prevent us from having a good time sexually. We satisfied each other and could lie in each other's arms for a long time afterwards, delighting in our proximity. It was not exhausting, frenzied lovemaking but gentle and tender, an absolutely happy state." The rumor persists that Fitzgerald suffered his fatal heart attack while in bed with Sheilah Graham. However, according to her he felt a pain while sitting in an easy chair reading the *Princeton Alumni Weekly*, tried to rise, and collapsed on the floor, dead.

QUIRKS: Sex was one of Scott's warm-up preparations for writing, and he often made love as though he had a deadline to meet. After spending a night with him, Lottie commented to a mutual friend, "He was nervous and I thought maybe that was why he was so quick about it. I asked him if that was his usual way and he said yes, so I didn't take it personally, like he wanted to get it over with." Lottie then gave Scott a few pointers, for which he was grateful.

A few of Fitzgerald's biographers have speculated that the author was a latent homosexual. A picture of Fitzgerald in drag for a college review prompted a burlesque house to offer him a job as a female impersonator. He once donned a gown and attended a University of Minnesota dance with a friend, Gus Schurmeier, but he did it as a prank. His transvestite experiences were apparently confined to his college years. Furthermore, a transvestite, whether prankster or princess, is not necessarily a homosexual.

Fitzgerald did have a fetish for which there exists more solid evidence. He was greatly excited by women's feet. His view of feet as sex objects, a self-described "Freudean [*sic*] complex," compelled Scott to keep his own bare feet modestly hidden. At the beach, he would bury them in the sand rather than expose them to public view.

Scott was likewise ashamed of another part of his body—his penis. Zelda once told him that he could never satisfy her or any other woman, saying his problem was "a matter of measurements." His ego shattered, he consulted Hemingway, who suggested that they compare organs and afterward declared that Scott's was normal-sized. Fitzgerald was unconvinced, so Hemingway took him to look at statues in the Louvre. But even this failed to restore Fitzgerald's self-esteem. Years later, he asked an experienced prostitute named Lottie how his penis compared to others, and she assured him that it was technique that mattered to women, not size. This opinion was later echoed by Sheilah Graham, who wrote a rather backhanded defense of Scott's dimensions. "Personally," she said, "given the choice between a donkey and a chipmunk, I might choose the latter."

HIS THOUGHTS: "This is a man's world. All wise women conform to the man's lead."

—*M.J.T.*

Scandalous Moralist

ANDRÉ GIDE (Nov. 22, 1869–Feb. 19, 1951)

HIS FAME: A towering figure in French literature, this Nobel Prize-winning writer is best known for his semiautobiographical novels (among them *The Immoralist* and *The Counterfeiters*), which deal with homosexuals and the duty of each individual to shape his own moral code. A champion of homosexuality, Gide gave literary respectability to this hitherto taboo subject.

HIS PERSON: Paris-born to both wealth and position, Gide lost his father, a law professor of Huguenot stock, when he was 11. His overprotective, puritanical mother dominated her only child. A sickly dunce in school, he was once expelled for masturbating in class. Weeping, his mother took him to a doctor who threatened to castrate him to make him desist. Neurotic and anxiety-ridden, at 13 Gide fell in love with his 15-year-old cousin, Madeleine Rondeaux, whom he called his "mystic lodestone" and worshiped all his life. At 20 he received his baccalaureate and thenceforth devoted his time to music, writing, travel, and social causes. At 25 he openly declared he was a pederast: a man whose object of desire is a male child or adolescent. Nonetheless, after the death of his mother, he married his cousin Madeleine. (The marriage was never consummated.) For the rest of his life he was torn apart by the polarization of the sensual and spiritual aspects of his nature. His writing was an attempt to reconcile the conflict. Gide's frankness, expressed in his works, shocked the public and deeply hurt his wife. Although he was a major literary influence of his time, the Catholic Church banned his works. Honors were withheld until 1947, when—at age 78—he received both a doctorate from Oxford University and the Nobel Prize for literature.

LOVE LIFE: Gide suffered from "angelism," an aberration which precluded intercourse with a beloved or idealized object; in his case the angel was his wife. Cultured, intelligent, almost saintly, she never complained about their platonic relationship, content with his spiritual half as long as she could believe it was all hers. But at 47 Gide fell in love with Marc Allégret, the 16-year-old son of the best man at the Gides' wedding. More than a casual affair, their liaison developed into an enduring relationship. Gide records that he experienced the torments of jealousy for the first time when Marc returned home late one night after visiting artist-writer Jean Cocteau. In retaliation for Gide's "spiritual infidelity," Madeleine burned all his letters to her. Throughout his life Gide maintained that he had loved her alone. She died, still devoted to him, in 1938.

SEX LIFE: His family's brutal attempt to repress his sexuality tended to link sensuality with guilt in his mind. Because of his mother's attitudes, he thought "good" women had no sexual feelings, and feared prostitutes as much as "vitriol throwers." Homosexual copulation he once described as being like "a huge vampire feeding upon a corpse." Because most forms of homosexual activity were repellent to him, when he discovered he was a pederast the solitary masturbation of his childhood was replaced by reciprocal masturbation with young partners.

After his mother died, Gide had agonized over his sexual identity and suitability for marriage. Sexual attempts with women continued to fail, whereas encounters with young boys had been consistently satisfying. He consulted a doctor about his tastes and confessed to what he thought was a hopeless perversion. The doctor examined him, listened to Gide's account of feeling sexually "normal" only in the arms of boys, and then gave him some optimistic advice: "Get married. Get married without fear. And you'll quickly realize that all the rest exists only in your imagination."

SEX PARTNERS: Gide's first sexual experience at 23 was with a 14-year-old Arab who loafed around his hotel in Tunisia. Ali offered himself in the sand dunes, and after a feigned hesitation, Gide submitted joyfully. Later he tried to "normalize" himself by having intercourse with Meriem, a 16-year-old female prostitute who resembled a child. While he was with her, he wrote, he had pretended she was her little brother, a young lad "black and slim as a demon." Meriem's "treatments" were terminated when Gide's mother came to Africa to nurse him through tuberculosis.

The following year, in Algiers, Gide met Oscar Wilde and his lover, Lord Alfred Douglas. One night Wilde procured a young musician, Mohammed, for Gide—an episode which ever after Gide regarded as the high point of his sexual experience. "After Mohammed had left me, I spent a long time in a state of quivering jubilation, and although I had already achieved pleasure five times with him, I revived my ecstasy over and over again, and back in my hotel room, prolonged the echoes of it until morning."

In Algeria Gide formed a strong attachment to his beautiful 15-year-old servant boy, Athman, whom he called a "black pearl." When he wrote his mother about bringing Athman back to Paris, to "help in the house," Mme. Gide wouldn't hear of it. For a month they fought, exchanging increasingly exasperated letters. At his mother's ultimatum that *her* servant would leave if a "Negro" were brought into the house, Gide relented. He was miserable at having to leave the boy, but four years later he returned to Algeria, found Athman, and took him back to Paris.

At 46 Gide began a heterosexual affair with Elizabeth van Rysselberghe, the daughter of a lifelong friend. He passed her a note saying he would like to give her a child, a wish fulfilled in 1923 when their daughter Catherine was born. He publicly acknowledged this child and lived to be a grandfather.

QUIRKS: As a boy Gide found that his sexual excitement was stimulated "by a profusion of colors or unusually shrill sweet sounds," and also by the "idea of destruction." He noted arousal when he spoiled a favorite toy or heard a story about crockery being smashed to pieces. Later he was attracted to crippled, deformed, or monstrous children, in whom he recognized some aspect of himself.

HIS THOUGHTS: "Rousseau says that he wrote his *Confessions* because he believed he was unique. I am writing mine for exactly the opposite reason, and because I know that a great many will recognize themselves in them.—But to what purpose?—I believe that everything that is true can be instructive."

"It is better to be hated for what one is than loved for what one is not."

—*M.B.T.*

Herr Nicefoot

JOHANN WOLFGANG VON GOETHE
(Aug. 28, 1749–Mar. 22, 1832)

HIS FAME: Most renowned for his verse drama *Faust*, the "German Shakespeare" also wrote 14 volumes of scientific prose, was a statesman in the Weimar court, and managed a theater. Yet in his 82 years of life he found time to fall in love over and over again, nearly always with Olympian passion.

HIS PERSON: The first-born child and only son of a highly cultured Frankfurt family, Goethe was accomplished in music, art, and six languages when he left home for law school in 1765. An attractive young man with a beaky nose and large, dark eyes, he affected a bohemian

Goethe, 26, with silhouette of Charlotte von Stein

appearance and manner in his student days at the University of Leipzig. This may have been what prompted one of his professors to remark: "It was the well-nigh universal opinion that he had a slate loose in the upper story." This "universal opinion" was, of course, dead wrong. Goethe functioned superbly throughout his life. His ability to revel in the empyrean realms of the imagination was balanced by his intense interest in the nuts and bolts of existence. Example: As bullets whined past him during a battle, he took his pulse to check his heart's performance under stress.

His short novel *The Sorrows of Young Werther*, written during the *Sturm und Drang* ("storm and stress") period, made suicide for love fashionable among the young in Europe and also established him as a popular novelist. Frankfurt society took him to its bosom, and the Duke of Saxe-Weimar invited him to join his court in 1775. After a few months of debauching with the 18-year-old duke (throwing plates from palace windows and perhaps engaging in orgies), Goethe settled down to serious work as chief minister of state (inspecting mines and issuing military uniforms) and an austere way of life (he gave up coffee and stopped wearing a wig). For the rest of his life, except for two journeys to Italy, Goethe lived at Weimar, where he wrote masterpieces, managed the theater, and studied science (he founded morphology and his work on plants foreshadowed Darwin's).

LOVE AND SEX LIFE: Goethe's emotional and literary lives were in constant embrace, and he wrote volumes about the state of his romantic feelings. The tension between polarities that helped to create greatness in his writing also existed in his love affairs; he was often involved in bizarre triangles with two different women (one innocent, one experienced, for example), and the course of his romances rarely ran smooth.

Freudian biographer K. R. Eissler postulates that Goethe may have had problems with premature ejaculation as a young man and did not have actual intercourse until he was 39. This has been neither proved nor disproved. Goethe did indeed have a free-flowing, intense personality and was deeply affected by the merest physical contact. A kiss could throw him into ecstasies.

The women Goethe loved were often unattainable; several were engaged or married to his friends. Charlotte Buff, who inspired *The Sorrows of Young Werther*, was engaged to Goethe's friend Johann Christian Kestner.

Though Goethe had relationships with aristocratic intellectuals, he had a predilection for competent, pretty, earthy women below him in social station. Round-faced Käthchen Schönkopf, an innkeeper's daughter and perhaps his first real love, was typical, as was the hot-and-cold course of their love affair. One moment he was indifferent to her, the next writing to a friend: "But I love her. I believe I would take poison from her hand…. We are our own devils, we drive ourselves out of our own Edens."

His passion for Friederike Brion, a parson's daughter, was a "magic garden," yet he wrote, "One isn't an atom happier when one gets what one wanted." Some biographers claim he left her not only brokenhearted but with child.

During his period as "Carnival Goethe" in Frankfurt society (toward which he had some uneasy contempt), he became engaged to Lilli Schönemann, a banker's daughter. After several dramatic breaks and reconciliations, the engagement reached an end when Goethe left for Weimar in 1775. Did they have intercourse? Lilli's later claim that she owed him her "moral existence" would indicate no, yet there is a puzzling entry in his autobiographical notes which reads: "Episode with Lilli. Prelude. Seduction. Offenbach."

At Weimar, Goethe had a 10-year, probably platonic relationship with Charlotte von Stein, married and the mother of eight, an intellectual, seven years older than Goethe. He sent her more than 1,500 letters, writing little else during this period.

After his journey to Italy in 1786-1788 to discover the classical world and the sensuousness of the south, he met Christiane Vulpius, a worker in an artificial-flower factory. Stocky and black-eyed, she loved the theater, dancing, clothes, wine, and Goethe. He called her his "force of nature." She moved in with him and stayed until the end of her life. They shared homely, simple things. When he was away on occasion, they wrote to each other. They alluded in their letters to an unborn child as *das Pfuiteufelchen* ("the little it's-a-damned-shame"), and Christiane referred to Goethe's penis as Herr Schönfuss ("Mr. Nicefoot"). When they had been together more than 15 years, he wrote asking for a pair of her "danced-out shoes" to "press against his heart." He married Christiane in 1806, after the French invasion of Germany, during which she had saved him from being shot by two soldiers. His marriage seemed to arouse in him yearnings for other women, among them Minna Herzlieb, who inspired "sonnet fever," and Marianne von Willemer, married to a friend, who shared his Arabic period. Christiane died in 1816. When Goethe was 74, he proposed to his "daughter-ling," Ulrike von Levetzow, then in her late teens. She turned him down.

HIS THOUGHTS: "Great passions are mortal illnesses. What might cure them makes them but more dangerous than before."

"So, lively brisk old fellow, / Don't let age get you down. / White hairs or not / You can still be a lover."

—*A.E.*

The 30-30 Shell

ERNEST HEMINGWAY (July 21, 1899–July 2, 1961)

HIS FAME: In a career spanning four decades, Hemingway established himself as one of America's greatest writers, and his macho approach to life is evident in both the style and substance of his work. His major novels, *The Sun Also Rises*, *A Farewell to Arms*, *For Whom the Bell Tolls*, and *The Old Man and the Sea*, often mirrored his adventurous life, re-creating his physical sensations while hunting big game, bullfighting, and soldiering. At the same time, his aesthetic sensibility drew wide critical acclaim and brought him both a Pulitzer Prize and the Nobel Prize for literature.

HIS PERSON: Hemingway's life has been called a "never ended rebellion" against his middle-class past. The son of a doctor, Hemingway was raised in a Chicago suburb in a family dominated by its women, including his four sisters, a nurse, and a cook. His mother made him wear girls' clothing for several years and held his elder sister Marcelline back a year so that the two could enter school together, as twins. At 15 he ran away from home but returned in order to finish high school. After WWI, during which he saw front-line action as an ambulance driver in Italy, he went to Paris as a journalist. There, under the guidance of writers like F. Scott Fitzgerald, Ezra Pound, and Gertrude Stein, Hemingway developed his crisp style and achieved initial fame and success as a novelist. He craved yet resented being in the limelight, carefully creating a virile public image of the withdrawn, macho man, seeking out adventure as a boxer, hunter, wartime correspondent, and soldier all over the world. In later years he enjoyed life at his beloved Cuban home, Finca Vigia ("Lookout Farm"). After Fidel Castro seized power in 1960, Hemingway moved to a house in Ketchum, Ida. There he became anxiety-ridden and depressed and was unable to write. He twice underwent electroshock therapy at the Mayo Clinic. Two days after returning to Ketchum from one of these sessions, he took his life with a shotgun.

SEX LIFE: In keeping with his masculine image, Hemingway portrayed himself as a great lover. He told Thornton Wilder that as a young man in Paris, his sex drive was so strong he had to make love three times a day; also he ostentatiously consumed sex-sedating drugs to quiet his raging libido. His family, however, reported that he didn't even begin dating until he was a junior in high school. ("About time," they said.) He was never comfortable with casual sex, although he later boasted he was "an amateur pimp." He compared intercourse to bicycle racing, in that the more you do it, the better you get at it.

Hemingway liked to dominate his women, believing that the man "must govern" sexual relationships. Three of his four wives appear to have accepted that rule. The exception was his third wife, Martha Gellhorn, who said afterward that "Papa" Hemingway had no redeeming qualities outside of his writing. (Hemingway called their marriage his "biggest mistake.")

In his letters, Hemingway told of having many unusual bed partners, including a black harem he maintained while on an African safari. His strident womanizing led contemporaries to question his manhood. Some observers, including former mentor Gertrude Stein, implied that he was a latent homosexual. In fact, on one occasion in Spain, while walking to the bull ring with his friend Sidney Franklin, the Brooklyn-born matador, Hemingway spotted a very obvious homosexual across the street "just minding his business." Hemingway snorted, "Watch this." He strode across the street and without warning smashed his fist into the man, knocking him down and hurting him. Satisfied, Hemingway rejoined Franklin. However, there is certainly no evidence to suggest that Hemingway ever had a homosexual relationship; he himself commented that he had been approached by a man only once in his life.

"'Course, Hemingway's big problem all his life, I've always thought," Sidney Franklin once told author Barnaby Conrad, "was he was always worried about his *picha* [penis]. The size of it, that is." "Small?" Conrad wondered. Sidney Franklin "solemnly held up the little finger of his left hand with his thumbnail at the base," Conrad reported. "He appraised it with a critical eye; then he raised his thumbnail up a fraction of an inch in reevaluation. ''Bout the size of a thirty-thirty shell,' he said."

Papa Hemingway was a straight man in bed, and he preferred women who "would rather take chances than use prophylactics." He abhorred any sexual arrangement that violated his sense of propriety. He wasn't always the best performer and sometimes experienced stress-induced impotence.

SEX PARTNERS: Hemingway boasted of his sexual prowess, claiming he had made love to a wide variety of women, including Mata Hari, Italian countesses, a Greek princess, and obese prostitutes in Michigan, where he spent many youthful summers. He also claimed he had made love to some of Havana's most outrageous prostitutes, who bore such nicknames as Xenophobia, Leopoldina, and the International Whore. In truth, his relationships were considerably more chaste than he portrayed them, and his attitudes toward sex were almost prudish. His "loveliest dreams" were inhabited by Greta Garbo and his friend Marlene Dietrich. In real life he preferred submissive, shapely blondes or redheads. Friends and acquaintances thought him "a Puritan," and Hemingway himself blushed when accosted by a prostitute, feeling that only those "in love" could make love. Married four times (and producing a total of three sons), he always regarded his divorce from first wife, Hadley Richardson, as a "sin" he could never expiate. Although their first few years together were nearly ideal, their marriage was doomed when Hemingway met and fell in love with Pauline "Pfife" Pfeiffer, a beautiful sycophant who was to become his second wife. Hadley agreed to a divorce only after she had forced Pauline and Ernest to stay apart for 100 days.

Hemingway's second marriage lasted 12 years on paper but far less in reality. The relationship ended for sexual reasons; after Pauline twice gave birth by Caesarean section, they had been forced to practice coitus interruptus because her Catholicism precluded the use of prophylactics.

Hemingway met his third wife, Martha Gellhorn, while reporting on the Spanish Civil War from Madrid. They were quickly drawn to each other, but their passions cooled after marriage, and they were divorced five years later, in 1945. It was Ernest's shortest marriage and a cosmic mismatch. Ernest did not like Martha's independence (she was an accomplished writer in her own right) or her sharp tongue. He wanted blind adoration and submission, which Martha could not give any man.

Hemingway's fourth wife, Mary Welsh, was in many ways made to order. She was patient, worshipful, and beautiful (and nine years younger than Hemingway). He called her his "pocket Rubens." The marriage lasted for the remainder of Hemingway's life largely because Mary overlooked his often difficult behavior. Hemingway continued to enjoy a number of dalliances and made no effort to keep them secret.

As a young man he had preferred older women (Hadley was eight years his senior). From middle age on, he enjoyed the company of much younger women. A number of these women seemed to be models for Hemingway's fictional characters—one may have inspired Brett Ashley in *The Sun Also Rises* and the other may have inspired Renata in *Across the River and into the Trees*, but none won his heart completely. He never let them get too close lest they try to run his life. "I know wimmins," he told one friend, "and wimmins is difficult."

QUIRKS: Hemingway had several unusual theories about sex. He believed that each man was allotted a certain number of orgasms in his life, and that these had to be carefully spaced out. Another theory was that if you had sex often enough, you could eat all the strawberries you wanted without contracting hives, even though you were allergic to the fruit.

HIS ADVICE: From *Death in the Afternoon*: "If two people love each other, there can be no happy end to it, for one of them must die and the other remain bereft."

—*J.A.M.*

The Indefatigable Egotist

VICTOR HUGO (Feb. 26, 1802–May 22, 1885)

HIS FAME: Hugo was known to his contemporaries as a champion of the Romantic movement, to literary critics primarily for his poetry, and to general readers then and now for his epic novels *Les Misérables* and *The Hunchback of Notre Dame*.

HIS PERSON: "Victor Hugo was a madman who believed himself to be Victor Hugo," said the poet Jean Cocteau in summing up the extravagances and contradictions of a man who was larger than life both in literature and in love. This supremely self-centered genius championed the rights of the poor and

the downtrodden at the same time that he emblazoned his walls with the motto *Ego Hugo* ("I, Hugo"). He amassed a fortune, yet insisted on being buried in a pauper's coffin.

He was one of the literary centerpieces in a nation and a century rich in writers, and a political force in a time of turmoil and change. An immense man of gargantuan energy and robust health, he slept less than four hours a night, wrote standing up, and boasted that he never had a thought or a sensation that was not grist for his writer's mill.

His disillusionment with the Second Empire of Louis Napoleon drove him into exile in 1851, and for nearly 20 years he lived and worked on the Channel Island of Guernsey, creating a bizarre and ornate personal environment of architectural whimsy, made up of secret staircases, hidden rooms, and eccentric decorations. Here he wrote feverishly and explored the occult.

When he finally returned to France, he was again active in politics and literature, vigorous almost to the end. His dying words echo the contradictions of his life: "I see a black light."

SEX LIFE: When Hugo married at the age of 20, he was a virgin, but on his wedding night he coupled with his unsuspecting young wife, Adèle Foucher, nine times. She became exhausted by his sexual athleticism, and after five difficult pregnancies in eight years, she called a halt to their sex life. The marriage was shaken further when Adèle fell in love with Hugo's friend, the famous literary critic Sainte-Beuve. Although the affair probably was not consummated, it nearly led to a duel between the two men.

The rupture with Adèle only temporarily disrupted Hugo's sex life. In fact, his appetite had merely been whetted by his wife. He had been married 11 years and was world-famous for *The Hunchback of Notre Dame* when in 1833 he began an affair with the raven-haired, dark-eyed beauty Juliette Drouet. An actress and the mistress of a series of famous and wealthy men, she taught him the varieties of sensual pleasure. He was soon able to boast, "Women find me irresistible."

And obviously they did. He began one of the most amazingly active sex lives ever recorded. It was not unusual for him to make love to a young prostitute in the morning, an appreciative actress before lunch, a compliant courtesan as an aperitif, and then join the also indefatigable Juliette for a night of sex. He maintained a certain level of activity almost to his deathbed; diary entries at the age of 83 record eight bouts of love over the four months before his death.

SEX PARTNERS: He craved affairs with women who were passionate, witty, and challenging, but he often settled for sheer numbers. His powerful personality and his fame were strong aphrodisiacs, and he enjoyed a dazzling parade of willing partners. They were almost exclusively young; in fact, as he grew older, often young enough to be his granddaughters. He was perfectly open to having liaisons with married women, but not if they were living with their husbands. Any other woman, or girl, who was young, amenable, and attractive was fair game.

Juliette, who was the great love of his life, tolerated his prodigious activity. But by the time she was in her 30s her beauty had begun to fade—no doubt in part because of the cloistered existence Hugo forced upon her. By 1844 she had been temporarily displaced by Léonie d'Aunet, a young noblewoman who had run away with a painter. The affair turned into a shocking scandal when Léonie's jealous husband arranged to have the couple tailed by the police, who caught them *in flagrante delicto*. Although Hugo escaped punishment by claiming his privileges as a member of the peerage, Léonie was thrown into jail for adultery. Upon her release from prison, Hugo divided his time equally for a while between Juliette and her. Eventually Juliette's absolute devotion won out, however, and Léonie was deposed.

Juliette's reinstatement as his primary love did not in any way limit the scope of Hugo's conquests. She herself estimated that he had sex with at least 200 women between 1848 and 1850. Even at age 70 he managed to seduce the 22-year-old daughter of writer Théophile Gautier, and it is possible that he was carrying on an affair with Sarah Bernhardt simultaneously.

Despite the myriad women who claimed his attentions, Hugo always returned to Juliette as his "true wife." Their love affair lasted 50 years. During most of that time they had to live separately. When possible, Hugo visited her every day. As for Juliette, her devotion was unswerving. She wrote him 17,000 love letters. At age 77 she died in his arms, and although his sex drive continued during the remaining two years of his life, her death seemed to break his spirit at last.

QUIRKS: Rumors abounded during his lifetime, as they have since, that he carried on an incestuous relationship with his daughter Léopoldine, but no conclusive proof of this exists. He was apparently a voyeur and something of a foot fetishist, and he was turned on by intrigue and mystery. He often admitted his mistresses through secret staircases and entertained them in hidden rooms even when this was not really necessary.

HIS THOUGHTS: "Love ... seek love ... give pleasure and take it in loving as fully as you can." And, to his young grandson, who walked in on the 80-year-old Hugo in the embrace of a young laundress: "Look, little Georges, that's what they call genius!"

—R. W.S.

The Gay Romantic

CHRISTOPHER ISHERWOOD (Aug. 26, 1904 –Jan. 4, 1986)

HIS FAME: British-born Christopher Isherwood, novelist, screenwriter, playwright, and essayist, is probably best known for his quasi-autobiographical "Berlin novels," one of which, *Goodbye to Berlin*, introduced the character Sally Bowles and was the basis for the hit musical *Cabaret*. The slender, 5-ft. 7-in. Isherwood spent time in pre-Hitler Germany and chronicled much of the decadence of that society in his fiction. With his good friend W. H. Auden, with whom he collaborated on several plays, Isherwood left Europe in 1939 and immigrated to the U.S. He settled in California and began working on films, including *The Loved One*. An

Isherwood, 48, with 18-year-old Don Bachardy

American citizen since 1946, Isherwood is a student of Vedanta and has written extensively on the various aspects of Hindu philosophy. He is also an active supporter of gay liberation, having openly admitted to his homosexuality in his book *Kathleen and Frank*.

LOVE LIFE: Asked when he first came to the realization of his own homosexuality, Isherwood replied, "Quite early—by the time I was 10 or so, in the sense of being physically attracted to boys at school. I managed to have orgasms with them while we were wrestling and I guess some of them had orgasms, too, but we never admitted to it. I fell in love a lot during my teens, but never did anything about it. I was very late in getting into an actual physical affair. That happened while I was in college."

It was his partner's idea. When Isherwood protested, the other young man locked the door and sat on his lap.

"Other experiences followed, all of them enjoyable but none entirely satisfying," according to Isherwood. This was because he was suffering from an inhibition common to upper-class homosexuals of the time; he couldn't relax with his British peers. He needed "a working-class foreigner."

Isherwood found his answer in Berlin when he visited Auden in 1929. The fact that the Germans were "simple and natural about homosexuality" was a welcome change. In one of Berlin's homosexual bars he found the type of blue-eyed blond boy who represented for him "the whole mystery-magic of foreignness."

After returning to England, he was hired as a tutor for a young boy in a remote village on the coast. Isherwood's autobiography, written in the third person, recounts the scene.

"While Christopher was there, he had his first—and last—complete sexual experience with a woman.... They were both drunk.... She liked sex but wasn't the least desperate to get it. He started kissing her without bothering about what it might lead to. When she responded, he was surprised and amused to find how easily he could relate his usual holds and movements to this unusual partner.... He also felt a lust which was largely narcissistic; she had told him how attractive he was and now he was excited by himself making love to her.... Next day, she said, "I could tell that you've had a lot of women through your hands.".... He asked himself: "Do I now want to go to bed with more women and girls? Of course not, as long as I can have boys. Why do I prefer boys? Because of their shape and their voices and their smell and the way they move. And boys can be romantic. I can put them into my myth and fall in love with them. From my point of view, girls can be absolutely beautiful but never romantic. In fact, their utter lack of romance is what I find most likeable about them. They're so sensible."

Back in Germany in 1930, Isherwood met the boy whom he was to call Otto Nowak in *Goodbye to Berlin*. Otto was a bisexual with a highly dramatic nature and "a face like a very ripe peach." By 1932 the affair had cooled and Otto was replaced by 17-year-old Heinz. After Hitler came into power, Heinz and Isherwood wandered around Europe from country to country, living like a "happily married heterosexual couple" until 1937, when Heinz risked a visit to Nazi Germany, where he was arrested and imprisoned for draft evasion and homosexuality. Heartbroken, Isherwood returned to London and allowed himself to be comforted by a variety of young men.

He also had the companionship of Auden. About his relationship with Auden, Isherwood has written:

Their friendship was rooted in schoolboy memories and the mood of its sexuality was adolescent. They had been going to bed together, unromantically but with much pleasure, for the past 10 years, whenever the opportunity offered itself.... They couldn't think of themselves as lovers, yet sex had given friendship an extra dimension.

When Isherwood went to Hollywood in 1939, he met Aldous Huxley and Swami Prabhavananda. For a while he stayed at the swami's monastery, where he and the other devotees pledged themselves to celibacy. But Isherwood did not completely forswear his love life. His boyfriends during the 1940s included William Caskey, a young photographer from Kentucky with whom he lived for several years.

In 1953 Isherwood met 18-year-old Don Bachardy, who collaborated with Isherwood on a play and some film scripts, and lived with him in Santa Monica for the rest of his life.

Isherwood has always maintained that he is very happy with his sexual preference. Although Auden once baited him by calling him a "repressed heterosexual," Isherwood offers his own definition of what it means to be a homosexual. "It seems to me that the real clue to your sex-orientation lies in your romantic feelings rather than in your sexual feelings. If you are really gay, you are able to fall in love with a man, not just enjoy having sex with him."

—*C.H.S.*

Ireland's Lost Sheep

JAMES JOYCE (Feb. 2, 1882–Jan. 13, 1941)

HIS FAME: Irish novelist and poet James Joyce was one of the most important innovators in modern literature, owing to his use of interior monologue, or "stream of consciousness." Among his greatest works are *Ulysses, Finnegan's Wake, Dubliners*, and *A Portrait of the Artist as a Young Man*.

HIS PERSON: When the elder Joyce, a Dublin tax collector, sank into alcoholism and eventually lost his job, young James was withdrawn from an exclusive Jesuit-run boarding school, and for two years the brilliant boy educated himself. At age 17 he entered another Jesuit institution, University College in Dublin, and briefly considered becoming a priest,

Joyce in Zurich

but rejected the idea because it required a vow of celibacy.

Joyce fell in love with a semieducated Dublin chambermaid, Nora Barnacle, on June 16, 1904, the date to which he assigned all the happenings in his novel *Ulysses*. Refusing to be married by "a clerk with a pen behind his ear or a priest in a nightshirt," Joyce took Nora as his common-law wife, and they left for the Continent in October, 1904. They eventually married in 1931, at the urging of their daughter, Lucia.

Joyce earned a precarious living by teaching conversational English and writing reviews in Trieste, Zurich, and Paris. Until 1912 he made rare visits to Dublin, which he considered stifling to artists like himself. After years of drudgery—and a series of 25 painful operations for iritis, glaucoma, and cataracts, which left him at times nearly blind—he finally began to enjoy a comfortable income from his writing. Lanky, bespectacled, and shy, Joyce never permitted himself an off-color remark in the presence of a lady. Yet he became famous for his unbuttoned prose, and in December of 1920 *Ulysses* was banned for its obscenity in the U.S. and England.

SEX LIFE: In his student days Joyce haunted Dublin's seedy "Nighttown" red-light district, where he lost his virginity at age 14. In his early 20s he gave up prostitutes, saying he longed to "copulate with a soul." The soul mate he chose, Nora Barnacle, remained his lifelong companion. He saw himself as a weak child in need of Nora's motherly discipline and once wrote to her: "I would be delighted to feel my flesh tingling under your hand.... I wish you would smack me or flog me even. Not in play, dear, in earnest and on my naked flesh. I wish you were strong, *strong*, dear, and had a big full proud bosom and big fat thighs. I would love to be whipped by you, Nora love!"

The small-breasted, boyishly built Nora adapted well to the role of dominatrix, addressing Joyce as "simpleminded Jim" and describing him to others as "a weakling." While Joyce's work earned him worldwide praise, Nora made no secret of her disdain for his writing. Despite the fact that *Ulysses* became famous for its psychological penetration of the female mind, Nora asserted that Joyce knew "nothing at all about women." Still, Nora was faithful to him throughout their long relationship, even though she confided to friends that Joyce wanted her to go to bed with other men "so he'll have something to write about."

Joyce was never at a loss for words in his letters to Nora. In 1909, when he was away from Ireland on business, he wrote her lusty letters packed with scatological endearments and praises for her soiled underwear: "The smallest things give me a great cockstand—a whorish movement of your mouth, a little brown stain on the seat of your white drawers ... to feel your hot lecherous lips sucking away at me, to fuck between your two rosy-tipped bubbies." When he didn't hear from her, he wrote again with words of apology: "Are you offended, dear, at what I said about your drawers? That is all nonsense, darling. I know they are as spotless as your heart." Nora's drawers, and what was in them, kept Joyce's pen quite busy. He was a dyed-in-the-wool underwear fetishist and even carried a pair of doll's panties in his pocket. Fortified by liquor, he would sometimes slip the tiny underpants over his fingers and cakewalk them across a café table, to the bewilderment of onlookers.

The author spent much of his time in cafés and bars, chatting with other writers and artists. It is believed that Joyce was less interested in exchanging ideas with his intellectual peers than in avoiding intercourse with Nora; drinking himself flaccid provided an effective means of birth control.

While teaching English in Paris, Joyce fell passionately in love with one of his students, Amalia Popper, the daughter of a wealthy Jewish businessman. It was an unrequited love affair that was thwarted by Amalia's father, who gently warned the author not to take advantage of his position of authority. The experience kindled in Joyce a nagging desire for a dark, Semitic woman.

In early 1919 Joyce found his ideal in a Zurich woman named Marthe Fleischmann. He described to a friend the circumstances under which he first saw Marthe: "She was in a small but well-lit room in the act of pulling a chain." Through this unabashed first encounter, Marthe had unwittingly endeared herself to the coprophilic Joyce, who later that night explored "the coldest and hottest parts of a woman's body."

MEDICAL REPORT: During Joyce's early forays into Nighttown he contracted syphilis, which he treated himself by cauterizing the chancre. The treatment eliminated the symptom but not the disease, and it is believed that the author's chronic eye trouble stemmed from it. However, he died in Zurich as the result of complications that followed surgery for a duodenal ulcer.

HIS THOUGHTS: "Love is a cursed nuisance when coupled with lust also."

—*M.J.T.*

"*Public Lover Number One*"

GEORGE S. KAUFMAN (Nov. 16, 1889–June 2, 1961)

HIS FAME: Unquestionably the most prolific and successful playwright of the American theater from the mid-1920s to the late 1940s, Kaufman had at least one play in performance on Broadway every year for over 20 years. Most noted for his satire, he was both a director and a writer, coauthoring two Pulitzer Prize-winning plays, *Of Thee I Sing* (1932) with Morrie Rys-kind and *You Can't Take It with You* (1936) with Moss Hart. He also coauthored *The Man Who Came to Dinner* (1939) and three of the Marx Brothers' most successful movies, *The Cocoanuts*, *Animal Crackers*, and *A Night at the Opera*.

HIS PERSON: The third of four children and the only male to survive infancy, George was born in Pittsburgh, Pa., to middle-class Jewish parents who "managed to get in on every business as it was finishing and made a total of four dollars." He went to public schools in Pittsburgh, then moved with his parents to Paterson, N.J. He tried law school for three months but dropped out and went through a succession of ill-suited jobs, including selling hatbands and pump ribbons. Outside of his salaried positions he did much better, making frequent contributions to the newspaper column of Franklin P. Adams, which soon led to his own column. Later he became drama editor for *The New York Times* (1917–1930).

The man whom the American press would eventually label "Public Lover Number One" certainly never looked the part. He was tall and lanky, had poor posture, always wore wire-rimmed glasses, and sported a bushy pompadour hairdo. At age 28 he married Beatrice Bakrow, who remained his wife and closest confidante until her death in 1945. Four years later, at age 59, he married 35-year-old Leueen MacGrath, an extremely beautiful Irish actress.

Kaufman was almost puritanical, seldom if ever using profanity, shying away from dirty stories, and taking great offense at any mention of the sex act. He hated to write love scenes, always deferring the privilege to his collaborators. A perfect Victorian gentleman, he exuded a quiet strength and a brilliant wit. Groucho Marx once remarked that "the perfect woman would look like Marilyn Monroe and carry on a conversation like George Kaufman."

SEX LIFE: In 1905, when he was 14 years old, Kaufman and six of his friends made a pact and signed their names to an oath swearing to remain virgins until they married. Although Kaufman didn't wed until he was 28, he kept his vow. Bea Bakrow commented later, "We were both virgins, which shouldn't happen to anybody!" Bea became pregnant during their first year of marriage and carried the baby well beyond term, giving birth to a stillborn child. The experience was so traumatic for Kaufman that he and Bea were never again sexual partners. They agreed to remain married, for in all matters other than sexuality they were well matched and content with each other. However, they also agreed to allow each other complete freedom in choosing sexual partners. In order to pursue his extramarital affairs in a comfortable manner, Kaufman rented a small apartment on 73rd Street in New York, which he maintained for many years. When his adopted daughter, Anne, heard about the apartment and its function years later, she said, "I wonder if Mummy furnished it?"

Once Kaufman had fulfilled the obligation of his adolescent vow, he wasted little time exploring the delights of the feminine body. Shortly after his stillborn child's birth, he opened up a charge account with Polly Adler, the famous madam of *A House Is Not a Home* fame. His account was not typical, however, for he never visited her business establishment. The call girls selected for him were instructed to wait under a specified street lamp between 73rd and 74th streets in New York's Central Park. Kaufman would walk by, return, and begin a conversation, then invite his young friend to dinner, and finally return with her to his 73rd Street apartment and attempt to "seduce" her. Naturally, he was always successful, noting her phone number before she departed and promising to meet her again. No money ever changed hands or was even mentioned. At the end of the month he would receive a bill from Miss Adler for services rendered.

As Kaufman's fame grew, he quickly learned that successful Broadway writers and directors did not have to pay beautiful women to sleep with them, and he capitalized on this fortuitous situation. Always discreet, always a gentleman, he dated some of the most beautiful women on Broadway: chorus girls, rising or established stars, and dancers. His appeal went far beyond that due to his fame. Kaufman never promised women parts in his plays in return for favors. He seemed to understand women, was charming, urbane, witty, warm, and honest. He paid attention to the woman he was with and remained her friend long after the fire of passion was extinguished. And although he seldom told stories about his many affairs, he couldn't resist recounting to his friends the evening he spent with one chorus girl, who throughout their lovemaking kept yelling, "Oh, Mr. Kaufman! Oh, Mr. Kaufman!" His friend Max Gordon called him a "male nymphomaniac."

Kaufman met movie actress Mary Astor in New York in the spring of 1933. He dazzled her and she "fell like a ton of bricks." To Kaufman, their relationship was just another sexual friendship, but to Mary Astor it was love. She knew that her love was not reciprocated, but she was thrilled each time they were together. "I am still in a daze—a kind of rosy glow," Mary wrote in her diary. "It is beautiful, glorious, and I hope my last love. I can't top it with anything in my experience." The blue-covered diary, one of a series Mary Astor had kept for five years, candidly recounted her love trysts with Kaufman. Unfortunately, the diary fell into the hands of her husband, Dr. Franklyn Thorpe, whom she was divorcing and who tried to use its contents against her during a bitter child-custody trial. The existence of the diary was brought to public attention in July, 1936, when it was reported that Mary Astor had had an affair with a mystery man named George. Early speculation centered on George Gershwin or writer George Oppenheimer as Mary's lover—until Dr. Thorpe's lawyers finally revealed that the George referred to in the diary was George S. Kaufman.

By this time various versions of the diary were showing up in print. One excerpt in particular caused a great sensation: "He fits me perfectly ... many exquisite moments ... 20—count them, diary, 20.... I don't see how he does it ... he is perfect." One New York newspaper suggested the passage might refer to "the number of clubs she and Kaufman visited one night," and playwright Moss Hart claimed the subject matter dealt with the string of Broadway hits Kaufman had enjoyed. But most Americans thought otherwise, and overnight George S. Kaufman became known as "Public Lover Number One." A publisher in the Midwest offered $10,000 for any photo of Kaufman in a swimming suit or gym trunks. When he was subpoenaed to appear at the trial, Kaufman fled Hollywood for New York and refused to talk to the press until the case was over. "You might say I did not keep a diary," he told reporters. Mary Astor and her husband reached a settlement in court, and soon the story dropped from the headlines.

Kaufman's wife, Bea, was embarrassed by the attention she and her husband received, but she stood by him throughout the ordeal. He continued his pursuit of beautiful women, but now he preceded his seduction with the line "Do you keep a diary?" Apparently he himself was not averse to putting his sentiments down in writing. Stage and film actress Claire Luce turned over a sealed envelope to the J. Pierpont Morgan Library in New York. Written on the envelope were her words: "To be opened 50 years from the above date. Contents: 68 tender and intimate pieces of correspondence from George S. Kaufman 1938–1953."

When Bea Bakrow died in 1945, Kaufman was grief-stricken and for some time withdrew from society. It was not until he met and married actress Leueen Mac-Grath in 1949 that he once again joined the social world of New York. Kaufman then devoted his energies to writing a play to showcase his beautiful wife's acting ability. As his health weakened, he urged her to take lovers. They divorced in 1957, but Leueen returned to Kaufman in the years just before his death, refusing to marry him again because people would think it was for financial gain. She remained with him until his death in 1961 and shared the bulk of his estate with his daughter.

HIS THOUGHTS: "The trouble with incest is that it gets you involved with relatives."

—*S.B.*

Prodigal Son

D. H. LAWRENCE (Sept. 11, 1885–Mar. 2, 1930)

HIS FAME: David Herbert Lawrence wrote the most outspoken novels of his day, books banned for their explicit descriptions of sexual activity. *Women in Love* (1920) had to be privately printed, and *Lady Chatterley's Lover* (1928) had to be expurgated until a landmark 1959 court decision allowed publication of passages featuring illicit intercourse. Today, few eyebrows would be raised by the following scene:

Lawrence at age 38

> For a moment he was still inside her, turgid there and quivering. Then as he began to move, in the sudden helpless orgasm, there awoke in her new strange thrills rippling inside her. Rippling ... like a flapping overlapping of soft flames, soft as feathers, running to points of brilliance, exquisite ... and melting her all molten inside....

HIS PERSON: Lawrence was the too dearly loved son of a proud, possessive mother who scorned her coarse husband, a Nottinghamshire coal miner. The frail and sickly "Bert" grew up surrounded by doting women, suffering agonies of frustrated "animal" feelings in the repressive late-Victorian atmosphere. At the age of 16 he suffered a severe sexual trauma, followed by pneumonia, after being cornered and threatened with exposure of his private parts by a rowdy group of factory girls.

"I loved my mother like a lover," Lawrence admitted after her death in 1910. Employed by day as a schoolteacher, he spent his nights working out his mother fixation in his early masterpiece, *Sons and Lovers* (1913), a classic variation on the Oedipus theme. Trying to exorcise his mother's influence, he elaborated a philosophy of sex as the motive force of life, a kind of morphia inducing a pseudoreligious state of grace.

Always thin and consumptive, never particularly virile, with tousled hair, a "flaming" red beard, and eyes "intense as blue stars," Lawrence attracted by the force of his personality a succession of wealthy, titled patronesses. "Income on two legs" he called these women, who subscribed to the Lawrencean sexual mystique and subsidized his nomadic lifestyle. (The writer repaid their devotion by satirizing female "culture vultures" in his novels.) So acutely sensitive that he could not tolerate the nerve-jangling excitement of city life, Lawrence roamed all over rural England and southern Europe. He also traveled to Ceylon, Australia, the American Southwest, and Mexico, which he described in travel essays. From 1928 until tuberculosis struck him down at age 44, Lawrence was constantly on the move. He was like John the Baptist, "crying in the wilderness," one devotee wrote.

LOVE LIFE: Lawrence's young manhood was dominated by the struggle (recounted in *Sons and Lovers*) between his first sweetheart, Jessie Chambers, and his mother, both possessive women who wanted to "wheedle the soul" out of him. He was first initiated into the "mystery of sex" at 23 by the local pharmacist's wife, Alice Dax, who has described how, finding him stuck over a poem, she "gave Bert sex" to prompt his creative imagination. Jessie may have surrendered to him physically, but the two were never able to overcome their sexual timorousness together. Lawrence abandoned Jessie for another friend, the more sexually alluring Louie Burrows, whom he had known since he was 15. "Strong and rosy as the gates of Eden," she too proved to be too "churchy" for the writer's taste.

Although all three women had good reason to feel ill used by Lawrence, so powerful was his influence on them that Jessie Chambers lived her whole life in the shadow of Lawrence's rejection, Alice Dax remained celibate in his memory, and Louie Burrows married only after his death.

In 1912 Lawrence fell in love and ran away with Frieda Weekley, a member of the aristocratic German Von Richthofen family, who was at the time of their meeting married to one of Lawrence's professors. Lawrence "touched a new tenderness in me," explained the buxom blond Frieda, who abandoned her husband and three children to follow and later marry the impoverished writer six years her junior. "There was nothing for me to do but submit."

Actually, Frieda was a handsome Aryan "giantess" of a woman, who had enjoyed sex with an earlier lover, Freudian psychologist Otto Gross. Anything but submissive, Frieda enjoyed a brawling love-hate relationship with Lawrence, a lifelong contest of wills punctuated by public quarrels and broken crockery. This because Lawrence, the messiah of sexual liberation, also espoused male chauvinism. ("I do think a woman must yield some sort of precedence to a man," he once said to British author Katherine Mansfield. "Men must go ahead ... women must follow, as it were, unquestioningly.") He even counseled beating recalcitrant wives. But Frieda, who was more than her husband's equal physically, refused to submit to such treatment. Sexually, also, there was evidence of incompatibility. They were never able to achieve simultaneous orgasm, complained Lawrence, who accused his wife, and *all* women, of having "sex on the brain"—a curious complaint for a man who was himself obsessed by the subject. But the Lawrences seem to have met one another's deepest-seated emotional needs. Frieda, who wore the long full skirts, aprons, and closely fitted bodices of his beloved mother, functioned as the writer's earth mother, a source of warmth and succor. "And I hope to spend eternity," Lawrence wrote in a poem, "with my face down-buried beneath her breasts."

Frieda was known to indulge in harmless dalliances with Italian peasants and Prussian officers, while Lawrence, the working-class guru of sex, was occupied with his rich benefactresses. These included the eccentric Lady Ottoline Morrell, who was supposed to reign over Lawrence's utopian colony of Rananim (founded on "the complete fulfillment in the flesh of all strong desire") but instead ended up as the sinister Hermione in *Women in Love*; Cynthia Asquith, an unattainable patrician beauty whom Lawrence is said to have made love to through his writings and paintings; and Mabel Dodge Luhan, an American heiress and writer who gave Lawrence a 166-acre ranch in New Mexico but failed in her attempt to "seduce his spirit." ("The womb in me roused to reach out and take him," wrote Mrs. Luhan, who was not physically attracted to Lawrence but sought physical union with him because the "surest way to the soul is through the flesh.")

In fact, Lawrence was something of a puritanical prude. He was offended by lewd tales and considered sexual intercourse indecent anytime except in the dark of night. He probably also suffered from impotence, which would have been aggravated by his exhausting bursts of creative energy and by his worsening tubercular condition. Dorothy Brett, one of his most devoted followers, has described how Lawrence climbed into her bed one night but was unable to consummate the relationship. Lawrence's "sexual potentialities," according to another friend, were "exclusively cerebral."

"Even if we can't act sexually to our complete satisfaction," Lawrence wrote apropos of *Lady Chatterley's Lover*, "let us at least think sexually, complete and clear.... This is the real point of this work. I want men and women to be able to think sex, fully, completely, honestly and cleanly."

HOMOSEXUALITY: Lawrence professed to be shocked by the effete homosexuality of the British intelligentsia, but would say, "I believe the nearest I have come to perfect love was with a young coal miner when I was about 16." Occasionally frustrated in his relations with women, he exalted a sort of mystical communion of men, a "blood brotherhood." He was also fascinated by the male physique, which he celebrated in the nude wrestling scene in *Women* *in Love.* In fact, Lawrence seems to have had more of his mother in him than his father; women may have worshiped him, but men considered him effeminate and joked about his domestic virtues. The messiah of sex was happiest when he was peeling potatoes or scrubbing floors, as the writer Norman Douglas once pointed out, not without malice. Lawrence's friend and biographer Richard Aldington said, "I should say DHL was about 85 percent hetero and 15 percent homo."

HIS THOUGHTS: "You mustn't think I advocate perpetual sex. Far from it. Nothing nauseates me more than promiscuous sex in and out of season."

—*C.D.*

The Call Of The Wild

JACK LONDON (Jan. 12, 1876–Nov. 22, 1916)

HIS FAME: Owing to such works as *The Call of the Wild,* Jack London was the most successful writer to emerge at the onset of the 20th century in America. He remains one of the most widely translated American authors, especially in the Soviet Union, where his socialist philosophy has had wide appeal.

HIS PERSON: Survival was taking shape as the theme of his life while he was still in the womb. "A Discarded Wife: Why Mrs. Chaney Twice Attempted Suicide," ran the *San Francisco Chronicle* headline seven months before Jack's birth. "Driven from House

London with Charmian Kittredge

for Refusing to Destroy her Unborn Infant—A Chapter of Heartlessness and Domestic Misery," it continued. The unborn baby was Jack. The abandoned mother-to-be was Flora Wellman and she was *not* Mr. Chaney's wife. Flora and W. H. Chaney, two beyond-the-fringe occultists of San Francisco, had been cohabiting during Flora's conception period, but Chaney claimed he was impotent at the time and furthermore did not want this out-of-wedlock child. Despite the publicity and the turmoil, Flora had a successful delivery, and Jack was raised on the tough waterfront by his stepfather, John London. An independent youth, he set out at 14—using his stepfather's surname—to see the world. He rode the rails as a hobo (and once spent a month in jail because of it), explored the Klondike for gold, and hunted seal in Siberia. Though he made California his home, the lure of travel and adventure never stopped calling him. He visited the slums of London, sailed the South Pacific, and was a war correspondent during the Russo-Japanese War. Refusing his doctor's orders to change his drinking habits and his lifestyle, he died from an overdose of morphine and atropine at the age of 40.

LOVE LIFE: "Prince of the Oyster Pirates," they called him when he sailed San Francisco Bay. It was with the "Queen of the Oyster Pirates," a girl named Mamie who came with the boat he bought at age 15, that he enjoyed his first sexual encounter.

Latently homosexual was how Joan London described her father's relationship with his best friend, George Sterling. But there was nothing latent about his heterosexual relations. His friends called him "the Stallion," and one biographer characterized him as "a sexual anarchist." The essence of man-woman sex for London was embodied in a story he told of meeting a woman on a train and romping in bed with her for three days while the train chugged east and a maid baby-sat the woman's child. When the train stopped, London bade the woman a final farewell, having got all he wanted.

London desired two things from a wife: a son and tolerance for his infidelities. The first great love of his life, the pale and delicate Mabel Applegarth, would also have given him a dictatorial mother-in-law. Mabel was one of the first "nice" girls London met in Oakland in the 1890s. She was from what he called the "parlor floor of society," as opposed to the "cellar," and he worked hard to raise himself to her social status. It was never high enough for her mother, though, and after London had courted Mabel unsuccessfully for several years, his ardor cooled.

The woman he married in 1900 gave him two daughters and a divorce. Bess Maddern, who was a good friend of Mabel's, could not tolerate his straying. (He believed that resisting the temptations of the flesh was a waste of willpower.) Bess named Anna Strunsky, Jack's longtime friend in the Socialist movement and his co-writer on *The Kempton-Wace Letters*, as the other woman, and the couple separated in 1903. Bess never suspected that the other woman was in fact Charmian Kittredge, who acted as Bess' confidante during the separation.

Jack married Charmian in Chicago in 1905, as soon as he had been granted a divorce in California. Illinois, which did not recognize divorce until a year after such decrees were granted, declared the marriage to Charmian invalid. In the uproar that ensued, the lecture tour Jack was on at the time was canceled, his books were banned in various parts of the country, and an organization called the Averill Women's Club passed a resolution condemning both college football and Jack London.

To London, Charmian was worth the tempest. She could box and fence like a man, enjoyed travel, and earned one of the highest appellations Jack could pin on a female—"Mate-Woman." But they did not live happily ever after. In 1911, when Charmian gave birth to a sickly daughter who lived only three days, a bitterly disappointed London became "one wild maelstrom," embarking on nightly debauches to assuage his grief at not being able to father a son. Charmian was aware of a world filled with "slim-ankled potential rivals" and began playing a game friends called "breaking it up," wherein she would not allow him to be alone with another woman for more than two minutes. But women continued to fling themselves at "God's own mad lover," as the blue-eyed, curly-haired, muscular writer referred to himself. The Londons' marriage deteriorated to a state of bitter coexistence. It was during his last few years, when his kidneys began to fail, that they journeyed to Hawaii, where Jack, depressed and ill though he was, met the last love of his life. He fell hard but never revealed a single detail about the woman. (George Sterling later told Joan London of the existence of that affair—but nothing else.) London couldn't bring himself to demand a separation from Charmian, having more or less given up on life. The Londons spent their final years sleeping in separate wings of their home in Glen Ellen, Calif., with Jack vowing that he would take to his bed any woman who might give him the son that he had always wanted. When he died, Charmian, who had suffered chronic insomnia through her fear of losing him to another woman, slept for a day and a half.

ADVICE: "A man should love women, and lots of them."

—*D.R.*

A Double Life

W. SOMERSET MAUGHAM (Jan. 25, 1874–Dec. 16, 1965)

HIS FAME: The most widely read British author since Charles Dickens, Maugham gained world renown for his novels, especially *Of Human Bondage*, *The Moon and Sixpence*, *Cakes and Ale*, and *The Razor's Edge*. He was also celebrated for numerous short stories, notably "Miss Thompson," upon which the play *Rain* was based, and for his plays.

HIS PERSON: Because his father was English solicitor to the British embassy in Paris, Maugham was born in France and French was his first language. When he was eight years old, his mother died of tuberculosis, and two years later his father died of stomach cancer. The loss of his mother scarred him forever. The orphaned boy was sent to England and placed in the care of his father's brother, a clergyman in the small town of Whitstable. The atmosphere seemed alien, bleak, and loveless, and Maugham suffered. Attending the strict King's School in Canterbury, he developed a stammer. Because of ill health, he was sent to Germany, where he enrolled in Heidelberg Univer-

W. Somerset Maugham (l) Gerald Haxton

sity. There his interest in literature grew, and he secretly began to write. At 18 he returned to England and was pressured by his uncle to take up medicine. Maugham reluctantly entered the medical school of St. Thomas' Hospital in London.

After five years, he was a doctor and on his own. Now he turned full-time to writing. He wrote and published short stories, and at 23 had already published his first novel, *Liza of Lambeth*. In the decades that followed he turned to playwriting, and when he was 34 he had four hit plays running in London at once. At 41 he returned to the novel and brought out his autobiographical *Of Human Bondage*, a modern classic.

He traveled constantly—to the South Seas, China, India, Italy, North Africa, Mexico. During WWI he served as a British espionage agent in Switzerland and Russia. In 1928 he bought a Moorish residence on the French Riviera, the Villa Mauresque at St.-Jean Cap Ferrat, his home for the rest of his life. Here he entertained his equals, greats of the world like Winston Churchill, H. G. Wells, and Noel Coward. Maugham's appearance, at his peak, was that of a natty gentleman, 5 ft. 7 in., with dark hair and mustache. His manner was diffident and remote, yet (despite his stammer) he was a witty storyteller. In his last years he was not afraid of death. "Death, like constipation, is one of the commonplaces of human existence," he told a friend. "Why shy away from it?" He didn't. In his 92nd year, partially demented, often angry, sometimes euphoric, he died of lung congestion and too many years.

LOVE LIFE: Maugham was bisexual. While most gossip made him out to be largely homosexual, one of his oldest friends, author Beverley Nichols, said he "was not predominantly homosexual. He certainly had affairs with women.... He had no feminine gestures nor mannerisms."

SEX PARTNERS: At age 16, while studying in Heidelberg, Maugham had his first sexual encounter. His mate was 26-year-old Ellingham Brooks, an attractive Cambridge graduate with a private income, who devoted himself to travel and reading. Returning to London, Maugham was afraid to consort with male homosexuals there because copulating with them was a criminal offense. Only five years before, Oscar Wilde had been sent to jail for two years for practicing homosexuality. So, while still a medical student, he cast his eye on women. "One Saturday night," he confessed, "I went down Piccadilly and picked up a girl who for a pound was prepared to pass the night with me. The result was an attack of gonorrhea.... Undeterred by this mishap, however, I continued whenever I could afford it." Shortly after, Maugham shared a flat with a friend, Walter Payne, an accountant who was good at obtaining girls, "small-part actresses, shopgirls, or clerks in an office." When Payne was through with each, he passed her on to Maugham, who would take her to dinner and then to bed. "There was no romance in it, no love, only appetite." In the two decades to follow, Maugham had a number of sexual affairs with well-known women. One was Violet Hunt, a feminist who edited *The Freewoman*. Violet was 41 and Maugham 29 when she confided in her diary that she had seduced him. Another was Sasha Kropotkin, daughter of Pëtr Kropotkin, the Russian anarchist who lived in exile in London.

There were two important mistresses in Maugham's life. One he loved, and the other he married. The one he loved was Ethelwyn Jones, known as Sue Jones, whom he always referred to as "Rosie," since he had used that name for her in his novel *Cakes and Ale*. A sparkling 23, the daughter of a successful playwright, she was a divorcée and a rising actress when Maugham met her. After a few dates, Maugham took her to his room and made love to her. He guessed she wanted to marry him. "I didn't want to do that," he wrote long after, "because I knew that all my friends had been to bed with her. That sounds as though she were something of a wanton. She wasn't. There was no vice in her. It just happened that she enjoyed copulation and took it for granted that when she dined with a man sexual congress would follow." Later, when Sue was doing a stage play in Chicago, Maugham had second thoughts. He pursued her and proposed. When she turned him down, he was stunned. But Sue was already pregnant by another man, and soon she married the son of the 6th Earl of Antrim.

The other mistress, the one Maugham married, was Syrie Barnardo Wellcome. Her father, a German Jew, had founded the orphanages known as the Barnardo Homes. At 22, Syrie, a shapely, lively young lady, met and married 48-year-old Henry Wellcome, an American-born pharmaceutical giant. The marriage was a disaster. Syrie had an affair with Gordon Selfridge, also American-born and a London department store tycoon. Annoyed, Wellcome had her sign a deed of separation. Maugham met Syrie in 1911 and found her gay, smart, charming. By 1913 they were sleeping together. She wanted a baby by Maugham, and eventually he gave her one, a daughter named Elizabeth. Wellcome, who'd hired detectives to detail his wife's adultery, now sued for divorce, naming Maugham as corespondent. Syrie tried to kill herself but survived. Once she was divorced, Maugham did what he felt to be the right thing. He married her on May 26, 1917.

It was a poor marriage. All the love was on her side. She constantly wanted sex with him. He wanted no more with her. In a letter to Syrie, Maugham cruelly outlined his complaints: "I married you because I thought it the best thing for your happiness and for Elizabeth's welfare, but I did not marry you because I loved you, and you were only too well aware of that." She was too shallow for him, he felt, interested only in "frocks and furniture." They went their own ways. She became a renowned interior decorator, doing houses for Tallulah Bankhead and Wallis Simpson. Syrie had her own big grievance. She had lost her husband to a man and to homosexuality. She asked for a divorce, and in 1929 she got it.

Unexpectedly, Maugham had found his greatest love in France during WWI. Gerald Haxton was born in San Francisco but had been raised in England. He was slightly taller than Maugham, brown-haired, blue-eyed, pock-marked, somewhat dissipated in appearance. Many women thought him handsome. Some men thought him evil. Haxton was 22 and Maugham 40 the night they met. Maugham asked him what he wanted out of life. Haxton said, "Fun and games. But I've not got a cent. So I want someone to look after me." They went up to Haxton's quarters, undressed, and got into bed. After they'd made love, Maugham whispered, "You needn't worry about the future, Gerald, because I'll look after you." For almost 30 years, until Haxton's death of edema of the lungs, Maugham looked after him. Haxton served as Maugham's secretary-companion on the Riviera and during his travels. Throughout the years Haxton—a drunkard, gambler, liar—held a strange dominance over the author. But he was cherished by Maugham as caretaker and lover. And in their travels, because he was a good mixer, Haxton provided Maugham with raw material for some of his best characters and stories. Also, to give his employer sexual variety, Haxton turned procurer. In 1924 Haxton found Maugham some lovely teenage boys in Mexico. In Indochina, Maugham had the happiest love encounter he had ever known, with a young boy in a sampan. In New York, in 1943, the 69-year-old Maugham had an affair with 17-year-old prep school poet and admirer David Posner. In his thorough biography, *Maugham*, author Ted Morgan quotes a letter from Posner on Maugham's lovemaking. "He wasn't particularly virile, but he was full of lust. He was rather businesslike about sex, but it's equally true that there were occasions when he spent a long time just fondling…. He profoundly disliked women sexually … he was very disturbed once when he saw me with a girl."

After Haxton's funeral Maugham took on a new secretary-companion. This was Alan Searle, a sweet, kind young man who'd been a hospital social worker and had once had an affair with Lytton Strachey. Searle adored Maugham, waited on him hand and foot, and considered him the best lover he'd ever known. In 1962, Maugham, upon hearing that his daughter Elizabeth might have him confined for incompetence, followed the advice of a French lawyer and adopted Alan Searle as his son, disowning Elizabeth as his legal daughter. Elizabeth hauled her father into court in Nice, proved her legitimacy, and had Searle's adoption nullified. On his deathbed, Maugham's last words were spoken to Searle: "I want to shake your hand and thank you for all that you've done for me."

—*I.W.*

The Tireless Frenchman

GUY DE MAUPASSANT (Aug. 5, 1850–July 6, 1893)

HIS FAME: He gained celebrity in his native France and throughout the world as the author of 300 popular short stories including, "*La Maison Tellier*" ["The Tellier House"] and "*Sur l'Eau*" ["On the Water"] and six novels, including *Bel-Ami* and *Pierre et Jean*.

Maupassant, age 40

HIS PERSON: Two occurrences in Maupassant's youth, spent near Dieppe, France, scarred him for life. One was the separation of his parents when he was 11 years old. Raised by his strong, neurotic mother, Maupassant adored her, hated his father, despised all husbands, and remained a bachelor. The other was the discovery that he had syphilis, which he had either inherited or contracted. He claimed he was cured of it, but in fact he wasn't, and in his later years it destroyed him. Living in Paris and studying law, he began to write on the side, with his mother's friend Gustave Flaubert as his stern mentor. Quitting law, Maupassant worked for 10 years as a government clerk, mostly for the Naval Ministry. When he was 30, his first published short story, "*Boule de Suif*" ("Ball of Fat"), caused a sensation, and three years later he published his first novel, *Une Vie* ("A Life"), called by Leo Tolstoi "the best French novel since

Les Misérables." After that, writing steadily, Maupassant became rich and famous, ultimately possessing four dwellings and two yachts. He was a powerful man, able to row a boat 50 mi. in a single day. But syphilis brought him down in the end. He became ill, began to hallucinate, and tried to cut his throat. Committed to a Paris insane asylum, he died there at the age of 42.

SEX LIFE: Guy de Maupassant was one of the most prodigious lovers in modern French history. In a quarter of a century of steady lovemaking, he reportedly had sexual intercourse with thousands of young women. He was prouder of his sex exploits than of his books. He possessed three qualities that made him a much-sought-after lover: the ability to go on and on in his couplings without coming, the ability to have multiple orgasms, and the ability to bring most women to a climax. He credited his carnal successes, above all, to his intelligence. He said, "Most people are inclined to think that the lower classes ... are better lovers than those who live sedentary lives. I don't believe that.... It needs brains to give another the greatest possible amount of pleasure."

From age 12 to 15 he masturbated "occasionally." Then he had his first love affair. "When I was about 16 I had a girl, and the delight she gave me cured me of self-abuse." He never forgot the feel of her loins or the way she gasped, "Enough, enough!" Later, he enjoyed consorting with prostitutes, and at the peak of his fame preferred wealthy young society women, favoring those who were married and Jewish.

Maupassant was very matter-of-fact about his endurance and insisted that successive sex bouts did not exhaust him. "I'm as tired after 2 or 3 times as I am after 20," he once said. "I've counted 20 and more. Surely you know that in 2 or 3 times you exhaust your stock of semen, so you can go on afterward without further loss." When Flaubert doubted his endurance, Maupassant had a bookkeeper accompany him to a Paris brothel as a witness, and there he "had six girls in an hour." Another time, to impress and "stagger" Bobukin, a visiting Russian writer, Maupassant picked up a dancer at the Folies Bergère, took her to a nearby brothel, and in front of his visitor had sexual intercourse with her six times in a row. When he finished with her, he went across the hall and had sex three more times with a young prostitute.

SEX PARTNERS: Whenever Maupassant saw an attractive woman, he wanted her. In 1889, on his only visit to London, he was taken to lunch at an Earl's Court restaurant by Henry James. Noting a beautiful woman at the next table, Maupassant asked James to "get her" for him. James was never more horrified. Most women Maupassant wanted only once, but there was a handful that he saw frequently. All of them were married. One affair—with Marie Kann, a wealthy young brunette—lasted eight years. Maupassant wrote her 2,200 steaming love letters. Another of his long-lived affairs was with Blanche Roosevelt Macchetta, born in Sandusky, O., who married a Milan nobleman and became a marchesa. She was a shapely redhead who made a brief singing debut at Covent Garden in London, then became a published novelist. She bedded down with Maupassant regularly at his country retreat in Étretat and admitted enjoying "the maximum of sensual pleasure" with him. For variety, Maupassant sometimes liked his women on the kinky side. After Gisèle d'Estoc, who affected close-cropped hair and men's clothes, had had an affair with Emma Bouer, a trapeze artist with the Cirque Medrane, and had stabbed her in a fight, Maupassant took up with Gisèle. Often Gisèle shared her broad-hipped lesbian ladies, as well as hashish or ether, with him.

QUIRKS: One day journalist Frank Harris went for a walk in the country with Maupassant. As Harris recalled it:

> "I suppose I am a little out of the common sexually," he [Maupassant] resumed, "for I can make my instrument stand whenever I please."
> "Really?" I exclaimed, too astonished to think.
> "Look at my trousers," he remarked, laughing, and there on the road he showed me that he was telling the truth.

HIS THOUGHTS: "The only woman I really love is the Unknown who haunts my imagination. She must be intensely sensuous, yet self-controlled; soulful, yet a coquette: to find her, that's the great adventure of life and there's no other."

—*I. W.*

The Last Samurai

YUKIO MISHIMA (Jan. 14, 1925–Nov. 25, 1970)

HIS FAME: The most colorful and prolific author to emerge in postwar Japan, Mishima wrote numerous plays, stories, novels, and journalistic pieces which earned him a worldwide reputation. Among his most famous works are *Confessions of a Mask* (novel, 1949), *The Temple of the Golden Pavilion* (novel, 1956), "Patriotism" (short story, 1960; film *Yukoku*, 1966), and *The Sailor Who Fell from Grace with the Sea* (novel, 1963).

HIS PERSON: Mishima's father was a minor bureaucrat who deeply admired Hitler and Nazism. His mother was a

Mishima, the year before he ended his life

second-class citizen in a household dominated by her dictatorial mother-in-law. Mishima was literally a prisoner in the possessive old woman's darkened sickroom until he was 12 years old; he grew into a brilliant, languid, morbid youth obsessed with fantasies of blood and pain.

He began to write during adolescence, and at 16 was already a central figure in the new romantic school of Japanese literature, having shunned his given name, Kimitake Hiraoka, and adopted his now famous pen name to conceal his writing from his antiliterary father. Later in life the author would write out "Yukio Mishima" in Japanese so that the characters also read "mysterious devil bewitched with death." As he told friends, "It's eerie, but that's the way to write my name."

Exempted from military service because of poor health, he worked in an aircraft factory during WWII. Afterward he studied law at the insistence of his father. Then he accepted a prestigious civil service job in the finance ministry, but quit in order to devote himself exclusively to writing. In 1949 *Confessions of a Mask*, a masterful autobiographical novel dealing with homosexuality, appeared, and Mishima became an international celebrity. He delighted in shocking the Japanese public and affected a hip, westernized demeanor. He was overjoyed when people mistook him for a gangster and relished the image so much that he played the lead in a Japanese film called *Tough Guy*.

In spite of his homosexuality, Mishima took a wife and had two children. He was fascinated with the physical activity he had missed as a boy and became an avid body-builder, attaining the fifth-rank black-belt grade in Japanese swordsmanship and the second-rank black belt in karate as well.

His many Western friends delighted in his imitations of Brando and Bogart. However, he retained an inner core of fanatic Japanese nationalism and became the leader of a private army of some 100 young, right-wing zealots, known as the Shield Society. In 1970 he led four members of this toy army in a suicide raid upon the office of a general of the Army Self-Defense Forces in Tokyo and took the general hostage. There, from a balcony, he exhorted a regiment of soldiers to revert to the prewar militarism and emperor worship he so admired. When the troops laughed at him, he disemboweled himself in the ancient ritual of seppuku, or hara-kiri. He was beheaded with his 17th-century samurai sword by a follower, who then committed suicide.

SEX LIFE: As a boy he drew pictures of beautiful knights dying of their wounds, and was appalled to learn that a picture he had mooned over represented Joan of Arc and not a young man, as he had thought. From that day forward he hated the sight of women in men's clothes and once angrily reprimanded his wife for appearing in slacks. At 12 he had his first orgasm, while looking at a picture of St. Sebastian bound and pierced by arrows. At about the same time he fell in love with a male classmate and developed three fetishes which stayed with him until death: masculine armpit hair, sweat, and white gloves.

He became a frantic masturbator, finding release in Marquis de Sade-like fantasies of death and cannibalism. In his youth he attempted to interest himself in the company of women, and while studying law was briefly involved with a woman to whom he assigned the fictional name Sonoko. On the day she married someone else, Mishima got thoroughly drunk for perhaps the only time in his life. With the celebrity he earned from *Confessions*, he more or less came out of the closet, and often entertained friends at Brunswick, a gay café on the Ginza in Tokyo. He favored young roughnecks, and on a trip to New York in 1952 he cruised gay bars looking for his ideal white male. From New York he went to Rio, where he spent the month before Carnival time. There he haunted city parks in the afternoons and often took young boys of 17 or so back to his hotel. When a friend asked how he managed to communicate with the youths, Mishima answered that in the world of homosexuality "you don't need a common language." He added that he was interested in the process of courting females but was entirely disinterested in performing "the final act" with a woman. As if to demonstrate the truth of this statement, Mishima later phoned his friend for help because a Japanese woman was trying to seduce him in his hotel room.

The author flew from Rio to Paris, where he became good friends with the composer Toshiro Mayuzumi. Mishima asked Mayuzumi to take him to a "bar for pederasts" and later got angry at the composer because Mayuzumi, who could speak French, monopolized all the boys.

Women tended to shy away from Mishima because of his odd physical appearance. He was 5 ft. 2 in., with a weight lifter's torso set on top of skinny, underdeveloped legs. A crew cut revealed that his head was shaped like a light bulb. In a magazine poll, 50% of the female readers questioned stated that they would rather kill themselves than marry the famous novelist. The girl who did become his wife in 1958, Yoko Sugiyama, was faced with the enmity of Mishima's mother, Shizue, who jealously treated him more like a lover than a son. Even in the presence of company, Mishima would address Shizue in intimate terms, causing a great deal of wonder about the extent of their mother-son relationship. Mishima regarded his pretty, round-faced wife as a near equal and often invited her to mix with his friends, thus breaking Japanese tradition. His only rule was that she not disturb him while he worked.

After he became a celebrity, Mishima found himself pursued by what he called "the literature virgins." He liked to tell the story of how he had almost been smothered to death in the breasts of a tall American woman who insisted on dancing with him at an embassy function.

However, Mishima's true erotic interest was in a painful, gory death, and sooner or later everyone who knew him heard him say that seppuku was "the ultimate form of masturbation." The author's companion in suicide was a 25-year-old "soldier" named Masakatsu Morita, who was once referred to by friends as Mishima's "fiancé." Morita, who was also fascinated by death, had pledged his life to Mishima.

HIS THOUGHTS: "I am desperate to kill a man. I want to see red blood."

—*M.S.*

Philosopher With A Whip

DONATIEN ALPHONSE FRANÇOIS DE SADE
(June 2, 1740–Dec. 2, 1814)

HIS FAME: Because Sade was imprisoned by royal decree for staging orgies during which he whipped and sodomized young women, his name has become synonymous with unlimited sexual license—especially the license to derive pleasure from inflicting pain. His life spawned the word *sadism*.

HIS PERSON: After two brief incarcerations for "outrageous debauchery," the young and handsome Marquis de Sade, lieutenant governor of four royal provinces, was forced to transfer his quest for strange pleasures from Paris to his ancesteral château in the south of France. When five Marseilles prostitutes accused him of attempting to sodomize and poison them, his mother-in-law obtained a *lettre de cachet* (a royal order for indefinite detention without trial) and eventually put him away in 1777 for 12 1/2 years.

In prison he became a prolific writer, churning out conventional works as well as frenzied erotica. At last the French Revolution freed him when the Constituent Assembly abolished *lettres de cachet*. He was now Citizen Sade, a pamphleteer, orator, and living legend for having incited, from his tower cell, the historic storming of the Bastille. Promoted to revolutionary judge during the Reign of Terror, he found himself incapable of demanding his mother-in-law's execution when her case came before him. He was denounced as a moderate, escaped the guillotine only by luck, and turned to a theatrical career. In 1801 he was prosecuted by the Napoleonic regime's censors, ostensibly for his erotic novel *Justine* but actually for a pamphlet lampooning Napoleon and his wife, Josephine. He was found criminally insane and lived out his life at the Charenton asylum, where the director allowed him to stage dramas in which he often acted the part of the villain.

SEX LIFE: On the evening of Oct. 18, 1763, Jeanne Testard, 20, a fan maker and part-time prostitute, entered a house of assignation with an elegant, auburn-haired young nobleman. He led her to a small inner room draped in black; its walls, on which religious art mingled strangely with pornography, featured a large collection of whips. Later, he explained, she would flog him with one of them, and she could choose one with which to be flogged. Meanwhile, perhaps an enema or a little sodomy? She declined both, but was forced at gunpoint to smash a crucifix.

Unfortunately for Sade's future victims, his in-laws, the Montreuils, were influential at court. After 15 days in jail, Sade professed repentance and was released. The Paris police warned brothel keepers not to supply him with any more prostitutes for his private orgies. As a result he began to pick up amateurs. On Easter Sunday, 1768, he accosted Rose Keller, a thirtyish widow lately reduced to public begging, politely conducted her to a house in the suburbs, and made her strip and lie facedown on a couch. He then began to beat her with a whip of knotted cords, pausing several times to rub a white ointment into the lacerations. Her screams for pity seemed only to energize him, until he stopped with an appalling, orgasmic cry.

Keller was able to escape and find help. Although she was bribed into silence by Sade's family, the authorities had already taken evidence. Sade was jailed as an example to the many other sexually depraved aristocrats. He earned a quick release by getting his wife, the uncomplaining Renée-Pélagie, pregnant again when she visited him at the jail. Paroled, he was ordered to live quietly on his estate in the south. He and his family went there, and for company invited his wife's lively younger sister, Anne-Prospère, who was soon his wife in all but name. That winter a private world of pleasure was created in the old château of La Coste; erotic spectacles were staged and the entire household, including not only Sade's sister-in-law but his wife, took part willingly in elegant indecencies. Too elegant, it seems, for when Sade visited nearby Marseilles to collect a debt, he instructed his valet Latour to procure several young women for the most violent orgy yet. Four water-front prostitutes, aged 18 to 23, were subjected by Sade to a complicated ritual in which each was in turn beaten and ordered to beat him; in between beatings they were offered various combinations of anal and vaginal intercourse with Sade and, alternately or simultaneously, Latour. All the women were continually offered handfuls of anise-flavored bonbons. That same evening Sade attempted a similar orgy with another prostitute. Hours later she and one of the girls used earlier were vomiting uncontrollably; they had overdosed on Spanish fly, a common aphrodisiac of the time. Sade and Latour fled the city but were condemned to death *in absentia* and executed in effigy. Caught and jailed in Sardinia, Sade escaped and lived the next few years as a fugitive.

In May, 1774, the *lettre de cachet* obtained by Mme. de Montreuil seemed about to lapse with the accession of a new king. Sade lost no time in realizing his latest fantasy: He would lure young girls to the château and personally undertake their sex education. Anne-Prospère had now left him, but his wife, Renée-Pélagie, was his ally in everything. With her support he engaged an experienced procuress who recruited five 15-year-old girls and a small boy, supposedly for domestic service. There were orgies that Renée-Pélagie may have directed. The outcome was more tragedy: two girls escaped, one needing medical treatment; the parents of three began legal action; the procuress had a baby by Sade, quit, and was jailed by *lettre de cachet* (Mme. de Montreuil's work) to stop her from talking, and the baby died of neglect. Undaunted, Sade found older replacements through a corrupt local monk, who assured anxious parents that the "discipline" at the château was well up to convent standards.

Early in 1777, news arrived from Paris that Sade's mother was dying. Although he had never cared for her, he set off at once. Since friends had warned him of Mme. de Montreuil's intentions, it seems likely that, in his heart of hearts, he wanted to get caught, and he was. In prison Sade discovered two enduring sources of sexual satisfaction: masturbation and literature. His imaginary orgies were so successful that he never attempted real ones again. Renée-Pélagie, loyal throughout his imprisonment, divorced him on his release. He soon formed a lasting relationship with the young actress Marie-Constance Renelle; he lived with her for a while in a hayloft at Versailles, baby-sitting her little son and earning a few sous as a stagehand. She followed him to Charenton asylum, and seems not to have minded when this fat, rheumatic, partially blind old man enlivened his last two years there with a pretty young woman from the asylum's laundry.

SEX PARTNERS: By the end of young Sade's military service as a cavalry officer, he was hiring one woman a day. His down-at-the-heels father was delighted when the bourgeois but wealthy family of Renée-Pélagie de Montreuil suggested her as a suitable bride; marriage would steady the boy, he thought. Meanwhile Sade had actually fallen in love with a count's daughter, Laure de Lauris. She left him with a beautiful memory and a venereal infection.

Renée-Pélagie was pious and frigid, but Sade favorably impressed her charming young mother and her blond and sexy younger sister (the story is told that he asked to marry the sister instead). His first arrest threw the entire family into shock. Almost with relief Mme. de Montreuil noted that, after his release, he followed the approved fashion and began keeping mistresses. There was Mlle. Colet, a popular actress at the Comédie Italienne; then another actress, the buxom Mlle. Beauvoisin, whom he took south and allowed to pass as his wife; then a *poule de luxe* ("fancy lady"), Mlle. Dorville; then several ballet dancers, one of them an expert flagellator. Renée-Pélagie knew nothing of these affairs, but Mme. de Montreuil did. What she did not know was that Sade had an isolated suburban fun house outside Paris where he regularly staged bisexual orgies; one of them, at which he had flogged four women and then served them dinner, was the talk of the sexual underworld. It was to this house that he took Rose Keller—for a job, according to her testimony, for a debauch, according to his.

We know little of the Marseilles victims except their names and ages: Mariette Borelly (23), Marianette Laugier (20), Rose Coste (20), and Marianne Laverne (18), of the morning orgy; and Marguerite Costa (25), of the one attempted in the evening. Marguerite brought the first complaint, followed by the other four together. Of Latour, Sade's partner in the affair, it is said that he was a nobleman's son; Sade would switch roles with him socially as well as sexually, addressing him as "monsieur le marquis." Latour and Anne-Prospère, who had stayed on at La Coste, accompanied Sade when he fled over the border to Italy. Renée-Pélagie, a woman of such saintly character that Sade must have worked hard indeed to corrupt her, was in the uncomfortable position of being her sister's rival. When

Sade was finally jailed, she became in good conscience what she had always tried to be to him: the perfect wife. The affair of the 15-year-old girls was so effectively hushed up that we cannot even be certain of their names. One of their successors was Catherine Trillet, known as Justine; promoted from the kitchen to Sade's orgies, she would not leave him even when her father turned up brandishing a pistol. Her predecessor as household favorite was Gothon, Renée-Pélagie's personal maid, who remained fond of him and sent him fruit and jam in prison.

During his early prison years Sade enjoyed, by letter, a platonic relationship with Marie-Dorothée de Rousse, his former housekeeper; he had always tended to separate sex from friendship. For a few months after his release he lived with a widow of 40, la Présidente de Fleurieu, but left her for the more sympathetic Marie-Constance Renelle, of whom he wrote, "This woman is an angel sent to me by heaven." In the asylum, with the director's connivance, she passed as Sade's daughter. Of his last mistress, Madeleine Leclerc, we know that she was only 12 when Sade's eye first lighted on her and 15 when she became his mistress (he was 72), that her mother hoped the marquis would launch her as an actress, and that she shaved her pubic hair.

MEDICAL REPORT: Sade claimed that the extreme thickness of his sperm made ejaculation painful for him. The diagnosis is unlikely, but the symptom may explain his algolagnia (i.e., pleasure in both receiving and inflicting pain).

—*J.M.B.E.*

The Non-Violent Sadist

WILLIAM SEABROOK (Feb. 22, 1886–Sept. 20, 1945)

HIS FAME: In the 1920s and 1930s Seabrook thrilled readers in Europe and America with books about his travels to exotic places. In *The Magic Island* (1929) he described his participation in *voodoo rites in Haiti*, and in *Jungle Ways* (1931) he told of eating human flesh in Liberia. His most lasting contribution was the 1935 bestseller *Asylum*, a frank description of the seven months he spent in a mental hospital, attempting to cure his alcoholism.

HIS PERSON: Born on Washington's Birthday in Westminster, Md., "Willie"

Seabrook was the oldest son of a lawyer turned Lutheran minister. After working as a newspaper reporter, city editor, and advertising executive, Seabrook enlisted in the French army and was gassed at the Battle of Verdun. Returning to the U.S., he became a reporter for *The New York Times* and then a feature writer for King Features Syndicate. In 1924 he and his first wife traveled to the Middle East. His account of this journey, *Adventures in Arabia*, was an instant success and launched him on a career of writing travel books. Seabrook enjoyed his celebrity and was excited by getting to know famous people. He maintained friendships with Aleister Crowley, Isadora Duncan, Gertrude Stein, Man Ray, Aldous Huxley, Emma Goldman, Jean Cocteau, and Thomas Mann.

Actually, he did not engage in a cannibal feast in Africa as he claimed. He recognized the meat served to him by a tribal chief as that of an ape and left Liberia frustrated because he had failed in his mission to taste a cooked human. Back in Paris, with the help of friends he acquired pieces of the remains of a young worker who had died in an accident. Seabrook had different parts roasted, broiled, and prepared as a ragout. He ate it all and then described the meal in *Jungle Ways* as if it had taken place in West Africa. After the book was published, word spread from Liberia that ape meat had been substituted for human flesh in the meal he had eaten there and Seabrook was forced to choose between being considered a sucker or a liar. He accepted the image of sucker until the publication of his autobiography in 1942 in which he confessed his role in the hoax.

HIS WIVES: There were three. The first was Katie Edmondson, the daughter of a Coca-Cola executive. They were married for 22 years, although for most of those years they were more friends than a couple. She operated a famous coffee shop on Waverly Place in New York City's Greenwich Village. And later she married the first husband of Seabrook's second wife.

Seabrook was introduced to novelist Marjorie Worthington at a bridge game in 1929. They lived together for five years before they married, and were married six years before they divorced. She was very jealous of his interest in other women and felt most at peace when they were both at work at their typewriters.

A few days after Seabrook met Constance Kuhr, she convinced him to plunge his elbows into boiling water so that he would be unable to lift a glass of liquor to his lips. They were married the following year and she gave birth to Seabrook's only child, William.

SEX LIFE: As Marjorie Worthington described it in her biography, *The Strange World of Willie Seabrook*, "Lovemaking, for Willie, was a complicated process, all mixed up with his complexes, fetishes, and compulsions." In fact, this hard-core Republican, Rotarian son of a preacher practiced a major sexual aberration, and a highly unusual one at that. He liked to tie up naked women and chain them to pillars or dangle them from the ceiling. He never hurt them and he paid them well, and he never made love to them. Seabrook claimed that a childhood in which he was pampered by five doting aunts had caused him to desire to torture women in a relatively benign manner. As a child he found no shortage of pictures of women in chains in books of mythology and history. When he was nine years old, a neighbor girl let him tie her hands behind her back with the ribbon from her hair. However, his special brand of soft sadism remained in the realm of imagination until he returned to New York after WWI. Then he met Deborah Luris, a Greenwich Village puppeteer, who was willing, indeed eager, to fit into his fantasy. "When people uncork parallel or complementary chimeric wish-fantasies," Seabrook wrote, "sparks generally fly. And so they did—for a week." Wife Katie was completely tolerant and even encouraged him. Once he brought Deborah to a costume party dressed as a prisoner, with her hands chained behind her back. When Seabrook fell in love with Marjorie Worthington, it was not Katie who became jealous, but Deborah Luris.

But it was Marjorie who had to endure Willie's greatest indulgences, as he lapsed into extended periods of avoiding writing by drinking a quart and a half of liquor a day and transforming his fantasies into reality with a succession of willing young hired houseguests. Once, in Paris, Seabrook invited a group of distinguished French businessmen to his studio for cocktails. Marjorie served aperitifs while Mimi, a Montparnasse call girl, wearing only a leather skirt, hung by her wrists, suspended from the balcony on a chain. None of the Frenchmen spoke a single word to or about Mimi.

Another time Seabrook asked Man Ray and his date to stay in his studio for four hours and watch over a girl he had chained to the newel of the staircase, while he and Marjorie went out to a dinner in the Seabrooks' honor. As soon as the Seabrooks left, Ray unchained the girl and invited her to join them at the dinner table. During the meal she explained that Seabrook liked to sit and drink whiskey and look at her for hours. When he went to bed, he chained her to the bedpost and she slept on the floor like a dog. She thought that Willie was impotent and she couldn't understand why Marjorie humored him.

When Willie became interested in witchcraft and the occult, he set up a "research laboratory" in the barn on his farm in Rhinebeck, N.Y. Willie stocked the barn with a cage and a witch's cradle and entertained a series of young women whom he called "research workers" and "apprentice witches." Marjorie, fretting and suffering in the main house, called them "Lizzies in chains." Some of the Lizzies stayed naked under voluntary domination in the barn for weeks, and Seabrook wrote of observing them experience mystical ecstasies like those of St. Theresa of Avila.

Eventually they emerged unharmed and the people of Rhinebeck excused the strange comings and goings at the barn by saying that Seabrook was writing a book about whatever was going on inside. They were right. But the book, *Witchcraft*, upset Seabrook, and despite his studies he was unable to exorcise the demons within him. At the age of 59 William Seabrook committed suicide by taking an overdose of sleeping pills.

—D. W.

The Chameleon

STENDHAL (Jan. 23, 1783–Mar. 23, 1842)

HIS FAME: "Literary fame is a lottery. I am taking out a ticket whose winning number is 1935," wrote Stendhal in his autobiographical work *The Life of Henri Brulard.* His "ticket" won. A French writer of the 19th century who wrote, he said, for the liberated "happy few," he has been appreciated far more in the 20th century than in his own, particularly for his two "realist" novels, *The Red and the Black* and *The Charterhouse of Parma.*

Stendhal at 57

HIS PERSON: Someone once asked Stendhal what his profession was, and he answered, "Observer of the human heart." The heart he observed was often his own; he described it with candor, accuracy, and much detail in his voluminous journals. It was partly because of his appearance that he was so self-conscious. Though he had a radiant smile and well-shaped hands, Stendhal was no beauty. He lost most of his hair at an early age and chose to cover his pate with a purplish wig; his nose was thick, his cheeks were fat, and his legs were short. In later life, he developed a paunch. Once he expressed the desire to be a tall, blond German.

To compensate for his unprepossessing appearance, he cultivated a brilliant wit. "I'd rather be a chameleon than an ox," was his motto, and a chameleon Marie Henri Beyle was, with more than 200 pseudonyms, among them Stendhal (his favorite), Dominique, Machiavelli B., Old Hummums, and Mr. Myself. In contrast, his writing was simple and direct, and he worshiped the truth.

When a boy of 16, he left his hometown of Grenoble and his materialistic father, who had raised him "under a bell jar," to study at the École Polytechnique in Paris. However, instead of enrolling, he lived in a garret and roved the streets expecting to find damsels to rescue. He himself was the one who was rescued—by a distant relative, Noël Daru, who found Henri ill, gave him a room in the Darus' Paris home, and got him a secretarial job with the ministry of war. In 1800 Stendhal traveled to join Napoleon's army in Italy, a country he adored for the rest of his life. Until 1814 he served on and off in the army; in 1812 he was with Napoleon during the retreat from Moscow. Battle disgusted him. After he rejected military life, he settled in Austrian-ruled Milan until 1821, when rumors claiming he was a French spy or an Italian revolutionary made him fear imprisonment. On returning to Paris, suffering from unrequited love for an Italian woman,

Stendhal contemplated suicide, but he immersed himself in his writing instead. A return visit to his adopted homeland ended abruptly in 1828 when the Austrian police expelled him from Milan as a subversive. A magnanimous Stendhal nevertheless published his enthusiastic tribute to Italy, *Roman Journal*, the following year. In 1831, after the Austrians found him unacceptable for a post in Trieste, Stendhal accepted a consulship in Civitavecchia, located in the Papal States. Here he felt intellectually isolated and bored. Although his official duties were light during the next seven years, he started three books which he never completed.

He died of a stroke at the age of 59, his *chasse de bonheur* ("pursuit of happiness") over. As he had requested, his tombstone was engraved with *Arrigo Beyle, Milanese, Visse, Scrisse, Amò* ("Henri Beyle, Milanese, He lived, He wrote, He loved"). It was a fitting epitaph for the creator of *Beylisme*, a method of deliberately cultivating the senses and the mind, which was expressed in the equation "Happiness = love + work."

SEX LIFE: Many of the women Stendhal loved were unattainable, including the first. He wrote, "I wanted to cover my mother with kisses, and that there not be any clothing.... I always wanted to give them to her on the breast." She died when he was seven.

As he walked with his tutor, his 12-year-old eyes "devoured" a good-looking nun who passed them. Noticing the boy's reaction, the tutor thereafter changed their route. Stendhal was also erotically aroused by paintings ("To bathe like that with lovely women!" he mused, standing before a landscape showing nudes in a stream), music, nature, and the glimpse of his Aunt Camille's thigh as she descended from a wagon.

When he was grown, his love objects were often married women who refused to sleep with him. This did not lessen his relentless, though awkwardly shy, pursuit of them. And while he couldn't always have what he wanted, he still enjoyed an active sex life. His first encounter, in Milan in 1800, was probably with a prostitute. He said of it, "The violence of my timidity and of the experience have absolutely killed my recollection." However, he never forgot the result; a venereal disease, possibly syphilis, plagued him intermittently for the rest of his life. In the spring of 1806 he recorded another casual sexual encounter, this one with a serving maid in a doorway. Afterward, he accompanied her to her room for more sex, then left in the morning "thoroughly disgusted and ashamed," but he also contemplated returning to her room to try anal intercourse.

His sexuality was affected by his state of mind. Of one sexual failure (followed in the morning by victory), he said that anxiety "agitated my mind too much for my body to be brilliant." In a depressed mood in the summer of 1821, he attended a party where the guests were young men and prostitutes. During the orgy, he was impotent with the prostitute Alexandrine—a "complete fiasco," he said. She rejected his offer to bring her to orgasm manually, and then reported his impotence to the rest of the company, thus generating a story that circulated around Paris. His novel *Armance* was about an impotent man. Yet he wrote of having intercourse with a woman seven times in a row and of additional many-times-in-one-night bouts with other women. At 50 he confessed his interest was waning, that he could "quite easily pass a fortnight or three weeks without a woman."

Although he was overwhelmingly heterosexual, an appreciator of women, he was once attracted to a Russian officer sitting next to him in a theater. "If I had been a woman, this lovable officer would have inspired me with the most violent passion."

He died a bachelor.

LOVE LIFE: In 1835, by the shores of Lake Albano, near Rome, Stendhal wrote in the sand the initials of his major loves:

$$
\begin{array}{cccccccccccc}
a & d & & i & l & ine & pg & de & & & r \\
V. & A. & A. & M. & M. & A. & A & .A & .M & .C. & G. & A.
\end{array}
$$

He mused on the "amazing follies and sillinesses" they made him commit and noted that he had not even possessed all of them. He loved one enough to list her twice. In his order, they most likely were:

V.—Virginie Kubly, a tall married actress whom he worshiped from afar while a teenager in Grenoble. Seeing her approach in a park, he fled from the "burn" of her closeness. He never spoke to her.

Aa. and *Apg.*—Angela Pietragrua ("Gina"), a married Milanese with flashing eyes whom he met in Milan in 1800. He was too shy to tell her of his love. In 1811, again in Italy, he pursued and finally made love to her. To mark the occasion, he had his suspenders embroidered: "AP 22nd-September, 1811," and wrote, "It seems to me that perfectly pure pleasure can come only with intimacy; the first time, it's a victory; in the three following, you acquire intimacy." Their affair was studded with quarrels, signals (half-open windows), and barriers (two nuns sleeping in an adjoining bedroom). Gina's performance in bed with another man, which he watched—unbeknownst to her—through a keyhole, made him think of "puppets ... dancing before my eyes." Initially it made him laugh, then depressed him. They broke up in an art gallery with Gina "clinging to my garments and dragging herself on her knees.... assuredly she never loved me more than on that very day."

Ad.—Adèle Rebuffel, whom he met while having an affair with her mother. She was then a child of 12. In his four-year pursuit of Adèle, the furthest he got was to put hand on her breast.

M.—Mélanie Guilbert (called Louason), an actress with whom he lived in Marseilles from the summer of 1805 to the spring of 1806. On an outing in the countryside, he saw her bathe nude in a river, a vision like the painted nudes that aroused him when he was a boy. After she went back to Paris, he wrote, in disillusionment, "I desired passionately to be loved by a melancholy and slender woman who was an actress. I was, and I didn't find sustained happiness."

Mi.—"Minette," or Wilhemine von Griesheim, blond daughter of a Prussian general, who rebuffed his advances.

Al.—Angéline Béreyter, an opera singer with whom he had a three-year affair, during which she taught him songs from various operas. Sometimes she had as many as nine orgasms a night, but he complained that their physical happiness robbed him "of much of my imagination." In another list of his lovers, he said he never loved her.

Aine.—Alexandrine Daru, wife of his cousin Pierre, double-chinned and decent, who never gave in to his blandishments, which included caressing her gloves as though they were her hands and tracing an *A* in the sand.

Mde.—Mathilde Viscontini Dembowski ("Métilde"), a sympathizer with the revolutionary movement in Milan, whom he loved unrequitedly from 1818 to 1821. For her he turned down other women—though not all, as a case of gonorrhea he contracted in 1819 attests. Once he undertook to follow her to another town, where he contrived to pass by her in a disguise consisting of green spectacles and a large overcoat. She inspired his book *On Love*, a "scientific" study of love, in which he explained his concept of "crystallization"—love so powerful it transforms one's beloved into a perfect being. The book sold 17 copies in its first ten years of publication. By the end of 1820, his pursuit of Métilde reached "*le dead-blank.*"

C.—Countess Clémentine Curial ("Menti"), married, 36 to his 41 when their affair began. Once for three days, he stayed cooped up in a cellar, while she brought food and emptied his chamber pot and provided sex. In love with someone else, she ended the relationship in 1826, causing him great pain. When she was 47, he tried to revive their affair, but she said, "How can you love me at my age?" and refused to consider it.

G.—In 1830, Giulia Rinieri, a 19-year-old aristocratic virgin, attempted to seduce Stendhal, saying, "I am perfectly aware, and have been for some time, that you are old and ugly," and then she kissed him. After hesitating for several months, he slept with her, then later that year asked for her hand in marriage but was rejected.

Ar.—Alberthe de Rubempré, married, witty, a little crazy, in love with the occult. Their affair lasted six months, but he was in love with her a "month at most." After he died, she tried, in a séance, to summon up the shade of "poor Henri."

HIS ADVICE: Aug. 1, 1801, from his diaries: "Like many others, I'm embarrassed when it comes to _____ a respectable woman for the first time. Here's a very simple method. While she's lying down, you start kissing her lightly, you titillate her, etc., she begins to like it. Still, through force of habit, she keeps on defending herself. Then, without her realizing what you're up to, you should put your left forearm on her throat, beneath her chin, as if you are going to strangle her. Her first movement will be to raise her hand in defense. Meanwhile, you take your _____ between the index and middle finger of your right hand, holding them both taut, and quietly place it in the _____.... It's important to cover up the decisive movement of the left forearm by whimpering."

—*A.E.*

The Tormented One

AUGUST STRINDBERG (Jan. 22, 1849–May 14, 1912)

HIS FAME: Considered Sweden's greatest playwright, Strindberg revolutionized the world's theater with a prolific outpouring of critical writings and dozens of plays that still are performed today, including the masterful *Miss Julie*.

HIS PERSON: The fourth child born to his parents—who had wed just a few months before his birth—Strindberg had a tormented youth. His father declared bankruptcy, and the family's poverty forced Strindberg to wear ill-fitting hand-me-downs and consequently suffer the taunts of his schoolmates. Strindberg adored his mother, but she clearly favored her eldest son over August and the others. Yet worse was to come. In 1862, when Strindberg was 13, his mother died. Within a year his father remarried, and Strindberg found himself in continuing conflict with his aloof father and a stepmother whom he jealously hated.

An obvious genius, Strindberg was bored at the University of Uppsala. He failed to earn a degree and turned to writing for his livelihood. Supplementing his meager literary earnings by working as a librarian, Strindberg labored long on *Master Olof*, his first play, and was crushed when the Swedish Royal Theater rejected it. He persisted at his writing, but for consolation turned to alcohol—he was a prodigious drinker—and to mystical pursuits including alchemy (he claimed he had discovered how to transform baser metals into gold). Those around him suspected that he was sinking into madness. He proclaimed that the spirit of Edgar Allan Poe, who had died in the year Strindberg was born, had migrated into his body. Through it all, however, his powerful, often viciously satirical writing continued, and it had won him, by the time of his death, the general respect of his fellow Swedes, who regarded him as their most brilliant writer.

SEX LIFE: Brought up in a family that adhered to Pietism, a gloomy hellfire Lutheran movement, Strindberg found that his early thoughts of sex were colored by his religious devotion. It horrified him when, at age 14, he stumbled upon a slim volume entitled *Warning of a Friend of Youth against the Most Dangerous Enemy of Youth*. Because he had masturbated, he feared he was "condemned to death or lunacy at the age of 25." To regain salvation, he immersed himself in a theology class. It was during this time that he had his first adolescent infatuation. The object was the 30-year-old daughter of Strindberg's landlord, a very cultured woman who was a member of the emotional Pietist sect. Ephemeral as that crush was, it paved the path for dozens more, and also for Strindberg's escape from the religious doctrines he found unsatisfying.

His independence growing, the blond-haired, blue-eyed teenager took to passing his evenings by dancing and flirting with a parade of young girls. He especially adored the fragile brunettes, perhaps because they reminded him of his beloved mother. Strindberg himself was aware of the possible link: "Are my feelings perverted because I want to possess my mother? Is that an unconscious incest of the heart?" Incestuous in origin or not, Strindberg's burning desire was to have a tranquil, married home life with a wife more devoted to him than his mother had been. He would have been happy, he once mused, if at 16 he had married a pleasant woman and taken a simple job.

SEX PARTNERS: While Strindberg married three times, the peaceful home life he yearned for was never his. Despite his avowed preference for old-fashioned women—he stridently denounced Henrik Ibsen's *Doll's House* for fomenting female emancipation—his enduring lovers were complex, ambitious, and independent.

When he met Siri von Essen, his first wife, it was—as it always would be for Strindberg—love at first sight. At the time, she was married to an army officer and coincidentally lived in Strindberg's boyhood home. Whereas Siri's rakish husband thought her frigid, Strindberg thought her chastely pure. Their two-year affair ended in marriage. Unhappily for Strindberg, Siri wished to pursue her theatrical ambitions, and as she won success as an actress, she lost Strindberg. He accused her of having affairs with both men and women and implored his friends to spy on her. Strindberg and Siri fought frequently and loudly. After 14 years and four children, their marriage ended in divorce, and Siri—to Strindberg's sorrow—retained custody of the children.

A year later he was romancing Frida Uhl, an Austrian journalist. Their embattled courtship augured the nature of their tempestuous marriage. Just days before the ceremony, the wedding was nearly halted because Strindberg (mistakenly) thought Frida had been the model for a scandalous painting of a bare-backed odalisque, or harem girl. With this rift mended, the marriage went forward, but only to dissolve within two years, owing in part to Strindberg's obsession with what he perceived to be Frida's promiscuity. They had one child, a daughter, who remained with Frida.

Strindberg was smitten by his last wife, Harriet Bosse, when he saw her acting the part of the playful Puck in Shakespeare's *Midsummer Night's Dream*. A few social meetings fired his desire for her, even though Harriet was 30 years younger than the 52-year-old playwright. "Would you like to have a baby by me?" he asked. She agreed, they wed, and she soon produced Strindberg's sixth child. But Harriet, like Siri, wanted an acting career, and Strindberg—as ever—wanted a domesticated wife. Again he imagined infidelities. When, after the birth of their child, Harriet bought a new cloak to show off her restored figure, Strindberg snappishly inquired if she had bought the garment "to walk the streets." She cried. They made up. That cycle, and the battles, continued for three years until this marriage, too, ended in divorce. Harriet kept the baby, a daughter, to whom Strindberg remained devoted until his death from stomach cancer eight years later.

HIS THOUGHTS: "We are all in quest of her, our mother. I imagine I shall always remain tied to mine. She died too early, and even while she lived, she did not give me my full share of love. I have something owing me."

"I am thoroughly independent, save in one point. I cannot make children alone. I need a woman for that."

—R.M.

The Remorseful Lover

LEO TOLSTOI (Sept. 9, 1828–Nov. 20, 1910)

HIS FAME: A writer, social reformer, and moral thinker, Leo Tolstoi is best known today as the author of such epic novels as *War and Peace* and *Anna Karenina*. He also wrote short stories and nonfiction. Popular throughout his long career, Tolstoi ranks as one of the world's greatest fiction writers.

HIS PERSON: Born into an aristocratic Russian family, Tolstoi was orphaned as a child and raised by relatives. He left Kazan University to manage the family estate but preferred the social whirl of Moscow and St. Petersburg, where he lived a profligate

Tolstoi when he was writing War and Peace

life. Disgusted with his aimlessness, Tolstoi went to the Caucasus in 1851 and joined the army. While there, he worked on his first novel, the semiautobiographical *Childhood*. When it was published a year later, Tolstoi became a literary celebrity.

In 1862, at the age of 34, Tolstoi married 18-year-old Sofya (Sonya) Andreevna Behrs, who bore his 13 children and encouraged him to write.

Although his novels and short stories made him rich and famous, and his family life was relatively happy, Tolstoi became dissatisfied with himself. During the last stages of work on *Anna Karenina*, he experienced a moral and spiritual crisis. He questioned the purpose of life and even contemplated suicide when the crisis came to a head in the late 1870s. His anguish ended after he became a Christian and discovered that faith in God could give meaning to one's existence and could unite people into a brotherhood of universal love and justice. He adopted the Sermon on the Mount as his personal credo. In order to live according to his new convictions, Tolstoi adopted peasant dress, worked as a farm laborer, and tried to dispose of his property. He eventually transferred his estate to his wife and children and gave Sonya the right to publish his earlier books. Turning away from his previous literary style, Tolstoi concentrated on writing moralistic fiction and social and religious essays. His teachings attracted many followers, called Tolstoyans.

To Tolstoi's great resentment, Sonya was unwilling to join him in his ascetic lifestyle. The household was in constant turmoil, and in 1910, at the age of 82, Tolstoi finally left his wife for good. Ill prepared both spiritually and physically for such a journey, he collapsed at the small railroad station of Astapovo. As he lay dying in the stationmaster's house, Sonya was not allowed to come to his bedside until he was unconscious and could no longer recognize her. Seven days later he was dead.

SEX LIFE: Tolstoi lost his virginity at the age of 16 in a way that was considered commonplace for a man in the 1800s—to a prostitute. As he recounted it later, "The first time my brothers dragged me to a brothel and I performed the act, I sat down afterward at the foot of the woman's bed and cried."

Throughout his life, Tolstoi's remorse and his sexual desires fed upon each other. "Regard the company of women," he wrote in his diary, "as a necessary social evil and avoid them as much as possible." He did not heed his own advice. As he later admitted to Anton Chekhov, he was "insatiable." While living on his estate in 1849, he seduced one of the servants, a dark-eyed virgin named Gasha. "What does all that mean?" he asked himself with distaste. "Is what has happened to me wonderful or horrible? Bah! It's the way of the world; everybody does it!" A short time later he became involved with another servant. At the age of 69 he remembered "Dunyasha's beauty and youth ... her strong womanly body. Where is it? Long since, nothing but bones." He also had an incestuous desire for a distant aunt, Alexandra Tolstoi. He called her "delicious" and "unique" and even dreamed of marrying her. "Where is one to look for love of others and self-denial, when there is nothing inside oneself but love of self and indulgence?" he wrote to her. "My ambition is to be corrected and converted by you my whole life long without ever becoming completely corrected or converted."

Prosperous and successful as a writer, Tolstoi began to look for a wife, even though he was not very confident of his appearance. (He had a broad nose, a toothless mouth, thick lips, and half-closed eyes.) After discarding Axinya, his peasant mistress of three years who had given him a son, he decided to marry Sonya Behrs, a young, serious girl who was proud to be the wife of a famous author. But the marriage was doomed to unhappiness when, shortly before the wedding, he forced Sonya to read his diary, where every one of his sexual exploits was described in explicit detail. He wanted her to know everything about him, but she interpreted his action as meaning that he had only a physical love for her. Their first night together was a confrontation between a satyr and a virgin bride. Two weeks after their wedding night, Sonya wrote that "physical manifestations are so repugnant," and throughout her married life she was never able to enjoy sex fully. His wife's innocence and apprehension only inflamed Tolstoi's lust. The seducer of coarse farm girls was to come to enjoy family life immensely, glorifying familial harmony and stability in the first of his masterpieces, *War and Peace.* Although he wrote in defense of individual freedom, he was a tyrant under his own roof and believed that a woman should devote herself to her husband's happiness. Sonya did her best to please him. She took care of the household and assisted him while he wrote. She copied *War and Peace* over seven times before he was satisfied with the draft.

In 1889 Tolstoi stunned Sonya with *The Kreutzer Sonata*, a work in which he urged people to renounce sex and adopt celibacy. Marriage, he explained, must be avoided, since a Christian should abstain from all sex. After the book's appearance, Sonya was mortified to find herself pregnant. "That is the real postscript to *The Kreutzer Sonata*," she wrote angrily. Try as he would to follow his new beliefs about sex, Tolstoi failed—again and again. His sexual drive remained undiminished, as indicated by Sonya's references to his passion in her diary. Not until he was 82 could he admit to a friend that he was no longer seized by sexual desire. Tolstoi blamed Sonya for making him want her and for letting him fall into sin. For her part, Sonya loathed his moral hypocrisy and disliked his constant advances. The fact that he smelled like a goat and had feet covered with sores and dirt did not make him more attractive to her. He later described to Maxim Gorky the remorse he felt about sex: "Man can endure earthquake, epidemic, dreadful disease, every form of spiritual torment; but the most dreadful tragedy that can befall him is and will remain the tragedy of the bedroom."

Seven years after the first publication of *The Kreutzer Sonata*, Tolstoi and Sonya suffered another marital crisis when Sonya fell in love with a longtime family friend, pianist and composer Sergey Tanayev. Her gay manner and the girlish attentions she paid to Tanayev infuriated Tolstoi. He called the relationship her "senile flirtation" and referred to her as a "concert hag." Hurt and humiliated, he was greatly relieved when her innocent passion began to wane a year later.

Tolstoi gradually confided less and less in Sonya, and she began to feel that he had rejected her as a wife, except for the sexual aspect of their relationship. They bickered more and more, their quarrels occasionally ending with threats by Sonya to run away and kill herself. Despite Tolstoi's guilt feelings, the mornings after nights of sex were about the only harmonious times they enjoyed. When she suspected that Tolstoi and his favorite disciple, Chertkov, were drafting a will bequeathing Tolstoi's works to the public, she became hysterical and accused her 81-year-old husband of having homosexual relations with Chertkov.

HIS ADVICE: Tolstoi's advice regarding lust is summed up in his diary: "The best thing one can do with sexual desire is (1) to destroy it utterly in oneself; next best (2) is to live with one woman, who has a chaste nature and shares your faith, and bring up children with her and help her as she helps you; next worse (3) is to go to a brothel when you are tormented by desire; (4) to have brief relations with different women, remaining with none; (5) to have intercourse with a young girl and abandon her; (6) worse yet, to have intercourse with another man's wife; (7) worst of all, to live with a faithless and immoral woman."

—A.S.M. and L.L.

The Man Who Loved His Wife

MARK TWAIN (Nov. 30, 1835–Apr. 21, 1910)

HIS FAME: One of the best-known American novelists and humorists, Twain wrote such enduring classics as *Tom Sawyer*, *Huckleberry Finn*, and *A Connecticut Yankee in King Arthur's Court*.

HIS PERSON: Samuel Langhorne Clemens was born in Florida, Mo. His pen name, Mark Twain, was derived from a call boatmen used when sounding water depths. He began his writing career as a journalist and eventually turned to fiction. Though he was a brilliant writer, there was a tragic side to his life. Yielding to convention, Twain funneled his writing into a socially acceptable mode; he did not complete or

Twain with two Angel Fish

attempt to publish many of his beloved creations. His work was successful financially, as were his many lecture tours, but he repeatedly lost fortunes by sinking money in bad business schemes.

LOVE LIFE: Twain's amorous life was dominated by a single figure—that of his wife, Livy Langdon. Although he had had sweethearts before he met her, he was probably a 34-year-old virgin when they married in 1870. Shown Livy's picture by her brother, he instantly fell in love with her. Her family was highly respectable, and even though Twain was making good money as a lecturer, it wasn't easy to convince her parents that he was worthy to marry their Livy. But marry her he did. Besides giving him three daughters, Livy set about reforming him. She waged war on all of his bad habits: tobacco (he had smoked since the age of eight), drink, cardplaying, and the irrepressible cussing that was his trademark. Looking upon him as a wayward child, her pet name for him was "Youth." Twain told a friend, "After my marriage she edited everything I wrote. And what is more—she not only edited my works—she edited me!" He added, "I would quit wearing socks if she thought them immoral."

Twain positively worshiped Livy. Believing her to be the essence of female perfection, he never criticized her. And though he delighted in teasing her and playing practical jokes on her, he generally obeyed her. Livy was a partial invalid all her life because of a fall on the ice in her youth, so Twain happily doted on his wife and nursed her. He remained madly in love with Livy until her death in 1904. The loss for Twain was enormous; he never recovered his happiness and barely wanted to live without her.

SEX LIFE: Twain may well have been impotent most of the time by the age of 50. This is strongly indicated in a number of his humorous writings which have not been widely read. But he never said it directly, stating in his memoirs that he would tell the truth about himself, but not the sexual truth, since Rousseau had taken care of that in his *Confessions*. He probably never made love to anyone but his wife, although his longtime personal secretary, Isabel Lyon, set her sights on him after Livy died. He found the woman repulsive and wrote to a friend, "I could not go to bed with Miss Lyon. I would rather have a waxwork." He explained that she was "an old, old virgin, and juiceless, whereas my passion was for the other kind."

QUIRKS: A curious fact about the great Mark Twain is that he delighted in writing obscene poems, ballads, and essays. He had them printed privately in very small quantities, if he had them printed at all. He complained, "Delicacy—a sad, sad false delicacy—robs literature of the two best things among its belongings: family-circle narratives and obscene stories."

The most famous of his sexual and scatological works is *1601: A Tudor Fireside Conversation*. This hilarious essay was written in Elizabethan language; in it, Queen Elizabeth I, Sir Walter Raleigh, and others exchange lewd tales and insults. Twain sent a copy of it to his dear friend Rev. Joseph Twitchell, and the two of them would take it to a favorite spot in the woods and roar with laughter over it.

One of Twain's poems begins, "Constipation, O constipation," and an address to be given to a men's club (the Stomach Club) is entitled *Some Remarks on the*

Science of Onanism. The Mammoth Cod is a song and speech written for another men's club, the Mammoth Cods, who were devoted to cod fishing, drinking, and revelry. (*Cod* is an old-fashioned euphemism for "penis.") From the song:

> *Of beasts, man is the only one*
> *Created by our God*
> *Who purposely, and for mere fun*
> *Plays with his Mammoth Cod!*

He called the song a hymn and imagined it "sung by hundreds of sweet, guileless children" in Sunday schools. In the Cod essay he wrote:

> I fail to see any special merit in penises of more than the usual size. What more can they achieve than the smaller ones? ... In this, as in everything else, quality is more to be considered than quantity. It is the searching, not the splitting, weapon that is of use.
>
> I really don't know whether I have such a thing as a "Cod" about me. I know there is a conduit about my person which is useful in conveying the waste moisture of the system, but that is the only use I have ever put it to, except the natural one of procreation. I may be excused for this, for it would be a shame to have the kind of man I am die out with myself. As for what men of the world call pleasure ... I know nothing about it and care less. My recollection of it is, that while it was, perhaps, pleasant, it was so brief and transitory that it was not worth my while to repeat.

Equally revealing is this excerpt from *Letters from the Earth*:

> During 23 days in every month (in the absence of pregnancy) from the time a woman is 7 years old til she dies of old age, she is ready for action, and *competent*. As competent as the candlestick is to receive the candle. Competent every day, competent every night. Also, she *wants* that candle—yearns for it, longs for it, hankers after it, as commanded by the law of God in her heart.
>
> But man is only briefly competent; and only then in the moderate measure applicable to the word in *his* sex's case. He is competent from the age of 16 or 17 thenceforward for 35 years. After 50 his performance is of poor quality, the intervals between are wide, and its satisfactions of no great value to either party; whereas his great-grandmother is as good as new. There is nothing the matter with her plant. Her candlestick is as firm as ever, whereas his candle is increasingly softened and weakened by the weather of age, as the years go by, until at last it can no longer stand, and is mournfully laid to rest in the hope of a blessed resurrection which is never to come.

Twain goes on to calculate that while a man is good for 100 acts of love a year for 50 years, a woman is good for 3,000 a year as long as she lives. This averages at 10 acts a day for her. And it puts man's lifetime total (according to Twain's arithmetic) at 5,000 "refreshments" and woman's at 150,000. Twain therefore recommended that men receive a one-fiftieth interest in one woman, while women receive a male harem.

Perhaps the most telling work of all is a poem entitled "A Weaver's Beam," which has a wonderful pun in the first line of its second stanza:

> Behold—the Penis mightier than the Sword
> That leapt from Sheath at any heating Word
> So long ago—now peaceful lies, and calm
> And dreams unmoved of ancient Conquests scored.

Twain possessed one other quirk. In his later years, he became obsessed with little girls. His interest clearly bordered on the sexual. He formed his favorite little ladies into a club and called them Angel Fish separately (each was given an angelfish pin) and the Aquarium en masse. The average age for an Angel Fish was 13, and girls over 16 were rarely eligible. When one Angel Fish abandoned Twain for the company of young men, Twain was extremely jealous. His secretary wrote, "his first interest when he goes to a new place is to find little girls" and "off he goes with a flash when he sees a new pair of slim little legs appear, and if the little girl wears butterfly bows of ribbon on the back of her head then his delirium is complete."

HIS THOUGHTS: "Love seems the swiftest, but is the slowest, of all growths. No man or woman really knows what perfect love is until they have been married a quarter of a century."

Written in his notebook during Livy's final illness: "Men and women—even man and wife are foreigners. Each has reserves that the other cannot enter into, nor understand. These have the effect of frontiers."

—A. W.

Domestic Claustrophobia

H. G. WELLS (Sept. 21, 1866–Aug. 13, 1946)

HIS FAME: Wells emerged from literary obscurity in 1895 with publication of *The Time Machine*, followed by *The Invisible Man* (1897) and *The War of the Worlds* (1898). But these science fiction endeavors were only a small part of his total output of over 100 books. Among his best-known works were *Kipps* (which established him as a novelist) and *The Outline of History* (an encyclopedic study a million words in length written in one year).

Wells at age 56

HIS PERSON: Born in Bromley, Kent, England, Herbert George Wells was the fourth and last child of Joseph and Sarah Wells. His easygoing and self-indulgent father ran a china shop and earned extra money by playing cricket. His mother was a rigid, domineering, deeply religious woman who constantly reminded her husband that his entire life was a failure. Wells once said that his parents had a foolproof method of birth control: They slept in separate rooms.

To escape the drudgery of his lower-middle-class surroundings, young Wells turned to reading books and daydreaming. His fantasies often centered on the glories of war—victorious battles with Wells as supreme commander. As he said: "I used to walk about Bromley, a small rather undernourished boy, meanly clad and whistling detestably between his teeth, and no one suspected that a phantom staff pranced about me and phantom orderlies galloped at my commands to shift the guns and concentrate fire on those houses below...."

After unsuccessful attempts at being a draper's—and then a druggist's—apprentice, the 17-year-old Wells was sent off to school in Midhurst, where he earned a scholarship to the Normal School of Science in London. There he came under the influence of Thomas Henry Huxley, otherwise known as "Darwin's Bulldog." Subsequently, Wells received a degree in zoology and taught in various schools before he became a full-time writer.

Wells was not a handsome man. He was 5 ft. 5 in. tall (he blamed his mother for that, claiming that she kept him in a short bed for too many years), with small hands and feet and a robust, heavyset body. His face sported a drooping mustache, bushy eyebrows, and penetrating blue eyes. His chestnut-brown hair usually looked as if it had been glued to his head. To his chagrin, Wells had a very high-pitched voice, and his speech was peppered with a cockney accent.

H.G. was self-centered, irascible, unpredictable, and upon occasion crude. His associates in the Fabian Society—like George Bernard Shaw—and his literary peers—like Joseph Conrad and W. Somerset Maugham—were sometimes exasperated, other times entranced, by his overpowering personality. As one of his biographers said: "With all his faults, you could not help loving him. Bursting with brains, bubbling with humor, he was full of a boisterous vital stimulating charm that made it nearly always a pleasure to be in his company, and you either rode the storm or were swept onto the rocks." There were many women who could have testified to the truth of that analysis.

SEX LIFE: Wells was obsessed with finding the ideal sex partner. As a young boy, "Bertie" was first sexually aroused by semidraped Greek statues, and he was to search forever for their real-life equivalent—his "Venus Urania." It was a quest that led him through two marriages, several serious affairs, and countless *passades* (defined by H.G. as "a stroke of mutual attraction").

At 25 Wells married his first cousin Isabel Wells, a dark-haired virginal beauty with a slim, graceful body. Except for one unfulfilling experience with an "unimaginative" prostitute when he was about 22, Wells was also a sexual novice. His physical craving for Isabel was almost unbearable as he prepared for their wedding night and "flame meeting flame." Unfortunately, the flames were quickly doused by Isabel's tears as she found herself incapable of responding to H.G.'s ardor. The embittered husband embarked upon a string of minor romances before the couple ended their four-year marriage in 1895. In his autobiography Wells concludes that Isabel was not only naive but book-shy and unable to stimulate him intellectually (another requisite of Venus Urania). However, for many years after the divorce Wells could not shake Isabel from his mind. Her second marriage, in 1904, threw Wells into fits of jealousy. He tore up all of her letters and photographs and refused to speak her name. Years later they once again became friends.

Amy Catherine Robbins was one of H.G.'s students at the University Tutorial College in London in 1892. He was immediately attracted to her fair hair, brown eyes, and delicate features. They married as soon as Wells was divorced. Wells, for no apparent reason, decided to call his second wife Jane.

H.G. and Jane remained married until her death in 1927. The 32-year marriage, which produced two sons, was an unusual one. Once again Wells had paired up with a woman "innocent and ignorant" of the physical necessities of life. The dissatisfied husband and the sympathetic wife reached a mutual understanding in which she agreed to give him all of the sexual freedom he desired. From then on, Wells was quite open about his relationships, even keeping pictures of his lovers in his room.

Jane was the most stabilizing factor in H.G.'s turbulent life. She reviewed and typed his books, invested his money, prepared his tax returns, and kept their home in perfect order. In 1908, 42-year-old Wells became involved with 22-year-old Amber Reeves, daughter of one of London's most prominent families. Jane's friends were stunned and appalled when Amber became pregnant. However, Jane—the sensible, all-enduring wife—went out and bought clothes for the new baby.

In 1912 Wells finally met the Venus Urania of his dreams. Her name was Rebecca West and she was to become one of England's foremost journalists and novelists. Writing in a small feminist magazine, West reviewed—and panned— H.G.'s book *Marriage*. Wells, usually thin-skinned about bad reviews, was intrigued by her humor and style. A year later Wells, then 46, and West, 20, began an affair that was to last for 10 years.

Wells had found the perfect mate. In addition to her beauty and sensuality, she was his equal in wit, imagination, and intelligence. He said, "She was the only woman who ever made me stop and wonder when she said 'Look.'" He wrote her many fervent love letters, professing his endless desire for her. On many of the letters Wells sketched a "picshua" of a panther and a jaguar (Rebecca was the panther, Wells the jaguar). They shared intense happiness and had one son, Anthony.

The break with Rebecca came after an incident involving Wells and another of his lovers, Austrian journalist Hedwig Verena Gatternigg. Following a row with Wells, the Austrian woman tried to kill herself in H.G.'s London flat. Wells wasn't there at the time, but Jane, who often visited her husband's home-away-from-home, discovered the woman and had her taken to a hospital. Rebecca's name appeared in the ensuing publicity. Although the episode was ultimately covered up, scandal had come too close to Rebecca's doorstep. But that wasn't her only reason for ending the affair. She had become increasingly intolerant of H.G.'s disregard for her career ("He never read more than a page or two of any of my books") and his restless, irritable moods. His continuing *passades* (which included birth-control advocate Margaret Sanger) and Rebecca's social isolation were also precipitating factors. Finally, there seemed to be no boundaries to H.G.'s self-centeredness. At one time he moved his ailing first wife, Isabel, into his home so that his second wife, Jane, could care for her, while he continued to see Rebecca.

After Rebecca, Wells sought comfort in the arms of Odette Keun, a Dutch woman then living in France. A former nun turned writer, Odette had sent Wells a copy of her book *Sous Lenin* ("Under Lenin"), which he favorably reviewed. They exchanged letters and finally met in Geneva in 1924. Their rendezvous took place in her hotel room. She shut off the lights before her Prince Charming arrived and then led him right into bed. Odette later recalled, "I did not know whether he was a giant or a gnome." The lovers built a house in the south of France, where they spent all of their time together—a situation which made Jane's life less complicated. H.G. remained a part of Odette's life for the next nine years.

In 1934 the 68-year-old writer began a full-time relationship with an old acquaintance, Moura Budberg, former secretary to Maxim Gorky. She refused to marry Wells and they kept separate homes in London, but they remained friends and confidants until his death in 1946.

Throughout his adult life Wells was rarely without a woman. Despite his poor health (tuberculosis, diabetes, and kidney afflictions), he was sexually active almost to his death at age 79. According to Somerset Maugham: "H.G. had strong sexual instincts and he said to me more than once that the need to satisfy these instincts had nothing to do with love. It was a purely physiological matter."

HIS THOUGHTS: Once, when depressed over problems with Rebecca, Wells wrote a letter to her in which he poured out his feelings: "I can't—in my present state anyhow—bank on religion. God has no thighs and no life. When one calls to him in the silence of the night he doesn't turn over and say, 'What is the trouble, Dear?'"

—C.O.

The Love That Dare Not Speak Its Name

OSCAR WILDE (Oct. 16, 1854–Nov. 30, 1900)

HIS FAME: Wilde was the best-known homosexual of the Western world, one of the most written-about authors in history, and one of the greatest wits of all time. He was the author of several plays, including *The Importance of Being Earnest*; a novel, *The Picture of Dorian Gray*; and poetry, essays, stories, and fairy tales.

HIS PERSON: Wilde was born in Dublin, Ireland, to eccentric parents. His mother badly wanted a daughter, so when a second son, Oscar Fingal O'Flahertie Wills Wilde, was born, she dressed the child like a girl. As a youth Oscar was

Wilde with Bosie (Lord Alfred Douglas)

tall, almost overgrown, yet somehow graceful and, in any case, always striking in appearance and dress. Leaving Dublin to attend Oxford, he began to develop the unique style of manners, garb, and wit which was later characteristic of members of the "aesthetic movement." His theory of "art for art's sake" developed further after he left Oxford, and soon he was the rage of London society as people strove to imitate his sensual velvet costumes and sparkling aphorisms. Oscar was the ultimate party entertainment, and he was in great demand. Wrote a contemporary, "He was, without exception, the most brilliant talker I have ever come across…. Nobody could pretend to outshine him, or even to shine at all in his company."

Wilde supported himself by writing art criticism and book reviews for ladies' magazines and other journals and by lecturing in England and America. He eventually moved on to plays, becoming England's foremost comedic playwright. He was extravagant, generous, outrageous, and, above all, happy. The story of his ruin sounds incredible today, but it remains one of the great modern tragedies.

SEX LIFE: As a young man Wilde was decidedly heterosexual, despite his affectations. In fact, he was mildly shocked at the idea of homosexuality. His earliest love was Florrie Balcombe, whom he met when he was 21. Wilde suffered his first heartbreak over her, when she decided to marry Bram Stoker, who went on to write *Dracula*. Some years later Wilde unsuccessfully courted society beauty and actress Lillie Langtry, who was married. He eventually became her good friend, and also became friends with the French actress Sarah Bernhardt.

In addition to a few youthful affairs, Wilde occasionally used prostitutes. One evening he announced to his friend Robert Sherard that "Priapus was calling" and went out and picked up a high-class whore. Meeting Sherard the next morning, Wilde said, "What animals we are, Robert." Sherard expressed his concern that Wilde might have been robbed, to which Wilde replied, "One gives them all in one's pockets."

In 1881 Oscar met Constance Lloyd, a sweet, pretty girl whom he courted with passionate, poetic letters. Madly in love, the two were blissfully married in 1884. They honeymooned in Paris, and the morning after the wedding night, while Wilde strolled with Sherard, he described so vividly the joys of the previous evening that Sherard was terribly embarrassed. Indeed, for the first few years Oscar and Constance were deeply in love. They had two sons, Cyril and Vyvyan. Though Oscar adored his children, he was not much suited for a life of domesticity.

The story of how Wilde drifted from heterosexuality to homosexuality is open to some debate. It is probable that while at Oxford he had contracted syphilis from a prostitute. The treatment at that time was mercury. (This caused severe discoloration of the teeth, which Oscar certainly suffered from.) Before proposing to Constance, he consulted a doctor, who assured him that he had been cured of his venereal disease. Two years later he discovered that the dormant spirochetes had broken out again, so he gave up sex with Constance and began to indulge his interest in boys.

Robert Ross, a lively, cultivated young man who remained Oscar's lifelong devotee, boasted that he was Oscar's "first boy," when he was 17 and Wilde was 32. However, it was not until 1891 that Wilde met the great love of his life, in the person of 21-year-old Lord Alfred Douglas, called "Bosie" by his friends and family. The attraction was immediate. Bosie was young (16 years Oscar's junior), a poet, from a prominent family, extraordinarily good-looking, passionate, impulsive, and proud—in short, everything that Wilde admired. And for Bosie's part, it was an incredible thrill to be admired by London's premiere playwright and wit. They both adored luxury and began their whirlwind friendship by dining daily at the best restaurants in England, completely inseparable. Even Constance liked Bosie.

According to Bosie's confessions later in life, he kept his sexual relations with Wilde to a minimum. He did not respond to Oscar's overtures for six months, and when he did, the extent of their activity was probably oral sex. Bosie insisted that no sodomy took place, that "Wilde treated me as an older boy treats a young man at school." (Bosie had had relations with both men and women before meeting Oscar.) Bosie's reticence was probably due to the fact that he too preferred boys. This is well illustrated in the story of their adventures on a trip to Algiers. By sheer coincidence, their hotel in the small town of Blida was occupied by an acquaintance of Wilde's, the younger writer André Gide. Gide had been struggling against his homosexuality for five years, and when he realized that Oscar and Bosie were guests at the hotel, he almost left. Preparing for an evening out, Bosie took Gide by the arm and said, "I hope you are like me. I have a horror of women. I only like boys. As you are coming with us this evening, I think it's better if you say so at once." A nervous Gide accompanied them on a tour of the Casbah, finally winding up in a homosexual brothel and bathhouse, where men danced together to the sounds of exotic music. There Wilde gleefully pronounced the sentence that sealed Gide's fate: "Dear, do you want the little musician?" And Gide's downfall was complete. As the vacation neared its end, Bosie was making arrangements to run off with an Arab youth he had purchased from the boy's family, but the lad left him for a woman.

In London, Wilde and Douglas were introduced to Alfred Taylor, a gracious gentleman and semiprofessional procurer, who enjoyed wearing ladies' clothing and burning incense in his dimly lit apartment. He acquired for Wilde a number of young boys—out-of-work clerks, grooms, and newsboys who were willing to sell their favors, and who in addition unexpectedly found themselves dining in the best restaurants in London with Wilde, drinking champagne, and receiving expensive gifts.

Although there was gossip surrounding Wilde and Bosie, all would probably have gone on happily had it not been for Bosie's father. The 8th Marquis of Queensberry was a short, coarse, nearly insane sportsman—he laid down the Queensberry Rules for boxing—who had been on a slow burn for years about his son's questionable friendship with Wilde. His rage vented itself in abusive letters to his son and finally culminated when he delivered a card to Wilde's club, which read, "For Oscar Wilde posing as a somdomite [sic]." Enraged himself, and fed up with the marquis' harassment, Wilde took a reckless action. With Bosie's encouragement, he pressed charges against Queensberry for criminal libel, having assured his lawyer that there was no basis whatsoever for the marquis' accusation. But to the prosecution's immense surprise, Queensberry had prepared his case well. Hiring a team of private detectives and paid informers, he had bought the testimony of many of the young boys Wilde had met through Taylor. When it was clear that the boys would be produced, the prosecution withdrew and the marquis was acquitted. Oscar's friends begged him to leave the country while he still could—even his wife hoped he would flee—but he refused. Within a month he was arrested, charged by Queensberry with committing acts of gross indecency with various boys. The procurer Taylor had also been arrested, having refused to turn state's evidence against Wilde.

During the second trial, one of the most sensational in English history, Wilde handled himself with great poise and wit, but they were not enough to save him. One by one the boys testified. "I was asked by Wilde to imagine that I was a woman and that he was my lover.... I used to sit on his knees and he used to play with my privates as a man might amuse himself with a girl.... He suggested two or three times that I would permit him to insert 'it' in my mouth, but I never allowed that," and so on. Hotel chambermaids even testified that they had found curious stains on the hotel sheets, though that evidence proved dubious. From these proceedings it emerged that the preferred form of lovemaking was mutual masturbation, or fellatio, with Wilde as the active agent. (He told a friend it gave him inspiration.) Sodomy was seldom, if ever, performed.

Wilde was also forced to defend his published writings, such as *Dorian Gray*, and his personal letters, which were accused of having homosexual overtones. It was in this context that he gave his now famous speech on the "Love that dare not speak its name" (a line from one of Bosie's poems), which was so moving that it brought spontaneous applause from the gallery. In the end the jury could not reach a decision, and a third trial was called. Between trials, Wilde again refused to attempt an escape. The outcome of the third trial was grim: Wilde and Taylor each received the maximum sentence—two years of hard labor.

Prison conditions in England at that time were extremely cruel, and the horror of the experience drove Wilde slightly mad. He wrote a long, scathing denunciation of Bosie, now published as *De Profundis*, accusing Bosie of having led him to his ruin. But despite all, Bosie remained completely loyal, unlike most of Wilde's other friends, and wrote, "Though he is in prison he is still the court the jury the judge of my life." In later years, Bosie turned the tables, writing several books whitewashing himself while viciously denouncing Wilde.

After Wilde's release he lived, broken and exiled, using the name Sebastian Melmoth, in France and Italy. Constance Wilde, Bosie's family, and numerous friends plotted to keep the two men apart, but their friendship and love prevailed. The last three years of Wilde's life were spent on and off with Bosie, both having returned to consorting with young boys.

While living in France, Oscar succumbed to an attempt to reform him. The poet Ernest Dowson took him to a brothel, hoping he might acquire "a more wholesome taste." When Wilde emerged, he remarked, "The first these ten years—and it will be the last. It was like cold mutton." But he asked Dowson to "tell it in England, for it will entirely restore my character."

THOUGHTS: Trying to explain in court the "Love that dare not speak its name," Wilde said, "It is beautiful, it is fine, it is the noblest form of affection. There is nothing unnatural about it. It is intellectual, and it repeatedly exists between an elder and a younger man, where the elder has intellect and the younger man has all the joy, hope, and glamour of the life before him. That it should be so, the world does not understand. The world mocks at it and sometimes puts one in the pillory for it."

—*A. W.*

The Giant And The Jew

THOMAS WOLFE (Oct. 3, 1900–Sept. 15, 1938)

HIS FAME: Wolfe was an American writer who established his literary reputation at home and abroad with four highly autobiographical novels. *Look Homeward, Angel* (1929) and *Of Time and the River* (1935) were published during his lifetime. *The Web and the Rock* (1939) and *You Can't Go Home Again* (1940) were issued posthumously.

HIS PERSON: The youngest of eight children, Wolfe could talk well at age one and do simple reading at age two. His father was a stonecutter, and his mother kept a boardinghouse in Asheville, N.C., where Wolfe was born and raised. Mama nursed him until he was three and a half, and they slept together until he was nine, at which time he was allowed to cut off his curly, shoulder-length hair. Wolfe took a lot of ribbing about his hair. Once, when two older boys began calling him a girl, Wolfe protested vigorously, then whipped out his penis to dispel all doubts.

He entered the University of North Carolina at 15, became editor of the school paper and magazine, and wrote several one-act plays. After graduation he enrolled at Harvard, with the intention of becoming a playwright, but he often said, "I'd rather be a poet than anything else in the world." In 1923, armed with an M.A., he went to New York, where he taught English at Washington Square College. In 1930, when royalties from *Look Homeward, Angel* started rolling in and a Guggenheim Fellowship came through, Wolfe quit teaching and from then on devoted himself to writing. While he made seven trips to Europe and also traveled in the U.S., he lived primarily in New York for the rest of his life.

Wolfe, whose powerful body stood at 6 ft. 5 in., had a mop of unruly black hair and dark, penetrating eyes. His giant appetite for food, sex, and alcohol was well known. He drank especially heavily when his writing was not going well. Normally, he would write for days on end, supported by nothing more than coffee, canned beans, and endless cigarettes. Wolfe died in Baltimore after surgery revealed tubercular lesions on his brain.

LOVE LIFE: With a combination of boyish good looks, masculinity, and fame, Wolfe appealed to a wide variety of women. Some were publicity seekers, some were literary groupies, and some primarily wanted to mother him. Said one of the women: "He was intolerable and wonderful and talked like an angel and was a real son of a bitch." Wolfe "loved women and was somewhat oversexed," wrote Elizabeth Nowell, his agent and one of his biographers. At a party, for example, Wolfe would take a receptive girl into another room and make love to her. Later that night, when someone pointed to the girl, he would shoot back, "Who's she?"

Wolfe lost his virginity and first experienced "the coarse appeasement of the brothel," as he put it, at age 16. With two fellow students from the university, Wolfe went to a Durham, N.C., whorehouse, where a prostitute named Mamie Smith took him to bed. She ignited "all the passion and fire," Wolfe said afterward. He soon made another visit to Mamie and was a steady customer for the next four years. During Christmas vacation back in Asheville that first year, he slipped away from a family gathering to be with a "red-haired woman" at a cheap hotel.

In the summer of 1917 Wolfe fell in love. "A nice young boy, here, the son of my landlady, has a crush on me," wrote 21-year-old Clara Paul to her sister. Since she was engaged, nothing came of it, but Wolfe recalled: "Clara—moonlight and the holding of a hand. How her firm little breasts seem to spring forward, filled with life…." Writing to a friend years later, he confessed that he had forgotten what the girl looked like but insisted that he had never quite got over the love affair.

On Wolfe's 25th birthday, Aline Bernstein, then 44, became his mistress. A highly successful theatrical designer, she was attractive and tiny, with streaks of gray in her hair. They had met one month before on a liner returning from Europe; both fell madly in love. That Aline was married and the mother of two grown children did not seem to matter. Their often stormy relationship continued for six years without protest from her worshipful husband, Theo, who remained devoted and compassionate throughout her turbulent affair with Wolfe. At first the pair would meet in Wolfe's New York apartment; then she rented a loft for them to share at 13 East 8th Street. They made love often, and Wolfe referred to her as his "plumskinned wench," his "dear Jew," and his "gray-haired, wide-hipped timeless mother." Aline would write, "He called me a lecherous old woman and cursed me that he could not get me out of his soul." He was insanely jealous of her. Sometimes he would call her at two in the morning to see if she was out on some "bawdy mission." Wolfe's compulsive whoring and his mother's anti-Semitic hostility toward Aline eventually diminished his sexual desire for her. Aline knew he was bringing girls into their loft. "You've gone with dirty, rotten women all your life," she would say, "and that's the only kind you understand!" At one point Wolfe asked her to marry him, but she refused. Before one of his European trips, Aline made him promise not to fool around. "By God, I kept the faith," he noted in his diary. At another time, however, both were in Paris. As soon as she left for New York, Wolfe headed for the nearest brothel. Aline mothered him and fostered his career, and when, at the urging of his editor, Maxwell Perkins, Wolfe finally broke away in 1931, she attempted suicide with sleeping pills. To console her, Wolfe wrote: "I shall love you all the days of my life, and when I die, if they cut me open, they will find one name written on my brain and in my heart. It will be yours." When she was 70, Aline suffered the first of a series of small strokes that eventually resulted in widespread paralysis. She was 75 when she died. Loyal Theo, aged and ailing, was with her till the end.

Besides Aline and countless one-night stands, there were at least three other women who briefly came into Wolfe's life. One was the actress Jean Harlow, whom he met on a Hollywood set one day in 1935. That evening both left in Jean's limousine, and they returned to the studio together the next morning. What happened in between is not recorded. Another woman was Thea Voelcker, a 30-year-old German artist, whom Wolfe met just before the 1936 Olympics in Berlin. He persuaded the tall, shapely divorcée to accompany him to the Austrian Alps, where they enjoyed themselves briefly. She was deeply in love with Wolfe and wrote affectionate letters to him after his return to New York. Wolfe, however, would have nothing more to do with her. While in Germany Wolfe was also in the company of Martha Dodd, the American ambassador's daughter. He was a bit in love with her, but there is no indication that sex was involved.

HIS THOUGHTS: Although Wolfe was a sexual athlete, he longed for family life and would often ask friends if they knew a nice girl he could marry. "I believe in love, and in its power to redeem and save our lives. I believe in the loved one, the redeemer and savior," he wrote when his love for Aline was at zenith. "I can always find plenty of women to sleep with, but the kind of woman that is really hard for me to find is a typist who can read my writing," he once said. To Wolfe, the ability to cook well indicated a sensual personality. He would often surprise women he was interested in by asking, "Are you a good cook?" Wolfe kept a list of women he had not yet slept with but intended to. He did not plan to marry until he was around 35, "after possessing hundreds of women all over the globe." In the end, still unmarried, his last thoughts were of Aline, his greatest love. Just before he died, Wolfe whispered, "Where's Aline? ... I want Aline ... I want my Jew."

—*R.J.R.*

The Chaste Pornographer

ÉMILE ZOLA (Apr. 2, 1840–Sept. 28, 1902)

HIS FAME: A writer and critic, Zola authored the famous open letter titled "*J'accuse*" ("I accuse") that defended Capt. Alfred Dreyfus, a French Jew falsely accused of treason. Zola's novels, like *Nana*, shocked France with their scatology and descriptions of sex, and this realism influenced the course of Western literature.

Zola with Jeanne Rozerot in 1899

HIS PERSON: Zola's father, an Italian engineer, died suddenly, leaving his French wife and their six-year-old son penniless in Aix-en-Provence. When he was seven Zola was sexually molested by a servant named Mustapha, and the experience left him with a lifelong loathing of homosexuals. In 1857 his mother moved to Paris, and Émile joined her the following year. During the next two years Zola failed his baccalaureate examination twice at the Lycée St. Louis.

During adolescence Zola was a romanticist who read and wrote poetry. After failing his graduation exams, the shy country poet lost his naiveté when unemployment forced him to live in a "louse-infested lodging house packed with thieves and prostitutes." The story that he avoided starvation by trapping sparrows on the roof and pawning his pants is undoubtedly an exaggeration, but it is indicative of his poverty.

In 1871 he published the first of his novels, which illustrated his theory of naturalism. This theory postulated that man's actions are determined by heredity and environment. One of his "obscene" (but best-selling) books, *La Terre* [*Earth*], even provoked a "manifesto" which suggested that the depravity in the novel was caused by "an illness of the loins" that had made the author impotent.

Zola was extremely nervous, a hypochondriac, and so sensitive that a pinprick would send shooting pains up his arm. He possessed "delicate, mobile, astonishingly expressive hands" and a similarly expressive nose with a highly developed sense of smell. He was nearsighted and he lisped, but he had a beautiful tenor voice. Zola was a solid man, 5 ft. 6 in. tall, with brown hair and beard, and a face that perpetually wore a melancholy expression. A gourmand, by middle age he tipped the scales at 224 lb., but after 1887 he lost much weight by following a low-liquid, no-wine diet.

LOVE LIFE: As a youth Zola was infatuated with Louise Solari, a friend's younger sister, but since she was only 12 when he left for Paris, a romantic attachment seems doubtful. Years later a story surfaced that Zola had courted a young girl called Jeanne (supposedly a pseudonym for Louise) by picking bunches of grapes because he was too shy to express himself verbally. She ate as many as she could, then thanked him and returned home.

During the years he lived in red-light districts, Zola no doubt learned much about sex from his noisy neighbors, and he might have had firsthand experience as well. Some biographers contend that he lived with a prostitute, who left the starving writer for more comfortable circumstances.

At the age of 25 Zola began courting Alexandrine Meley, a tall, striking brunette a year older than he, who worked as a seamstress. The manner of their meeting is unknown. One story says they were introduced by Paul Cézanne, who had been Alexandrine's lover. In another version, she attracted Zola's attention because she was weeping hysterically over her previous lover's desertion. In any event, Alexandrine became his mistress, and four years later, in May, 1870, they were married.

The marriage was not sexually successful. Just five years later Zola confided to male friends that they had intercourse only every 10 days. Even this periodic passion was soon spent. Zola's repressed sexuality twisted him with guilt, and his conflict was augmented by his belief that sex without procreation was reprehensible. He and Alexandrine never had children, even though both desperately wanted a family, and this surely contributed to the marital coldness and discord.

Physically faithful to Alexandrine, Zola poured his repressed passion into his work, producing over 20 books, such as *Nana* and *Pot-Bouille*, where vivid descriptions of nakedness and copulation aroused the critics if not Zola himself. After 18 years of a marriage that provided little in the way of either sex or love, Zola at 48 was fat, unhappy, and aged. He confessed he was "plagued by the desire to go to bed with a very young girl … who had not yet reached puberty."

Beginning in 1887, his life changed incredibly. He started losing weight and, the following year, he met Jeanne Rozerot. She was just 20 years old, tall, dark-eyed, and modestly surprised that Zola noticed her. He rapidly fell in love and moved her into an apartment.

Jeanne bore Zola two children, Denise and Jacques. He was as devoted to them as he was to their mother, who gave him a happiness he had never known and, presumably, a satisfactory sex life. Zola was very protective and loving toward Jeanne. He disliked the fact that she was forced to live as a recluse because of him, but Jeanne seems to have been content, calling him her "Prince Charming."

After years of juggling two households successfully, Zola was aghast when an anonymous letter informed Alexandrine of his mistress and children. Alexandrine raged and threatened separation, but eventually her tirades subsided. She met the children, and after Jeanne's death she watched over them, legally gave them Zola's name, and made them her heirs.

Zola's affair ended when he died accidentally (some suggested it was murder by political enemies) as the result of carbon monoxide poisoning.

—*P.A.R.*

VI

Poetic Licence

Scotland's Bawdy Bard

ROBERT BURNS (Jan. 25, 1759–July 21, 1796)

HIS FAME: Recognized as Scotland's national poet, Robert Burns earned his greatest acclaim for his first published volume, *Poems, Chiefly in the Scottish Dialect.* He is best known as the author of such widely quoted lines as "The Best Laid schemes o' mice and men / Gang aft a-gley"; "O my Luve's like a red, red rose, / That's newly sprung in June"; "Man's inhumanity to man"; "Oh wad some power the giftie gie us / to see oursels as ithers see us!"; and the ever popular

> *Should auld acquaintance be forgot,*
> *And never brought to min'?*
> *Should auld acquaintance be forgot,*
> *And days o' auld lang syne?*

One of his collections of songs, *The Merry Muses of Caledonia*, which contains his bawdiest lyrics, was not published for the general public in uncensored form until 1965.

HIS PERSON: Robert Burns was the oldest of seven children born to William and Agnes Burnes (Robert changed the spelling in 1786), who leased a small farm in the county of Ayrshire. Robert received most of his formal education from John Murdoch, a tutor hired by the local farmers, who encouraged him to study literature.

At 22 Robert left home for Irvine to study to be a flax dresser, but he was forced to return after his patron's shop burned down. His father died two years later, and Robert and his brother Gilbert moved the family to a new farm. He earned a local reputation for his poetry and in July, 1786, he arranged for *Poems* to be printed in Kilmarnock. Near the end of the year, the young poet set out for Edinburgh, where he received honor, praise, and 100 guineas for the copyright to his popular book. He made several tours of the Scottish countryside, working on two collections of traditional songs, without pay, considering it a duty to his country. By then he had a wife and several children (legitimate and illegitimate) to support, and the family farm was close to failure. So in September, 1789, he accepted a position with the excise service as a tax inspector. He did well at this job and earned a promotion in 1792. But these years were marred by rumors of his drinking and controversies over his support of the French Revolution. He continued to write poetry until he suffered a severe attack of rheumatic fever and died in 1796.

At 5 ft. 10 in., Robert Burns was above average in height, and he had a large build. But his most striking feature was his wide, deep-set eyes, which gave a look of innocence to the "peasant poet." Burns' legendary drinking habits have been refuted by most biographers, but his sexual reputation is well substantiated by personal letters, legal records of paternity suits, and his poems.

SEX LIFE: To Robert Burns, love and poetry were inseparable. Consequently, many of his poems chronicled his experiences, relationships, and rejections. At 15, his first love, by his own account, was Nelly Kirkpatrick, his partner in the traditional harvest festivities and the subject of the first poem he ever wrote, "Handsome Nell." Their relationship was quite innocent, and his affection mostly unrequited, as was also the case with his later courtship of Alison Begbie. He wrote Alison a series of romantic, but very proper, love letters, leading up to a proposal of marriage, followed by a polite acknowledgment of her rejection. But during a brief stay in Irvine, he became friends with a sailor, Richard Brown, who encouraged him toward looser ways and, in Burns' words, "did me mischief."

Rural society in Scotland was sexually quite open, and marriage usually occurred after the woman became pregnant. Both common-law and trial marriages were frequent. And even the Church would forgive fornication for a small fine and the acceptance of a rebuke before the congregation. However, it was not until after his father's death that Robert dared to make love to Elizabeth Paton, a servant girl working in his mother's household. Their relationship was short, passionate, and fruitful; a daughter was born in May, 1785. He wrote a poem to mark the occasion, "Welcome to a Bastart Wean." The child was named Elizabeth. (In his lifetime Burns had three daughters out of wedlock, each by a different woman, and all three daughters were named Elizabeth.) Miss Paton did not demand marriage, but after *Poems* was published, she sought and won "a certain sum," then disappeared from Burns' life, leaving behind their little girl. Another of his poems, "The Fornicator," chronicled the whole affair, including the rebuke he received in Church.

> Before the Congregation wide,
> I passed the muster fairly,
> My handsome Betsy by my side,
> We gat our ditty rarely;
> But my downcast eye by chance did spy
> What made my lips to water,
> Those limbs so clean where I, between,
> Commenc'd a Fornicator.

The poet blithely went on to his next affair. Jean Armour, six years younger than Burns and probably one of the most beautiful women in his life, was well aware of the reputation he had already earned. In February, 1786, she informed him that she was pregnant, and they signed a document recognizing each other as man and wife. But Jean's father, a master mason, preferred having an illegitimate grandchild to an impoverished son-in-law. He had a lawyer destroy the signed document and sent Jean to live with relatives. Feeling quite betrayed, Burns made plans to leave Scotland for Jamaica with another woman, Mary Campbell. Little is known about "Highland Mary," except that Burns considered her the personification of innocence and purity. That may have been a poor judgment, since there is evidence that she was the same Mary Campbell who had been mistress to several notable Scotsmen of the time. She was pregnant by Burns, but died suddenly, possibly in childbirth, just after his poems had been published.

During the months spent in Edinburgh and in touring the Scottish countryside, Robert Burns had a wide assortment of relationships with women whose social status varied sharply. He had a long and loving correspondence with Mrs. Frances Dunlop, a prominent widow with 13 children, to whom he confided his other affairs. He proposed marriage to Margaret Chalmers, daughter of a gentleman farmer, who turned him down in favor of a banker. A brief encounter in Edinburgh with May Cameron, a servant girl, resulted in another paternity claim and his second daughter Elizabeth. However, his most unusual relationship was that with Agnes Maclehose, an Edinburgh woman whose husband lived in Jamaica. Burns wrenched his knee before he was to meet Mrs. Maclehose, and their rendezvous had to be postponed. Instead she wrote to him, and their correspondence turned very romantic. They even gave each other mythical names. He was "Sylvander," she was "Clarinda." But after Robert was back on his feet, Clarinda would allow the relationship to go no further, so he sought out a servant girl, Jenny Clow, who bore him a son. Jenny later made a claim for additional support, contacting a surprised Robert Burns through Mrs. Maclehose.

Meanwhile, Burns was reunited with Jean Armour. He briefly visited his home during his first tour in June, 1787, and found that Mr. Armour had changed his opinion of the newly successful poet. In fact, he locked Robert and Jean in her bedroom that night, to insure "a happy reunion." When Burns returned again the next spring, Jean was nine months pregnant and in a foul mood. He wrote to a friend that he cheered her up with vigorous lovemaking "till she rejoiced with joy unspeakable and full of glory." Then the author of the poem "Nine Inch Will Please a Lady" commented: "O, what a peacemaker is a guid weel-willy pintle! It is the mediator, the guarantee, the umpire, the bond of union, the solemn league and covenant, … the sword of mercy, the philosopher's stone, the horn of plenty, and the Tree of Life between Man and Woman." That same day, Jean gave birth to twins (both of whom died in infancy), and Robert and Jean were married a month later. They had four more children.

But neither married life nor his position with the excise service could fully control Burns' passions. In 1791 there was another claim, this one from Anne Park, the barmaid at a local inn. Jean was totally understanding and ended up raising the child, the third Elizabeth. Burns was a frequent guest of the area's richer families, including the Riddells of Woodley Park. Mrs. Maria Riddell was one of his most fervent admirers, and there were rumors that their relationship was extremely intimate. One evening near Christmas, 1793, Burns attended a party at Woodley Park. Everyone was drinking heavily, and someone suggested that they amuse themselves with a mock "Rape of the Sabine Women." Burns went after Mrs. Riddell with more enthusiasm and realism than the other guests could accept; for the first time in his life, Robert Burns had compromised himself with a woman whose status was higher than his.

One of his letters, published posthumously, was addressed to his younger brother William. In this he advised William to "try for intimacy as soon as you feel the first symptoms of the passion," since it was "the best preservation for one's peace." He considered himself "a very Poet in my enthusiasm of the Passion," and declared that "the welfare & happiness of the beloved Object, is the first & inviolate sentiment that pervades my soul." But toward such matters as marriage he was totally practical and unsentimental. "To have a woman to lye with when one pleases, without running any risk of the cursed expense of bastards.... These are solid views of matrimony."

In his short lifetime Robert Burns successfully broke all of his own rules.

—*C.L.W.*

The Bride Of Silence

EMILY DICKINSON (Dec. 10, 1830–May 15, 1886)

HER FAME: Dickinson was something of a literary sphinx. Working alone, completely outside the mainstream of American life and art, she composed some of the finest poetry ever written by a woman. Her most famous poems include "I Never Saw a Moor," "I Died for Beauty," and "Because I Could Not Stop for Death." There have been several dramatized versions of her life, including *The Belle of Amherst* (1976).

HER PERSON: Emily Dickinson grew up in high-minded gentility in the remote college town of Amherst, Mass. Her father, whom she adored, was treasurer of Amherst College, a lawyer, and a U.S. con-

Dickinson at 17

gressman; her mother was nervous, sickly, and retiring. The Dickinsons were a closely knit family, remaining together until Emily's parents died. Neither Emily nor her sister, Lavinia, ever married, and when their brother, Austin, did, he simply moved next door.

Emily was plain and shy, "small, like the wren," with little to distinguish her except her "bold" red hair and "eyes like the sherry in the glass," as she wrote Thomas Wentworth Higginson. When she returned home after a year at Mount Holyoke Female Seminary, she apparently enjoyed the customary dancing parties and the attentions of young beaux for a time. Gradually, however—amid rumors of thwarted love—she became a recluse, communicating with dearly beloved friends by letters, poems, and gifts of posies or cookies. Alone, she thrilled to the novels of the Brontë sisters; identified vicariously with Aurora Leigh, Elizabeth Barrett Browning's poetic heroine; and wrote her own poems, which she bound into precious hand-sewn booklets. It was in 1862 that she first sought the advice of Thomas Wentworth Higginson, a prominent literary figure who was to become her "preceptor." He continuously advised against publication of her poems, which he considered "strange" and "peculiar."

During the last 20 years of her life, Emily scarcely left her childhood home. She began to dress exclusively in white, moving like a diaphanous ghost in a Gothic legend, all the while distilling her intense inner life into short poems which read like telegrams sent by the mind's eye. After her death from Bright's disease, her family found some 1,800 poems and a wealth of correspondence. Published posthumously, her work included love poems and love letters from the 30-year-old poet to an anonymous "master." "Wild Nights—Wild Nights!" she had written, inviting intense speculation over spinster eccentricity; "Were I with thee / Wild Nights should be / Our Luxury! ... Rowing in Eden— / Ah, the Sea! / Might I but moor—Tonight— / In thee."

LOVE LIFE: A mystery of the first order, the identity of Emily Dickinson's "master" has given rise to volumes of biographical, literary, even psychoanalytic detective work. The mystery was deepened by Dickinson family lore that Emily "met her fate" in the person of the Rev. Charles Wadsworth, an eloquent preacher whom she encountered on a rare visit to Philadelphia. Wadsworth was married, as were the other possible "masters," but he had the virtue, as far as the family was concerned, of being physically removed from Amherst. The supposed lovers met only twice, briefly, but Emily continued to correspond with her "dearest earthly friend"—largely about spiritual matters.

According to another source, Emily's star-crossed lover was a brilliant young army officer who was also the husband of her friend Helen Hunt Jackson. A somewhat more plausible candidate was Samuel Bowles, editor of the *Springfield Republican*, with whom Emily corresponded for years and to whom she sent many of her love poems. But while the poet undoubtedly displayed an exaggerated affection for the editor, she may also have had professional motives. A few of her poems were published anonymously by Bowles, who took the liberty of "correcting" them, so little did he esteem the poet's skill or reciprocate her feelings.

Whoever the "master" was, it is known that at the age of 48 Emily enjoyed a "December romance" with 64-year-old Otis Lord, a distinguished jurist and lifelong friend of the family, whose wife had just died. One biographer has even constructed a convincing case for Lord's being the elusive "master," speculating that a secret passion may have blossomed 14 years earlier when Emily was undergoing medical treatment in Cambridge and the judge was holding court nearby. If Lord was Emily's "master," she was his Ophelia in the Shakespearean symbolism in which they communicated. ("Exultation floods me," Emily wrote. "I cannot find my channel, the creek turns sea at thought of thee.") The two never married, whether because their love was frowned upon by both families, or possibly because they had become too set in their separate ways.

But Emily was in any case probably incapable of consummating her sexual passion, according to one psychoanalytic biographer. Suffering from an unresolved Oedipal conflict, an abnormally prolonged period of "sexual latency," and an uncertain self-image as a woman due to her estrangement from her mother, she is said to have compensated by working out an elaborate love fantasy in her writings.

Finally, it has even been argued that Emily's "master" was really a "mistress." Citing her ardent correspondence with her female friends and the occasional use of feminine pronouns and bisexual symbolism in her love poetry ("Ourselves were wed one summer, dear" was addressed to her friend Kate Scott Turner), proponents of this view hold that Emily was a lesbian and that her life was ruined by the restrictions of a heterosexual society.

—*C.D.*

The Snow Princess

EDNA ST. VINCENT MILLAY (Feb. 22, 1892–Oct. 19, 1950)

HER FAME: At the age of 20 Millay became an overnight literary sensation with the publication of her poem "Renascence." She went on to produce some of the greatest love poetry in the English language. Writing from a uniquely feminine point of view, she enjoyed popular as well as critical acclaim. In 1923 she received a Pulitzer Prize, the first ever awarded to a woman.

HER PERSON: The eldest daughter of a divorcée, Millay grew up in a remote town on the Maine seacoast as "Vincent," the surrogate man of the family. Her mother was a free-spirited woman

Millay, photographed by Carl Van Vechten, 1933

who worked as a nurse to raise her three daughters as a tight little band of creative women. Thanks to a benefactress, the young poet was able to enter Vassar College—belatedly—when she was 21. Rebelling against this "pink and gray college" where men were excluded, she smoked secretly, disregarded campus rules, and escaped after graduation to the uninhibited freedom of New York's Greenwich Village. There she worked intermittently as an actress while writing poetry and the pseudonymous magazine articles which paid the rent. "My candle burns at both ends," Millay wrote in *A Few Figs from Thistles* (1920), and it became the epigraph of the dawning decade. The petite red-haired poet, half Irish and half Yankee, was, at her best, an enchantingly beautiful fairy-tale princess. But she was also intense, high-strung, and prone to mental and physical breakdown. In 1923 she married Eugen Boissevain, an importer of Dutch-Irish ancestry, who waited on her hand and foot during the 25 years of their marriage. "Anybody can buy and sell coffee," Boissevain explained. "It seemed advisable to arrange our lives to suit Vincent."

SEX LIFE: Millay had an intoxicating effect on both men and women. Her sexual ambivalence revealed itself when she was young in attachments to older women. "Anybody reading this would think I was writing to my sweetheart," she wrote to her mother. "And he would be quite right." A young doctor once suggested that her recurrent headaches might stem from "an occasional erotic impulse towards a person of [her] own sex." Millay replied, "Oh, you mean I'm homosexual! Of course I am, and heterosexual too, but what's that got to do with my headache?"

Her first serious lover, the playwright and radical Floyd Dell, described her as a "Snow Princess, whose kiss left splinters of ice in the hearts of the mortal men who loved her." Equally fearful of desertion and of the confines of traditional femininity, incapable of emotional surrender, she rejected Dell and a rapid succession of other lovers. At one point Dell unsuccessfully tried to persuade her to enter therapy to deal with what he called her "sapphic tendencies," which to him meant her compulsive plunging into one love affair after another.

An exception to her usual pattern was poet Arthur Davison Ficke, who was already married and hence safely unattainable. They consummated their passion during a whirlwind 36 hours in the midst of WWI and then remained lifelong admirers. However, to Millay it seemed only proper that Ficke would always be unattainable. When he proceeded to fall in love with another woman after divorcing his first wife, she accepted it complacently and even became friendly with his new sweetheart.

Another lover was author and literary critic Edmund Wilson, who became infatuated with the poet at first encounter. "Edna ignited for me both my intellectual passion and my unsatisfied desire, which went up together in a blaze of ecstasy that remains for me one of the high points of my life," Wilson wrote in his memoirs. He was able to joke about her many lovers (the "alumni association," he called them), and on one occasion Wilson and his friend John Bishop playfully divided her in half for the evening, Wilson embracing the lower part of her body and Bishop the upper half. But Millay's extreme promiscuity wounded Wilson deeply. "What my lips have kissed, and where, and why," she wrote in one poem, "I have forgotten...."

Eugen Boissevain, whom she finally married, represented to her a safe harbor, the supremely indulgent parent figure. (The tall, handsome, spirited Boissevain had played the same subordinate role with his first wife, feminist Inez Mulholland, before her premature death.) He nursed Millay back to health, bought her a farm in the Berkshires and an island off the Maine coast, and managed every domestic detail down to washing his wife's hair. "To be in love is a terrific and continuous excitement," Boissevain once confided to Alan Ross Macdougall. "I want to keep that excitement, never being quite sure, never knowing, so that I can ask myself: Does she love me? And have the answer: I don't know."

Theirs was an "open marriage," Boissevain insisted, but Millay was so fiercely protective of her privacy that the identity of the extramarital lover described in the sonnets in *Fatal Interview* (1931) remains unknown. In a sense, the identity of her lovers was subordinate to the feelings they engendered within her. As Edmund Wilson observed, "She did not ... give the impression that personality much mattered for her or that, aside from her mother and sisters, her personal relations were important except as subjects for poems...." In the end she always returned to her deepest love—what she called her "soul's chastity"—poetry.

HER THOUGHTS:

> My candle burns at both ends;
> It will not last the night;
> But ah, my foes, and oh, my friends—
> It gives a lovely light!
> —from Millay's "A Few Figs from Thistles"

—C.D.

The Mad Poet

EZRA POUND (Oct. 30, 1885–Nov. 1, 1972)

HIS FAME: Pound was a master of poetic style and form. His most famous work is *Cantos*, an autobiographical multivolume epic 40 years in the making.

HIS PERSON: An eccentric figure with a billowing cape, a "fox's muzzle" beard, and one long, dangling earring, Pound affected a personal style as distinctive as his verse. After abandoning his doctoral studies at the University of Pennsylvania, he worked briefly as a professor of Romance languages at Wabash College in Crawfordsville, Ind., then left for Europe in 1908. While teaching at London's Regent

Street Polytechnic Institute, he developed a nonacademic interest in one of his pupils, Dorothy Shakespear. They married in 1914. After WWI they moved to France, and later to Italy. Meanwhile, Pound was working on *Cantos* and lending invaluable support to Ernest Hemingway, T. S. Eliot, James Joyce, and other struggling writers. He was also developing a reactionary philosophy which eventually led to his conviction that "usury is the cancer of the world" and that the Jews were the prime perpetrators of this evil. By the time the first rumblings of WWII were heard, he was acclaiming Mussolini as a genius and Hitler as "a

Pound just before his 28th birthday

Jeanne d'Arc, a saint." Pound's vehement denouncements of the American war efforts over Rome Radio resulted in his being indicted by the U.S. on 19 counts of treason. Arrested outside his home at Sant' Ambrogio, Italy, in April, 1945, he spent six months in an American army stockade before being shipped back to the U.S. At his trial in Washington, D.C., in February of 1946, he was judged of "unsound mind" and was confined to St. Elizabeth's Hospital for the criminally insane. Finally released in 1958, he returned to Italy, worked sporadically for a few years, then lapsed into silence for the last decade of his life. At the end he lamented, "Everything that I touch, I spoil. I have blundered always."

LOVE LIFE: Getting engaged was one of Pound's favorite pastimes as a young man. When he was 19 he established a liaison with 34-year-old concert pianist Katherine Ruth Heyman, who gave him an heirloom diamond ring. At about the same time, he became engaged to poet Hilda Doolittle (pen name H. D.), who recorded in her journal that Pound's "fiery kisses" were "electric, magnetic." Another young poet to fall under Pound's sway was Hilda's friend Frances Gregg. After his relationships with Frances and Hilda cooled, he became engaged to Mary Moore and gave her the diamond ring entrusted to him by Miss Heyman. Complications with the opposite sex continued to dog his steps. His landlady found a woman in his bed one morning after he had left for his teaching duties at Wabash College, and as a result of the incident Pound lost his job. Although he claimed that the girl was merely a destitute actress on whom he had taken pity, members of the community were outraged.

Leaving the tangled skein of his romances behind him, Pound sailed for Europe, where he served as Katherine Heyman's concert manager before meeting Dorothy Shakespear, whose mother was a close friend of the poet William Butler Yeats. Dorothy had all the requisites for a wife. She was "beautiful and well-off" and had "the most charming manners." But Pound was not destined to settle into a conventional marriage for long. In 1922, eight years after he had wed Dorothy, he was introduced to fellow American expatriate Olga Rudge, a pretty, dark-haired concert violinist in her mid-20s. She thought him "the handsomest man she had ever seen" and he considered her "a great goddess." When the goddess became his mistress, Pound began leading a double life, spending winters with Dorothy and summers with Olga. In 1925 Olga gave birth to his daughter, Mary, and the following year Dorothy bore his son, Omar. In 1944, when the Germans forced Pound and his wife out of their home in the Italian seaport of Rapallo, they moved in with Olga in Sant'Ambrogio for the remainder of the war. Although no angry words were ever spoken in the household, Pound's daughter recounts that the air was always heavy with tension because Dorothy and Olga despised each other. During the final stages of his life, as his health declined and he became increasingly reclusive, Dorothy proved physically unable to care for him. Consequently, his last years were spent with Olga, who would accompany him to the Montin trattoria in Venice. According to one restaurant employee, "he never said a word and always sat with his chin on his chest, sometimes muttering." After his death at 87, Olga Rudge stayed on in Italy, and today, according to one Venetian, "she listens all day, at the loudest volume, to tapes of Ezra Pound reading his poetry; perhaps not having heard his voice much when he was alive, she wants to do so now."

HIS THOUGHTS: "It is more than likely that the brain itself is, in origin and development, only a sort of great clot of genital fluid held in suspense or reserve.... There are traces of it in the symbolism of phallic religions, man really the phallus or spermatozoid charging, head-on, the female chaos.... Even oneself has felt it, driving any new idea into the great passive vulva of London, a sensation analogous to the male feeling in copulation."

—The Eds.

The Santa Claus Of Loneliness

RAINER MARIA RILKE (Dec. 4, 1875–Dec. 29, 1926)

HIS FAME: Rilke was a German poet whose lyric and finely crafted verses gained him international acclaim. His most famous works are the *Duino Elegies* and *Sonnets to Orpheus.*

HIS PERSON: Born in Prague, Rilke was raised by his unbalanced mother as a girl for his first six years. Later his father sent him to a military school, but he dropped out because of poor health. He also quit a commercial school in Linz, Austria, and the University of Prague. Rilke published his first volume of poems at 19, then went to Munich to devote himself to writing. All his life Rilke traveled constantly in Europe, producing a steady stream of poetry. He also visited North

Africa and Egypt, and he called Russia—where he met Tolstoi—his spiritual home. But actually he preferred Paris. For a time he was Auguste Rodin's secretary. Then members of the European aristocracy took Rilke under their wing, putting him up in a series of villas and castles. Princess Marie von Thurn und Taxis-Hohenlohe became his lifelong patroness in 1909. Rilke found in her the mother figure he had longed for, and to her he opened his heart. During WWI he briefly served as a clerk in the Austrian army. Intellectual and artistic women were always drawn to the graceful Rilke, although he was no Adonis. With his

long head, large nose, receding cleft chin, and droopy mustache, he seemed "ugly, small, puny" even to Princess Marie. Rilke preferred the company of women, yet he would bolt as soon as he felt his solitude and work threatened. He practiced nudism, flirted with the occult, and believed in nature cures. Images of virgin girlhood, death, and roses run through much of his poetry. "The Santa Claus of loneliness," as poet W. H. Auden called him, died near Montreux, Switzerland.

LOVE-LIFE: "I am no good at love, because I did not love my mother," Rilke once confessed. At other times he complained about the suffering and despair that his erotic relationships had brought. Because he found very little pleasure in sex, with many women he preferred the role of a good friend. But there certainly were exceptions.

At 16, while at the commercial school in Linz, he had a love affair with an instructor several years his senior, and they eventually ran away together. The next year he fell in love with and became engaged to Valerie von David-Rhonfeld, an aspiring artist a year older than he. Three years and 130 love letters later, Rilke broke off the engagement.

In 1897 Rilke met Lou Andreas-Salomé, a well-known author and the daughter of a Russian general. Although she was married and 13 years his senior, they quickly became lovers. Rilke's diary suggests that she may even have borne his child. Rilke, Lou, and her husband made a trip to Russia, and a short time later the two lovers returned to Russia, this time passing themselves off as cousins. This was Rilke's most enduring relationship with a woman, not counting Princess Marie's purely nonsexual friendship. Even after Rilke and Lou officially parted, they continued to see each other and corresponded for the rest of Rilke's life. Lou, an amateur psychoanalyst, wrote years later that of the "many fears" in Rilke, his biggest was the girlish fear of his penis. She alluded to Rilke's sexual infantilism and revealed that a physical difficulty with his genitals made erections painful for him. She also interpreted his fears as a "displaced, converted guilt over masturbation."

Rilke married German sculptor Clara Westhoff in 1901. Their daughter, Ruth, was born the same year. But the Rilkes soon went their separate ways without bothering to get divorced.

In 1914 pianist Magda von Hattingberg considered living with Rilke forever, but then decided that she did not love him as woman loves man. "For me he is the voice of God, the immortal soul," she said. The following year the flamboyant painter Loulou Albert-Lazard became his mistress in Munich. In the winter of 1918 Rilke wrote impassioned letters to poet Clair Studer, with whom he had a "short ecstatic flowering of physical love." Then there was 17-year-old Marthe Hennebert, a pathetic Parisian waif with whom Rilke carried on a lover-father affair from 1911 to 1919. And in Switzerland in 1921 he had an erotic liaison with the Russian painter Baladine Klossowska.

Rilke also was linked romantically, but not necessarily sexually, with many other women, including poet Regina Ullmann and Countess Francesca von Reventlow. His last love was a young Egyptian beauty, Mrs. Nimet Eloui Bey, whom Rilke met shortly before his death. It is said that while picking roses for her, Rilke pricked his finger. An infection developed, and while treating it doctors discovered by chance that Rilke had leukemia. He was dead within weeks.

HIS THOUGHTS: Rilke once confided to Princess Marie, "All love is an effort for me, a difficult task...." Among the manuscripts unpublished at his death were seven poems glorifying the human phallus; in these the sexual act is extolled in religious metaphors. The essence of earthly splendor is our "lovely" sex, which Christianity has always sought to suppress. "Why did they make our sex homeless for us?" Rilke asked.

FROM THE PHALLIC POEMS: The fourth in the series of seven poems was written in October, 1915.

> You don't know towers, with your diffidence.
> Yet now you'll become aware
> of a tower in that wonderful rare
> space in you. Hide your countenance.
> You've erected it unsuspectingly,
> by turn and glance and indirection,
> and I, blissful one, am allowed entry.
> Ah, how in there I am so tight.
> Coax me to come forth to the summit:
> so as to fling into your soft night,
> with the soaring of a womb-dazzling rocket,
> more feeling than I am quite.

> —R.J.R.

The Whippingham Papers

ALGERNON CHARLES SWINBURNE (Apr. 5, 1837–Apr. 10, 1909)

HIS FAME: An innovative writer of the Victorian era, he gained fame with the poetic drama *Atalanta in Calydon* (1865) and notoriety with the sensual lyrics in *Poems and Ballads* (1866). Later he produced several volumes of literary criticism.

HIS PERSON: Born of noble ancestry in London, the eldest child of a naval captain, Swinburne cut an odd-looking figure. He had a puny physique, an oversized head covered with carrot-colored hair set atop severely sloping shoulders, and a springy gait. His high-pitched voice turned into a falsetto during times of excitement, and a nervous constitution produced an effeminate manner, trembling hands, and cataleptic fits. Yet his ambition was to be a soldier, until his father prudently scotched the idea. In 1861 Richard Monckton Milnes introduced Swinburne to the writings of the Marquis de Sade, whom he emulated thereafter. He lived for a time with artist Dante Gabriel Rossetti and befriended a number of homosexuals and unusual types. His first success, *Atalanta*, was followed by volumes of poetry generally criticized for their obscene content. Heavy drinking and carousing so undermined the poet's fragile constitution that in 1879 he lay near death. At that time he was "adopted" by Walter Theodore Watts (later Watts-Dunton). Watts-Dunton was a critic, poet, and novelist whose works include *The Coming of Love and Aylwin*. Swinburne was nursed back to health at the Pines, Watts-Dunton's estate, where he resided until his death 30 years later. During that time he produced numerous volumes of poetry and criticism. Although Watts-Dunton clearly saved the dissolute poet from an early grave, some critics charge that his incessant mothering smothered Swinburne's genius.

SEX LIFE: Swinburne was a masochist who acquired a taste for flagellation at Eton's infamous flogging block. He once rinsed his face with cologne just before a whipping in order to heighten his senses. He later was a regular customer at a flagellation brothel in the St. John's Wood section of London. Euphemistically referred to as the "Grove of the Evangelist," the house featured rouged blond girls who whipped to order while an elderly lady collected clients' fees. Swinburne observed, "One of the great charms of birching lies in the sentiment that the floggee is the powerless victim of the furious rage of a beautiful woman."

He shared his love for the lash with his cousin Mary Gordon, but there is no evidence that they did anything more than talk about it. Swinburne may have proposed to Mary, and he reportedly was crushed at the announcement of her marriage to another. Later she denied that they had ever been lovers.

Swinburne was positively obsessed with flogging. It dominated his whole life, his every fantasy, and a great deal of his writing. His widely published poems were shocking enough to earn him insults, full as they were of heterosexual sadomasochistic fantasy and references to death, delirium, and hot kisses. *Punch* magazine called him "Swine Born"; one literary critic accused him of "groveling down among the shameless abominations which inspire him with frenzied delight"; and Thomas Carlyle described him as "standing up to his neck in a cesspool, and adding to its contents."

But his unpublished and underground works would have been the real shockers to the critics, had they read them. They bore such titles as *The Flogging-Block, Charlie Collingwood's Flogging,* and *The Whippingham Papers.* Some of these writings appeared anonymously in *The Pearl,* an underground journal of Victorian erotica.

Swinburne, wistfully pining after the glorious Eton beatings, once wrote in a letter to his homosexual poet friend George Powell, who was at the college: "I should like to see two things there again, the river—and the block." He asked for news of Eton whippings: "the topic is always most tenderly interesting—with an interest, I may say, based upon a common bottom of sympathy." Powell sent him a special present: a used birch rod. Swinburne was delighted and wrote that he only wished he could be present at an Eton birching. "To assist unseen at the holy ceremony ... I would give *any* of my poems." Powell next sent him a photograph of the flogging block. Swinburne was happy but wished for an action picture. "I would give anything for a good photograph taken at the right minute—say the tenth cut or so." An 1863 letter to his friend Milnes finds Swinburne irritated that Milnes would stoop to flogging a boy of the lower classes. Birching, he chastised, was an aristocratic sport.

There is no concrete proof that Swinburne was gay. However, besides his friendship with Powell, he was close to the homosexual painter Simeon Solomon, who sent him drawings depicting flagellation. Swinburne was once seen chasing Solomon around the poet Rossetti's home while both were naked. And his letters imply homosexuality. At an Arts Club dinner Swinburne got drunk and professed a horror of sodomy, but wouldn't stop talking about it. He appears to have been impotent with women. In an attempt to cure him of his bad habits, Rossetti once paid Adah Isaacs Menken, a popular entertainer and lover of the period, £10 to sleep with Swinburne. After several attempts she returned the fee, explaining that she had been "unable to get him up to scratch" and couldn't "make him understand that biting's no use!" Perhaps to refute rumors of his homosexuality, Swinburne boasted to friends of the "riotous concubinage" he had enjoyed with Adah. The nature of the relationship between Swinburne and his mentor Watts-Dunton remains unclear. In Swinburne's last will, he named the poet his sole heir.

QUIRKS: Flagellation was not Swinburne's only quirk. He also was inordinately fond of babies, especially plump, cherubic ones. He loved to cuddle and caress them. He collected baby pictures and kept on his desk a figurine depicting a baby hatching from an egg. Although there are no grounds for believing that he ever sexually abused an infant, his close relationship with Bertie Mason, the five-year-old nephew of Watts-Dunton, so alarmed Mrs. Mason that she temporarily removed her son from the Pines. The lad's absence inspired Swinburne's book of poems *A Dark Month*.

An extraordinary account of Swinburne's experiences with George Powell in a French cottage is given by the writer Guy de Maupassant, who visited them when he was 18. After lunch "gigantic portfolios of obscene photographs" were produced, all of men. Maupassant recalled one of an English soldier masturbating. At a second luncheon, Maupassant tried to decide if the two men were really homosexuals. His conclusion was that they had sex with their pet monkey and with clean-cut 14-year-old servant boys. The monkey, he further reported, had been hanged by one of the jealous servant boys.

Another young man claimed to have visited Swinburne when he was living in a tent on the Isle of Wight, again with a monkey, which he dressed in women's clothes. Swinburne made advances toward the boy after expounding on "unisexual love." At this, the jealous monkey attacked the visitor. Swinburne persuaded his young man to return for a second lunch. This time the main course was grilled monkey. Hearing these rumors, Oscar Wilde said that Swinburne was "a braggart in matters of vice, who had done everything he could to convince his fellow citizens of his homosexuality and bestiality, without being in the slightest degree a homosexual or a bestializer."

HIS THOUGHTS: Russian novelist Ivan Turgenev once asked Swinburne to name the most original and unrealizable thing he would like to do. "To ravish St. Geneviève," the poet replied, "during her most ardent ecstasy of prayer—but in addition, with her secret consent!"

—W.A.D. and A.W.

The Sexual Vagabond

PAUL VERLAINE (Mar. 30, 1844–Jan. 8, 1896)

HIS FAME: One of the great French writers of the 19th century, Verlaine expanded the rhythmic and harmonic frontiers of French poetry. He was also well known for his bohemian way of life and bisexual love affairs, including one with the poet Rimbaud.

Verlaine at age 49

HIS PERSON: His father was an army officer who amassed a comfortable nest egg, his mother a simple woman who kept the fetuses of her three stillborn infants in glass jars and jealously indulged her only surviving child. Throughout his life Verlaine would remain his mother's beloved son, weak and irresponsible, demanding yet submissive, sexually ambivalent.

He was "overcome by sensuality" at the age of 12 or 13, Verlaine remembered, but his personal slovenliness and ugliness aroused antipathy rather than attraction. His face was broad and flat with narrow slanting eyes set under thick brows. Children taunted him, and a teacher said he looked like a degenerate criminal.

At school he was attracted to younger boys, with whom he formed "ardent" friendships. One of them, Lucien Viotti, has been described as a pretty youth with "an exquisitely proportioned body." At about the age of 17 Verlaine became a regular patron of female prostitutes, exploring with great relish the borders of illicit pleasure and pain. He also demonstrated a weakness for alcohol, with a preference for the deadly green absinthe. After an extended period of debauchery, he met and in 1870 married a young girl, Mathilde Mauté, who seemed the epitome of unsullied virginity.

Verlaine settled down briefly to a civil service job, but the Franco-Prussian War soon broke out, and the arrival in Paris of Arthur Rimbaud in 1871 ended forever any semblance of bourgeois respectability in Verlaine's life. His affair with Rimbaud lasted two years, followed by 18 months in prison for having assaulted the younger poet. While in jail, Verlaine consoled himself with religion.

From then on Verlaine lived as a sexual vagabond, wandering from one disastrously messy relationship to another, alternating between violence and penitence, sobriety and debauchery, quarrels and reconciliation—all the while distilling the essence of his experience into verse. Even during affairs he lived with his mother in a tempestuous love-hate relationship which frequently erupted into open battles.

After his mother's death in 1886, Verlaine returned to heterosexuality for the first time since his marriage. His health was declining (his many complaints included cirrhosis of the liver, a heart condition, and a "bad leg," possibly caused by tertiary syphilis), and he spent nearly half of his last years happily ensconced in public hospitals, where he was cared for like a baby and regaled as a celebrity. Two years before his death from pneumonia, he was elected "prince of poets," by the young poets of Paris.

MATHILDE: For Verlaine, it was love at first sight when he met the proper 16-year-old girl who admired his poetry. Having already seen the poet in literary circles, Mathilde was not put off by his appearance. Indeed, the infatuated Verlaine was so happy, Mathilde later wrote, that "he ceased to be ugly, and I thought of that pretty fairy tale, 'Beauty and the Beast,' where love transforms the Beast into Prince Charming."

During their 10-month engagement Verlaine remained adoringly devoted and chaste, writing trite poetry which idealized love. Marriage, however, revealed "Beauty" to be a vain and snobbish bourgeoise, while "Prince Charming" reverted to the "Beast." He began to drink again, acting out his ambivalence, alternating between gentleness and brutality. He once tried to set his wife's hair on fire, and in a burst of rage hurled his infant son against a wall. Finally, he ran away with the 17-year-old poet Rimbaud. After an unsuccessful attempt to seduce her errant husband into returning home, Mathilde obtained a formal separation and eventually divorced him. It had been a mere three years from her first encounter with Verlaine to his final desertion.

RIMBAUD: He was the evil boy-genius of French poetry, a beautiful, precocious teenager who wrote startlingly original verse, ascribing colors to vowels and feelings to inanimate objects. He was also, by all accounts, an insufferable hooligan, ruthlessly perverse, gratuitously sadistic. His philosophy of exploring every form of love, suffering, and madness in order to achieve poetic "truth" made him sexual fair game for Verlaine.

Preceded by some of his poems and a letter of introduction sent to Verlaine, Rimbaud arrived in Paris dirty and penniless. Verlaine put him up at his in-laws', where he was living at the time, then housed him with a succession of friends. (One of them, a homosexual musician, introduced the boy to the mind-expanding experience of hashish.) Day and night the two poets caroused, drinking and engaging in deliberately provocative displays of public affection. Privately, Verlaine introduced Rimbaud to "nights of Hercules" and the exhilarating "love of tigers."

Of the two, Rimbaud was clearly the dominant partner. Verlaine, who considered himself "a feminine" seeking love and protection, fell under the spell of the "infant Casanova" with his irresistible combination of beauty, genius, and violence. Rimbaud, testing his powers, slashed Verlaine with a knife just to amuse himself, and taunted him about his marital respectability.

In July, 1872, the two poets ran away together, apparently with the financial assistance of Verlaine's mother, who was jealous of Mathilde. "I am having a bad dream," Verlaine wrote to his wife from Brussels. "I'll come back someday." Recovering, he invited her to join them: "Rimbaud would be very happy to have you with us." The escapade lasted for the better part of a year, which Verlaine would forever remember as a time of "living intensely, to the very top of my being." They explored the Belgian countryside, then crossed the channel to London, living in cheap hotels and rooming houses. They made a perfunctory effort to support themselves by giving French lessons, but were glad to fall back on Verlaine's indulgent mother, who estimated bitterly that Rimbaud cost her 30,000 francs.

It was a period of great creativity for Verlaine. Rescued from bourgeois captivity, he wrote his *Romances without Words*. But it was also a time of constant bickering and vituperation, as Rimbaud vented his self-disgust and his hatred of being dependent on the older poet. Unable to bear it any longer, Verlaine left abruptly in July, 1873, for Brussels. Dispatching suicide notes to all concerned—including his wife—he waited to be rescued. Verlaine's mother arrived first, followed by a truculent Rimbaud. In the drunken emotional disorder of the occasion, Verlaine turned his suicide weapon on Rimbaud, shooting him in the wrist. Threatened again and fearful of another attack, Rimbaud called the police, who arrested Verlaine and proceeded to investigate his sexual proclivities. Medical examination revealed signs of homosexual intercourse. Verlaine was subsequently sentenced to two years in prison for attempted manslaughter.

Released in January, 1875—he got six months off for good behavior—Verlaine sought out Rimbaud. The latter repulsed these advances by knocking him out and leaving him by the roadside. Rimbaud soon abandoned poetry and lived the rest of his short life as a mercenary adventurer, dying of cancer in 1891. Verlaine, never one to harbor a grievance, would remember their time together as the peak experience of his life—intellectually, emotionally, and physically—a time of pleasure so intense it bordered on pain.

SURROGATE LOVERS: Verlaine spent the rest of his life divided between demon-lovers and mother figures, the opposite poles of sexual attraction for him. While teaching in a provincial school in 1879, he met a young student whose impudence and opportunism reminded him of Rimbaud. Lucien Létinois at 19 was a handsome and straightforward peasant. (A friend of Verlaine's described him maliciously as a "musical-comedy shepherd.") Lucien accepted the effusive affection and financial support of the 35-year-old poet, only to complain privately that he wished they had never met.

Verlaine maintained the sentimental fiction that Lucien was his adopted son. He took him to England and paid his expenses in London while he (Verlaine) taught at a private school in Hampshire. The poet later gave up his teaching post and rushed to London to rescue Lucien upon learning that he had fallen in love with a young British girl. Then Verlaine bought a farm in France and installed Lucien's family to help run it. The venture was a romance of rural life that ended in bankruptcy. When Lucien went into the army, Verlaine became a camp follower, composing fatuous verse about "the handsome erect soldier sitting his steed." Yet Verlaine, fortified by his religious conversion in prison, seems to have stopped short of sexually seducing his "son." When Lucien died of typhoid in 1883, the poet had him buried in a coffin draped in the white cloth indicative of a virgin. He then launched into a period of drunken homosexual vagabondage.

A young Parisian artist and writer named F. A. Cazals became for a time the poet's platonic friend, heir, and obsession. Liberated by the death of his mother, Verlaine spent his last years—when not in the hospital—alternating between two aging prostitutes. Philomène Boudin and Eugénie Krantz were both slatterns who satisfied his adolescent craving for tainted sex and stimulated his masochism with their physical and verbal abuse. They were also greedy, urging him to write poetry which they exchanged for cash at his publisher's office. Composed under the influence of absinthe and the broomstick, these poems reveal a preoccupation with thighs, breasts, and buttocks.

Philomène came equipped with a pimp, who extended his protection to the poet, but Eugénie, who was semiretired, provided him greater stability. Eugénie was with Verlaine when he died and presided over his funeral in widow's weeds. She soon drank herself to death with the proceeds from a lively trade in bogus literary souvenirs.

—C.D.

VII

Let's Make Music

The Moody Bachelor

JOHANNES BRAHMS (May 7, 1833–Apr. 3, 1897)

HIS FAME: Renowned as one of the "three great *B*'s," along with Bach and Beethoven, Brahms is considered the major orchestral and nonoperatic vocal composer of the late 19th century.

Brahms in his early 30s

HIS PERSON: Brahms was raised in the poverty-stricken red-light district of Hamburg, and this environment left its effects upon both his personality and his love life. At an early age he played the piano in taverns in order to earn money, and most of his audiences consisted of prostitutes and their clients. His mother, a lame and homely woman, was 17 years older than his father, who was a timid orchestral musician, and she lavished her affections on her young son. Maintaining an unnaturally strong attachment to her until her death in 1865, Brahms cried out over her grave, "I no longer have a mother! I must marry!"

This was not to be, however. He moodily vacillated between protecting his bachelorhood and considering marriage. An infinitely kind man who secretly supported struggling musicians when he was able, Brahms was also subject to fits of temper, and he was singularly lacking in tact and the social graces. Although he enjoyed bawdy nights of beer drinking and folk songs, his music tended to reflect his darker side. While he was serving briefly as a conductor in Vienna, his programs were so invariably serious that people joked, "When Brahms is really in high spirits, he gets them to sing 'The Grave Is My Joy.'"

His first few recitals brought him little public attention. But after his initial concert tour, at age 20, he met composer Robert Schumann in Düsseldorf, and Schumann was so greatly impressed by Brahms' compositions that he recommended that they be published. Schumann also wrote about Brahms for a music magazine. His article created a sensation, and the young composer's fame and reputation began to spread throughout Europe. Eventually Brahms adopted Vienna as his home, where he produced his four symphonies and the famous *German Requiem.*

LOVE LIFE: As a lover, Brahms led a double life; he fell in love with numerous respectable women (always singers or musicians) but slept only with prostitutes. One possible exception to this was Clara Schumann, the charming and beautiful wife of Robert Schumann. When Schumann suffered a nervous breakdown and was confined to a mental institution, Brahms stayed at Clara's side. Her appeal as a mother figure (she had seven children) was combined with that of friend and musical adviser (she was an accomplished pianist). His feelings for her quickly deepened, as their correspondence shows. Addressed at first to "Dear Frau Schumann," Brahms' letters soon were being sent to a "Most Adored Being." During Schumann's confinement, the conflict Brahms felt between his friendship for Schumann and his passion for Clara made him so miserable that he gave only occasional concerts. He later described the mood of a quartet he started during this period as that of "a man who is just going to shoot himself, because nothing else remains for him to do." When Schumann died after two years in the mental institution, however, the couple shied away from further romantic involvement. They remained close friends for the rest of their lives, and Brahms rarely published any music without Clara's approval.

Brahms' other affairs went much the same way. Unable to resist a comely figure or a beautiful voice, he had at least seven major, unconsummated relationships, but he always bolted before exchanging marriage vows. The objects of these romances often appeared in his music. After his affair with Agathe von Siebold, a fiery singer with lustrous black hair, he immortalized her in a sextet in which the first movement evokes her name three times by using the notes A-G-A-D-H-E (H is the German designation for B-natural). Another of his passions was Schumann's daughter, Julie. When she became engaged to a count, the miserable Brahms presented her with his famous *Rhapsody* (Opus 53), a piece highly evocative of loneliness, and referred to it as *his* wedding song.

Yet he remained single. A fellow bachelor once remarked: "Brahms would not have confided to his best friend the real reason why he never married." He may have been scarred by his relationship with Clara or by his strong attachment to his mother. His early exposure to the "singing girls" of Hamburg had certainly left its mark. He occasionally burst into tirades against women in general, and in an attempt to explain his behavior to a friend, he spoke of his early encounters with the tavern prostitutes: "These half-clad girls, to make the men still wilder, used to take me on their laps between dances, and kiss and caress and excite me. This was my first impression of the love of women. And you expect *me* to honor them as you do!" Always courteous to prostitutes, who found him an eager if awkward lover, his caustic side was more likely to surface with society women. In his relationships with women, Brahms liked to do all the wooing; he was put off if the object of his affection displayed any initiative. A flirtatious woman once asked him if he thought she resembled a famous beauty, and Brahms growled: "I simply can't tell you two apart. When I sit beside one of you, I invariably wish it were the other!"

While he longed for domestic happiness and often complained bitterly of having missed the best part of life, Brahms continued to fall in love well into his 50s, only to abort the affairs before they threatened his bachelorhood, and he continued to immortalize his feelings in the rich, darkly passionate music for which he is known today.

HIS THOUGHTS: "I feel about matrimony the way I feel about opera. If I had once composed an opera and, for all I care, seen it fail, I most certainly would write another one. I cannot, however, make up my mind to either a first opera or a first marriage."

—J.H.

Life Of The Party

FRÉDÉRIC CHOPIN (Mar. 1, 1810–Oct. 17, 1849)

HIS FAME: As a pianist, Chopin amazed all who heard him; he was an innovator who made the piano sing in romantic style. He also gained lasting fame as the composer of bittersweet, deceptively simple, short pieces for the piano—the first Polish music to be played worldwide.

HIS PERSON: A musical prodigy, Chopin debuted with a concert at age eight and became a local celebrity in his early teens. Warsaw then was a musical backwater, and Chopin's father, a French-born high school teacher, had little money. In 1830 the young Chopin left Poland forever to seek his fortune as

Chopin in his last year

a traveling virtuoso, though he lacked the physical strength to give public concerts. He settled in Paris, where he found a niche as piano teacher to rich men's wives, composer of best-selling sheet music, and recitalist to the elite; a gifted mimic, he also became the life of fashionable parties. The social round wore him down and he contracted tuberculosis. In 1848 revolution drove his pupils out of Paris and forced him, despite his coughing up blood, to play for his supper in the stately homes of England and Scotland. He returned to Paris a total invalid and died there after months of suffering.

SEX LIFE: Most women were as charmed by Chopin's romantic good looks as by his music. Chopin, in turn, was drawn to women, but not sexually; their tender adoration reminded him of his mother and sisters. In his late teens he pestered a male friend, Tytus Woyciechowski, with girlish mash notes. He was obsessed with kissing the reluctant Tytus' lips. "Give me your mouth," Chopin wrote, and once, while waiting for lunch, he said, "In a while, the semolina!

But for now, your mouth!" With girls he showed no such aggressiveness. Imagining himself in love with a fellow music student named Constantia Gladkowska, he could not even bring himself to write her a letter. Constantia soon married someone else and was amazed to learn many years later what she had meant to Chopin.

The temptations of Paris did not appeal to Chopin, but he appears to have caught a mild dose of venereal disease from a woman named Teressa. Perhaps this confirmed his distaste for sex. Still, ever since his death, there have been rumors—possibly supported by a cache of erotic letters—of an affair between him and one of his first pupils, the musical and sexually liberated Countess Delfina Potocka. "I would like again to plop something down your little hole in D-flat major [a black key between two white keys]," he wrote in one of the alleged letters, of which only a photocopy remains. The document may well have been faked by its "discoverer," one Pauline Czernicka, who committed suicide in 1949.

Chopin had always wanted a family life of his own. In 1836 he proposed to Maria Wodzinska, the pretty and musically accomplished daughter of a Polish count. Maria accepted him, but the countess, disturbed by his evident poor health, made them keep their engagement secret. Chopin ignored the countess' pleas to take better care of himself, and soon Maria's letters stopped. Either unwilling or unable to protest this rejection, he abandoned all hopes of marriage.

In this frame of mind, he met the free-living novelist George Sand (née Amandine Aurore Dupin), who admired him and pursued him. Chopin was not immediately attracted to her, declaring to a friend, "What a repellent woman that Sand is. Is she really a woman? I am very much inclined to doubt it." Eventually he did succumb to her advances, but she appears to have broken off sexual relations after the first year or two of their nine-year association despite Chopin's complaints that abstinence would kill him. His bedroom performance, she let it be known, was corpselike, and contrary to his protests, he showed little interest in lovemaking. Preoccupied with raising her two children, she was prepared to make him the third. Chopin enjoyed his part-time family, especially little Solange, the daughter. As she grew up she took to flirting with him, calling him "no-sex Chopin." When, in his absence, Sand married her off to a rascally sculptor known for his suggestive nudes, Chopin was aghast. In a violent quarrel between Sand and Solange's husband, Chopin was tricked by Solange—a pathological liar—into siding against her mother, who then broke off with him. Chopin's conscious feelings for Solange remained paternal.

The last woman who seriously tried to attract him was his wealthy pupil and financial savior Jane Stirling, of whom he remarked, "I would as soon marry death." Chopin dreamed in his music of a love that life denied him. Jane Stirling knew this when she said, "He had such a noble idea of what a woman should be!"

—J.M.B.E.

The Temperamental Diva

MARIA CALLAS (Dec. 3, 1923–Sept. 16, 1977)

HER FAME: One of the foremost sopranos in 20th-century operatic history, Maria Callas reigned as a leading diva for more than a decade. She was particularly renowned for her desire to try new roles and the resultant variety of her repertoire.

HER PERSON: She was born in Manhattan, the daughter of two recent Greek immigrants, Georges and Evangelia Kalogeropoulos. Her father changed the family name to Callas when he opened a drugstore in the borough. The Callases already had a daughter—Jackie—when Maria was born, and had hoped for a son to replace one who had died earlier. Consequently, Maria never felt wanted.

Callas, 30 as Alceste

It is quite possible she was *not* wanted. An overweight, myopic child, she was shy and unpopular. In 1929 her father lost his drugstore at the outset of the Depression, and her mother, realizing that both Jackie and Maria had musical ability, set out to find them fame. When Maria was 13, Evangelia took her daughters back to Greece.

The Callas women lived in Greece during WWII and became friendly with some Italian army officers stationed in the country. Maria would delight them by occasionally singing arias from Italian operas; in turn, the officers taught her how to converse in their native tongue. During the war she also acquired some formal musical training by studying with the well-known soprano Elvira de Hidalgo, but her career didn't really get started until her triumphant performance in *La Gioconda* at Verona, Italy, in 1947. Throughout the 1950s her success was constant.

Slimmed to 135 lb. by the time she was an international star, Maria Callas was relatively tall for a woman—5 ft. 7 in.—and prone to fragile health. Nevertheless, she had one of the most penetrating voices of modern opera.

LOVE LIFE: Despite the publicity her private life received, Callas was involved with only two men in her adult life. While singing in Verona in 1947, she met Giovanni Battista Meneghini, an Italian industrialist and opera patron 30 years her senior, who was not put off by the fact that she weighed 230 lb. She later remarked, "I knew he was *it* five minutes after I first met him…. If Battista had wanted, I would have abandoned my career without regrets, because in a woman's life love is more important than artistic triumph." Their marriage plans were complicated by the fact that both families were opposed. Meneghini's family feared that he would immerse himself in operatic matters and neglect the family business. Maria's mother was upset because of the age difference and because Meneghini was not a Greek. With no family members in attendance, the two were wed on Apr. 21, 1949, in Verona. Maria's new husband immediately took over the guidance of her career. Under his tutelage the overweight bride quickly grew trim and learned to dress with style. Her debut at La Scala, the famous Milanese opera house, in 1950 was a triumph. Meneghini would not let his wife bear children because it might harm her career, but their marriage seemed to be on smooth ground until they took a fateful sea cruise in the summer of 1959.

That cruise was aboard the *Christina*, a yacht owned by Aristotle Onassis. The Meneghinis boarded with Onassis, his wife Tina, and Sir Winston and Lady Churchill. Throughout the 2 1/2-week voyage Maria vented the full force of her hot temper on her husband. Meanwhile she and Onassis grew closer, often taking side trips to the Mediterranean ports, leaving the others behind. By the end of the cruise both the Meneghini marriage and the Onassis union were destroyed.

Maria and Meneghini separated a month later. He claimed, "I created Callas and she repaid my love by stabbing me in the back." She alternated between such public statements as a shrill "To hell with him" and a more subdued "The breaking of my marriage is my greatest admission of failure." Tina Onassis divorced Ari; however, it was not Callas who was named as corespondent, but Jeanne Rhinelander, a Riviera socialite with whom Ari had had an affair much earlier.

Callas had met Onassis before; he was the uncle of one of her classmates. Although she claimed he was her "best friend," their subsequent spats were legendary. He admired her talent but fell asleep when she sang. After Callas was freed from Meneghini in 1966, she and Ari discussed marriage, but two years later Onassis married Jacqueline Kennedy instead. Callas was stunned. She felt that Onassis had taken their nine-year affair for granted. In addition, she believed that the former First Lady was all wrong for Onassis. As Callas later explained to her accompanist Robert Sutherland: "The Gold Digger [Jacqueline Kennedy] doesn't understand him. She's always away attending some American anniversary or other. He's married a national monument! She was never right for him. She tried to change his whole way of life. It's typical that she redecorates everything— even the yacht. That's a big mistake. It's like taking away his past. I never did that—I wouldn't have dared." Eight days after Onassis married Kennedy, Callas said that the groom was "back at my door. But I wouldn't let him in."

Afterward her temper cooled, and she and Onassis resumed their relationship, creating quite a splash in the newspapers when they were photographed kissing under a beach umbrella. Looking back on her years with Onassis, Callas once commented, "We were doomed, but oh how rich we were."

Callas' last years were lonely. She had more or less abandoned her singing career, and she had also rejected Meneghini's offer of a reconciliation after Onassis' death in 1975. Callas died in September, 1977, still a legendary opera figure and an object of public interest.

The Operatic Lover

A.L.G.

ENRICO CARUSO (Feb. 25, 1873–Aug. 2, 1921)

HIS FAME: Enrico Caruso was one of the most popular opera singers the world has ever known. A lyric tenor noted for his strong, romantic voice, Caruso captivated audiences with his musical range and depth of feeling. He is generally credited with being the first singer to recognize the value of the phonograph as a means of recording one's voice for posterity and making a great deal of money while doing it.

HIS PERSON: Born in the slums of Naples to a family with 21 children, young Enrico escaped a life of poverty on the strength of his voice. While singing in the church choir, he realized his voice was golden because young suitors were willing to pay him to serenade their sweethearts. Tutored by the great singers of Italy, Caruso achieved an unequaled prominence in both England and America. Commanding large sums for his performances, the tenor enjoyed an opulent life and spent a fortune surrounding himself and his loved ones with luxury. A man of tremendous appetites, Caruso risked losing his voice by smoking two packs of Egyptian cigarettes a day (but sought to protect his throat by wearing fillets of anchovies around his neck). In later life he suffered from a variety of physical afflictions, but he continued to sing until he succumbed to pleurisy.

LOVE LIFE: A dumpy little man with a barrel chest and an absurd waxed mustache, Caruso enchanted women with the magic of his voice. Early in his career he was betrothed to the daughter of an opera theater manager. At the last moment he broke the engagement and fled with a ballerina, the mistress of an elderly opera director, for a torrid but brief fling.

Attracted to older women, Caruso fell in love with Ada Giachetti, a voluptuous opera singer 10 years his senior. Responding to her young lover's passion, Ada sacrificed her own singing career to care for him. In turn, Caruso turned down countless offers of liaisons from his female fans, although his constant flirtations drove Ada wild with jealousy. Their affair, marked by numerous separations and mutual accusations of infidelity, lasted for 11 years. They had two sons out of wedlock.

Caruso's jealousy finally was justified when Ada ran away with their young chauffeur. Shocked but still in love with Ada, Caruso suffered a nervous breakdown that nearly cost him his career. Then, seeking revenge, Caruso plunged into a brief, turbulent affair with Ada's younger sister. When this tactic did not bring Ada back, Caruso threw himself into a series of casual romances with the female opera lovers who flocked around the stage door after each performance. Ada responded by suing Caruso for "stealing" her jewelry, but she settled out of court for a monthly allowance.

Caruso had once said, "I am a great singer because I have always remained a bachelor. No man can sing unless he smiles, and I should never smile if I were married." And for years he skillfully avoided marriage.

Then, at the age of 45, Caruso shocked the opera world by marrying Dorothy Benjamin, a quiet, prim woman 20 years his junior. The product of an old New England family, Dorothy was not a music lover; in fact, she considered opera "noisy and unnatural." Her father immediately disinherited her, and friends of the passionate singer thought he would soon wear her out in bed. But Dorothy bore Caruso a daughter, and they remained devoted to each other for the rest of their lives. Frequently Caruso exhorted her to "become very fatty so no one else will look at you."

QUIRKS: One of the most popular figures of his age, Caruso made headlines in 1906 when he was arrested in New York City for pinching a strange woman's bottom while strolling through Central Park Zoo. In what became known as the Monkey House Scandal, Caruso was attacked by the press as an "Italian pervert" who was intent on seducing innocent American women.

At the trial a mystery witness, dramatically veiled in white, testified that Caruso had fondled her at the Metropolitan Opera House. Furthermore, a deputy police commissioner claimed that he had built up a file on Caruso as a frequent molester of strange women. Caruso was convicted and fined despite the fact that the arresting policeman had often been accused of filing trumped-up charges and had been the best man at the wedding of the "victim"—30-year-old Hannah Graham of the Bronx—who refused to take the stand.

Caruso steadfastly maintained that he had been framed by enemies in the operatic world who were trying to sabotage his popularity with the American public. Caruso's friends pointed out that the singer had just returned from a tour of Latin America, where pinching women in public was considered a casual sport for the elite, and suggested that Caruso simply forgot where he was.

Worried that the Monkey House Scandal would ruin his career, Caruso hid for a time from the hounding press, but he finally returned to the New York stage, where he was greeted by wild applause from enthusiastic opera lovers who cared more about his voice than about his peccadilloes.

—R.S.F.

Musical Chairs

CLAUDE DEBUSSY (Aug. 22, 1862–Mar. 25, 1918)

HIS FAME: Acclaimed for *Clair de Lune* ("Moonlight"), *Prelude to the Afternoon of a Faun*, and his single completed opera, *Pelléas et Mélisande*, Debussy was a composing giant and a major influence on 20th-century music. He was also a minor playwright and critic.

Debussy taken by Félix Nadar

HIS PERSON: Debussy was both intensely brilliant and highly emotional. While he gratified his whims when it came to women and expensive baubles, he could never quite indulge himself in happiness. Claude Achille Debussy was born in Saint-Germainen-Laye, France, to a poor china-shop owner. He entered the Paris Conservatory of Music at age 10 and studied there for 11 years. In 1884 his cantata *L'Enfant Prodigue* won him the Grand Prix de Rome, a coveted award which gave musicians three undisturbed years to work at the Villa Medici in Rome.

Debussy's country upbringing and disinterested attitude made him unpopular with his teachers and fellow musicians, so he made his few friends among the progressive painters and poets of his time. He never had money, never went to see a single performance of his own opera, and rejected the moderate degree of fame he received in his 50s (he hated to be called a professional musician). After he had endured several years of treatment and private suffering, cancer of the rectum killed him at 55.

LOVE LIFE: Many women succumbed to Claude Debussy's genius and dark, brooding character; two wives and a mistress loved him deeply; twice, a self-inflicted gunshot was the recourse taken by his women scorned.

While studying at the Paris Conservatory, 17-year-old Debussy took a summer job as music teacher to the children of Russian millionairess Nadezhda Filaretovna von Meck, who was also Tchaikovsky's patroness. In his third summer with her, Debussy asked Mme. von Meck for permission to marry her daughter and heiress, Sonia. Mme. von Meck pointed out that, as a musician, he was obviously an unsuitable prospect for an heiress and then she dismissed him summarily. In disgrace, Debussy returned to Paris.

Sex, however, was not to be denied him. His next job was as accompanist for an amateur singer whose husband could only suspect what was being taught in the private room he provided for their rehearsals. While working for Mme. Vasnier, Debussy won the Grand Prix de Rome but put off moving to the Villa Medici for seven months because he didn't want to leave his comfortable situation at the Vasniers. Vasnier, suspecting the affair between his wife and the 21-year-old musician, persuaded Debussy that the opportunity was too great to pass up. He hated the Villa Medici and quit after only two of the resident three years. But when he returned to Paris, his affair with Mme. Vasnier was quietly and amicably relegated to the past.

The next two years of Debussy's life are lost to history because of his bohemian ways. Passing time in coffeehouses with the likes of writer Marcel Proust and avant-garde pianist Erik Satie, Debussy had no fixed address until he moved in with a pretty young blonde named Gabrielle Dupont. "Gaby," as he called her, worked at odd jobs to support him for the 10 years they were together. Although Debussy was constantly unfaithful to Gaby, she stayed with him even during the time he was engaged to singer Thérèse Roger. That engagement was abruptly broken off when Thérèse and Debussy were performing in Brussels and she apparently learned of a one-night stand he enjoyed there.

Gaby's patience was remarkable, but even she had her limits. Her affair with Debussy finally ended not long after an argument caused by a note she found in his coat pocket which spoke of yet another affair he was having. Gaby shot herself, although not fatally. After her release from the hospital she lived with Debussy several more months, and he behaved as if the whole scene had never happened. Then Gaby became friendly with Rosalie "Lily" Texier, a young, simple, dark-haired beauty, who was a dressmaker in a small Paris shop. She and Gaby often met in the coffeehouses, their friendship marred only by the way Gaby's composer boyfriend mocked Lily's way of talking. But his ridicule soon turned to flattery, and Gaby was supplanted. Debussy and Lily were married in October of 1899. They started married life literally without a sou, Debussy giving a piano lesson on their wedding day to pay for their breakfast.

Lily was absolutely devoted to Debussy, but youth, devotion, and beauty were not enough. After four years of marriage Debussy began seeing Emma Bardac, an amateur singer and the wife of a wealthy banker. On July 14, 1904, the composer went out for his morning walk and did not return. Weeks later Lily heard from friends that Emma had deserted her husband and that Debussy was with her. On October 13 Lily could stand it no longer and shot herself twice, once in the groin and once in the breast. She was found by Debussy, who had come home because she had sent him a suicide note. Lily recovered from her wounds with no help from Debussy, but she carried the bullet in her breast the rest of her life.

Debussy was divorced from Lily on Aug. 2, 1904, and Emma had his daughter out of wedlock in the autumn of 1905. (She was named Claude Emma, but they called her "Chou-Chou.") When Emma's divorce was settled in January of 1908, she and Debussy married. The marriage appeared to be a good one for both of them, though some people unfairly accused Debussy of marrying for money. Emma was not young or beautiful, but she had intellect and culture, and sustained Debussy as he aged and grew ill.

Debussy died in 1918 in Paris, while the city was under fire from German guns. Emma lost her daughter to diphtheria the following year. Gaby lived out her life in luxury as the mistress of an aristocrat. And nine years after Debussy's death, in 1927, Lily could be found at every lecture that the biographer Léon Vallas gave about the life of Claude Debussy, trying to understand the genius of the man she still loved.

—J.M.

The Duke

DUKE ELLINGTON (Apr. 29, 1899–May 24, 1974)

HIS FAME: Edward Kennedy Ellington was one of the foremost jazz composers, orchestra leaders, and musicians of the 20th century, writing such classics as "Mood Indigo," "Black and Tan Fantasy," "Bojangles," "A Drum Is a Woman," and "Concerto for Cootie." In addition he composed music for several films (including *Anatomy of a Murder*) and for the theater, and later in his career he wrote and performed so-called "religious jazz."

HIS PERSON: Duke (a nickname given him by childhood friends because of his elegant dress and aristocratic manner) Ellington was born in Washington, D.C., to middle-class parents. His father, James Edward, was a blueprint maker for the Dept. of the Navy and a sometime butler who occasionally worked in the White House. The family was devoutly religious, and young Ellington was "terribly spoiled" by his mother, Daisy, to whom he was devoted throughout her life. Ellington showed an early talent in art and won a poster contest sponsored by the National Association for the Advancement of Colored People. Subsequently, he was even offered an art scholarship. But Ellington, who'd taught himself to play the piano by imitating ragtime piano rolls on the family's player piano, was far more interested in music and chose to pursue that as a career. He put together a band and played at various functions in Washington before finally traveling to New York, where he became a mainstay at nightspots like the Cotton Club in Harlem. Soon he and his band were touring the country, garnering great critical acclaim. In 1918, shortly after his 19th birthday, Ellington married a childhood friend and neighbor, Edna Thompson, and less than a year later they had a son whom they named Mercer. Another child born shortly thereafter died in infancy. The marriage to Edna was not a happy one. Duke remained with her several years before they permanently separated, and he continued to support her generously after the breakup. Though it was often rumored that he had two other wives, Ellington remained married to Edna until she died in 1966. Enormously respected throughout his life, Ellington died of cancer in New York City at the age of 75.

Duke with Beatrice Ellis, who for 37 years was known as Elvie Ellington

SEX LIFE: Duke stood 6 ft. 1 in. and weighed 185 lb., though his weight fluctuated wildly, for he loved to eat. Extremely urbane and gracious in his manner, he was a great ladies' man, a charmer and flatterer who tossed off phrases like "You make that dress look so beautiful" or "Does your contract stipulate that you must be this pretty?" Even while he was still living with Edna he had numerous affairs, and according to his son, Mercer, during an argument over one of them Edna slashed his face with a knife, leaving a permanent scar. Duke always loved the attention women paid him, and his son believed that at least part of the reason he went into show business was because it was "a good way to get a girl to sit beside you and admire you as you played the piano." Ralph Gleason, writer and jazz critic, recalled the time he stood with Ellington in the wings of a theater while his band was playing. A trumpet solo was in progress, and as Duke watched, two of his musicians who had a reputation for using drugs sat in their chairs, heads drooping, nodding off. Duke shook his head and said, "I don't understand it at all. I'm a cunt man myself." Another time, Gleason recalled, Duke turned to a script girl working on the documentary *Love You Madly* and remarked, "Sweetie, I don't know your name. You must tell me right away because last night when I dreamed about you I could only call you baby." But Ellington, according to Mercer, "never seemed to be interested in the perfect woman. If she had a scar, or was slightly misproportioned—big-busted, big-hipped, or a little off balance—then he was more interested." But women definitely did interest him. At the notorious House of All Nations in Paris, after the spectacle was over and the girls had lined up, he was asked by a friend to take his pick. Ellington replied, "I'll take the three on this end." He had so many women that he had to develop tricks to deal with all of them. He got into the habit of giving everybody four kisses, thus making it impossible for anyone to know with whom he was actually involved. When someone would ask about the unusual number of kisses, Duke's standard reply was "Once for each cheek." In 1972, during a week-long festival, so many of his women showed up—and stayed in the same hotel that he was at—that he would get a friend to take two of them out to dinner while he took yet another one up to his room.

SEX PARTNERS: In 1929 his marriage to Edna ended in separation after Duke had a passionate affair with an attractive actress. Although Mercer calls it "one of the most serious relationships of his life," the anonymous woman left Duke because he refused to divorce Edna and marry her.

Mildred Dixon, who caught Ellington's eye from the chorus line at the Cotton Club, moved in with Duke in 1930 and stayed for almost a decade. Personable and intelligent, Mildred was Duke's "Sweet Bebe," but her charms paled next to those of Beatrice Ellis, a half-black, half-Spanish show girl who also worked at the Cotton Club. Strikingly beautiful, she spent the next 37 years answering to the name of Evie Ellington and patiently waiting for Duke's infrequent trips to their lavish New York City apartment. Even when the globe-trotting Ellington breezed in to relieve Evie's loneliness, they rarely were seen together in public. His sister Ruth was the "official" hostess, and her possessiveness and Evie's greed were the major reasons that Duke never married Evie. Until Edna died in 1966, he maintained that a divorce would be very expensive, and Evie wanted to keep her deluxe standard of living. After Edna's death, when Evie was certain Duke would marry her, he flatly refused, even when she pulled a gun on him. Evie resigned herself to a solitary life without a marriage certificate, and Duke called her daily, wrote her touching notes, and showered her with flowers, candy, and fruit.

In 1959 Duke met nightclub singer Fernanda de Castro Monte, who later became Madame Zajj in "A Drum Is a Woman." Tall, blond, and fortyish, Fernanda accompanied Ellington on many of his world tours and was introduced as "the Countess." Mercer remembers the farewell she gave Duke after they met in Last Vegas: "She was very smartly dressed in a mink coat. Just as the train was about to pull out, she opened the coat. She had nothing at all on under it, and she wrapped it around him to give him his good-bye kiss. With that, she left him to cool off." Fernanda had expensive tastes and introduced Duke to vodka and caviar (which he touted as an aphrodisiac). When she started making demands, Ellington told her that he was legally married to Evie, who was so jealous of Fernanda that she threatened Duke with her gun a second time.

Fernanda de Castro Monte was the final woman of influence in Ellington's life. He had affairs with many other women (some of whom divorced their husbands for him), but none of them made much of an impact on Duke's life. To the end he insisted, "Music is my mistress, and she plays second fiddle to no one."

—*C.H.S. and the Eds.*

The Music Lover

GEORGE GERSHWIN (Sept. 26, 1898–July 11, 1937)

HIS FAME: One of the most significant and popular American composers, Gershwin wrote the musical score for such classic musicals as *Funny Face* (1927), *Of Thee I Sing* (1931), and *Porgy and Bess* (1935). A posthumous film biography, *Rhapsody in Blue* (1945), helped to cement and preserve his fame.

HIS PERSON: Born Jacob Gershvin in a tough Jewish section of Brooklyn, Gershwin gave no hint of his extraordinary talent during his early years. But at the age of 10 he happened to hear the sounds of a violin drifting through an open window and instantly succumbed

to the charms of music. "It was, to me, a flashing revelation of beauty," he later said. Enraptured, Gershwin took up the piano. In 1913 he quit school to become a staff pianist with a Tin Pan Alley publishing firm and soon began issuing his prolific stream of compositions. His 1919 hit, "Swanee," sung by Al Jolson, established his fame and allowed him to pursue more ambitious undertakings, including scoring Broadway shows and Hollywood movies, often with his older brother, Ira, as lyricist.

Despite his successes, Gershwin was plagued by nervous and digestive disorders. He rigidly limited his diet to easily digested foods—cereals and the like. To combat constipation and chronic depression, he entered psychoanalysis with Dr. Gregory Zilboorg. He saw Zilboorg five times a week for a year, and they got along so well that they even went on vacation to Mexico together.

Gershwin was hardly all gloom and constipation, however. He was the life of many parties and enthusiastically plunged into a variety of projects, from juggling to painting. His vitality remained undiminished until his sudden death, at 38, from an inoperable brain tumor.

SEX LIFE: Gershwin brought his full enthusiasm to sex. Women by the score were attracted to his dark, athletically trim good looks. He slept with many of them, but, unsated by the flood of women who pursued him, he also indulged in frequent trips to brothels, where he gladly bought more sex. He even asked a friend how one went about "keeping" a woman. When informed of the cost involved, he dropped the subject.

A scorecard of Gershwin's lovers would list hundreds, even thousands, of partners, and he often bragged of his conquests and his bedtime prowess; for example, he occasionally enjoyed sex with two women at the same time. Aware of his sexual reputation, he once offered to bestow upon a young woman the privilege of sleeping with him before her marriage. She declined. But one trip to a bordello undid his boasting. While having his pleasure in a Parisian brothel, a pair of his friends—unbeknownst to Gershwin—bribed the madam for a look through a peephole which gave a clear view of Gershwin's performance. What they saw, they reported later, was mechanical sex hastily consummated. Gershwin's interest in lovemaking, despite a multitude of lovers, was perfunctory. But that is not unexpected. Although he believed that sex stimulated his creativity, Gershwin's chief interest—always—was music. Once while at a party, for example, Gershwin sat with a pretty girl ensconced on his lap. Invited to play a few tunes on the piano, Gershwin bolted from his chair so rapidly that the young lady tumbled to the floor. He had simply forgotten her presence when music was mentioned. In another instance, after learning a woman he had loved had married another, Gershwin commented, "If I wasn't so busy, I'd be upset."

Ironically, despite his vigorous pursuit of sexual pleasures, Gershwin retained some prudishness. His sister Frances discovered that part of his nature when she once said "darn" in public and Gershwin slapped her for uttering the expletive. And he frequently rebuked her for wearing her skirts above her knees.

SEX PARTNERS: Because of Gershwin's many lovers, his biographers inevitably seek to identify *the* woman of his life, the one he loved best. Dozens of candidates for *the* woman are championed, including composer Kay Swift, to whom he dedicated his *Song-Book* compositions; actress Paulette Goddard, whom he urged to leave her spouse, Charlie Chaplin; French starlet Simone Simon, who presented Gershwin with a gold key to her Los Angeles home; and dancer Margaret Manners, whose son took the name Alan Gershwin and, in 1959, authored an article for *Confidential* magazine entitled "I Am George Gershwin's Illegitimate Son." Was he? The evidence on both sides is unconvincing. But it would still be irrelevant to the issue at hand, since there are no signs Manners played a major role in Gershwin's life. Only one fact is certain: Gershwin never loved one woman enough to marry her.

With some insight, wit Oscar Levant, a close Gershwin friend, once quipped, "Tell me, George, if you had to do it all over again, would you fall in love with yourself again?" Levant's sharp tongue perhaps cuts unfairly. Gershwin did love himself. But he loved music even more.

HIS THOUGHTS: "I think that the reason why I've never gotten married is that I'm always looking for a woman like my mother—and there just *isn't* another like her."

"Why should I limit myself to only one woman when I can have as many women as I want?"

—*R.M.*

Lady Day

BILLIE HOLIDAY (Apr. 17, 1915–July 17, 1959)

HER FAME: "Strange Fruit" was the first hit record of this black singer of jazz and blues, who became famous for her passionate and touching vocal renditions, which transformed even the most banal lyrics into sheer poetry. As her career blossomed, she progressed from Harlem nightclubs to concert stages with jazz greats Benny Goodman, Artie Shaw, and Count Basie, and from live performances to movie roles.

HER PERSON: Billie wrote, "Mom and Pop were just a couple of kids when they got married. He was 18, she was 16, and I was 3." Pop was an itinerant guitarist, and, although they were poor, Mom would feed any musician who drifted through Baltimore. A childhood experience traumatized Billie; her great-grandmother died in her sleep, and her stiffened arm had to be broken in order to release the just-awakened Billie from its grasp.

Eleanora Fagan Holiday was a tomboy, and her father called her Bill. She called herself Billie after her favorite movie actress, Billie Dove. She attended school only through the fifth grade, and she secretly loved comic books as an adult. After a lifetime of tragic heroin addiction, police harassment, and jail terms, she died at age 44 of heart and liver failure.

SEX LIFE: Ten-year-old Billie was sentenced by a judge to a Catholic reform school. Her crime: being raped by a middle-aged neighbor, Mr. Dick. The event was "bloody and violent," as was her first voluntary sexual encounter two years later with an older musician on her grandmother's parlor floor. Around that time she started running errands for a whorehouse, where she heard her first jazz records. As a teenage prostitute in New York City, she preferred white customers because the blacks took too long. A black man she refused to service tipped off the cops about her, and she was jailed for prostitution. Later she admitted to having had lesbian relations in prison, but claimed she had taken a passive role.

In her first singing job she refused to pick up customers' tips from the table in the customary manner—using her vaginal lips—and the other girls started calling her "Lady." Yet she wore no underwear onstage, and one night she expressed her sentiments to an unappreciative audience by raising her skirts as she stalked off.

"Lady Day" could really sing the blues with passion, and the men she chose to sleep with gave her violent inspiration. She liked them big and pretty. Of one drummer she remarked: "They don't call him 'Big Sid' because he's six foot three, you know." In her 20s she had many musician-lovers and often sang with her pretty face marred by black eyes and her body covered with bruises. If her friends warned her away from a bad character, she usually went after him with more determination than ever. Men used her and spent her money; before long she had a reputation as an easy mark.

LOVE LIFE: The dates of various events in Billie's life are cloudy; for example, that of her engagement to a young pianist named Sonny White. Their relationship was no rougher than most of Billie's casual affairs, but both of them supported their mothers and eventually the problems involved ended the romance.

Tenor sax player Lester Young was the best friend Billie ever had. His obbligato solos matched Billie's moods so perfectly that the records they made together are considered her finest. Lester shortened her last name and called her "Lady Day"; she affectionately called him "Pres," short for "President Roosevelt." It is interesting that through all their years together—recording, on the road, nightclubbing—their friendship was never physical. The music they made together shows that Lester touched Billie as no other man could, and years later, when they had parted ways, an old Lester told a writer, "She's still my 'Lady Day.'"

In 1941 Billie met her husband-to-be, handsome businessman Jimmy Monroe. Jimmy "smoked something strange." When their marriage began to founder, she thought that joining Jimmy in his opium smoking would restore the lost magic, but before she was 30 she was separated from him and living with trumpeter Joe Guy, then 25 years old. That relationship was a triangle— Joe, Billie, and her heroin.

Drug busts and touring eventually separated them, and Billie's next choice of a lover, John Levy, proved a disaster. Levy managed a nightclub and gave her a singing job when nobody else would. He bought her nice clothes, gave her wholesale jewelry, and gradually took over her finances. Although she was making $3,500 a week, she had to beg him for pocket money. Levy eventually left Billie and her band stranded and broke during a tour in the South.

The year 1956 brought a second marriage for Billie, to Louis McKay, a club owner and her manager. She was devoted to Louis, but they filed for divorce in California in late 1958. "Lady Day" died before the divorce decree was finalized.

—J.M.

The Virtuoso

FRANZ LISZT (Oct. 22, 1811–July 31, 1886)

HIS FAME: Renowned as the foremost piano virtuoso of his era, Liszt revolutionized the piano recital genre and spent a lifetime promoting the musical arts in Europe.

HIS PERSON: The son of a Hungarian nobleman's servant, Liszt was a child prodigy. The European aristocracy, for whom he would spend his life playing, was impressed by the boy's talents and financed his musical education. Acknowledged as the greatest pianist of the day, he led an exciting life traveling from Portugal to Turkey to Russia, and achieved widespread fame in the process. In 1848, at the peak of his career, he accepted the directorship of the Weimar court theater. During the next 13 years he instilled new life into European music, not only with his concerts and operatic productions but also through his encouragement of such new composers as Richard Wagner. After leaving Weimar, Liszt spent eight years living and working in Rome, where he became an abbé of the Roman Catholic Church. (This entitled him to perform the rite of exorcism.) The next 17 years he spent playing, teaching, and directing in Rome, Weimar, and Budapest. Liszt's genius brought him such great wealth that midway in his career he ceased to work for money, devoting his efforts instead to fund-raising for worthy causes. In his waning years, the rigors of traveling for these charitable enterprises weakened him, and in 1886 he died of pneumonia in Bayreuth, Germany.

Throughout his career, Liszt demanded respect from his aristocratic audiences and constantly sought to elevate the status of artist above that of superservant. On one occasion he refused to play for Isabella II after he was denied a personal introduction to her majesty because of Spanish court etiquette. Another time he halted a performance in mid-flight and, with head bowed and fingers poised above the keyboard, waited until Czar Nicholas I of Russia ceased speaking. Despite these flashes of hauteur, his passionate style ensured his popularity. Striding forcefully to the stage, his long mane of whitening hair flowing behind him, he would tear off his doeskin gloves and toss them dramatically to the floor, seat himself as he flipped back his coattails, and address the keyboard with lips pressed and eyes blazing.

LOVE LIFE: Like the rock stars of today, Liszt was smothered with feminine adulation. His appearances caused a sensation as his female admirers sought souvenirs; one lady even stripped the cover from a chair that had held the revered posterior. Lovers were his for the taking, and he had dozens, especially among the noblewomen who made up his audiences and pupils.

Crushed at 17 when he was forced to break off a budding romance with Caroline di Saint-Crieg, one of his aristocratic piano pupils, Liszt withdrew into a period of fierce practice that yielded the extraordinary skills that were to bring him society's adoration. His earliest substantial liaison was with the Countess Adèle de la Prunarede, but he broke off the affair upon learning that the countess had a second lover. Liszt's first long-term relationship began in 1835, when Countess Marie d'Agoult left her husband and children in Paris to join Liszt in Switzerland, where she bore him three children. (Their daughter Cosima later became Richard Wagner's wife.) In 1839, however, the couple separated, their relationship strained by Liszt's loss of interest and his friendship with Frédéric Chopin's mistress George Sand, a cigar-smoking writer of risqué novels who loved to sit under the piano while Liszt played. When the countess challenged Sand to a duel at one point—the chosen weapon was fingernails—Liszt locked himself in a closet until the ladies calmed down.

Liszt's name was soon linked with that of Lola Montez, a hot-blooded and beautiful-bodied Spanish dancer who had achieved notoriety by baring her breasts when introduced to King Ludwig I of Bavaria. When Liszt tired of their stormy affair, he deserted Montez while she was napping in a hotel room and left money to pay for the furniture he knew she would destroy in her rage. Liszt's sexual peccadilloes were the talk of European musical society. His mistresses included the eccentric Italian-born Princess Christine Belgiojoso, who once had the body of a deceased lover mummified and kept it at home in a cupboard; the Russian Baroness Olga von Meyendorff, known as the "Black Cat" because of her tight-fitting black clothing; the young Polish Countess Olga Janina, who threatened to shoot and poison Liszt when he broke off their relationship; and the famous courtesan Marie Duplessis, who inspired *Camille*.

The longest affair of Liszt's life, extending through his Weimar and Roman periods, was with Princess Carolyne von Sayn-Wittgenstein. This intellectual Polish noblewoman left her Russian husband and her feudal estates to join Liszt in Weimar, where she spent hours lying on a bearskin rug wearing a turban and smoking a hookah while Liszt played the piano. Liszt hoped to marry the princess and went to Rome to seek papal approval for her divorce, an approval thwarted by her Russian husband's influential connections. By this time Liszt's feelings toward Carolyne had begun to cool, and he was relieved that the divorce was denied.

Liszt's sexual exploits continued into his autumn years, and he was frequently involved with a pupil young enough to be his granddaughter. He claimed, however, that because of his reverence for virginity he had never "seduced a maiden." Even though he feared impotence—and used a variety of stimulants to prevent its onset—he had a longer list of lovers than almost any of his contemporaries. Liszt's only comment was, "I didn't take a big enough bite of the apple."

—*J.Z.*

Warmhearted Wunderkind

WOLFGANG AMADEUS MOZART (Jan. 27, 1756–Dec. 5, 1791)

HIS FAME: Considered the purest example of "raw genius" in history, Mozart was the greatest musical technician of all time and one of the world's supreme creative artists. Master of all forms, he composed over 600 works, including choral and chamber works, symphonies, sonatas, concertos, and operas. Critics call his *Don Giovanni* and *The Marriage of Figaro* the most perfect operas ever written.

HIS PERSON: This most prodigious of all child prodigies, born in Salzburg, Austria, began music lessons at four with his violinist father, Leopold, a stern but loving disciplinarian. Composing from the age of five, Mozart at six astonished the royalty of Europe as he and his gifted sister made the first of many arduous concert tours. A virtuoso on violin, organ, and harpsichord, he was called "*Wunderkind*" ("marvelous child") and showered with attention. Yet he remained completely natural and affectionate.

His adult life was a sharp contrast to his younger years. Short, pale, insignificant in appearance, he could not command the interest of aristocratic and ecclesiastical patrons as a serious and mature composer. He never found an official post that paid enough to enable him to devote himself fully to the major works he longed to write. Precious time was wasted giving perfunctory lessons and grinding out charming potboilers. His life was a long losing struggle against jealous rivals, illness, and poverty. He and his wife, Constanze, did not live within their financial means. Pleasure-loving, they were unable to keep money from vanishing, not the least because of their generous handouts to every comer.

Mozart died at 35 of kidney disease brought on by overwork and malnutrition. He was in debt to his tailor, the druggist, the upholsterer, as well as his friends. Working feverishly, he tried unsuccessfully to finish his great *Requiem* before his own funeral. A heavy rainstorm prevented his wife and friends from accompanying the coffin to the graveyard. Not until 17 years later did Constanze realize that Mozart's remains had been dumped into an unmarked pauper's grave.

LOVE LIFE: Pampered by women as a child, he was precociously aware of their looks. He once wrote his father, "Nature speaks as loudly in me as in any man, perhaps more forcefully than in many a big strong oaf." Mozart enjoyed flirting, saying that if he had had to marry every girl with whom he flirted, he would have been a husband 100 times. At 21 he carried on a playfully indecent correspondence—full of double meanings—with his favorite cousin, Maria Anna Thekla Mozart.

While on tour Mozart stayed with the musical Weber family of Mannheim and seriously lost his heart for the first time. The object of his affections was Aloysia Weber, 16, a lovely girl who was studying to be an opera singer. Encouraged by her designing mother, she flirted with Mozart, who was enchanted. They played and sang together by the hour. Wolfgang's father heard about it and ordered him summarily back on his tour since he thought the "loose-living" Weber clan was socially beneath the Mozarts. Some months later Wolfgang returned to Mannheim to find that Aloysia, now ensconced as a member of the Munich opera, had forgotten him. Their meeting was so awkward that Mozart sat down at the piano and played a ribald song to cover his hurt feelings. Long after Mozart's death, when Aloysia was asked why the relationship had cooled, she replied, "I did not know, you see. I only thought he was such a *little* man."

At 25 Wolfgang transferred his affection to Aloysia's younger sister—uneducated, unmusical Constanze. When writing to his father, Mozart described her as plain but with a good heart and wonderful housekeeping skills. This time Mother Weber used strong tactics to keep Mozart in the family. She spread the story that he was being too familiar with Constanze, then told him that people were talking and that she feared for her daughter's reputation. The conniving mother engineered an ultimatum for Mozart: either he must stop seeing Constanze or sign a marriage contract which stipulated that if he defaulted he would have to pay 300 guldens ($150) a year. Wolfgang certainly had no intention of giving up Constanze, and she proved her good heart by tearing up the contract as soon as he had signed it. Their wedding took place when he was 26, she 19. Leopold's grudging consent came in the mail the next day, but he never approved of Constanze.

The nine-year marriage was genuinely happy; the Mozarts were companionable and physically compatible. Constanze was easygoing, tolerant, uncomplaining, and usually pregnant and ailing (only two of their six children survived). A visitor once found the couple dancing around their living room in each other's arms to keep warm as they had no money to buy wood.

When Mozart died, Constanze was hysterical with grief. Later she scrupulously paid off all his debts. She was married a second time, to one of her lodgers, Danish diplomat Georg Nikolaus von Nissen, and went to live in Copenhagen. Nissen helped her write the first biography of Mozart, whom she survived by 50 years.

Legend attributes many extramarital affairs to Mozart, but most stories seem to be mere gossip.

Mozart was no Don Juan like the hero of his opera (when he and librettist Lorenzo Da Ponte required a living model for that character, they called in Casanova for advice). His strenuous work habits were not conducive to dalliance. Until the end of his life he wrote to his wife almost daily whenever they were separated. His letters brim with warmth and affection: "Adieu, my dear, my only love! Hold your hands in the air—2,999 1/2 kisses are flying from me to you and waiting to be snapped up." In the letters Mozart seems the ideal of marital fidelity. Also, by his own admission, he avoided promiscuity because of the perils of venereal disease.

QUIRKS: In his youth Mozart wrote a great many letters to his mother and his favorite cousin, Maria, which indicated that he was something of a coprophiliac, or human-waste fetishist. In one letter, he wrote Maria: "Oh, my ass is burning like fire! ... Perhaps some muck wants to come out? ... What is that?—Is it possible ... Ye gods!—can I believe those ears of mine? Yes indeed, it is so—what a long, melancholy note! ... I shit on your nose and it will run down your chin.... Do you still love me?" As soon as Mozart began writing home to his father asking for permission to marry Constanze, he ceased to discuss his bowels in his letters.

HIS THOUGHTS: "A bachelor, in my opinion, is only half alive."

—*The Eds.*

The Sensuous Soprano

ADELINA PATTI (Feb. 19, 1843–Sept. 27, 1919)

HER FAME: A coloratura soprano, Patti reigned for 56 years as undisputed queen of world opera, the most popular and richest prima donna of the late 19th century.

HER PERSON: She came from a completely musical family. Her father was Sicilian, her mother Roman, and Adela Juana Maria Patti was born in Madrid while her parents were on tour. She was only a few years old when her father moved the family from Italy to America, where he helped manage New York's Astor Place Opera House. Patti made her U.S. singing debut at the age of eight.

After a decade of small tours, she made her London debut at Covent Garden in *La Sonnambula* at the age of 18. She was an overnight sensation. Soon she took Brussels, Paris, St. Petersburg, Milan, Monte Carlo, and Madrid by strom.

She was a quick study. She could sing a role to herself twice and know it. At the height of her career she had a repertoire of 42 operas. Her most acclaimed roles were Rosina in Rossini's *Barber of Seville* and Zerlina in Mozart's *Don Giovanni*. Chiefs of state showered her with diamonds. In 1881, using her own luxurious private railroad car, she began to give concerts (at $5,000 a performance) around the U.S., featuring popular songs like "Comin' Thro' the Rye." Summoned to Windsor Castle, Patti sang "Home, Sweet Home" for Queen Victoria, who wept at its conclusion. On another occasion, Jenny Lind was also moved to tears upon hearing Patti's soaring voice. Giuseppe Verdi proclaimed Patti the greatest singer he had ever heard. The elderly French composer Daniel Auber said of her, "I have never heard so perfect an artist as Patti." There were few dissenters; one of them, George Bernard Shaw, said: "She seldom even pretends to play any other part than that of Adelina, the spoiled child with the adorable voice."

In her prime Patti was described by an admiring critic as a young woman with a "delicately chiseled head, fine mobile features, and the guileless eyes of a doe—white marble turned into flesh, surrounded by a dark frame of hair." A male friend spoke of her as "a child of nature, half timid and half wild ... good-humored and violent." Poorly educated, Patti was nonintellectual. Another friend said he had "never perceived in Adelina the least interest in the higher problems of mankind—in science, politics, religion, not even in belles lettres."

SEX PARTNERS: The major interest in her life, next to singing, was men. In 1868, when she was 25, she married Henri, the Marquis de Caux, equerry to Napoleon III. The emperor had seen Patti perform in Paris and had sent the marquis backstage to convey his congratulations. Middle-aged, dapper, refined—but with an income of only 10,000 francs a year—Henri became enamored of Patti. She rather liked him, liked the idea of a title, although she never loved him. At their Catholic wedding in England, Patti wore a virginal white satin gown trimmed with lace and designed by Worth of Paris. But she was anything but a virgin. One of the guests at the wedding breakfast was Giovanni Mario, the handsome 58-year-old Italian tenor who had played opposite Patti in many operas. During the breakfast, Mario leaned over to British music critic Sutherland Edwards and whispered, "The marquis, much as he might be attached to his fascinating bride, has never made love to her as much as I, her constant lover, have done."

The marriage produced no passion and no children. After seven years Patti fell in love with her new leading man, the Italian tenor Ernesto Nicolini. The pair played Romeo and Juliet onstage, and offstage as well. Nicolini's wife and five children were distressed. The Marquis de Caux was furious. He forbade his wife ever to appear on a stage with Nicolini again. Patti ignored her husband and appeared with Nicolini in *La Traviata* in St. Petersburg. Enraged, the marquis cornered Patti in her dressing room and shouted that her adultery had besmirched the title he had given her. "You can take your title back!" Patti cried, scooping up a handful of jewelry and throwing it in his face. The marquis hit her. She screamed. Stagehands had to break down her door to evict her husband. The pair separated in 1877. It took Patti eight years to get a French divorce, and she got it then only after she agreed to give the marquis half her fortune. His share came to 1.5 million francs.

Even before the divorce Patti and Nicolini had been scandalously living together in Craig-y-Nos Castle on their magnificent rural estate in South Wales. He had his billiard room illuminated by the first electric lights to be installed in a country house in Britain, and she had her private theater. He was 52 and she 43 when they finally were wed in a Protestant ceremony in June, 1886.

The happy union lasted a dozen years, until Nicolini's death in 1898. Less than a year later Patti, almost 56, married her third husband, Baron Rolf Cederström of Stockholm, who was 30 years younger than she was. They remained together until her death 19 years later. The baron lived until 1947.

QUIRKS: Adelina Patti was not as sexually straight as she seemed. Occasionally she fancied something different in a heterosexual partner. One day in 1882, when she was 39, she was riding in her carriage in New York, gazing out at the storefronts. Momentarily, her eyes held on Bunnell's Curiosity Dime Museum, for something in the window caught her attention. She stopped her carriage, stepped down, and walked to the window. She stared at a photograph advertising the appearance of an attractive male midget named General Mite. The midget's actual name was Dudley Foster, and he came from Nova Scotia. He was 20 years old, less than 2 ft. tall—actually, his height was 22 in.—and he weighed 10 lb. Something about him excited Patti. She went into the museum and told Foster she would like to take him home for a while. The midget was delighted. Patti made arrangements with the proprietor and then carted the tiny Foster off to her boudoir. Their subsequent coupling (or whatever) and bizarre affair became the talk of show business for years.

—I. W.

Sparrow

ÉDITH PIAF (Dec. 19, 1915–Oct. 11, 1963)

HER FAME: A cabaret singer who rose from the streets to receive worldwide acclaim, Piaf was the beloved of her fellow Frenchmen because she was the very voice of romance. "La Vie en Rose," "Les Trois Cloches," and "Non, Je ne Regrette Rien" are just a few of the hundreds of songs she sang about the suffering and sweetness of love.

Piaf with her own true love, prizefighter Marcel Cerdan

HER PERSON: Édith Giovanna Gassion was born on a sidewalk in a poor district of Paris. She was promptly deserted by her mother, and later by her acrobat father as well. Consequently Édith and her half sister, Momone, were raised in their grandmother's house of prostitution. Momone, who was younger, became Édith's confidante and alter ego; they remained close in later life.

Édith was discovered and renamed by her first impresario, Louis Leplée, who took her off the streets to sing in his cabaret. To him she looked like a sparrow, so he used the French slang term for that bird—*piaf*—for her stage name. She had an emotionally powerful, rich, throbbing voice which often reduced audiences to tears. Maurice Chevalier, when he heard her sing, exclaimed, "*Cette môme; elle en a dans le ventre*" ("That kid, she's got it inside").

Thin, only 4 ft. 10 in. tall, Piaf looked plain and frail. But her passion for life and love shone in her large, luminous eyes. "I've got sagging breasts," she said, "a low-slung ass, and little drooping buttocks ... but I can still get men!"

She drank enthusiastically and excessively for years, and alcohol—combined with drug problems, several auto accidents, and a turbulent emotional life—killed her at 47. Thousands paid homage at her Paris funeral, and a generation later fans were still placing flowers on her grave in Père Lachaise Cemetery.

SEX LIFE: Piaf's sexual activity was prodigious. She had already slept with many men before she was 15, and couldn't remember the first one. Like a romantic schoolgirl she fell desperately in love with each of them. Although she made millions of francs and thousands of dollars singing in Europe and the U.S., she gave most of it away; she bought wardrobes for her lovers and provided generous financial assistance to friends—like Charles Aznavour—and lovers alike. When Piaf died, she left nothing.

She was attracted to all kinds of men and jokingly subdivided her affairs into "the streets," "the sailors," "the pimps," "the flings," "the professors," and "the factory" group (so named for her part in turning out new singing talent, notably Yves Montand). "You never know a guy till you've tried him in bed," she said. "You know more about a guy in one night in bed than you do in months of conversation. In the sack, they can't cheat!"

SEX PARTNERS: Regardless of the circumstances, Édith Piaf enjoyed her innumerable lovers. During her early days of singing in the street, all she could afford was a hotel room with one bed. One young lover, Louis Dupont, didn't object to sharing the bed with Édith and Momone. "There was a deep purity in Édith," said Momone, "which nothing ever spoiled. Three in a bed may not be right, of course, but at 17 and as poor as we were, love is so marvelous, it's made silently. It lulled me and I dropped off to sleep like a little kid."

Despite the many men in her life, there was but one true love, a shy, muscular, and graceful Arab-French prizefighter. Marcel Cerdan already had a wife and three sons. Called the "Moroccan Bomber," he took the middleweight crown from Tony Zale at Madison Square Garden on Sept. 21, 1948. Even when Cerdan was in training for the Zale return fight, Piaf needed to be with him constantly. She took a room in the Waldorf-Astoria for appearance' sake, but it was Momone who used it. Hiding in the trunk of Cerdan's car, Édith was smuggled into his training camp, where she stayed in a shabby bungalow that smelled of sweat and liniment, but she did not dare open the windows. Marcel joined her there during breaks in his grueling training. One day they chanced a relaxing afternoon in the open air. A friend walked by and warned them of an approaching group of reporters. Luckily there was a large willow basket close by. Cerdan stuffed Édith inside and sat down on the lid just as the reporters arrived. For the next three hours he answered questions without moving. When Piaf, cramped beyond endurance, groaned aloud, Cerdan growled a Moroccan curse and silenced her by digging his heel into the basket. She didn't complain when she finally crawled out. For Marcel she had only embraces.

A year later Piaf was in New York while Cerdan held boxing exhibitions in Europe. She missed him terribly and persuaded him to visit her, insisting that he travel by plane rather than by ship. He was killed when his plane crashed in the Azores. Momone had to have her sister sedated to prevent suicide.

Among Piaf's other lovers were actors Eddie Constantine, Yves Montand (one of the few men she was faithful to), and John Garfield. She spotted Garfield when he was in a play in Paris, and sat through the performance every night for weeks, entranced by this "handsome beast." Finally she spent the night with him. He didn't try to see her again until months later, and by then she had lost interest.

Piaf claimed not to believe in marriage, but she was married twice. In 1952 she wed Jacques Pills, a singer. They divorced five years later. In the last year of her life she married Theo Sarapo, a 26-year-old Greek hairdresser and singer, who was deeply devoted to her. After she died, he cradled her body in his arms for hours.

QUIRKS: For Piaf, men with blue eyes were especially irresistible, but she was not indifferent to the charms of any man. Each time she fell in love, it was love at first sight. Her need for love produced such tension that she slept with her hands clenched into fists. She was so obsessed by love that, as Momone said, "She went wild. She ate her heart out, she was jealous and possessive ... she howled, she locked her guys up. She was demanding, she was unbearable; they slapped her around and she cheated on them."

Whenever her lover was a blue blood, she itched to provoke him into coarse behavior. Of Paul Maurisse she said, "He's an iceberg ... a handbook of etiquette ... I'm going to make him forget his good breeding. He's going to smack me yet, do you hear? I'll get my smack out of him."

HER THOUGHTS: Édith Piaf valued love above all. Her songs and her life were full of the search for it and the pain of its loss. She said to her sister, "Can't have a house without a man, Momone. It's worse than a day without sunshine. You can get along without the sun—there's electricity. But a house without some guy's shirt lying around, where you don't run across a pair of socks, or a tie ... it's like a widow's house—it gets you down!"

—*B.J. and K.P.*

Bighearted Bessie

BESSIE SMITH (1894?–Sept. 26, 1937)

HER FAME: Bessie Smith is regarded by many as the greatest blues singer in history. Columbia Records released 44 of her recordings during her lifetime, some of which were million-sellers, and 8 posthumous LPs. Smith toured with her own vaudeville-type show and performed as a special guest in others. Her accompanists included such jazz notables as Louis Armstrong, Fletcher Henderson, Coleman Hawkins, and Benny Goodman. In 1929 she starred in a short sound film called *St. Louis Blues*, a musical dramatization of the famous W. C. Handy song. Her career

Smith by Carl Van Vechten in 1936

declined in the 1930s, primarily because of widespread economic disaster brought on by the Depression, evolution of musical tastes from blues to swing, and the advent of movies and radio as cheap entertainment. She continued to perform, but never again for the big crowds and money.

HER PERSON: Bessie Smith was born into total poverty in Chattanooga, Tenn. Her birth date is unknown, although Apr. 15, 1894, appears on her marriage license. Smith's appearance was striking, for she was a tall, heavy, very dark black woman who wore strange hats and colorful costumes onstage. She had a quick temper and would not hesitate to attack a man or woman with her bare fists. Bessie especially hated to see black people behave with servility toward whites. Occasional bouts with alcoholism were a problem in her personal life, although they rarely affected her performances. She never learned the value of money and would hand out cash to strangers. At the same time she was tightfisted about paying her own performers and crew. Despite her lusty, violent, pleasure-seeking ways, Smith was religious and would attend church whenever possible.

HER DEATH: The rumor that Smith died because a white hospital refused to treat her after a car accident is false, but this story has persistently been used as an example of Southern racism. The facts are that Bessie—who hated racism as much as anyone—died at the Afro-American Hospital in Clarksdale, Miss., where she had been taken after receiving first aid from a white doctor who happened on the scene of the auto accident.

LOVE AND SEX LIFE: Smith was married young to Earl Love, who came from a prominent black Mississippi family. The wedding took place following WWI (the exact date is unknown), and Love died soon after.

In 1922 Bessie met Jack Gee, a watchman who falsely claimed to be a policeman, and moved in with him. Although Gee was illiterate, he wanted to manage Smith's career, and did so for a while. Because of his carelessness, Bessie received only $125 per recording, and not a penny of royalties during her entire career.

In fairness to Gee, it should be remembered that while he did take advantage of Bessie later on, their affair began before Bessie was discovered. On June 7, 1923, they married in a simple ceremony. The marriage was good in the beginning but deteriorated into wild jealousy in less than three years. One time, while on tour, Bessie heard that Gee was "messing around" with a chorine in her show. Without bothering to verify the story, Bessie beat up the girl and threw her out of their railroad car onto the tracks. Gee appeared on the scene and stopped to comfort the bleeding and bruised chorine. An outraged Bessie emerged from the car and emptied Gee's own pistol in his general direction as he fled down the tracks. The train left without Gee.

Bessie was not innocent of indiscretions herself. She had her own lover on tour, a young male dancer named Agie Pitts. Bessie's affair with Pitts ended when Bessie was jailed for beating another chorine. Pitts, entrusted with the $1,000 bail money to free Bessie, skipped town instead and was soon jailed himself.

Despite their violence and infidelities, and Gee's opportunism, the couple seemed unable to break up. Whenever Gee was around, the fun-loving, carousing Bessie would be on her best behavior. They never divorced, but a final separation did occur. In early 1929 Gee financed a show with Bessie's money, making his girl friend, Gertrude Saunders, the star. This hurt Bessie more deeply than anything else Gee had done. When she read about the show in a newspaper, she took a cab from Cincinnati to Gee's hotel in Columbus, O. Fortunately, Saunders was out when Bessie arrived, for the ensuing fight with Gee left the furniture in the hotel room in a shambles, and Bessie emerged bleeding. Though Gee reunited briefly with Bessie, he returned to Gertrude. Bessie's married days were over.

She took the breakup very hard and began drinking heavily. A brief affair with blues singer Lonnie Johnson did not relieve her loneliness. The Great Depression finally began to affect Bessie, a year and a half after most other performers had been forced to give up. But she still toured, and when her troupe stopped in Chicago in the summer of 1939, an old platonic friendship with bootlegger Richard Morgan grew into the love she had never had before. Morgan genuinely admired Bessie both as an artist and as a person, and she was happier than she had ever been. Morgan was tall, handsome, a sharp dresser, and he liked having a good time as much as Bessie did. His profitable bootlegging operations, and his management of Bessie's business affairs, helped end her financial decline. He also filled the void left by Gee and Bessie's adopted son Jack, Jr. (whom Gee had kidnapped and placed in foster homes). Bessie and Morgan lived together happily until Bessie's death in 1937.

It is not known when Bessie began to enjoy sex with women, but the first provable affair was in late 1926. Lillian Simpson was a young chorine in Bessie's show, and she regularly slept in Bessie's room on the railroad car. One night Bessie kissed Lillian publicly in the car, and the girl objected. Bessie threatened to throw her out of the show, saying, "The hell with you, bitch. I got 12 women on this show and I can have one every night if I want it." Simpson attempted suicide four nights later. Bessie saved her life, and the episode seemed to release Lillian's inhibitions, for she never complained again. But the whole troupe feared Gee might visit the tour at any time, as he usually did when he ran out of money, and discover the lesbian affair. Gee finally did catch Bessie in a compromising situation with another chorine named Marie. He chased them through the hotel corridors, and Bessie hid in a girl friend's room, terrified as only Gee could make her. When Gee ran down the street thinking Bessie had escaped from the hotel, Bessie quickly told the entire troupe to grab what they could carry and run for the train depot. Still in pajamas, the entourage quietly slipped out of Detroit in a darkened railroad car.

Another of Bessie's fears was that Gee would discover her visits to "buffet flats." Buffet flats were small, private establishments run by women which featured gambling, sex shows, and kinky or straight sex for the customers. Bessie went only to watch, afraid word would get back to her husband if she participated.

HER SONGS: The lyrics of Bessie's songs, some of which she wrote, were masterpieces of the sexual double entendre. A classic example is "Kitchen Man," written by Razaf and Belledna, in which "Madame Bucks" who is "quite deluxe" receives notice from her cook:

> *His frankfurters are oh so sweet;*
> *How I like his sausage meat;*
> *I can't do without my kitchen man.*
>
> *Oh how that boy can open clams;*
> *No one else can touch my hams;*
> *I can't do without my kitchen man.*
> *When I eat his donuts, all I leave is the hole.*
> *Anytime he wants to, why he can use my sugarbowl.*

—*J.M.*

The Maestro Seducer

LEOPOLD STOKOWSKI (Apr. 18, 1882–Sept. 13, 1977)

HIS FAME: A flamboyant showman, Leopold Stokowski served as conductor or music director for the Cincinnati, Philadelphia, NBC, Hollywood Bowl, New York Philharmonic, and Houston Symphony orchestras during his 75-year career. He popularized avant-garde compositions, instituted "pops" and youth concerts, and introduced modern technology to the concert hall.

Stokowski at age 54

HIS PERSON: Born in London, England, Stokowski was the son of an immigrant Polish cabinetmaker and his Irish wife. By the age of seven Leopold was introduced to music, and he learned to play the violin, piano, and organ before he was 13. While working as a church organist, Stokowski was discovered by a wealthy member of the congregation, who sponsored him at the Royal College of Music, after which he entered Queen's College, Oxford.

Stokowski then studied in France and Germany before playing as an organist in prestigious churches in London and New York City. In 1909 the ambitious young musician became the conductor of the Cincinnati Symphony Orchestra despite the fact that he had no experience as a conductor. From Cincinnati he went to Philadelphia, where in the next three decades he created a symphony orchestra that gained world renown.

A great experimenter, Stokowski was one of the first conductors to record classical music and the first to introduce electrical instruments in the orchestra. Working in Hollywood during the late 1930s, he was musical supervisor for Walt Disney's *Fantasia* and performed in two other films.

After an amazingly productive and creative career, Stokowski died in his sleep in Nether Wallop, England, at the age of 95.

SEX LIFE: Tall, handsome, slender, and blond, Stokowski devoted almost as much time and energy to the seduction of women as he did to his music. Of his early affairs we have only rumors until 1906, when he met concert pianist Olga Samaroff—born Lucie Hickenlooper in San Antonio, Tex. After five years as lovers, they married. Stokowski demanded that his new wife give up her career to help further his. For a decade she used her time and influence to secure his advancement. However, upon moving to Philadelphia Stokowski began his bedroom wanderings, and in 1923 Olga—tired of her husband's domineering personality and sexual escapades—sued for divorce.

After Olga's departure, Stokowski conducted his sexual affairs openly. In his bedroom with its chartreuse walls, he entertained Philadelphia society women, actresses, and chambermaids. Also, he became well known for his labors with the teenage female student body of Philadelphia's prestigious music school, the Curtis Institute. His liaisons with these students became so notorious that the local citizens often referred to Curtis Institute as Coitus Institute. Stokowski showed little prejudice in his selection of bedmates, sleeping with single and married women alike. He referred to his sex companions as "nurses" because, in his words, "They are angels of mercy who rejuvenate us." (Stokowski's sex partners praised his general performance but complained of his sporadic impotence.)

In 1926 at the age of 44, Stokowski suddenly dropped his 19-year-old debutante girl friend to marry Evangeline Johnson, an heiress to the Johnson and Johnson fortune, whom he had known for three weeks. A liberated woman active in social causes, Evangeline accepted her new husband's claim that he needed his sexual maraudings to stimulate his musical creativity.

During the 1920s and 1930s, Stokowski's musical fame and reports of his bedroom conquests raised him to the rank of a national sex symbol. This was reinforced in 1937, when Stokowski seduced Greta Garbo, who reported, "I felt the electricity going through me from head to toe." During this tumultuously romantic affair, the couple resided in Italian villas, where Stokowski—a health fanatic—introduced Greta to yoga. However, after 10 months the flame suddenly died, and so did Stokowski's second marriage. Complaining of her husband's oppressive personality, long absences, and headline affairs with movie stars, Evangeline sued for divorce.

Stokowski continued his libertine ways until 1945, when he stopped off in Reno, Nev., on his way from New York to Los Angeles. There he married Gloria

Vanderbilt, who had just divorced her first husband. Like his two previous wives, Gloria was beautiful, young (23 years old), and rich (two years earlier she had inherited $5 million). At the age of 63, Stokowski had changed little. In 1956 *Look* magazine reported that Gloria's position in the marriage was "like that of an Arab wife: obedient, almost slavish, doing everything for her husband and her children and nothing for herself." Stokowski's demands on Gloria led her to a psychiatrist, who helped her become more assertive, which, in turn, ended the marriage. In 1962 she sued Stokowski for a divorce.

After this last divorce, Stokowski's sexual adventures decreased in frequency, probably because he was then over 80. However, until his death 15 years later, Stokowski continued to have occasional affairs.

HIS THOUGHTS: When asked by a friend whether he felt guilt over the fact that he was sleeping with a fellow musician's wife, Stokowski replied, "None. Conscience is that which hurts when everything else feels marvelous. The percentage is against it!"

—*R.J.F*

The Closet Z

PËTR ILICH TCHAIKOVSKY (May 7, 1840–Nov. 6, 1893)

HIS FAME: By composing such works as *Swan Lake, The Nutcracker, Sleeping Beauty*, and his Sixth Symphony, known as the "Pathétique," Tchaikovsky established a reputation as one of the world's great musical geniuses.

HIS PERSON: Though strong, handsome, and abundantly talented, Tchaikovsky suffered from neurasthenia throughout his life. This precarious emotional condition was touched off when his governess, Fanny Durbach, left the family employ in 1848. This was the first in a series of painful separations from mother figures which he was to experience. His

Tchaikovsky in 1868

actual mother died when he was 14, leaving him so inconsolable that 25 years later he wept uncontrollably for days after coming across a packet of her letters.

Following a miserable four-year stint as a clerk in the ministry of justice in St. Petersburg, he turned his full attention to music in 1863. He taught at the

Moscow Conservatory of Music and threw himself into Moscow nightlife, becoming a gay young fop who was popular at parties for his ability to create spontaneous melodies on the piano. But even his successes had a pathetic side. The first time he conducted a piece of his own in public, he hallucinated that his head was going to come off unless he held it absolutely rigid. He didn't conduct in public again for 10 years. In 1866 he suffered a nervous breakdown one night while composing and was so frightened by the experience that he gave up nocturnal composing forever.

SEX LIFE: He called the murky undercurrent of his sexual life Z, using the letter in his diaries to refer to his homosexuality (alternately called "This" in letters to his homosexual brother, Modest). "Z tortures me unusually today," reads one diary entry. Another reads: "Was very tortured, not by the sensation of Z itself, but by the fact that it is in me." Who his homosexual lovers were is uncertain since he so feared exposure that he kept his activities extremely circumspect. One likely candidate, however, is Vladimir Shilovsky, his favorite student at the conservatory and his frequent, often secret, traveling companion, to whom he dedicated two of his early piano pieces. Another is Vladimir "Bob" Davidov, his nephew, whose attraction for him is made clear in a number of diary entries. "Oh, how perfect is Bob," he wrote in one. "Am terribly reluctant to go away from here. I think it's all on account of Bob," he wrote in another. Havelock Ellis called the Sixth Symphony, which Tchaikovsky dedicated to Davidov, "the homosexual tragedy."

His agonizing homosexuality, and the earlier heartbreak at losing Fanny and then his mother, made it just about impossible for him to have a normal relationship with a woman. The closest he came to such a thing was with Désirée Artôt, a French opera singer he met in 1868, while she was touring Russia. He fell madly in love with her and they became engaged, but his friends' concern that he would fall into Désirée's shadow awakened his own fears and caused him to postpone the wedding. Artôt resumed her tour and almost immediately married a Spanish baritone. Tchaikovsky was crushed.

In 1877 he married Antonina Ivanova Milyukova, a student of his at the conservatory. Antonina had professed an undying love in her letters, and she determined to marry him despite his admission of homosexuality. By all accounts she was deluded and stupid, constantly imagining that men were trying to seduce her and unable to name a single piece of her husband's music. Tchaikovsky married her out of pity, confusing her with Tatyana, the victim of love in Pushkin's *Eugene Onegin* (the basis for an opera Tchaikovsky produced in 1877-1878). Three months after the marriage the composer fled, and he spent the rest of his life trying to extricate himself from the commitment. He attempted suicide, standing up to his armpits in the Moscow River one October night in hopes of catching pneumonia. He tried confessing to adulteries he hadn't committed in order to secure a divorce, but she wouldn't hear of it. He even contemplated murdering Antonina. Finally he learned of her own adultery in 1881, but now he hesitated to seek a divorce for fear she might tell the world about him. In the ensuing years she became increasingly deranged and carried on an endless string of affairs which resulted in several children. Nonetheless, Tchaikovsky faithfully supported her until his death in 1893. Three years later she was committed to an asylum, where she died in 1917.

As odd as his marriage was, it was no more bizarre than his relationship with Nadezhda Filaretovna von Meck, a wealthy widow nine years Tchaikovsky's senior, who had such an addiction to music that she included pianists (among them Debussy) as members of her household staff. She fell in love with Tchaikovsky's music and was his patron for 14 years. They communicated solely by letter, filling three volumes of oftentimes intimate correspondence. Even while he occupied an apartment of hers in Italy and she lived but a half-mile away in a villa, the two never spoke. In 1890, for some unknown reason, she broke off all communication with Tchaikovsky, and when he lay dying of cholera in St. Petersburg three years later, he repeated her name over and over again in what his brother Modest described as a "reproachful tone."

HIS THOUGHTS: When asked by Nadezhda Filaretovna von Meck if he had ever experienced love, he replied: "If you had phrased your question differently, if you had asked me whether I had ever discovered complete happiness in love, I should have answered no, and no again…. If, however, you ask me whether I have ever experienced the entire power and inexpressible tension of love, I must answer yes, yes, yes. For time and again I have labored to render in music all the anguish and ecstasy of love."

—D.R.

The Cocksure Composer

RICHARD WAGNER (May 22, 1813–Feb. 13, 1883)

HIS FAME: A multitalented genius, Wagner was the leading German composer of the late 19th century, and his revolutionary composition techniques crucially affected the development of modern opera. His magnum opus is *The Ring of the Nibelung*, a four-opera series based on Norse mythology.

HIS PERSON: Wagner was an arresting figure, with piercing blue eyes set in a large head, severe features, and an initially reserved manner. He had little formal musical education but was adept at reading music in his childhood. Skilled as a writer and poet, he became his own librettist, and his operas are recognized as much for their poetry as for their musical scores. Unfortunately, his amazing knowledge doomed Wagner to continual disappointment when his works were produced, because no musician or performer could conduct, act, or sing them as well as he.

Wagner was well aware of his capabilities and was noted for his conceit. He regularly regaled friends with dramatic readings of his writings, and these—plus his incessant, passionate conversation—ensured that he was always the center of attention. One evening when his guests were peacefully chatting, Wagner was so annoyed that he screamed until all eyes were once again riveted on him.

Wagner sincerely believed that, owing to his genius, it was the duty of others to support his extravagant lifestyle. "The world ought to give me what I need. Is it an unheard-of demand if I hold that the little luxury I like is my due? I who am procuring enjoyment to the world and to thousands?"

Cosima and Richard Wagner

His standard of living required a lot of money, which was provided by friends, admirers, patrons, and his salary from conducting jobs. Wagner's creativity demanded sensuous surroundings. No angular objects, such as books, no noise or commonplace odor was allowed to remind him of the real world. Rooms were draped with varicolored satins and silks, with violet and red predominating. Thick carpets covered the floors, perfumes scented his chambers, and natural light was muted. He dressed in similar luxury, favoring lace shirts, satin pants, fur-lined slippers, and satin or silk dressing gowns. His preferred colors were yellow and pink.

The combination of his opulent tastes and financial irresponsibility put Wagner in constant debt. He spent one night in debtors' prison and had to leave two cities hastily to avoid arrest. (One of these escapes required that he, his wife, and their dog cross the Russian border; if caught, they would have been shot.)

In later years Wagner adopted a vehement anti-Semitism that sometimes embarrassed his family and his benefactors. He was much more talk than action, though, and the three men who were responsible for his last production—*Parsifal* in 1882—were Jews.

LOVE LIFE: The composer's attraction to women began when he was a boy and became aroused at the touch of his sisters' clothing. At 13 he boarded with another family and enjoyed "pretending to be too sleepy to move so that I might be carried to bed by the girls." Wagner detested being alone and constantly sought out feminine company. He felt that women, much more than men, had the capacity to understand and sympathize with him and with his art. His fondness for the opposite sex carried him through many affairs, both before and after his marriage. He was always searching for a "love that knew no bounds in the way of trust and self-surrender." He wanted a woman who was unquestioningly devoted to him and willing to be devoured in return. His lovers ranged from intellectuals to maids and covered all age groups. They included one amiable young woman who also served as his housekeeper and cooked and cleaned in her pink pantaloons to please him.

However, his most notorious attachment was not to a woman but to 18-year-old Ludwig II, king of Bavaria. (Wagner initially avoided his messenger, fearing the stranger was a creditor.) The blatantly homosexual king idolized Wagner's music and provided the composer with housing and money. Infatuated with the older man, Ludwig addressed Wagner in letters as "My loved one" and "Darling of my soul." Wagner reported spending hours with the king engaged in earnest conversations about art and music or simply sitting in enraptured silence. He was sufficiently involved to write: "Shall I be able to renounce women completely? With a deep sigh I confess I could almost wish it! ... Now he is everything to me, world, wife and child!" The king evidently wasn't enough, however, for Wagner was simultaneously living with Cosima von Bülow (later his wife). The royal liaison was ended after a year and a half by the king's advisers, who objected to Wagner's "unwholesome influence" on the monarch.

SEX PARTNERS: In 1836 Richard married Christiane Wilhelmine "Minna" Planer. She was 27 and he was 23. The pretty, sedate leading lady of a regional theater troupe had been ardently pursued by its young conductor for two years and had rejected his proposals several times. Their marriage contained early bright spots, but was largely composed of 25 years of fights, jealousy, intellectual and emotional differences, and separations. Minna steadfastly stood by Wagner during his poverty-stricken early years, but his inability to remain debt-free and his flights of imagination alienated her sensibilities. Moreover, Wagner expected her to be content housekeeping while he pursued his extramarital loves and his work. In 1847 Wagner tried to convince 37-year-old Minna that she was too old and frail for sex. He wrote her, "What is a young passion compared to an *old* love such as ours? Passion is only fine when it ends in love in this sense...." Minna finally agreed with him 11 years later, when her heart trouble was aggravated by the discovery of her husband's affair with Mathilde Wesendonk.

In April of 1848 Wagner met Jessie Laussot, a beautiful 21-year-old English-woman whose husband financially supported Wagner. Jessie's intellectual capacities endeared her to Wagner, and they plotted to flee to Greece together. But her husband discovered the plan, threatened to shoot Wagner, took his wife to the country, and, when Richard followed, had the police run him out of France. (His visa had expired.) In the end Wagner felt that Jessie had failed him by not rushing to his side against all odds.

Several years later Wagner, in his early 40s, became enamored of another patron's wife, Mathilde Wesendonk, his inspiration for *Tristan und Isolde*. He revered her as his muse and insisted that their relationship was on an otherworldly plane and totally virtuous. Of course, he also declared, "she is and remains my first and only love," and stated that her love was his highest possession. Scrupulously honest, Mathilde made her husband her confidant and convinced him to support Wagner financially, provide him with a house next to their own, desist from sexual relations with her, and maintain warm, friendly relations with the composer. Wagner regularly crossed the garden to converse with her, and servants also ferried messages. Minna Wagner did not agree that their love was pure after she intercepted a hotly worded letter. In a rage, she went first to her husband and then to Mathilde. Mathilde, aghast that Wagner had neither been honest with his wife nor mollified her anger, became estranged from the composer and returned to her husband's bed. Minna moved out, and except for brief periods the Wagners did not live together again.

At 50 Wagner became the lover of 25-year-old Cosima von Bülow, whom he had known for 10 years. She was the daughter of his friend Franz Liszt and Countess Marie d'Agoult, and the wife of his favorite pupil and dear friend, Hans von Bülow. Five years earlier Wagner had been involved with her older sister, Blandine, who was prettier, but Cosima was to become his true love.

On their honeymoon the Von Bülows went to Zurich, where they visited Wagner at the Asyl, the country home of Mathilde Wesendonk, with whom the composer was in love at the time. His wife, Minna, was there also. When Mathilde visited the Asyl, the trio of women Wagner loved—Minna, Mathilde, and Cosima—was assembled under one roof.

In the beginning Cosima was openly shared by Wagner and Von Bülow, but eventually she left her husband, taking their two children, and went to live with Wagner and the two children she had borne him. After Minna died and Von Bülow sued for divorce on grounds of infidelity, Cosima and Richard were married in 1870. She ran the household and Richard's life efficiently, and emerged as the woman who was best suited to live with the genius on a daily basis.

Wagner died in Cosima's arms after a heart attack. She clung to his body for 24 hours, then cut off her long hair and placed it in the coffin on his heart.

HIS THOUGHTS: "Soul, character, talent—everything, in fact, shrivels up unless new and extraordinary relations, and always highly passionate ones, are entered into."

—P.A.R.

VIII

Rockin' and Rollin'

"God Is Gay"

KURT COBAIN (Feb. 20, 1967–Apr. 5, 1994)

HIS FAME: Every generation, it seems, demands its dead idols. The lead singer of the grunge band Nirvana, Cobain rose to fame by mainstreaming the underground post-punk and hardcore sound of the 1980s, causing an unprecedented sea change in popular music and the self-image of the American teenager— yet in addition to the revitalizing energy he poured into rock music, his suicide in 1994 would cast an even greater pall over popular music, lasting for more than a decade.

HIS PERSON: The man who put Seattle on the map as a cultural mecca, Kurt Cobain was born in Aberdeen, Washington. His parents divorced when he was a child, an act that profoundly scarred him. An unenthusiastic student, Cobain spent his time pursuing art and baiting the other students by spray-painting messages like "God is Gay" and "Homo Sex Rules" across town, for which he was briefly arrested. Given his first guitar by an uncle at 14, Cobain trained himself to play with determination before meeting bassist Krist Novoselic. The duo instantly gelled, forming the first incarnation of Nirvana. Going through a *Spinal Tap*-worthy succession of drummers, Nirvana would eventually settle on Dave Grohl, shortly thereafter finding overnight international success with their hugely popular second album, *Nevermind*. It was at this time that Kurt found his Yoko: actress, performer, stripper and seasoned rock-star succubus Courtney Love. The two bonded over post-punk music and, especially, heroin, and were married within the year. Love was already pregnant with the couple's daughter, Frances Bean (allegations that Love had not ceased using heroin during the child's pregnancy would soon sweep the press). Cobain himself had likely been a user since 1986, and a fully-fledged addict since 1990; he spent most of Nirvana's successful years nodding out at the wheel and more-than-occasionally overdosing. The stresses of fame mounting through the release of *In Utero*, the band's tormented 1994 follow-up to *Nevermind*, found Cobain in a suicidal mood. An unsuccessful suicide attempt in March of the year was followed by a successful attempt in April, when Cobain escaped from rehab and was subsequently found dead in his Lake Washington home with a shotgun wound to the head. Although his death was ruled a suicide, many fans believe that he was murdered. Though many blame heroin for Cobain's downward spiral, he had often remarked that heroin was the only thing keeping him from the grave.

LOVE LIFE: Cobain's first and most formative sexual experience was with a developmentally disabled girl. Already suicidal at age 16, and determined to lose his virginity before he went, Kurt followed a "half-retarded" girl home with two of his friends. After they left, he stayed. "I tried to fuck her, but I didn't know how," he wrote later. "I got grossed out very heavily with how her vagina smelled and how her sweat reeked, so I left." Later interrogated by the police after the father claimed his daughter had been molested, Kurt escaped charges when it turned out the girl was over 18, and not legally mentally disabled. Kurt was deeply scarred, however, and incessantly tormented over the scandal. Furthermore, he was friends with a gay student and, though not gay himself, he remarked "I Am Not Gay, Although I wish I were, just to piss off homophobes." Cobain was famous for wearing dresses onstage, leading to further rumors.

He was a relentless troublemaker on the behalf of the downtrodden, and he carried this role with him into his adult career, most famously in the lyrics of one of his finest songs, "All Apologies": "What else could I say? Everyone is gay." Some have suspected that Cobain was indeed homosexual and struggled to hide it behind a sham family life and drugs and, eventually, his possible suicide; what is certain, however, is that heroin at times took much of the place of sex for Cobain, gay or straight. Cobain's sexuality, like that of many addicts, was somewhat less than heroic. He gave up sex completely for a period at the age of 23 and stopped masturbating for months, writing in his journal that "I am a male age 23 and I'm lactating. My breasts have never been so sore, not even after receiving titty twisters from bully schoolmates. I haven't masturbated in months because I've lost my imagination. I close my eyes and I see my father, little girls, German Shepherds, TV news commentators, but no voluptuous pouty-lipped naked female sex kittens wincing in ecstasy. I see lizards and flipper babies." His meeting with Love, however, changed that—Kurt had had a few short, emotionally traumatic relationships previously (including six months with Bikini Kill's Tobi Vail), but Courtney was the one. He often spoke in interviews of the couple's exhibitionist penchant for copulating against walls in public, among many other less-than-appetizing displays (both individuals bore the look of homeless squatters throughout the early nineties; Radio One DJ John Peel once remarked of Love's appearance, shortly after Cobain's death, that she "would have drawn whistles of astonishment in Bedlam." By many accounts, Cobain's relationship with Courtney Love was a downward spiral of drug abuse and psychodrama, with Love continually pushing him further down into the depths and stripping away his self-confidence. Seattle Police Department reports from the couple's many domestic disturbance calls reek of animalistic rage—Courtney throws a glass at Kurt's face; Kurt chokes her on the floor and slashes her arms with the broken glass; both parties refuse any medical treatment. The situation only worsened. Drugs and despair took Cobain's sex drive in turns; after a suicide attempt it had vanished altogether. As Love later told *Spin* magazine, "I

tried to have sex with him in the hospital afterward. He was just gone. Gone."
In his "suicide" note, Cobain poured out his feelings of self-loathing and unworthiness, and proclaimed "I have a goddess of a wife who sweats ambition and empathy and a daughter who reminds me too much of what I used to be, full of love and joy, kissing every person she meets because everyone is good and will do her no harm. And that terrifies me to the point where I can barely function."

HIS THOUGHTS: "I started being really proud of the fact that I was gay even though I wasn't."

—J.L.

Are You Experienced?

JIMI HENDRIX (Nov. 27, 1942–Sept. 18, 1970)

HIS FAME: Jimi Hendrix has been hailed as the greatest rock 'n' roll guitar virtuoso in history. *Life* magazine called him "a rock demigod," *The New York Times* called him "the black Elvis," and John Lennon called him the "Pied Piper of rock." Among his many hit songs were "Hey Joe," "Foxy Lady," and "Purple Haze." Among his hit albums were *Are You Experienced?* and *Electric Ladyland.* All these remain classics of acid rock.

HIS PERSON: As a guitar player, Jimi was unique, outstandingly daring and ground-breaking. As a performer, he was, well … you had to see it to believe it. He wore outlandish, crazy clothes. He writhed, he snaked, he moaned around the stage. He played his guitar at earsplitting volume with his teeth, his tongue, his elbow; but mostly, it seemed, with his crotch. One of the most sexual performers in history, Hendrix thrust his guitar madly against his groin and rubbed it between his thighs, often ending these orgasmic episodes by smashing the guitar to bits in an explosion of love and fury. At the Monterey Pop Festival of 1967, after a particularly explosive performance, he caused a sensation by dousing his guitar with lighter fluid and setting it on fire. He eventually grew tired of all these histrionics and wanted to be appreciated purely for his musical ability.

Onstage, Jimi was a wild man. Offstage, he could be anything—polite and gentlemanly, someone you could bring home to your mother (except for his clothes and general appearance), or angry and destructive. He was a true enigma. Everyone describes him differently. Sometimes he was painfully withdrawn, shy, and inarticulate. And then again he could be voluble and gregarious. Some who knew him claim it was impossible to get really close to him; others speak wistfully of the deep intimacy they shared with him. But who knew what he was really like? Possibly Jimi was as confused about himself as everyone else. He frequently had fits of violence and tears, beating up girl friends and smashing furniture, for which he would apologize abjectly afterwards. His song lyrics ranged, like Jimi himself, from the cosmic:

> *Purple Haze was in my brain*
> *Lately things don't seem the same*
> *Actin' funny, but I don't know why*
> *Scuse me while I kiss the sky.*
> *to the fleshly*
> *But first are You experienced?*
> *Ah! have you ever been experienced?*
> *Well, I have.*

He certainly frequented parts of the mind that most of us have never visited once.

Jimi Hendrix's cultural heritage may be a key to his many-sidedness. His father was an easygoing black gardener in Seattle, his mother was a hard-drinking American Indian, and his stepmother was Japanese. For most of his life Jimi was not especially conscious of his "blackness" and chose his friends and lovers from all races and nationalities. He picked up the guitar at an early age, left home to join the army, became a parachute jumper, and was discharged when he was injured. Then he began his travels, playing backup guitar for such greats as the Isley Brothers, B. B. King, Sam Cooke, Wilson Pickett, Ike and Tina Turner, King Curtis, James Brown, and Little Richard.

In 1966 he was discovered in New York by Chas Chandler, formerly of the Animals. Chandler took him to England, put him together with two English musicians, and managed the Jimi Hendrix Experience. They took England by storm but scandalized mothers and teenyboppers in America, where they opened the show for the clean-cut Monkees. The Experience was thrown off the tour, which was great publicity. *Rolling Stone* called Jimi "the first black performer to take on white rock 'n' roll head-on and win."

Jimi handled success relatively well at first, but eventually business and legal difficulties, the pressures of the road, and the breakup of the band exhausted and depressed him. Popular opinion holds that Jimi was a heavy drug abuser. And he did try everything—LSD, uppers, booze, even snorting a little heroin. The manner of his shocking, sudden death at 27 added to the reputation. He took too many sleeping pills and died of suffocation, having inhaled his own vomit. Some called it suicide, but it was undoubtedly at least as much an accident as Janis Joplin's tragic drug death three weeks later.

The loss of Jimi Hendrix truly rocked the rock 'n' roll world. A genius was dead.

SEX LIFE: The consummate superstud, Hendrix is something of a sexual legend today. His appetite was voracious, and he often indulged it with three or more girls at a sitting (or lying). He was exotically good-looking, *very* famous, and so sexy. Women flocked to him like bees to honey. And what a honey he was reputed to be! One girl said his member was "damn near big as his guitar." He was one of the major black sex symbols for white women of the 1960s.

Jimi started early. Never shy about finding women, although self-conscious about his skinny chest and long arms and legs, he had his first sex at age 12. At age 15 he was expelled from high school for holding hands with a white girl during class. When his teacher confronted him with this crime, he replied, "What's the matter? Are you jealous?"

Jimi's immense popularity and his cooperation with groupies (he called them "Band-Aids") led to an unusual experience. In Chicago two chubby teenaged groupies devised a scheme to make themselves something special on the competitive market. They called themselves the Plaster Casters, dedicated to making molds and then true-to-life reproductions of rock stars' penises. Although one of the girls performed fellatio prior to the casting, it was often difficult for the stars to sustain their erections in the wet plaster. But not Jimi. One of the Plaster Casters wrote, "He has got just about the biggest rig I've ever seen! … He even kept his hard for the entire minute. He got stuck, however, for about 15 minutes (his hair did) but he was an excellent sport—didn't panic … actually enjoyed it and balled the impression after it had set. In fact, I believe the reason we couldn't get his rig out was that it wouldn't GET SOFT!"

SEX PARTNERS: Despite his rampant promiscuity, Jimi had a number of intimate relationships. Today some of these girls vie for the envied historical position of having been the greatest love in Jimi Hendrix's life. Any girl who attained this status would still be second to Jimi's guitar, which he called his "Electric Lady." His greatest human love was probably Kathy Etchingham, an attractive redheaded English girl with whom he lived on and off in London for over three years. She said that Jimi "used girls like some people smoke cigarettes," and that he had children in Sweden, the United States, and Germany. Kathy usually didn't mind his groupie infidelities. There were occasions, though, when one or the other got jealous, and there were fights. During one of these, Jimi fractured Kathy's nose with his foot. She took her revenge by hitting him over the head with a frying pan while he was asleep. Once she was attacked and viciously beaten by four jealous groupies. Later, when Kathy married, her husband agreed that she could still go out with Jimi.

There were a number of other girls with whom Jimi had involved relationships; some he lived with, but never monogamously. "If I stay with one person too long," he said, "I feel more obligated than I do pleased."

One long-lasting, unconventional relationship was with groupie Devon Wilson. Devon was black, tall, voluptuous, regal (she looked like Jimi), bright, and wily. She was totally into sex, and also totally into heroin (which Jimi did not approve of). She had been a teenage prostitute, had been rescued by composer Quincy Jones, and eventually turned Queen of the Groupies. She served for years as Jimi's lover, pimp, secretary, drug procurer, and girl Friday. In return he gave her companionship, a salary, sex, love of a sort, and a distinguished position among her peers. He wrote a song about her, half-erotic, half-sardonic—called "Dolly Dagger"—(a word play on her on-off affair with Mick Jagger, of whom Jimi was a little jealous) which went: "… her love's so heavy / Gonna make you stagger."

One unconsummated passion (these were rare) was with singer Marianne Faithfull, then Mick Jagger's girl friend. One night after playing in a London club, Jimi seated himself between Mick and Marianne at their table. According to biographer David Henderson, Jimi turned his back to Mick and whispered in Marianne's ear that he "wanted to fuck her and that she should leave Mick who was a cunt and come with him, right now." A tempted Marianne refused.

When Jimi met Monika Danneman, a tall German ice-skating instructor, he played a whole concert to her in the midst of a crowd of thousands. Naturally, it thrilled her, but she played it cool for a while. Monika did fall madly in love with Jimi, and he was her first lover. She claimed they were going to be married, which friends doubted. True love or not, it was Monika who was with him the night he died.

HIS THOUGHTS: "It was fun. I didn't know it was anger until they told me that it was—all that destruction. Maybe everybody should have a room where they can get rid of all their inhibitions. So my room was a stage."

—*A.W.*

Take My Breath Away

MICHAEL HUTCHENCE (Jan. 22, 1960–Nov. 22, 1997)

HIS FAME: The lead singer of Australian chart-toppers INXS, Michael Hutchence was one of the most prominent, charismatic and successful rock musicians of the 1980s. He rode high throughout the '80s, dating supermodels and actresses and launching his own acting career before crashing in the '90s and, eventually, committing suicide in 1997 in an act of autoerotic asphyxiation.

HIS PERSON: Born in Sydney and raised in Hong Kong, Hutchence was the son of a model-turned-makeup artist and a businessman. Returning to Sydney in his teens, he befriended Andrew Farriss—along with Farriss' brothers and friends, the duo would form the band The Farriss Brothers, which would soon change its name to INXS with the release of their first album in 1980. It was under this name that Hutchence proceeded to co-write and perform, with Farriss, some of the most crowd-pleasing rock songs of the 1980s, such as "New Sensation," "Devil Inside" and "Need You Tonight." Producing several *Billboard* smash albums, their popularity peaked with 1987's album *Kick*. In many ways INXS had found themselves in the right place at the right time: instead of remaining another Stones knock-off Australian pub-rock band, INXS was perfectly suited to capitalize on the new medium of the music video. Both Hutchence's mother and sister were actresses and he had spent much of his youth on film sets. Combined with the looks and fashion sense he had inherited from his model mother, Hutchence was the nascent MTV network's dream come true. By the 1990s, however, the band's

slick and accessible style was on the way out: attempts to experiment with the band's sound met with complete critical and financial disaster in the United States, despite success in the UK and Europe. A 1997 comeback effort, *Elegantly Wasted*, completely tanked in the U.S. yet again; it was tragically followed by Hutchence's probably accidental death in November of the year—he was found hung by a belt in his Sydney hotel room, ruled the result of autoerotic asphyxiation.

SEX PARTNERS: If Hutchence's final moments were lonely ones, such was not the case throughout the preceding years. One of the most recognizable sex symbols of the decade, Hutchence's every move was trailed by the Australian tabloids as he dated a string of actresses, supermodels and singers—most famously the nascent Aussie diva Kylie Minogue in 1989, whom he helped to transform from an innocent soap actress into the internationally-worshiped sex-bomb performer she quickly became. Hutchence penned the song "Suicide Blonde" about her. Of the pair's relationship, Minogue later stated, "Everything I know about sex, I learned from Michael." Their life together fell apart after Kylie caught Michael cheating on her with the supermodel Helena Christensen. Other romances included the transsexual model April Ashley, 25 years his senior, and British television presenter Paula Yates, whom he began dating after his relationship with Kylie Minogue fell by the wayside. Yates left her husband, Boomtown Rats frontman and humanitarian bard Bob Geldof, for Hutchence in 1995, after almost a decade together. Divorce was finalized within months—Hutchence and Yates' daughter, Heavenly Hiraani Tiger Lily Hutchence, was born shortly thereafter. Their couplehood was short-lived—Yates spiraled into depression after Hutchence's death, refusing to accept the suicide verdict, and subsequently found herself locked in a custody battle with Hutchence's mother and sister for the custody of her daughter. Kylie Minogue has claimed at times to the press that she believes that Hutchence's ghost still watches over her. "People might think I'm mad," she stated in the years following his death, "but I feel his presence. It's very personal. He checks in with me and it's typical of him that I feel his presence just when I need him most. It's not spooky, it's reassuring, although the force of his presence can be scary."

HIS THOUGHTS: "Fame makes me feel wanted and loved. Everybody wants that."

—J.L.

Victim Of The Kozmic Blues

JANIS JOPLIN (Jan. 19, 1943–Oct. 4, 1970)

HER FAME: Janis' whiskey-drenched, gutbucket brand of blues singing earned her comparison with the likes of her idols, Bessie Smith and Billie Holiday. She is remembered for her version of "Ball and Chain" and her four albums: *Big Brother and the Holding Company*, *Cheap Thrills*, *I Got Dem Ol' Kozmic Blues Again Mama*, and *Pearl*.

HER PERSON: Born into a middle-class family in the conservative backwater of Port Arthur, Tex., Janis was made to suffer for her nonconformity at an early age. She had an artistic bent and liked to read and paint, but neither activity was accorded much respect by her high school peers. Her "beatnik" lifestyle, coupled with the fact that she was overweight and had severe acne, earned her the cruel nickname of "Pig Face." In college she was nominated for "Ugliest Man on Campus." In turn, she adopted a self-defensive pose which stayed with her for the rest of her life—that of a hard-drinking, shoot-up-anything, good-time mama. Ever trying to become one of the boys, she often crossed into nearby Louisiana for the honky-tonk life. It was there that she discovered the blues. She began imitating the style of Bessie Smith and performed for free, or for the price of a drink, in cafés and roadhouses near Port Arthur.

She left home to join Big Brother and the Holding Company, a San Francisco based rock band, as their lead singer. Janis' virtuoso performance at the first Monterey Pop Festival (captured in the film *Monterey Pop*), coupled with the success of Big Brother's second album, *Cheap Thrills*, pushed Janis into the nations spotlight and made a cult figure of her. She used drugs and alcohol daily and made no secret of it. Janis pressured the manufacturers of Southern Comfort into giving her a fur coat for all the free publicity she'd given them. Her hell-bent image was adored by her fans and feared by her promoters. Yet at the height of her fame she often wistfully confided to friends that what she really wanted was a home life: "Just give me an old man that comes home, like when he splits at nine, I know he's gonna come back at six for me and only me, and I'll take that shit with the two garages and two TVs." When friends pleaded with her to stop using hard drugs, she told them, "Let's face it, I'll never see 30." While recording her third album in 1970, she returned to her room at the Landmark Hotel in Hollywood and mainlined a large shot of unusually pure heroin. A member of her entourage found her the next morning, dead from an overdose at age 27.

SEX LIFE: When Janis was 18, she made an ill-fated first trip to San Francisco in search of the bohemian life she had dreamed of as a high school student. She moved in with a man who soon tired of her and walked out. Throwing her arms around his knees as he walked up a San Francisco hill, she begged him not to leave her. He kept walking, dragging Janis behind him. It was a cathartic moment for her. She picked herself up, said, "O.K., Daddy, what the fuck," and resolved never again to beg for love. Strung out on Methedrine, broke and alone, she tried to sell her body for five dollars a trick and was devastated when prospective johns either laughed at her or ignored her completely. She eventually returned to Port Arthur to lick her wounds. She said of herself in this period: "I'd've fucked anything, taken anything ... I did. I'd take it, suck it, lick it, smoke it, shoot it, drop it, fall in love with it...."

In 1966 she made her second trip to San Francisco with an emissary from Big Brother, who made love to her in order to secure her services as a singer. Later, she delighted in telling people how she had been "fucked into being in Big Brother." Her constant and graphic remarks about her love life became a Joplin trademark.

Although her primary interest was heterosexual, Janis often enjoyed sex with women, and sometimes liked to indulge in threesomes with her girl friends and men she picked up at random. She had a come-on style all her own and frequently panicked potential sex partners with the directness of her approach: "I thought we'd go back to the dressing room and get it on." For these casual encounters she favored "pretty young boys" of 16 or 17.

The schoolyard taunts she had suffered stayed with her to the extent that she was unable to handle her sexy, onstage image, although her performances had the same effect on men that Jimi Hendrix's and Mick Jagger's did on women. She frequently commented that she was too ugly to attract men, and was heard to lament, "I'm a big star and I can't even get laid." Actually, she got laid quite a lot, but seldom more than a few times by the same person. Once, after a long train trip, she complained that there were over 365 men on board and she'd had sex with only 65 of them. Terrified of rejection, she histrionically faked orgasm at times, feeling that if she didn't have one it was *her* fault. On other occasions she wore partners down with demands for nonstop sex. She never let pickups become too close, because she feared being financially exploited.

Janis made a distinction between sex for the hell of it and serious relationships, and even considered marriage with one of her lovers. Her most serious relationship with a "star" involved Kris Kristofferson, with whom she fell in love. Unfortunately, a romantic triangle occurred when one of Janis' female lovers fell for him too. She also had a four-month affair with singer Country Joe McDonald, who described her as "pretty" and "a very feminine woman." According to Peggy Caserta in her book, *Going Down with Janis*, she also slept with a number of other well-known personalities.

HER THOUGHTS: "My music isn't supposed to make you wanna riot! My music is supposed to make you wanna fuck!"

"Onstage I make love to 25,000 people, then I go home alone."

—*M.J.T.*

Ride The Snake

JIM MORRISON (Dec. 8, 1943–July 3, 1971)

HIS FAME: The lead singer of The Doors, Jim Morrison remains an enduring symbol of priapic adolescent lust (rock critic Lester Bangs called him a "Bozo Dionysus"), his burning gaze staring forth from the wall of suburban teenage bedrooms, his throne in the Valhalla of Dead Rock Stars secured for eternity.

HIS PERSON: The son of an admiral, Morrison was raised throughout the United States, never settling in one place for long. However, it was the landscapes and mythology of the Southwest that left the most lasting mark on the young man, and would later come to haunt his lyrics. After studying film at UCLA, Morrison lived itinerantly on Venice Beach, writing poetry. After showing some of it to fellow student Ray Manzarek, the two formed a pact to start a band, taking the name The Doors from a line in William Blake's *The Marriage of Heaven and Hell*: "If the doors of perception were cleansed everything would appear to man as it is, infinite." After the quick addition of musicians Robby Krieger and John Densmore, the band was complete; their initial gigs at the Whisky-A-Go-Go in Los Angeles put them well on the road to stardom; they were signed to Elektra

Records in 1967. Their first album, *The Doors*, was a massive black sheep in an era of flower power, charting Morrison's excursions into his id with murder ballads like "The End," a long Oedipal freak-out in which he fantasizes about murdering his father and fucking his mother "all night long." In a career-making appearance on *The Ed Sullivan Show*, Morrison scandalized the nation by clearly singing the word "higher" in "Light My Fire." They were soon one of the most popular bands in the country, soundtracking the country's dark passage through war and assassination. His Dionysian good looks didn't last for long, however; fame and alcoholism took their toll and Morrison was smashed on the rocks, a corpulent Rasputin, by 1969. At a concert in Miami he finally "gave the audience what they wanted" and exposed himself on stage, for which he was arrested. The band split up the following year, and Morrison moved to Paris with his common-law wife Pamela Courson to pursue his writing career. He was dead by June 1971, at the age of 27 (there are persistent rumors that he faked it), found by Courson bloated and KO'd from a heroin overdose in his bathtub. His gravesite in Père Lachaise cemetery in Paris remains one of the most frequented, and vandalized, plots in the world, haunted by generation after generation of devoted fans.

SEX LIFE: What can be said about the man who made leather pants fashionable, and who had over 20 paternity suits pending against him at the time of his death? The Doors shot to prominence largely because the Whisky nightclub in Los Angeles continually booked them due to female frenzy—Elmer Valentine of the Whiskey recalls "The chicks, the chicks, the chicks all asking 'Is that horny motherfucker in black pants there tonight?'" Some of these calls were arranged by the band themselves; in a brilliant PR moment, Morrison dubbed the band "erotic politicians." Despite his revelry, Morrison remained in a relationship with L.A. groupie Pamela Courson from before the time of his success to the time of his death (she overdosed and died a few years after him). They maintained an open, and frequently tense, arrangement. Though he slept with numerous groupies and celebrities—including Grace Slick of Jefferson Airplane, *16 Magazine* editor-in-chief Gloria Stavers, Janis Joplin and Nico, who was utterly obsessed with him—the real "other woman" in his relationship was rock critic, science fiction writer and witch Patricia Kennealy. Kennealy played High Priestess to Morrison's High Priest, bewitching him with tales the old Goddess Religion, of her status in her coven, and of her hereditary connection to old witch and shamanic lineages, something she shared in common with Morrison. Jim was so impressed and so sought a deeper connection with Kennealy that he regularly removed her diaphragm before sex—this would eventually result in the conception of a child that Kennealy aborted. In her memoir of the relationship, *Strange Days*, Kennealy spoke of wanting "molecular fusion" with Morrison. The two were wedded in a Celtic Pagan handfasting ceremony, and their relationship soon ratcheted Morrison's darkside trip up even further. His increasing involvement in the occult wound up in blood-drinking rituals—coked out of his mind, Jim spent an evening quaffing blood out of the wrists of a Scandinavian groupie named Ingrid Thompson. Kennealy, however, blamed Courson's heroin death trip for

Morrison's end; the triangle between Morrison, Kennealy and Courson was vicious to say the least (Kennealy called Courson "The Redheaded Remora").

HIS THOUGHTS: "Sex is full of lies. The body tries to tell the truth, but it's usually too battered with rules to be heard, and bound with pretenses so it can hardly move. We cripple ourselves with lies."

—*J.L.*

I'll Be Your Mirror

NICO (Oct. 16, 1938–July 18, 1988)

HER FAME: Singer, musician, fashion model, actress and Warhol icon Nico cast a long shadow over the New York artistic underground of the 1960s and, by proxy, the world art scene. Most famous for her appearance on the Velvet Underground's first album at Andy Warhol's request, Nico proceeded to quietly record several solo albums that are remembered as bleak masterpieces that predated or, more accurately, created Goth.

HER PERSON: Born out of wedlock in Cologne in 1938, Christa Päffgen came into the world just in time to be conscious through the horrors of the fall of the Third Reich. She left school at the age of 13 to sell lingerie, and was soon discovered by the fashion industry, taking the name Nico while on shoot in Ibiza. Nico moved to Paris to model for the top fashion magazines of the 1950s, and made her way into commercials and films, most notably Federico Fellini's 1959 film *La Dolce Vita*. Making her way to New York, her interest soon shifted to music, and a 1965 meeting with the Rolling Stones' doomed psychedelic pioneer Brian Jones produced the inspiration for a single, "I'm Not Sayin'." As a singer Nico was unearthly, almost flat, her voice carrying the alluring songline of a ghostly and mechanical deathmarch. Her disaffection was perfect for what would become her greatest role, that of a fixture at Andy Warhol's Factory, one of the brightest superstars in the pop artist's constellation. Nico was soon partnered with the freshly-minted Factory house band the Velvet Underground. She shared billing on their first album, but only sang three songs—"I'll Be Your Mirror," "All Tomorrow's Parties" and "Femme Fatale"—all of which retain legendary status in the annals of pop music. It was also at this time that Nico began to develop the heroin addiction that would rule her life until her death. The Velvets went on to develop their often abrasive sound on several more albums and through several more lineup changes, and Nico went on to launch her solo career, although both Reed and Cale would continue to assist her. Her initial solo album *Chelsea Girl* was written almost totally by other songwriters of the day, incuding Reed, Cale, Dylan, Tim Hardin and Jackson Browne, who penned the best two songs on the album ("The Fairest of the Seasons" and "These Days"). With Cale's assistance in fleshing out the music, Nico wrote and recorded three more albums in the next decade, as well as a portion of a live album. Nico staged her 1980 comeback at New York's CBGB to critical raves; the following years produced two more albums, both highly experimental even by her standards. While riding her bicycle with her son Ari in Ibiza in 1988, Nico suffered a minor heart attack, falling and hitting her head hard enough to cause severe internal bleeding. She died shortly thereafter, at the age of 49, and was buried by her mother in Berlin.

SEX LIFE: Just as her career was beginning in 1962, Nico had her son, Ari. By her own claim, the child was fathered by the legendary French actor Alain Delon. Delon disputed the claim, though the child was subsequently raised by his parents. Jean-Marc Billancourt, a French civil servant, later claimed paternity of the child, claiming that he was a perfect body double of Alain Delon and had seduced Nico under the pretense that he was, in fact, Delon, only telling her of his real identity after she announced that she was pregnant. Ari became the youngest of Warhol's superstars when he appeared in *Chelsea Girls* in 1966; by the time of his adolescence he had grown into the mold of a perfect Factory superstar, having developed a heroin addiction just like his mother, who introduced him to the drug.

Throughout the sixties, Nico shared her bed with many of the brightest musical talents of the decade. Her affair with Lou Reed ended when she entered a roomful of people and announced, "I cannot sleep with Jews anymore." Other lovers were Brian Jones, Lou Reed, John Cale, Jackson Browne (only 17 at the time—Nico was 12 years his senior), Tim Buckley, Iggy Pop and Jim Morrison. It was Morrison that she was obsessed with over all others; the Lizard King allegedly tried to kill her during a sex magick ritual, which she claimed to have enjoyed immensely. It is also rumored (and backed up by Clinton Heylin in *Behind the Shades*, his biography of Bob Dylan) that Nico bagged Dylan for one night in 1964, after Dylan met her in Paris shortly after the beginning of her recording career. He demoed the song "It Ain't Me Babe" for her, and then penned the song "I'll Keep It With Mine" in tribute to her. Yet though Nico knew everybody, nobody truly knew her. In life, as in death, she was an enigmatic, ethereal, almost untouchable figure; despite her broad range of affairs, she despised sex, associating it with horror and madness.

The Nico biography by James Young, *The End*, recounts Nico's self-mythologizing story of her being raped by a black American sergeant when she worked as a young teenager for the American Air Force stationed in Germany. Nico also claimed the sergeant was shot for the offense, and that this episode destroyed her interest in sex for the remainder of her life. It is instructive that the subtitle of another Nico biography is *The Life and Lies of an Icon*. No American serviceman was ever shot for the crime of rape. It's also doubtful that a 15-year-old German girl was employed by the Air Force.

As Carlos Maldonaldo-Bostock remarked of her in the 1995 film *Nico Icon*, "No one loved Nico and Nico loved no one… she was just alone… she couldn't bear for anyone to touch her… Nico had sex with no one." Already distanced from herself and her reality by her rape, her experiences as a girl in the wreckage of Nazi Germany, and her shame at being an illegitimate child, Nico spent decades vanishing bit by bit into the heroin void while her physical beauty decayed and finally went completely. She had already grown to resent her looks by the mid-sixties, considering them more a liability than an asset; in the age of the "serious singer-songwriter" she felt her looks doomed her to remain seen as only a pretty face instead of a serious artist like, for instance, Janis Joplin. Her relationship to her body, and her life, was antagonistic to say the least. Had Nico passed from death directly into undeath, those around her would have in all likelihood have barely noticed, a fitting finale for the template from which every Goth that has ever existed has been drawn.

HER THOUGHTS: "You are beautiful and you are alone."

—J.L.

All Shook Up

ELVIS PRESLEY (Jan. 8, 1935–Aug. 16, 1977)

HIS FAME: Even in star heaven, Elvis is a special luminary. His importance extends way beyond his fame as the so-called "father of rock 'n' roll" or as a sex symbol. He is a god to his millions of fans the world over, his life an almost mythical rags-to-riches story.

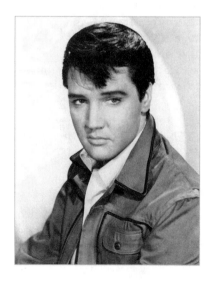

HIS PERSON: Born to a dirt-poor Mississippi family, Elvis received a guitar when he was 11 because his parents couldn't afford to give him the bicycle he wanted; the guitar was also intended to keep him out of trouble. Wanting to be different, young Elvis began to embody a duality: the Rebel and the Good Boy. On the one hand, he wore sideburns and wild pink-and-black clothes and worshiped James Dean. On the other, he was deeply religious (and would remain so), going to church regularly with his parents. After high school, he got a job as a truckdriver. It cost him $4 to make his first record, which was a birthday present for his mother. When Sam Phillips of Sun Records heard Elvis, Phillips' dream came true. He had often said, "If I could find a white man with the Negro sound and the Negro feel, I could make a billion dollars."

It all began with Sun, and Elvis' sexy, powerhouse performances. The curling lip, the sultry hooded eyes, the virile animal sexuality of the gyrating hips have been described by countless writers. Elvis Presley's performances elicited from women of all ages what can only be described as erotomania—mass sexual frenzy. As the authors of *Elvis: Portrait of a Friend* put it: "He was genuine and honest in his appreciation of girls; there were no games, just an open, sincere, sexual attraction between one boy and millions of girls." In 1955 "Colonel" Tom Parker became Elvis' adroit manager; that same year Presley signed with RCA and bought his first Cadillac—pink—for his family.

Elvis' scandalous behavior outraged the world. Hedda Hopper called him "a menace to young girls." (She later reversed her position and did the twist with him at a Hollywood party.) He was given such nicknames as "Elvis the Pelvis" and "Sir Swivel Hips"; and worst of all for Elvis, he was denounced from countless pulpits.

Billy Graham said he wouldn't want his daughter to meet Elvis. Elvis just didn't understand it; gospel singing and revival meetings were his musical roots. Deeply hurt, he defended himself by saying, "I never tried to hurt teenagers. When I sing I start jumpin'. If I stand still I'm dead." In a conversation with his mother, Elvis further explained, "I don't feel sexy when I'm singin'. If that was true I'd be in some kind of institution as some kind of sex maniac." In 1955 the Florida police forced him to perform without moving. By 1956 he had made his first million; by 1957 he had moved his parents and grandmother into a 23-room Memphis mansion called Graceland; by 1965 he was the highest-paid performer in the history of the music business. During his lifetime he grossed more than a billion dollars. Shown on the *Ed Sullivan Show* from the waist up, he was viewed by 54 million Americans, and his TV ratings were higher than President Eisenhower's.

Between 1961 and 1967 he gave no public performances. After finishing a two-year stint in the army in 1960, Elvis concentrated on making a stream of stunningly corny movies in Hollywood. Then in 1968 he reappeared on the musical scene with an NBC TV Christmas special before a live audience and began to perform in public again. But there was another side to this strange embodiment of the American Dream: flying a thousand miles with his entire entourage for a peanut-butter-and-jelly sandwich; living by night (Elvis could never go out, ever—he'd have been mobbed); shooting out TV sets during his violent outbursts. He surrounded himself with up to 15 Southern buddies—dubbed the "Memphis Mafia"—who were employed as bodyguards, valets, and royal jesters to "the King." Causing the King any slight displeasure could result in a terrifying fit of temper. Graceland became a weird prison and Elvis' life grew increasingly bizarre.

Elvis' drug use—one of his employees called him "a walking drugstore"—had begun in the army with Dexedrine. He later took uppers, downers, and painkillers in pill form or as injections, and in his last years lived in a total narcotic haze. He developed a number of classic macho obsessions; he loved guns, motorcycles, badges, uniforms, and police paraphernalia. In addition, he had severe health problems and was unquestionably fat. Knowledge of these difficulties drove fans crazy; a god was not allowed to decay. Elvis had become a kind of one-man Decline and Fall of the Roman Empire. At the age of 42 he was found dead of a heart attack in his Graceland bathroom. Technically, Elvis did not die from an overdose, although 10 different kinds of drugs were found in his bloodstream. President Carter eulogized him, saying, "He was a symbol to people the world over of the vitality, rebelliousness, and good humor of his country." Mass hysteria followed Elvis' death. Girls claimed to be making love to his ghost. The Graceland lawn was covered with fainting women who did not want to live in a world without Elvis. In a single anguished cry, millions mourned their lost youth and vowed to keep Elvis' memory alive. The King is dead, long live the King.

LOVE LIFE: Numerous biographers have insisted that Elvis' greatest love was his mother, Gladys. She lived for her son and always told him that even though he came from poor country people, he was as good as anybody. When she died in 1958, Elvis was crushed.

Apart from his mother, there was one great love in Elvis Presley's life: Priscilla Beaulieu. While stationed in Germany as a soldier, Presley met a pretty little 14-year-old, the daughter of a U.S. Army officer. "Cilla," as he called her, was feminine, unspoiled, and remarkably mature for her age—exactly suited for the pedestal upon which Elvis liked to place the women he loved best. He talked her father into allowing her to be shipped to Graceland, where Elvis installed her, sending her to Catholic school and then to finishing school. Before her arrival, Elvis had shown a snapshot of her to his stepmother and said, "I've been to bed with no less than 1,000 women in my life. This is the one, right here."

According to Elvis' secretary, he started sleeping with the 15-year-old girl right away. Years later Priscilla made a discreet mention of their premarital relationship in a *Ladies' Home Journal* interview. But Elvis had his cake and ate it too. He usually did not allow Priscilla to accompany him to Hollywood, where he had constant affairs. The list of stars with whom Elvis has been linked is virtually endless, and includes Ann-Margret, Juliet Prowse, and Tuesday Weld. Elvis' amours were not always with the famous. One woman, Virginia Sullivan, a cashier in a movie theater, claimed to have been his lover for 14 years, from 1953 to 1967. They had what she described as "comfortable sex."

Elvis married Priscilla in 1967, when she was 21. Exactly nine months later their daughter, Lisa Marie, was born. While the marriage was good in the beginning, it was subject to increasing strains. Priscilla was tired of waking up to face the Memphis Mafia at her breakfast table; she was tired of living at Graceland and going weeks without seeing her husband. And he was still sleeping around, while the Memphis Mafia was expected to cover it up. Worst of all, when Elvis was home, he and Priscilla had no privacy; he even took his entourage along on their vacations.

After five years of marriage Priscilla announced to Elvis that she had fallen in love with another man and was leaving. The rival was Mike Stone, her karate teacher. Elvis was shattered; he had lost his most valuable possession. The couple separated in 1972 and divorced in 1973. Priscilla's final settlement was $2 million. Although the divorce was relatively amicable, Elvis was deeply wounded.

He sought to balm his wounds with drugs, women, work, and food. The most important woman to come down the pike after Priscilla was the tall, willowy Miss Tennessee of 1972, Linda Thompson. She was model-beautiful and utterly devoted to the King. She was a virgin when she met Elvis, and a gracious, good-humored Southern belle. She moved into Graceland, and the relationship lasted several years. When Elvis started dating other women—and invited Linda along as a third—the affair petered out.

In the last year of his life Elvis had an affair with 19-year-old Ginger Alden, Miss Memphis Traffic Safety of 1976. He gave her the customary Cadillac and an $85,000 ring. She was with him the night of his death.

SEX LIFE: Elvis probably wasn't lying when he told his stepmother that he had slept with more than 1,000 girls. And *that* was before he married Priscilla. In the beginning of his career he was shy, and more interested in succeeding for the sake of his mother than in busying himself with sex. But he soon got the hang of it. Elvis had access to countless women, all over the world, who were dying to make love to him. Between the ages of 20 and 30, when he was young and in good health, he frequently had two or three women a day. Toward the end of his life drugs dampened his desire for sex ("Bed," he would say, "is for sleeping on"), and sometimes angry, unravished dates complained to the Memphis Mafia. However, it was strictly understood that the boys were not to fool around with a girl Elvis might still want, although their dates were fair game for Elvis.

According to the authors of *Elvis: What Happened?*, a biography written by three of Elvis' ex-bodyguards, the King had some distinctive sexual preferences. He was not a breast man and did not like a large bosom, but preferred shapely legs and buttocks. He liked his women petite and feminine ("girl-type girls"), and his biggest turnoff was big feet. He also detested male homosexuals. Another thing that turned him off sexually was the knowledge that a woman had been married or had had children. He once dropped a girl friend flat when he discovered she was a mother. He was also a passionate peeker. He had a one-way mirror in his bedroom so that he could secretly watch other couples; he had mirrored ceilings; and he liked to videotape his sex.

According to *Elvis: What Happened?*, Elvis had another quirk. He would give his girl of the moment a sleeping pill and put her in his bedroom. Then he would go to a nearby room, where he would watch two especially pretty prostitutes have sex. When this show had sufficiently excited him, he would "make a dead run to his bedroom and make it with his girl."

His overall preference in women ran to the young and inexperienced, because they were less likely to compare him with other men or reject him. The King, for all his glory, was terribly insecure.

—*A.W.*

California Love

TUPAC SHAKUR (June 16, 1971–Sept. 13, 1996)

HIS FAME: The son of black revolutionaries, Tupac Shakur was, and is, the
number one hip-hop artist of all time,
both in sales records and in social
importance. A thinking man's rapper, the
socially conscious and fiercely intelligent
Shakur showed promise beyond that of
just a hip-hop artist and actor, but as a
leader of the black community, all the
way up to his untimely assassination in
the East Coast-West Coast rap wars at
the age of 25.

HIS PERSON: Born to Black Panther Alice Faye Williams, who took the name
Afeni Shakur (he never knew his father), Tupac was raised as an intellectual. Tupac
considered himself effeminate and unmanly; and in the hard times of his youth he
turned to acting with a theater group in Harlem at the age of 12. At 15, with the
family relocated to Baltimore, he discovered his route to manhood—rap. By 1990,
he had scored a gig as a backup dancer for Digital Underground; his apprenticeship
was short-lived, and his first solo album, 1992's *2Pacalypse Now*, established him as
a major voice in the new genre of gangsta rap. He starred in the gang film *Juice* in
the same year, simultaneously establishing himself as a major new talent in both
mediums. 1993's *Strictly 4 My N.I.G.G.A.Z.* was released the following year, along
with Shakur's headlining role across from Janet Jackson in John Singleton's *Poetic
Justice*; a star had been born. However, the long shadow of his medium had followed him—Pac had found himself on the wrong end of the law after allegations of
sexual misconduct and an attack on an off-duty police officer. Violence followed
Tupac in higher and higher-cresting waves but he sprang back with the climax of his
short career, the powerful masterworks *Me Against the World* and *All Eyez on Me*,
which sold two and three million copies each, respectively. Yet it was at his pinnacle
that the final blow came: after leaving a Mike Tyson fight he attended with notoriously mercenary Death Row Records president Suge Knight, Tupac was shot four
times in a drive-by; he died shortly thereafter of cardiac arrest. Conspirators have
suspected the involvement of not only the Southside Crips, but also Las Vegas P.D.,
rival rappers Puff Daddy and the Notorious B.I.G. and even Knight himself—not
to mention the persistent conspiracy theory that 2Pac somehow remained alive.

In contrast to his Thug persona, Tupac wrote sensitive and vulnerable love
poems to girls, many of which were published after his death in the book, *The
Rose That Grew From Concrete*.

SEX PARTNERS: Tupac more than lived up to the virile self-image he constructed for himself in his lyrics, engaging in such legendary antics as having sex with almost all of the women who appeared in the promotional video for "How Do U Want It?" and subsequently collapsing from exhaustion. On a darker note, Shakur was controversially charged with sexual assault in December 1993; a 19-year-old woman he had previously received oral sex from in a club (half an hour after meeting her) and then had consensual sex with in his hotel room complained that Shakur had later forcibly sodomized her and then egged members of his entourage on in gang-raping her. Under testimony, the woman stated she had rendezvoused with Shakur four days after their initial sexual encounter in order to reclaim items she had left in his hotel room; after beginning a second sexual round with Tupac, his three friends allegedly barged into the room and began fondling her while Shakur grabbed her hair and stripped her clothes off, telling her that she'd been selected as a reward for his three friends and that "millions of other women would be happy to be in her situation." Shakur maintained he had slept through the act and had failed only in leaving her alone with his friends; the judge was not particularly sympathetic to his claims. The defense's only witness was Talibah Mbonisi, Tupac's publicist, who stated that Tupac had been with another woman that night, and that she (Mbonisi) had been talking to Shakur later when his accuser burst into the room demanding to know who was the woman that Shakur had been with. The defense's main argument was that Tupac's accuser had been motivated to make false claims because she had been spurned for another woman (one of many other women). After both sides concluded their arguments, Shakur was convicted of "sexual abuse (forcibly touching the buttocks)" and sentenced to one-and-a-half years in prison; he was wheeled into the courtroom to receive his sentence the day after being shot in the lobby of Quad Recording Studios in Manhattan (as with the shooting that killed him, Shakur suspected the involvement of Sean "Puffy" Combs and Christopher Wallace, a.k.a. the Notorious B.I.G.—Shakur, as part of his ongoing feud with Wallace, claimed to have had sex with his wife, R&B singer Faith Evans, in the track "Hit 'Em Up.") He was released on bail pending appeal after serving part of his sentence. Yet more than any sexual relationship, it was with the young actress Jada Pinkett (later to marry Will Smith) that Tupac formed his most lasting bond; the two were classmates at the Baltimore School for the Arts. Pinkett recalled of him at the time, "When I met Tupac, he owned two pairs of pants and two sweaters. He slept on a mattress with no sheets." Shakur said of the pair's apparently Platonic relationship in the posthumous documentary *Tupac: Resurrection*: "Jada is my heart. She will be my friend for my whole life"; and Pinkett said of Shakur that he was "one of my best friends. He was like a brother. It was beyond friendship for us. The type of relationship we had, you only get that once in a lifetime."

HIS THOUGHTS: "I'm somewhat psychotic... I'm hittin' switches on bitches like I been fixed with hydraulics."

—*J.L.*

IX

Command
Performances

The Little Corporal

NAPOLEON BONAPARTE (Aug. 15, 1769–May 5, 1821)

HIS FAME: In 1804 Napoleon became France's first emperor, thus climaxing his military triumphs on European battle-fields. His rise to power was aided by timely political patronage from French revolutionary leaders. During his rule he birthed the modern nation of France by bringing major reforms to the country's judicial, financial, and administrative institutions.

HIS PERSON: A relatively obscure artillery officer in his early military career, Napoleon won distinction—and a general's rank—by capturing Toulon (1793) from British forces aiding the French royalists. Called to Paris in 1795, his ruthless suppression of a rebel mob saved the new republic, and he was given command of French armies in Italy. There, in battles against the Austrian armies, Napoleon's outstanding victories made him a national hero. Returning secretly to Paris after his Egyptian campaign (1799), Bonaparte took advantage of the Directory's internal dissension and, aided by Abbé Sieyès, executed a coup d'état. The Consulate was then created, and as first consul Napoleon became master of France at age 30. He set up a military dictatorship, camouflaged by a constitution that gave him unlimited political power. Continental Europe fell under his domination during the ensuing Napoleonic Wars. His efforts to exclude British goods by boycott caused Spain to revolt, and other nations joined in. A disastrous Russian campaign (1812) and a crushing defeat at Leipzig (1813) led to a forced abdication and his banishment to Elba. Although Bonaparte escaped briefly to wage the "Hundred Days" struggle, his effort to regain the French throne ended in his defeat by the Duke of Wellington at Waterloo (1815). Exile for life on the island of St. Helena followed.

SEX LIFE: During his two official marriages, Napoleon had a dozen known mistresses. Another 20 were said to have shared his bed before he was sent into exile. By his own admission, he lost his virginity at 18 to a prostitute he picked up on a Parisian boulevard. This commercial experience did little to overcome the future emperor's timidity toward women. In 1795, eager to wed, he courted his first real love, his sister-in-law Eugénie Désirée Clary, hoping that his brother Joseph, who was married to Eugénie's older sister, would smooth the way. Joseph's effort failed, and Napoleon withdrew the marriage proposal abruptly, possibly fearing he would be impotent with the young beauty who was destined to become Sweden's future queen. Thereafter, he shifted his wooing to more mature women, making firm offers to at least five. Two were old enough to be his grandmother and mother, respectively: Mademoiselle de Montansier (age 60) and Madame Permon (age 40). Both were shocked to learn that he was deadly serious.

His frantic search for a suitable wife finally ended when Count Paul Barras, seeking to rid himself of his expensive and aging Creole mistress Joséphine de Beauharnais, arranged for the two to meet. Relying on the count's assurance that the match would have great benefits both monetarily and socially, on March 9, 1796 Napoleon married the "28-year-old." (She knocked four years off her age on the marriage certificate and he added two to his to make the gap between them less obvious.) Their marriage night proved to be an unexpected shocker. Engaged in vigorous intercourse, the bridegroom suddenly uttered a shriek as Joséphine's pet pug, Fortuné, joined the act. Believing his mistress was being attacked, the dog had jumped on the bed and bitten *le petit général* on his bare left calf. Two days later the wounded warrior cut the honeymoon short and left for Italy, freeing the lusty Joséphine—who rarely slept alone—to resume her liaisons with standby lovers.

Irked by Joséphine's constant unfaithfulness—a contemporary once smirked that the empress seemed to believe "farsighted nature had placed the where-withal to pay her bills beneath her navel"—Napoleon took Pauline Fourès as his mistress during the Egyptian campaign of 1798. He soon became smitten with the 20-year-old blonde, who had disguised her boyish figure in male attire to be with her soldier-husband. The cuckolded lieutenant was cunningly sent back to Paris with dispatches, and Pauline moved into a house near Napoleon's Cairo headquarters. Nicknamed "Our Lady of the Orient" and *"Madame la Générale,"* she heightened the general's passion by wearing plumed hats, gold-braided coats, and skintight white pantaloons, which stoked his buttocks fetish into a near frenzy. (A lifelong connoisseur of bottoms and buttocks, he had once fondly described Joséphine's rump as "the prettiest little backside imaginable.") The notorious affair was spiked by the British, who captured the ship on which Lieutenant Fourès had sailed and maliciously returned him to Egyptian soil to play the role of outraged husband.

For Napoleon's casual romps, Géraud Duroc, his chief aide-de-camp and intimate confidant for 15 years, served as pimp. The overnighters were brought to a bedroom adjacent to Napoleon's study in the Tuileries. Duroc admitted the girls secretly and gave orders for them to strip and slip beneath the bedcovers, to be ready for instant sex once Bonaparte's workday was over. Some intrigues of longer duration, like those with court ladies-in-waiting Eléonore Denuelle and Marie Antoinette Duchâtel, were deliberately arranged by conniving members of Napoleon's family, eager to sponsor any mistress who could prove the hated Joséphine to be barren. They succeeded with Denuelle. In 1806 she gave birth to a son, Léon, and Napoleon proudly claimed credit as the father. Although Bonaparte preferred to keep his trysts secret, the affair with Mademoiselle George (real name: Marguerite Weymer, later called "the Whale" because of a huge gain in weight) erupted publicly, to his great embarrassment. An erotic book surfaced, with illustrations showing his mistress engaged in graphic homosexual acts with her lesbian lover, Raucort.

Napoleon's favorite partner, Marie Walewska, was an unsolicited "gift" from her fellow Poles, who needed France's might to achieve independence for their homeland. The liaison began unevenly. Taken to Napoleon's private apartments in Warsaw, the nervous young countess fainted when he became sexually aggressive. Undeterred, Napoleon raped her. Regaining consciousness, she quickly forgave him, and the affair flourished for over three years. Her quiet charm and devotion captivated the emperor, and Marie left her mark on history as the only woman he ever really loved. In 1810 she gave him his second son, Alexander, further proving that he was far from impotent.

Meanwhile, the problem of producing legally acceptable offspring became of even greater concern. In 1809, after his tempestuous marriage to Joséphine failed to result in a much-wanted heir, Napoleon reluctantly annulled the union. Out of political necessity, he chose as his second wife Archduchess Marie Louise of Austria, an 18-year-old virgin so sheltered during childhood that all male animals were kept from her view. Checking over her prolific ancestors like a farmer seeking a prize brood mare, the heirless emperor concluded that she had "the kind of womb I want to marry." Marie Louise proved true to her breeding and presented Napoleon with a son a year after their marriage in 1810. Both wives were showered by thousands of love letters while he was absent on campaigns during their marriages, letters worded so passionately that they seemed unreal. The flaming prose often closed with such provocatives as "I kiss your breasts, and lower down, much lower down!" or "I kiss the little black forest."

Napoleon not only tolerated homosexuality among his associates but also refused to permit punitive legislation against its practice. His habit of caressing his soldiers intimately while tweaking noses or pulling ears hinted strongly at his own homosexuality. Aides were often chosen for both their youth and their effeminate behavior. To one, Napoleon himself gave the nickname "Miss Sainte Croix." Another, Baron Gaspard Gourgard, was the emperor's personal orderly for six years. Gourgard was furiously jealous of any who dared to pay undue personal attention to "Her Majesty," his affectionate name for the master he curried. After age 42, the question of Napoleon's true gender did not matter. He became impotent, fulfilling Joséphine's derisive charge of earlier years that "*Bon-a-parte est Bon-à-rien*" ("Bonaparte is good-for-nothing").

MEDICAL REPORT: Napoleon's known loss of sexual potency, combined with a pronounced lemon-yellow cast to his skin in his last years, hinted at a progressively fatal malfunctioning of the endocrine glands. The medical examination and autopsy performed by Dr. Antommarchi, witnessed by several English doctors, provided further evidence that Napoleon's pituitary, thyroid, renal, and gonad glands had been rapidly failing and were almost certainly tumorous. A huge gastric ulcer and extensive calcium deposits throughout the urinary system were found to be the primary causes of his lifelong indigestion and painful urination. The urethral obstruction probably was responsible for his complaint of being afflicted by *la chaude pisse* ("burning urine"). The ulcer was seen to be cancerous, although it had not yet spread elsewhere in the body. Napoleon's penis had shrunk to an inch in length and both testicles were minuscule, showing an advanced case of hypogonadism. The body hair was almost nonexistent, and the pubis was feminine in appearance. Glandular changes had produced softly rounded, creamy-textured breasts that many women would have envied, and had reduced the hands and feet to an abnormally small size. Napoleon's final height, as recorded in the autopsy, was 5 ft. 2 in., perhaps reduced several inches because of the ravages of his multiple ailments.

—*W.K.*

Reclining Venus

PAULINE BONAPARTE (Oct. 20, 1780–June 9, 1825)

HER FAME: Pauline Bonaparte belongs to history mainly because she was Napoleon's favorite sister, one of the classical beauties of her time, an unremitting nymphomaniac, and the model for Antonio Canova's most popular sculpture.

HER PERSON: Pauline came from Ajaccio, Corsica, the sixth of her parents' 13 children. When she was 12, her family moved to Toulon, France. As her older brother moved up in the world, she was right behind him, transformed from a peasant to a princess. When Napoleon graduated from general to emperor, his pet sister, Pauline, also stood in the limelight of Parisian society.

Men of the top rank constantly pursued her. According to the French dramatist Antoine Arnault: "She was an extraordinary combination of perfect physical beauty and the strangest moral laxity. If she was the loveliest creature one had ever seen, she was also the most frivolous." After she was married, Napoleon wrote her: "Love your husband, make your household happy, and above all do not be frivolous or capricious. You are 24 years old, and ought to be mature and sensible by now." Of her, Countess Anna Potocka wrote: "With the finest and most regular features imaginable she combined a most shapely figure, admired (alas!) too often."

Pauline loved fornication and luxury. She owned 600 dresses and millions of dollars' worth of jewels and traveled in a carriage drawn by six horses. In a time when most French women did not bathe frequently, Pauline made a fetish of cleanliness because her body was constantly exposed. She bathed every morning in a tub filled with 20 liters of milk mixed with hot water. After disrobing, she had her young black servant, Paul, carry her to the tub. When onlookers were scandalized, Pauline said, "But why not? A Negro is not a man. Or are you shocked because he is unmarried?" To remedy this, she married Paul off to one of her white kitchen maids—and he continued to carry her to the tub. To immortalize her perfect body, Pauline commissioned Antonio Canova, the Italian sculptor who had done statues of Pope Clement XIV and Napoleon, to do her in marble as a nude Venus. Afterward, when someone asked how she could pose naked, she answered, "It was not cold. There was a fire in the studio."

When Napoleon fell, Pauline was the only one of his siblings to join him in exile—for four months—on the isle of Elba.

SEX LIFE: At 15 she fell in love with 40-year-old Louis Fréron, an intelligent but unscrupulous political adventurer who was called the "king of the dandies." He gave up his mistress, a Parisian actress, to devote himself to Pauline. "I swear to love but you alone," Pauline promised in return. Napoleon was ambivalent about the match, but their mother, Letizia, was certain Fréron was wrong for her daughter and he was sent away. With Fréron eliminated, Pauline began to flirt with most of Napoleon's general staff. In order to end this, Napoleon sought a husband for Pauline. He found one in an army comrade. Charles Victor Leclerc was blond, clean-cut, and serious, the son of a wealthy miller. Napoleon handed him Pauline *and* a promotion to brigadier general. Pauline accepted Leclerc's proposal amiably, and they were married in June, 1797. While she had no great passion for Leclerc, he satisfied her in bed and that was enough. The next year, when she was 17, Pauline bore her husband a son, whom Napoleon named Dermide. (The child would die in his sixth year.) In 1801, when the rich French colony of St. Domingue—now Haiti—in the Caribbean was threatened by the Spanish, the English, and soon enough by the independence-minded Toussaint L'Ouverture, Napoleon sent Leclerc at the head of 25,000 troops to restore order. Pauline was forced to accompany her husband. Just as Pauline was beginning to enjoy the social amenities of Haiti, her husband came down with yellow fever and died in November, 1802.

Back in Paris, Pauline's mourning was short-lived. She wanted to play. To prevent this, Napoleon found her a second husband. He was 28-year-old Prince Camillo Borghese, an attractive, dark-haired, empty-headed, elegant Italian who owned one of the world's biggest diamond collections and countless properties, including the art-laden Villa Borghese in Rome. Pauline was not terribly interested in Borghese, but she liked the wealth and the title that came with him. A papal cardinal officiated at their wedding in August, 1803. From the wedding night on, their sexual union was a disaster. What ruined their coupling for Pauline, as one biographer put it, was that Prince Borghese "somewhat disappointingly had a very small penis. Pauline, whose nymphomania was periodic but intense, scorned all but very large ones." Disgusted, Pauline wrote an uncle, "I'd far rather have remained Leclerc's widow with an income of only 20,000 francs than be married to a eunuch."

After that, she separated herself from Prince Borghese and went on a hunt for men of the proper proportions. By 1806 she had found what she wanted in Paris. A tall, muscular, society painter, Louis Philippe Auguste de Forbin was 30 years old and mightily endowed. Pauline made him her royal chamberlain and copulated with him daily—endlessly. This ceaseless fornicating at last began to affect Pauline's health, and at the urging of her doctors and mother, Forbin left to enlist in the French army. Long after, he became director of the Louvre.

Despite her physical exhaustion, Pauline's sexual activity rarely abated in the next 15 years. In Nice she took up with a mild-mannered young musician, Felix Blangini. She hired him to "conduct her orchestra." She had no orchestra, but she had her bed, and there they enjoyed duets. In 1810 she tried out an aide to Napoleon's chief of staff, a sensual ladies' man aged 25. Her affair with Col. Armand Jules de Canouville was passionate and wild. To nip any potential scandal Napoleon had the colonel transferred to Danzig. In 1812 he was killed near Moscow, a locket containing a miniature of Pauline pressed against his chest. For days Pauline sobbed with grief. Finally, she distracted herself with other affairs, including a loveless one with the celebrated actor François Talma. After Waterloo and St. Helena, she had a brief reconciliation with Prince Borghese, and in the Villa Borghese, mirror in hand, she died of cancer at 44. Her last wish was that her coffin not stand open at her funeral, but that the Canova nude be brought out of storage to represent her.

MEDICAL REPORT: Pauline Bonaparte's case was an unusual one—that of a woman suffering from excessive sexual intercourse. The problem first appeared during her mating with Forbin, whose organ was so often inside Pauline that she suffered acute vaginal distress. Her unhealthy state, said one biographer, "was based on nothing but undue friction, mostly brought on by M. de Forbin, who was endowed with a usable gigantism and very hard to get rid of." When Pauline's vaginal distress worsened, her doctor called in France's leading gynecologist, Dr. Jean-Noël Hallé, to have a look at her. Hallé did so twice and then wrote the following memorandum to Pauline's physician.

Her general appearance indicates … exhaustion. The womb was still sensitive, but somewhat less so; and the ligaments still exhibited signs of the painful inflammation for which we prescribed baths last Thursday. The present condition of the uterus is caused by a constant and habitual excitation of that organ; if this does not cease, an exceedingly dangerous situation may result. That is the source of her trouble, and I hinted at its causes when speaking to the Princess last Thursday. I blamed the internal douches, and spoke in a general way of possible causes of an irritation of the womb.... The douche and its tube cannot always be held responsible. One is bound to assume a continuous cause for such exhaustion in the case of a young and beautiful woman living apart from her husband. If there is anyone who shares the fault for these indulgences, this person would not accuse himself. We would be blamed for seeing nothing and permitting everything. I've no wish to pass for a fool nor be accused of base and stupid complacency. But quite apart from that, there is the necessity of saving this unfortunate young woman.

The doctors acted. Forbin was sent away. And Pauline rested—but not for long. Soon the inflammation reappeared, as it would continue to do for the rest of her life.

—*I.W.*

No Horsing Around

CATHERINE II OF RUSSIA (Apr. 21, 1729–Nov. 6, 1796))

HER FAME: Catherine the Great, a German princess with a French education, ruled the vast Russian empire as an autocrat for 34 years.

HER PERSON: Married at 16 to her 17-year-old cousin Peter, who was the nephew and heir of Russia's reigning Empress Elizabeth, Catherine was under notice to produce children. (Elizabeth was herself childless.) Unfortunately, Peter was crazy, impotent, and sterile. Catherine contemplated suicide, then sought escape in voracious reading and long strenuous hours on horseback. At last, after nearly 10 years of marriage, she gave birth to a

Catherine at 15

son—probably by her first lover, Sergei Saltykov, a young Russian nobleman. Since Peter was growing crazier and more unpopular each day, Catherine's own chances of succession looked hopeless too; moreover, Peter was threatening to divorce her. She decided that she could and would plan a coup d'état. In June, 1762, Peter had been emperor just six months and was absent planning an insane war against Denmark. Catherine donned a lieutenant's uniform, rode into St. Petersburg (then the Russian capital) at the head of a detachment of imperial guards, and had herself proclaimed empress. Peter, shattered by the news, was quickly arrested and murdered. Catherine's chief accomplices had been her lover

Count Grigori Orlov and his two brothers, all officers in the Horse Guards. In the course of her long reign she broke the power of the clergy, put down a major rebellion, reorganized the civil service, forced the Ukrainian peasants into serfdom, and added more than 200,000 sq. mi. to Russian territory—at the expense of the 95% of the population which worked the land.

SEX LIFE: Catherine before marriage was innocently sensual; at night she masturbated with a pillow between her legs. To her bridegroom, however, bed was where one played with toys. At 23 she was still a virgin.

One stormy night on an island in the Baltic Sea her lady-in-waiting, very likely on the empress' instructions, left Catherine alone with Saltykov, a hardened young seducer. He had promised her rapture, and she was not disappointed. Neither was Empress Elizabeth. The affair with Saltykov unleashed Catherine's sexuality. After two miscarriages, Catherine again became pregnant and this time was ordered to take life easy. No sooner had her son Paul been born than the empress snatched him away. Catherine lay unattended in a drafty room while Russia celebrated. Her second child, also officially Peter's, was a girl, who died soon after the actual father, a young Polish nobleman employed by the British ambassador, was sent home in disgrace. Peter was overheard muttering, "I don't know how it is that my wife becomes pregnant."

Catherine's three remaining children, all boys, were fathered by Grigori Orlov. They were born in secret, Catherine's hoop skirts having successfully concealed each pregnancy. The first birth occurred while Peter was still alive. In order to lure him away from the palace as she went into labor, Catherine had a faithful servant set fire to his own house, which was nearby. (Peter never could resist a good fire.) The other two children, brought up for a while in the homes of servants, were not introduced into the court nursery until they were at an age where nobody could be certain whose they were. These maneuvers were necessary because Catherine, not wanting to end the Romanov dynasty, had refused to marry Grigori. He retaliated by making the ladies of the court his harem. Nevertheless, Catherine stayed faithful to him for 14 years and turned him out only when he seduced his 13-year-old cousin.

Catherine was now 43. Her thick brown hair, expressive blue eyes, and small, sensual mouth had lost none of their appeal, while her figure was more voluptuous than in her youth. One of her protégés and original supporters, a cavalry officer named Grigori Potëmkin, had already declared his loyalty to her and then retired to a monastery (he had once studied to be a priest). Potëmkin was canny enough not to return to secular life until Catherine promised to appoint him her "personal adjutant general" (i.e., official favorite); first, the current favorite had to be dismissed. For two years thereafter the empress and her 35-year-old lover enjoyed a tumultuous affair, filled with quarrels and reconciliations. When the sexual passion died, Potëmkin, willing to give up Catherine but not his influence at court, convinced her that her favorites could be replaced as easily as any other servants. To make sure that they were, he added, he would select them himself.

Amazingly, the new system worked quite well until Catherine was 60. A potential favorite was first examined by Catherine's personal physician for signs of venereal disease. If pronounced healthy, he was then given a different kind of "physical"; his virility was tested by a lady-in-waiting appointed for that purpose. The next stage, if he reached it, was installation in the favorite's special apartment, located directly below Catherine's and connected to it by a private staircase. There he would find a large monetary gift. Repeat performances with the empress brought additional rewards and honors, while his main job remained that of being her adjutant general and "emperor of the night." On dismissal he might receive anything from additional money to an estate complete with 4,000 peasants. In this way Catherine ran through 13 men and a great deal of public money in 16 years. Growing old at last, the 60-year-old empress succumbed to the wiles of 22-year-old Platon Zubov, an officer of the Horse Guards, whom Potëmkin disapproved of because he was too ambitious. Zubov was her main sexual interest until her death at 67. Contrary to the age-old rumor that she died while attempting intercourse with a horse, Catherine expired two days after suffering a massive stroke.

SEX PARTNERS: Peter's impotence seems to have been due to an operable malformation of the penis. One story is that Saltykov and his friends, having got Peter drunk, persuaded him to undergo corrective surgery and so become accountable for Catherine's pregnancies. But we do not know whether Peter ever had sex with her, though he did begin having mistresses. Polish Count Stanislas Poniatowski, Catherine's second lover, was caught leaving her country retreat in disguise. When Peter accused him of having intercourse with Catherine, he indignantly denied it, whereupon Peter dragged her out of bed. Later he forced the lovers to join him and his mistress at supper. In 1764 Catherine had Poniatowski made king of Poland, as Stanislas II, but when he proved unable to control the Polish nationalists, she wiped the country off the map by annexing part of it and giving the rest to Prussia and Austria. He seems to have loved her deeply.

Grigori Orlov, a baby-faced colossus, flourished on physical danger but went to pieces as a courtier. He became a political liability to Catherine after mishandling some important peace negotiations with the Turks; his sexual exploits, however, had already become more than Catherine could stand. He died mad, haunted by Peter's ghost though it was his brother Alexei who had planned the murder. Of Alexei Vasilchikov, Grigori's amiable replacement, Catherine wrote to Potëmkin: "If that fool had stayed with me another year and you had not come … it is quite likely that I should have grown used to him." Potëmkin was a potbellied, hypocritical, one-eyed boor who wolfed huge midnight snacks in the palace sauna after frolicking there with Catherine in the steam. Perhaps he and Catherine were secretly married; she certainly called him "husband" in her letters. (She also called him such names as "my marble beauty" and "golden rooster" and "wolfbird.")

There is little to be said about Potëmkin's handpicked successors, except that they were all handsome guard officers in their 20s and none lasted. The gentle Alexander Lanskoy, Catherine's favorite of favorites, died of diphtheria after undermining his health with aphrodisiacs. Ivan Rimski-Korsakov—grandfather of the composer—disgraced himself by returning to the "virility tester," Countess Bruce, for additional "tests." The countess subsequently was replaced by an older woman. Alexander Dmitriev-Mamonov was allowed to resign in order to marry a very pregnant court lady; Catherine sulked for three days, then gave them a generous wedding present. Most of the royal favorites enjoyed successful careers in later life.

HER THOUGHTS: Catherine wrote in her memoirs: "I was attractive. That was the halfway house to temptation, and in such cases human nature does the rest. To tempt and be tempted are much the same thing." Her favorite toast was "God, grant us our desires, and grant them quickly."

—*J.M.B.E.*

Old Rowley Himself

CHARLES II (May 29, 1630–Feb. 6, 1685)

HIS FAME: Charles II, King of England, Scotland, and Ireland, was the "Merry Monarch" who returned after 14 years of exile during Oliver Cromwell's Puritan rule to create the cultured, witty, and often decadent "Restoration" court.

HIS PERSON: Charles' first adviser and tutor, the Earl of Newcastle, told the teenage prince that he would learn more from men than from books. The lessons that the boy learned during the tumultuous, dangerous years of his teens and twenties were lessons of intrigue, political maneuvering, and all the other skills needed to survive as an exiled, uncrowned king. In 1646, during England's bloody civil war, Prince Charles took his father's advice and fled, first to the Scilly Islands and then to Jersey and France. While in exile in 1649, he learned that his father had been beheaded by Oliver Cromwell's forces.

His years of waiting and plotting were rewarded when, in 1660, he returned to take advantage of the struggle between Cromwell's successors. Britain welcomed him back. He was crowned and married to Catherine of Braganza, the daughter of the king of Portugal. The queen was never able to bear children, but Charles steadfastly refused to divorce her.

He was a shrewd politician, a charming man who was loved by most of his subjects, much interested in horse racing, fishing, and naval matters, and even tolerant of rival religions. The "Merry Monarch" was, all in all, a good king.

SEX LIFE: The Puritans chose to represent Charles as a sexual monster, but in the intervening years, especially in biographies written in our own time, another picture of the "Merry Monarch" emerges. The man did indeed enjoy sex enormously; he was good at it, well equipped for it, pursued it vigorously, and, as a handsome man and king, was never short of willing partners. He didn't, however, cross the fine line between being very active and being compulsive. His standards were high; he did not bed every available woman. And despite his energetic extramarital sex life, he was always attentive to Catherine, who quickly learned that forbearance and tact were the best means of exerting influence on her husband. Although they had no heir, it was not through lack of trying. They made love regularly, and Catherine was said to have suffered two miscarriages in her futile attempt to provide him with legitimate offspring.

Charles' code of sexual ethics was summed up in his belief that God would never damn a man for "allowing himself a little pleasure" and that "to be wicked and to design mischief is the only thing that God hates." He lived up to his code, allowing himself much more than a little pleasure and yet not causing intentional harm to any of his partners. Where other powerful men discarded their mistresses, Charles pensioned his off with an income and a title and did the same for their children.

He loved what might be called elaborate sexual games, little dramas incorporating more or less consciously arranged role-playing, with Charles himself as the central character. He loved to see women dressed as men, a taste which did not hint at all at homosexuality but sprang rather from the many "breeches parts" written into Restoration plays, roles intended to allow shapely young actresses to scamper about the stage in tight-fitting breeches rather than skirts. Charles loved it on stage and in the boudoir.

As part of the game playing, he was in a position to indulge in the creation of complex sexual "menus." Two mistresses at the same time, for example, in separate residences, one of whom was a highly sexual and sensual libertine, and the other a coy virgin playing with dolls and whetting the king's appetite but refusing to satisfy it. Or an elegant lady and a saucy actress. Charles' sex life seems to have been one in which, literally, there was never a dull moment. When boredom did threaten, the king relied on Will Chiffinch, his trusted private messenger, to arrange for the secret nocturnal visits of nameless but highly attractive wenches.

As a young man of 15 he was introduced to sex by his former governess, Mrs. Wyndham, after which he indulged an early taste for older women. Eventually his partners got younger and his sexuality more adventuresome, and then in his later years he tended to seek more settled relationships, usually one at a time in what might be called "serial monogamy."

Although he didn't consider himself handsome (he once exclaimed, "Odd's fish, I am an ugly fellow!" upon examining a quite realistic portrait), women found his tall, strong frame and dark sensual visage to be exciting. He loved his reputation as a sexual animal. The king was often called "Old Rowley," after a famous stallion, well endowed and in great demand as a stud. While passing through the halls of his palace one day, Charles heard a young woman singing a satirical ballad entitled "Old Rowley, the King." He immediately knocked on the door of her apartment, and when she asked who was there he replied, "Old Rowley himself, madam." According to the wit and poet John Wilmot, Earl of Rochester: "Nor are his high Desires above his Strength; / His sceptre and his p—k are of a length, / And she that plays with one may sway the other...."

SEX PARTNERS: Nell Gwyn's rise to fortune was a storybook affair. Her father was an inveterate ne'er-do-well who breathed his last in debtors' prison. Her mother was an alcoholic, whose contribution to her daughter's future was to get her a job as a barmaid in her bawdy house, and who eventually died brandy-besotted and ditch-drowned. Sweet, saucy Nell became one of the first English-speaking actresses in history (since before that only preadolescent boys had played women's roles) and therefore one of the first to use her sprightly antics on the stage to catch the eye, and other more private parts, of a king. Her king was Charles II, although she called him her "Charles the Third" because she had already had two lovers named Charles before him. She provided the perfect mingling of sugar and sauce to the sensual banquet that Charles devoured. Witty, playful, coarse, flashing sweet and vulgar in turn, stimulating Charles with mock coyness and then satisfying him with her own very real sexuality, she was a perfect mistress to the king. Another of her charms was her perfect calves and thighs, which she bared on stage—and Charles was a leg man.

The common people loved Nell because she was one of them, a "girl of the London streets" made good. One afternoon as she rode along in the handsome carriage Charles had given her, she was suddenly the target of the jeers and curses of the unwashed rabble. Her carriage had been mistaken for that of Charles' other mistress, the elegant, haughty, and strikingly beautiful Louise de Kéroualle, who, because she was French and Catholic, many suspected of being little better than a spy for King Louis. Nell poked her head out of the carriage window, smiled winningly, and cried out: "Pray good people, be civil! I am the *Protestant* whore!" The people were delighted. It also pleased the king and the people that Nell did not care to enter into politics. As an anonymous poet of the period put it:

Hard by Pall Mall lives a wench call'd Nell;
King Charles the Second he kept her.
She hath got a trick to handle his prick
But never lays hands on his sceptre.
All matters of state from her soul she does hate,
And leave to the politic bitches.
The whore's in the right, for 'tis her delight,
To be scratching just where it itches.

Charles reveled in the contrast between the saucy Nell and the cultured Louise. He also enjoyed the contrast between two of his other playmates, the shy, demure, virginal Frances Stuart, who apparently never gave in to Charles although she was much pursued, and the rapacious, voluptuous Barbara Palmer (also known as Lady Castlemayne), of whom diarist Samuel Pepys wrote: "My Lady Castlemayne rules him, who hath all the tricks of Aretino [a 15th- and 16th-century pornographer] that are to be practised to give pleasure—in which he is too able, having a large—; but that which is the unhappiness is that, as the Italian proverb says, 'A man with an erection is in no need of advice.'" Pepys was more than a little jealous.

The unattainability of Lady Castlemayne's opposite—the virginal Frances—was mirrored to some extent in his bittersweet relationship with his sister, Henrietta Anne. Fourteen years his junior, she was a frail, beautiful woman with an exceptionally kind and loving nature. Shortly before Charles' coronation she married Philippe, Duc d'Orléans, a petty and spiteful man who was jealous of his wife's natural charm and well known for his interest in members of his own sex. Forced to look elsewhere for understanding and affection, she turned to Charles and served as his intermediary, or "private channel," to her brother-in-law, King Louis XIV. When Henrietta Anne died at age 26, the last words she whispered were, "I have loved him [Charles] better than life itself and now my only regret in dying is to be leaving him." On learning of her death, Charles became ill with grief and suffered an unprecedented physical collapse.

The rest of Charles' partners fall into two categories, those such as Moll Davis and Catherine Pegge whom he publicly acknowledged and by whom he had a dozen children, and the numerous passions of the moment by whom he fathered many unacknowledged children. As the Duke of Buckingham put it, a king is supposed to be the father of his people, and Charles certainly was father to a good many of them.

HIS THOUGHTS: "I never interfere with the souls of women but only with their bodies when they are civil enough to accept my attentions."

—*R. W.S.*

The Sexual Politician

CLEOPATRA (69-30 B.C)

HER FAME: The last queen of Egypt, Cleopatra has come to be identified with decadence, cunning, and exotic beauty. For 30 years she was a dominant figure in Mediterranean affairs of state, using her personal attractions to further her political ambitions.

HER PERSON: Cleopatra was a Macedonian Greek descended from Ptolemy, one of Alexander the Great's generals, who ruled Egypt upon Alexander's death. An intellectual by nature, she was the first member of the royal family who bothered to learn the Egyptian language, and she reportedly was fluent in many

other tongues. She was educated in Hellenistic as well as Egyptian traditions, and was considered culturally superior to some of the greatest statesmen of Rome. With a long hooked nose and a large mouth, Cleopatra was not especially beautiful, but her body was slender and well proportioned and she was a master of the cosmetic arts. She was an enchantress by virtue of her mannerisms, movements, and moods, and it was said that the sweetness of her melodic voice resembled the sound of a lyre.

SEX LIFE: Historians have recorded that Cleopatra staged weeks of nightly orgies, at which those in attendance engaged in various forms of debauchery. The lascivious atmosphere of her court during her love affair with Roman leader Mark Antony showed how she played to his notorious taste for obscene jokes and sexually provocative conversation. For his entertainment she kept a performer of erotic dances at court. Cleopatra and Antony visited the pleasure resorts outside of Alexandria, and they formed a dining club, the Inimitables, where guests participated in lewd theatricals. One Roman guest played Glaucus the sea god, dancing and crawling on his knees, his naked body painted blue. The orgies led to a rash of scandals about Cleopatra's personal sex life. Rumors spread that she promiscuously indulged in fellatio; some Greeks called her Meriochane, which means "she who gapes wide for 10,000 men." In one account she was supposed to have fellated 100 Roman noblemen in a single night. The idea that Cleopatra was a harlot was developed by her enemies, one of whom, King Herod of Judea, claimed that she attempted to seduce him. His assertion is probably false, because Cleopatra's principal aim was to keep in the good graces of her lover, Antony, a formidable political ally.

SEX PARTNERS: In accordance with the Egyptian custom of marriage between royal siblings, Cleopatra was married to two younger brothers: first to Ptolemy XIII in 51 B.C., when she was 18, and shortly after his death in 47 B.C. to the 12-year-old Ptolemy XIV. There was no physical consummation of these marriages, which were arranged only because a male co-ruler was necessary for her to be queen.

Although some sources maintain that Cleopatra began her sex life at the age of 12, it is entirely possible that she took her first lover nine years later, choosing the 52-year-old dictator of Rome, Julius Caesar. Fleeing her country amidst a power struggle with her brothers and sisters, the 21-year-old queen presented herself to Caesar at his palace in Alexandria, smuggled past guards in a carpet or a roll of bedding. She quickly captivated the notorious womanizer and their love affair began, thus ensuring her political position. Even though he was already married, an Egyptian marriage possibly took place between Caesar and Cleopatra, and he soon moved her and their son, Caesarion, to Rome, installing them in one of his homes. He publicly proclaimed her influence over him by placing a statue of her in a temple dedicated to Venus, thus arousing Rome's anger by deifying a foreigner. Because Caesar had no legitimate son, the possibility of an Egyptian successor caused much resentment toward the queen, and she was often referred to as a whore in the bawdy songs sung by Caesar's soldiers.

Upon Caesar's murder by his political adversaries, Cleopatra returned to Egypt, where she learned of the emergence of a new Roman leader. Ruggedly handsome, with a muscular build, broad forehead, and aquiline nose, Mark Antony, like Caesar, had a weakness for the opposite sex. Determined to seduce him, Cleopatra sailed to Tarsus in an opulent barge with purple sails, silver oars, and a poop deck of gold. The music of lutes and flutes announced the arrival of the queen, who was dressed as Venus and surrounded by attendants dressed as cupids and the Graces. For several days she staged elaborate banquets and bestowed expensive gifts upon the somewhat unsophisticated soldier-statesman and his officers. By the time a power struggle with Caesar's nephew, Octavian, forced Antony back to Rome, she had conceived twins by him. Several years later he left his new wife, Octavia—sister of Octavian—and returned to Cleopatra's side. The rupture in his relations with Octavian led to two years of war, which culminated in Antony's and Cleopatra's defeat at Actium.

After Octavian's forces reached Egypt, Cleopatra fled to her mausoleum, barricading herself inside with three attendants. Antony received a report that she had committed suicide, and in his grief he stabbed himself. Mortally wounded, he was informed that she was still alive and was transported to her mausoleum, where he died in her arms. Cleopatra was soon captured by Octavian, and for once her seductive powers proved unsuccessful. She took her own life upon learning that she was to be paraded as a captive in the streets of Rome upon Octavian's triumphant return.

—*L.A.B.*

The Royal Rake

EDWARD VII (Nov. 9, 1841–May 6, 1910)

HIS FAME: Albert Edward, who ascended to the throne in 1901, ruled Great Britain as one of its most popular kings. As Edward VII, his personal style of diplomacy helped gain acceptance of the *Entente Cordiale*, an agreement between Great Britain and France for closer diplomatic cooperation, and earned him the nickname "Edward the Peacemaker."

HIS PERSON: The eldest son of Queen Victoria and Prince Consort Albert, "Bertie," as Edward was called, had a bleak and lonely childhood. Hoping to turn him into a paragon of virtue, his

King Edward and Queen Alexandra

parents separated him from other children. Victoria wanted her son to grow up as good as her beloved Albert, in spite of the fact that she believed that no one could be "so great, so good, so faultless" as the prince consort. Bertie set about to prove that she was right. He completely rebelled against his parents' strict moral code. He turned a deaf ear to his tutors' lectures on morality and ignored his father's memoranda on propriety. The pursuit of pleasure in all its forms became his life's goal. He was addicted to cigars before he turned 20. A man of gargantuan appetite, he ate several meals a day, sometimes consuming as many as 12 courses in a sitting. He paid so much attention to clothes—he was a stickler for proper attire down to the last button—that even tea was a full-dress affair.

Bertie occupied himself with "bachelor outings" (even after his marriage to Danish Princess Alexandra) which lasted several months of every year and consisted of visits to Paris, Bad Homburg, and the Riviera, or hunting and shooting at his country estates. He was usually surrounded by his aristocratic friends of the "Marlborough House set," forerunners of the modern jet set, who joined him for gambling at baccarat parties or at the horse races at Ascot or Epsom. Bertie's own horses won the Derby three times.

Because of Edward's frivolous ways, Victoria would not allow him to assume any governmental responsibilities. He was the official host and tour guide for visiting dignitaries, and Victoria's stand-in at public ceremonies. When his "eternal mother" finally died in 1901, he dropped the name Albert and the following year was crowned Edward VII. He was 60 years old.

SEX LIFE: Bertie became king 40 years after his father had died. It was Bertie, Victoria believed, who had caused her dear husband's death. While serving with the British army in Ireland, 19-year-old Bertie lost his virginity when fellow officers smuggled actress Nellie Clifden into his bed. Albert passed away soon after hearing of his son's "fall into sin." It was decided that Bertie should marry immediately to remove him from further temptation.

Victoria chose Princess Alexandra as her son's bride, and he accepted the selection. The beautiful teenage princess and the stocky, handsome Prince of Wales were married in 1863. Alexandra bore five children over the next six years, and with marriage as a "cover" Bertie played the field for over 40 years. In spite of her husband's wanderings, Alix—as Alexandra was called by friends and family—always believed he loved her best and said that "if he *was* a cowboy I should love him just the same." In a sense he was a cowboy; he put his brand on women all across Europe. As prince and king, he took frequent trips to German spas, where he indulged himself with steam baths, high colonic enemas, and sex. His favorite watering holes were in Paris. French police recorded Edward's comings and goings at hotels and intimate restaurants where he enjoyed the company of actresses, courtesans, and noblewomen. At one Parisian dinner, a huge covered serving tray was set before the prince. When the lid was lifted, Bertie happily discovered he had been presented with the infamous and beautiful Cora Pearl, clad only in a sprig of parsley and a string of pearls. Giulia Barucci, who called herself the "world's greatest whore," let her gown slide to the floor when she first met Bertie. He was pleased, and when her escort upbraided her she replied that she had only "showed him the best I have—and for free." He dallied with stage star Hortense Schneider, Moulin Rouge cancan dancer Louise Weber, known as *La Goulue* ("The Greedy One"), actress Sarah Bernhardt, and courtesan La Belle Otero.

Not all of the king's lovers were notables. He often cavorted at Le Chabanais, a Parisian brothel, where the chair upon which he sat with his lady of the evening became a conversation piece for the establishment's proprietor. It was said that King Edward, when he was a bit too rotund to enjoy the pleasures of the bed, would lounge in this chair and be fellated by a young woman. In spite of Bertie's tendency to stoutness, he was by all accounts a very virile man. He had great sexual stamina and staying power. No woman ever gave him poor marks; he was a "very perfect, gentle lover," said his mistress Daisy Brooke, Countess of Warwick.

According to the Duke of Cambridge, in his later years Bertie had a special liking for young girls. Three young women he frolicked with became known as "H.R.H.'s virgin band." However, his favorites by far were married beauties. In general, their husbands were from his inner circle of friends and considered it their duty to be cuckolded by Bertie. His schedule usually consisted of visiting a woman's home in the afternoon while her husband was away, joining his regular mistress in the evening, and often meeting his latest actress friend later in the night. The Marlborough House set was usually sufficiently discreet, but the arrangement caused a nasty scandal at least once. When Lady Harriet Mordaunt had a child that was born blind, she believed that this was God's curse and confessed to her husband that she had "done very wrong ... with the Prince of Wales and others, often and in open day." Bertie was forced to swear in court that he had not been the woman's lover.

Bertie's lengthy affair with professional model Lillie Langtry was severely chilled when the scandal sheets started rumors that her husband was about to divorce her and name the Prince of Wales as corespondent. His five-year liaison with the "Jersey Lily" began in 1877, and it was a very special one. She was independent, never subservient, and different from Alix in that she was punctual. (Because Alexandra was always late, Bertie, who was a fanatic about punctuality, kept the royal clocks set half an hour fast.) Even Alix became fond of Lillie and spoke of her in glowing terms. The princess seldom became jealous of her husband's other women, knowing that they posed no threat to her marriage, but she didn't take too kindly to an American actress named Miss Chamberlain, whom she disparaged as "Miss Chamberpots."

In the late 1880s Bertie fell deeply in love with Daisy Brooke, the Countess of Warwick, a seductive beauty 20 years younger than he. Their relationship worried Alexandra more than any of her husband's other dalliances. Bertie and Daisy exchanged rings, and he addressed her as his "little Daisy wife." He became involved with her when she went to him for help in a personal matter, her lover of the moment having had the nerve to make his own wife pregnant. Daisy was a volatile woman who couldn't stand such "infidelity," but that didn't prevent her from taking the Prince of Wales into her own bed. Their affair lasted almost seven years, but he began to see less of her when, in spite of her wealth and class standing, she lectured him on the economic exploitation of the lower classes.

The king's last long-term mistress was Mrs. Alice Keppel, who was Edward's junior by 30 years. During Edward's 12-year romance with her, both Mr. Keppel and Alexandra fully accepted Mrs. Keppel's role as second wife to Bertie. Mrs. Keppel often called at Windsor Castle, where she became Alexandra's good friend, and Edward frequented the Keppel home and played with Keppel's two daughters. Alice Keppel was the first person Alexandra notified when Bertie lay dying of bronchitis at age 68. Alice's daughter Sonia later wrote about "kingy's" visits and remembered the game she played with him. They would race buttered toast, buttered side down, along the king's trousers, he betting a penny on one leg, she betting that the toast on the other leg would be the first to slide to the floor. Bertie was, as Prime Minister Gladstone once wrote, "kept in childhood beyond his time."

—R.J.F. and V.S.

The Abdicating Lover

EDWARD VIII (June 23, 1894–May 28, 1972)

HIS FAME: King of England for only 327 days in 1936, Edward gained a renown that stemmed not so much from his short reign as from his abrupt abdication in order to marry "the woman I love." After leaving the throne, Edward became the Duke of Windsor, a title he held until his death.

Edward VIII and Wallis Simpson

HIS PERSON: Edward was born to be king. As George V's eldest son, Edward (David to his friends) passed his youth preparing for his turn to rule. But his childhood was not a happy one. His father, a strict disciplinarian, showed his children no affection. (Edward even admitted to a friend, "My father doesn't like me…. Not at all sure I particularly like *him*.") He preferred his mother, but their relationship was never close either and Queen Mary confessed to her intimates a distaste for raising children.

Nor was Edward's youth otherwise auspicious. He completed his prescribed schooling, but did so lackadaisically. During WWI he clamored for a demanding military assignment, but his royal position made that impossible. When the war ended, however, Edward began to come into his own. Dispatched as an unofficial roving ambassador, Edward (as Prince of Wales) toured the globe, and his unaffected bearing and abundant native charm soon made him one of the world's most popular figures. Even after his abdication he retained his popularity, and his personal wealth (an estimated $15 million) allowed him to pursue a leisurely luxurious life as a resident of France, where he frequented the nightclubs upon which he doted and immersed himself in golf and gardening. A heavy smoker, he died of throat cancer in the arms of the woman he loved and for whom he had abdicated his throne. He was a month shy of his 78th birthday.

SEX LIFE: Edward's rank, wealth, and charm cinched for the 5 ft. 6 in. slender young man acclaim as the world's most eligible bachelor. He reveled in that role and enjoyed the women it brought him. His affairs, or at least the bulk of them, were brief. An acquaintance once remarked that Edward "reset his watch by every clock he passed," and where women were concerned, his fickleness was undeniable. Only four women succeeded in engaging him in lengthy affairs.

He met the first, Lady Coke, when he was 21. Although 12 years older and married, Lady Coke was deluged with Edward's love for three years. When in England, he strove always to be with her. When he was abroad, Edward's letters cascaded upon her home by the score. Whether Lady Coke reciprocated his strong affection is unknown. What is known is that her marriage remained firmly intact throughout Edward's courtship.

When Freda Ward entered the scene, Lady Coke exited. Edward met Freda (who was married to a member of Parliament) in 1918 when an air raid drove the two strangers to seek shelter in a cellar. They conversed, and at the raid's end Edward insisted that she join him at a party, where they danced for hours. That began their 16-year relationship, during which Edward fell "abjectly" in love, as friends put it, with the learned and witty Freda. He underlined his devotion with telephone calls each morning (calls referred to by Mrs. Ward's staff as "the baker's") and whenever he was in London they invariably met for the evening at 5:00 P.M. sharp.

Occasional flings took Edward away from Freda, but their relationship remained strong, continuing even after he met the beautiful Thelma Furness. The 24-year-old "Toodles," who was Gloria Vanderbilt's twin sister, was married to Lord Marmaduke Furness, a British shipping tycoon. Theirs was a marriage of convenience, destined to end in 1933 after seven years of mutual infidelity. Physical passion, not the intellectual conviviality he found with Freda, fueled Edward's intense five-year affair with Thelma. But, despite their selection of the affable teddy bear as an emblem of their love, their liaison was not a thoroughly happy one. Edward, Thelma later complained, suffered from chronic premature ejaculation. (One of Edward's friends further impugned his sexual prowess, saying, "To put it bluntly, he had the smallest pecker I have ever seen.")

But both Freda and Thelma slipped from Edward's life within months of his meeting Wallis Simpson, an American divorcée who, like her predecessors, was currently married. Wallis entered Edward's life in 1931, when Thelma made the double mistake of introducing her to Edward as well as angering Edward by spending time with playboy Aly Khan. Wallis proceeded to take over Edward's life. The pair became inseparable. While not a beauty, Wallis' playfulness captivated Edward, as well as her ability to engage him in talk about his work. "I made an important discovery," Edward subsequently said, "that a man's relationship with a woman could also be an intellectual partnership." Edward soon helped Wallis arrange a quick divorce while he set his sights on marriage.

Edward was king at this point, however, and he had vastly underestimated the royal family's opposition to Wallis, a woman his mother condemned as "an adventuress" and whose two divorces smacked of scandal. Parliament, too, was unwilling to see Mrs. Simpson become queen, a title that, barring a constitutional change, automatically went to the king's wife. As the crisis heightened, Edward confronted his options. Either Wallis or the throne had to go. In an emotional speech on BBC radio, Edward announced his decision to abdicate in favor of his younger brother, Albert.

Six months later Edward and Wallis wed, despite continuing disapproval from the royal family and Parliament (the Cabinet withheld from Wallis the title of "Her Royal Highness," a slight that forever irked Edward). Nonetheless, to all appearances theirs was a storybook romance. Their lavishly opulent life filled the pages of every tabloid, and on the private level their love flourished too. Rare was the evening, even after many married years had passed, that Edward did not place a flower on Wallis' pillow. But there were discordant undertones in their love as well. Wallis was a hard-edged woman—"If she happened to be hungry, she might have taken a bite out of you," observed actress Lilli Palmer—and Edward was not spared. During one spat he exclaimed, "Darling, are you going to send me to bed in tears again tonight?" Edward, for his part, upbraided Wallis only once—when rumors reached his ears that Jimmy Donahue, the couple's frequent nightclub companion and an heir to the Woolworth fortune, had become her lover. Happily, however, the rumors were false, and Wallis could assure him (truthfully) that Donahue was a homosexual, adding, "His friends call me Queen of the Fairies."

Wallis dominated Edward's life, that much is certain. And for the man who once was king, it was exactly the way he wanted things to be. His love for Wallis was unwavering. At a 1970 White House dinner hosted by Richard Nixon, Edward offered this apt autobiographical summary: "I have the good fortune to have had a wonderful American girl consent to marry me and have 30 years of loving care and devotion and companionship—something I have cherished above all else."

—R.M.

The Royal Tease

ELIZABETH I (Sept. 7, 1533–Mar. 24, 1603)

HER FAME: The last Tudor monarch and one of England's best-loved and most able rulers, Elizabeth reigned for 44 years, a period of unprecedented national peace, prosperity, creative vigor, and geographical exploration.

HER PERSON: Elizabeth Tudor, the daughter of Henry VIII and Anne Boleyn, endured an emotionally battered childhood marked by the execution of both her mother and her stepmother, Catherine Howard, by the headsman's ax. Ascending the throne in 1558, she strove to reconcile the country's fierce

religious divisions and she built the nation into a major sea and colonial power. She condemned both her cousin, Mary, Queen of Scots, and her favorite, Robert Devereux, the Earl of Essex, to the chopping block, but only after exhausting every other means of subduing them. Physically expressive with her intimates, she often caressed men and struck women; she laughed much and also frequently wept. While she encouraged some personal familiarity, even flippancy, in her courtiers, she would not tolerate disrespect to the throne, and her chilling oath "God's death, my lord!" usually preceded a royal chewing out that reduced many an arrogant knight to abject trembling. Though not beautiful, she was certainly attractive. Her slender medium stature, shapely hands, pale oval face, and auburn hair were celebrated by poets of the time. Highly educated, she spoke five languages and was an expert rider and dancer. And she thrived on flattery. Even as she faded into a haggard, mirror-hating old woman decked with false red hair and plastered with cosmetics, she maintained her court of blazing young studs, all competing to praise her fantasied physical charms. But her intelligence and razoredged wit never faded, and English veneration for the "Virgin Queen" crowned her with the aura of a surrogate Virgin Mary. "Though God hath raised me high," she said in 1601, "yet I count this the glory of my crown, that I have reigned with your loves." She died at 69, apparently of an infection resulting from pyorrhea.

LOVE LIFE: For 30 years Elizabeth kept Englishmen and European courts frothing in a perfect stew of "does she or doesn't she?" The question of if, when, and whom the queen would marry persisted during most of her reign, and it kept many a powerful man, both at home and abroad, on his best behavior. Basically and always, she didn't want to marry and frequently said so. Yet she constantly invited men—young, athletic, handsome ones—to chase her. She loved the foreplay of passionate letters, ribald jokes, and heaps of gifts, and at times it seemed she had half the princes of Europe panting to share her bed and kingdom. But if she often hinted yes, she seldom went so far as to say it. She was an expert tease, who always found excellent reasons to delay consummation. Strangely, few of her cocky suitors learned her game, even after years of playing it. She winked and they came with tails wagging, eager to devour crumbs of ecstasy and chunks of exasperation from her lily-white hands—and she loved it. But she had seen too much of what had happened to the royal wives in her own family. To her, a husband represented at best the sharing of her throne; at worst, usurpation of her power.

Her first romance at age 14 was with Lord Admiral Thomas Seymour, younger brother of England's lord protector and a handome rake "of much wit and very little judgment," as she later described him. Seymour habitually romped into her morning bedroom, where the couple played slap-and-tickle. It was expensive dalliance, eventually costing Seymour his head when his motives—to marry her and stage a palace coup—became known. Elizabeth, under suspicion as heir apparent and ill that summer, may have had a miscarriage. According to biographer Alison Plowden, this was the only time in her life when a pregnancy might have passed undetected. Whatever trouble Seymour caused her, he set the favorite male prototype for her future romances—young, dashing, and usually somewhat longer on muscle than brains.

English noblemen by the dozen courted Elizabeth after she became queen. These included Sir Christopher Hatton, Sir Walter Raleigh (who named colonial Virginia for her), and, most enduringly, Lord Robert Dudley. "Sweet Robin," she called him and nicknamed him her "Eyes." She tickled his neck during his solemn investiture as the Earl of Leicester, and he teased her openly about their wedding date. Even though married to Amy Robsart, he pursued Elizabeth with such ardor that their eventual marriage seemed likely. They visited each other's bedchambers, and rumors flew that "Lord Robert did swyve [copulate with] the queen" and had fathered her child. But after Amy's suspiciously timely death, Elizabeth dared not marry him since this would seem to confirm that Dudley had poisoned his wife. Yet he stayed, a master intriguer who tried to steer her toward suitors he knew she couldn't marry. Their 30-year affair flamed hot and cold, but not even his secret marriage to Lettice Knollys, which infuriated the queen, interfered for long. Believing herself dying of smallpox in 1562, she swore that "as God was her witness, nothing improper had ever passed between them." Of all the men in her life, he probably knew her best. And when he died in 1588, she shut herself up for grief-stricken weeks and kept his last letter by her bedside until her own death.

At stake in her numerous foreign courtships was the balance of European power. Philip II of Spain, her former brother-in-law and a future enemy, pursued her; and the Archdukes Ferdinand and Charles of Hapsburg, the princes of Denmark and Sweden, Charles IX of France and his sulky homosexual brother, the Duke of Anjou, all sent proxies to woo her. At 49 she probably came closest to actual marriage. The 27-year-old Duke of Alençon, the younger brother of the Duke of Anjou, was not much to look at, but he was charming, was considered "apt for the getting of children," and was the only prince who actually came in person to see her. She called him her "Frog," but she kept him, like the others, on the burner too long (11 years) and she danced for joy when he finally died. Conveniently for her, the European courtiers who sought her Protestant hand usually were Catholic, so she always had a bottom-line escape clause.

Her sex life became a favorite topic for gossip. In 1581 it was charged that Dudley "hath five children by the queen," and that she never left long "but to be delivered." But squads of foreign ambassadors inquired closely and often into her sexual morals, and none ever produced a shred of evidence for scandal. Elizabeth maintained that if she "had ever found pleasure in such a dishonorable life ... she did not know of anyone who could forbid her; but she trusted in God that nobody would ever live to see her so commit herself," and she wanted her epitaph to "declare that a queen, having reigned such a time, lived and died a virgin."

MEDICAL REPORT: Was Elizabeth really a lifelong virgin? The best contemporary sources indicate that, unlikely as it sounds, she was. A sexual liaison simply could not have been kept hidden in her unprivate milieu. Was she a sexually normal woman? Lord Burghley, after thorough consultations with her doctors, concluded that she was "very apt" for procreating children, and he recommended marital intercourse to cure her of "such dolours and infirmities as all physicians do usually impute to womankind for lack of marriage." A contradictory report came from Elizabeth's physician, Dr. Huick, who advised her against marriage owing to a "womanish infirmity." Playwright Ben Jonson, a contemporary, claimed she "had a membrana on her, which made her uncapable of man, though of her delight she tryed many." A current theory has been advanced by endocrinologist Dr. Robert B. Greenblatt. He speculates that Elizabeth suffered from Rokitansky's syndrome, a congenital defect which produces a very shallow vaginal canal and an undeveloped uterus. This posthumous diagnosis could be true only if Elizabeth had never menstruated. A 1559 medical report written by Sir James Melville stated that "she had few monthly periods or none." This may be explained by another conjecture suggesting that Elizabeth suffered from anemia which started during puberty. In any case, sex for the queen was verbal and vicarious, and delightfully so. But no evidence exists that it ever got beyond adolescent slap-and-tickle. For her, that was close enough.

HER THOUGHTS: "I hate the idea of marriage for reasons that I would not divulge to a twin soul."

"I am already married to a husband, which is the people of England."

"I will have here but one mistress and no master."

—J.E.

The Polygluttonous King

FAROUK I (Feb. 11, 1920–Mar. 18, 1965)

HIS FAME: The last monarch to rule Egypt, Farouk (or Faruk) was known for his gluttony, his promiscuity, his capriciousness, and his kleptomania. While he began his reign at age 16 with high ideals, these quickly deteriorated under the impact of his monumental physical and emotional problems. He could weep over the death of a rabbit one moment, then pick a cat up by the tail and dash it against a wall the next. One of his first acts as king was to have his cars (more than 100 of them) painted fire-engine red, and then to make it illegal for any other cars to be that color, so that he could speed through the

Farouk and Irma Capece Minutolo in 1963

countryside without police interference. In a short time he had alienated his allies and his own army to such a degree that revolutionaries were able to take over in an effortless coup. Farouk went into exile at the age of 32. The deposed king's possessions, including a vast amount of pornography and the world's largest stamp collection, were auctioned off, bringing over a million dollars into the coffers of the new Egyptian republic. Farouk's erotica—the "nudie" playing cards, the pulp porn, the X-rated films, and even the manacles which he supposedly used to chain women to his bed—were a small part of his vast hoard. During his reign he had filched enough to fill several storehouses: bottle caps and toothpaste tubes, clocks and coins, a ceremonial sword and assorted medals stolen from the dead body of Riza Shah Pahlevi of Iran as it passed in state through Cairo, and even Winston Churchill's heirloom gold pocket watch.

SEX LIFE: At 18 Farouk fell in love with and married pretty 17-year-old Safinez Zulficar, whose name he legally changed to Farida ("The Only One"). Within a few years he began having other women and made no effort to hide the fact. By creating for himself an image as an insatiable lover, Farouk successfully hid from his subjects the embarrassing truth that he had underdeveloped genitals and a low sex drive.

He began each day with a banquet of not only eggs but countless dishes of meat and fish, and he swilled soda pop by the gallon, but his inevitable obesity was forgivable. It was even considered admirable for the 6-ft.-tall ruler to weigh in at 300 lb. A lack of virility, however, was another matter. Though he began having bouts of impotence at 23, he attempted sexual intercourse with an estimated 5,000 women in his lifetime. He consulted hormone specialists and hunted for aphrodisiacs, trying amphetamines, hashish mixed with honey, and caffeine pills, stopping only at powdered rhinoceros horn. While pelting other guests at nightclubs and gambling casinos with spitballs, he flirted with desirable women. Those who resisted his invitations were captured and deposited in "harems" at any one of his five palaces. He often coveted married women and tried to blackmail them into divorcing their husbands. He flaunted women in front of his wife; girls would, according to biographer Hugh McLeave, "scamper up the backstairs and make merry with the king until sunrise." None of those who became his mistress stayed long.

After nearly 11 years of marriage and three daughters—but no son—Farouk divorced the estranged Farida. According to rumor, Farida asked him to go ahead with the divorce after a French opera singer was seen leaving Farouk's bedchamber one night. In a futile attempt to regain the affection of the Egyptian people, he later married a commoner, Narriman Sadek, a 16-year-old who reminded him of another woman he had once desired. Narriman went with him into exile in Italy in 1952, but she returned to Egypt and obtained a Muslim divorce in 1954. Faruk established himself in Rome, settling into the role of European playboy on a dwindling fortune. There he met aspiring 18-year-old actress Irma Capece Minutolo when she appeared in a beauty contest. She lost the contest, but as a consolation prize Farouk took her under his wing. He paid for her singing lessons and moved her into his apartment building. Irma remained his friend until his death, but his infatuation did not prevent him from prowling the cabarets of Rome in a constant search for additional female companionship. Farouk died at age 45, after a night of sheer gluttony at his favorite restaurant. It was a fitting end.

—J.H.

The Lady-Killer

HENRY VIII (June 28, 1491–Jan. 28, 1547)

HIS FAME: The king of England from 1509 to 1547, Henry VIII is known for having had one of the most dramatic reigns in British history, during which he married six women and divorced or beheaded four of them. The divorce from his first wife necessitated severing the English church from Roman papal authority, which brought about the Reformation and changed the course of history.

HIS PERSON: The second son of Henry VII, Henry Tudor was blessed with magnificent looks. He was 6 ft. tall, fair, and powerfully built, and he had a formidable mind. In his teens he became the embodiment of the Renaissance man, excelling not only at tennis and jousting but also in music, art, philosophy, and other scholarly pursuits. Foreign ambassadors vied with native eulogists in praising his auburn hair, his golden beard, his "extremely excellent calf." He loved dancing and feasting, pageantry and fine dress. Sir Thomas More said of him that he "has more learning than any English monarch ever possessed before him," and asked, "What may we not expect from a king who has been nourished by philosophy and the nine muses?"

Henry, however, was also self-righteous, willful, and temperamental. During the first 20 years of his reign he drained the royal coffers to finance court entertainment and warfare. (He more than replenished them later when he broke off religious contact with Rome and confiscated the wealth of the monasteries.) Toward the end of his life he developed syphilitic leg ulcers, which prevented him from taking any physical exercise. The man who could tire four or more horses in a day and was considered the leading athlete in the nation became an obese, piglike man who walked with a limp and had to have his legs, of which he had been so proud, constantly bandaged. This affliction, plus repeated disappointments in love, turned Henry into an irascible and unpredictable monarch. Weakened by a number of illnesses, including malaria and alcoholism, he died at 55. Despite his failings, he left England a stronger, more unified kingdom than it had ever been, and he is remembered as one of its greatest rulers.

LOVE LIFE: At 12 Henry was betrothed to Catherine of Aragon, who was the 18-year-old widow of his brother Arthur. (They had been married six months when Arthur died.) But Henry did not wed Catherine until his succession to the throne two months before his 18th birthday. His first sexual experiences were with peasant girls when he was 16. Six weeks after he was crowned, Henry married Catherine, who wore white to show the world that, though she and Arthur had been briefly married, she was still a virgin and fit, therefore, to be Henry's wife.

When Catherine was young, she was quite beautiful. The daughter of King Ferdinand of Spain, she was dainty and graceful, loved to dance, and dressed in bold, bright colors. She was also Henry's intellectual equal. She taught him Spanish and decided to learn English herself. Henry loved her with the ardor of first love. He linked her initials with his in the royal monograms, wore her colors at tournaments, and ran to her with every new happening, saying, "The queen must hear of this!" or "This will please the queen!"

But soon Catherine's troubles began. Her first child, a girl, was stillborn; then a son died shortly after birth. Henry grieved, especially over the son, but soon turned his attentions toward consoling his wife. A second son was stillborn; a third was born prematurely and died. Finally Catherine gave birth to a healthy baby daughter, Mary, who would one day become Queen Mary Tudor. Despite his disappointment at the child's gender, Henry was delighted to be a father at last, saying, "If it is a daughter this time, by the grace of God the sons will follow." But during the next three years Catherine had two more miscarriages and another stillbirth; then, at 35, she stopped conceiving.

So much childbearing took its toll on Catherine's appearance; her figure had thickened and her face had a heavy look. Henry, at 25, was in the prime of life and had begun an affair with 17-year-old Elizabeth Blount, one of Catherine's ladies-in-waiting. Henry was ecstatic to have a young lover, and England was never so tranquil as when he carried on with his "Bessie." Six months after Catherine's last baby, Elizabeth gave birth to a male child, who was christened Henry Fitzroy and taken away to be raised in semiroyal privacy as the Duke of Richmond. He died in 1536.

When Henry stopped seeing Elizabeth, he began an affair with Mary Boleyn, daughter of Sir Thomas Boleyn and Lady Elizabeth Howard. Mary, at 18, had just returned from the French court, where she had lost everything but her heart for loving. Two years later, her sister Anne, aged 15, also returned from that court and became one of Catherine's ladies-in-waiting. During the next four years, while Henry slept with Mary, Anne fell in love with a young courtier named Sir Henry Percy, who was banished from court soon after the king became infatuated with Anne. As Anne reached her 19th year, Henry realized that he was in love with her.

Anne Boleyn was not beautiful but she was bewitching. She was small, with long dark hair and fiery eyes, and she was said to have three breasts. Anne had become sophisticated at the French court and had been hardened by her heartbreak over Sir Henry Percy. Moreover, she had learned by her sister's example. Anne refused to become Henry's mistress and thereby changed the course of history. Henry decided that he must have a divorce.

Henry's self-righteousness would not allow him to admit that he wanted to exchange his old, worn-out wife for a new one. Instead, he quoted the Bible: "If a man shall take his brother's wife, it is impurity; he hath uncovered his brother's nakedness; they shall be childless." He informed Catherine that for the last 20 years they had been living in sin. Catherine, who loved Henry, insisted that she was a virgin when she married him and would not agree to a divorce. Henry waited unsuccessfully for the pope to approve his divorce, which would insure the legitimacy of his future issue in the eyes of the English people. "The king's great matter," as it came to be called, dragged on for six years, while Anne held Henry at bay.

Finally, Henry divorced the English Church from Roman Catholicism, making himself head of both Church and State. He married Anne Boleyn, who had at last become his mistress and was pregnant. The English people would not accept Anne as queen—their loyalty remained with Catherine—and a reign of terror began, in which anyone who opposed Henry's marriage or his being the sovereign ruler of both Church and State was tortured and burned, drawn and quartered, or boiled to death.

As Henry's wife, Anne began to show the sharper edges of her tyrannical nature. Henry was soon advising her to "wear the bridle of reason." When Anne's first child was a daughter, Henry was bitterly disappointed. If his first wife had not been a good "broodmare," Anne apparently was no better. Three miscarriages and one stillborn son later, Henry was through with her. Five men—including her own brother—were accused of having had sex with the queen (they were all, in fact, innocent), and all five were sent to the block along with Anne. Anne would not be blindfolded, and the executioner found her eyes so disarming that he had someone distract her while he took off his shoes and stole up beside her to cut off her head.

For some time Henry had had his eye on Jane Seymour, one of Anne's ladies-in-waiting. Jane was as plain as Anne had been sparkling. She was simple, sweet, and good-natured, and her submissive ways greatly appealed to Henry after Anne's domineering nature. They married, and Jane gave birth to a boy, later to become Edward VI, but she herself died soon afterward. Henry was devastated. Of the four wives whom he outlived, Jane was the only one for whom he wore black.

Within a few years Henry wanted to make Germany an ally and therefore began to look for a German bride. Anne of Cleves was one prospect. Holbein painted a flattering portrait of her, and Cromwell, Henry's chief administrator, recommended her heartily. By the time she arrived from Germany, Henry was lusty for love; he traveled, laden with presents, to meet her boat. When he saw this Anne, he was immediately repulsed by her appearance. She was tall and spoke a guttural German, and her face was pitted from smallpox. Though they went through with the marriage, it was never consummated. When Henry asked Anne to resign her title, she was so relieved that she wasn't going to be beheaded that she instantly agreed.

Meanwhile Henry had become taken with yet another lady-in-waiting. Catherine Howard was the most beautiful of Henry's wives. At 18 she was fair, slender, merry, and light on her feet, and her pretty, tinkling laughter was often heard echoing down the castle halls. When her uncle informed her that she was to marry Henry, Catherine protested that she was in love with Thomas Culpeper, who happened to be the king's favorite courtier. Her uncle convinced her, however, that her personal wishes did not matter. Her fate had already been decided, and besides, she owed it to her family.

Henry felt that he was in love for the first time. At 50 he was having an Indian summer, and his lust for Catherine was insatiable. He caressed her in public much more than he had his other wives; in fact, he could not keep his hands off her. Catherine was his "rose without a thorn." He did his best to be her gallant bridegroom.

Catherine tried to please Henry. She avoided Culpeper as best she could, while poor Tom, as the king's favorite, was often called to his bedside when he was not with Catherine; there Henry would recall the joys he had shared with his fresh, young wife in excruciating detail. But soon rumors began circulating about Catherine. Henry's archbishop discovered that as a teenager she had been rather wild, had even been sexually involved with one of the boys who would pay nightly visits to her boarding school. Henry laughed it off at first. But when the court began to pour forth its evidence, he aged before their eyes. He cried in public for the first time. Wanting desperately to find a way to overlook Catherine's premarital indiscretions, he prolonged her life. But when it was discovered that she was currently in love with Thomas Culpeper, he flew into a rage. Catherine, her former lover, and Culpeper were all executed. Before the block Catherine announced: "I die a queen. But I would rather die the wife of Thomas Culpeper." She was buried near Anne Boleyn, her cousin.

His last tangle with romantic love had left Henry a very old and broken man. He had given Catherine his all, only to discover that she had never really let him into her heart. She was the first woman for whom he had not come first. But a year and a half later fortune smiled on him again in the form of yet another Catherine. Catherine Parr had a long hooked nose, a short neck, a respectable body, and a well-shaped, even ardent mouth. At 31 she had been widowed twice. She was cultured, graceful, and tactful. When, in 1543, Henry proposed marriage, she let out a shriek, saying that it would be better to be his mistress. But she soon took pity on the aging monarch, and pity developed into warm affection. She was a patient nurse for him in his old age, when Henry had grown fat and needed constant care. They were married for four years before Henry succumbed to his many illnesses. Though he had loved his last Catherine well, he asked to be buried next to Jane Seymour, "the woman who died in order to give me a son."

—J.H.

Muhammadan Heaven

KING ABDUL-AZIZ IBN-SAUD OF SAUDI ARABIA
(1880?–Nov. 9, 1953)

HIS FAME: Known as the King of the Desert, this magnetic charmer was the first leader to succeed in uniting all the warring nomadic tribes and sects of Arabia. In 1932 he bestowed his family name on the new nation, calling it Saudi Arabia and proclaiming himself its absolute ruler. The following year he flung open the doors of his desert kingdom and admitted Western developers, who rushed in to tap the lakes of oil beneath the Saudi sands. During his lifetime, while sharing 50-50 with his new friends, Ibn-Saud—whose official car had been a battered Studebaker—saw his personal income catapulted to a dizzying $2.5 million weekly. This sum provided tidily for his innumerable wives, concubines, slaves, and children.

HIS PERSON: The Sauds had ruled much of Arabia for 100 years, but soon after Ibn-Saud's birth the family was ousted from power by their rivals, the Rashids, and the future king spent his youth as an impoverished exile in Kuwait. During these refugee years, Ibn-Saud's father toughened the boy for desert fighting, ordering him to ride untamed horses bareback and forcing him to exercise every midday by walking barefoot over scorching rocks and sand. At 20 Ibn-Saud was pronounced groomed for revenge against the Rashids. He was 6 ft. 4 in., lean and muscular, and thirsty for battle. One black night, accompanied by 40 camel-borne men, he sneaked into his father's former capital of Riyadh, shot the governor, and occupied the castle. Overjoyed, onetime followers of the Saud dynasty rallied to him, as did nomadic tribesmen and religious leaders. It took him only two years to recapture half of Arabia. Subsequent battles eliminated remaining rivals, and Arabia became his. Ibn-Saud promptly proclaimed himself king and renounced further conquest. The arrival of oil revenue, and the problem of spending it, bewildered him. He regarded this income as his own, built no schools because he believed all learning was in the Koran, and no hospitals because Saudi Arabia had no doctors. Instead he acquired a stable of 500 luxury automobiles (one a green Rolls-Royce from Winston Churchill complete with a sterling silver ablution bowl), a trailer furnished like a throne room, and a fleet of airplanes.

Ibn-Saud's devotion to his Islamic faith was total. Five times daily he humbly bowed toward Mecca and prayed. He did not drink, smoke, gamble, or view motion pictures. And in rigid observance of the Koran, he never permitted himself more than four wives at a time.

The standards he set for his sons were equally puritanical. When the oilmen introduced alcohol to the country, he was appalled. After one of his sons embarked on a drunken binge, his father had him publicly flogged. Another son, following a night of boozy revelry that had seen him ousted from the British vice-consul's home, reappeared at his host's residence demanding an English girl for his

King Ibn-Saud with two of his more than 100 children

collection. When his request was refused, the young prince shot the consul dead. Ibn-Saud promptly ordered his son's arrest and invited the bereaved consul's widow to choose the method of execution, throwing in a promise that the prince's head would be stuck on a pike outside the British embassy. The widow declined the privilege, whereupon the sorrowful father sentenced his son to prison and commanded that he receive 20 lashes monthly. Dismayed by his sons' behavior, Ibn-Saud banished alcohol, and Saudia Arabia remains a dry country to this day.

SEX LIFE: By the grace of Allah—who had spoken through the prophet Muhammad—Ibn-Saud enjoyed sanctioned polygamy. By murmuring "I divorce thee" three times, he created frequent vacancies in his harem, always discarding one wife before a journey in anticipation of replacing her with a new discovery while on the road. He was forgivably vain about his sexuality. Aided by close to 200 wives, he fathered 44 legitimate sons. He is thought to have had 64 daughters, but the figure may be inexact since no one bothered to count girls. Sometimes new brides were chosen by emissaries. Brought to him veiled, they were taken immediately to the bridal chamber. If they displeased the king, they were divorced on the spot and sent away—still veiled.

Yet, in surprising recognition of women's rights, Islamic law decrees that each wife receive her share of connubial bliss. Obedient to his faith, Ibn-Saud made his rounds without protest. His duties accomplished, he then visited with his concubines and slaves.

His first bride, the beautiful Bint al Fiqri, whom he wed in Kuwait when he was 15, remained the love of his life although she died just six months after their wedding. Only one wife, Munaiyir, survived all the harem shuffles. She gave the king seven sons and also some daughters. He divorced Munaiyir once, but after her marriage to another man he realized that he missed her. Ibn-Saud demanded that she shed her new husband, then gratefully rewed her.

Ibn-Saud's last children were born when he was 67. His subsequent sterility depressed him, and in a final stab at youth he dyed his graying hair black. A heart attack took his life but it may not have ended his sexual career. He had prayed that God would allow his six favorite wives to join him in paradise. Perhaps God did.

QUIRKS: He considered morning sex unhealthy.

He despised communism, not ideologically, but because he believed Communist men slept with their mothers and sisters.

Shortly before each of his babies was to be born, he left the palace grounds and refused to view the infant until it was several days old. Following Islamic practice, he avoided the new mother sexually for 40 days.

HIS THOUGHTS: "The longest winter night is too short for me."

"Sleep is but a slice of death inserted into life; why have too much of it?" (True to his credo, he never slept more than five or six hours a day, dividing his sleep into three periods.)

—S.W.

The Sun King

LOUIS XIV (Sept. 5, 1638–Sept. 1, 1715)

HIS FAME: Known as "the Sun King" for the opulence and grand decadence of his reign, Louis XIV at the height of his power ruled every aspect of French life. A patron of artists, writers, and scientists, Louis led his army to victories over the other great nations of Europe. Although he created one of the most grandiose civilizations in history, he left his country impoverished, and his political and religious persecutions led to the French Revolution.

HIS PERSON: Whether or not Louis himself believed that he was a "visible divinity," he insisted that his subjects so regard him. He taxed the French people mercilessly to support the ostentatious life of his royal court and nearly bankrupted France to build the incomparable pleasure palace at Versailles.

The monarchy Louis inherited from his father was plagued by rebellious nobles, who in 40 years had fought 11 civil wars against the throne. Louis XIV brought the French nobles under royal control by offering them positions at his court, where he seduced them with wine, women, and fortunes. His elaborate system of patronage extended beyond politics to the ladies at court, where it was estimated there were never fewer than 300 of them scheming for the king's attentions. He was not reluctant to bestow wealth and prestige upon those women who participated in his dalliances.

Although facially scarred by a childhood bout with smallpox, Louis XIV was an athletic and witty charmer and an indefatigable lover. Married twice, he had innumerable affairs with noblewomen and palace servants alike and was generous to them all, ignoring scandal while he rewarded them with jewels, estates, and rank. His women were confidantes as well as lovers, and he decreed legitimate his many children born out of wedlock. However, torn between his licentious nature and the constant urgings of his religious counselors to atone for his many sins, Louis was often as harsh in his punishment of others' sins as he was lax in controlling his own. In 1674 he ordered the noses and ears cut off all prostitutes found servicing the soldiers stationed within 5 mi. of Versailles.

SEX LIFE: Although he was sexually initiated at 16 by a court seamstress who threw herself naked into his arms, Louis' first real love was Marie Mancini, a niece of his closest political adviser, Cardinal Jules Mazarin. Their affair of the heart lasted two years, until the entreaties of both Mazarin and Louis' mother convinced him to send her away from court. To bring about peace between France and Spain, Louis married Marie Thérèse of Austria, the daughter of the Spanish king.

Queen Marie Thérèse was a plain if not an ugly woman, devoutly religious but determined to do her "duty"—at least twice a month—by her husband, even if it meant sharing their living quarters with his mistresses. She bore six of Louis' children, although only one, the Dauphin Louis, survived infancy. The solitary suggestion of scandal to mar her married life occurred when a rival for Louis' affections, Madame de Montespan, claimed that Marie Thérèse had borne a black child after being given a black dwarf by an African prince. The queen said that during her pregnancy the dwarf once frightened her, and that that incident caused the child to be born black. The queen generally tolerated Louis' many transgressions, but her temper erupted one night when the king failed to return to their chamber. She had the entire palace searched, and every woman in Versailles was interrogated to find out whether she had the king in her bed. Marie Thérèse died in the convent in which she spent most of her later years.

Louis, of whom Voltaire said, "He liked the ladies, and it was reciprocal," conducted his court as a never-ending party. Surrounded by fawning attendants from the time he woke in the morning until he retired at night (when he used Versailles' labyrinth of secret passages to visit one of his current lovers), Louis directed every detail of the continuous round of hunts, dances, and royal dinners that established his court as the center of European culture. A court observer wrote, "One should have some indulgence for this prince if he should fall, surrounded as he is by so many female devils, all seeking to tempt him." And the women were encouraged in their prestige-seeking flirtations by "their families, fathers, mothers, even husbands."

While romancing his homosexual brother's wife, Louis fell in love with one of her attendants, Mme. Louise de La Vallière, who became his secret, then official, mistress. A frail, almost homely woman, La Vallière's place in the king's heart and court was usurped by one of her closest friends, Madame de Montespan, wife of the Prince of Monaco. A woman of intelligence and voluptuous beauty, the Marquise de Montespan used her influence as Louis' mistress to rule the social life of the palace for many years.

Since she had gained the king's affection and ascended to his bedchamber by treachery, Madame de Montespan was well aware that there would be romantic plottings against her by the other women of the court. Her attempt to keep Louis faithful led to the most famous scandal of their day, the "affair of the poisons."

In her anxiety, Madame de Montespan first resorted to love potions and charms. Then, despairing of their effectiveness, she submitted to Black Masses conducted by a mad priest. During these secret ceremonies, she would lie naked on an altar (with her face and breasts covered in deference to her rank) while priests chanted and fondled her body. It was alleged that she even participated in the sacrifice of infants, whose hearts and entrails were burned, powdered, and added to love potions which were slipped into the king's food.

Finally Madame de Montespan was accused of attempting to poison her rivals and of planning, out of frantic jealousy, to poison the king himself, reasoning that if she couldn't have him, no one else would either. Louis never gave public recognition to these accusations, but he dismissed her from his bed and court after providing her with an ample estate as a token of their affair.

There followed numerous short-lived romances before Louis became enthralled with Madame de Maintenon, widow of satirist Paul Scarron and former governess of the king's children. A deeply religious woman who had been disgusted by the sexual demands of her crippled husband (in his partially paralyzed state, he was forced to consummate their marriage orally), Madame de Maintenon at first rejected Louis' attentions and his request that she become his mistress.

Because she burned all of their love letters following Louis' death, it is only speculation that they slept together before they were secretly married, when she was 48 and he 45. (It has even been suggested that she was technically a virgin when they married.) Their morganatic marriage ceremony, during which the king gave her his left hand instead of his right, entitled this woman of common birth to be the king's wife without the rights or inheritance claims of a queen.

Considered frigid by nature and morally repulsed by Louis' extramarital affairs, Madame de Maintenon struggled to reform the king and save his soul, while still satisfying his amorous nature. "Imagine," she said, "the slavery of having to amuse a man who is incapable of being amused."

Still, the "peasant queen" did her best, and she shared the king's bed until he died of gangrene five days before his 77th birthday. A true voluptuary, Louis XIV remained lusty and vigorous until the end, both in and out of bed.

—R.S.F.

The Well-Beloved

LOUIS XV (Feb. 15, 1710–May 10, 1774)

HIS FAME: King of France from the age of five until his death at 64, Louis XV was a relatively passive ruler under whom the monarchy suffered a number of blows, including the loss of its North American colonies to England and an involvement in various debilitating wars. This paved the way for the revolution that toppled his successor, Louis XVI. When young, Louis was affectionately nicknamed "the Well-Beloved" by his people. Toward the end of his reign, however, his scandalous private life made him very unpopular. His fame today derives more from his love affairs than from his political achievements.

HIS PERSON: Because Louis inherited the throne as a child, the first years of his reign saw a regent and ministers in control of France. As a youth Louis dedicated himself to hunting and regular church attendance, pursuits he followed throughout his life. Official occasions required, however, that the boy-king appear before his thronged subjects. Those appearances scarred the child, leaving him forever fearful of crowds, extremely shy, and consistently aloof in his dealings with strangers.

In 1723, under prevailing French law, Louis reached his majority. Two years later, at the bidding of his chief minister, the Duc de Bourbon, Louis wed Maria Leszczyńska, daughter of Stanislas I, the deposed king of Poland. Adult or no, Louis still did not assume the full duties of the throne. In 1743, upon the death of Cardinal André Hercule de Fleury, who had replaced the Duc de Bourbon as chief minister, Louis insisted he would take complete control. Nonetheless, Louis still preferred pursuits more pleasurable than ruling—in particular, making love. His mistresses, and there were many, often meddled in the affairs of state. The Marquise de Vintimille is blamed for France's involvement in the War of the Austrian Succession (1740-1748).

SEX LIFE: Strikingly handsome, Louis had a sensuous face and a well-developed body. At 15 his sexual maturity was apparent. Since he loathed his five-year-old fiancée, the Spanish infanta, his chief minister affianced him instead to the 23-year-old Maria Leszczyńska. While preparations were under way for the scheduled wedding, Louis' tutors worried about how he could be taught the art of lovemaking. They decided to hang pictures of sex acts on the walls of his study. For firsthand instruction, Louis turned to a certain Madame de Falari and lost his virginity in her bed. Although Louis' intellect is occasionally belittled, he learned the subject of sex thoroughly. On his wedding night, Louis made love to his wife seven times.

Maria dutifully gave Louis 10 children (seven survived childhood), but her enthusiasm for sex paled beside his hearty appetite. As she pointed out, she was always "in bed, or pregnant, or brought to bed." She retreated within a small circle of staid intimates to whom she complained that Louis came to her in the night stinking of champagne, and soon she bored the king.

Maria and Louis remained wed until her death in 1768; however, their marriage, for all practical purposes, ceased to be in 1738. Maria, having suffered a miscarriage, was told by her doctor to refrain from sex. As a result she locked Louis out of her bedroom. Shortly thereafter he made public his affair of some duration with Madame de Mailly, one of the five De Nesle sisters. Within months Louis' fickle affections had turned to Madame de Mailly's sister, the Marquise de Vintimille. That affair ended when she died giving birth to his child. Louis turned next to a third De Nesle sister, the dazzling Madame de Châteauroux. She, too, soon died, after emerging from a sickbed to heed Louis' call. The youngest sister amused Louis briefly but found herself rewarded by being married to a duke. Only one sister escaped Louis' attentions. Her husband objected to sharing her with the king.

In 1745 Louis took as his mistress Jeanne Poisson, who became the Marquise de Pompadour—perhaps the central figure in his life. Pompadour, an accomplished and charming woman (even Maria liked her and said, "If there must be a mistress, better this one than any other"), had long dreamed of becoming part of the royal family. When she was nine, a fortune-teller thrilled her by predicting she would one day be the king's mistress. After contriving to draw Louis' attention to her at a ball, she became his "official mistress." Her husband grudgingly accepted a legal separation from her. Besides sharing the king's bed, Pompadour shared the secrets of state and the resources of the nation's treasury. Her love of luxury and her interference in politics caused the people to resent her as well as the king. Described by Louis as "the most delicious woman in France," Pompadour valiantly tried to keep pace with his unflagging sex drive. She took aphrodisiacs and lived on a diet designed to heighten her passion—a menu of vanilla, truffles, and celery. It was to no avail. As she herself confessed, she was "very cold by nature." In 1751, her health weakened by a chest infection, she ended her sexual relations with Louis. It was not the king's body she wanted—"it's his heart," she said. She got her wish. Pompadour remained Louis' closest confidante and, until her death in 1764, lived in apartments connected to his by a staircase.

After the break in physical relations with Pompadour, the virile king turned to a succession of lovers—often young prostitutes. At the Parc aux Cerfs, a four-room hideaway in Versailles, a parade of mistresses satisfied him. Very few knew that their lover was the king. They were told that he was a rich Pole. Girls were nearly always in residence there, but few stayed long; new lovers moved in to replace old ones whose charms had waned. Only Louise O'Morphi, a former model for the painter Boucher, achieved a long tenure at the Parc aux Cerfs. The libertine Casanova claimed in his memoirs that he had procured her for the king, but she may have been brought to Louis by his regular pimp, his valet Lebel. She arrived when she was 15 1/2 years old and instantly captured the king's affection. Several years and one or two children later, however, she indiscreetly asked the king about Pompadour. "On what terms are you, then, with your precious old girl?" she inquired. Louis sent O'Morphi packing for her boldness, although he did arrange a marriage for her with a minor noble.

In 1768 Louis took his last mistress of importance, the voluptuous Comtesse du Barry. The reputed daughter of a monk and—or so Parisian gossips claimed—a former prostitute, Du Barry's affair with Louis outraged the French. Louis was not to be shaken, however. When the Duc de Richelieu asked why he kept her, Louis replied: "She makes me forget that soon I will be 60." Du Barry remained with Louis until his death from smallpox.

HIS THOUGHTS: In inquiring into the attributes of a woman touted to him by a courtier, Louis asked whether she had "a good bust." The official admitted that he had not looked. "You are a booby!" Louis rebuked the man. "That is the first thing one looks at in a woman."

—*R.M.*

Spain's Doña Juana

QUEEN MARIA LOUISA OF SPAIN (Dec. 9, 1751–Jan. 2, 1819)

HER FAME: Maria Louisa, who was queen of Spain during the turbulent era of the French Revolution, scandalized the courts of Europe by using her royal bodyguards as a recruiting ground for sexual playmates. She elevated her most enduring paramour, Manuel de Godoy, from guardsman to prime minister of Spain. When the Spanish monarchy was overthrown in 1808, the queen went into exile accompanied by not only her husband but her lover as well.

HER PERSON: Maria Louisa was a Bourbon by birth and by marriage. Her father was the brother of Charles III, king of Spain; her mother was the eldest daughter of Louis XV of France; and Maria Louisa was married at the age of 14 to her cousin Charles, heir to the Spanish throne. Having been educated by the philosopher

Étienne Bonnot de Condillac, the aggressive and articulate Maria Louisa was considered twice the man her amiable but slow-witted husband was. She was also said to be an imperious woman with an unquenchable sexual appetite—the "degenerate offspring of an illustrious race." As a young woman she was shapely and graceful, with fetching black eyes, but she became old and haggard by her mid-30s owing to her many pregnancies (she gave birth to 12 children, losing five in infancy and miscarrying several others), dental disease (she lost her teeth by the time she was 37), and, it was widely believed, sexual excesses. According to the Russian ambassador in Madrid, "Her complexion is now greenish, and the loss of almost all her teeth—which have been replaced by artificial ones—has given the *coup de grâce* to her appearance." While all Europe seethed around her with revolutionary discontent, the queen of Spain sought solace for her lost beauty with a long succession of lovers.

HER LOVERS: Maria Louisa's infidelities were the scandal of Spain, a very prim country in matters of morality. Soon after her marriage she created her own court in the Casita del Principe ("Little Prince House") and began deceiving her husband with grandees such as the Count of Teba, the Duke of Abrantes, and Don Juan Pignatelli, exiling the latter to France because of his partiality to a fairer face. Other lovers were banished by Maria Louisa's sternly reproving father-in-law, Charles III. Only her husband, who became Charles IV on the death of his father in 1788, remained happily oblivious to his wife's promiscuity. "If queens felt tempted to sin," this true naïf who passed his days hunting and tinkering once remarked, "where would they find the kings or emperors to sin with them?"

Hitherto sovereign in her sexual caprices, Maria Louisa became enthralled at 37 by handsome 21-year-old guardsman Manuel de Godoy, an impoverished provincial nobleman whose brother had preceded him into the royal bed (and thence into exile). Godoy, amusing, indolent, sensual, aroused in her a grand passion compounded of lust, maternal instinct, hero worship, and jealousy. The balance of sexual power shifted to Godoy, who in 1792 at the age of 25 became prime minister of Spain. "It is difficult to imagine," French Ambassador Bourgoing wrote to Paris, "that a young man without any previous political experience could have been appointed to one of the most important ministries; a man whom the queen's love demands leave little time to dedicate to government affairs." Three years later, after concluding a catastrophic war against France, he was elevated to "Prince of the Peace," second in stature only to the king of Spain.

Most of Godoy's diplomacy was devoted to handling the queen. The Prussian ambassador described their typical day thus:

At eight o'clock in the morning Godoy goes to his country house riding school where the queen joins him every day at nine o'clock, while Charles IV is away hunting. The riding takes place until eleven. At one o'clock in the afternoon Godoy returns to the palace to be present during the queen's lunch, which is one of his "duties." Afterward, he goes to his rooms, which are located under the queen's. Maria Louisa soon joins him, using a secret staircase.

Aristocratic ladies vied for Godoy's favors, emerging rumpled and flushed from the prime minister's chancery, while their husbands contributed to his growing personal fortune. There was also Josefa "Pepita" Tudo, a beautiful, plump, dark-haired commoner who bore Godoy two children out of wedlock. It was to break up this affair that Maria Louisa arranged for her lover's marriage to the king's cousin, Maria Teresa de Vallabrige, Countess of Chinchon, in 1797. The countess, however, could not abide her husband, who continued to sleep with the comely Pepita.

Jealousy drove the aging, toothless queen, absurd in her girlish frocks, into even further sexual excesses. "To appease the queen's unnatural sensuality," the French ambassador reported, "the assiduity of the king, the fleeting attentions of the Prince of Peace, and the frequent assistance of the choicest of the bodyguards are all required." During periods of estrangement from Godoy, Maria Louisa consoled herself with fresh young bodies: an Italian named Malaspina, whom she goaded to intrigue against Godoy; Don Luis de Urquijo, who was promoted by the queen to first secretary of state; and Don Manuel Malló, another handsome guardsman, who was rewarded for his services with a carriage and horses so splendid that even the phlegmatic Charles took notice. Seated with Maria Louisa and Godoy, the king one day asked, "Manuel, who is this Malló whom I see every day with a new carriage and horses?" Replied Godoy, "Your Highness, Malló does not have a penny, but it is well known that Malló is kept by some toothless old woman who robs her husband to enrich her lover." The king laughed and turned to the queen. "What do you think of this, Louisa?" Flushed, the queen replied, "Charles, you know that Manuel is always joking!"

Godoy is even said to have provided the queen with lovers. Whatever the case, the bond between Maria Louisa and her favorite was so compelling that it lasted the rest of her life. Godoy fathered two of the queen's children, a son named Francisco and a daughter named Maria Isabella. Far from being suspicious, the complacent Charles was genuinely fond of Godoy, to whom he abdicated all power and responsibility. This aroused the undying enmity of the heir apparent, Ferdinand, who conspired to overthrow the regime. The French intervened, Napoleon installed one of his brothers as king of Spain, and Maria Louisa and Charles were dispatched into exile. With them, as the fulcrum of the royal sexual triangle, went Godoy and his assorted children, legitimate and otherwise. They were joined by Pepita shortly afterwards. This complicated ménage survived until the death of Maria Louisa in Rome, followed by that of her husband just three weeks later. Free at last, Godoy moved to Paris, where he married his Pepita in 1828. Bored and weary of their poverty, Pepita left him and went back to Spain in 1833.

—C.D.

The Monk And The Harem

KING MONGKUT OF SIAM (Oct. 18, 1804–Oct. 1, 1868)

HIS FAME: This king of Siam is known to the Western world as the inspiration for the Broadway musical *The King and I*. In Asia his popularity was due to his ability to befriend foreigners, thus sparing his people the violence that accompanied the coming of the Europeans to the rest of the continent. He was a progressive leader who initiated many democratic reforms before his subjects even asked for them. After his death he was called Rama IV.

HIS LOVES: Few people in history have gone through such a sudden and radical change in their sex lives as did Mongkut at the age of 46. He began normally enough, marrying early and fathering two children. When he turned 20 he followed tradition by leaving his family to become a monk, intending to return in a few months. However, while he was away his father died, and Mongkut's elder half brother was chosen to replace him as king. In order to avoid any hint of political intrigue, Prince Mongkut remained a monk and spent the next 26 years practicing celibacy in the priesthood.

In 1851 his half brother died, and it was Mongkut's turn to be king. He moved from his simple quarters in a monastery to the luxurious accommodations of the Inner Palace in Bangkok, which he shared with 3,000 women. No other men were allowed in the Inner Palace except priests and an occasional doctor, and these visitors had to be escorted by members of the all-female palace guard.

Assuming the throne in early April as Phra Chom Klao, Mongkut wasted little time returning to action after two and a half decades of abstinence. By mid-August he had taken 30 wives, and early in 1852 royal children began appearing at a rapid pace. By the end of his 17-year reign he had fathered 82 children, 66 of whom were alive at the time of his death.

The rigid laws of custom stipulated that he spend the period between 11:00 A.M. and 1:00 P.M. each day being "attended by the ladies of the palace." Unlike his predecessors, Mongkut felt that he had more than enough wives and concubines. In the most dramatic reform of his career he announced that his wives and concubines, if they so desired, could leave the palace to return to their parents or to marry other men. Only the mothers of his children could not remarry. Very few women took advantage of the king's offer.

—*D. W.*

The Passionate Prude

VICTORIA (May 24, 1819–Jan. 22, 1901)

HER FAME: The longest-reigning monarch in English history (1837–1901), Victoria became symbolic of the era of prudery and sexual repression which bears her name. There is increasing evidence, however, that Albert, her adored husband and stern consort, was the true inspiration behind Victorianism.

Queen Victoria and Prince Albert

HER PERSON: Victoria's father, fourth son of King George III, died when she was an infant. She grew up simply at Kensington Palace, sharing a room with her mother and companionship with her German governess, Baroness Lehzen. Despite a solitary childhood, she was a merry, mischievous, and willful little girl; her imperious tendencies were reinforced on becoming heir apparent to the throne at age 11 and queen at 18.

The young Victoria was a romantic figure. Although only 5 ft. tall ("Everybody grows but me," she lamented) and with a hearty appetite that early portended stoutness, she was fair, charming, and as sprightly as a hummingbird. During the first visit of her cousins Ernest and Albert, 16-year-old Victoria danced and romped to her heart's content. "All this dissipation does me a great deal of good," she remarked.

LOVE LIFE: In her time the most prized match in the world, Victoria was courted by a succession of royal suitors, many of them her cousins. She described them all in her diary with enthusiastic approval, particularly the tall, dashing Grand Duke Alexander, heir to the Russian throne, with whom she fell just a little in love. But the dominant male figure during her first years on the throne was Lord Melbourne, prime minister of England, a gallant, sophisticated man of great erudition who educated the young queen in her public role and took private pleasure in gossiping with her on the sofa at Windsor Castle. The widowed Melbourne, who was 40 years older than his pupil, has been described as "more than a father, less than a lover" to Victoria. They spent several hours a day together, obviously delighted with one another's company, and corresponded when they were separated even briefly.

Although she was susceptible all her life to strong men with roguish charm, Victoria chose to marry her cousin Albert, a young German princeling with operatic good looks, because she found him pure and fair, gentle and winning. As queen she was the one to propose marriage, and she maintained her ascendancy during an engagement otherwise noted for fervent embraces and ecstatic letters. "I am the Sovereign," Victoria reminded her betrothed, denying his request for a quiet honeymoon. Shortly after the 20-year-olds were wed, Albert complained to a friend that he was only "the husband, not the master of the house." But his influence grew with every day, and with every night, and with every royal pregnancy, of which there were nine. By the second child, Albert had succeeded in supplanting the governess, Baroness Lehzen; by the third, the royal "I" had been changed to "we."

Was Victoria a true Victorian or not? The evidence is contradictory. The wedding night injunction to "Close your eyes and think of England" has been attributed to her; but she also wrote with such frankness of the delights of the marriage bed that her journal was destroyed after her death. She hated pregnancy ("a complete violence to all one's feelings of propriety") and complained of the "shadow side of marriage," i.e., the sexual slavery of woman to man; yet she liked to call Albert her angel, worshiped him effusively, and presented him with gifts of nude works of classical art. When advised to have no more children, she is said to have replied to her doctor, "Oh, Sir James, can I have no more fun in bed?" However, Victoria was naive about some aspects of sexuality. In 1885, when presented with the anti-homosexual Criminal Law Amendment, she crossed out all references to females. Lesbianism simply did not exist, insisted the queen.

Victoria and Albert had, by any account, an intimate companionship. What the straitlaced and abstemious consort lacked in passion he made up for in devotion, calling Victoria "little wifey" in German, choosing her bonnets, and even putting her stockings on for her. He knelt at her feet and held her hand even while enduring her emotional outbursts. The two shared a mutual love for music, mountains, history, and family. Both were jealous and possessive—Albert of influence over his wife, Victoria of attractive women, even her oldest daughter. For it was the queen who was the child in the royal family, enjoying in her patient and protecting husband the father she never knew.

Albert's public role was to foster the national climate of piety and prudery which typified "Victorianism." Lacking the queen's natural vigor, he damaged his health irreparably in a fit of hysterical indignation over the Crown Prince Bertie's illicit escapades. After Albert's sudden death at the age of 42, Victoria was consumed with grief and longing. "Poor Mama," her daughter Vicky said, "has to go to bed and has to get up alone—for ever." Not quite alone. There were Albert's nightshirt clutched in her plump arms, a portrait of him on his pillow, and a cast of his hand nearby.

A WIDOW'S CONSOLATIONS: The usual image of the widowed Victoria is a plump, plain figure with bulbous eyes and a little kerchief on her head, mourning for her sainted Albert. Remarriage was unthinkable, but there were diversions. Chief among these was John Brown, a burly, brusque Scots manservant who became the queen's closest companion after Albert's death. "Wumman," he would say familiarly, "what's this ye've got on today?" Victoria's son and successor, Edward, was appalled at her attachment to Brown. He ordered a wooden pavilion dismantled which had been a favorite resting place of his mother's when she went on outings with Brown. Victoria promptly commanded that it be rebuilt, and retaliated by giving Edward the silent treatment for several weeks. The pavilion most likely harbored drinking buddies and not lovers, since Victoria and Brown shared a fondness for whiskey. Victoria for her part publicly acknowledged Brown as her "friend and most confidential attendant," refusing to give him up despite scandalous rumors that they were secretly married. (It has even been argued that Victoria bore Brown a son, who died a recluse in Paris at the age of 90.) Brown himself died in 1883.

One of Victoria's last conquests was Benjamin Disraeli, who as prime minister (1868, 1874–1880) became the queen's close friend and confidant. Also a bereaved spouse, Disraeli was a romantic who consoled and flattered Victoria, restoring her taste for power by making her empress of India. Although Victoria once paid "Dizzy" the honor of visiting him at his country house, he declined another royal visit from her on his deathbed, saying, "No, it is better not. She will only ask me to take a message to Albert."

—C.D.

X

Follow the Leader

The Master Of Monticello

THOMAS JEFFERSON (Apr. 13, 1743–July 4, 1826)

HIS FAME: The third president of the U.S. wrote his own epitaph. It reads, "Here was buried Thomas Jefferson, Author of the Declaration of Independence, of the Statute of Virginia for Religious Freedom, and Father of the University of Virginia."

HIS PERSON: Irony and ambivalence were as much a part of his makeup as were his red hair and 6-ft. 2-in. stature. One of history's most complex characters, he once asked the Virginia legislature for permission to free his slaves and later in his first draft of the Declaration of Independence he condemned slavery. However, in his *Notes on Virginia* of 1785, he compared blacks to whites unfavorably, citing "a very strong and disagreeable odor," laziness, and the inferior intellect of the former. Furthermore, he said, blacks themselves prefer the beauty of whites much like "the preference of the orangutan for the black women over those of his own species."

Psychohistorians have suggested that his role in the rebellion against the mother country was due in large part to hostile feelings toward his own mother, Jane Randolph Jefferson, who was widowed when Tom was 14 and with whom he lived until he was 27. Jefferson once told John Adams that if he had to live his life over again, he'd skip the first 25 years, and in a letter to his mother's brother in England, dated May, 1776, he dismissed news of his mother's death the previous March with three unsentimental lines.

LOVE LIFE: His first love was Rebecca Burwell. He was 19 and she was 16, and the relationship had a certain adolescent air about it. She gave him a silhouette of her profile, and he referred to her in code in his letters. But because he failed to make his intentions clear, he lost her to another man. "Never again," says biographer Fawn Brodie, "would he fall in love with a virgin with whom marriage would be in every case socially acceptable."

His first nonvirgin was Betsey Walker, wife of his friend and neighbor John Walker. Jefferson had been a member of the Walker wedding party in 1764 and was named executor in Walker's will, but in 1768, while Walker was away for the summer, Jefferson made advances to Betsey. She admitted that much to her husband almost 20 years later. In 1802 the Walkers and President Jefferson became the object of a national sensation over the President's past relationship with another man's wife. Only through the mediation of mutual friends was the President able to avert a duel with John Walker, who—34 years after the fact— had become the most famous cuckold in the land.

Martha Wayles Skelton's husband had also been a friend of Jefferson's. After Skelton's death Tom and Martha were married, on New Year's Day, 1772. Jefferson virtually removed himself from politics during the marriage, preferring his gentleman-farmer pursuits at Monticello, his Virginia estate. Martha was a bit of a Tory and historians contend that Jefferson never would have become president had she lived longer. But she was not a healthy woman. She lost three children in infancy and after giving birth to their third daughter she herself died in 1782, leaving Jefferson with a suicidal sadness and a deathbed promise that he'd never marry again.

After overcoming his grief he agreed to succeed Benjamin Franklin as minister to France, and he set sail for the Continent in 1784. The carefree lifestyle he encountered was a revelation to him, and everywhere he looked it seemed that men such as his friend Lafayette and his aged countryman Benjamin Franklin were in joyous pursuit of women. In 1786 Jefferson, too, succumbed. He met Maria Cosway, a 27-year-old artist and the unhappy wife of English miniaturist Richard Cosway. Their mutual attraction was immediate, and their private correspondence, including Jefferson's famous "My Head and My Heart" letter, reflects the emotional depth of their relationship. Part of that 12-page letter reads: "Deeply practised in the school of affliction, the human heart knows no joy which I have not lost, no sorrow of which I have not drank! Fortune can present no grief of unknown form to me." Maria left her husband in London and spent almost four months in Paris in the fall of 1787, but because of her Catholicism or her fear of Cosway or simple confusion, she returned to London in December, leaving Jefferson with a letter of good-bye. She was to write him many more letters, almost until the day he died. Most of her letters the heartbroken Jefferson left unanswered.

"It is well known that the man, whom it delighteth the people to honor, keeps, and for many years has kept, as his concubine, one of his slaves. Her name is SALLY." Thus scandalmonger James T. Callender, writing in the *Richmond Recorder* on Sept. 1, 1802, launched one of the most blistering attacks ever leveled at the private life of an American president. "Sally" was Sally Hemings, the beautiful mulatto daughter of slave Betty Hemings and her master John Wayles, Jefferson's former father-in-law. Sally had accompanied Jefferson's daughter Polly to France in 1787 when she was 14 years old, and she remained with Jefferson, occupying a place of special privilege at Monticello, until his death 39 years later. Only recently have white historians begun to accept what black historians have maintained for years, that Thomas Jefferson was the father of Sally Hemings' seven children, and that there was some truth to a ballad that made the rounds during his presidency. Sung to the tune of "Yankee Doodle" and presented from the point of view of Jefferson, it included the following verses:

When press'd by loads of state affairs,
I seek to sport and dally,
The sweetest solace of my cares
Is in the lap of Sally.
She's black you tell me—grant she be—
Must color always tally?
Black is love's proper hue for me—
And white's the hue for Sally.

—*D.R.*

Bachelor President

GROVER CLEVELAND (March 18, 1837–June 24, 1908)

HIS FAME: New Jersey-born Stephen Grover Cleveland, the only president in U.S. history to serve two nonconsecutive terms (1885-1889 and 1893-1897), is remembered for his opposition to that era's tariffs and for his prolific use of the veto— 413 times in his first term alone. Many thought of him as an uncouth, uneducated, barroom ruffian, while others saw him as an honest statesman and a man one could count on. As sheriff of Erie County, N.Y., in 1871, "Big Steve" was required by law to fill in when the usual hangman wasn't available. Twice Cleveland threaded the noose around a murderer's neck and sprang the gallows trapdoor. This attention to duty provoked

his enemies to dub him "the Hangman of Buffalo." He was described as unimpressive and charmless, but his physical size was notable. Short and stocky, he weighed 250 lb.

HIS LOVES: While Cleveland was an unlikely choice for the role of president, let alone paramour, he began his first term amid the hubbub of a sex scandal. His trudging efficiency and integrity as governor of New York State had at first made him the perfect Democratic opponent to Republican nominee James G. Blaine in the 1884 election because Blaine's political career had been tainted with corruption. Early on in the campaign, however, the Republican party revealed that Cleveland had fathered a son out of wedlock. Apparently Cleveland had regularly enjoyed the company of women during his years in state and local politics, for his saloon pals took no special notice of a tall, slender widow named Maria Crofts Halpin. The 35-year-old mother of two was different from most of Cleveland's female friends in that she seemed cultured and educated, never swore, and seldom drank. Then, in 1874, she bore a son. Although he wasn't certain the child was his, Cleveland never denied that he was the father. Desperate for a husband, Widow Halpin tried to cajole Cleveland into marrying her. He refused and the despondent woman turned to drink. Ever conscientious, Cleveland placed the boy in an orphanage until foster parents could be found, and when Maria protested, she was committed to a Buffalo asylum for five days. Later, she tried to win legal custody of her son until Cleveland gave her $500 to drop the suit. Maria moved to Niagara Falls, where she started a small business with more of Cleveland's money, and ultimately remarried. A wealthy couple was located to adopt the boy, who grew up to become a doctor. The gossip faded out until 1884. Then the Republicans—taunting Cleveland with their "dirty tricks" campaign slogan, "Ma, Ma! Where's my Pa? Gone to the White House, ha, ha, ha!"—brought the long-dead affair into the open. When his campaign workers asked how they should respond, Cleveland commanded them, "Tell the truth." This they did, right down to the fact that Cleveland had financially supported the mother and child. Such unprecedented honesty turned the scandal into a political asset.

Two years after the election, the first presidential marriage to occur in the White House united Grover Cleveland and 22-year-old Frances Folsom. The daughter of Oscar Folsom, Cleveland's law partner, she was the youngest, and many said prettiest, First Lady ever. Cleveland had looked after her in the years following her father's death. He once confided to his sister that he was "waiting for his wife to grow up." A regular visitor to the Folsom house, Cleveland had taken young Frances toys, once surprising her with a pet terrier. While at Wells College, her room was kept bright with flowers from "Uncle Cleve." Although only 31 guests attended the wedding ceremony, the Chief Executive's romance captured the public's fancy. The newspapers wanted to squeeze every possible headline out of the event, and despite efforts to keep the presidential honeymoon plans secret, reporters trailed the newlyweds to Deer Park, Md. The next morning, Cleveland was infuriated to discover his honeymoon lodge surrounded by newsmen equipped with powerful field glasses. Marriage had a settling influence on the President, and Frances brought a social elegance to the White House that the bachelor executive had not achieved. Their second child, Esther, was the first baby born in the White House. Their first child was born between Cleveland's two terms.

Unable to attack Cleveland's politics successfully, the Republicans kindled rumors about his private life toward the end of his first term. Opponents accused Cleveland of drunken rages that led to wife-beating. Frances repeatedly denied such allegations, standing by her husband until he died of a stomach ailment at age 71.

—T.C.

Supreme Commander

DWIGHT DAVID EISENHOWER (Oct. 14, 1890–Mar. 28, 1969)

HIS FAME: Supreme Allied Commander of the European theater in WWII, Eisenhower masterminded the Normandy invasion and liberated North Africa and Italy; it was to him that the Germans surrendered on May 7, 1945. His wartime military feats and his winning personality made him a popular hero; he capped his career by serving two terms as president of the U.S., 1953-1961.

Eisenhower and Mamie in the beginning

HIS PERSON: Eisenhower was raised in Abilene, Kans., the son of a poor dairy worker. "Ike," as he was called, entered West Point after working to help pay for a brother's college education and graduated in 1915. While stationed in San Antonio, Tex., he met Mamie Geneva Doud, who was vacationing there with her parents. The young couple was married in 1916. One month later Ike put his arms around his new wife and said, "Mamie, there's one thing you must understand. My country comes first and always will. You come second." The couple had two children, David Dwight, who died young, and John Sheldon Doud, born in 1923. As a professional officer, Eisenhower never remained in one post very long; by the time he became president, he had moved 34 times, serving in posts in Panama, France, the Philippines and elsewhere. But none of these assignments seems to have changed his provincial outlook—the French were always "frogs" to Ike. In the peacetime army, his rise through the ranks was painfully slow; he was only a colonel at the outbreak of WWII. But his singular diplomatic gifts, including a marked skill at cards, won him rapid promotion during the war, with some assistance from friends like Generals George Marshall and Douglas MacArthur. Promoted for his ability to put strategic theory into action, Eisenhower always allowed himself free time to play bridge and read pulp magazines. As a general and as president, he delegated as much work as he could.

His domestic life was far from tranquil. Mamie, the favorite daughter of a wealthy Denver meat-packer, often refused to live in army housing at distant outposts. She later cited squalid living conditions as the reason. Ike once had to protect her from an attacking bat by lunging at it with his dress sword, "just like Douglas Fairbanks," she said. The death from scarlet fever of their beloved first son, "Icky," was a blow from which they never fully recovered; they drifted apart as Ike was shuttled from post to post. During WWII, their separation for over two years while Ike led the Allies to victory in Europe prompted bitter correspondence ("please try to see me in something besides a despicable light," he pleaded; "... you don't really think of me as such a black-hearted creature as your language implies").

After the war there was less moving around. The marriage settled down and Ike became involved in civilian politics, seeking and winning two terms as president. In office, Ike steered a moderate-conservative course and tried to leave as much time open for golf as he could. When chipmunks disturbed his putting on the White House lawn, he had them box-trapped and carted away. He left the White House in 1961, retiring to his farm near Gettysburg, where he died nine years later, following a heart attack. Mamie was by his side.

LOVE LIFE: As a young man Ike had a reputation as a woman hater; wife Mamie once said that this made him intriguing, and added that he was a "bruiser," being well built and handsome. As a military hero during WWII he still retained some of those qualities and won the heart of Kay Summersby, an aristocratic young Irish woman who served as his staff driver. "His kisses absolutely unraveled me," Summersby wrote afterwards. "Hungry, strong, demanding." Their affair, hotly denied by the Eisenhower family, was unconsummated because the general was impotent, according to Summersby's memoirs. After an attempt at lovemaking, the general reportedly confessed, "It's too late." On another occasion Ike told her his marriage to Mamie "killed something in me. Not all at once, but little by little. For years I never thought of making love, and when I did ... I failed." However, ghostwriter Sigrid Hedin says that Summersby told her that Ike was not totally impotent, although Summersby had to teach him about lovemaking. But Kay loved him: "I wanted to hold him ... I wanted to lie on some grassy lawn and see those broad shoulders above me, feel that hard body against mine." According to Harry Truman, Eisenhower wrote to General Marshall right after the war, asking to be relieved of duty so he could divorce Mamie and marry Kay. Truman said that Marshall sent a sizzling reply to the effect that, if Eisenhower ever did such a thing, Marshall would personally "bust" him out of the army and make his life hell.

Eisenhower was not about to let romance ruin his budding political career. But the aborted affair haunted the general and his family for years to come and would have surfaced in the 1952 election had Truman not destroyed the incriminating Marshall-Eisenhower correspondence. Ike and Mamie went on to share a king-sized, pink-ruffled bed during their White House years, though it was doubtful that sleep in a pink bedroom was pleasant for the general, who had once changed his suite in Claridge's of London because the bedroom was "whorehouse pink."

QUIRKS: While Mamie later claimed, "Ike took care of the office, I took care of the house," she knew so little about housekeeping when they were first married that Ike had to do the cooking and cleaning. To save money when they were living on an officer's pay of $100 a month, Ike also hemmed her dresses and showed enough skill with a needle to perk up a frock.

—*J.A.M.*

The Indiscreet President

WARREN G. HARDING (Nov. 2, 1865–Aug. 2, 1923)

HIS FAME: The 29th president of the U.S., Harding led the country during the restless years following WWI. Elected by the widest popular margin recorded up to that time, he was the only president to state that he lacked the stature for such an office and that he didn't want the job.

Harding and his wife, Florence

HIS PERSON: Born in Blooming Grove, O., the son of a farmer turned doctor, Harding attended Ohio Central College, where he showed ability in public speaking and writing. After a brief stint as a schoolteacher, he purchased the *Marion Daily Star*, an unsuccessful small-town newspaper. The young publisher caught the attention of Florence Kling DeWolfe, an unattractive divorcée with one child and the daughter of the wealthiest man in Marion. The strong-willed Florence pursued Harding with a vengeance until he married her in 1891. Florence, a shrewd businesswoman, took the reins of the newspaper into her own hands, and its circulation soon increased. Harding was then able to devote more time to the community, and he became an important figure in local organizations and fraternal orders. He allied himself with the powerful Ohio political machine and was elected state senator in 1898 and U.S. senator in 1914. When the time came to select a presidential candidate, Harding's political cronies in the Republican party knew that he was their man: a middle-of-the-road midwesterner whom war-weary Americans would rally around. Strikingly handsome and with an imposing stature, he looked the part. But most important, he was easily manipulated. He was decidedly lax in supervising his political appointees, many of whom were personal friends. By 1923 the gross misconduct in his administration had surfaced. The Teapot Dome scandal involved California and Wyoming oil reserves, which Secretary of the Interior Albert Fall secretly leased—in return for $400,000 in bribes—to oil barons Henry F. Sinclair and Edward L. Doheny. While Harding was not personally involved, the news of such corruption overwhelmed him. He became ill and died in San Francisco after eating spoiled shellfish. Some speculated that he was murdered, but no autopsy was performed and the cause of death was officially recorded as a sudden stroke.

LOVE LIFE: Harding's character was best summed up by his father: "If you were a girl, Warren, you'd be in the family way all the time. You can't say no." A relentless womanizer, Harding's lecherous desires led him from pleasure palaces to clandestine rendezvous, while his wife was left brooding over his infidelities. He was not physically attracted to Florence Harding, and it was common knowledge among their friends that Harding sought sexual fulfillment outside his home. The couple's domestic life was a dramatic cat-and-mouse game. She spied on him and had him followed, castigating him with her evidence, while he remained impenitent, carrying on two long-term love affairs with women from Marion, O. The first of these women, Mrs. Carrie Phillips, the beautiful wife of a prominent local department store owner and a friend of the Harding family, was said by Warren's intimates to have been the most important love of his live. Before Harding became president, the two couples traveled together extensively and their friendship appeared innocent. Eventually Mr. Phillips discovered the love affair, and when downtown Marion was decorated in bunting the day Harding's presidential campaign opened, Phillips' store remained conspicuously bare. Throughout the 15-year liaison, which continued until 1920, Harding wrote ardent love letters, clumsily describing his lover's physical attributes and his strong sexual urges. In a letter dated Christmas, 1915, headed "The Seventh Anniversary," he included this poem:

> I love you more than all the world
> Possession wholly imploring
> Mid passion I am oftime whirled
> Oftimes admire—adoring
> Oh, God! If fate would only give
> Us privilege to love and live!

Carrie saved all of his letters, using them for blackmail when he refused to divorce his wife and marry her. In 1920 the Republican National Committee paid Carrie Phillips $20,000 and guaranteed her a monthly stipend of $2,000 as long as Harding held public office.

While Harding was still a U.S. senator, he began an affair with Nan Britton, the daughter of an old family friend. He had developed a more than paternal interest in her when he was in his mid-40s and she was a flirtatious 13-year-old, physically mature for her age and so obsessed with winning Harding's attentions that Mrs. Harding asked Nan's mother to restrain her from climbing on Harding's lap, and to stop her from following him around town. When the pretty, voluptuous young girl finished college, Harding saw to it that she secured a secretarial job in New York. Unlike his clandestine behavior with Carrie, his conduct with Nan was extremely indiscreet. He met her regularly in New York and Washington hotel rooms, tucking $30 into her silk stocking during their first rendezvous. He wrote to her on Senate Chamber stationery, and after he became president he entertained her intimately at the White House, having sexual intercourse with her in a closet on one occasion and barely escaping a confrontation with his wife. In January, 1919, Nan became pregnant and later gave birth to a daughter, Elizabeth Ann Christian. Nan claimed that Harding was the father, and he provided $500 a month for the child's support until his death. When the Harding family refused to recognize the deceased Harding's paternity, Nan sought other means of supporting her child. She published her memoirs, detailing her intimacy with the late President. As no publisher would risk a lawsuit by printing her story, *The President's Daughter* was published privately by the "Elizabeth Ann League," which Nan formed to sponsor the cause of unwed mothers and their children. Nan Britton's last known place of residence was Chicago.

—*L.A.B.*

The Philandering President

JOHN F. KENNEDY (May 29, 1917–Nov. 22, 1963)

HIS FAME: One of America's most charismatic leaders, John F. Kennedy was also the nation's youngest elected chief executive and the first Roman Catholic to become president. After Kennedy was gunned down by an assassin in Dallas, Tex., near the end of his first term, his time in office came to be characterized as the "1,000 days of Camelot."

HIS PERSON: Born into the wealthy and tightly knit Irish Kennedy clan, the man who would become president 42 years later was instilled from birth with a fiercely competitive spirit that was fueled by a demanding father who wouldn't

President John F. Kennedy and family in Hyannis Port

accept second best from any of his four sons. Jack Kennedy was a quick study with a voracious memory and graduated cum laude from Harvard. He was plagued with a weak back all of his life and also suffered from Addison's disease. But despite the fact that "at least one half of the days that he spent ... were days of intense physical pain," Kennedy refused to act the part of an invalid and carried on an active life, enjoying sailing, swimming, and other sports. A casual dresser who favored loafers without socks and old tennis sweaters, Kennedy nevertheless carried his 6-ft. 1-in., 175-lb. frame with a certain elegance, and when he became president he took great care to look good. The cool gray-eyed Democrat enjoyed laughing at himself and was fond of telling about the time his father sent him a telegram during an election. It read: "Dear Jack, Don't buy a single vote more than necessary. I'll be damned if I'm going to pay for a landslide." After serving as U.S. senator from Massachusetts, Kennedy narrowly defeated Richard Nixon in the 1960 presidential race. Part of his appeal was his talent for expressing grand-sounding ideals, epitomized by his famous remark, "Ask not what your country can do for you, but what you can do for your country." On the one hand Kennedy was a serious-minded politician, who readily admitted his mistakes and took full responsibility for the Bay of Pigs fiasco. However, he was also capable of projecting a lighthearted devil-may-care attitude, prompting one of his aides to remark, "This administration is going to do for sex what the last one did for golf."

SEX LIFE: Kennedy prided himself on being a sexual athlete and was well known for his popularity with women. He viewed sex as a natural need and once offhandedly remarked to British Prime Minister Harold Macmillan that if he went too long without a woman he suffered severe headaches. One of his closest friends in the Senate, George Smathers, described his colleague as having "the most active libido of any man I've ever known."

Kennedy's initiation into the sexual world took place in a house of prosti-tution in Harlem with a school buddy at the age of 17. Although his reputation as a playboy still was developing during his college days, he managed to get in trouble at least once for having girls in his room, which was not permitted. From there he progressed to a more dangerous female entanglement, which nearly jeopardized his naval career. While stationed in Washington, Kennedy became involved with Danish journalist Inga Arvad, whom he affectionately called Inga-Binga and who was suspected in certain intelligence circles of being a Nazi spy. After cold water was thrown on the affair by government officials, Kennedy rapidly moved on to other conquests.

During his congressional years, Kennedy was dubbed "the gay young bachelor" and was rarely at a loss for female companionship, although the word among some Georgetown women was that the senator was a disappointment in bed and had a talent for making love with one eye on the clock. Indeed, former Senator Smathers commented that "just in terms of the time he spent with a woman, he was a lousy lover. He went in more for quantity than quality." Others indicated that Kennedy enjoyed the pursuit and conquest almost more than the act. Kennedy himself once told reporters, "I'm never through with a girl until I've had her three ways."

According to Smathers, "No one was off limits to Jack—not your wife, your mother, your sister." During their Senate days, Kennedy and Smathers shared a *pied-à-terre* where they could carry on discreet affairs. Once, when Smathers was called away to the Senate, leaving Kennedy with both of their dates, he returned to find the ambitious senator chasing both girls around the apartment. Having two girls at once was one of Kennedy's "favorite pastimes," Smathers said.

When Kennedy finally decided in his mid-30s that he needed a wife, he went far afield from the voluptuous starlets and model types he usually was attracted to and chose Jacqueline Bouvier. A nervous Thoroughbred with an impeccable family background, the elegantly attractive Jackie was an ideal wife for a presidential candidate. However, marriage did not mean monogamy to Jack Kennedy, and the opportunity for sexual liaisons was wide open on the campaign trail. Kennedy maintained a cool nonchalance about the potential stir his meanderings might cause. Some years before, when aides became frantic over a picture showing Kennedy lying next to a nude and very buxom brunette on a Florida beach, the senatorial candidate merely smiled and remarked, "Yes, I remember her. She was great!" Another time, when a landlady took pictures of Senator Kennedy leaving the apartment of his 21-year-old secretary, with whom he was having an affair, he simply brushed the incident aside.

Kennedy also refused to let anything cramp his style. Fond of swimming in the nude in the White House pool, Kennedy was even fonder of being accompanied by well-endowed beauties similarly unattired. A number of women were reportedly smuggled in and out of the White House when Jackie was absent, and two secretaries, referred to by Secret Service agents as "Fiddle and Faddle," were reputedly kept on the staff for Kennedy's personal convenience.

That Jackie knew of her husband's infidelities seems fairly certain, and it was reported that Kennedy's father offered her a million dollars not to divorce his runaround son on the brink of the presidential campaign. Friends said Jackie would often turn a blind eye on Kennedy's affairs, although once, upon discovering a pair of panties stuffed in a pillowcase, she icily asked him, "Would you please shop around and see who these belong to? They're not my size." However, despite all of Kennedy's wanderings, the two shared a certain intimacy, and the White House staff had strict orders not to disturb them when they retired to their quarters in the early afternoon while their children were napping.

SEXUAL PARTNERS: While he was still alive, John F. Kennedy's sex life was considered a taboo subject by the world press, but 12 years after his death, with the U.S. in a post-Watergate mood, women began appearing from every direction to tell their stories of indulging in pleasures of the flesh with the martyred President. Kennedy's taste in women ran the gamut from starlets to society women to obscure secretaries and airline stewardesses. Stripper Blaze Starr claims to have spent 20 minutes making love to Kennedy in a closet in a New Orleans hotel suite in 1960, while her fiancé, Gov. Earl Long, held a party in the next room. In the closet, Kennedy found time to tell Blaze the story of President Harding's making love to Nan Britton in a White House closet. Divorced painter Mary Pinchot Meyer, wife of CIA operative Cord Meyer, said that she had a sexual affair with Kennedy in 1962. They smoked marijuana together in the White House and he wrote her love letters. She kept a diary of the affair, but it disappeared after she was murdered in October, 1964.

Kennedy's most notorious affair involved a dark-haired beauty who was later investigated for having close connections with the Mafia. Judith Campbell Exner met Kennedy before he became president, but continued her affair with him during his early days in the White House. Kennedy was generous and once insisted on buying her a fur coat, Exner said, but his generosity did not carry over to the bedroom. His favorite way of making love was on his back, which was partially due to his back problem but which made it seem to her as if the woman was there "just to satisfy the man." Kennedy tried to talk her into a *ménage à trois* one night while a tall, thin woman waited for them in the bedroom. But Judith refused, even though he told her, "I know you, I know you'll enjoy it."

Part of Kennedy's attraction was his humor, according to one former mistress, who says she enjoyed Kennedy, "not because he was so great in bed, although he wasn't bad, but because he had such a great sense of fun." This stood Kennedy in good stead when he encountered an infrequent rejection. After he had attempted unsuccessfully to seduce Pulitzer Prize-winning historian Dr. Margaret Louise Coit, she asked him, "Do you do this to all the women you meet?" "My God, no," he replied, "I don't have the strength."

The young President's name was linked with those of many movie stars and Hollywood actresses, including Gene Tierney and Jayne Mansfield. But his most famous liaison was with sex goddess Marilyn Monroe. Monroe, who sang a sexy happy birthday in her breathy whisper at Kennedy's 45th birthday party in Madison Square Garden, was reportedly sneaked aboard Kennedy's plane after their affair began in 1961.

Despite his profligate affairs, Kennedy maintained a certain detachment and rarely became emotionally involved with his women. As he himself readily admitted, he never lost himself in passionate affairs, explaining, "I'm not the tragic-lover type."

—*L.K.S.*

The Elusive Extrovert

FRANKLIN DELANO ROOSEVELT (Jan. 30, 1882–Apr. 12, 1945)

HIS FAME: A believer in progressive reform, he was president of the U.S. for 12 years, through most of the Great Depression and WWII.

HIS PERSON: Charismatic and handsome, though partially paralyzed by polio in 1921, Franklin Roosevelt was a strangely elusive apparent extrovert. Behind the jauntiness exemplified by his up-tilted cigarette holder and sweeping cape was a man who did not often indulge in confidences. His son James, referring to his father's "rigid, Hyde Park

upbringing" (Hyde Park was the site of the family estate), once said, "Of what was inside him, of what really drove him, father talked to no one."

An only child, Franklin was the product of an aristocratic and traditional family. He was adored by his mother, Sara, who later interfered constantly in his marriage. At Harvard he was active in the Missionary Society but was not invited to join the exclusive Porcellian Club, which was a great disappointment to him. Some of those in his social circle considered him a lightweight and called him "the feather duster."

In 1905 he married a distant cousin, Eleanor Roosevelt, by whom he had five children who lived to maturity. He went on to law school and a political career, which was interrupted by his bout with polio at age 39. He fought his way back from the life of an invalid by exercising, particularly in the mineral waters at Warm Springs, Ga. (He established the Warm Springs Foundation for paralytics in 1927.) Never again able to stand without braces or support and afraid of dying in a fire, he practiced crawling as an escape measure.

He campaigned for governor of New York in 1928 from a specially equipped car. His promise: to help "the forgotten man at the bottom of the economic pyramid." He won the election and four years later was elected president of the U.S. His New Deal included an alphabet soup of reform agencies—Civilian Conservation Corps (CCC), Tennessee Valley Authority (TVA), and Works Progress Administration (WPA) among them. He also introduced Social Security. In his inaugural address he quoted the maxim "the only thing to fear is fear itself," often requoting it as he led the country through the Second World War.

Roosevelt liked martinis (which he prided himself on mixing well), collecting (stamps, books, naval prints), and sailing. Only once was he known to cry—when, after the death of his mother, he came upon the mementos of his life that she had saved.

LOVE LIFE: Roosevelt had a patrician handsomeness—firm jaw, finely chiseled nose (with pince-nez accentuating it), level brow—and a flirtatious magnetism which appealed to many women. The women who attracted him tended to be tall and straitlaced, even prudish. Eleanor Roosevelt had been brought up as a Victorian young lady and was, perhaps, even more the product of old-fashioned virtues than her contemporaries. Lucy Mercer, with whom Roosevelt had an affair, and Marguerite "Missy" LeHand, with whom he *may* have had an affair, were products of Catholic childhoods and noted for their reticence.

He proposed to Eleanor on a walk, admired her mind, wrote her poetry, was in love with her. On their honeymoon he had a vivid dream about a beam that revolved dangerously over Eleanor's head. When she woke him, he exclaimed, "Don't you see it?" (He also was a sleepwalker.)

In 1916 he began an affair with Lucy Mercer, who was originally hired as Eleanor's secretary. Lucy came from a Social Register family which had suffered financial reverses. Stately, with a rich, velvety voice, she had an air of mystery and elegance about her. She accompanied Franklin (without Eleanor) on a weekend yacht cruise up the Potomac, and the two of them registered one night as man and wife at a Virginia Beach motel. When Eleanor wrote him letters reflecting her suspicions of why he chose to remain in Washington while she was at Campobello, their summer place in Canada, he answered ingenuously, "I really can't stand that house all alone without you, and you were a goosy girl to think or even pretend to think that I don't want you here *all* the summer, because you know I do!"

When Franklin returned from a trip to Europe as assistant secretary of the navy in 1918, he was ill with pneumonia. Eleanor sorted his incoming mail for him and found Lucy's love letters. In a family conference, with Sara Roosevelt present, Eleanor offered him his freedom, but they decided to stay together, perhaps for political reasons, on the proviso that Franklin never see Lucy again. In 1920 Lucy married, but much later, shortly before Franklin's death, they met without Eleanor's knowledge, though probably not for sexual intimacy. Lucy, along with several other people, was with Franklin at Warm Springs when he died. Eleanor wasn't.

According to most sources, Franklin and Eleanor, who had never kissed before their marriage, stopped having sexual relations sometime between 1916 and 1918. Their relationship was cool, though not without affection. James Roosevelt, their son, recalls an incident where "she went to father and said simply, 'Hall [her brother] has died.' Father struggled to her side and put his arm around her. 'Sit down,' he said, so tenderly I can still hear it. And he sank down beside her and hugged her and kissed her and held her head to his chest...." Franklin's pet name for her was Babs, which meant baby; in the latter part of their marriage he called her "my missus," usually with pride.

In 1923 Missy LeHand, 23 years old and somewhat good-looking, became his secretary. She went everywhere with him, waited on him, and was probably in love with him. On more than one occasion, while they were cruising on the *Larooco*, the Roosevelt houseboat, she was seen sitting on his lap. When Eleanor was away, Missy acted as hostess for Franklin; she was his companion, listener, conscience. One Roosevelt son, Elliott, believes she was Franklin's mistress; his son James does not. At 41 Missy was felled by a stroke, which left her without speech. In despair she swallowed chicken bones in an abortive suicide attempt. For a while she lived at the White House, and Franklin wheeled himself into her room often to see her. In his will he left her half the income from his estate to pay her medical bills. Though she died before he did, he did not change his will.

Other women named as FDR's possible lovers were Dorothy Schiff, once owner and publisher of the *New York Post*, and Princess Martha of Norway, who lived in the U.S. during WWII and called him "dear godfather" at his request. Roosevelt was certainly capable of sexual activity in spite of his paralysis. In 1932 three doctors testified to that in writing: "No symptoms of *impotentia coeundi* [inability to copulate]."

HER SEX LIFE: To compensate for her loneliness and to fulfill her need for human warmth, Eleanor undertook a relationship of her own. In 1932 she met Associated Press reporter and possible lesbian Lorena Hickok, to whom, over the next 30 years, she wrote more than 2,300 letters, a few passionate. For example, shortly after the Roosevelts moved into the White House, she wrote: "Hick darling, … Oh, I want to put my arms around you. I ache to hold you close. Your ring is a great comfort. I look at it and think she does love me, or I wouldn't be wearing it." On Nov. 27, 1933, the First Lady penned: "Dear one, and so you think they gossip about us, well they must at least think we stand separations rather well! I am always so much more optimistic than you are—I suppose because I care so little what 'they' say." A few weeks later Lorena received this note: "Dear, I've been trying today to bring back your face—to remember just how you look. Funny how even the dearest face will fade away in time. Most clearly I remember your eyes, with a kind of reassuring smile in them, and the feeling of that soft spot just northeast of the corner of your mouth against my lips. I wonder what we'll do when we meet—what we'll say. Well, I'm rather proud of us, aren't you? I think we've done rather well." Drawn together by a mutual sense of unattractiveness (Lorena wore her hair in a bun and was overweight) and humanitarian causes, they may have become lovers. At least one Roosevelt scholar, Rhoda Lerman, discounts the idea, but Lorena Hickok did live at the White House for four years, and Eleanor always made sure she was financially secure.

HIS THOUGHTS: "Nothing is more pleasing to the eye than a good-looking lady, nothing is more refreshing to the spirit than the company of one, nothing more flattering to the ego than the affection of one."

—A.E.

WORLD LEADERS

The Jewish Lion

BENJAMIN DISRAELI (Dec. 21, 1804–Apr. 19, 1881)

HIS FAME: One of Britain's greatest statesmen, Disraeli served in Parliament for 30 years and twice became Queen Victoria's prime minister (1868; 1874–1880). His domestic and foreign policies, implemented by debate and oration, eventually led to the founding of the United Kingdom's present-day Conservative party.

HIS PERSON: The youthful Disraeli, heavily in debt after stock-market losses and a disastrous publishing venture, became a writer out of sheer desperation. To call attention to his literary efforts, he set his black hair in ringlets and frequented the London salons of the 1830s clad in green velvet

trousers, an embroidered canary-yellow waistcoat, silver-buckled black shoes, and white wrist lace. A master of flattery and the witty, foppish reply, Disraeli conned his aristrocratic friends into furnishing the colorful "inside" tidbits that he used for *Henrietta Temple* and other novels. In 1832, sensing a greater challenge, he entered the political arena. His unsavory reputation—for extravagance and sexual encounters—caused four successive defeats before he finally sat in the House of Commons in 1837. During the next decade Disraeli used his literary talent to advance his political, social, and religious convictions simultaneously, writing the trilogy *Coningsby* (1844), *Sybil* (1845), and *Tancred* (1847). After his political star brightened, he abandoned his peacock style of dress in favor of a dark suit, conservatively cut. Indispensable as a leader, yet distrusted by his colleagues, Disraeli was called both a man of genius and a self-serving opportunist during his long tenure in Parliament.

LOVE LIFE: Disraeli's *modus operandi* was simple and direct: "Talk to women as much as you can.... This is the way to gain fluency, because you need not care what you say, and had better not be sensible." At age 21 he used the ploy to launch his first novel, *Vivian Grey* (1826–1827), while having an affair with Mrs. Sarah Austen, wife of a family friend. His barefaced flattery so charmed the impressionable lady that she not only fell madly in love with the callow youth but also persuaded her gullible husband to lend the young Jew turned Christian large sums of money. To keep the author's identity secret (the novel's characters were thinly disguised and unflattering portraits of prominent society figures), Mrs. Austen laboriously transcribed Disraeli's entire holographic manuscript in her own distinctive handwriting before convincing a prominent publisher friend to buy it. Later, Disraeli would discard anonymity to trumpet his authorship of each new novel.

Seeking an entrée into London's drawing rooms in 1832, Disraeli utilized his mistress, Mrs. Clara Bolton, a vivacious, party-giving doctor's wife with impressive literary and political connections. Within the year, he had exchanged her for the oversexed and dazzling Lady Henrietta Sykes, a mother of four who fluttered obediently into his reach. Their passionate affair throbbed steadily for the next four years, aided conveniently by Henrietta's husband, Sir Francis, whose frequent out-of-town grouse shooting was combined with a roving eye for a pretty ankle. Henrietta's initial worries over being found out were forever banished when she caught her husband dallying with her lover's former mistress Clara. A triumphant Henrietta secured Sir Francis' promise that their extramarital couplings would be mutually ignored. Disraeli moved in with Lady Sykes at her London residence, but her incessant sexual demands began to ruin his health. According to contemporary rumor, Disraeli struck a unique pact with Lord Lyndhurst, a notorious womanizer and then leader of the Tory party. Lyndhurst—who fervently believed in platonic relationships "after, but not before" sexual intercourse—supposedly was eager to take on the willing Henrietta and in return sponsored Disraeli's political career.

In 1839 Disraeli married Mary Anne Lewis, a wealthy widow some 12 years older than he. His year-long courtship nearly ended in disaster when he demanded she become his wife immediately to end snickers that he was merely her paid lover. Indignant, she threw him out, but the resourceful suitor spent the night composing a masterful 1,472-word plea for reconsideration. Tearfully, Mary Anne changed her mind even though his letter candidly admitted that originally he had been solely interested in her money and devoid of all "romantic feelings." Surprisingly, their marriage became one of history's greatest love matches, lasting over 33 years. As Mrs. Disraeli, Mary Anne kept all of London in a continuous state of shock with her titillating double-entendre remarks and her outrageous costumes, which defied the current fashion. But even as she played the role of a flirtatious featherbrain, Mary Anne shrewdly kept her husband constantly in the public eye, an accomplishment which greatly helped to retain Disraeli in office. She paid his enormous debts, personally cut his hair, and mothered him through endless crises. Dying of stomach cancer (both thought they were concealing the fact from each other), she gave her beloved "Dizzy" written permission to seek another mate after she was gone.

In 1873, a year after Mary Anne's death, Disraeli began his last affair, a bizarre romance with Lady Bradford. He chased her ardently for years, scribbling passionate notes daily while he listened absentmindedly to boring speeches in Parliament. His cause was hopelessly lost from the beginning; Lady Bradford was happily married and a grandmother. In desperation, believing forlornly that the status of brother-in-law might allow closer contact with Lady Bradford, he even proposed formally to her 71-year-old sister, Lady Chesterfield. Tactfully, she turned him down.

HIS THOUGHTS: When William Gladstone publicly commented that Disraeli would "probably die by the hangman's noose or a vile disease," Disraeli promptly replied, "Sir, that depends upon whether I embrace your principles or your mistress."

—*W.K.*

The Politics Of Sexual Sublimation

MOHANDAS KARAMCHAND GANDHI (Oct. 2, 1869–Jan. 30, 1948)

HIS FAME: He ranks with Jesus Christ and Buddha as a great religious teacher, a prophet with the spiritual force to transform the lives of his followers. Politically, his gospel of militant nonviolence—inspired by the passive resistance of his child-bride—brought independence to India and influenced the great nationalist revolutions of the 20th century.

HIS PERSON: He was the youngest, smallest, and favorite child of the middle-aged prime minister of the minor principality of Porbandar in western India and the minister's fourth wife. Solitary, shy, and sweet-tempered, homely

Gandhi and Kasturbai, both age 45

with his big nose and jug ears, he enjoyed a close relationship with both his parents, particularly with his deeply religious mother.

The turning points of his childhood were his marriage at the age of 13, in the Hindu tradition, and the death of his father three years later, at the very moment Gandhi was sexually importuning his pregnant child bride. This left him with a lifelong sense of sexual guilt that would eventually be sublimated in political activism.

At 18, after taking a vow not to touch wine, women, or meat, he went alone to study law in England for three years, a formative period for the young Indian. He had great difficulty satisfying his hearty appetite with British vegetarian cuisine. But despite temptation, particularly at the hands of middle-aged landladies eager to assuage his needs, he succumbed to nothing more than a temporary case of fashion-consciousness.

Gandhi came into his own during 21 years spent in South Africa, arriving in 1893 as attorney for a Muslim firm and becoming a leader of the Indian community there through his protests against racial discrimination. He began to experiment with "nature cures" and communal living. And at the age of 37 he took the Hindu vow of *brahmacharya*, or celibacy, to free himself for a lifetime of political and religious leadership.

Gandhi called his political philosophy *satyagraha*, a combination of truth and force, which has been variously translated as passive resistance or militant nonviolence. By means of civil-disobedience campaigns and symbolic protest demonstrations—and later by dramatic public fasts—he would counter might with right and return good for evil, compelling the strong to acknowledge the force of the weak.

In 1915 Gandhi returned to India to take on the question of colonialism. Rejecting all Western influences, he established a simple, austere lifestyle in his ashrams, or communal retreats. He adopted the spinning wheel as a symbol of traditional self-sufficiency, making homespun cloth to replace imported fabric. And he devised a series of symbolic confrontations with the British which culminated in 1947 in Indian independence. Soon afterward, while working to bring peace between Hindus and Muslims, he was assassinated by a Hindu fanatic.

With his small, frail body—naked except for a loincloth and metal-rimmed spectacles—Gandhi confronted the key issues of his time: tradition and modernization, colonialism and nationalism, identity and faith. The one question he was never able to resolve, and which would continue to plague him into old age, was sex.

CHILD MARRIAGE: Marriage at the age of 13, Gandhi recalled, meant at first only the acquisition of a "strange girl to play with." It also meant that, assuming the traditional authority of the Hindu husband, he might dictate when and where his bride might play. But Kasturbai Makanji, also 13, was stubborn and strong-willed; she spent nearly half of her first two years of marriage at home with her parents. She was submissive only when it came to sex.

For Gandhi, who had been coached by his brother's wife, marriage launched a period of lascivious sexual self-indulgence. He was constantly preoccupied with erotic urges, and his schoolwork suffered. Kasturbai remained illiterate ("lustful love left no time for learning") and Gandhi would henceforth seek intellectual companionship elsewhere.

Sex was always a source of guilt and conflict for Gandhi, as epitomized by the circumstances of his father's death. He shared the Hindu concern with digestion and excretion, and the worship of semen as the vital life force, loss of which is debilitating to body and mind. Celibacy, in fact, is not uncommon among older Hindu males. But for Gandhi, who was highly sexed and in his mid-30s when he adopted it, it involved a great struggle.

A combination of factors motivated Gandhi's final resolve to forswear sex. Abstinence is the only morally acceptable form of birth control, he believed, and after five sons (one died in infancy) he wanted no more children. He wished to conserve all his energy for a life of service. Also, as psychohistorian Erik Erikson points out, racial repression in colonial South Africa may have reminded him of the sexual chauvinism in his marriage.

In Gandhi's thinking, there was a parallel between sexual and political exploitation. His philosophy of passive resistance, he wrote, was inspired by the indomitable Kasturbai. "Her determined resistance to my will … made me ashamed of myself and cured me of my stupidity in thinking I was born to rule over her." Celibacy was simply a form of nonviolence between the sexes. But until her death in 1944, while she and Gandhi were serving time in prison for civil disobedience, Kasturbai reserved a peasant distrust of the women who surrounded her husband. For although the traditional Hindu vow required a celibate to avoid the opposite sex altogether, Gandhi spent the rest of his life tempting fate.

GANDHI'S WOMEN: He was a great flirt who adored women, William Shirer wrote. Moreover, they were useful to his movement. Beginning in South Africa with 17-year-old Sonja Schlesin, he had a long line of secretary-nurses who served him with great devotion and slavish obedience. Over the years, in addition to taking dictation, these women assumed the duties of massaging him, bathing him, and even sleeping with him.

Some of Gandhi's women were famous in their own right, for example, Sarojini Naidu, "the Nightingale of India," a poet from a wealthy, cosmopolitan Brahmanic family. She became one of Gandhi's most devoted converts, enjoying a relationship of great personal affection with the Mahatma, or "Great Soul," whom she called "our Mickey Mouse." ("You will never know how much it costs us to keep that saint, that wonderful old man, in poverty," she joked.)

Such was Gandhi's appeal that women came from far and wide. Madeleine Slade, a 33-year-old Englishwoman, daughter of an admiral, and a former devotee of Beethoven, arrived in 1925 to prostrate herself at Gandhi's feet. "You shall be my daughter," he welcomed her. But Mirabehn, as she was renamed, was in love and wanted more; Gandhi simply advised her to sublimate her love in service instead of "squandering" it on him. There remained a special empathy between the two, William Shirer observed, while biographer Louis Fischer described their relationship as "one of the remarkable platonic associations of our age." Not all of Gandhi's relations with the opposite sex, however, were entirely platonic.

GANDHI'S GIRLS: The struggle to remain sexually pure, he wrote, was "like walking on the sword's edge." He continued to be tormented by nocturnal emissions, which he confessed publicly as a form of atonement, into his late 60s. Then there was the scandal of the naked young girls he slept with, to keep him warm and "test his resolve."

He had been experiencing "shivering fits" in the night, so he asked young women in his inner circle—all virgins or young brides—to warm him with their bodies. Sushila Nayar, who first arrived at the ashram at 15 and went on to become Gandhi's physician, masseuse, secretary, and bedmate, thought no more of it than of sleeping with her mother. But for some of the others it was an ambivalent experience. Abha Gandhi, the wife of a grandnephew who began sleeping with the Mahatma when she was 16, eventually was asked to remove all her garments. Her husband was so upset that he offered to keep the old man warm himself. Gandhi refused his offer, saying he wanted Abha for the *brahmacharya* experiment as well as for the warmth.

Some of Gandhi's girls were motivated by jealousy of one another and their fear of losing favor. Manu Gandhi was a distant cousin, raised from childhood by Kasturbai, who bathed and shaved the Mahatma and from the age of 19 slept with him. He would lean on her and Abha, his "walking sticks," when he went out; and during his fasts Manu would monitor his vital signs and administer enemas. "She rejoiced in her servitude and was proud of her special place in his affections," Gandhi biographer Robert Payne wrote of Manu.

"The, more they tried to restrain themselves and repress their sexual impulses," Raihana Tyabji, one of Gandhi's disciples, said about the women in his entourage, "the more oversexed and conscious they became." Ironically, Gandhi once scolded Raihana, also a celibate and a healer, for sleeping naked with one of her patients. In fact, in matters of sex as well as politics, the Mahatma simply wrote his own rules.

—C.D.

Mysterious Bed Partner

ADOLF HITLER (Apr. 20, 1889–Apr. 30, 1945)

HIS FAME: One of the most powerful leaders of the 20th century, Adolf Hitler was also the titular head of the National Socialist German Workers' Party, or Nationalsozialistische Deutsche Arbeiterpartei. (The shortened name "Nazi" is derived from the syllables *Nat* and *zi*.) His infamous dictatorship, lasting for only 13 years, created a permanent shift in world politics and was directly responsible for the deaths of over 30 million people.

HIS PERSON: Born at Braunau am Inn (Austria-Hungary), Hitler originally dreamed of becoming an artist, but twice (1907, 1908) flunked the entrance examinations for Vienna's Academy of Fine Arts. The future dictator of Nazi Germany moved frequently around the Austrian capital to evade military service, while he supported himself by painting postcards and posters. When WWI began, he enlisted in a Bavarian infantry regiment and survived four years of front-line combat, serving with distinction (wounded, gassed, twice awarded the Iron Cross). In 1920 Hitler joined the German Workers' party and turned the tiny, ineffective group into a formidable, paramilitary organization. At Munich on Nov. 8, 1923, he tried to force the Bavarian government into a full-scale revolution against the Weimar Republic, but his beer hall putsch failed and Hitler was sentenced to five years' imprisonment for high treason. Released nine months later, he emerged with a rambling manuscript outlining his plan for Germany's domination of the world. Titled *Mein Kampf* ("My Struggle"), it became the Nazi party bible.

Aided by Germany's internal chaos and worsening economic condition, Hitler schemed his way into authority and in 1933 was named chancellor. His hypnotic oratory won him the enthusiastic support and adoration of the masses. Political opponents were either brutally murdered or permanently jailed. He purged potential threats to his leadership from within his private army of 100,000 men—the brown-shirted Sturmabteilung ("Storm Troopers")—by ordering the bloody massacre (June 30, 1934) called the "Night of the Long Knives." His policy of Aryan supremacy sent over 6 million European Jews, Gypsies, and political dissidents to the gas chambers and crematoriums. Hitler rearmed Germany, reoccupied the Rhineland, took over Austria, and seized Czechoslovakia's Sudetenland as preliminary steps toward conquering first Europe, then the world.

On Sept. 1, 1939, his armored columns rolled across the Polish border, triggering WWII. *Der Führer* ("the Leader") personally directed overall military strategy, often rejecting the advice given by his experienced top commanders. When battlefield casualties numbering in the millions provoked an unsuccessful assassination plot on his life in 1944, he sadistically condemned the men responsible to a slow—and deliberately prolonged—death by piano-wire strangulation while hung on meat hooks. As they were about to expire, they were cut down, revived, and then rehung—repeatedly. (The gruesome spectacle was filmed in graphic detail for Hitler's later enjoyment.) In 1945, with his armies facing total collapse on both the eastern and western fronts, Hitler fled to a concrete bunker beneath the Berlin Chancellery. There on April 30 he committed suicide, ending a reign he had boasted would last for a thousand years.

SEX LIFE: Dr. Leonard L. Heston, professor of psychiatry at the University of Minnesota, investigated Hitler and came to one conclusion.

> Sexual deviations of several kinds have been suggested, but the fact remains that very little is known about Hitler's sex life. Ignorance has fostered blatant speculation. The evidence is: He was regarded as sexually normal by his physicians and by those who knew him through the war. Eva Braun, his mistress, was thought by all to be a thoroughly normal young woman. Hitler was an emotional person who certainly grieved deeply and appropriately following the death by suicide of an earlier mistress, Geli Raubal. Eva Braun voluntarily came to Berlin during the last days, elected to marry Hitler, and then to die with him. Hitler was certainly capable of sustaining for a lengthy period a relationship involving profound affectional ties. Saying more would be sheer speculation.

Gossip that Hitler might be homosexual was scoffed at by his colleague Albert Speer. "Such accusations have no truth in them. Hitler's worries and long hours often made his sex drive taper off and he would request drugs ... to help, but as

Eva Braun—photo by A. Hitler

to being a homosexual—no!" According to Glenn B. Infield, in his study of Hitler's secret life, the Führer was normal. "The testimony of the women he slept with, and many are still alive, proves that he appreciated female flesh. They laugh at the accusation that he was a homosexual, and their evidence is convincing."

The preponderance of evidence suggests that Hitler's longest and most publicized love affair—with Eva Braun, who was to become his wife—involved little more than sexual intercourse.

Some 23 years younger than Hitler, Eva Braun became his mistress-in-residence in 1932. Intellectually a zero, the Bavarian beauty compensated for her lack of brains with a shapely, athletic body that had but one flaw: a vagina too small for normal sex. Eva underwent painful corrective surgery, doggedly enduring secret and lengthy postoperative treatments. (Her gynecologist promptly died in a car accident shortly after announcing that a full recovery had been achieved.) As Hitler's mistress, Eva kept a confident but low profile, seldom appearing with her lover in public. In her diary she was less sure, writing that "he needs me only for certain purposes ... this is idiotic." Otto Skorzeny, Hitler's chief of commandos, once reported a conversation in which Eva had confided, "He doesn't even take his boots off, and sometimes we don't get into the bed. We stretch out on the floor. On the floor he is very erotic." Indoors, Hitler encouraged Eva to cavort in the buff by hinting that she seemed "too hot in her clothes." He preferred to strip her himself, removing her garments with fumbling fingers that nearly drove her crazy with frustration. Outdoors, he insisted she swim or sunbathe nude, while he took photographs to add to his huge pornographic collection. Usually the shots were close-ups of her buttocks. He declared this peculiar angle was necessary to prevent her from being recognized if the prints should fall into "the wrong hands."

Trapped in his Berlin bunker, while the Russians were about to overrun the city, Hitler married Eva in the early morning hours of Apr. 29, 1945. The following day, in a suicide pact, Eva took her life with cyanide and Hitler ended his life with a bullet.

SPECULATIONS ON HIS SEX LIFE: Underground rumors swept Germany during the 1930s suggesting that the real reason for the Nazi party leader's fanatical devotion to duty was that he was impotent. Jokingly, the wags pointed to his typical pose at public functions, during which he clasped his hands protectively in front of his genitals, and wisecracked that he was "hiding the last unemployed member of the Third Reich." The small group of women who became intimate with Hitler and survived the experience assured interrogators that he was anything but impotent.

Subsequent to their affairs with the Führer, many of his mistresses either committed suicide or were murdered by the Gestapo to protect Hitler's reputation. This appears to be a fact. What seems not to be absolute fact—maybe true, maybe not true—based mostly on shreds of gossip and guesswork—is that Hitler's chosen females learned that their revered leader specialized in coprophilic sadomasochism.

Hitler's one true love appeared to be Angela "Geli" Raubal, the 21-year-old daughter of his half sister. In September, 1929, the attractive brunette went to join her mother, then the housekeeper at Hitler's sumptuously furnished Prinzregentenplatz apartments in Munich. Forty-year-old "Onkel Adolf" promptly appointed himself guardian-protector, gave her an adjacent bedroom, and jealously assigned guards to keep the Viennese girl a virtual prisoner, under continual observation. Flattered by the attention, Geli reveled in the uncle-niece relationship on public occasions, and privately they became lovers, but possibly with bizarre twists she didn't expect. According to rumors, along with the coprophilic demand, Hitler claimed artistic privilege to draw precisely detailed, pornographic sketches of Geli, posing her in every obscene position he could devise. "My uncle is a monster," she reputedly sobbed to friends; "you would never believe the things he makes me do." Terrified, yet unable to escape, Geli endured the sadomasochistic perversions for two years. The chambermaids responsible for tidying up the bedroom could only gossip among themselves over the "very strange and unspeakable" abnormal sex relations that had taken place. As a compensation and to even the score, Geli not only seduced Hitler's longtime companion and chauffeur, Emil Maurice, and made love with the willing security guards assigned to her, but she had sex with every young man with whom she could secretly establish a liaison. In 1931, unable to accept the gilded-cage captivity any longer, she shot herself through the heart, using Hitler's personal 6.35-mm. Walthur pistol. Ironically for the millions of people who later died because of Hitler's rule, a despondent Führer had to be closely watched to ensure that he, too, did not commit suicide.

In the mid-1930s, Hitler met Renate Müller, then 29 and an established star in German movies. The petite, blue-eyed blonde—a typically Aryan beauty—

accepted a command invitation for sex in the private quarters of Germany's master. In October, 1937, the meetings ended abruptly. Renate Müller either jumped 40 ft. from her Berlin apartment window or was thrown out on Gestapo orders, after being charged with secretly having a Jewish lover.

Other female intimates met equally tragic fates. In 1939 Englishwoman Unity Mitford shot herself while in Munich. With a bullet lodged in her brain, she lingered on as a human vegetable for 9 years. Earlier, Suzi Liptauer had hanged herself after an overnight rendezvous. Maria "Mimi" Reiter attempted a like fate but miraculously survived.

The reasons behind these strange suicide attempts and deaths? Hitler's unnatural bedroom behavior? Possibly. But unproved—and the truth remains unknown.

MEDICAL REPORT: Soviet doctors, after performing an official autopsy on Hitler's burned corpse, reported a curious fact: "In the scrotum, which is singed but preserved, only the right testicle was found. The left testicle could not be found in the inguinal canal." Seemingly, Hitler was born with but one.

Of the seven children conceived by his mother, Klara, four died prematurely, one was moronic, and another was hidden from public view as an idiot. Her marriage was so close to being labeled incestuous that the pope had to give the couple a special dispensation. This inbreeding led Hitler to fear that his own blood was "tainted." He used leeches to "purify" it, and had numerous samples drawn so he could visually reassure himself. His pathological, festering hatred of the Jews was perhaps due to a suspicion that his paternal grandmother, Anna Maria Schicklgruber, had been seduced by her Jewish employer's student son. While an unmarried servant girl, she had produced Hitler's father, Alois.

—*The Eds.*

The Fornicating Fascist

BENITO MUSSOLINI (July 29, 1883–Apr. 28, 1945)

HIS FAME: Dictator of Italy for over 20 years, Mussolini was idolized by his countrymen. However, when Italy faced certain defeat by the Allies during WWII, the Fascist Grand Council demanded his "resignation," and *Il Duce*'s ("the Leader's") reign came to an abrupt end.

HIS PERSON: Mussolini was born in the northern Italian town of Dovia in the province of Forlì, the son of a blacksmith and a schoolteacher. An unruly child, he was expelled from two elementary schools after attacking fellow students with his penknife. Still, he was an intelligent boy and managed to get both an education and a teaching certificate. At age 18 he worked as a

schoolteacher in a small village near his hometown, until his reputation as a young satyr cost him his teaching contract. Mussolini gained a modicum of fame as a Socialist orator, journalist, and general rowdy. By the time he was 26 he had been jailed six times for inciting violence against authority. He was expelled from the Socialist party for advocating war with Austria. When WWI began, Mussolini enlisted in the army and was wounded by shrapnel. When Benito came marching home again, he was doing the Fascist goose step.

Mussolini founded the Fascisti to fight socialism and bolshevism, accumulating over 300,000 devoted followers. By 1922 the Fascists were powerful enough to intimidate King Victor Emmanuel III into appointing Mussolini, then 39, as the youngest prime minister in Italian history. Under Mussolini's dictatorship, Italy's economy was stabilized, public works were started, and the country prospered. But Mussolini's desire for expansion, coupled with his ill-fated alliance with Hitler, proved fatal, and in 1943 he was ousted from power. Two years later, when he was no longer protected by the Germans, Mussolini and his faithful mistress, Clara Petacci, were shot to death by Italian partisans.

A superstitious man, *Il Duce* might well have attributed his downfall to plain bad luck. He had a deathly fear of hunchbacks, cripples, and open umbrellas. He painted shamrocks on the hood of his red Alfa-Romeo and never ventured anywhere without a small statue of St. Anthony, the patron saint of healing, in his pocket. He fainted at the smell of either incense or ether, and though he was involved in several duels, not to mention battles, corpses made him squeamish. Blessed with a speaking voice that could charm the multitudes, Mussolini was less charismatic close up. He seldom bathed or changed his shirt, and he once offended Queen Elena of Italy by attending a reception with two days' growth of beard. An avid fan of Wallace Beery, the Keystone Cops, and Laurel and Hardy, *Il Duce* enjoyed their antics at nightly film screenings.

SEX LIFE: Initiated into the world of the flesh by a prostitute at age 16, Mussolini never tired of the pleasure women afforded him. During his teens, he admitted to "undressing every girl I see with my eyes." When he did undress a woman, it was seldom all the way, since most of his early encounters took place on staircases, against trees, or on the banks of the River Rabbi. The undisputed master of the "quickie," Mussolini as prime minister would receive female petitioners in his office and seduce them on a window seat or on the floor, rarely taking the trouble to remove his pants and shoes. He was loath to let women spend the night beside him, afraid they would laugh at his nightshirt. Actually, it would have been grossly unwise for any woman to laugh at him, since his violent nature ignored gender. When he was 18, he stabbed a woman with the pocket knife he always carried. And once when Clara Petacci angered him, he struck her soundly enough to send her flying against a wall. He viewed women as mere "objects to plunder," and plunder them he did, sometimes seven in rapid succession. He only asked that they be plump and wear no perfume, criteria which were easily met by Italian peasant girls.

SEX PARTNERS: In his teens Mussolini frequented prostitutes. But he soon discovered that he had a way with women and could charm them into bed for free. He seduced his cousin and several of her friends, as well as any country girl who caught his fancy. His first steady partner was Angelica Balabanoff, a Russian Socialist agitator 14 years his senior. She lost interest in the egotistical 19-year-old because she doubted his sincerity as a Socialist. While he was a schoolteacher in the town of Tolmezzo in the Alps, Mussolini carried on an affair with his landlady, a woman named Luigia. She was extremely jealous and would burn pages she found in his notebooks on which he had scribbled the names of women he had read about in history books. The fact that Luigia had a husband did not bother Mussolini.

In 1909 he fell in love with Rachele Guidi, one of his former students, who was working as a barmaid in his father's inn. As a Socialist, he was ideologically forbidden to marry, and when he proposed that they live together out of wedlock, Rachele's mother would not hear of it. So Mussolini produced a pistol and said, "You see this revolver, Signora Guidi? It holds six bullets. If Rachele turns me down, there will be a bullet for her and five for me. It's for you to choose." At that, the signora gave them her blessing. They finally did marry several years later, during the First World War, for practical reasons. One of Mussolini's mistresses, Ida Dalser, bore him a son and began calling herself Signora Mussolini. Moreover, she began running up bills using that name. So *Il Duce* wed Rachele and clarified the situation for all concerned. Ida died in a mental institution in 1937; her son, Benito Albino, was killed during WWII.

Though a devoted family man, Mussolini was still a Fascist. He bossed and occasionally beat Rachele, and even threw things at his beloved daughter Edda. However, Rachele was equally capable of violence. When *Il Duce* returned home drunk one night and ran amok in their apartment, smashing what few furnishings they had at the time, Rachele warned him the next day, "If ever you come home again in that state, I'll kill you." Knowing she meant it, he gave up alcohol for good. On the other hand, Mussolini was never so intimidated by his mistresses. Magda Fontanges, a French journalist with whom he had an affair, wrote in *Liberty* magazine that one of Mussolini's first acts of courtship was to choke her jokingly with a scarf.

Of all *Il Duce's* mistresses, the dark beauty Clara Petacci was by far his favorite. Their relationship lasted over 10 years. Although he loved her dearly, he was permanently bound to Rachele and his family and refused to leave them.

Clara understood this and managed to console herself with the luxurious apartments Mussolini provided for her. It was in one of these love nests that Rachele finally confronted Clara. Livid throughout the brief meeting, Rachele sarcastically noted the luxury in which her husband kept his "whore," and told Clara that one day "they'll take you to Piazzale Loreto"—a meeting place for down-and-out prostitutes. It was an accurate prediction, for the Piazzale Loreto was the place Clara's and *Il Duce*'s bodies were hung by their heels after their execution. For a while, Clara's skirt dangled around her face, until it was tied in place for the sake of modesty. She and Mussolini had spent their last night together in a farmhouse, and although the partisans would have let her live, she insisted on dying with her lover. Loyal to the end, she flung herself in front of Mussolini at the instant the first shots were fired.

MEDICAL REPORT: Mussolini contracted syphilis while living in Tolmezzo, perhaps from his landlady Luigia. He was so distressed about having the disease that he almost shot himself. A friend intervened at the last minute and convinced him that it would be wiser to see a doctor. He was never cured, and it has been speculated that his bungled war efforts resulted from brain damage caused by the disease. Syphilis, unless properly treated, is known to result in megalomania and exaggeration of emotions, traits which were plainly visible in *Il Duce*'s character.

HIS THOUGHTS: "Woman is to me an agreeable parenthesis in my busy life; they never have been more, nor can they ever be less. Today [1927], I have no time to punctuate my life with other than work, but in the past, now the long-ago past, when I was free to pick and choose my style of writing, I often found the parenthesis a pleasant way to punctuate."

—*M.J.T.*

Evita

EVA PERÓN (May 7, 1919–July 26, 1952)

HER FAME: A legendary Argentinean political figure, Eva Perón, popularly called "Evita" ("Little Eva"), was the wife of dictator Juan Perón. She wielded unprecedented power for a woman in her country, acting as de facto minister of health and labor from 1946 to 1952.

HER PERSON: María Eva Duarte was born in Los Toldos, a poverty-stricken village on the pampas, about 150 mi. from Buenos Aires. Eva was the fourth child born to Juana Ibarguren as the result of her unmarried liaison with Juan Duarte, a married minor landowner.

Faced with a bleak future, Eva left for Buenos Aires at age 14 hoping for a theatrical career. At first her regional accent and undisciplined manner worked against her, but eventually she became one of the leading actresses on the radio. She was tall for an Argentine woman—5 ft. 5 in.—with dyed honey-blond hair, large dark-brown eyes, an attractive face, and a tendency toward plumpness, which she determinedly controlled. She was barely literate.

Juan and Eva Perón in 1945

Her ambitions led her to cultivate the company of Juan Perón, a widower and a colonel, whom she met in 1943. She moved in with him and two years later married him on Oct. 21, 1945. With Eva at his side, Juan Perón became president-dictator of Argentina. Not content to be a conventional first lady, Evita unleashed her venom on the rich and her personal enemies alike, but she won the hearts of the poor of Argentina, whom she called *los descamisados* ("the shirtless ones"). They revered this peasant who stood before them in regal attire, and backed her as she promoted women's suffrage, organized workers, and under the guise of the María Eva Duarte de Perón Welfare Foundation pumped millions of dollars of government money into welfare programs (and her Swiss bank accounts). When she died of cancer of the uterus at age 33, Evita was mourned as a saint.

SEX LIFE: Eva Perón had a very complex personality, being as vindictive as she was charismatic, and she used sex as a means to obtain wealth and power, which were no doubt her true loves. With little chance of advancement from the lower classes a woman in Argentinean society had only one tool—sex—and Eva knew how to use it. When she married Juan Perón, she sought to conceal all evidence of her past, and what remains is often mere rumor and gossip.

It has sometimes been assumed that she began her career in Buenos Aires as a prostitute, but despite the fact that she later tried to legalize the red-light district, it is unlikely that she ever worked the streets. Instead, she became the mistress of a series of men in an upwardly mobile progression. It is known that she posed for cheesecake photographs, which were later rounded up and destroyed, and she was supposed to be "good on her knees." In other words, she offered her men fellatio.

Nevertheless, she was unable to shake off the tag "little whore." There is a story—possibly apocryphal, but still illustrative—told about an incident which occurred on an official trip to Milan, Italy. While traveling in an automobile with a retired admiral, she was jeered by an angry mob. She turned to her companion and cried, "Do you hear that? They're calling me a whore." To which the admiral allegedly replied, "I understand perfectly. I haven't been to sea in 15 years, and they still call me admiral."

SEX PARTNERS: Information on the men in her life is less clouded, but there are still discrepancies. At age 14 she offered her sexual services to a second-rate tango singer named José Armani, if he would take her to Buenos Aires. Armani agreed and she was on her way. (The story was later changed, and popular singer Agustin Magaldi became credited as her first lover.)

Eva soon realized that a tango singer was not much help in the big city, and by the time she was 15 she had latched onto Emilio Karstulovic, the owner of an entertainment magazine and a man-about-town. Soon she gravitated toward more useful men, like photographers and producers. Those who knew her say Eva was basically a shrewd, cold, asexual woman whose interest was power, not love. Yet she did have charm, and she used it on Rafael Firtuso, the owner of the Liceo theater, who cast her in one of his productions, and on a soap manufacturer, who provided her with the best in cosmetics.

Then came Perón. Juan Perón was a handsome ladies' man with a penchant for teenage girls. Eva was 24 and he 48 when they met. They made love their first night together and before long she had convinced her new lover—a man who supported Hitler and Fascism—that he could rise from the military to be head of government. She became not only his inspiration and champion but his brain trust.

After Eva's death Perón founded the infamous Union of Secondary School Students, which quickly became the means by which young girls were procured for his pleasure and that of his officers. The union was highly organized, with branches in every secondary school in the country. Officers scouted comely prospects and sent the most alluring to regional "recreation centers." These centers included luxurious quarters and a permanent staff of doctors to handle pregnancies and venereal diseases. Perón had his own private recreation center, where he often spent his afternoons with some teenage girl far from home and unable to resist the powerful president of the country. In 1955 Perón was ousted from Argentina by a coup and settled in Madrid. He returned to power for a brief period in 1973, but without the figure of his wife in her furs and diamonds, he could regain little popularity.

Although most evidence indicates that Eva was faithful to her husband during their marriage, there was one instance where a man's power and wealth were too great to resist. She first met Aristotle Onassis during WWII, in connection with sending food parcels to Nazi-occupied Greece. When Eva was traveling through Europe in 1947, Onassis made a special effort to meet her. After a formal lunch he asked one of her escorts to arrange a more private meeting with Eva. He was promptly invited to her holiday villa on the Italian Riviera. No sooner had he arrived than they got into bed and made love. Afterward, she cooked him an omelet and Onassis gave her a check for $10,000 to donate to one of her favorite charities. He later described the omelet she had cooked that afternoon as "the most expensive I have ever had."

The legend of Evita continues, and in the late 1970s a musical play based on her career, written by Andrew Lloyd Weber and Tim Rice, won international acclaim. In *Evita*, Eva Perón captures her audience singing, "Don't cry for me, Argentina. For the truth is I shall not leave you."

HER THOUGHTS: "If a woman lives for herself, I think she is not a woman, or else she cannot be said to live … we women carry things to greater extremes than men."

"It is natural for a woman to give herself, to surrender herself for love, for in that surrender is her glory, her salvation…. No woman's movement will be glorious and lasting … if it does not give itself to the cause of a man."

—*A.L.G. and the Eds.*

The Red Book With The Plain Brown Wrapper

MAO TSE-TUNG (Dec. 26, 1893–Sept. 9, 1976)

HIS FAME: The principal architect of modern China, Mao rose from the peasantry to rule a quarter of the world's people for a quarter of a century, and he left a body of political writings that insured his place in history as one of the leading Communist philosophers.

Mao and Chiang Ch'ing in 1945

HIS PERSON: Born in the village of Shaoshan in Hunan Province, Mao was the oldest son of wealthy peasants. After graduating from Hunan Normal School in 1918, he went to Peking, where he studied Marxism. Three years later he became one of the founders of the Chinese Communist party. Mao turned his attention to the peasants and organized them into an army skilled in the tactics of guerrilla warfare. By 1934 Chiang Kai-shek's rival Kuomintang forces had surrounded the peasant Red Army. To escape, Mao led his 100,000 followers on a 6,000-mi. retreat marked by starvation, battle, disease, and death to a safer area in northwest China. When the "Long March" was over a year later, only 5,000 of those who started had survived the journey. Mao eventually emerged as the most powerful man in the party, and in 1949 he defeated Chiang and established the People's Republic of China.

A good part of Mao's success as the foremost leader in China's long revolutionary struggle can be attributed to his unwavering identification with the masses. Though he personally deplored the harsh life he saw around him, he retained many peasant habits, and he articulated the discontent and longings of his people. He was also a serious student of the Chinese classics, a heavy reader, and an accomplished speaker and writer. Despite his accomplishments, he was a bit of a slob. He cared nothing for his personal appearance (and during his youth he didn't care about his body odor), was indifferent to what he ate, smoked until his teeth blackened, talked openly about his bowel movements, and once even dropped his pants while in the company of Europeans to cool off on a hot day. Yet he turned these evident drawbacks into strengths. He inured himself to physical hardships and deprivations, was largely impervious to personal criticism, and retained a strong sense of humor. He was probably one of history's least egotistical great leaders.

LOVE LIFE: By his own admission, he was a somewhat introverted youth, and several times he endured periods of sexual abstinence while concentrating on political problems, but he appears to have been a wholly heterosexual male who appreciated beauty, femininity, and intelligence in his women. His first adult relationship with a female was an odd one which contributed greatly to the shaping of his political thought. By the time he was 14, he had alienated his taskmaster father with his idling and dreamy devotion to romantic literature. To jar the boy out of his indolence, Mao's father arranged a marriage for him with an older girl. Though appalled by the situation, Mao went through the traditional wedding ceremonies (perhaps the only time he did so in his four marriages) but then refused to live with his bride. Later he claimed that he had never touched her. This act of rebellion inaugurated his lifelong fight against Chinese traditions.

A decade of spasmodic education and odd jobs followed, after which Mao settled down to serious journalism and incipient revolutionary work in Peking. He said of his early life, "I was not interested in women," but he seems to have had a few romantic involvements. Still, he probably remained a virgin until he met Yang K'ai-hui, a beautiful fellow revolutionary. According to Edgar Snow, an American journalist who interviewed Mao extensively during the late 1930s, Mao and Yang joined in a "trial marriage" before formalizing their bonds around 1921 in a wedding whose exact date no one bothered to remember. By freely choosing each other, they flouted tradition. Their radical peers thought them the ideal revolutionary couple. During the fighting with Chiang Kai-shek's Kuomintang forces in 1927, Mao left Yang and his children in Changsha for safety. Three years later the Kuomintang captured Yang there and publicly executed her for refusing to renounce Mao, who was by then a major Communist leader. Many other members of Mao's family were killed over the next 20 years, and he lost track of most of his children (whose number is not known) in the upheaval of the times.

Although Yang had never disavowed Mao, by the time of her death he was already living with another beautiful corevolutionary, Ho Tzu-chen, a girl about half his age. They married soon after Yang's death. When the Long March started in 1934, she had two children and was pregnant with a third. She was severely wounded, and the rigors of the march also destroyed her mental balance. Ho was sent to Moscow for psychiatric treatment, but her condition only worsened. Eventually she was placed in a mental hospital in Shanghai.

Before breaking completely from Ho, who he divorced in 1937, Mao flirted with several presumably promiscuous women. Lily Wu, a graceful actress and interpreter, captivated him and was charged by Ho with alienating Mao's affections. In 1938 he shocked the Chinese Communist party leadership by taking up with a movie actress whose reputation was even less savory and whose commitment to the revolution was suspect. This was Lan Ping ("Blue Apple"), who soon changed her name to Chiang Ch'ing ("Azure River"). She was a poor but ambitious actress who had resorted to Shanghai's casting couches to get better parts. Rumors spread that she had been the mistress of Chang Keng, a director and Communist party official, and the wife of Tang Na, an actor and film critic. When she jilted Tang Na, leaving their two children with him, he threatened to kill himself. After marrying Mao in 1939, Chiang became an obscure housewife—a role said to have been ordained by the party leaders. Chiang later revealed something of her relationship with Mao in a famous epigram: "Sex is engaging in the first round, but what sustains interest in the long run is power." Chiang Ch'ing's quest for power began during the 1960s, when she resurfaced as the driving force behind the Cultural Revolution. By the 1970s Mao was clearly estranged from her (she had to apply in writing to see him), but kept up.

Mao's personal physician from 1954 until his death in 1976, Dr. Li Zhisui, brooke long-suppressed information in his 1994 memoir, The Private Life of Chairman Mao, about the leader's occasional concerns of impotence and his use of his personal bodyguards in a similar way to rock stars use roadies: rounding up potential bedmates among young, beautiful and sometimes married starry-eyed fans. Dr. Zhisui mentions how cuckholded husbands often considered it "an honor to offer his wife to the Chairman," a carrier of *Trichomonas vaginalis*.

Writes Dr. Zhisui, "the young women were proud to be infected."

"I suggested that he should at least allow himself to be washed and cleaned. Mao still received only nightly rubdowns with hot towels. He never actually bathed. His genitals were never cleaned. But Mao refused to bathe. 'I wash myself inside the bodies of my women,' he retorted."

MAO AND WOMEN'S LIBERATION: Paradoxically, Mao, who one way or another abandoned four wives, was always a crusader against the oppression of women. The essence of Mao's ideas about woman's liberation was that the "double standard" had to be eliminated in order to give women the same freedom that was enjoyed by men. Further, Mao recognized that while all Chinese peasants had been exploited, women had suffered the additional exploitation imposed upon them by men, making them an even more potent revolutionary force.

HIS THOUGHTS: In one of his poems, Mao referred to his second wife, Yang K'ai-hui, as a proud woman. When a friend wondered why he had described her as proud, Mao replied: "A woman got her head cut off for the revolution. Isn't that something to be proud of?"

—R.K.R./A.P.

XI

Make Love
Not War

The Agreeable Sea-Wolf

JOHN PAUL JONES (July 6, 1747–July 18, 1792)

HIS FAME: John Paul Jones is best known as the naval hero of the American War of Independence.

HIS PERSON: "He was," wrote Samuel Eliot Morison, "one of the most paradoxical and fascinating figures in all American history." His real name was simply John Paul. Born to a gardener and his wife in Kirkcudbright, Scotland, he left home at the age of 13 to become an apprentice seaman. After several years as a mate on slave ships, he commanded a merchant vessel to Tobago in 1773. While in port, when he postponed paying the crew, they mutinied and he killed their leader. Convinced that he could not get a fair trial on the island, he fled to Fredericksburg, Va., and changed his name to John Jones.

When the Revolutionary War broke out, John Paul Jones, Esq., as he then called himself, was commissioned as a first lieutenant in the Continental Navy. By 1776 he was the captain of his own ship and on Sept. 23, 1779, Jones' *Bonhomme Richard* engaged the British *Serapis* off the east coast of Yorkshire. During a 3 1/2-hour engagement at close quarters Jones answered an enemy question about the sad condition of the *Richard* with the memorable "I have not yet begun to fight!" and proceeded to win a stunning victory. He was a hero to the colonists, a pirate to the British, and "Vindicator of the Freedom of the Seas" to Louis XVI. Nonetheless, after the war, Jones couldn't find a suitable job. This led him to become *Kontradmiral Pavel Ivanovich Jones* in Catherine the Great's Russian navy during her war against the Turks. After a few engagements and an incredible scandal, he returned to Paris, sick and embittered, "like a wineskin from which the wine is all drawn," as Thomas Carlyle later wrote. He died in 1792 at the age of 45 of a kidney ailment and pneumonia and was buried in a Paris cemetery. More than a century later, bones believed to be his remains were shifted to the U.S. Naval Academy in Annapolis, Md.

SEX LIFE: "I love women, I confess," Jones—a confirmed bachelor—wrote Prince Grigori Potëmkin, "and the pleasures which one enjoys only with their sex." Short and a little homely, his "stature" increased miraculously after his naval exploits earned him friendship with Benjamin Franklin, Thomas Jefferson, and the Marquis de Lafayette. Jones offset a fierce visage and towering temper with a sentimental nature that produced some fine verse. "A poet as well as a hero," one admiring woman wrote of him. With his men he was a haughty tyrant who displayed an enormous ego and what he termed "infinite" ambition, but the meticulous Jones was almost too tender with the women who flocked around him. Abigail Adams clearly found him to be a "dandy" who understood "all the etiquette of a lady's toilette as perfectly as he does the mast and sails and rigging of his ship." She was impressed by the fact that he knew "how often the ladies use the baths, what color best suits a lady's complexion, what cosmetics are most favorable to the skin." Because of his charms he had an active sex life, usually with married and, whenever possible, titled women. That he never wed can be attributed to his rival passion—the sea.

SEX PARTNERS: Although he visited the high-class prostitutes of Soho during his youthful years, his first love was Dorothea Dandridge, a cousin of Martha Washington's who dashed Jones' "prospects of domestic happiness" when she married someone of her own class—Gov. Patrick Henry. But Jones had no trouble getting over her; in Holland he flirted with Anna Dumas, a 13-year-old he dubbed "the Virgin Muse," and in France took up with Madame Le Ray de Chaumont, the wife of an influential businessman. (Ben Franklin had advised him that the fastest way to learn French was to find a "sleeping dictionary.") During the spring of 1780 he was toasted wherever he went in Paris. "The men of France I esteem," Jones wrote in his journal. "But the women of France! what words can I find to express my homage, my worship, my devotion!" He reveled with the beautiful friends of Ben Franklin, and at the salon of the famed courtesan Madame d'Ormoy (known as Madame la Présidente), and also with the ladies of the court of Louis XVI. In June of 1780 he spent five love-filled days at a secret rendezvous with the married Countess de Nicolson—"Delia" in his many passionate letters. But while Delia was sure that the "tender Jones is as faithful [a] lover as [he is a] valiant warrior," he was also courting another married lady, Madame Charlotte de Lowendahl, a woman of royal birth, who called him "the most agreeable sea-wolf one could wish to meet with." (Her portrait of him now hangs in the U.S. Naval Academy.) Though he pursued Charlotte assiduously, she shied away from his sexual maneuvers; in order to remain in her good graces, he was forced to assure her that "Friendship has nothing to do with sex." But if one woman could be called the "love of his life," it would be "Madame T." Shrouded in history, she has now been identified as a widow named Thérèse Townsend, who claimed to be the daughter of Louis XV. From 1784 to 1790 they maintained contact through letters, often carried by Thomas Jefferson, and it is thought that she had a son by Jones.

They finally broke off their correspondence—perhaps because he discovered she had no royal blood, after all—and Jones then became involved in a scandal in Russia, when a 10-year-old girl accused him of rape. Jones offered at least three versions of the event, the most plausible of which held that while the child had "lent herself to do all that a man would want of her," Jones had *not* "deflowered" her. Catherine the Great eventually cleared him of the charge but hastened his departure from Russia. Jones believed there had been a "complot" against him devised by Potëmkin or his other rivals in the Russian navy. Another explanation, based on one of Catherine's diaries, held that the jealous empress had turned on Jones when she learned of his affair with a blue-eyed, golden-haired lady-in-waiting, Princess Anna Kourakina, who supposedly bore Jones a son (and later died in a convent). This tale is now regarded as untrue.

Following his retreat from Russia, Jones returned to France, where he died a lonely man. A decade earlier, when asked if he'd ever been wounded, Jones had replied: "Never on the sea but on the land I have been bled by arrows which were never launched by the English."

HIS ADVICE: In his last years, in response to a letter from a woman who had concluded that he preferred "love to friendship," Jones replied: "You may be right, for love frequently communicates divine qualities, and in that light may be considered as the cordial that Providence has bestowed on mortals to help them to digest the nauseous draught of life."

—G.A.M.

Lawrence Of The Birches

T. E. LAWRENCE (Aug. 15, 1888–May 19, 1935)

HIS FAME: He was known to history as "Lawrence of Arabia—the uncrowned king of Damascus." Originally a mapmaker for British Intelligence, Lawrence succeeded in rallying factious Arabian princes around his own personal banner to battle the German-allied Turks during WWI.

Lawrence of Arabia in India

HIS PERSON: Lawrence was short (5 ft. 5 1/2 in.) and born out of wedlock—both of which could have contributed to the overall quirkiness of his life. His Anglo-Irish father, Sir Thomas Chapman, had run off to Wales with Sarah Maden, the governess hired to care for his daughters. Known as "Mr. and Mrs. Lawrence," the couple had five sons, the second of whom was T.E. There has been speculation that Lawrence's heroic drive was in part an attempt to redeem his mother's name. In any case, he so impressed the Bedouins with his zest for

Dahoum, the donkey boy

their austere desert life—driving his camel hard, walking the hot sands in his bare feet, and facing violent desert storms head on—that they followed him on numerous guerrilla raids against the Turkish-controlled railroad and during the seizure of Aqaba. After the war he served as a technical adviser to the British delegation at the Paris Peace Conference of 1919 and lobbied strongly for Arab independence. Between 1919 and 1920 he wrote his war memoirs, *The Seven Pillars of Wisdom*, twice, having burned the notes and lost the final draft of the first copy. His exploits and writings brought him to the attention of such men as Lowell Thomas, Winston Churchill, and George Bernard Shaw, all of whom lionized him and indirectly drove him back into the ranks of the military in a search for anonymity. He joined the Royal Air Force as Pvt. J. H. Ross in 1922, but was exposed by the press and had to leave. He then joined the Royal Tank Corps as T. E. Shaw (a name he assumed legally in 1927), and by 1925 had worked his way back into the RAF, where he remained as an aircraftman until his death. He died in a motorcycle accident near Bovington Military Camp in Dorset at age 46. The controversy surrounding his death was appropriate to the life he led. One story had him being run off the road by a black mystery car driven by British agents because the government feared his political views and ambitions. Another story had his death being faked by the British so that they could smuggle him into the Middle East to do espionage work.

SEX LIFE: Fellow Oxford student Vyvyan Warren Richards first declared his love for Lawrence in 1905. But later Richards told biographers Phillip Knightley and Colin Simpson that Lawrence "had neither flesh nor carnality of any kind.... He received my affection ... my total subservience, as though it was his due. He never gave the slightest sign that he understood my motives or fathomed my desire ... I realize now that he was sexless—at least that he was unaware of sex." Lawrence did, however, try to form a serious relationship with a woman while he was an undergraduate. Janet Hallsmith, his childhood friend, was surprised when he abruptly proposed to her. She laughed at him, for they had not even kissed or discussed their feelings and she had hoped to marry his brother. Lawrence was hurt, but they remained friends. How much more aware of sex Lawrence was six years later during an archaeological dig in Asia Minor (now in Turkey) is still uncertain. But he did enjoy the company of a teenage donkey boy named Dahoum, whom he took camping and hiking and later took home to England in the summer of 1913. And he did adorn his house in Carchemish with a statue he had carved of Dahoum in the nude. He most likely dedicated *The Seven Pillars of Wisdom* as well as his efforts in the Arabian campaign to Dahoum, who died of typhus in 1918. From the dedication:

> *I loved you, so I drew these tides of men into*
> *my hands and wrote my will across the sky in stars*
> *To gain you Freedom, the seven-pillared worthy house,*
> *that your eyes might be shining for me.*

The crucial sexual encounter of Lawrence's life may or may not have happened as he described it in *The Seven Pillars of Wisdom*. He told many versions of the story, and he was an "infernal liar" according to Charlotte Shaw, wife of George Bernard and a mother figure to Lawrence. The crux of the story as it appears in the book is that Lawrence was captured by the Turks while on a reconnaissance mission in Deraa in 1917; then he was sexually molested by the Turkish bey and beaten by the bey's guards. In a confessional letter to Charlotte Shaw, however, Lawrence admitted to having given away his "bodily integrity" in order to "earn five minutes' respite from the pain." And he told Col. R. Meinertzhagen that he allowed himself to be sodomized not only by the bey but by his servants as well. The factuality of the account seems almost secondary to the vivid, almost loving detail with which Lawrence described the incident in his book. Speaking of a Turkish corporal who had just kicked him "yellow" with a spiked boot, Lawrence wrote, "I remember smiling idly at him, for a delicious warmth, probably sexual, was swelling through me."

QUIRKS: Lawrence liked to be beaten—spanked with a birch rod on his bare buttocks—to the point of seminal emission, according to one friend. Whether it was to "purify" himself after his degradation at Deraa or to atone for his parents' scandalous relationship, he went to great, imaginative lengths to keep himself "birched." He went to "beating parties" in Chelsea organized by an underworld figure named Bluebeard, and his arrangement with John Bruce, a young Scots bunkmate, is well documented. Lawrence told Bruce that a relative, whom he called "the Old Man," was keeping him on a financial string and threatening to expose his bastardy if he didn't do as he was told. In 1968 Bruce detailed the beatings:

> … before Lawrence left for India there had to be another beating … on the Old Man's orders [it] was a ferocious one…. Twelve strokes. When Lawrence returned from India in 1929 it was another 12…. In September the same year he had a flogging at my house in Aberdeen … he came all the way from Cattewater, Plymouth, had breakfast and a flogging and caught the next train back. The worst beating of all was in 1930…. There was another beating in 1931 … and another in 1934…. On this last occasion the Old Man made him travel … on his motor bike.

Bruce was also told to describe the birchings—and Lawrence's reactions to them—in letters which Lawrence said he himself would deliver to the Old Man. As it turned out, the Old Man never existed. He was a figment of Lawrence's imagination, and the letters' only purpose was to excite Lawrence further.

HIS THOUGHTS: "Marriage-contracts should have a clause terminating the engagement upon nine months' notice by either party."

"The period of enjoyment, in sex, seems to be a very doubtful one. I've asked the fellows in this hut ... they all say it's all over in ten minutes: and the preliminaries—which I discounted—take up most of the ten minutes. For myself, I haven't tried it, and hope not to."

—*D.R.*

Big Mac

GENERAL DOUGLAS MacARTHUR (Jan. 26, 1880–Apr. 5, 1964)

HIS FAME: A flamboyant leader, General MacArthur headed the Allied troops in the Southwest Pacific theater during WWII. He presided over the postwar occupation of Japan and commanded the U.N. Army at the outset of the Korean War in 1950.

HIS PERSON: MacArthur was an imposing figure. Nearly 6 ft. tall with a spare build, his battered cap, sunglasses, and corncob pipe became his trademarks. Enemies considered him imperious, cold, calculating; friends regarded him as warm, understanding, brilliant. Everyone knew he was vain. Biographer William Manchester noted that General MacArthur, as Chief of Staff, "sat at his desk wearing a Japanese ceremonial kimono, cooled himself with an Oriental fan, smoked cigarettes in a jeweled holder, increasingly spoke of himself in the third person ... and had erected a 15-foot-high mirror behind his office chair to heighten his image." When asked to explain his numerous successes, MacArthur said, "I believe it was destiny."

He was born in the armory building at Fort Dodge in Little Rock, Ark. His father had been a Civil War general. His dominating mother supported MacArthur's military ambitions from the time he was a child. Inevitably,

MacArthur went to the U.S. Military Academy at West Point, where he graduated first in his class. Eventually he commanded the 42nd Infantry (Rainbow) Division in France in WWI. Following this conflict, MacArthur served successively as President Herbert Hoover's Army Chief of Staff for four years and as President Franklin D. Roosevelt's Army Chief of Staff for one year.

Retiring from the U.S. military in 1937, MacArthur accepted Philippine President Manuel Quezon's appointment as field marshal of the Philippines, thereby becoming the highest-paid military officer in modern history. In 1942, with America's entry into W.W. II, General MacArthur was made commander of all Allied forces in the Pacific arena. He accepted the Japanese surrender in 1945 and became virtual dictator of Japan during the postwar reconstruction period. In 1950 he was called upon to lead U.N. troops in defense of South Korea against North Korea and China. Eager to expand the war, MacArthur came into direct disagreement with President Harry Truman, who wanted to limit the conflict. In April, 1951, President Truman fired MacArthur and had him recalled to the U.S. Returning to a hero's welcome, MacArthur briefly considered running for the U.S. presidency. However, he spent his final years in seclusion, living at the Waldorf Hotel in New York City.

LOVE LIFE: General MacArthur was the most decorated man in U.S. military history, but in love he lost two major battles before achieving victory. As a West Point cadet, with his mother living nearby, MacArthur dated girls from colleges in the area. Credited with engagements to eight different young women, MacArthur often denied this, saying, "I do not remember being so heavily engaged by the enemy."

His first love was Louise Cromwell Brooks, a divorcée, socialite, heiress to millions, who liked parties, jazz., and bathtub gin during Prohibition. MacArthur met Louise at a party. He immediately proposed marriage, and she accepted. They had a large wedding on St. Valentine's Day in 1922. MacArthur's mother refused to attend. The couple settled down in Manila, where MacArthur liked to spend his leisure time with President Quezon and his Filipino circle. The high-society whites with whom Louise associated found MacArthur's friends unacceptable. This led to a marital rift, and during the next five and a half rocky years Louise constantly tried to persuade MacArthur to leave the military. When he refused, she left him. In June of 1929 she sought a divorce. MacArthur agreed, on "any grounds that will not compromise my honor." The heiress went to court in Reno and cited MacArthur's "failure to provide." Granted the divorce, Louise returned to her social set and eventually had two more marriages and two more divorces. In his memoirs, MacArthur summarized their union briefly. "In February, 1922, I entered into matrimony," he wrote, "but it was not successful, and ended in divorce years later for mutual incompatibility." He did not mention his wife's name.

The general's next skirmish with the opposite sex was also unsuccessful. In Manila, five months before being transferred to Washington, D.C., MacArthur had quietly taken on a gorgeous young Eurasian mistress, Isabel Rosario Cooper.

The daughter of a Chinese woman and a Scottish businessman, she had danced in a Shanghai chorus line and was calling herself an actress when MacArthur met her. In her chiffon tea gowns, she was exquisite. A lobbyist who met her recalled, "She looked as if she were carved from the most delicate opaline. She had her hair in braids down her back." MacArthur moved her to Washington and installed her in a suite at the Hotel Chastelton on 16th Street. He supplied her with kimonos, black lace underthings, and a fur coat, but almost no street clothes. He did not want her to go out. He gave her a poodle to keep her company. He wrote her love letters, and while on state visits to Paris and Vienna he sent her postcards. Isabel complained, and at last MacArthur gave her a car and chauffeur and a large sum of money. When MacArthur was abroad, Isabel visited local nightclubs and seduced several men. She also went to Havana and blew all her money. MacArthur continued to keep her presence his secret.

MacArthur made one mistake. He provoked the enmity of the country's leading political gossip columnist, Drew Pearson, who with Robert S. Allen wrote the widely read national column *Washington Merry-Go-Round.* The two columnists had been particularly rough on MacArthur. In 1932, when 15,000 war veterans—the "Bonus Marchers"—converged on the capital and camped there with their families, MacArthur personally led the troops that drove them out by force. Pearson and Allen promptly described his tactics as "unwarranted ... harsh, and brutal." Later, learning of MacArthur's vanity and arrogance, the columnists called him "dictatorial" and "disloyal." Infuriated, MacArthur sued his attackers for $1,750,000.

By then, tired of Isabel's infidelity and extravagance, MacArthur had broken with her. However, Pearson, investigating MacArthur, uncovered the secret. Pearson located Isabel, who was in need of money. He "rented" six letters the general had written her. Several of them were love letters, dating back to late 1930, in which MacArthur pledged unlimited devotion. One letter was in response to Isabel's request that the general secure a job for her brother, and it contained an enclosure from MacArthur of "Help Wanted" ads from a newspaper. The last letter from MacArthur, postmarked Sept. 11, 1934, carried a chilling dismissal and a plane ticket back to the Philippines. Isabel made it clear she had no intention of returning to her native land. Besides paying her to copy the letters, Drew Pearson bought her some new street clothes and found her a hiding place in Baltimore.

After spending $16,000 in legal fees (a tidy sum in those Depression years), General MacArthur suddenly dropped the lawsuit against Drew Pearson. No further explanation was given. Obviously, a compromise had been reached. On Christmas Eve, 1934, MacArthur's representative gave $15,000 in $100 bills to Drew Pearson's agent, who acted on Isabel's behalf. In return, MacArthur received his original letters back, although Pearson kept copies. With the $15,000 in hand, Isabel moved out of Washington and opened a beauty shop somewhere in the Midwest. Then she moved to Los Angeles, where in June, 1960, she committed suicide. Shortly after his tangle with Pearson, MacArthur was relieved of his post as Chief of Staff and transferred to the Philippines.

General MacArthur's mother died in 1935, but this period of heavy grief was alleviated by an encounter that brought the general the beginnings of happiness. On a ship bound for Shanghai, he met a petite, vivacious, cultured Southern belle named Jean Marie Faircloth. By the time the ship docked, MacArthur and Jean were in love. After a year and a half of courtship, the general won her. They had a small wedding in New York on April 30, 1937. Their honeymoon was cut short because the groom had to hurry back to Manila to oversee the graduation of his newest Filipino recruits. Jean understood and did not mind. She loved the military life. Jean bore the general a son, Arthur, in 1938. She was the best wife the general could hope for, and he knew it. After their wedding breakfast, MacArthur had told reporters, "This job is going to last a long time."

—*J.M.*

The Salacious Soldier

PANCHO VILLA (June 5, 1878–July 20, 1923)

HIS FAME: A military genius and a bloodthirsty marauder, Villa won worldwide recognition as a courageous leader for his guerrilla activities during the Mexican Revolution that began in 1910. Because he plundered the estates of the rich and often shared the spoils with the poor, he is sometimes described as a real-life Robin Hood.

Villa and Luz Corral

HIS PERSON: Christened Doroteo Arango by his peasant parents, the boy took the name "Francisco Villa" (and later "Pancho") from a feared Mexican bandit chief of an earlier era. He needed the protection of a pseudonym because, legend has it, he had to flee from his home in 1894 after killing the wealthy seducer of his sister Mariana. Straightaway, Villa turned to crime for his livelihood. He robbed hundreds of foreigners, particularly Chinese merchants living in Mexico; rustled cattle; looted trains and mines; and murdered scores of innocent people. Arrested in 1903, he avoided lengthy imprisonment by volunteering for the Mexican cavalry, where he found his calling.

A bold military strategist, Villa aligned himself with Mexico's revolutionaries. While distinguishing himself on the battlefield, he harbored a desire to be Mexico's president. At times he could be brutal, reportedly killing 80 women and children living in his own camp because they slowed down his troop movement. In 1916, in revenge for U.S. support given one of his rivals, Villa invaded Columbus, N.M., and killed 17 Americans on U.S. soil. U.S. Gen. John J. Pershing, who was dispatched to punish the raider, ventured deep into Mexican territory, dispersed all but a handful of Villa loyalists, but nonetheless failed to capture Villa. Despite the loss to the better-equipped Pershing, Villa emerged a hero. His escape sealed his reputation as a wily guerrilla, and in 1920 he was retired as a general at full pay and with honors. But in 1923 Villa, whose ruthless exploits had also won him many enemies, was assassinated as he rode through Parral, Mexico, in his Dodge motor car.

SEX LIFE: The intensity and brutality of Villa's military exploits carried over to his affairs with women. A self-described "son of a bitch with the ladies," Villa was never a gentle lover. When the pretty Petra Espinosa spurned the young Villa's advances, he raped her. On occasion Villa and his soldiers overtook a town not to rob its citizens but to rape its women. In one instance, Villa had a father tied to a chair while—in full view of the man—he raped his young daughter. A Juárez pawnshop owner was bound and compelled to watch while his wife was raped repeatedly by Villa and his men. Then the man was shot numerous times, and when he died his wife was ordered to clean up the bloody mess.

But countless other women happily submitted to the overtures of this stocky, 5-ft. 10-in. *bandido* with wavy hair and a smile cemented beneath his black mustache. (He had an adenoidal condition that prevented his lips from completely closing.) He was "married," in spurious ceremonies, perhaps as many as 75 times. Asked how he managed to find an official to oversee these rituals, Villa offered this explanation: "Just threaten to put a bullet through his head. You'll see how fast he comes around."

Villa frequently married women within hours of meeting them. His first wife, Luz Corral (who claimed, "I was the only woman that Pancho really loved"), met Villa when she was doling out provisions to his men. They talked briefly, and the next day he impulsively returned to ask for her hand in marriage.

Six more women, at the least, *legally* became his wife, despite Mexican laws prohibiting bigamy. When Villa tired of a woman—even if she had borne him a child, as many of his wives and mistresses did—he simply mounted his white horse and rode away. But Villa's wives did not, in their husband's eyes, enjoy the same liberty. Villa abandoned his third wife, Pilar Escalona, when he stumbled upon a bundle of old photographs and letters to her from a former lover. He banished from his sight his sixth wife, Maria Amalia Baca, when—after an absence of several years—he returned to find she had married another man. While she escaped with her life, Villa never forgave what he considered treachery on her part.

Villa observed his own version of morality. While he was romancing a woman named Adelita, her fiancé—one of Villa's soldiers—walked in on the couple. The shocked soldier promptly drew his pistol and shot himself through the head. Chagrined, Villa banished Adelita. And throughout his wandering life, Villa did manifest a curious devotion to his first wife, Luz, who steadfastly remained faithful to him. Villa sporadically returned to her for a night or two of lovemaking.

Ironically, just as sex played an immense part in Villa's life, so it proved instrumental in his death. After his retirement Villa regularly—and predictably—appeased his lusty romantic appetite during trysts in Parral with his mistress, Manuela Casas. Those appointments were inviolable, a fact his assassins used to their advantage in masterminding the scheme that saw Villa fatally sprayed with 13 bullets as he began the drive home after an afternoon with Manuela.

HIS THOUGHTS: "It is a natural law of man to go after women—even married women. Of course it may be true that he has little respect for them after. But why bother your head about that? There's something else: women who are unfaithful should be shot."

—*R.M.*

The Angriest Black Man In America

MALCOLM X (May 19, 1925–Feb. 21, 1965)

HIS FAME: One of the greatest activists and black leaders of the twentieth century, Malcolm X rose from a small-time pimp, drug dealer and burglar to becoming a leader of the Nation of Islam and Pan-African spokesman. Famous as "the angriest black man in America" at the time of his assassination in 1965, he is now remembered as perhaps the most enduring symbol of black nationalism.

HIS PERSON: Characterized by the massive shifts and identity overhauls, Malcolm X's life was a study in extremes. Born Malcolm Little to a Baptist preacher and follower of Marcus

Garvey, he survived the murder of his father by whites and the subsequent insanity of his mother, fostering an extreme hatred of white society. In order to survive, Malcolm Little became "Detroit Red," a street hustler, drug dealer and racketeer. The "Red" moniker came from Malcolm's hair, which carried a reddish tinge—his maternal grandfather was white, which meant that Malcolm also had a light-skinned complexion, a fact that he was initially proud of but later grew to passionately resent. Sent to Massachusetts State Prison in 1946 for burglary, he subsequently converted to the Nation of Islam and found a surrogate father in the movement's leader, Elijah Muhammad. After prison he changed his name to Malcolm X and by the sixties had become the most prominent leader of the movement after his mentor. In 1964, when it was revealed that Elijah Muhammad indulged in multiple extramarital affairs, despite the fact that such affairs were expressly forbidden by the Nation of Islam, Malcolm left the movement and founded Muslim Mosque, Inc., emphasizing black nationalism instead of the Islamic unity preferred by the Nation of Islam. During and after pilgrimages to both Mecca and Africa, Malcolm laid the groundwork for international pan-African connections, founding the Organization for Afro-American Unity. Always a fiery, vitriolic speaker, Malcolm was tagged early by the FBI as a radical and classified as mentally ill. After his split with the Nation of Islam, he also made violent enemies within the movement. On February 21, 1965, Malcolm was shot 16 times in the chest at the Audubon Ballroom in Manhattan; three men were charged and convicted.

SEX LIFE: Malcolm's iconic autobiography was written as object lesson of how he learned from hard life lessons; how he overcame a lowly street life consorting with pimps, living with prostitutes, selling drugs and numbers and other mob rackets. After having a lengthy affair with a married white woman, Malcolm came to believe it was the result of self-hatred of his own black skin, and transformed himself into an advocate of Islam as a result.

Malcolm married Betty Sanders (who subsequently took his last name of X) in Lansing, Michigan, in 1958. The marriage produced six daughters, including twins who were born after Malcolm's death. According to a biography published in 1991, Bruce Perry's *Malcolm: The Life of a Man Who Changed Black America*, Malcolm worked as a male prostitute from the age of 20, and at one point was employed as a butler for William Paul Lennon, a rich bachelor in Boston, who he was also paid to sprinkle with talcum powder and then service, giving him hand relief until orgasm. Friends have related many stories of Malcolm's youthful sexual encounters, including with a local boy he discovered masturbating and then ordered to give him a handjob before performing oral sex on him, as well as a transvestite named Willie Mae with whom he had an affair in Flint, Michigan. Biographer Bruce Perry surmises that his homosexual activities may have functioned as a release valve, without the risk of becoming overly entangled with women, which the young man may have viewed as making him that much less effective. It is this discomfort with his desires which would find its apotheosis in radical Islam and black nationalism; his religious conversion in particular may have been motivated to some extent by a need to burn out and purify his natural inclinations. Malcolm spoke of his shame at his criminal background in his autobiography and the pride he felt at his conversion; his urge to "become a man" on all levels speaks to some modicum of sexual self-suppression. Whether by inclination or design, apparently his homosexual liaisons, if not impulses, ceased after he joined the Nation of Islam. The Qu'ran itself is somewhat confused on the subject of homosexuality—Mohammed prohibits sodomy in practice ("If two men among you are guilty of lewdness, punish them both"—Qu'ran 4:16) but then goes on to say that Muslims will be able to enjoy it in paradise ("Round about them will serve boys of perpetual freshness"—Qu'ran 56:17). However, the Nation of Islam is hardly so conflicted, expressly forbidding homosexuality as the work of Satan (and, at times, the Jewish people).

—*J.L.*

XII

Getting Down to Business

Contradictory Car-Maker

HENRY FORD (July 30, 1863–Apr. 7, 1947)

HIS FAME: A pioneer in automotive design and mass-production methods, Ford revolutionized industry and transformed the world. He epitomized a traditional American hero—the self-made man. Born on a farm near Dearborn, Mich., he left school at 16 and died a billionaire at 83. His life abounds in contradiction. An enlightened employer who doubled the minimum wage and shortened the workday, he devised the five-day week to speed up production, hired informers to spy on workers, and fought unions with terror tactics. Inherently magnanimous, he often treated people with contempt and alienated his friends. A philanthropist, he published virulent anti-Semitic articles and in 1938 was awarded a medal by Adolf Hitler.

Henry and Clara Ford

SEX LIFE: Contradiction extends to Ford's love life. He was a straitlaced guardian of sexual morals, yet evidence suggests the possibility that he fathered a son whose mother was another man's wife.

Ford's marriage seemed ideal. It had been love at first sight when he met pretty Clara Jane Bryant, a farmer's daughter, at a village ball. They wed when he was 24 and she 22. One child, Edsel, was born after four years. Smart, even-tempered, unselfish, Clara would go along with her husband's enthusiasms even if it meant letting him run a gasoline motor in her sink or serving meals composed mainly of soybean products. He called her "the Believer" because of her complete faith in him. (However, in domestic matters her word was law.) When in one rare instance she "interfered" in his business affairs, begging him to end his resistance to unions and avert bloodshed, he followed her advice.

Spending millions in charitable undertakings, Clara detested waste. She mended her petticoats and underdrawers and continued to darn Ford's socks after he was a millionaire. The Fords enjoyed simple pleasures together: family gatherings, picnics, bird-watching, dancing, or just listening to the radio. Clara died in 1950, three years after Ford.

A different picture emerges from John Dahlinger's *The Secret Life of Henry Ford* (1978). Dahlinger asserts that he is Ford's son, born in 1923.

John Dahlinger (center) with Ray Dahlinger and the man he claims was his real father, Henry Ford

According to Dahlinger, his mother, beautiful Evangeline Côté (a cousin of Tyrone Power), caught Ford's eye when, still in her teens, she began working in an office at his plant. Clara's polar opposite, Evangeline charmed Ford, 30 years her senior, with her headstrong and vivacious ways. (She later became a licensed pilot and harness-racing champion.) Ford arranged her marriage to one of his executives, Ray Dahlinger. He built the Dahlingers a magnificent home adjoining his, with a secret stairway leading to Evangeline's bedroom. Ford shocked nurses by visiting her new baby at the hospital. Little Dahlinger was showered with gifts and attentions by Ford and encouraged to play with Ford's grandchildren. Once when an artist needed a model for the tycoon as a boy, Ford asked young Dahlinger, not one of his own grandsons, to pose for the portrait.

Both Evangeline and her husband held important positions with the Ford company until Mrs. Ford's death. The new regime headed by grandson Henry Ford II, Dahlinger says, aware of gossip concerning the Dahlingers, tried to suppress all traces of Ford's association with them.

—M.B.T.

The Sugar Daddy And The Show girl

WILLIAM RANDOLPH HEARST (Apr. 29, 1863–Aug. 14, 1951)

HIS FAME: Hearst was a publishing titan whose empire at its peak included a chain of 28 newspapers, 13 magazines, 8 radio stations, and 2 movie companies. He pioneered a brusque, sensationalized form of journalism stressing concise writing, bold headlines, lurid sex and crime stories, and constant public-service crusades. One of America's most powerful and controversial men, he served in the U.S. House of Representatives (1903–1907) and at his death left behind a combined personal and publishing estate of $220 million.

Hearst with his good friend Marion Davies

HIS PERSON: An only child, Hearst was breast-fed by a wet nurse until he was 14 months old. Although a shy, spoiled youngster, he concocted some original and mischievous antics. In his junior year, he was expelled from Harvard after presenting his professors with a bedpan adorned with each instructor's name and photograph.

In 1887 Hearst persuaded his father, Sen. George Hearst (a man who amassed his fortune from gold, silver, and copper mines), to put him in charge of the faltering San Francisco *Examiner*. Within two years young Hearst had raised the paper's circulation and turned it into a profit maker.

He fashioned a newspaper style known as "yellow journalism," a lurid editorial stance aimed at boosting circulation. Most Hearst city rooms carried placards bearing the motto "Make 'Em Say, 'Gee Whiz.'" Hearst reportedly goaded President McKinley into entering the Spanish-American War by running a series of front-page articles (not all of them accurate) in the New York *Journal* describing atrocities committed by the reigning Spanish government on the citizens of Cuba, and by exploiting the battleship *Maine* disaster in his papers. Likewise, Hearst was blamed for the 1901 assassination of President McKinley because of his anti-McKinley cartoons, articles, and editorials—particularly one editorial published five months before the shooting, approving political assassination under extreme circumstances.

As powerful as his news empire made him, Hearst did not always get what he wanted. He had been disappointed at age 10 when his mother would not buy the Louvre in Paris for him. And his disappointments continued; he lost several political races, including the Democratic presidential nomination in 1904. Still, Hearst had other dreams. He wanted to be a movie mogul and build castles. He succeeded at the first; during the early years of filmmaking, he was one of the most powerful men in the industry. He started producing newsreels in 1913, and later used his Cosmopolitan Pictures company (and favorable publicity in his newspapers) to promote his mistress, actress Marion Davies. His other dream was never completed; in fact, he believed that if he ever finished building his 146-room castle at San Simeon, Calif., he would die. And so for 30 years architect Julia Morgan redesigned his "living museum" and redecorated it with ancient tapestries, rare objets d'art, and even ceilings taken from centuries-old monasteries. But Hearst couldn't buy immortality; his 88-year-old heart gave out in 1951.

LOVE LIFE: He was extremely devoted to his mother, who called him "Sonny" or "Billy Buster." Phoebe Hearst even became involved in her son's romances. In 1884, when Hearst announced his engagement to aspiring actress Eleanor Calhoun, Phoebe first convinced the couple not to marry and then supposedly paid for the girl to study drama—in Europe. It might also have been Phoebe's money that influenced her son to terminate a relationship of several years' duration with Tessie Powers, a Cambridge waitress Hearst had met while at Harvard. He flaunted the affair, taking Tessie with him to Europe and Egypt and buying her a house in New York. But at a crucial point in his career in the 1890s, when he was entering politics and trying to borrow millions from his mother for his enterprises, he stopped seeing Tessie.

In spite of his political career, Hearst could not stay away from show girls. In 1897 he began courting *two*—sisters Millicent and Anita Willson, who were dancers in a current Broadway musical. Theatergoers were amazed to see 34-year-old Hearst escorting the young ladies, one of whom (Millicent) was only 16. This time Phoebe didn't get involved in her son's love life. On April 28, 1903, the day before his 40th birthday, Hearst married 22-year-old Millicent Willson.

The stocky, 6-ft. 2-in. Hearst fathered five children but grew bored with his wife, who had put her fun-loving past behind her for the sake of her social position. Though the marriage officially lasted their lifetimes, Hearst saw little of Millicent during his final 30 years. Instead, he returned to dating show girls (who called him "the Wolf") and became involved with a number of them. But it was the gorgeous Marion Davies who stole his heart.

Born in Brooklyn on Jan. 1, 1897, Marion Davies (née Douras) was educated in a Hastings, N.Y., convent. She followed her three older sisters onto the stage and pursued a dancing career. While she was performing as a chorus girl in *Stop! Look! Listen!* in 1915, her affair with Hearst began.

Hearst, 34 years her senior, installed Marion as his protégée and mistress. She entertained his guests at San Simeon (except when presidents or royalty visited, on which occasions Millicent was flown in to preside as hostess). Marion starred in a slew of Hearst-funded films, including *The Cardboard Lover* (1928), *Show People* (1928), and *Blondie of the Follies* (1932). Hearst never allowed her to play any roles that would tarnish his virginal image of her. It was for this reason, not particularly for her lack of talent, that he lost $7 million on her films.

Throughout their relationship there was widespread belief that Hearst was "keeping" other women and had fathered a number of children born out of wedlock. And there were rumors that perhaps Hearst's twin sons by Millicent were really Marion's. Marion once even recommended to a friend, whose girl friend was in need of an abortion, the name of a doctor who, she said, "took care of all mine." Though she enjoyed their early sexual encounters, Marion and Hearst slept in separate bedrooms and she referred to him as "Pops." Marion often formed a "crush" on her leading men, and Hearst, aware that he couldn't always satisfy her sexually, "allowed her an occasional truancy from fidelity," according to Marion's biographer Fred Guiles. Sex, for Marion, was just another pleasurable pastime, "less exhilarating than a fast Charleston or even a particularly gamey joke." An irrepressible romantic, she always tried to be discreet in her affairs. Marion, who called herself "just another dumb blonde," shared her intimate love with actor Dick Powell and had a brief romance with actor Leslie Howard, but it was her fling with Charlie Chaplin that aroused the most interest.

Approximately 15 celebrities, including Chaplin and producer Thomas Ince, were aboard Hearst's yacht *Oneida* on Nov. 18, 1924, for an impromptu party. Within a few days, Hollywood was mourning Ince's death. Most experts contended that Ince died from heart failure brought on by acute indigestion. However, stories surfaced that during the celebration Ince slipped off with Marion and tried to seduce her. Hearst, pistol in hand, discovered them in a dimly lit cabin below deck, mistook Ince for Chaplin, and unloaded a bullet in Ince's head. The scandalous story was denied by those on board, Ince's body was cremated, and Hearst, it was said, provided Ince's widow, Nell, with a trust fund.

Acutely jealous of his winsome blond beauty, on numerous occasions Hearst hired detectives to spy on her. A thinly veiled reconstruction of their 36-year-affair served as the story line for the 1941 cinema classic *Citizen Kane*. Hearst and Davies were outraged by the depiction of their romance, but all attempts to purchase and destroy the prints of the Orson Welles film failed.

Several times Hearst attempted to secure a divorce from Millicent. Once he even hired a detective in the hope of catching her in an adulterous affair. Millicent responded to his pleas for a divorce by purchasing a pearl necklace priced in six figures from Tiffany's and ordering the clerk to "send the bill to my husband's office." Hearst and Marion resigned themselves to a lifetime affair. Though Hearst could never give Marion a wedding ring, he lavished jewels and money on her, which she parlayed into a vast fortune in real estate. Hearst, who spent half a billion dollars in his lifetime, once had to borrow a million dollars from his mistress.

During his last four years, after the onset of illness, Hearst lived with Marion in her Beverly Hills mansion. Two months after Hearst died, on Oct. 31, 1951, Marion ran off to Las Vegas and married merchant marine Capt. Horace Brown, a man who bore an uncanny resemblance to the younger-day Hearst. It was Marion's first marriage. Ten years later, at the age of 64, Marion succumbed to cancer.

QUIRKS: Hearst loved to see Marion in costumes. Once, after a long separation, she received this message from an exuberant, randy Hearst: "Patient is on the blink ... [bring] your nurse's uniform."

—A.K. and V.S.

The Sex Investor

HOWARD HUGHES (Dec. 24, 1905–Apr. 5, 1976)

HIS FAME: American billionaire Howard Hughes gained fame as a business entrepreneur, Hollywood film mogul, pioneer airplane designer, and record-breaking experimental aviator. Later in life, he achieved notoriety as a recluse who lived in near isolation for more than one and a half decades.

HIS PERSON: The son of a millionaire who manufactured oil-drilling equipment, Howard Hughes was born in Houston, Tex. An only child, he was spoiled by both of his parents but especially by his mother Allene, who worried and fretted over the young

Hughes with Ava Gardner

Hughes constantly. Allene instilled in her son her own phobias, including a profound fear of germs, which years later would dominate Hughes' life. During his childhood, Hughes had only one close friend and rarely took part in any group activities at school. A loner even as an adolescent, the thing he liked most was to ride his horse around the countryside.

As a teenager, Hughes was a poor student who appeared to have little ambition or direction. But after his mother died suddenly when he was 16 and his father died two years later, the orphaned Hughes revealed a strong-willed personality. He had a court declare him legally an adult, bought out his relatives' shares of the Hughes Tool Company, and thus took over total control of the family business. A millionaire at the age of 19, he moved to Hollywood, where he directed and produced films, including the WWI aerial epic *Hell's Angels*.

By the early 1930s Hughes had a new passion—aviation. He founded the Hughes Aircraft Company, bought control of Trans World Airlines (TWA), and personally designed new, experimental aircraft. Serving as his own test pilot, he set a new airspeed record in 1935, and within three years broke the transcontinental and transworld records. He also crashed three times, suffering serious injuries.

As early as 1944, Hughes suffered his first nervous breakdown. While his economic empire grew over the next two decades, Hughes' mental condition deteriorated dramatically. Surrounded by aides who never suggested he seek psychiatric help, Hughes withdrew into bedrooms in mansions and penthouses where he used box after box of Kleenex—spreading the tissues over everything he came in contact with—in his obsessive war against germs. For at least the last decade of his life he was a chronic paranoid, addicted to codeine and Valium. Weighing less than 100 lb., with long shaggy hair, Hughes died at the age of 70 while en route from Acapulco, Mexico, to a hospital in Houston, Tex. He left an estate valued at $2.3 billion.

SEX LIFE: A very shy teenager, Hughes had few if any dates and little experience with women. After his father's death he decided to marry, choosing Ella Rice, a young Houston socialite. A vivacious extrovert, Ella turned down his proposal. However, Hughes had his aunt, who had married into the Rice family, intervene on his behalf. Finally Ella's mother agreed that Hughes would be an asset to the family and arranged the marriage.

After the wedding Hughes and his bride moved to Los Angeles, where the marriage proved to be a disaster. Intoxicated with the excitement of Hollywood, Hughes paid little attention to his new wife, while spending an increasing amount of time in the company of people involved in the film industry. After three years Ella left for Houston and sued for divorce. (This was but the first of many times that Hughes proved himself incapable of maintaining an intimate, permanent relationship with a woman.) Hughes' reaction to Ella's rejection set a pattern for the future; feeling betrayed, he never saw or spoke to her again.

After Ella's departure Hughes began a pursuit of Hollywood film stars which was to continue for 30 years. Actress Billie Dove was his first conquest, but Hughes did not want their affair publicized. When he learned that Dell Publications had printed a one-shot "magazine" featuring himself and Billie on the cover, Hughes bought the entire printing before it could be distributed. Billie Dove was genuinely in love with the 6-ft. 4-in., dark-skinned, lanky young Texan. This was unfortunate, since he dropped her for no apparent reason after a short affair and never spoke to her again. Katharine Hepburn was another love. When she went on the road with a show, Hughes followed her across the country in his private plane. In the end, Hepburn terminated the romance after explaining to a friend that Hughes bored her.

Ginger Rogers was also linked with Hughes. But their relationship ended when she found Hughes in bed with another actress. One actress widely assumed to have been romantically involved with Hughes was Jane Russell. Although they had a close relationship for a number of years, they never made love. Hughes was particularly concerned, however, with Jane Russell's breasts and how they appeared on screen. After viewing rushes of the film *Macao* starring Russell, Hughes wrote a three-page memo describing in detail the kind of brassiere she should wear to enhance her assets. "What we really need is a brassiere of a very thin material.... This brassiere should hold her breasts upward but should be so thin that it takes the natural shape of her breasts." Other movie actresses associated with Hughes included Marian Marsh, Hedy Lamarr, Jean Harlow, Ida Lupino, Ava Gardner, Lana Turner, Terry Moore, Yvonne Schubert, and Carole Lombard.

Probably no other person in history invested as much money in his sex life as did Howard Hughes, who obsessively searched for the woman with the perfect face, body, and especially breasts. For besides his heavily publicized affairs with well-known actresses, Hughes established another outlet for his sexual urges. Over the years he developed a system for procuring young women for what was to become a veritable harem. Hughes operatives across the country were told of their boss' need for new faces and bodies. These agents found likely candidates, promised them screen tests and movie careers, and then shipped them off to Los Angeles. At one time Hughes owned or leased five houses in different areas of Los Angeles. Each one was occupied by a hopeful starlet or show girl, who was kept on salary. Thus, whichever neighborhood Hughes found himself in, he would have privacy and a girl.

Hughes, himself, was constantly looking for talent in magazines, on television, and on the streets. He set up his own detective agency to research and contact these prospects. One friend, studio executive William Fadiman, was sent to check out the star of the Ballet de Paris, Zizi Jeanmaire, after Hughes saw a picture of her. When Fadiman heartily approved of what he saw, Hughes bought the entire ballet company and installed it on the second floor of the RKO Writers Building. He hired a writer to do a screenplay for the company and set about to seduce Jeanmaire. After two years of failure, Hughes abruptly dropped the ballet and the planned film project.

Another victim of Hughes' obsessional desire was Italian actress Gina Lollobrigida. When she was approached by a Hughes agent and asked to go to Hollywood to act, she was thrilled. But when she arrived, she was whisked off to the Town House Hotel, where she was kept a virtual prisoner; she had a 24-hour guard and was permitted to see no one. Happily married to a dentist in Italy, she wanted no part of Hughes' advances. Lollobrigida finally escaped and returned to Italy, commenting, "I was not free in the time I spent there."

Beauty contests were always a good source for Hughes' reconnaissance missions. In 1960, after viewing the Miss Universe pageant on television, Hughes ordered his detectives to contact seven of the finalists, who were subsequently registered in Los Angeles hotels. The operation failed, however, when the seven became suspicious of the promises of stardom and bolted for home. At one point during the 1950s, a Hughes aide claimed there were 108 active files on various candidates for Hughes' bedroom. After reading the files and looking over the photographs of these women, Hughes decided which were to be contacted—his favorites being teenage brunettes with large breasts.

The case of one Riverside, Calif., 15-year-old who won a local beauty contest was typical. She was investigated, contacted, moved to Los Angeles, and given a house in Coldwater Canyon. Chauffeured by Hughes' drivers, she was given singing, voice, acting, and dancing lessons. At the same time, she was cut off from old friends, especially men. Forced to live a life of seclusion, she became lonely. Hughes waited for that vulnerable moment, stepped into her life, and began taking her to dinner. Soon they were lovers. But the girl from Riverside realized that, although she lived in luxury, her movie career was still nonexistent. It took her five more years to realize that Hughes had never intended to make her a star.

At least one of these operations at seduction backfired. A 16-year-old blond with a 40-in. bust was brought to Hollywood from North Carolina. Her mother, who had also gone west, suggested a trip to Palm Springs, Calif., for her daughter, herself, and Hughes. He readily agreed and once there took the girl to bed. In the middle of their lovemaking, the mother burst into the room, claiming her daughter had been ruined. To avoid statutory rape charges, Hughes was forced to settle out of court for $250,000.

In 1957, at the age of 51, Hughes married 31-year-old movie star Jean Peters, whom he had dated off and on for 11 years. He would not allow her to shave her body hair, because he liked hair on women. (When Peters posed in bathing suits for fan magazines, her legs and thighs had to be retouched.) Why the couple married remains a mystery. Hughes was already mentally unbalanced, and Peters had to give up her career and live in seclusion with him. Sometime during the early 1960s, Hughes' sex life ended when his overwhelming fear of germs precluded physical contact with another person. Sex was replaced by drugs and his around-the-clock viewing of movies and television. Finally, in 1970, Jean filed for divorce, not having seen Hughes for over three years.

MEDICAL REPORT: In the early 1940s Hughes had a big chow named Chang. One morning Chang got into a fight with another dog. When Hughes tried to separate them, the other dog bit him on the penis. It took six stitches to sew up the wound. Although he was temporarily disabled, the injury didn't seem to have any lasting effect. However, Hughes never owned another pet.

—R.J.F.

The Golden Greek

ARISTOTLE ONASSIS (Jan. 20, 1906–Mar. 15, 1975)

HIS FAME: Upon his controversial marriage to Jacqueline Kennedy, Aristotle Socrates Onassis—the richest and most flamboyant of the "golden" Greek shipowners—became one of the most publicized figures of the 20th century. A friend of such eminent men as Winston Churchill, he mingled smoothly with world leaders, royalty, and the very well-to-do.

Onassis with his wife, Jacqueline

HIS PERSON: Onassis was the son of a prosperous Greek tobacco merchant in Smyrna, Turkey. A likable but rebellious youth, he was suspended from several schools, once for administering a firm pinch to the backside of a woman teacher. In 1922, when the Turks launched brutal attacks on the resident Greek population, the 16-year-old Onassis and members of his family fled to Athens. Although he hoped to immigrate to the U.S., he was discouraged by a potential wait of several years and instead set sail for Argentina. He arrived in Buenos Aires with only a few hundred dollars in his pockets. By means of personal daring and astute business acumen, he first established himself in the tobacco business and then branched out to his real love, shipping. He became a millionaire by age 25, and through investments in shipping—especially oil tankers—he amassed one of the great personal fortunes of the postwar era, if not of all time.

LOVE LIFE: As a youngster Onassis was sexually precocious. He had to be restrained from seducing the family laundress at the age of 11. A few years later he received his initiation from his 25-year-old French teacher, whose scanty dress, owing to the scorching weather, fired his lust. "Mademoiselle, you are arousing me against my will ... nothing can stop me from violating you!" was his winning approach. Needless to say Onassis proved to be a most ardent student. The women of Argentina found him, with his astonishingly intense black eyes, irresistible. Later, as a young man-about-town, he savored New York City nightlife during the 1940s in the company of his tall blond mistress, Ingeborg Dedichen. Ingeborg was an aristocrat who helped advance Onassis' career as well as smooth his rough social edges. Of this period Ingeborg has written: "He would lick me between the toes.... He would embrace every part of my body and cover me with kisses." Yet as passionate as it was, this affair descended into a series of beatings administered by the jealous Onassis and an attempted suicide by Ingeborg.

Following a brief Hollywood fling with a number of screen stars, Onassis finally married for the first time at 40. Tina Livanos, the petite 17-year-old daughter of a rival shipowner, was to bear his two children, Alexander and Christina. But this idyllic existence was shattered by the appearance of the greatest love of his life, opera singer Maria Callas. For Callas and Onassis, it was love at first sight. Their affair was conducted openly, and they understood each other emotionally, intellectually, and sexually. Although opera bored him, Onassis deeply enjoyed the worldwide success and fame of his fiery theatrical lover. Their relationship never led to marriage, but they remained close until the day of Onassis' death.

On Oct. 20, 1968, Onassis (who had been divorced from Tina for some years) stunned the world by wedding the beautiful widow of a beloved, slain president of the U.S. That widow, of course, was Jacqueline Kennedy. Onassis had known her casually for some time, but Kennedy-watchers around the world thought he was "too short, too old, too dark, and too coarse" to be a suitable successor to John F. Kennedy. The eyes of the world were focused on the isle of Skorpios, the site of the wedding, and from that moment on, this May-December couple (Jackie was a generation younger than Ari) found itself bathed in an unending glare of publicity. One portion of the marriage that particularly intrigued everyone was the famous prenuptial contract, which quickly became one of the most discussed and speculated-about financial and legal documents of our time. The text allegedly contained over 100 clauses and covered everything from money to sleeping arrangements. Christian Cafarakis, a steward formerly employed by Onassis, claimed that the contract provided for separate bedrooms for the couple at all times and released Jackie from any obligation to bear Onassis' children. Onassis offered affection and the protection of wealth to a woman who had been shattered by the violent death not only of her husband but of her brother-in-law, Sen. Robert Kennedy, as well. In return, Jackie offered Ari warmth and the companionship of one of the most glamorous of women. But their carefully constructed relationship was soon shattered by the death of Onassis' only son. Thrown into a deep depression, Onassis grew irritated by Jackie's extravagant and capricious ways. He turned to Callas for comfort and contemplated a divorce. However, death in the form of myasthenia gravis put an end to his plans.

QUIRKS: Onassis could be described as a "roaring" heterosexual. His boudoir humor tended toward the explicit. Once he asked Ingeborg Dedichen to examine him for piles. As she investigated, Onassis wafted a not so gentle breeze in her startled face. On another occasion, when harassed by a photographer, Onassis took him into the washroom, where he said he would show him the secret of his success. Unzipping his fly, he revealed an asset that may best be described as physical rather than fiscal.

HIS THOUGHTS: "I've always been attracted to tall, statuesque women. I guess I should have been a sculptor."

—*J.M.M.*

XIII

Bed Sports

The Other Don Juan

JUAN BELMONTE (Apr. 14, 1892–Apr. 8, 1962)

HIS FAME: More than 45 years after his death, Spanish-born Juan Belmonte is still considered one of the two greatest bullfighters who ever lived.

HIS PERSON: The eldest of 11 children, he was raised in abject poverty in a Seville slum. He grew up scrambling in the streets, and at the age of 11 he joined a gang of "guttersnipes," whose members taught him "to smoke, to drink ... , to play cards, and to go with women." Small, ugly, virtually a cripple, and a stammerer, Belmonte resolved at the age of 16 to become the world's greatest matador. His early attempts were met with jeers and laughter; during his first professional fight, an exhausted Belmonte begged the bull to kill him. Because of his physical limitations, he revolutionized bullfighting techniques; since he could not jump out of the way of a 1,200-lb. charging bull, he used his fantastic control of the cape to make the bull swerve away from him.

Belmonte was an enormous success, and soon nearly every matador was trying to imitate this new style. Many were killed in the attempt. Even the great "Joselito," who learned and perfected Belmonte's innovations well enough to become his rival, was killed by a bull in 1920 at the age of 25.

But Belmonte went on and on; his stamina was unbelievable. He fought 109 times in 180 days one season, and soon was earning $10,000 for each performance. He figured prominently in many books, including Ernest Hemingway's *Death in the Afternoon* and *The Sun Also Rises*. Fame did not come without sacrifice, however. Fear was his constant companion, and when Belmonte was asked how many times he had been gored, he replied, "Say 50 times, including three times where a man appreciates it least."

LOVE LIFE: His first love was a married woman who was "adept in the arts of pleasure." Convinced he would be fatally gored in Valencia during his second professional fight, Belmonte gallantly burned the lady's letters (written in red ink, which she swore was "her own heart's blood") to spare her reputation after his death.

As his fame as a bullfighter grew, Belmonte was delighted to observe a dramatic increase in his appeal to women. Once a woman named Chivita (which translates as "nanny goat") "suddenly started to make love" to him in a tavern. Her date, an aficionado, didn't mind relinquishing her to the great bullfighter, but Belmonte, probably put off by her aggressiveness and the accompanying public attention, considered the incident "one of the most unfortunate things that ever happened to me."

He first saw Julia Cossio at a bullfight in Lima, Peru. His love for the socialite grew, but the shy Belmonte dreaded participating in a wedding ceremony. Finally, he discovered that a proxy marriage could be performed while he was fighting bulls in Venezuela, so his stand-in married Julia in 1918. They had two daughters before they were estranged.

Belmonte was a womanizer, and females of every social level were his great joy after—and even before—his almost daily encounters with bulls. By a servant girl he had a son, whom he ultimately acknowledged. Juan Belmonte, Jr., became a good matador, but he lived in the shadow of his father's legend until he gave up bullfighting.

A millionaire, Belmonte owned a great estate in Spain and made up for his limited schooling (which had lasted only four years) by undertaking his own education. He had affairs constantly with wealthy women from the international jet set. One famous and beautiful actress who lives in California recently recalled, "Even the sound of the footsteps of that ugly-beautiful, bandy-legged little man coming down the hotel hall to my bedroom would set me aquiver!" She went on to explain: "The same energy that went into his conquering a bull also went into his conquering a woman, and he was the greatest lover I ever had."

Although Belmonte retired from bullfighting in 1935, he kept returning to the ring, and was performing in exhibitions well into his 60s. One of his favorite companions during these later years was an exquisite Chinese woman who wanted to be a matador.

In the spring of 1962, a depressed Belmonte told his friends: "My doctor has forbidden me to do the three things I love most in the world—fight bulls, ride horses, and mount women. It's time to go." So one Sunday, six days before his 70th birthday, he drove to his ranch near Seville, rode his horse, Maravilla, out into the fields, and proceeded to cape seven fierce bulls. Then, after attending mass, he spent two hours of pleasure with his mistress of 12 years. Finally, exhausted, he returned to his luxurious home and shot himself to death.

HIS THOUGHTS: "Like a soldier in wartime, or anyone else who is living dangerously, a bullfighter is always preoccupied with women. The sexual explanation is simple enough."

—*B.C.*

Wilt The Stilt

WILT CHAMBERLAIN (Aug. 21, 1936–Oct. 12, 1999)

HIS FAME: One of the best basketball players in NBA history, Wilt Chamberlain played for the Philadelphia/San Francisco Warriors, Philadelphia 76ers, Los Angeles Lakers and the Harlem Globetrotters. Though he holds many all-time records in the NBA—including being the only player in history to average more than 50 points in a season or score 100 points in a game—his most enduring record was made off the court; Wilt is remembered for having slept with upwards of 20,000 women (and never letting one of them take his lifelong bachelor status).

HIS PERSON: Born in Philadelphia, Wilt was one of nine children, and enjoyed a cozy middle-class childhood, attending the largely Jewish Overbrook High School, where he soon excelled in track and field and basketball. By the time he graduated, 200 universities tried to recruit him. As a player for the University of Kansas Jayhawks, Chamberlain was already overachieving: he had appeared on the covers of *Time, Newsweek, Life* and *Look* magazines by the time he was 21. As a professional player, the 7'1" Chamberlain became the object of scorn, ridicule and fantasy, often seen as a monstrous giant or Goliath and subject to hard fouls by other players and jeering from fans. Yet by the beginning of the 1960s, Chamberlain was setting records that remain unbroken—that remain *unthreatened*—to this day. Chamberlain was bigger (7'1" and 300 lbs. in muscle at his peak), stronger, faster and more coordinated than almost anybody he was matched against on the court; his offensive power was so overwhelming that the NBA changed many rules to help hedge the curve against him. Despite his strength, and the scorn heaped against him both on the court and from the stands, Chamberlain was a man fully in control of his emotions; he did not foul out once in his 14-year stint in the NBA, in more than 1,200 games. After retiring at the end of the 1972–73 season, Chamberlain spent time coaching professional players, but after becoming bored with the role turned to acting (he played the villain Bombaata in the 1984 Arnold Schwarzenegger vehicle *Conan the Destroyer*), big-league volleyball, tennis, marathons, polo and, at one point, even planned to challenge Muhammad Ali to a fight, though this never came off. Rumors of an NBA comeback never ceased, even into Chamberlain's fifties; he contented himself with authoring several books instead and resting on the laurels of his hard work before his death of heart failure in 1999, at the age of 63.

SEX PARTNERS: Chamberlain's infamous 20,000-women figure was self-reported in his 1991 autobiography *A View From Above*, a bold statement (as he wrote, "At my age, that equals out to having sex with 1.2 women a day, every day since I was 15 years old"), and one that caused immense controversy in the African-American community for reinforcing old stereotypes—especially coming shortly before Magic Johnson's announcement of his HIV+ status. "Whites didn't like it," Chamberlain stated, "and people of color wanted me to be more attentive to my own kind so they could be 'proud' of me... I was just doing what was natural—chasing good-looking ladies, whoever they were and wherever they were available." It was his early stint with the Harlem Globe-trotters that first opened the world of the infinite sexual possibility of the public figure to Chamberlain; often a Globetrotter wouldn't have to do much more than hand out game tickets to women they saw on the street while on tour in order to sleep with them, even if they didn't speak any English whatsoever, or stand shirtless on their hotel balcony flexing his pecs. Though his extreme height likely contributed to his attractiveness to women, it also made sex difficult, particularly in tight quarters. During his second season with the Lakers, at the age of 33, Chamberlain tore a tendon in his knee and was put in a cast; he wrote that, combined with his height, "trying to drag that cast around without breaking [a] girl's leg (or decapitating her) was a real effort," though, in best Chamberlain style, he found that in many cases the exotic quality of the cast made him even more attractive. Chamberlain narcissistically boasted of the high quality of the women he attracted, stating that "I am a man of distinctive taste and most of the women I have encountered, the average Joe would have proposed marriage to on the first date." He also maintained that not one woman he slept with was married, a point on which he was unwavering. He developed his own 20-point rating system for women (he cited Raquel Welch and Jennifer O'Neill as among the only 19s he ever saw, and said he never saw a 20 in his life)—and liked his women "bright, pretty, well read, widely traveled, interested in good food and good times... white, black, red, yellow or green." He preferred women to be 5'4" to 5'6", ironically finding tall women unattractive, and was firmly an ass man rather than a breast man—"I'm a pragmatist at heart," he stated, "and I can't see where big breasts have any function as useful as walking or sitting." Chamberlain lived alone in a palace he built himself in Beverly Hills; the media called it a "sybaritic paradise." Wilt wrote that "I must admit that my favorite form of entertainment is still me and a pretty girl and a big bed—and I can think of no better, more romantic place for that entertainment than my own bedroom." Chamberlain's bed was situated atop a 13' x 25' platform, underneath a triangular mirrored ceiling which would slide back to reveal the sky with the flick of a switch. Another switch would close the drapes and lock the room into pitch darkness. Another room downstairs, the "X-rated room," was designated for the sexual frolics of guests. Despite or because of his priapic exploits, Chamberlain remained a bachelor his entire life. Questioning the modern relevance of marriage, he stated "I've always thought that weddings—like funerals—are more for the friends and families of the principals than the principals themselves." Chamberlain's longest relationship lasted exactly three weeks—"I get tired of a girl fairly quickly, and when I do, I 'fire' her... who knows—I may already have fired one or two girls who would have made ideal wives for me if I'd kept them around long enough to really get to know them." He reported that there had been exactly five women in his life (that is .025% of his total yield) that he loved enough to marry, though he never committed; as he commented in a 1991 interview, "The women who I have been the most attracted to, the most in love with, I've pushed away the strongest."

HIS ADVICE: "With all of you men out there who think that having a thousand different ladies is pretty cool, I have learned in my life I've found out that having one woman a thousand different times is much more satisfying."

—J.L.

The Black Hope

JACK JOHNSON (Mar. 31, 1878-June 10, 1946)

HIS FAME: He was the first black heavyweight boxing champion of the world. In 48 years he engaged in 113 bouts and lost only 7. Ring historian Nat Fleischer called him "the greatest heavyweight of all time."

HIS PERSON: Raised in a poor family of nine in Galveston, Tex., Johnson ran away from home at 12, and in five years on the road he learned to be a boxer. He was soon beating the best fighters around and was in line for a shot at the heavyweight title held by a tough Canadian, 5-ft. 7-in. Tommy Burns. But Burns flung insults at Johnson and ignored him, until baited by a $35,000 promoter's offer. The match was held outside Sydney, Australia, with Burns a 7-to-4 favorite. In the 14th round, a venomous right from Johnson knocked Burns flat. A black man ruled the fistic world.

Champion Jack Johnson returned to a segregated, racist America, refusing to play Uncle Tom, flashing his power and arrogance. The seething press and boxing crowd sought a "white hope." Johnson crushed them all. Novelist Jack London begged in print: "Jeff, it's up to you!" and the undefeated, invincible white Jim Jeffries came out of five years' retirement to take care of the black upstart. The fight of the century was staged on the blazing afternoon of July 4, 1910, in Reno, Nev. The 6-ft. 2 1/2-in. Jim Jeffries squared off against the 6-ft. 1/4-in. Jack Johnson. "The great Jeffries was like a log," reported the Associated Press. "The reviled Johnson was like a black panther." In the 15th round, Johnson knocked out Jeffries.

Race riots exploded throughout the U.S. Johnson ignored them. In his beret and silk suits, sipping wine through a gold straw, enjoying his own Chicago cabaret, driving a Stutz Bearcat, starring in *Othello*, making love with endless white women, he was on top of the world. The whites had to get rid of him. They found him guilty on a phony morals charge, but Johnson escaped to European exile for five years. Eager to return home, Johnson defended his crown against lumbering 6-ft. 6-in. Jess Willard in Havana on Apr. 5, 1915. Johnson was knocked out by Willard in the 26th round. Johnson claimed he'd thrown the fight to get back to America and obtain a pardon. Experts claimed Johnson lost because he was out of shape. He got no pardon. He spent a year in Leavenworth Prison, working as athletic director. He died at 68 in an auto accident.

SEX LIFE: When Johnson boasted, as allegedly he once did, "I can get any white woman in Chicago I want"—or when the press reported his affairs and marriages with young white ladies—the white population of America became inflamed and enraged. Once, 100 Texans prepared to converge on Chicago to lynch Johnson. In Congress, Rep. Seaborn A. Roddenberry of Georgia introduced a constitutional amendment banning intermarriage between blacks and whites, shouting, "No brutality, no infamy, no degradation in all the years of southern slavery, possessed such villainous character and such atrocious qualities as ... states which allow the marriage of the Negro, Jack Johnson, to a woman of Caucasian strain." Race riots set off by Johnson's knocking out white men and bedding white women caused the deaths of 19 persons nationwide in seven years.

Johnson's explanation for his behavior was a simple one: "I didn't court white women because I thought I was too good for the others. It was just that they always treated me better. I never had a colored girl that didn't two-time me."

Most white men felt threatened by Johnson's sexual prowess. They imagined he had a gigantic penis that their white women loved. When Johnson heard this, he laughed and decided to threaten his white tormentors further. Dressing to spar in public, he would wrap gauze bandages around his penis to enlarge it and then go out before the spectators in the skintight trunks of the time, displaying the mammoth bulge at his crotch. There was talk of forcing Johnson to wear loose boxing trunks instead of skintight ones. But former bareknuckle heavyweight champion John L. Sullivan announced, "The size of a nigger's penis is not to be discussed in public."

SEX PARTNERS: At 20 Johnson married a childhood sweetheart, a lightly colored girl named Mary Austin. When he refused to quit prizefighting, she divorced him in 1901. Then he began living with Clara Kerr, an attractive black girl. They traveled everywhere together until Clara ran off with a white man in Johnson's entourage, taking with her all of Johnson's clothes and handy cash. Years later, Johnson heard Clara was in a New Jersey jail for murdering her husband. Learning that she had killed in self-defense, Johnson helped her win acquittal and bought her a small hotel.

Disenchanted by black women, Johnson turned to white ones. He became involved with an Irish girl from New York, Hattie McLay, daughter of a respectable jeweler. He took her along with him to Europe and on to Australia, where he won the championship. When he got back to Chicago with Hattie, he broke with her because she was an alcoholic and had been sleeping with his manager. After Hattie's departure, Johnson fell for a girl of German descent, Belle Schreiber, brought up in Milwaukee and called "the prettiest white whore" in Chicago. Belle worked in the classiest bordello in America, the Everleigh Club, run by two young Kentucky-bred sisters, Aida and Minna Everleigh. The club featured 30 exotic boudoirs furnished with marble-inlaid brass beds covered with white cashmere blankets, perfume sprays over the beds, and mirrored ceilings. The tubs in the bathrooms were gold. Among the club's regulars were James J. Corbett, Ring Lardner, and John Barrymore. Belle Schreiber was one of the higher-paid prostitutes, receiving $50 a tumble. Meeting Johnson, she offered to live with him, and he accepted. Soon Belle accompanied Johnson to San Francisco. There, at his hotel, he found Hattie had just arrived for a reconciliation. The women ran into each other and began some hair pulling, but Johnson parted them and promised to keep each one happy. He would make love to Hattie, then to Belle, and to avoid the press he would use a rope outside Belle's window to get down and back to his quarters. One night as he descended the rope, the hotel owner's daughter pounced on him, grasping for his crotch. "She wanted the sight and feel of my privates," Johnson said. "Like she thought I was built of leather down there. I've never seen a girl get so frantic." To prevent her from screaming, Johnson had intercourse with her. When she wanted a repeat performance the next night, Johnson refused, insisting he could not satisfy three women. Furious, the girl told her father the champion had raped her. Her father confronted Johnson, accusing him of "ruining his poor little baby, with his gigantic, oversized thing." Johnson paid off the hotel owner to suppress any bad publicity.

Shortly afterward, at the Coney Island racetrack, Johnson met a 28-year-old white woman, Etta Terry Duryea, a tall, slender blond who had recently divorced an eastern horse-racing tycoon. Johnson began living with her, truly loved her, gave her a $2,500 engagement ring, and finally married her in Pittsburgh in 1909. The press was in an uproar, coast to coast, about this marriage. The pressure began to get to Etta, and she suffered long spells of depression. Johnson wanted children by her. Etta refused. Fearful of pregnancy, she began to sleep in a separate bedroom. Johnson then became the first black regular at the Everleigh Club. At heart he was devoted to his wife, yet on Sept. 11, 1912, Etta put a gun to her head and committed suicide. (When Johnson died, he was buried beside her in Chicago's Graceland Cemetery.)

Three months after Etta's death, a pretty 19-year-old white girl from Minneapolis, Lucille Cameron, applied to Johnson for a job as his secretary. He hired her. They lived discreetly apart but slept together. Lucille's mother heard about it and came screaming into town to stop it. She insisted Johnson be charged with abducting her underage daughter. Headlines condemned Johnson. Lynch crowds gathered. Defiantly, Johnson married Lucille Cameron. The reformers decided to get Johnson once and for all, and for that purpose they employed the Mann Act, the federal white slavery law of 1912 that made it a crime to transport a woman across state lines for immoral purposes. But the government needed a witness. They found one in Belle Schreiber, who was determined to have her revenge on Johnson for discarding her. She told authorities that Johnson had taken her over one state line after another for the purposes of debauchery, prostitution, unlawful sexual intercourse, and crimes against nature. On May 13, 1913, a jury found Johnson guilty. He was sentenced to one year and one day in a federal penitentiary. Out of jail on bail, Johnson, at the urging of his mother, posed as a Canadian baseball player and skipped the country.

With Lucille, Johnson spent five years of exile abroad. In France Johnson had love affairs with the leggy star of the Folies Bergère, Mistinguette, and with actress Gaby Deslys. In Germany he had a love affair with Mata Hari. Later, in Hollywood, he had an intense relationship with actress Lupe Velez. After 12 years of marriage, his third wife, Lucille Cameron, quietly divorced him. In August, 1925, Johnson married the last of his white wives, Irene Marie Pineau, another blond who divorced her white husband, an advertising man, to wed him. His love for her, Johnson said, knew no parallel in his life. By this time, there was no public fuss. Despite his arrogance, Jack Johnson was an easygoing, affable fellow. He just had the misfortune of being born in the wrong time.

—I. W.

The Bambino Of The Bed

GEORGE HERMAN "BABE" RUTH (Feb. 6, 1895–Aug. 16, 1948)

HIS FAME: The best-known baseball player in the history of American sports, he was the first one to gain world renown. In WWII, when Japanese troops charged a U.S. Marine emplacement, they shouted, "To hell with Babe Ruth!" Babe Ruth *was* America. Born into an impoverished family in Baltimore, he was saved from becoming a juvenile delinquent when his exasperated parents sent him to St. Mary's Industrial School. Excelling in baseball, he was hired by the minor-league Baltimore Orioles, then signed by the major-league Boston Red Sox, and finally sold to the New York Yankees. From the best left-handed pitcher in the American League, he was transformed into a full-time outfielder and hitter. At his peak he was 6 ft. 2 in. and weighed between 215 and 240 lb., and his fame came from his ability to lash out home runs. He led his league in home runs for 12 years, slugging a record-making 60 in 1927 (broken by Roger Maris during a longer season in 1961). He was called "the Sultan of Swat" and "the Bambino." Lovable and sentimental, he was also undisciplined, crude, bawdy, vulgar. Although a selfish

Ruth and Claire Hodgson on their wedding day

hedonist, Babe Ruth never forgot the advice Mayor Jimmy Walker of New York gave him: to remember that he was the idol of millions of "dirty-faced kids" out there, and that he must behave accordingly. After retiring from the Yankees in 1934, Ruth's one ambition was to become a team manager. But no team would hire him as manager because of his irresponsibility. His last years were embittered, before he died of throat cancer at 53. Over 100,000 fans paraded past his bier in Yankee Stadium, "the house that Ruth built."

HIS LOVES: His appetites were gargantuan. His excesses included eating (a stack of mutton chops for breakfast, endless hot dogs throughout the day), gambling, drinking, partying, spending, and copulating. Hardly a day passed during his career that he did not have sex with at least one woman. He liked women as much as baseball. He had no favorites, bedding tall women, short ones, fat ones, thin ones, beautiful ones, ugly ones, socialites, film starlets, secretaries, other men's wives, and whores in every big city of the U.S. Whenever the team arrived in a new town and checked into a hotel, Babe Ruth left his suitcase with teammate Ping Bodie and hastened out to find some young woman. He was usually gone all night. When a reporter asked Bodie what Ruth was really like, Bodie said he did not know. "But you room with him," the reporter persisted. Bodie shook his head. "I don't room with him. I room with his suitcase." Other times Babe Ruth entertained women in his hotel. In Detroit once, he rented four adjoining rooms, purchased a piano, and invited teammates and stray women to his party. After a while, Babe Ruth stood on a chair, waving his beer mug, and bellowed, "All right, ladies, any girl who doesn't want to fuck can leave right now!"

When it came to sex he was insatiable, and he possessed great stamina. In St. Louis he took over a whorehouse for an entire night, stating he was going to have sex with every woman in the house. After that he took them on one by one, made love to each successfully, and in the morning celebrated by consuming an omelet made with 18 eggs.

Robert W. Creamer researched and described Babe Ruth in action—sexually—in his excellent biography, *Babe*:

One teammate, asked if Ruth had an exceptionally big penis, frowned a little as he searched his memory and shook his head. "No," he said. "It was normal size … Babe's wasn't noticeably big. What was extraordinary was his ability to keep doing it all the time. He was continually with women, morning and night. I don't know how he kept going." He was very noisy in bed, visceral grunts and gasps and whoops accompanying his erotic exertions. "He was the noisiest fucker in North America," a whimsical friend recalled.

All this carnal activity got Babe Ruth into trouble from time to time. Biographer Ken Sobol noted, "The circumstances of one unsavory rape in which he had been involved were already known to several sportswriters." Late in 1922 Babe Ruth was slapped with a breach-of-promise suit for $50,000, filed on behalf of Dolores Dixon, a teenage employee in a Manhattan department store. She claimed that she had become pregnant by Ruth, that he had promised to marry her, and that he had committed statutory rape. Ruth called it blackmail, his lawyer called it extortion. The matter went to trial in 1923, but the case was settled out of court.

The tragic part of Ruth's sex life was that during his busiest years in bed with other women he had a wife whom he sorely neglected. Helen Woodford, an auburnhaired Texas girl and quite pretty, was a waitress in a Boston café when Ruth fell in love with her. They were married in 1914 in a Catholic church just outside Baltimore. He was 19 and she 17. Throughout their 14 years of marriage, Helen's life with Ruth was hell. He gave her furs, an 80-acre farm, and an adopted daughter named Dorothy, but he gave her neither time nor fidelity. His affairs with other women caused her to have a nervous breakdown. She left Ruth in 1928, and the following year—while living with a dentist in Watertown, Mass.—she died in a house fire. Ruth mourned her briefly. Three months later he wed Mrs. Claire Merritt Hodgson, who had married a Georgia cotton broker at 14 and had had a child named Julia before divorcing him. She was classy, well-off, and still a beauty when she moved to New York to become a model and part-time actress. Ruth had been introduced to her at a ball game, had been smitten, and was having an affair with her when Helen died. He married Claire in April, 1929. Claire tamed him, changing his entire lifestyle. She put him on a strict diet. She curbed his drinking. She saved his money. She forced a ten o'clock curfew on him when he went to parties, and she knew about all the other women. "The Babe brought out the beast in a lot of ladies the world over," she wrote in her autobiography, "and I enjoyed very much setting them straight on their problem." To the end, the marriage was a happy one.

—I. W.

Net Loss

WILLIAM TILDEN, JR. (Feb. 10, 1893–June 5, 1953)

HIS FAME: In 1950 a poll conducted by the Associated Press proclaimed that "Big Bill" Tilden was the greatest tennis player of the first half of the 20th century, and some of America's leading sportswriters called him the greatest U.S. athlete in any sport at any time. Perhaps these writers hoped to bring solace to a onetime giant—a closet homosexual revealed—who was suffering his last years in disgrace and near oblivion.

HIS PERSON: He was Mr. Tennis to the world and to himself, a dazzling star fiercely dedicated to the game he dominated. Yet from the moment of his conception he was marked for personal

tragedy. Seven years before his birth, Selina and William Tilden had watched in horror as all three of their babies—two girls and a boy—died one by one during a diphtheria epidemic. The following year Selina Tilden bore their fourth child, Herbert. Still stunned by her loss, and longing for a daughter, Selina yielded Herbert's upbringing to his father. With the appearance of another son, Selina's maternal instincts resurfaced. She named her new baby William Tilden, Jr., but from the beginning she called him "June" (short for Junior) and he became her obsession. To keep him close, she convinced herself he was a sickly child. When June reached school age Selina refused to relinquish him, hired tutors for his lessons, and deprived him of playmates. June adored his mother and absorbed every word she uttered. When she spoke to him of sex, it was to warn him of the frightful venereal diseases that could result from genital contact. Not until he was 18, when a crippling illness confined Selina to a wheelchair, was June released—to become Bill, at last.

Young Tilden moved in with two maiden relatives and was sent to school for the first time. Starting at Germantown Academy, he moved on to the University of Pennsylvania. During his freshman year in college, news of his mother's death affected him so severely that he withdrew from Penn U. and returned to Germantown Academy as a tennis coach. There his two lifetime passions merged: the need to excel at tennis and the desire to cultivate the affection and playing skills of young boys. His own game remained unspectacular until he broke through at 27. For the next six years he never lost a championship match. When he was 29, an operation that amputated the tip of a middle finger seemed only to improve his game. In 1920 he became the first American to win the men's singles at Wimbledon, England. Between 1920 and 1930, he led the U.S. Davis Cup team to victory in seven consecutive years.

Success transformed him into an egocentric prima donna. Dubbed "Big Bill" although he was no more than 6 ft. 1 1/2 in. tall, he became arrogant, opinionated, and belligerent. He was also messy, unwashed, and frequently smelly. After sweaty matches he would return to the locker room but refuse to disrobe and shower in the presence of his teammates. Not one of them ever saw his naked body. He chainsmoked, drank strong black coffee, and ate almost nothing but steak and ice cream. With growing fame, he affected a British accent as he consorted with the world's notables, including four U.S. presidents. In Hollywood he was partnered with Errol Flynn, Spencer Tracy, and Montgomery Clift on Charlie Chaplin's tennis court. At Clifton Webb's he coached Greta Garbo, Katharine Hepburn, and Tallulah Bankhead.

After his first arrest on Nov. 23, 1946, and subsequent detention in a California honor farm for "contributing to the delinquency of a minor," most of Tilden's acquaintances fell away. Despite his considerable professional earnings and two inheritances, this tormented man died alone in a Hollywood side-street apartment with $10 in his pocket. His money had long since been dissipated on a pashalike lifestyle, ungrateful little boys, and disastrous investments, most notably a brief stage career wherein he financed and played the lead in Bram Stoker's *Dracula*.

SEX LIFE: In his autobiography, *My Story*, Tilden spoke of boyhood crushes on pretty girls. He claimed that upon reaching manhood he considered marriage, and later suffered from unrequited love at the hands of some of Hollywood's most famous women—all a pathetic fabrication. Actually, he recognized early on that he was "different." At age 10, somehow escaping Selina, he embarked on a five-year fondling affair with another boy. Traumatized by his mother's preachings, living as he did at a time when words like *pregnancy* and *menstruation* hid behind such euphemisms as "with child" and "the curse" and homosexuality was an absolute taboo, he fought to sublimate his sexual urges in tennis. Sadly, he never enjoyed a fulfilling homosexual love affair, and it is unlikely he ever had complete physical contact with another human body, male or female. Mostly he fondled his boys and masturbated privately, increasing this activity as his career faded. Although he minced onto the tennis court before launching into his powerful game, very few knew his secret. Ty Cobb called him "that fruit," and in *Lolita* Vladimir Nabokov's nymphet takes tennis lessons from Ned Litam ("Ma Tilden" spelled backwards), but no one openly exposed his problem.

Describing the incident that led to his downfall, Tilden wrote: "I met one lad on the court who showed unusual promise.... Somehow we drifted into a foolishly schoolboyish relationship.... Coming home from a movie ... we indulged in horseplay.... We were stopped by the police in Beverly Hills." As a consequence, Tilden spent almost eight months at a California honor farm, polishing kitchen pots, setting the table, and serving other inmates. Arrested a second time after he violated a five-year parole by consorting with a minor, Tilden protested, but to no avail. The youth he had pursued identified Tilden unhesitatingly, using that missing fingertip as a clincher. He also testified that Tilden "was playing with my privates." This time Tilden was sent to a road camp. Released in time for Christmas, he returned alone and abandoned to his apartment, where six lonely months later, fully dressed, he stretched out on his bed to rest, and quietly died. In his sensitive, definitive biography, *Big Bill Tilden*, Frank Deford wrote of Tilden's Philadelphia funeral: "He was placed ... at the feet of his mother, so that at last he could be her child again, for good, at peace."

—*S. W.*

XIV

Holier Than Thou

The Papal Bull

POPE ALEXANDER VI (Jan. 1, 1431–Aug. 18, 1503)

HIS FAME: Pope Alexander VI's corrupt, worldly, and ambitious papacy contributed to the decline of the Catholic Church's prestige and paved the way for the Protestant Reformation.

HIS PERSON: The scion of Spain's powerful Borgia family, Rodrigo was the protégé of his uncle, Alfonso Borgia, Bishop of Valencia. Uncle Alfonso supervised Rodrigo's education, and after becoming Pope Calixtus III, he wangled his 25-year-old nephew into the College of Cardinals. Young Rodrigo so exuberantly enjoyed the trappings of wealth and power that he greatly scandalized the Church and embarrassed his uncle, not an easy thing to do in those freewheeling days. Rodrigo himself was never embarrassed by anything, least of all the vast number of children that he sired during his career as a churchman. A fully accurate roster of his offspring cannot be compiled.

Rodrigo's own bought-and-paid-for tenure as Pope Alexander VI began in 1492. Once installed, he and his son Cesare commenced a campaign of diplomacy, assassination, strategic marriage, and treachery that brought the whole of northern Italy under Borgia control. Rodrigo and Cesare outflanked and routed the powerful Orsini and Colonna families and successfully resisted the reform movement of the Dominican monk Girolamo Savonarola, whom they burned at the stake as a heretic.

Folklore has made much of the Borgias' reliance upon poison as a political tool, painting Rodrigo's daughter Lucrezia as a specialist in its use. Actually, there is no evidence that she ever poisoned anybody. Her duty was to marry anyone Rodrigo told her to, whether she felt like it or not. As for the poison, the Borgias used it sparingly, preferring instead a straightforward strangling or bludgeoning carried out by hired thugs.

Although intrigue was Rodrigo's lifeblood, he was given to spasms of repentance. But these were usually short-lived, thanks to the many temptations that accompany great wealth. Most of Rodrigo's riches stemmed from his efforts to put Catholicism on a cash-and-carry basis. He was a foremost practitioner of simony, the buying and selling of religious favors. For 24,000 gold pieces Rodrigo, with the help of a bishop and a secretary, once sold a nobleman permission to commit incest with his sister.

Rodrigo was a great patron of the arts. He coaxed Michelangelo to undertake the rebuilding of St. Peter's Basilica and supported many other Renaissance artists in projects that were intended to glorify his reign. Still, toward the end of his life, it was popularly thought that he had made a pact with the devil, a notion which the manner of his death did little to dispel. Rodrigo fell ill following a banquet and died shortly thereafter. In death, his corpse immediately grew bloated and blackened, as if to underscore his corruption in life.

SEX LIFE: As a young cardinal, Rodrigo did his best to emulate the virility of the bull featured on the Borgia family escutcheon. He is said to have been a handsome youth, tall and robust, with penetrating bedroom eyes. His contemporaries called him an irresistible conqueror. But then, who would have dared resist? One of his mistresses, Giulia Farnese, was 16 and already married when he became her lover. The Romans sarcastically called her the "bride of Christ." Another woman, Vannozza dei Cattanei, bore Rodrigo four (some say five) children before he became pope. Three of those—Lucrezia, Cesare, and Giovanni—followed in their father's footsteps. Lucrezia may have been sexually available to both Rodrigo and Cesare, among others, and to this day historians debate whether her child was the issue of her father or her brother. Probably she couldn't have said herself. The family's notorious preference for sexy entertainments kept the clan's blood boiling, and tended to obscure trifles such as questions of parentage.

At the age of 29 Rodrigo was rebuked by Pope Pius II for appearing at an orgy in his cardinal's robes, although he probably retained only his red hat as the evening wore on. This pattern of behavior continued until his death. Rodrigo had the instincts of a Florenz Ziegfeld, and he delighted in sponsoring entertainments featuring lots of nude and nubile dancers.

It was not unusual for him to obstruct the solemn high mass. During one mass he brought giggling women up to the altar, and on another occasion he carelessly trampled the sacred host underfoot. He would celebrate at any excuse, bringing a rowdy crew of prostitutes into the papal apartments. During festivals, an average of 25 courtesans a night was provided for the pope's entertainment. Discretion was never one of Rodrigo's strong points, and he used to scandalize Christendom with his traveling arrangements, which often included a coterie of scantily clad dancing girls.

One of the pope's banquets was chronicled by his master of ceremonies, Johannes Burchard, Bishop of Ostia, who wrote in his *Diarium Romanum*: "... 50 reputable whores, not common but the kind called courtesans, supped [at the Vatican], ... and after supper they danced about with the servants and others in that place, first in their clothes and then nude ... candelabra with lighted candles were set on the floor and chestnuts were strewn about and the naked courtesans on hands and feet gathered them up, wriggling in and out among the candelabra.... Then all those present in the hall were carnally treated in public...." The pope, Cesare, and Lucrezia gave prizes to the men who copulated the most times with the prostitutes.

On the eve of one of Lucrezia's marriages, Rodrigo arranged a demonstration of the facts of life for her. The pope's men-at-arms commandeered several mares belonging to some passing merchants. The mares were brought into the papal compound, along with some of the pontiff's stallions. While the stallions fought among themselves for the mares, the pope and his favorite daughter stood on a balcony and laughed uproariously.

Unlike a previous pope, Sixtus IV, Rodrigo was a heterosexual. But legend persists that Rodrigo and Cesare imprisoned and raped the most beautiful young man in Italy. Proof, however, is lacking, since the victim was found in the Tiber with a stone around his neck before he could talk. Such evidence as there is seems to indicate that Rodrigo preferred women. In addition to the army of courtesans constantly at his command, he maintained a private harem, and his sons Giovanni and Cesare vied with each other for the pope's favor by sending him exotic beauties for his collection. At one point Giovanni scored a coup over his brother by scouting up a Rubenesque Spanish beauty who moved Rodrigo to ecstasy. Cesare, jealous of his brother's secular glory, had Giovanni stabbed and thrown in the Tiber. The murder of his favorite son caused the pope such distress that he briefly reformed. But this reformation turned into more of a rest period, and soon he was back to his decadent ways.

—M.J.T.

Hymn To Pan

ALEISTER CROWLEY (Oct. 12, 1875–Dec. 1, 1947)

HIS FAME: Dubbed by the British tabloid press "the wickedest man in the world," Aleister Crowley used his inherited fortune to blaze trails in every form of consciousness expansion available to a repressed Edwardian gentleman, making headways in mountain-climbing, drugs, the occult, sex and all-around perversity.

For a time a powerful spiritual figure, Crowley dead-ended in personal dissolution after founding his personal religion of Thelema, based on the individualist credo "Do What Thou Wilt Shall Be the Whole of the Law." Named one of the 100 greatest Britons in history by the BBC in 2002, his myth casts a long, and dark, shadow over popular culture.

HIS PERSON: Born Edward Alexander Crowley in Leamington Spa, Warwickshire in 1875, Crowley was raised in the Plymouth Brethren, a radically conservative Christian sect. After his father's death, his faith began to curdle, and Crowley rebelled; his mother referred to him as the "Beast" in the Book of Revelations. A deep chord was struck in the young Crowley: the man would spend the rest of his life trying to fill the abyss left in him by the death of his father, outdoing his father's with his own proselytizing of a new religion, Thelema, based around the apocalyptic narrative of the Book of Revelations. At Cambridge, Crowley dallied with prostitutes and began to realize homosexual desires before an undefined spiritual crisis in Stockholm led him to believe he was chosen to embark on the Great Work of Magick, as he spelled it; of attaining enlightenment. After school he filled his time writing turgid poetry and applied his fortune to mountain-climbing—he still holds unbroken records—and the pursuit of occult power, ingratiating himself with the infamous Victorian secret society the Hermetic Order of the Golden Dawn.

He married Rose Kelly in 1904, and they honeymooned in Cairo, spending a night of nuptial bliss in the Great Pyramid. Shortly thereafter Rose went into a trance and instructed Crowley that a spirit was attempting to communicate with him and to go to a certain place at a certain time, where an apocalyptic document called *The Book of the Law* was "dictated" to him. The long poem prophesied both World Wars, the downfall of all world religions, and 2,000 years of bloody strife and warfare on the world stage. Deciding he had reached the peaks of spiritual attainment, Crowley blew the last of his family fortune on publishing, setting forth his theories and methods in the massive series of books he titled *The Equinox*, and establishing a magical order, the A.A.o., with his friend George Cecil Jones. Bereft of money by the outbreak of the First World War, Crowley set into a cycle of itinerancy and leeching off students. He also developed a heroin addiction after the drug was prescribed to him for his chronic asthma. The remaining years of Crowley's life were not kind to him—nor was Crowley himself particularly kind to the women and adoring students who surrounded him, looking for a piece of his mystique. Crowley maintained to the end that the great mission of his life was to prove, via the existence of *The Book of the Law*, that there were disincarnate beings or extraterrestrials of much greater intelligence than human beings living and operating in the world. His last words were, "I am perplexed."

SEX MAGICK: One of Crowley's great projects was taking both theology and religious practice and reinterpreting them in sexual terms. Initiated into the German occult order the O.T.O. after the 1909 publication of *The Book of Lies*, in which he intuited the details of the group's secret sexual practices, Crowley was given a stack of sexual magick techniques by the order and proceeded to spend a year in New York testing them along "scientific lines" on one or more prostitutes a night. Sexual fluids were also used as a holy sacrament; Crowley believed that regularly consuming semen commingled with vaginal fluid after intercourse would gradually make him superhuman. He regularly sought out hunchback dwarf women, had intercourse with them inside a magic pentacle, then extracted their commingled ejaculations from the woman's vagina, made the mixture into pills, and sold them as cures for male impotence.

Crowley treated his string of "Scarlet Women"—mistresses and spiritual wives—with disdain, invariably leaving them in the lurch after chemical and ritual overload, coupled with Crowley's gutter lifestyle and insufferable high dramatics, caused breakdowns in his followers. Much of his infamy comes from his time at the "Abbey of Thelema" in Cefalu, Sicily, more or less a classic experiment in drug-based communal living—with Crowley as the guru. Accompanied by one of his favorite "Scarlet Women" Leah Hirsig, their multiple small children, and his followers, Crowley aimed to break down the barriers of perception. In practice, this meant feeding people mescaline and locking them in his "Chamber of Nightmares," a room covered with Crowley's childlike drawings of demons. On one lively night at the Abbey, Crowley talked Hirsig into being sodomized by a goat, and slashed its throat at the moment it orgasmed, drenching her in its blood. He was expelled from the country by Mussolini shortly thereafter. He also rewrote the O.T.O.'s rituals to incorporate anal sex; homosexual sex magick was one of Crowley's fortés.

In 1907, after he had lost his child with Rose Kelly and then lost Rose to alcoholism, Crowley engaged in a long series of homosexual magickal operations with the young poetry student Victor Neuberg in the Algerian desert. Crowley took the passive role in the sexual rites, always preferring for the young, reedy Neuberg to sodomize him. Crowley struggled with his bisexuality from an early age. He barely mentions his countless homosexual affairs in his autobiography, although his surviving diaries are much more candid: in *De Arte Magica*, he recounts the details of his "9=2 Magus Initiation," in which he was cluster-fucked by nearly two dozen men in a New York bathhouse. He took to cross-dressing at many points in his life; while in drag referring to himself as "Alys Cusack," one of many pseudonyms he used throughout his writings. Androgyny, of course, is a recurring, and crucial, theme in the alchemical and shamanic traditions of the world, and in this respect, Crowley was hardly an exception. Despite his infamously bad behavior and reputation, however, Crowley's writing reveals him as something of a closet romantic. He suffered many unrequited loves and heartbreaks in his life. Magick was Crowley's great love, and it never abandoned him, even as it dragged him through hell after hell. It is no wonder that his chosen symbol for the Great Work was Babalon, the Whore of Revelations who must take the Adept's every last drop of blood and utterly destroy him before he attains.

HIS THOUGHTS: "I slept with faith and found a corpse in my arms on awakening; I drank and danced all night with doubt and found her a virgin in the morning."

—*J.L.*

John Doe, Alias God

FATHER DIVINE (1877-Sept. 10, 1965)

HIS FAME: He was the founder of the Peace Mission cult, which eventually numbered over a million members. Many of his followers considered him God incarnate, an opinion with which he agreed, and many also thought that those who were true believers, i.e., "angels," would never die.

HIS PERSON: Although Father Divine carefully blurred the events of his early life, he was apparently born George Baker, the son—appropriately—of Joseph and Mary, Georgia sharecroppers. This semiofficial version conflicts with his own later account that he had been "combusted"

Father Divine and 21-years-old Edna Ritchings

one day in 1900 on the corner of Seventh Avenue and 134th Street in Harlem. After serving his gospel apprenticeship in Baltimore, he returned to Georgia to promote himself as a "Live Ever, Die Never" black evangelist, but intolerant officials arrested him as a public nuisance, booked him as "John Doe, alias God" (he was already insisting on his divinity), and suggested he leave the state. With 12— it had to be 12, of course—followers, he made his way to New York and set up on West 40th Street the first of many communal living arrangements, or "heavens," as they came to be known. He found jobs for his little band as cooks, waiters, valets, etc., and accepted their wages in return. Four years later he moved them, now 20 strong, to a house in Sayville, Long Island. There his movement grew rapidly, especially after 1931, when his godly powers were "proved" by the death (of a heart attack) of a local judge who four days before had sentenced Divine to six months in jail for disturbing the peace. "I hated to do it," Divine lamented from his cell. During the Depression thousands of down-and-outers became angels. (Angelic requirements included abstention from smoking, drinking, swearing, movies, cosmetics, and sex; depositing of all wages in the communal coffers; and a willingness to adore Father properly.) In Sayville, and later in heavenly annexes opened in Harlem, thousands feasted daily on fried chicken banquets that were absolutely free. In subsequent years, rural farms and urban hotels were acquired, all of which Divine visited regularly, descending from a chauffeur-driven Rolls-Royce or Duesenberg although he claimed to own nothing himself and paid no income tax. When he died at Woodmont, his 32-room chateau on Philadelphia's Main Line, at about age 90, he was to his followers across the country truly "God."

SEX LIFE: A realistic man, Father Divine must early on have accepted the fact that he was not the average woman's idea of a lover. Barely 5 ft. tall, squat, bald, he suggested at best a dark-complexioned Cupid. He was attracted to tall women; his two wives—Sister Peninah, later known as Mother Divine, who was black, and Edna Rose Ritchings, "Sweet Angel," who was not only white but golden blond as well—were considerably taller than he was. Both were, however, wives in name only; the discipline of the cult demanded unswerving celibacy from all. Men slept on one side of heaven, women on the other, and sex was strictly forbidden. The question was whether the Father applied the ban to himself, and more than one angry and grudge-bearing deserter from the flock declared otherwise. Tales of seduction regularly surfaced. In 1937 a woman identified as "Faithful Mary" broadcast an account of orgies in which young female converts ("Rosebuds," as they were known) were deflowered to such whispered phrases as "Your body belongs to God" and "Mary wasn't a virgin." An eager press gobbled up such allegations, but "Faithful Mary" later retracted her statement, so the truth of such charges remains doubtful. More than one D.A. assigned a female undercover agent to pose as a new disciple and obtain conclusive evidence of immorality in the heavens, but not one of these attempts was successful. Family court judges regularly branded the Father a "home breaker," but that was because of his habit of welcoming to his fold every unhappy wife who abandoned married life for the nearest heaven.

Why did Father Divine insist that married couples, too, abstain from sex— that this natural function be declared taboo? First because he was determined to achieve racial equality and real integration in the Peace Mission. He was well aware that in the 1920s and '30s and '40s the slightest trace of sexual impropriety in an interracial setting would be disastrous. At the first hint of miscegenation, every heaven would have to close down. Better forbid sex entirely than risk that. True, his own second wife was white, but he had made it clear that Sweet Angel, who was 21 when he, in his late 60s, married her, was and would remain his "spotless virgin bride," which apparently she did. Besides, she was, he said, the reincarnated spirit of his first wife, Mother Divine. The notion of "spotless virginity" fascinated the Father. His 26 secretaries—13 black, 13 white, mostly young—were known as "Father's Sweets" and were all virgins, at least theoretically. He had been known to "restore virginity" to a particularly attractive young convert with good typing and shorthand skills who otherwise would have been barred because of an unfortunate indiscretion in her past. The secretaries adored Father—purely, of course; otherwise this inner circle was not unlike a harem, with all the jealousies and intrigues peculiar to such.

The second reason for the sex ban was simply Father Divine's own basic need to be the one and only with his disciples. He wished to be a father-husband-lover-God. Female angels in particular, denied the catharsis provided by their former sexual outlets, tended to form passionate emotional attachments to him. A physical expression of that emotion, known as "vibrating" and resembling an extraordinarily sensual ballet, was an approved sex substitute for those who required it. It allowed for a sublime spiritual climax, and at times an actual physical orgasm. Father Divine—the exalted, the beloved, the God incarnate—would watch complacently.

HIS ADVICE: "The spirit of the consciousness of the presence of God is the source of all supply and will satisfy every desire and it does."

—*N.C.S.*

The Infallible Healer

MARY BAKER EDDY (July 16, 1821–Dec. 3, 1910)

HER FAME: Mary Morse Baker Eddy was the founder of the Christian Science Church. Her book, *Science and Health with Key to the Scriptures*, which at the time of her death had appeared in 160 editions, was the basic tract for her church and dealt in large part with mental healing. Mrs. Eddy was also responsible for establishing the newspaper *The Christian Science Monitor*.

HER PERSON: Mary Morse Baker, the youngest of six children divided equally between boys and girls, was born in Bow, N.H. Her father, Mark, was a pious, hardworking farmer. Mary was small, delicate, and rather pretty, with wavy brown hair and striking blue eyes. She was a sickly child who suffered from hysterical seizures, often throwing tantrums to get her way. As a result, she was sometimes treated by the family doctor with mesmerism and mental suggestion. Mary was also a romantic child with a penchant for writing flowery verse, and in adulthood she fancied herself an author.

In 1843 she married George Washington Glover, a hearty building contractor, and they moved to Wilmington, N.C. There, after less than a year of marriage, Glover died of yellow fever, and Mary, pregnant, was forced to move back to her father's home in New Hampshire. In 1844 she gave birth to a son, George Washington Glover II. Mary did not take well to motherhood, and at the age of 6 George was sent off to Minnesota to live with foster parents. Mary did not see him again for 23 years. (Her father said: "Mary acts like an old ewe that won't own its lamb.") In Bow, Mary became a chronic invalid, having to be rocked to sleep in her father's arms. Her sister Abigail had a huge cradle constructed for her, and neighborhood boys often earned extra money by rocking Mary to sleep.

In 1862, still suffering from extreme hysteria, Mary visited Phineas P. Quimby, a famous Maine faith healer, and was at least temporarily cured. She was much taken with Quimby's methods and studied with him for a time. In 1866 she fell on an icy sidewalk and was once again incapacitated. This time, however, she was able to "cure" herself by reading the Bible. Her recovery eventually led to the development of her Christian Science Church. In 1875 she published *Science and Health*, and through the strength of her personality as much as the merits of her book, she managed to gain adherents

Asa Gilbert Eddy become Mary's third husband

throughout New England. By the time of her death at 89, she'd earned more than $400,000 in book royalties and left behind a flourishing church.

SEX LIFE: Her first love came when she was 15. Andrew Gault, her neighborhood swain, was 21. Though Mary went so far as to write him a love poem, the only one she ever wrote, Andrew married someone else. Her marriage to George Washington Glover having ended tragically, she went into a mental and physical tailspin.

Nine years later she married Dr. Daniel Patterson, an itinerant dentist who had a reputation as a philanderer. He was off on trips much of the time, and Mary spent most of their married life as an invalid. During the Civil War Dr. Patterson joined the Union Army, was captured by the Confederates, and passed most of the war in prison. Shortly after returning to his wife, Patterson left home for good in 1866, and Mary, now deeply involved in her mental healing, took on several protégés, including young Richard Kennedy, with whom she set up a profitable "healing" business. She also took on the writing of her book, *Science and Health*, and finished the first draft in 1870. In 1873 she finally divorced Patterson on grounds of desertion, though she later insisted that it was because of adultery. Patterson sent Mary an allowance of $200 a year. In 1896 he died in a Maine poorhouse.

In 1877 Mary was wedded to Asa Gilbert Eddy, a sewing-machine salesman who became the first person to announce publicly that he was a Christian Scientist. On their marriage certificate, the 56-year-old Mrs. Eddy gave her age as 40. The presence of a new husband seemed to aggravate Mary's various illnesses. More and more often she found Eddy irritating. Said biographer Dakin: "He was constant in his efforts to please her and to anticipate her whims; but she showed an increasing annoyance at his slowness, his round awkwardness, and his rather rustic manners and appearance." She did not have to put up with him too long. In 1882 Eddy died of organic heart disease.

But Mary had become used to having a man nearby, and the same year as Eddy's death a young machinist named Calvin Frye entered her life. He served as her steward, secretary, bookkeeper, and footman until her death. In 1888 she met Dr. Ebenezer Johnson Foster, a homeopathic physician, and adopted him as her son. In Mary's later years, all the men close to her seemed to have one thing in common: They were inferior to her and she could easily manipulate them. When she couldn't, she got rid of them by accusing them of being "mesmerists."

QUIRKS: She believed fervently in something she called "malicious animal magnetism" (M.A.M.), which she thought her enemies were using to destroy her. (When her last husband, Asa Gilbert Eddy, died, she insisted that the cause was arsenic poisoning at the hands of the "mesmerists," by the use of M.A.M.) In order to protect herself, she created a select bodyguard of "watchers" to ward off these attacks of mental mesmerism. As Mrs. Eddy's stature in the community grew, she found it necessary to institute numerous lawsuits (all of which were thrown out of court) against her enemies and their use of M.A.M. In fact, one of the reasons she took on Calvin Frye was his supposed efficacy as an "antimesmerist."

Eventually Mrs. Eddy began to think herself infallible and became extremely autocratic in her rule. She preferred that her followers call her "Mother," and she wrote memos about controlling the weather through mental processes. Continuing to suffer from bouts of hysteria, she took morphine to ease her physical pain. She advised complete celibacy as the only true spiritual state.

HER THOUGHTS: About marriage she said, "it is often convenient, sometimes pleasant, and occasionally a love affair. Marriage is susceptible of many definitions. It sometimes presents the most wretched condition of human existence." Her last written words were "God is my life."

—*C.H.S.*

Tempted By The Devil

MARTIN LUTHER (Nov. 10, 1483-Feb. 18, 1546)

HIS FAME: A strong-willed monk, Luther challenged the Roman Catholic Church and inaugurated the 16th-century Protestant Reformation. Following his excommunication, Luther startled theologians by marrying a nun and dedicating his life to the establishment of a religious movement that took a more personal approach to presenting the gospel. Lutheran churches still flourish, using as their foundation the precepts the founder originally laid down in the 100 volumes he wrote.

HIS PERSON: Dominated by auto-cratic parents, Luther was often beaten by his father, a copper miner. As a result Luther suffered through a sickly and sad childhood. While growing up, he joined his impoverished family members as they slept together naked—thus providing the impressionable youngster an opportunity to witness sexual acts.

Although he found school boring, Luther readily submitted to his father's suggestion that he enter law school. However, he quickly abandoned his legal education and entered an Augustinian monastery. Ordained in 1507, his order sent him to the University of Wittenberg, where, in 1512, he received the degree of Doctor of Theology.

Luther gradually developed hostilities toward the Church. On Oct. 31, 1517, he posted on the door of the Castle Church in Wittenberg his scandalous 95 Theses. In the theses, Luther denounced the church practice of selling indulgences. (An indulgence was sold to a sinner by the Church to lessen the punishment for a sin.)

Labeled a "drunken German" by Pope Leo X, Luther appeared before an ecclesiastical court and shocked the assembled clergymen by accusing the pope of being "no better than any other stinking sinner." Luther was excommunicated and faced probable execution, but he escaped and was harbored by German knights who supported his cause. He resurfaced as a folk hero a year later and became the acknowledged leader of the Reformation.

Throughout his life Luther suffered from indigestion, constipation, kidney stones, and hemorrhoids, but his painful ailments didn't slow his crusade to reform the Catholic Church. He was supported by a vociferous following, and his profound religious impact was still evident even after his death.

SEX LIFE: As spiritual head of a new church that celebrated but two sacraments—baptism and communion—Luther advocated the elimination of clerical celibacy. He believed sex was not sinful, and insisted intercourse was as necessary as eating and drinking.

Luther supported wedlock for the clergy, and he practiced what he preached. Shortly after severing ties with the Catholic Church, he established an underground railroad to help nuns escape their cloisters. One of them, Katharina von Bora, became his wife after another of the other nuns he had aided rejected his offer of marriage. Luther married the reddish-haired runaway nun to spite the pope, to avenge his hatred for the devil, and to please his father, who was concerned that the family name would die out. The excommunicated monk insisted nothing could cure his lust, not even marriage. Luther learned to live with this lust, and apparently he was never unfaithful to Katharina. Reflecting on his marriage, he once said: "Man has strange thoughts the first year of marriage. When sitting at the table he thinks, 'Before I was alone; now there are two.' Or in bed, when he wakes up, he sees a pair of pigtails lying beside him which he hadn't seen there before."

Prior to marrying Katharina, Luther spoke openly of his "temptations of the flesh" and said that he and many of his fellow monks at the Augustinian monastery in Erfurt, Germany, had experienced "nocturnal pollutions." Luther frequently waited more than a year to change his bed sheets, permitting them to become saturated with the foul smell of sweat, and after his marriage he often touched "specified parts" of his wife's body while being tempted by the devil. The devil lost his greatest battles "right in bed, next to Katie."

Throughout his life Luther staged a haunting personal battle with Satan, who manifested himself in a variety of disguises. Luther was known to cry out to the devil, "I have shit in the pants, and you can hang them around your neck and wipe your mouth with it," and he boasted he could drive away the evil spirit "with a single fart." He had an intimate relationship with his bowel movements and regularly wrote home giving a box score of his defecations.

Although he believed women were emotionally weaker than men, and craved sex more intensely then their male counterparts, Luther confessed in a 1519 sermon that his own sexual desires were overpowering. He considered sex a natural function ordained by God and therefore supported the idea that an impotent man should supply a sexual partner for his wife.

Luther and his wife had six children of their own and raised 11 orphans as well. Their marriage lasted 21 years, from 1525 until Luther died of a stroke in 1546. Despite his religious radicalism, Luther wasn't ready for a domestic reformation. He believed the man was to rule his wife, and she was to give him not only love but also honor and obedience. In Luther's eyes women were meant to stay at home. "The way they were created indicates this, for they have broad hips and a wide fundament to sit upon." He preferred bigamy to divorce and thought that if a married man needed another female companion to satisfy his sexual needs, he should feel free to take a second woman as a mistress. History does not record Katharina's position on this patriarchal philosophy, but she may have deferred to it to preserve domestic harmony.

—A.K.

The Lord's Ringmaster

AIMEE SEMPLE McPHERSON (Oct. 9, 1890–Sept. 27, 1944)

HER FAME: As founder of the International Church of the Four-Square Gospel, "Sister" Aimee was the spiritual leader of thousands and one of the foremost big-money evangelists of the early 20th century.

HER PERSON: Aimee Elizabeth Kennedy spent her childhood near the rural hamlet of Ingersoll in Ontario, Canada, in an atmosphere of religious fervor. Her father was a Methodist farmer, her mother a Salvation Army zealot who consecrated Aimee's life to the Lord's service a few weeks after she was born. As a teenager, Aimee shocked her pious parents with her desire to become an actress. She eventually managed to satisfy all concerned by combining religion and show business in a successful, money-making formula that is still widely emulated.

Aimee first hit the revival circuit with a fiery Pentecostal preacher named Robert Semple, whom she married at age 17. Semple died of typhoid fever in Hong Kong, where the young couple had gone to set up a mission. The 19-year-old widow returned home with her infant daughter, Roberta, and shortly thereafter married Harold McPherson, a grocery clerk. After the birth of a son, Rolf, Aimee coaxed her reluctant husband into accompanying her and the children on the hallelujah trail. But McPherson quickly became disgusted with life under Aimee's revival tent and ordered his wife to settle down. In response, she cut loose from him and continued her wanderings. He divorced her in 1921 for desertion.

In 1918 Aimee set up her headquarters in Los Angeles, then as now a hotbed of religious cults, She began to receive invaluable newspaper publicity for her faith-healing services and quickly accumulated a large following. An attractive, dynamic woman, she was widely criticized for her Paris gowns, makeup, and tinted blond hair. Her massive concrete church, called the Angelus Temple, was famous for its theatrical religious spectacles. On one occasion Sister Aimee donned a policeman's uniform and rode a motorcycle down the center aisle to introduce a sermon on the consequences of breaking God's law.

During the 1930s her Four-Square Church was the center of a series of internecine intrigues and lawsuits. In a celebrated fight with her mother, Aimee broke the old woman's nose. After a third unhappy marriage, Aimee began to shy away from publicity. Her death from an overdose of barbiturates in an Oakland, Calif., hotel room was ruled an accident.

SEX LIFE: Aimee used to declare that her ideal man would be 6 ft. tall, have wavy hair, and play the trombone. In fact, her men adhered to no such specifications. Kenneth Ormiston, a radio engineer for her church station, was tall and slender, but he had a receding hairline and bat ears. If he played the trombone, he kept it to himself. Ormiston was already married. In addition, he was an agnostic who refused to treat Sister Aimee with the respect she was accustomed to receiving, and this she found attractive.

On May 18, 1926, the superstar evangelist was reported missing while swimming in the ocean off Venice, Calif. For days her followers searched for her body, and two of the faithful died during the search. Five weeks later Aimee turned up in Agua Prieta, a town near the Mexico-Arizona border, and she spun a fantastic tale of having been kidnapped and held captive in Mexico. Her clean clothes and fresh appearance gave little credence to her story, and a county grand jury decided to investigate. It was revealed that during the time Aimee claimed she was held by hoodlums in a shack in the Sonora Desert, she was actually enjoying an idyllic month with Ormiston in a rented cottage in Carmel, Calif. Aimee was forced to sever her relationship with Ormiston to preserve her career.

By her own admission, she was often lonely, and the tenets of her church forbade a divorced person to remarry while an ex-spouse was still living. Nevertheless, Aimee eloped in 1931 with 30-year-old David Hutton, Jr., a 250-lb. baritone. They met when he sang the role of Pharaoh in one of Aimee's biblical stage productions. The couple had been married for just two days when Hutton was named as defendant in a $200,000 breach-of-promise suit, initiated by a woman who worked in a massage parlor. The plaintiff was awarded damages of $5,000, and when Aimee heard the news she pitched forward in a faint, fracturing her skull. After her recovery, she left on a European tour without Hutton. He divorced her during her absence, and for a time eked out a living as a nightclub singer billed as "Aimee's man."

She indulged herself in discreet affairs in a special, out-of-the-way apartment in Los Angeles. One of these was with a Hearst reporter she had hired to ghostwrite her autobiography. Another was with a rising young comic named Milton Berle. He remembers her as a worldly and passionate woman who charmed him into her apartment and made love with him in front of a homemade altar—candles, crucifix, Calvary scene, and all.

In 1936 the *Los Angeles Times* reported that unknown persons were demanding money to refrain from releasing nude photographs of the evangelist, but the pictures never surfaced. Still, she was often a target for innuendo and obscene phone calls. Like it or not, Aimee had become a sex symbol, "the evangelist with pulchritude," as one reporter called her.

HER THOUGHTS: "I have never yielded one inch to a man … I have beaten the men at their own game. Who ever heard of a woman preacher, and a successful one at that?"

—*M.J.T.*

The Lustful Monk

GRIGORI RASPUTIN (1871?–Dec. 30, 1916)

HIS FAME: Born a rustic Siberian peasant, Rasputin had a combination of charisma, keen opportunism, and sexual prowess that helped him rise from the status of an unwashed back-country healer and mystic to a position of power and influence with the ruling families of prerevolutionary Russia.

HIS PERSON: Rasputin was born in the village of Pokrovskoye, the third and last child of Efim Akovlevich Rasputin, a farmer, and Anna Egorovna, who may have been a Mongol from Tobolsk. As a young man, Grigori gave every appearance of growing up to be a peasant farmer, with a farmer's appetite for work, hard drinking, and loose women. At 20 he married a local girl, Praskovia Feodorovna Dubrovina, and fathered four children, three of whom lived to adulthood. Around 1900 he had joined a heretical religious sect known as the Khlisti. These flagellants believed that man must sin first in order to be redeemed later, so they practiced an incredible variety of bizarre sexual customs and rites. Pushed out of his native village for these practices, Rasputin wandered through rural Russia, performing cures and initiating hordes of women into the rituals of the flagellants. By 1905 he had settled in the capital, St. Petersburg, where tales of his "miraculous" healing powers brought about an audience with Czar Nicholas and Czarina Alexandra. The imperial couple had a son, Alexis, who was a hemophiliac, and Rasputin's apparently genuine ability to ease the boy's suffering won him immense favor, especially with Alexandra. Rasputin used the czarina's protection to build his own influence, and at the same time scandalized St. Petersburg with his wild sexual antics. In 1916 a conspiracy of conservative noblemen assassinated him. After drinking poisoned wine, and being shot and beaten, Rasputin was tied up and thrown into the icy Neva River, where he finally died from drowning.

Rasputin with devoted followers

SEX LIFE: Rasputin was undoubtedly one of the most profligate sexual adventurers in history. He seems to have been born with an overabundance of natural lust, a lust which, according to his daughter Maria, seemed to "radiate" from his 13-in. penis. Even as a young boy his magnificent phallus was the delight of all the village girls, who observed him swimming in the nude—as they were—in a local pond. But his real initiation into the world of sex came at the hands of Irina Danilova Kubasova, the young and beautiful wife of a Russian general. She enlisted the help of six of her maids in a mass seduction of the 16-year-old Rasputin. With suggestive moves, Irina lured him into a bedroom. When he stripped and followed her to the bed, the maids suddenly leaped out of hiding, dousing him with cold water and grabbing his penis. Following this episode, he sported with prostitutes in his native village, even after his marriage to Praskovia Feodorovna. A sexual frolic with three Siberian peasant girls whom he chanced on while swimming in a lake led Rasputin to a religious revelation of sorts, and he soon joined the Khlisti, who not only allowed but actively encouraged the indulgence of the flesh. Thus converted, Rasputin embarked on a journey through Russia, during which he gathered women "about him through the magnetism of his animal attraction," celebrating his peculiar rites. These included enormous bacchanalian orgies, complete with partner-swapping "in any convenient place, the woods, a barn, or the cottage of one of his converts." His doctrine of redemption through sexual release allowed a multitude of guilt-ridden women to enjoy themselves sexually for the first time, despite the grubby, slovenly appearance of the "holy satyr." As biographer Robert Massie noted, "making love to the unwashed peasant with his dirty beard and filthy hands was a new and thrilling sensation." Even the sophisticated women of St. Petersburg fell under Rasputin's sexy sway. He set up shop in an apartment, and the ladies gathered about his dining room table to wait for an invitation to his bedroom, which he called the "holy of holies." So fashionable did his attentions become that the husbands of his conquests sometimes bragged to one another that their wives had "belonged" to the incredible Rasputin; one of his steady customers, an opera singer, often telephoned her mentor for no other reason than to sing him his favorite songs. Typically, he could be found in his dining room, surrounded by lovely "disciples," sometimes sitting with one of them on his lap, stroking her hair and whispering softly of the "mysterious resurrection." He would begin to sing, and eventually the ladies would join in. Soon the singing would erupt into wild dancing, which itself often led to passionate swoonings and trips to the "holy of holies." At one of his sessions in St. Petersburg, Rasputin abruptly launched into a graphic description of the sex life of horses. He then roughly seized one of his distinguished guests and said, "Come, my lovely mare."

Even Rasputin's death had sexual overtones. Described by biographer Patte Barham, in collaboration with Rasputin's daughter Maria, the mystic's murder was plotted by men jealous of his power. His assassins invited him to a midnight repast and fed him poisoned cakes and wine. One of the murderers, Felix Yussupov, was a prince, reputedly with homosexual tendencies, who had been rebuffed several times for his advances to the mystic. When Rasputin grew dazed from the poison, Yussupov sexually used him and then shot him four times. Rasputin fell, still alive, and another attacker pulled out a knife and "castrated Grigori Rasputin, flinging the severed penis across the room." A servant recovered the penis and turned it over to a maid, who, at last account, was living in Paris in 1968. Inside a polished wooden box she preserved the organ which looked "like a blackened, overripe banana, about a foot long."

SEX PARTNERS: Rasputin's willing sex partners—often anonymous—constituted a large tribe. He had probably been enjoying himself with the village girls long before Irina Danilova came on the scene. Dunia Bekyeshova, who at 14 was one of the girls who helped Irina seduce Rasputin, later became a servant of the priest's family and his lifelong mistress. Another of the many conquests noted by Rasputin's daughter was Olga Vladimirovna Lokhtina, the wife of a minor nobleman. The list goes on and on, including actresses, military wives, and—when no one else was available to quell his mighty lust—chambermaids and prostitutes. But the most famous of Rasputin's ladies—the czarina herself—was probably never a conquest, despite her flowery letters to the priest in which she vowed to "kiss your hands and lean my head on your blessed shoulder." Certainly the most patient of all his women was his wife, Praskovia, who suffered his lifelong infidelities without complaint, shrugging them off by saying tolerantly: "He has enough for all."

HIS THOUGHTS: "So long as you bear sin secretly and within you, and fearfully cover it up with fasting, prayer, and eternal discussion of the Scriptures, so long will you remain hypocrites and good-for-nothings."

—W.L.

The Passionate Philosopher

PAUL TILLICH (Aug. 20, 1886–Oct. 22, 1965)

HIS FAME: An eminent 20th-century Protestant theologian and existential philosopher, Paul Tillich was a central figure in the intellectual life of Europe and America. *The Courage to Be* (1952) and *Dynamics of Faith* (1957) remain his most widely read works.

HIS PERSON: Tillich's involvement with Protestantism began in the rustic town of Bad Schönfliess, Germany, where his father was a Lutheran minister. As a chaplain and gravedigger during WWI and a socialist professor during the Marxist revolution which followed, Tillich never lost his faith in man's

Tillich at age 33

"religious center." Out of those shattering times emerged his fundamental "Protestant principle," the idea that freedom and faith will resolve the conflict between personal needs and universal realities.

After the war, a love triangle involving his first wife, Margarethe Wever, and his best friend, Carl Richard Wegener, led to a divorce. In 1921 Tillich fell in love with Hannah Werner, an art teacher whom he met at a masked ball Ten years younger than he and unconventional in outlook, Hannah was engaged to Albert Gottschow, also an art teacher. She fell in love with Tillich but married Albert anyway, because she considered him such an affectionate lover. Hannah continued to see Tillich. When she became pregnant by Albert, she decided sex was not enough; she would leave him for someone who could inspire her intellectually. She became Tillich's wife in 1924.

During the next eight years Tillich, happily but turbulently married, dedicated himself to professorships at important German universities, and to lecturing and publishing over 100 articles. Outspokenly critical of Hitler's rise to power, Tillich was dismissed from the University of Frankfurt and exiled by the Nazi government in 1933—a deportation he considered an honor. In the same year, Tillich and his wife immigrated to New York City, where Reinhold Niebuhr had secured him a post at Union Theological Seminary.

Besides holding subsequent teaching positions at the University of Chicago and at Harvard, he published many popular and influential books. In 1940 he and Hannah became American citizens. The third volume of his magnum opus, *Systematic Theology*, was published in 1963, bringing him recognition as a world-renowned philosopher. A paradoxical and complex man, Tillich was not ultimately freed by his faith or his tragic burden of guilt. He died in Chicago of a heart attack at the age of 79.

SEX LIFE: While a seminary student in Germany, Tillich had a priggish attitude toward sex. His group of friends took a vow of chastity, which Tillich, an ordained minister, kept with difficulty until his marriage at 28. His first wife hurt him by scoffing at his belief in monogamy and his wish to be faithful to her. This led to her affair with Wegener and the divorce. His wife's desertion inspired him to plunge into a bohemian life in Berlin, seemingly bent on making up for lost time. He too began to consider monogamy unrealistic and unnatural. In his second marriage, he insisted on the freedom to be open to all experience. Possessive, jealous, and spiteful, Hannah begrudgingly accepted her husband's need for other women but sought equality in her own series of extra-marital affairs.

Hannah was the great love of Tillich's life; he needed her for stability and order. But he could not live without his passionate relationships with other women, believing that his work would suffer without the excitement and stimulation of new sexual encounters. Tillich had a genius for friendships with women and a healthy appetite for play. He cast an erotic spell. Hannah liked to say she had turned him into a "boy Eros." Wherever he lectured in Germany and the U.S., women swarmed around him. Some wrote him poetry, many became his lovers. Tillich also enjoyed good pornography, which he felt venerated the female body and the phallus. Both lusty and reverent in regard to lovemaking, with women he was able to achieve a spiritual transformation, a union with the divine. "Women are closer to God," he once said.

In the 1920s, Tillich's "erotic solution" became a moral imperative. Having already experienced one tragic love triangle, he was determined to avoid jealousy and guilt in his second marriage. He accepted Hannah's lovers and expected her to extend him the same courtesy. Since her schoolgirl days, Hannah had formed erotic alliances with men and women alike. She was introduced to lesbian love at 15 by a young woman named Annie, who was so seductive that for years afterward Hannah sought the charms of women. Once Tillich took a lesbian friend of Hannah's to bed while Hannah tried to enjoy her lover Heinrich in the next room. The situation was painful for Hannah, however, and she brought it to a halt. On another occasion, Tillich necked with a woman in full view of his wife. As he grew older he became more reliant on Hannah, until their interdependence finally superseded every conflict and bound them closely together.

Self-doubt and inner conflict persisted, however, until Tillich's dying day. Once he admitted to a friend that he was a great sinner. When asked why, he said, "Because I love women, drinking, and dancing." To all who knew him, Paul Tillich remained paradoxically Christian and pagan.

QUIRKS: Tillich was aroused by women's feet. He himself traced this fetish to one of his most erotic childhood memories: the sight of a friend of his mother's walking barefoot on the beach. Hannah wrote of a walk she once took with her future husband in the woods: "When I took off my shoes, Paulus became ecstatic about my feet. In later years I often said that if I hadn't walked barefoot with him that day, we would never have married."

—A.S.M.

The Polygamous Preacher

BRIGHAM YOUNG (June 1, 1801–Aug. 29, 1877)

HIS FAME: Quickly taking command as the second president of the Mormon Church upon the death of Joseph Smith, Young held the post for 33 years. He was instrumental in leading the church to Utah, where it established enduring roots, and in making polygamy an official Mormon doctrine.

HIS PERSON: Born into a puritan New England household, Young spent an impoverished childhood, which instilled in him a respect for physical labor—he prided himself on his skills as a carpenter and painter—and an austere morality, which his father reinforced with whip-

Young with Margaret Pierce, wife #17

pings whenever the motherless boy (Abigail Young had died when Brigham was 14) broke even minor rules. A self-taught reader (by age 16 he had attended school only 11 days), Young discovered the *Book of Mormon* in 1830 and soon embraced the religion founded by Joseph Smith. He was baptized in 1832, and, once commissioned to preach, he zealously fulfilled his missionary assignments as he rapidly climbed in the church's hierarchy.

When anti-Mormon feelings culminated in the 1844 murder of Smith in an Illinois jail, Young succeeded him as president, a position he held until his own death from natural causes. His authority soon pervaded all aspects of life in the flourishing Mormon communities and industries he helped found in the Utah desert to which he and his followers had fled. A strict disciplinarian, Young unsparingly wielded his powers; dissidents often found themselves dispatched on far-flung "missions" to convert the unfaithful. Only once was his will widely ignored, when Mormon women were as one in opposing his proposal that they dress in a "Deseret costume" of his own design (an ungainly ensemble that united an 8-in.-high hat, a baggy calf-length skirt over trousers, and an antelope-skin jacket). But that was one of the rare times women—or indeed, any Mormons—disobeyed the "Lion of the Lord."

SEX LIFE: Much of the Mormon Church's troubles in Illinois and points east stemmed from polygamy, a principle Joseph Smith claimed was "revealed" to him as a divine truth. Young insisted that, upon learning "plural" marriages were necessary for salvation, "it was the first time in my life that I had desired the grave ... knowing the toil and labor that my body would have to undergo." Nonetheless, it was Young himself who in 1852 officially incorporated polygamy into the church's canon—a move that led some members to resign, since the *Book of Mormon* itself forbids plural marriages. And it was also Young who most fervently practiced what he preached. No Mormon had more wives than Young, a man who wed so frequently that a precise accounting does not exist. Conservative counts give him 19 wives, possibly 27. The Mormon Genealogical Society credits him with 53 wives. Others peg the total at 70 or higher. No matter the precise count, Young indisputably and enthusiastically fulfilled his "duty" to marry often.

Nor had Young waited until 1852 to begin. His first wife, whom he married when he was 23, died soon after the pair joined the church. Two years later, in 1834, Young wed again, and then waited only until 1842 to take his initial "plural" wife. By the time he issued his official blessing of polygamy in 1852, Young had wed at least 22 times. Many of the older women were not his mates; he merely wanted to give them his name and financial support.

Was polygamy simply a tool to satisfy male lust? This was what one of Young's daughters-in-law suggested when she said, "If Salt Lake City were roofed over, it would be the biggest whorehouse in the world." But lust had nothing to do with it in Young's eyes. "There are probably few men in the world who care about the private society of women less than I do." Polygamy, he proclaimed, was a divinely sanctioned way to enhance the church's population and to eliminate prostitution, spinsterhood, and adultery. But when a pretty girl caught Brigham Young's eye, he was quick to invoke his orthodoxy. "You must be my wife," he told one. "You cannot be saved by anyone else.... If you refuse, you will be destroyed, both body and soul." Few women resisted the potent advances of the barrel-chested (44 in. around), 5-ft. 10-in., blue-eyed, robust Young. Only one, the beautiful actress Julia Dean Hayne, whom he unembarrassedly pursued, is known to have successfully spurned him. But, even with Hayne, Young had the last word. After the death of this woman, in whose honor he had named an ornate sleigh, he had a "proxy" marriage performed so that they could be together eternally in heaven. But Young also had no aversion to fleeting temporal weddings; while staying with the Sioux in 1847, for instance, he happily accepted the company of two young squaws, who, at least for the length of his encampment, were married to him.

His other marriages proved more lasting. One home held most of Brigham Young's wives. This was the Lion House (named after the reclining stone lion set over the entrance), located in a central block of Salt Lake City. No more than

12 of Young's wives ever slept in the Lion House at the same time. A New England-style structure, it was connected by a corridor to the adjacent Colonial abode known as Bee Hive House. However, most of Young's wives had their own private, monogamous-type residences scattered throughout the city.

The Lion House was the heart of Brigham Young's harem. The second floor was sectioned into a central parlor for prayers and entertainment and a series of bedroom suites for wives with children. The third floor contained 20 smaller bedrooms for the childless wives and older children. When Young decided upon a bed partner for the night, he made a chalk mark on the selected wife's door. He fortified himself for each amorous visit by eating large numbers of eggs, which he believed enhanced virility. Later, he would quietly go down the row of doors, find the one with the chalk mark, and slip inside. Upon completing his husbandly duties, Young invariably returned to his own bedroom for a solitary night's sleep.

His virility was never in doubt. He fathered 56 children. He had his first child, a daughter, when he was 24, and his last, also a daughter, when he was 69. In a single month of his 62nd year, three of his wives gave birth to children. He had long sexual relationships with a number of his wives. Lucy Decker, the third wife, had her first child by Brigham in 1845 and her seventh by him 15 years later. Clara Decker, the sixth wife, had her first child by him in 1849 and her fifth child by him 12 years later. Emily Dow Patridge, the eighth wife, had her first child by him in 1845 and her seventh child by him 17 years later. Lucy Bigelow, the 22nd wife, had her first child by him in 1852 and her third child by him 11 years later.

SEX PARTNERS: "I love my wives ... but to make a queen of one and peasants of the rest I have no such disposition," Young claimed. But many of his wives (along with other Mormon women) "whined" about his lack of attention, and Young responded by offering to divorce any of them that so wished. None did at that time. Certainly, however, Young had his favorites, and for nearly two decades Emmeline Free was his chief lover. They wed when she was 19 (and he 44), and over the years Emmeline bore him 10 children. She was, the other wives whispered, awarded the best quarters—a room that featured a private stairway Young could secretly use for his frequent visits.

But Emmeline's reign ended soon after 1860 with Young's first sight of Amelia Folsom, a 22-year-old who stubbornly resisted his advances and announced her love for another man. However, that rival stepped aside when threatened with a lengthy church mission, and Amelia surrendered to Brigham's wishes. But not fully. Unlike Emmeline, Amelia relished her role as Young's favorite. When he gave her a sewing machine, she pushed it down the stairs; it was the wrong brand, she huffed. Young bought her the right brand. When he lectured her on her sins, she scoffed, and on one occasion punctuated his sermon by pouring a pitcher of milk and an urn of hot tea on his lap. Never one to tolerate disobedience from anyone, Young nonetheless suffered it from Amelia until his death.

Troublesome as Amelia proved, it was Ann Eliza (wife number 27 by some counts; 51 by others) who proved the most rebellious. This wife, too, rejected the aging Young's advances. "I wouldn't have him if he asked me a thousand times—hateful old thing," she told friends. But she underestimated Young's determination; in 1869, a year after the courtship commenced, the 24-year-old bowed to family pressure and married him. But Young got more than he bargained for. Ann Eliza complained about his inattention; castigated him for his frugality (despite his riches, Young doled out slender provisions to his wives); and, in 1873, listing neglect and cruelty among the causes, she escaped Salt Lake City and filed for divorce. Young found himself forced to contest her claim strenuously, for only a year earlier federal charges of polygamy had been dropped because of a technicality. By conceding that Ann Eliza could sue for a divorce, Young would be admitting that he was a polygamist, and the federal government, he was sure, again would pounce on him. After years of bitter legal wrangling, Young won his case. He told the court that he was legally married to Mary Ann Angell (his second wife and his senior living spouse) and that he could not, therefore, have legally married Ann Eliza. But, in splitting this legal hair, Young had in effect repudiated his cherished doctrine of polygamy—a practice that soon after his death was to be formally abandoned by the Mormon Church.

HIS THOUGHTS: "Some want to marry a woman because she has got property; some want a rich wife; but I never saw the day I would not rather have a poor woman. I never saw the day that I wanted to be henpecked to death, for I should have been if I had married a rich wife."

"Make haste and get married. Let me see no boys above 16 and girls above 14 unmarried."

—R.M.

XV

Heads You Win

The Impotent Educator

HAVELOCK ELLIS (Feb. 2, 1859–July 8, 1939)

HIS FAME: Called "the Darwin of sex," Havelock Ellis was principally known as a sex educator and the author of a seven-volume work issued between 1897 and 1928 entitled *Studies in the Psychology of Sex.*

HIS PERSON: The son of a sea captain and a doting mother, Ellis was born in Croydon, Surrey, England. He attended private schools in London. At 16, suffering poor health, he was sent to Australia on his father's ship. There he worked as a teacher—part of the time in remote areas—for four years, too shy to be effective. Returning to London, he entered St. Thomas' Hospital at 22 to take up

medicine. After graduation, he practiced briefly in the London slums. Because he loved books, he gave up medicine for literary pursuits.

At 30 he published his first book, *The New Spirit.* Shortly after, Ellis became interested in sex, then a forbidden subject. Through interviews and research reading, he gathered material on human sexuality and wrote about it. The first volume of his *Studies in the Psychology of Sex* series was entitled *Sexual Inversion* and dealt with homosexuality. The book was banned in England for "obscene libel." Nevertheless, Ellis continued to pour out books about various aspects of human sexuality. Although widely known, he lived close to poverty most of his life. He was 64 when he had his first commercial success with *The Dance of Life,* an immediate hit in the U.S.

During his lifetime, Ellis defended the rights of women and homosexuals, and pioneered open discussions on sex. He gave free advice on sex to anyone who wanted it, and he could not understand why Sigmund Freud charged patients for the same help. Ellis was a sweet and humane man, part scientist, part mystic. Birth-control crusader Margaret Sanger found him a "tall angel," blue-eyed, handsome, with his trademark flowing white beard. He died in Washbrook, Suffolk, of a throat ailment at the age of 80.

SEX LIFE: Not until he was 25 did Havelock Ellis have any sexual experience with a woman. It came about by accident. He had read a novel, *The Story of an African Farm* by Ralph Iron, and wrote a fan letter to the author. The author proved to be an attractive, lusty woman named Olive Schreiner, a 29-year-old feminist and well-known novelist. They corresponded and then they met. Olive, who wanted to be dominated, expected a strong man and found in Ellis an awkward and withdrawn intellectual. They became friends, and he gave her his daily journal to read. Going through it, she realized that he was totally inexperienced in sex. Olive, who'd had several affairs with men, decided she could rectify that and eventually marry Ellis. She lured him to the Derbyshire countryside for a weekend. During their first walk together, she put her hand on his crotch to feel his penis. Determined to consummate their love, she lay nude with him on a sofa. He caressed her and kissed her vagina. He could not get an erection and finally suffered premature ejaculation. Time and again they tried, with the same result. "She possessed a powerfully and physically passionate temperament," Ellis admitted, and he could not match her sex drive. They settled for a close and enduring friendship. She was ever uninhibited with him. Once, in Paris together, observing some bronze vessels in the Louvre, Olive spoke seriously of the handicaps women suffered. "A woman," she said, "is a ship with two holes in her bottom." Eventually Olive returned to South Africa, married a farmer-politician, and endured a less than successful marriage.

Havelock Ellis was 31 when he became involved in his greatest love affair. Edith Lees, a 28-year-old former social worker, was curly-haired, pretty, under 5 ft. tall, and outspoken. Edith was drawn to Ellis upon reading his first book. He in turn liked her brightness and intelligence. When she proposed marriage, he worried about his privacy and his low financial state. Edith promised him privacy and agreed to share all their expenses. (She was running a girls' school at the time.) They went out for a wedding ring, and she paid for half of it. The marriage took place in December, 1891.

Edith did not know Ellis was impotent. On their honeymoon in Paris she found out. He did not even attempt to have intercourse with her. While she had told Ellis she'd had affairs with several men, she had not told him she liked women more. Edith mourned the baby she could never have with Ellis and settled for his fondling her in bed, still thinking him "beautiful" and her spiritual lover. She agreed to a marriage of companionship, but not for long. Three months after their wedding, she informed him that she was having a torrid affair with a woman named Claire. Unhappy but tolerant, Ellis interviewed Edith on lesbianism for a book he was writing on homosexuality. After breaking with Claire, Edith had another affair with a fragile painter named Lily. When Lily died, Edith turned her attentions back to her husband.

Their 25-year marriage was a stormy one. It turned out that Edith was a manic-depressive. When manic, she fixed up and rented cottages, gave lectures as Mrs. Havelock Ellis (her favorite lecture was on Oscar Wilde), wrote books and plays, and founded a film company. When depressed, she sat at her female lovers' graves, had several nervous breakdowns, and three times tried to commit suicide. When she resumed her lesbian affairs, Ellis continued to love her and resumed his own sexless affairs. He outraged his wife when he fell in love with the 24-year-old daughter of a chemist friend, a woman he referred to as Amy (her real name was Mneme Smith) and continued to be close to until she married another man. He was 57 when he met and became enchanted by Margaret Sanger. This intimate relationship brought Edith back from a lecture tour in the U.S. and gave her one more nervous breakdown. Ellis was constantly attentive to Edith. Her doctor told him she was on the verge of insanity. In September of 1916 she died in a diabetic coma.

Shortly afterward, a charming young Frenchwoman, Françoise Cyon, entered Ellis' life. Françoise wanted to collect her fee for having translated one of Edith's books into French. Drawn to Ellis' kind understanding, she returned to him for marital advice. She'd had a child by an earlier lover, and a second son by her husband, Serge Cyon, an insensitive Russian journalist whom she had recently left. During her treatment by Ellis, Françoise fell in love with him. On April 3, 1918, she wrote him, "I am going to write a very difficult letter. Yet it must be written if I want to find peace of mind. The truth is, Havelock Ellis, that I love you." He tried to warn Françoise of his impotency. He wrote her that he had many dear women friends. "But there is not one to whom I am a real lover.... I feel sure that I am good for you, I am sure that you suit me. But as a lover or husband you would find me very disappointing." Puzzled, she replied, "I will have nothing but what you offer; it is the very flower of love."

On going to bed with him, she learned his problem but was undeterred. They masturbated each other. She lavished love on him unconditionally, treating him as a virile male, a potentially good lover. And miracle of miracles, he responded. Aged 60, he had his first erection with a woman, and then another and another, and found himself enjoying sexual intercourse at last. Their relationship was idyllic, marred by only one bad incident. Ellis had asked her to be friendly with one of his admirers, an urbane minor novelist and advocate of free love named Hugh de Selincourt. While Ellis was out of town, Françoise allowed De Selincourt to seduce her. He was a mighty lover. He hated to wear a contraceptive device and had trained himself to copulate at great length, bringing his women to orgasm without ejaculating himself. Françoise lost herself in pleasure. Then Ellis learned about the affair and was wounded, feeling she had found a younger and better lover. Françoise tried to gloss over the physical aspect of her affair. Ellis answered, "Do you imagine that coitus is unimportant? Olive said to me once that when a man puts his penis into a woman's vagina it is as if (assuming of course that she responds) he put his finger into her brain, stirred it round and round. Her whole nature is affected." Françoise pleaded with Ellis, writing him, "You have been the beloved, the lover, the friend most divine. You are still this, will always be." She gave up De Selincourt and returned to Ellis. She worked as a teacher and at first lived separately with her sons. She wanted to move in with Ellis, but he could not support her. Then, from America, Margaret Sanger offered her a salary as Ellis' secretary. Françoise, at last able to pay her share of their expenses, joined him for what was left of his life. They had 22 warm years together. Françoise, keeper of the flame, died in 1974.

QUIRKS: Ellis asked many of his new women friends for photographs of themselves in the nude.

At the age of 12, while accompanying his mother to the London Zoological Gardens, Ellis saw her pause and urinate on an isolated gravel path. Hearing of this, his favorite sister told him, "She was flirting with you." Decades later, after lying down fully clothed to pet with Françoise the first time, he followed her into the bathroom to watch her urinate. He enjoyed having Françoise urinate when they went walking in the rain. She termed his interest in urolagnia a "harmless anomaly."

—*I. W.*

It's All In Your Head

SIGMUND FREUD (May 6, 1856–Sept. 23, 1939)

HIS FAME: The father of psychoanalysis, Freud established new directions for understanding and treating mental illness. His theories concerning the development of personality and the sexual origins of neuroses have been absorbed into our everyday speech in such terms as "Oedipus complex," "libido," "repression," "penis envy," and "death wish."

Freud and Martha Bernays in 1885

HIS PERSON: Sigmund Freud was his mother's firstborn and her favorite of eight children; his father, however, had two sons by a previous marriage. Always an excellent student, Freud attended the University of Vienna. It took him eight years to graduate since he could not settle on one course of scientific study. Ambitious as well as intellectually curious, Freud finally chose medicine because, as a Jew in Vienna, his opportunities in his first career choice—politics—were limited. He was not religious, but he retained strong ties to his heritage and was a lifelong B'nai B'rith member.

His research into the nervous system led to the study of related diseases and their possible cures. He experimented with hypnosis, became enthusiastic about cocaine as a therapeutic substance, and in 1886 established a private practice specializing in nervous disorders. That same year he married Martha Bernays. He was 30.

In the late 1890s Freud suffered a serious psychoneurosis, precipitated by the agonizing death of his father and his own fading interest in sex after the birth of his last child. In the process of analyzing his disturbing dreams at the time, he began making use of the "talking cure"—psychoanalysis—which had been developed by his teacher and friend Josef Breuer. For the next 40 years Freud lived a life of domestic stability and formidable achievement, gathering around him a circle of disciples, notably Carl Jung, Alfred Adler, Sándor Ferenczi, Helene Deutsch, and Ernest Jones.

When the Nazis came to power in 1933, they burned Freud's works as "Jewish pornography," but not until 1938 did he escape to London. Princess Marie Bonaparte of Greece, a friend and former patient, paid £20,000 ransom to the Third Reich for his safe passage. Freud spent his last year in London, deteriorating from cancer of the jaw and palate, and died there in 1939.

SEX LIFE: Freud made a career of sifting through the sexual secrets of others, yet he took pains to conceal his own private life. He destroyed many letters; some that survived are in the Library of Congress, unavailable to scholars until the year 2000.

At 16 his first love, Gisela Flüss, rejected him; he responded by getting a crush on her mother. Until he was 26 he showed no renewed interest in women. In 1882 Freud met Martha Bernays, a slim, pretty 21-year-old girl from a traditional Jewish family. They became engaged and remained so for four years, exchanging hundreds of letters and seldom meeting, although he was a resident at a nearby hospital. Freud was a passionate and jealous suitor in his correspondence. In 1884 he wrote, "Woe to you, my princess, when I come. I will kiss you quite red and feed you till you are plump. And if you are forward you shall see who is the stronger, a gentle little girl who doesn't eat enough or a big wild man who has cocaine in his body."

They finally had enough money to marry in 1886, and eventually settled into the Vienna apartment they would occupy until 1938. Within nine years Martha had six children. In 1895 her sister Minna Bernays came to live with them. Evidently Freud was faithful, but he became a distant husband. He was devoted to his work, and Martha was absorbed by domestic duties deemed proper to a wife and mother. She arranged the entire household for her husband's convenience, keeping children and servants out of his way, tending to his meals and wardrobe, even putting the toothpaste on his toothbrush. Looking back, Freud admitted that Martha never seemed at ease around him.

During Freud's self-analysis he developed dramatic emotional ties to Dr. Wilhelm Fliess, a Berlin ear, nose, and throat specialist. There was a strong attraction between the two men; they wrote constantly and met occasionally for "congresses," as they termed their out-of-town rendezvous. Freud wrote, "I am looking forward to our congress as to a slaking of hunger and thirst … I live gloomily … until you come and then I pour out all my grumbles to you, kindle my flickering light at your steady flame and feel well again." Fliess was receptive and caring. He tried to persuade his friend to give up smoking 20 cigars a day. (Freud never analyzed his habit, although he had observed that smoking, drugs, and gambling were substitutes for the "primal addiction"—masturbation.) At one of their congresses Freud fainted, and later remarked about the incident, "There is some piece of unruly homosexual feeling at the root of the matter." The friendship ended in 1903, largely owing to Freud's complicated reaction to Fliess' theory of a universal bisexual impulse. At first Freud rejected the idea, then claimed it as his own, and planned to write a major book on it, giving Fliess only nominal credit. Freud came to believe in a strong bisexual aspect to every personality and said, "Every sexual act is one between four individuals."

It has been speculated that Freud and his sister-in-law Minna were lovers. Indeed, for 42 years Minna's bedroom was accessible only through that of Sigmund and Martha. Larger and heavier than her sister, Minna was, according to one neighbor, also prettier than Martha. Of the two she was considerably more intellectual, and Freud found her a good conversationalist and a sympathetic ear for his thoughts on psychoanalysis. Minna was known for her pungent wit and strict discipline with the children. Freud once described Minna as being like himself; they were both "wild, passionate people, not so good," whereas Martha was "completely good." Freud loved to travel, and when he took his extended summer vacations, Minna often accompanied him. Martha stayed home.

The main source for the story that Freud actually had a love affair with Minna was Freud's disciple Carl Jung. Reportedly, Jung said that Minna and Martha had separately approached him about the problem of Freud's passion for Minna. Jung told an American professor that on one occasion in 1907, when Jung had been Freud's houseguest in Vienna, Minna came to him and poured out her secret. Said Jung, "From her I learned that Freud was in love with her and that their relationship was indeed very intimate." Upset, Jung confronted Freud about the matter and suggested that he be analyzed by an outside therapist. Jung offered himself as the analyst. Freud coldly rejected the suggestion.

Freud had a huge appetite for sex, but mainly as an intellectual pursuit. When he was only 41 he wrote to Fliess, "Sexual excitation is of no more use to a person like me." He lived by a thoroughly Victorian moral code. Even though his theories stressed the power of unconscious sexual impulses, Freud edited such wishes out of his own behavior. He was, after all, a married man, and he had said that no marriage was secure until the wife had succeeded in making herself a mother to her husband. After six children in rapid succession, his desires may have been quenched by anxieties about contraception. In 1908 he said, "Marriage ceases to furnish the satisfaction of sexual needs that it promised, since all the contraceptives available hitherto impair sexual enjoyment, hurt the fine susceptibilities of both partners, and even actually cause illness."

There was one instance when Freud admitted he dreamed about other women. In 1909 he traveled to the U.S. with Jung and other colleagues to deliver a series of lectures. One morning upon awakening, Freud confided to Jung he was having erotic dreams about American women. "I haven't been able to sleep since I came to America," confessed Freud. "I continue to dream of prostitutes." "Well, why don't you do something about it?" said Jung. Freud recoiled in horror. "But I am a married man!" he exclaimed.

Freud's theories described the forces shaping human behavior as sexual. But culture siphoned off the instinctual energy of sex and sublimated it into social functioning. Freud's own life epitomized the viewpoint he thought tragic but true: "The sexual life of a civilized man is seriously disabled."

HIS THOUGHTS: It is hard to imagine anyone having more thoughts on sex than Sigmund Freud. While some psychiatrists have observed the penis attached to the boy, Dr. Freud found the boy attached to the penis. Indeed, the penis was the axis of Freud's universe. Not having a penis, he thought, implied lack of the masculine virtues of strength and rationality, and his view of women as inferior to men bears this out. "Penis envy" was the basic factor in Freud's psychology of women; they could feel compensated for their deficiency only by having children. Woman's highest role was that of "beloved wife" in a marriage based on sexual inequality.

Freud warned of "the harm that is inherent in sexuality, [it] being one of the most dangerous activities of the human being." Since "our civilization is built up entirely at the expense of sexuality," Freud concluded that the cultured individual was necessarily repressed. Sex, by its power to reassert primal urges, had the potential to undermine society. In spite of such dire views, Freud claimed to "stand for an incomparably freer sexual life," but chose not to partake of that freedom. He saw no implications for himself when he said, "Sexual love is undoubtedly one of the chief things in life … apart from a few queer fanatics, all the world knows this."

—K.P.

The Beloved Of The Jung-Frauen

CARL GUSTAV JUNG (July 26, 1875–June 6, 1961)

HIS FAME: A German-Swiss contemporary of Sigmund Freud, Jung was the creator and father of analytical psychology, which incorporated many of his theories, including those of collective unconscious, the attitude types (extrovert and introvert), and the four function types (thought, intuition, feeling, and sensation).

HIS PERSON: A strange and imaginative minister's son, as a child Carl had visions, one of God defecating on a cathedral. He developed a lifelong interest in folklore from listening to peasants' tales and claimed he had two personalities.

Though he wanted to be an archaeologist, he chose medicine as a profession for practical reasons. In 1903, married and practicing psychiatry at a Zurich clinic, he began a study of word association, which led him to correspond with

Jung in 1912, just before his mental crisis

Sigmund Freud. The two met in 1907. Jung thought Freud "the first man of importance I had encountered"; Freud thought Jung "magnificent." They had their differences; for example, Freud wasn't keen on Jung's interest in parapsychology, and Jung was not a total believer in Freud's sexual theories. Of Freud's "Little Hans" theory (which contended that children believe that girls are castrated boys), Jung said, "Agatha [his little daughter] has never heard of Little Hans." When their close collaboration came to a bitter end in 1913, Sándor Ferenczi, an associate of Freud's, quipped, "The Jung no longer believe in Freud."

Jung went on to develop his own "school," run his institute, write his books, and travel to New Mexico and Africa to study primitive cultures. From these studies he formulated his theory of mythological archetypes common to all cultures. At his retreat in Bollingen, on Lake Zurich, he himself built a tower-shaped house and annex to which he could withdraw. When there he led a simple life—cutting his own wood, carving stone, and meditating.

Jung was a bull of a man, 6 ft. 1 in. tall with rough-hewn features, visionary eyes, and an imposing physicality. His sense of humor was robust (Freud once defended its coarseness) and witty ("Show me a sane person and I'll cure him for you"). He had a ferocious temper and a tendency to be callous; he once called a patient with a syphilis phobia a "filthy swine." His leaning toward the grandiose may have inspired his initial admiration of Hitler ("a spiritual vessel") and the Nazis ("the twilight of the gods"), which earned him just reproach from Jews; his reply was that they were paranoid. By 1939 he had changed his mind about Hitler and deemed him "more than half crazy."

His son Franz called Jung "maddening and marvelous." He cheated at games and was a poor loser, walked around the garden dressed only in ragged shorts, was a gourmet cook. He loved detective novels and dogs. "The Sage of Zurich" died at age 85.

LOVE LIFE: It was 22 years after its occurrence that, in a letter to Freud, Jung finally confessed to one of the significant events in his sex life: "My veneration for you has something of the nature of a 'religious crush' because of its undeniable erotic undertone. This abominable feeling comes from the fact that as a boy I was the victim of a sexual assault by a man I once worshiped." The man has never been identified. The incident, he felt, made the transference of his male patients repugnant to him. He and Freud had a stormy relationship, marked by intense quarrels and emotional reconciliations, during one of which Freud fainted and was carried to a couch by Jung. Both admitted the homosexual overtones in their natures, never given physical expression; both were basically heterosexual beings.

Jung's early loves included a village girl he met only briefly but with whom he was enraptured; a friend's good-looking but slightly cross-eyed mother; and a French-Swiss girl he nearly became engaged to in his student days.

Emma Rauschenbach, whom he married on Feb. 14, 1903, was the major love of his life. When he was a young medical student, visiting family friends, he caught sight of her—a 15-year-old in braids, standing on a staircase—and remarked to a friend, who did not take him seriously, that she would be his wife. It was six years before his prophecy was fulfilled. Emma was an intelligent and pretty girl who had been burdened at 12 by her father's dependence upon her when he suddenly went blind. Jung, eloquent and intellectual, represented an exciting escape. Their courtship was romantic (boating picnics and love letters), but they probably didn't sleep together before they married. Jung later wrote of their honeymoon at Lake Como: "My wife was apprehensive—but all went well. We got into an argument about the rights and wrongs of distributing money between husbands and wives. Trust a Swiss bank account to break into a honeymoon in Italy." They had five children—four girls and a boy. It is not known whether they practiced contraception, though Jung wrote Freud that he tried "every conceivable trick to stem the tide of these little blessings."

At first their marriage was idyllic. By 1906, however, Jung was having dreams, one of which, about two horses, was interpreted by Freud as "the failure of a rich marriage." Jung replied, "I am happy with my wife in every way … there has been no sexual failure, more likely a social one." The dream held, he believed, "an illegitimate sexual wish that had better not see the light of day."

In 1907 he became briefly infatuated with a woman he met while traveling with Emma in present-day Yugoslavia. In 1909 one of his patients wanted him to impregnate her, and he confessed that his professional relationship with her had "polygamous components." However, these two experiences only set the stage for the other important woman in his life—Toni Wolff, 13 years his junior, who came to him as a patient in 1910. Later, during his "confrontation with his unconscious," a near breakdown which began in 1913 and lasted several years, she helped him search out his *anima*, the female element of his nature. In Jung's typecasting of the women in his life, she was the "*femme inspiratrice*" ("female inspiration"), while Emma was wife and mother. Toni was elegant, with a delicately modeled face. At Jung's insistence she became a friend of the family, coming to Sunday dinner at the big house at Küsnacht on Lake Zurich. Emma was jealous, but Jung had his heart set on a triangle, which he later justified in theories about marriage in which the "many-faceted gem" (Carl), needing more than the "simple cube" (Emma), looks outside of the marital relationship for satisfaction. (According to biographer Barbara Hannah, Jung felt that fathers must live "the whole of their erotic life" or the "unlived life is then unconsciously displaced onto the daughters.") So powerful was his personality that he came close to convincing both women that the triangle was an ideal situation. It lasted for almost 40 years. Emma and Toni both became practicing analysts. Emma gave lectures on the Holy Grail and exchanged advice with Freud; Toni developed original theories about female function types. However, Toni, restive in her role as mistress in straitlaced Zurich, began to demand that Jung divorce Emma. He refused, and his own disenchantment expressed itself in criticism of her; for example, when he saw her new apartment he said, "Only Toni would have gone to live in a place with marble pillars and a study like Mussolini's." Toni, heartbroken, drinking and smoking too much, died at 64 of a heart attack. Emma died two years later in 1955. She and Jung had been married 52 years. "She was a queen! She was a queen!" cried Jung after her death.

Many of his followers were young female intellectuals, known jocularly as the "Jung-Frauen." Though only a few may have slept with him, they tended to adore him for his bearlike appeal, his sensibility, his empathy for women. He saw beneath the surface, an endearing quality. One old patient of Jung's, whom Freud called a "phenomenally ugly female," was to Jung a pleasant woman who "had such lovely delusions and said such interesting things."

Among his women friends was Olga Fröbe-Kapteyn, a flamboyant creature and supposedly an ex-circus rider, who created Eranos, a discussion group for intellectuals which met at her home. The meetings at least once degenerated into debauchery; an anonymous participant said it was the "nearest I ever came to wicked abandonment in my life." Jung was there, "bubbling over with wit, mockery, and drunken spirit." Some of these women claimed to have been his lovers. One gave him poor marks in lovemaking while another, Jolanda Jacobi, claimed he was undersexed. A cynical Jungian countered, "Presumably *she* hadn't been his mistress anyway."

Ruth Bailey, an Englishwoman he met in Africa who was his friend for more than 35 years, became his housekeeper and companion after Emma died. He was then over 80 and cantankerous. After a quarrel over two tomatoes, he advised her, "All you have to remember is not to do anything to make me angry."

HIS THOUGHTS: "The prerequisite for a good marriage ... is the license to be unfaithful."

—*A.E.*

Crusader For B. C.

MARGARET SANGER (Sept. 14, 1883–Sept. 6, 1966)

HER FAME: Margaret Sanger was among the foremost pioneers of sexual freedom and enjoyment and of birth control in the early 20th century. She faced extraordinary opposition—and triumphed over it—in her campaign to educate doctors and laymen, change laws, popularize the use of diaphragms, and start birth-control clinics throughout the world. She also contributed vitally to the development of the pill.

HER PERSON: Margaret Sanger, a fiery, petite, redheaded woman, was the daughter of a pious Catholic mother and a tyrannical, freethinking Socialist Irish father. One of 11 children, Margaret grew up in Corning, N.Y., watching her mother's tuberculosis worsen with each child she bore and each of her seven miscarriages. When Margaret was 16, TB killed her mother. This, plus her childhood privations as part of an over-large, poor family, inspired Margaret toward her crusade for birth control, or B.C., as she called it. A significant turning point occurred for her when, working as a maternity nurse in New York, she tended

a woman hemorrhaging as the result of a self-induced abortion. As the attendant doctor was leaving, the patient pleaded with him desperately, begging for contraceptive advice. He laughed and advised her to make "Jake [her husband] sleep on the roof." Months later, the woman died after another self-induced abortion. From then on, Margaret resolved to get to the root of the problem. And with her ceaseless work, she truly turned the tide for the women of her time.

SEX LIFE: "Saint Margaret," as she was called by a grateful correspondent, was a very complicated woman, and not always a saint to her two husbands and her many lovers. Throughout her entire life she repeated a trying emotional pattern, being generally in love with some man who was just out of reach, sexually or emotionally, and bored with the one who was too easily within her grasp.

Margaret not only was a proponent of B.C. but also vigorously espoused "free love" and sensual, spiritual sex. She told her first husband, William Sanger, an architect, that she must be free to make love with other men if she wished. It was for "the cause," she explained; and furthermore, although she and Bill were often separated by their careers, sex was the only thing that could put her to sleep at night when she was tense and nervous. He responded tartly, "I still hold that intercourse is not to be classed with a square meal." Eventually she divorced Sanger and more or less took custody of their children, while continuing to take a dazzling series of lovers.

In 1922 Margaret married again—this time a fabulously rich, uncultured Dutch businessman from South Africa. J. Noah H. Slee was 64 and she was 39. Margaret demanded a marriage contract that allowed her a private apartment in their home and the freedom to come and go as she pleased, with no questions asked. He very reluctantly agreed. And she, after teaching him how to make love more artfully, continued to take lovers until he died in 1941. Nonetheless, Mr. Slee called her "the adventure of my life" and remained sexually vigorous throughout the marriage, although he found her neglect maddening. Margaret Sanger could never be truly married to a man, for she was married first to her cause.

SEX PARTNERS: The list of her lovers is long, for Margaret loved sex, passion, romance, *and* adoration from several men at a time. Her partners ranged from a hot-blooded Spanish anarchist to an editor of the *London Times Literary Supplement.* For much of her life she had an intimate friendship with the great sexologist Havelock Ellis, whom she called "the King." Whether or not they were actual lovers is unknown, for Ellis was essentially impotent until he was in his 60s. Nonetheless, Margaret practiced what Ellis preached—free love. She had serious affairs with diverse men—Herbert Simonds, a chemical engineer; Angus Snead MacDonald, a lusty architect from Kentucky; and Hugh de Selincourt, a cultured but mediocre novelist who practiced "Karezza," an East Indian method of male sexual control. Her most celebrated lover was the English writer H. G. Wells. Although married, he was a notorious womanizer. He was 53, she 42, when in 1921 they began a passionate affair that continued on and off for years. In 1924, after a night of sex in London, she received a two-word note from Wells in the morning: "Wonderful! Unforgettable!" Margaret described Wells as "a sort of naughty boy-man." Once, when they spoke together at a B.C. conference, she feared that the ribald things Wells whispered in her ear onstage could be heard over the PA system throughout the hall.

HER ADVICE: Margaret wrote numerous books full of advice about sex, love, and birth control, as well as an autobiography. At one point she wrote that the male sex urge is "blind, imperious, and driving," and in a book entitled *Happiness in Marriage* she advised men to be tender on their wedding night and to delay their climaxes. She likened the sex act to a musical symphony, culminating in the bliss of simultaneous orgasm. "To be the master of his passion instead of its slave is the first essential rule in love etiquette every young husband must learn," she said, and outlined these nuptial rules: "(1) Avoid hurry. (2) Avoid violence. (3) Seek first of all to allay nervous fears and apprehension."

HER THOUGHTS: "There are three uses or purposes for sexual intercourse—physical relief, procreation, and communion. The first two have little to do with the art of love. Power, says Balzac in his *Physiology of Love*, does not consist in striking hard and often, but in striking properly."

"Never be ashamed of passion. If you are strongly sexed, you are richly endowed."

"Especially in the case of women may the damage entailed by too long continued abstinence bring about deep disturbances."

As an old woman, she told her 16-year-old granddaughter: "Kissing, petting, and even intercourse are all right as long as they are sincere. I have never given a kiss in my life that wasn't sincere. As for intercourse, I'd say three times a day was about right."

—*A. W.*

The Frustrated Sex Expert

MARIE STOPES (Oct. 15, 1880–Oct. 2, 1958)

HER FAME: A contemporary of the American birth-control crusader Margaret Sanger, Stopes established the first birth-control clinic in Great Britain, where, through her numerous writings, she advocated healthy pleasurable sex lives for women.

HER PERSON: She and her younger sister were the product of an essentially sexless marriage. Her mother, who was 40 when Marie was born, confused sexual ignorance with virtue, and because of her influence Marie went through the first 36 years of her life, including a five-year marriage, as a virgin. At this unhappy juncture in her life, Marie turned from botany and coal research, in which fields she was a recognized authority, to write a manual called *Married Love*. In 1918 this book and its companion work, titled *Wise Parenthood*, created an international sensation, mostly for discussing the subject of birth control openly. (Both books were banned by the U.S. postal authorities as "obscene.") The publication of her books, and the largely positive public response to them, inspired Stopes to found the Society for Constructive Birth Control and Racial Progress. She also engaged the religious establishment, especially the Catholic Church, in a vicious battle for the minds of the masses. That battle reached its climax in a prolonged libel suit brought by Stopes against the Catholic doctor Halliday Sutherland. In a book of his own on birth control, he had questioned Marie's qualifications for dealing with the subject and accused her of "exposing the poor to experiment" in offering them the means to control birth. On a third appeal before the House of Lords, the suit was settled in favor of Sutherland. Stopes was made to pay a modest fine and court costs, but she more than made up for her losses since the publicity surrounding her trial generated an enormous sale of her book.

SEX LIFE:

> Q.—With regards to your husband's parts, did they ever get rigid at all?
> A.—On hundreds of occasions on which we had what I thought were relations, I only remember three occasions on which it was partially rigid, and then it was never effectively rigid....

Q.—And he never succeeded in penetrating into your private parts?
A.—No.

Stopes was a certified virgin when she gave this testimony in a London divorce court in 1916. A sympathetic court annulled her marriage to Dr. Reginald Gates, who in five years had failed to consummate their marriage.

In truth, most of Marie's sex life was deserving of sympathy. She didn't get her first kiss until she was 24, and then it was from a married Japanese who was culturally opposed to kissing and had to be shown how. She'd met Kenjiro Fujii in 1904 while they were both researchers at the University of Munich. She played down her interest in him by ridiculing his shortness in letters written home to her mother, but in private she'd wrap herself tightly in a girdle to simulate the feeling of his arms around her. After five "physically pure" years, the relationship ended when Fujii, who was by then divorced, developed a psychosomatic illness at the thought of marriage to Marie.

Although against lesbianism throughout her career, Marie nonetheless attracted the attention of two older women. Clotilde van Wyss, one of Marie's teachers at North London Collegiate, and Dr. Helen McMurchy, a Canadian she met in 1908, both took a passionate interest in Marie; however, biographer Ruth Hall doubts that either relationship ever became overtly sexual since Marie was so naive she didn't even know what masturbation was until she was 29.

Marie finally learned about sex from books and Aylmer Maude, a translator of Tolstoi 22 years her senior. He had come to live with Marie and Reginald Gates a year after their 1911 marriage, and it was he who first pointed out the abnormality of her relationship with Gates. For this observation Maude became Marie's confidant and platonic lover, until Reginald Gates threw him out of his house.

Marie finally lost her virginity in 1918 to Humphrey Verdon Roe, her second husband and partner in her birth-control campaign. The Roes viewed birth control as a means of purifying their race; Marie at one point even suggested that Britain pass a bill to "ensure the sterility of the hopelessly rotten and racially diseased." In the latter group she put her daughter-in-law Mary Wallis, who married Marie's only child, Harry Roe. Mary suffered from nearsightedness, and Marie therefore railed against the marriage as a eugenic disaster.

In reality it was Marie's second marriage that was the disaster. In 1938, after years of frustration, she demanded and received from Roe a letter in which he confessed his own sexual inadequacy and granted her the right to carry on extramarital affairs. Despite the existence of such a letter and the mutual attraction that existed between Marie and younger men, it seems probable that she lived vicariously, and that the high point of her sexual life may well have been 1918.

QUIRKS: Even as a septuagenarian, Marie maintained that her real age was 26. On her 70th birthday, her son wrote to her: "Darling Mummy, Very many happy returns on your 26th birthday. Isn't it funny that never again will we be the same age, and that from next March on I will be older than you."

—D.R.

The Devoted Physicist

ALBERT EINSTEIN (Mar. 14, 1879–Apr. 18, 1955)

HIS FAME: In a succession of scientific papers authored during the 20th century's first two decades, Albert Einstein revolutionized physics. His theories of special and general relativity rank among science's most profound achievements, and he accordingly is considered to be among history's greatest thinkers.

HIS PERSON: Despite the universal acclaim for his genius that was to come, Einstein's early school years in Germany proved inauspicious and his parents at first feared he was a bit below normal in intelligence. In 1895 his application to Zurich's prestigious Polytechnic Academy was rejected. It took a year of remedial schooling before Einstein was accepted by that institution. In 1900 he graduated, but his request for an academic appointment was denied and he soon found it necessary to take a job as an examiner in the Swiss patent office in Bern. In 1905 he wrote "A New Determination of Molecular Dimensions," which was published in a scholarly journal. For this thesis the University of Zurich awarded him a Ph.D. That same year he published a paper on the special theory of relativity, and soon afterward he embarked on his career as a university professor.

A few years after the 1916 publication of his work on the general theory of relativity, Einstein found himself accorded "superstar" status. Universities clamored for him to join their faculties, fellow scientists sought his advice, and political and charitable groups competed for his support. But Einstein, true to his image as the genius lost in thought, restricted his nonscientific involvements to two causes that remained dear to him: pacifism and Zionism.

LOVE LIFE: Einstein's love life, what is known of it, starts with his 1903 marriage to Mileva Maric, a mathematics student he met while both were university students in Zurich. Their marriage was ill starred. For Einstein, physics came first; the demands made by a wife ranked a distant second. Yet Einstein soon fathered two sons—Hans Albert and Edward. In many respects the marriage seemed stable. In time, however, Mileva's moody, introverted personality clashed with Einstein's vitality and humor. Finally, in April of 1914, Einstein accepted a position at the Prussian Academy of Sciences in Berlin. Mileva and the boys went along to the capital but decided to vacation in Switzerland during the summer. When the eruption of WWI prevented them from rejoining Einstein in Berlin, they stayed in Zurich. Einstein remained in Berlin and, during the war's course, made only a few trips to visit his family in Switzerland. After a final visit in 1916, Einstein confided to a friend that his decision never again to see Mileva was "irrevocable." She interfered, it seems, with his ability to concentrate on physics, his greatest love. In 1919 they were divorced, and Einstein confidently pledged to Mileva the proceeds of the Nobel Prize he anticipated. That confidence was well placed. He won the prize in 1921 and promptly delivered on his promise. It is not known whether he fulfilled a second, more mysterious, promise: "You will see," he wrote Mileva, "that I will always remain true to you—in my way."

Meanwhile in Berlin, Einstein had been spending increasing amounts of time in the company of the daughter of his father's cousin, Elsa Lowenthal, the widowed mother of two girls. Elsa and Einstein had known each other as children and had corresponded sporadically over the years. When, in 1917, Einstein fell seriously ill with stomach trouble, he had already moved in with Elsa, who nursed him back to health. After his recovery Einstein stayed on, and within months of divorcing Mileva he married his former "nurse." Although Einstein accepted Elsa's children as his own, all accounts point to his relationship with their mother as one rooted not in passion but in convenience. She kept the material aspects of his life in order, taking responsibility for feeding and clothing him and maintaining his home. Once, when asked what he gave in return, Einstein cryptically commented, "My understanding."

After Elsa's death in 1936, Einstein—by then a resident of Princeton, N.J.—remained a widower until his own death. He remained close, in those years, to his elder son, Hans Albert, and saw to it that his younger son, Edward, who suffered from serious emotional disorders, received proper care in the institutions where he passed much of his adulthood.

HIS THOUGHTS: "Don't have any children. It makes divorce so much more complicated."

"When women are in their homes, they are attached to their furniture. They run around it all day long and are always fussing with it. But when I am with a woman on a journey, I am the only piece of furniture that she has available, and she cannot refrain from moving around me all day and improving something about me."

"Falling in love is not at all the most stupid thing that people do—but gravitation cannot be held responsible for it."

"It is a sad fact that Man does not live for pleasure alone."

—*R.M.*

Women Versus The Wireless

GUGLIELMO MARCONI (Apr. 25, 1874–July 20, 1937)

HIS FAME: The Italian electrical engineer's invention of wireless transmitters and receivers pioneered longdistance wireless telegraphy and opened a new era in communications.

HIS PERSON: Marconi struck many people as a dull, humorless man obsessed with his work and interested in little else. While his public presence was usually formal and preoccupied, there was another side of his personality, replete with volatile moods, sudden sunburst smiles, and paranoiac tantrums. Lionized for most of his life, he could be surprisingly reckless in his treatment of those who cared the most for him. The son of well-to-do parents (Irish mother and Italian father), Marconi worked out the technology for his basic achievements by age 21, and the attic of his family's house in Bologna became the world's first radio station. Incredible as it seemed, the Italian government showed no interest in his invention, so Marconi traveled to London to continue his experiments. In 1901 he received the first transatlantic wireless signal at St. John's, Newfoundland. Even though he won the Nobel Prize for physics in 1909, it was the 1912 *Titanic* disaster that vividly dramatized the importance of his work. The *Titanic's* SOS was heard by a rescue ship, and 711 of the passengers were eventually saved. (Marconi had booked passage on the *Titanic*, but had canceled at the last moment.) That same year Marconi lost his right eye in a head-on auto collision in Italy. Fitted with a glass eye, he soon resumed his frenetic pace and after WWI conducted most of his work on the steam yacht *Elettra*, his floating laboratory. Despite his brooding nature and polite taciturnity, Marconi was an honored guest of government officials as well as of the international celebrity set. Intensely patriotic if politically naive, he became a strong Fascist supporter of Mussolini, who sent him on numerous political missions. His later years were occupied by research on shortwave and microwave transmission. When he died in Rome at age 63, radio transmitters throughout the world shut down in tribute, and for two minutes in this century the ether was silent.

LOVE LIFE: "My father's eye for feminine beauty was unerring," wrote Marconi's daughter Degna, and he lost his heart "with fair regularity," but seldom impulsively. Shipboard romance was a recurring motif of his love life, partly because he spent so much time afloat and also because he seemed able to unbend at sea more than anywhere else. Women chased him, perhaps because of his intriguing Valentino-like features and air of moody disdain. His first serious love affair was with Josephine B. Holman, a rich girl from Indianapolis, whom he met on a transatlantic liner in 1899. They were engaged before the ship docked, and remained so for two years. Josephine broke it off, apparently after realizing that this strange, driven man would never make an Indianapolis-style husband.

In 1903 he met another beautiful American woman, Inez Milholland, on board the *Lucania*. However, her beauty was about all that he could relate to. A dedicated feminist and pioneer suffragist, she embodied "everything he basically disapproved of," wrote Degna. He proposed and she accepted, but the romance quickly died and instead became an enduring friendship.

Marconi met his first wife, 19-year-old Beatrice O'Brien, daughter of an Irish peer in the House of Lords, when he was 30. The courtship was strictly old-world, grave and formal. She refused his first proposal but, despite a disapproving family and the fact that the couple scarcely knew each other, accepted his second. "I don't love him," she wrote her sister. "I've told him so over and over again; he says he wants me anyhow and will make me love him. I do like him so much and enough to marry him." They married in 1905 and produced four children, of whom three survived infancy. From the outset, however, Bea often found herself abandoned for long periods as "Marky" pursued his work. When present, Marconi constantly rocked the marriage with his explosive jealousy and possessiveness. Not exactly the domestic housewife type, Bea was an extrovert and "born flirt" who could no more resist smiling at a handsome man than her husband could stop fiddling with transmitters. At one point he taught her Morse code, hoping to give her a hobby to occupy her free time. The couple underwent years of tense separations and hopeful reconciliations. Beatrice tolerated his extramarital flings because they always "ended in home-comings," wrote Degna. As their daughter further explained: "She played on the side of his nature that dreaded permanence, fearing that it would trap him." Joining the first *Elettra* cruise in 1920, Beatrice learned that her husband's latest paramour was also aboard. Marconi made no attempt to hide his newest love, and Beatrice was no longer able to remain deaf and blind to his indiscretions. "A man like Marconi should never marry," Queen Elena of Italy sympathetically told her. Still beautiful at 38, Beatrice soon began to see other men, divorced Marconi in 1924, and then promptly married the Marchese Laborio Marignoli. Marconi, whose *Elettra* affair had ended, became much more friendly and wrote long, confidential letters to his ex-wife. His sporadic diaries indicate that he sometimes had several affairs going at once, but he never seemed terribly passionate about any of them. Women came so easily to him that, though necessary, they were a distinctly secondary pursuit.

In 1925, at 51, he became engaged to 17-year-old Elizabeth Paynter, a Cornwall debutante. Beatrice was astonished and wondered "after all the years we were together when your own desire expressed continually was for freedom ... as your family impeded and oppressed you, why you should suddenly find … this craving for fresh ties!! I fail to understand." The engagement lasted only a few months.

His next one, however, led to marriage. He met Christina Bezzi-Scali, a quiet, serious, blue-eyed Italian of 25, on the *Elettra* and promptly took her into the solitary wireless room. Because she was Catholic—her parents of Vatican nobility—Marconi had to construct an elaborate ruse, with Bea's ironic complicity, to annul his first marriage. Both had to swear that they had wed with mental reservations, as in a virtual "trial marriage," thus providing grounds for lack of consent. In an impressive wedding ceremony, with Mussolini as his best man, Marconi married Christina in 1927. Several months later he suffered the first in a series of heart attacks. A daughter, Maria Elettra, was born in 1930. In declining health, Marconi pushed away from his first family, virtually ignored them in his will—leaving most of his $25 million fortune to Maria Elettra—and spent his last years as an apparently faithful if semi-invalid husband.

HIS THOUGHTS: Not given to intimate expressions on paper, Marconi usually wrote several drafts of his love letters before sending them. Probably his most typical and self-revealing line was "In very great haste. Yours affectionately, Guglielmo."

—*J.E.*

The Virgin Genius

SIR ISAAC NEWTON (Dec. 25, 1642–Mar. 20, 1727)

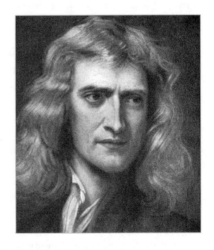

HIS FAME: Newton was an English physicist and mathematician whose discoveries earned him a place as one of the greatest scientists in history. He is perhaps best known for his formulation of a theory of gravitation.

HIS PERSON: Newton was born three months after the death of his father, a poor farmer. Until he was three years old he had no rivals for the love and attention of his mother, Hannah. Then she married Barnabas Smith, a minister, and the newly wedded couple moved away to a nearby village. Newton was left in the care of his grandmother for the next eight years. He remained absolutely devoted to his mother, even in the face of seeming abandonment, but he hated his stepfather.

Later he remembered "threatening my father and mother Smith to burne them and the house over them." Hannah had three children by Smith. When Smith died, she and 11-year-old Isaac were reunited. Perhaps his fixation on her developed new dimensions at that point. Regardless, she remained the central figure in his life.

He grew into an almost stereotypical recluse, an absentminded, ascetic, and devoted scientist. He lived in the world of the mind, often simply forgetting to sleep or eat.

LOVE LIFE: Newton apparently experienced some sort of tender feelings for Anne Storey, the stepdaughter of a family he boarded with while he was in school. They may even have been formally engaged for a short time, but almost certainly they did not have a sexual relationship. They parted in 1661, when Newton went off to Cambridge University, but remained friends over the years.

Historians who have studied Newton are divided into two schools of thought concerning his sex life. Some insist he died a virgin. Others, referring to the rumors that circulated during and after his life, believe that he had at least one great love affair.

It seems that Newton did indeed love Fatio de Duillier, a handsome young Swiss mathematician. The two men were inseparable companions for several years, starting in 1687, when Fatio was 23. They shared a burning interest in science and mathematics; whether they also shared a bed is speculation. For reasons known only to them, Newton and Fatio broke off their intense relationship in 1693. For the next 18 months Newton suffered a complete mental breakdown. He was depressed and hostile and had delusions that his friends had abandoned him. He reacted by writing poisonous letters, accusing them of betrayal and deceit. To John Locke he wrote, "Sir, being of opinion that you endeavored to embroil me with women and by other means, I was so much affected by it … 'twere better if you were dead." When Locke calmly and kindly replied, Newton apologized, explaining that he had been delirious from lack of sleep and didn't know what he was writing. Newton and Fatio exchanged occasional letters for the rest of their lives, but the friendship remained distant.

A rather mysterious "love triangle" involved Newton with the young, witty, and beautiful Catherine Barton, who was Newton's niece and lived in his London home for over 20 years, and Charles Montague. Contemporary observers believed that Newton may have connived at an affair between Catherine and the increasingly influential Montague (later Lord Halifax) in order to gain a highly paid position as master of the mint. Later historians, putting the theories of Freud to work, have suggested that Newton enjoyed the affair between Montague and Catherine because he identified with Montague and saw Catherine as an embodiment of his own mother. He could thereby enjoy a vicarious sexual relationship with his mother, a woman whom, although she deserted him early in life, he loved deeply. Some have even suggested that he himself actually had an affair with Catherine. The most reasonable consensus, however, seems to be that Newton had no sexual interest in women.

—*R. W. S.*

The Bourgeois Communist

KARL MARX (May 5, 1818–Mar. 14, 1883)

HIS FAME: Revolutionary theorist Karl Marx was the source of some of the most powerful ideas of modern times, ideas that have inspired revolutions and that permeate governments in countries all over the world.

HIS PERSON: Descended from a long line of rabbis, Karl was baptized at age six in the Evangelical Church in his hometown of Trier, Prussia, at the request of his father, who had repudiated the family faith. Later Karl himself rejected all religion ("Religion is the opium of the masses") and has been accused, probably justly, of anti-Semitism.

Marx in his early 30s

At 16 he fell in love with aristocrat Jenny von Westphalen, whom he married eight years later, after completing his education. (He received his doctorate from the University of Jena, something of a diploma mill.) The inflammatory articles he wrote for literary and cultural magazines in several European cities were partly responsible for his expulsion from three of those cities—Paris, Cologne, and Brussels. He was also active in the underground Socialist movement. In Paris he met Friedrich Engels, son of a wealthy textile manufacturer, who became his lifelong collaborator. Among their joint works is the *Communist Manifesto* (1848), written for the Communist League.

In 1849 Marx moved to London, "where the next dance [revolution] begins," he said hopefully. Engels went, too, to work at his father's textile firm in Manchester. Their hopes for revolution ended in disappointment when the stolid British showed little interest.

Money was Marx's *bête noire*. He refused to be a "money-making machine," so he and his family lived on what he earned writing and on handouts from Engels and relatives. The Marx children were trained to say to bill collectors, "Mr. Marx ain't upstairs." (Later, family fortunes improved.) Only three of the seven children grew to maturity, and of those three, two committed suicide.

Marx spent his days in the reading room of the British Museum doing research for his major work, *Das Kapital,* and for the articles and editorials he and Engels wrote for the New York *Daily Tribune.*

His physical condition was poor. Run-down and nervous, he rarely took baths, and for the last 20 years of his life he was afflicted with boils all over his body. In addition, he suffered from liver and eye problems.

A Victorian autocrat, Marx was not above faking a fit of temper and shouting, "I will annihilate you!" during arguments. He was prone to sarcasm and intolerant of others' opinions. Nicknamed "the Moor" for his swarthiness, he grew a flowing beard to point up his resemblance to a statue of Zeus he kept in his study. His brown eyes were passionate and defiant, his laugh was infectious.

LOVE LIFE: The only serious romantic love of Marx's life was green-eyed, auburn-haired Jenny, four years his senior and daughter of a baron. Gentle and scholarly, she also had style and a streak of vanity. Named "Queen of the Ball" one year in Trier, she was pursued by suitors but chose Karl, whom she called pet names, like *Schwärzwildchen* ("little black wild one"). Both families were against their marriage. In her extravagant and well-written love letters to him, she talked of "all the bliss that was and will be," though their passion for each other was not consummated until after their marriage. Once she spoke of how she would "lay down" her head for him, "sacrificing it to my naughty boy," and she called him a "wicked rascal" for flirting with a certain Madame Hermann while on a steamer.

On June 19, 1843, Karl and Jenny were married in a Protestant church. The couple honeymooned in Switzerland, a trip financed by Jenny's mother. They carried their spending money in a two-handled strongbox, which they purposely left open in hotel rooms so that anyone could take from it.

Their first child was born in Paris. Jenny took the baby girl home to show her off and wrote to Karl that she was afraid to return to Paris for fear that they would make more babies, which, of course, they did. Fear of pregnancy—and another mouth to feed—haunted their marriage.

Marx was a family man. Though he referred to Jenny as "mercurial" and complained in letters of her "floods of tears," he also said, to Engels, "When I see the sufferings of my wife and my own powerlessness, I could rush into the devil's jaws." They faced evictions for nonpayment of rent and even had to borrow the money to pay for a coffin when one-year-old Franciszka died. In happier moments, on Sundays, the whole family went for picnics in London parks, and Marx told stories as they walked along. In a graphic account of the Marx ménage, a Prussian police spy once told of an oilcloth-covered table littered with sewing, manuscripts, toys, and chipped cups, and of how he was offered a chair from which "the children's cooking [playthings]" was not removed.

The only known scandal that touched the family was Karl's affair with the family servant, Helene "Lenchen" Demuth, a delicately beautiful peasant girl who had joined the Von Westphalen family as a maid at age 11 or 12 and was "given" to Jenny in 1845 by her mother. Lenchen ruled the family with an iron hand and could beat Marx at chess. In 1851 she gave birth to a child, Henry Frederick, fathered by Marx. The child was raised by a foster family and never acknowledged by Marx—perhaps out of fear that it would destroy his marriage. Marx met the boy only once, in 1882. Lenchen worked for the Marx family until Karl's death, in 1883, two years after Jenny died. Then she went to work for Engels.

Marx had at least two minor flirtations—one with 33-year-old Frau Tenge, a cultured Italian married to a wealthy landowner, and another with his cousin, Antoinette Philips, 19 years younger than Marx, who in 1863 nursed him through a painful bout with boils. During his recovery, Marx wrote of Antoinette's "dark eyes shining dangerously as she pampers me."

He was paternal, and the practice of wife-beating so enraged him that he would have flogged a wife-beater "to the point of death," he claimed. Politically, he was against bourgeois marriage (though he had such a marriage himself) because it kept women in a state of slavery. Ironically, he deeply disapproved of Engels' mistress because she was of the lower classes.

The reverse side of Marx shows a corresponding vulgarity. He was fond of erotic French poetry of the 16th century, used words like *cock* and *toss-off*, and enjoyed telling dirty jokes, though never in mixed company.

HIS THOUGHTS: In 1856 Marx wrote to Jenny, "I have the living image of you in front of me, I hold you in my arms, kiss you from head to foot, fall before you on my knees and sigh, 'Madam, I love you.' … But love—… not of the proletariat, but love of one's darling, namely you, makes a man into a man again. In fact there are many women in the world, and some of them are beautiful. But where can I find another face in which every trait, even every wrinkle, brings back the greatest and sweetest memories of my life?"

—*A.E.*

The Objectivist

AYN RAND (Feb. 2, 1905–March 6, 1982)

HER FAME: Philosopher and novelist, Ayn Rand was the founder of the individualist, a quasi-libertarian school of thought she dubbed "Objectivism." She summed up her system thusly: "My philosophy, in essence, is the concept of man as a heroic being, with his own happiness as the moral purpose of his life, with productive achievement as his noblest activity, and reason as his only absolute." Rand is probably best remembered as the author of novels *The Fountainhead* (greatly popularized by the movie—with Rand's script—starring Gary Cooper and Patricia O'Neal) and *Atlas Shrugged.*

HER PERSON: Born Alisa Zinov'yevna Rosenbaum in Saint Petersburg to an agnostic Jewish family, Rand filled her young life with an early-developing love of literature, writing novels and screenplays from the age of seven and immersing herself in the works of Victor Hugo, Alexandre Dumas and other writers of the Romantic period. The 1917 Russian Revolution, which erupted when Rand was 12, financially crippled her family—they were forced to flee to Crimea—and left Rand with a permanent hatred for Communism. After returning to St. Petersburg to complete a university education, Rand gained an American visa to visit relatives at the age of 21. She never looked back, seeing in America the pinnacle of man's moral development and the antithesis of everything she had despised about the Soviet system. Taking the name Ayn Rand after stepping off the boat to New York, she made her way to Los Angeles, and, after a chance meeting with Cecil B. DeMille, broke into Hollywood as a script reader and, subsequently, as head of RKO Studio's costume department. There she met her future husband, actor Frank O'Connor, whose quiet dignity and exceptional good looks caused her to fall in love at first sight. After early successes with screenplays, Rand turned to writing novels—her early works, *We the Living* and *Anthem*, are still cherished by her fans if less known to the wider public. However, it was the 1943 publication of *The Fountainhead*, which champions the uncompromising character of its young architect hero, Howard Roark, who refuses to compromise his artistic vision despite having to languish in obscurity, and who ultimately destroys one of his own buildings, which made Rand's name. The follow-up publication of her masterwork *Atlas Shrugged* (which depicts a worldwide strike by the industrialists and innovators of America), in 1957, cemented her reputation. Her novels were universally panned by the literati and remain virtually blackballed by the academic world, but she remains one of the most influential authors and thinkers in print, especially with the young. After a decade's battle with lung cancer, Rand died of heart failure in March 1982 in her New York home. A dollar-shaped floral arrangement was placed by her coffin, because to Rand, the dollar sign represented the heroism of capitalism.

LOVE AND SEX LIFE: Essential to Rand's philosophy was the idea that sexuality is an expression of a human being's highest values; she depicted characters who were attracted to those who embody their highest values (it is an idea similar to ones advanced in Plato's *Symposium*). She summarized her views succinctly in a *Playboy* interview—"I say that sex is one of the most important aspects of man's life and, therefore, must never be approached lightly or casually. A sexual relationship is proper only on the ground of the highest values one can find in a human being. Sex must not be anything other than a response to values. And that is why I consider promiscuity immoral. Not because sex is evil, but because sex is too good and too important." Some of her views on sex, however, were more controversial—she believed that women's attitude toward men should be one of hero worship; homosexuality she viewed as an aberration and moral failure. Yet, she defended the rights of the individual to practice as they saw fit. Meanwhile, Rand's own marriage to Frank O'Connor was a largely unfulfilled one. An intensely focused and powerful woman, Rand found herself dominant in every aspect of the relationship, much in contrary to her ideal that men should be the subject of female worship; she also found O'Connor far from being her intellectual equal. Barbara Branden, one of her young students and, later, biographer, wrote of the split between Rand's theory and practice: "[Rand's theory of sex was] potentially a dangerous one, which already had had explosive effects on Ayn's life. It had led her to wildly aggrandize the men who were *her* sexual choices... and it would continue to do so in the future; if the men to whom she was attracted were not heroes, then what would her choices say about *her?*" Ironically, it would be Barbara Branden's husband Nathaniel, a Rand obsessive since his teens and longterm acolyte—her junior by two and a half decades—who would become her next lover in early 1955.

The affair was reluctantly "approved" by both Branden and Rand's respective spouses, though in truth the rejected spouses were in agony. While Nathaniel wanted to have sex with Rand in a hotel, she insisted on her apartment. Thus husband and lover often passed politely in the elevator. Frank and Barbara took to sharing their troubles in bars, and Frank eventually developed a serious drinking problem. Barbara Branden later wrote that the affair was "agonizingly painful" for both her and O'Connor.

Nathaniel Branden later recalled of his mistress, "What she wanted was a man whose esteem would take the form of reducing her to a sex object. This seemed so simple and natural to me." Ayn favored having sex with Nathaniel on the mink coat her husband had bought her (with the money from her successes). Like the aggressive and violent nigh-on-rapes that Rand made of her hero and heroines' sexual encounters in her novels, Ayn liked it rough and demeaning. Wrote Nathaniel Branden: "'What's happening to me?' Ayn would say. 'You're turning me into an animal.' And I would grin mockingly and answer, 'Really? What were you before?' 'A mind,' she would say. And I would reply, 'Really? Do you have a mind? Who ever told you that?'" After the release of *Atlas*, Rand fell into deep post-partum depression.

Her sexual affair with Branden ended histrionically. Brandon had fallen in love with a new woman, and hid the truth from Rand. Finally he revealed his secret, and confessed to Rand that he was no longer attracted to her because of her age. In front of a roomful of people, Rand furiously slapped Nathaniel and spat out a curse that he be impotent for the rest of his life. (Apparently the curse was ineffectual.) She stated that Branden had betrayed his highest value, Rand,

and expunged him from her life, removing her dedication to him in *Atlas Shrugged*. They never spoke again. Branden then divorced Barbara and married the young actress Patrecia Gullison Scott. He remains a pariah in the Objectivist community but has gone on to a successful career as a writer of Objectivist self-help books on relationships.

HER THOUGHTS: "Tell me what a man finds sexually attractive and I will tell you his entire philosophy of life. Show me the woman he sleeps with and I will tell you his valuation of himself."

—J.L.

The Man Who Confessed Everything

JEAN-JACQUES ROUSSEAU (June 28, 1712–July 2, 1778)

HIS FAME: The Swiss-born French philosopher, novelist, and political theorist authored such works as *Julie, or The New Héloïse*; *Émile, or A Treatise on Education*; *The Social Contract*; and his autobiographical *Confessions*. His writings on romance, education, government, and morality greatly influenced the leaders of the French Revolution and the Romantic movement. His philosophy is best epitomized in the concept that man is naturally good and that all contact with society is corrupting. So controversial and influential was Rousseau that George Sand called him "St. Rousseau," Voltaire and David Hume called him "a monster," and Tolstoi said that Rousseau and the gospel were the two greatest influences in his life.

HIS PERSON: After a dispute forced Rousseau's widowed watchmaker father to flee Geneva, Jean-Jacques and his brother François were left with an uncle. François was soon apprenticed, and Jean-Jacques was sent to live with a minister who taught him the classics. At the age of 16 he left Geneva to embark on a lifetime of traveling. In love with nature, he tramped about the countryside taking odd jobs. He worked variously for a notary, an engraver, and a lackey, and eventually became a music teacher. At age 37 he won an essay contest and turned to writing, and by 46 he was famous. He became immensely popular in high society despite the fact that he railed against the oppression of the masses by the upper classes. In 1762, when his book *Émile* was condemned by both Church and State, he escaped Paris, was expelled from Bern, and found refuge in London, where he stayed for a year. Toward the end of his life, his tendency toward paranoia and reclusiveness grew worse. He was sure that his friends were plotting to discredit him. In part, his fears were well based, for he had repeatedly outraged his best friends either with insults or with his wildly extravagant ideas. A lonely and melancholic man, troubled for most of his life with physical and emotional pain, he sank into intermittent periods of mental illness before his death outside Paris.

LOVE AND SEX LIFE: Good-looking, charismatic, and gushingly romantic, Rousseau was attractive to the ladies. But his love life was a complete mess. His first profound sexual experience was as a child. Having committed some minor offense, he received a spanking from his teacher, Mademoiselle Lambertier. He later wrote, "Who would believe that this childhood punishment, suffered at the age of eight at the hands of a spinster of 30 [he was in fact 11 and she 40], was to determine my tastes, my desires, my passions, my very self for the rest of my life?" He was left desperately craving more of the same. However, the astute teacher, realizing what she had started, never spanked him again. For poor Jean-Jacques, however, the damage was done. He suffered "erotic frenzies" which led him to intense fantasies of being spanked. But worse than these troubling frenzies were the long-term effects of The Spanking. "I have passed my life in silent yearning among those I loved most. Never daring to mention my peculiar taste, I achieved at least some satisfaction from relationships which retained a suggestion of it.... To lie at the feet of an imperious mistress, to obey her orders, to be forced to beg her forgiveness—this was for me a sweet enjoyment."

There was only one person with whom Rousseau truly lived out his masochistic dreams. In his brief youthful liaison with the 11-year-old Mademoiselle Goton, he was satisfied. She "played the schoolmistress" with him and spanked him, though "this was a favor which had to be begged for on bended knees." To his delight, she "allowed herself to take the greatest liberties with me without permitting me to take a single one with her. She treated me exactly like a child." After a short time, the two precocious youngsters were separated.

During his youth he was given to extravagant, unconsummated crushes on older women. And in due time he did learn about the birds and bees from the buxom Madame de Warens. He received an introduction to her house at Chambéry, Savoy, and lived there with her and her lover-caretaker, Claude Anet. Rousseau grew very devoted to her, calling her "mama" while she called him "little cat." Five years later, "mama" offered Rousseau her favors, to be shared, of course, with Anet. The "little cat" was 21 and she was 34; it was time for him to become a man. She gave him a week to consider the proposition. He consented, but rather than being excited, he was repelled at the thought of having sex with her. After five years, Rousseau felt more like her son than her lover, saying, "I loved her too much to desire her." It turned out that Mme. de Warens was a cold fish in bed, and Rousseau didn't enjoy himself. "Twice or thrice, as I pressed her passionately to me, I flooded her breast with my tears. It was as if I were committing incest." He turned to fantasizing about other women while he was making love to her. The *ménage à trois* continued until Anet died in 1734. Rousseau stayed with Mme. de Warens for three more years, finally leaving to seek his fortune when she brought in another young lover to live with them.

Rousseau's next romantic adventure began in 1745. At a hotel in Paris, he became infatuated with the chambermaid, 24-year-old Thérèse le Vasseur. Their affair lasted for the rest of his life. He told her from the start, "I shall never leave you, but I shall never marry you." After 23 years, he did marry her, in a spur-of-the-moment ceremony which he conducted himself. In a letter to a friend, he recommended a quarter of a century as a sensible length of time for a trial marriage.

Thérèse was pretty and kind and a good cook, but completely unsuited intellectually to Rousseau. She could barely tell the time, never learned to spell correctly, was unable to remember the months of the year or count money. She was remarkably devoted to Rousseau, considering his difficult nature and his cruelty regarding their five children born out of wedlock. Despite her protests, Rousseau insisted that each one be given at birth to a foundling hospital. His rationales were absurd; for example, since they weren't married, he argued, it was the only way to "save her honor." In later years he was racked with grief over his actions. Although his pet names for Thérèse were "aunt" and "boss," he never asked her for a spanking, and reported that she too was cold in bed. Interestingly, this was not the report of James Boswell (an ardent admirer of Rousseau) who constituted, as far as is known, Thérèse's only infidelity. Boswell wrote that he and Thérèse "mated" 13 different times. Thérèse told Boswell that while he was "vigorous" in bed, his lovemaking lacked "art."

Rousseau's wildest passion hit him when he was 44. The inspiration was the Countess Sophie d'Houdetot, a not especially pretty married woman. The problem was not Sophie's husband, but that she was devoted to her lover, an officer friend of Rousseau's who was often away. As usual, Rousseau "loved her too much to possess her." But that didn't stop him from trying. "The continuance over three months of ceaseless stimulation and privation threw me into an exhaustion from which I did not recover for several years and brought on a rupture [a hernia] that I shall carry with me to the grave ... such was the sole amorous gratification." All in all, he decided that it was the first and only time he had truly fallen in love; and Sophie served as inspiration for the terrifyingly moral Julie in his novel *The New Héloïse*.

QUIRKS: Rousseau was possessed of numerous sexual eccentricities. He had the odd habit of going into raptures over inanimate objects. When living with Mme. de Warens, he would wander through her apartment kissing her armchair, her bedcurtains, even the floor she walked on. Another female friend sent him "an under-petticoat which she had worn and out of which she wanted me to make myself a waistcoat.... It was as if she had stripped herself to clothe me.... In my emotion I kissed the note and the petticoat 20 times in tears." (Thérèse thought he was mad.)

As a young man Rousseau went through a period of exhibitionism. He would hide in dark alleys, and when a woman passed by he would expose his buttocks, hoping that one day some bold female would spank his behind in passing. Another time he flashed before some girls fetching water at a well, admitting in *Confessions* that the sight was "more laughable than seductive." When one of the girls gave the cry of alarm, Rousseau was confronted by an intimidating posse consisting of an angry man and several old women brandishing brooms, but he managed to worm his way out of trouble.

One of Rousseau's most incredible sexual escapades occurred while he was living in Venice, Italy, as a young man. Although he claimed to loathe prostitutes, he occasionally visited them. One such local beauty was Zulietta, a woman he elevated to goddesslike proportions in his mind. But on his first visit to her, as he was about to "pluck the fruit," he became deeply upset and began to cry. How, he wondered, could it be that this divine being was a mere prostitute? He decided there must be something wrong with her, "a secret flaw that makes her repulsive."

She managed to cheer him up, but as he was about to enter her he suddenly discovered the secret defect. "I perceived that she had a malformed nipple; I beat my brow, looked harder, and made certain this nipple did not match the other." Casanova had enjoyed Zulietta three years earlier and mentioned no such flaw. But Rousseau "started wondering about the reason for this malformation.... I was struck by the thought that it resulted from some remarkable imperfection of Nature.... I saw clear as daylight that I held in my arms some kind of monster rejected by Nature, man, and love." When he pointed this out to her, she scornfully told him to "leave the ladies alone and go study mathematics."

MEDICAL REPORT: Much of Rousseau's unhappiness was directly traceable to an extremely painful bladder ailment which troubled him all his life. He suffered a congestion of the trigones, or posterior part of the urethra, and inflammation of the bladder, which caused frequent, incomplete, and painful urination and fever. He needed a chamber pot constantly when his bladder was acting up, and Thérèse had to insert a catheter into his penis, but this often did not work. Sex became so painful for him that he gave it up entirely for the last 13 years of his life, returning to masturbation.

—*A. W.*

The Randy Lord Russell

BERTRAND RUSSELL (May 18, 1872–Feb. 2, 1970)

HIS FAME: Bertrand Russell, British philosopher, mathematician, and peace activist, achieved scholarly renown with the mind-bending classic *Principia Mathematica* (1910–1913), which he coauthored with Alfred North Whitehead. Russell also wrote numerous more popular works, including *Marriage and Morals* (1929), *History of Western Philosophy* (1945), and his *Autobiography* (1967–1969).

Russell and Alys Pearsall Smith

HIS PERSON: Russell, like Voltaire, was the "laughing philosopher" of his generation. An elfish, mischievous face resembling that of Sir John Tenniel's Mad Hatter surmounted his lively sparrowlike body. His irreverent wit and huge personal magnetism marked a bottomless appetite for life. Yet, also like Voltaire, he was a deeply passionate man whose rage at public policy often gave him, in news photos, the aspect of an avenging angel. Throughout his life he attacked conventional wisdom on everything from sex, education, and religion to woman's rights, politics, and nuclear arms.

Born into one of England's oldest families and raised by his austere Presbyterian grandmother, Russell was a shy, oversensitive child much concerned with his "sins." His precocious and gifted mind rejected religion at age 18, and led him to mathematics in search of "whether anything could be known," a lifelong pursuit. As an outspoken pacifist, he was jailed as a security risk in 1918 but supported the allies in WWII. Russell had almost achieved an affectionate popular following by the time he won the Nobel Prize for literature in 1950. His controversial stands on the Vietnam War, John F. Kennedy's assassination, and nuclear testing increased his following. In his late 80s he led protest marches and sit-down demonstrations and was again jailed. "I do so hate to leave this world," he said shortly before he died peacefully at 97.

SEX LIFE: At 15, Russell wrote, he was "continually distracted by erections," and "fell into the practice of masturbating." He suddenly dropped the practice at age 20 because he was in love. Alys Pearsall Smith, from a prominent Philadelphia Quaker socialist family, was five years older than Russell. He determined to marry her and first kissed her four months after he proposed. His grandmother vigorously fought the match, calling Alys a "baby-snatcher" and "designing female" and whispering dire stories of insanity in both families. The couple speculated about the frequency of their future sexual intercourse, but both remained virgins until their marriage in 1894. Their sexual difficulties during their honeymoon "appeared to us merely comic," Russell reported, "and were soon overcome." Alys, educated to think of sex as God's grudge against women, supposed that her carnal desires would be properly infrequent, but Russell "did not find it necessary" to argue the matter. Though both gave lip service to free love, neither practiced it, and their first five years together were happy and highly moral.

About 1901, however, Russell fell in love with Evelyn Whitehead, gifted wife of his collaborator Alfred North Whitehead. This relationship, though never physical, came as an "awakening" to Russell, who underwent an almost mystical "change of heart" in many of his feelings and views. Suddenly realizing—during a solitary bicycle ride—that he no longer loved Alys, he quite promptly told her so. "I had no wish to be unkind," he wrote, "but I believed in those days (what experience has taught me to think possibly open to doubt) that in intimate relations one should speak the truth." For nine more years Russell and Alys maintained the facade, but occupied separate bedrooms and were thoroughly miserable. "About twice a year," Russell wrote, "I would attempt sex relations with her, in the hope of alleviating her misery, but she no longer attracted me, and the attempt was futile."

One of his first tentative flings involved a young secretary with a matchless Victorian name, Miss Ivy Pretious. In 1910 he met Lady Ottoline Morrell, wife of Liberal M.P. Philip Morrell. Russell described Lady Ottoline as "very tall, with a long thin face something like a horse, and very beautiful hair." Their sexual relationship was furtive since Ottoline had no desire to leave or embarrass her husband. Philip appreciated their discretion. Russell left Alys that spring and did not see her again until 1950, when they met as "friendly acquaintances." Lady Ottoline "made me much less of a Puritan," he wrote, but he resented not being her sole interest. They had stormy quarrels but remained lovers until 1916 and close friends until her death in 1938.

Russell stopped being "a Puritan" with a vengeance. After 1910—though married three more times—he was never again monogamous until extreme old age. His private life was a chaos of serious affairs, secret trysts, and emotional tightwire acts that constantly threatened, if never quite exploded into, ruinous scandal. In his letters to Ottoline and other lovers, his conscience drove him to confess, even though he "made little of," his escapades with other women. More surprising is that most of his lovers tolerated his wanderings and each other so well.

During his first American lecture tour in 1914, a new Russell, turned on by any pretty woman within earshot, emerged full-force. He became intimate with Helen Dudley, daughter of a Chicago surgeon, and invited her to England, "My Darling," he wrote to Ottoline, "please do not think that this means *any* lessening of my love for you." When Helen actually arrived, however, Russell felt "an absolute blank indifference to her." By this time he had taken up with Irene Cooper Willis, a talented beauty whom he hired as a research helper. But she feared scandal and Russell hated caution. "I wish to goodness I had not made love to her," he told Ottoline.

In 1916 Russell met Lady Constance Malleson, a 21-year-old auburn-haired actress who used the stage name "Colette O'Niel." Her marriage to actor Miles Malleson was "open" by mutual agreement, and Russell remained her lover until 1920, often spending holidays with the couple. They renewed their affair three times over the next 30 years, and Colette always sent him roses on his birthday. But his affections for Colette "could never make a *shadow* of a difference to what I feel for you," he wrote to Ottoline.

Russell desperately wanted children. In 1919 he met Dora Black, a suffragist who was also interested in having children without the fetters of marriage and monogamy. Still in love with Colette, and regularly pouring out his heart to Ottoline, Russell went to China to take a post at Peking University, and Dora went with him. She was eight months pregnant when they returned to England in August of 1921. "From the first we used no precautions," said Russell. Having agreed on a marriage "compatible with minor affairs," and with their baby due in one month, they were wed. After a second child was born, the Russells established the experimental Beacon Hill School. Its liberal policies included advocacy of free love for those on the staff, and Russell enjoyed several affairs with young female teachers. While he was philandering at school and during lecture tours in the U.S., Dora had an affair with American journalist Griffin Barry and bore him two children. Russell clearly resented this particular application of his free-love theories. Moreover, he had said in their marriage contract, "If she should have a child that was not mine there would be a divorce." Strained beyond endurance, the marriage ended in 1935.

Russell felt that he didn't know any woman until he had slept with her. In *Marriage and Morals* he advocated both trial and open marriage, exceedingly radical proposals for 1929. He did not think he could "remain physically fond of any woman for more than seven or eight years." Dora wanted another child by him, but he "found it impossible." His affair with 21-year-old Joan Follwell was typical. "My only fear," he told her, "is lest you may find me inadequate sexually, as I am no longer young ... but I think there are ways in which I can make up for it." She reported years later, "I had dinner with him and the third time I slept [with him] ... this lasted over three years. But the sleeping wasn't a success so I gave him up." For all his galloping satyriasis, Russell apparently suffered frequently from impotence.

In 1930 he began a long affair with Patricia "Peter" Spence, the young governess of his children. He was determined to marry her, and finally did in 1936. A son was born the next year.

The family spent the war years in the U.S., where "Peter" Spence became increasingly unhappy. Russell's daughter recalled their unpleasant domestic life. "She had found marriage to the great man something of a disappointment. His passion cooled and was replaced by kindly courtesy and a show of affection thinly unsatisfying to a romantic young woman." By 1946, now in his 70s, Russell took up with the young wife of a Cambridge lecturer; their relationship lasted three years. Colette, whom he saw for the last time in 1949, wrote him bitterly, "I see everything quite clear now, and it seems a dreary end to all our years.... Three times I've been drawn into [your life] and three times thrown aside."

"Peter" Spence divorced Russell in 1952. Later that year he married his old friend Edith Finch, an American teacher and author. Russell, cooled at last from his self-declared inability to damp his "abnormally strong sexual urges," finally enjoyed a successful marriage. And Colette sent him red roses on his last birthday.

HIS THOUGHTS: "It is better to control a restrictive and hostile emotion such as jealousy, rather than a generous and expansive emotion such as love. Conventional morality has erred, not in demanding self-control, but in demanding it in the wrong place."

"It is clear that the Divine purpose in the [Bible] text 'it is better to marry than to burn' is to make us all feel how *very* dreadful the torments of Hell must be."

—*J.E.*

An Open "Marriage"

JEAN-PAUL SARTRE (June 21, 1905–Apr. 15, 1980)

HIS FAME: French existentialist philosopher Jean-Paul Sartre produced nine plays, four novels, five major philosophical works, and countless articles on every conceivable subject. As a major proponent of existentialism, a philosophy that holds that people are responsible for their actions, even in a random, absurd universe, Sartre had an international influence on the post-WWII generations.

Sartre and Simone de Beauvoir

HIS PERSON: Born the son of a French naval officer who died a year after Sartre's birth, the philosopher was raised by his mother, Anne-Marie Schweitzer (a first cousin of Albert Schweitzer's), in his grandparents' Parisian home. A timid, ugly child, Sartre had virtually no childhood friends and retreated into fantasy, especially after he discovered books at the age of four. Reading, writing, and studying occupied Sartre's youth. Even though he was over-protected by his mother and dominated by his authoritarian grandfather, he developed a strongly assertive personality.

After he entered the École Normale Supérieure, Sartre rejected his mother's and her parents' influence and middle-class way of life. After graduating, he became a leftist schoolteacher and writer. While serving in the French Army as a weatherman in 1940, he was captured by the German invaders and put in jail. Six months later he was released and joined the Resistance as a propagandist. After WWII, Sartre's genius flowered and his reputation—based on plays like *No Exit* and novels such as *Nausea*—became international.

Politically, Sartre was associated with communism and advocated proletarian revolution. He wrote political pamphlets, demonstrated, and even rioted. After the Hungarian Revolution of 1956, he broke with the Stalinists and later drifted toward Maoism. In 1964 he was awarded the Nobel Prize in literature, but refused it because he felt it was being offered by the forces of conservatism.

A man who had renounced materialism for the world of ideas, Sartre, who chain-smoked and constantly took amphetamines, died of pulmonary congestion after a heart attack in 1980 at the age of 74.

SEX LIFE: At 19, Sartre met named Camille at a public gathering. The 22-year-old Camille had been seduced by a family friend as a child and had worked in brothels since the age of 18. For four days and nights the young lovers stayed in bed, until relatives finally forced them apart. Their relationship lasted on and off for over five years, until Camille tired of Sartre's poverty and found a wealthy older lover.

In 1929, while in college, Sartre met Simone de Beauvoir, an intelligent and attractive fellow student who was to become a famous feminist writer. Sartre was infatuated, and Simone was overwhelmed by the 5-ft. 4-in, walleyed man with the tremendous intellect. They quickly became lovers and began a relationship that would last over 50 years. However, Sartre hated what he called "bourgeois marriage" and renounced the institution along with parenthood. During the early years of their romance, Sartre and Simone discussed extensively their ideas about love, commitment, marriage, and sex. They agreed that their relationship would be an open one in which they would support each other in times of need, but also allow each other "contingent loves."

In 1934, while studying in Berlin, Sartre exercised his rights for the first time and had an affair with Marie, the young wife of another student. Back in Paris for Christmas, Sartre informed Simone of the affair. By February, Simone told the supervisor where she was teaching that she was having a nervous breakdown and needed a leave of absence. Heading directly for Berlin, she met Marie, and her fears were removed when Marie and Sartre explained that theirs was only a temporary relationship which did not threaten Sartre's commitment to Simone.

Back in Paris, Simone took one of her students under her wing, tutoring her and allowing her to live in her apartment. When Sartre returned to Paris, he also took a liking to this Russian emigrant teenager named Olga Kosakiewicz. At this time Sartre experimented with mescaline and for months after had temporary hallucinations. Olga would accompany Sartre on walks during which he would vividly describe giant lobsters that were following them. This nurse-patient relationship developed into a sexual relationship and a subsequent living arrangement that included Simone. In her autobiographical novel, *She Came to Stay*, Simone tells how the younger woman usurped her lover and states, "There is something absolutely valid and true in jealousy." Finally, after four years, Olga found another lover and left Sartre. However, Simone and Sartre continued to support Olga, emotionally and financially, for the next 30 years.

During the second half of the 1940s, Simone had an affair with American writer Nelson Algren. This affair seems to have rid her of jealousy and also rejuvenated her sexually. She wrote, "His lust transfigured me; I who for so long had had no taste, no form, I again possessed breasts, a belly, a sex; flesh." At the same time Sartre, who never seems to have been afflicted with any jealousy, had an affair with a New York woman identified only as Dolores.

Although they had their "contingent loves," Sartre and Simone always nurtured their own relationship. But during the 1950s the couple moved farther apart then they had ever been before. Simone developed a relationship with Claude Lanzmann, a journalist who was 17 years younger than she. Although de Beauvoir and Sartre still traveled together, Simone lived with Lanzmann.

Sartre, who constantly sought female companions, explained his behavior by stating, "But the main reason I surround myself with women is simply that I prefer their company to that of men. As a rule I find men boring." Therefore, while Simone was cohabiting with Lanzmann, Sartre chose as his companion a 17-year-old Jewish Algerian girl named Arlette Elkaim. When Sartre almost married Arlette to protect her from deportation and because he thought her pregnant, the relationship between Sartre and Simone was nearly destroyed. However, Sartre did not marry the girl but instead adopted her, which improved communications with Simone.

After Lanzmann left Simone in 1958, Sartre and she became constant companions, more deeply in love than they had ever been before. During the last two decades of Sartre's life, they traveled together and took care of each other. Their unique, 51-year love affair ended when Sartre died with Simone at his bedside.

HIS THOUGHTS: "The association of a man with a woman always has sexual implications."

"Relations with a woman—even if one is not sleeping with her, but if one has slept with her, or if one could have—are richer."

—*R.J.F.*

Pessimist With Passion

ARTHUR SCHOPENHAUER (Feb. 22, 1788–Sept. 21, 1860)

HIS FAME: Called "the Philosopher of Pessimism," Arthur Schopenhauer is best known for his book *The World as Will and Idea*, in which he challenged the dominant idealism of his time with the concept of the "will to live" as the prime mover of human life and the basic cause of human suffering.

HIS LIFE: Physically, Arthur Schopenhauer fit the stereotype of a serious philosopher, small and slightly built, with a large head and piercing blue eyes, and always well dressed. He was a man of intense moods, extreme pride, and little patience for anyone who dared to disagree with him.

Both his parents were headstrong, intelligent, and short-tempered. His mother, Johanna, was jealous of her son's talents, and they fought constantly. Once she threw him down the stairs in a fit of rage. His father, Heinrich, was a stern, successful Danzig businessman who apparently committed suicide in 1805. Schopenhauer had admired his father and tried to continue the family business, but he hated it. When his mother encouraged him to study philosophy, he eagerly became a student. The widowed Johanna moved to Weimar, "the city of poets," where she became a popular novelist and salon hostess. Although disapproving of her "frivolous" lifestyle, the young Schopenhauer followed her to Weimar in 1813. He was shocked to find a young man, Müller von Gerstenberg, living in her house. Despite Johanna's insistance that theirs was a platonic friendship, in her son's eyes she had committed a grave sin: indiscretion. He told her, "Choose between Von Gerstenberg and me!" She chose Von Gerstenberg, and Schopenhauer never saw his mother again.

LOVE LIFE: At the same time he was battling with his mother in Weimar, Schopenhauer had a quiet affair with Karoline Jägermann, leading actress at the Court Theater and the recognized mistress of Duke Karl August. Few details are known of their relationship, except that Schopenhauer thought of her more romantically than of any other woman in his life. He wrote, "I would take her home though I found her breaking stones in the street."

When *The World as Will and Idea* was published, Schopenhauer moved to Italy. There he indulged his strong sensual nature. Believing that sexual passion was "the most distinct expression of the will," he gave it free rein, admitting, "I am not a saint." In Italy, where "the only sin is not to sin," he met a rich, distinguished, and beautiful woman, known today only as Teresa. He considered marriage, meticulously weighing her faults and virtues, but decided against it when she embarrassed him publicly by swooning over another man, Lord Byron. Schopenhauer wrote, "I was afraid of the horns of cuckoldry."

Schopenhauer returned to Germany to teach at the University of Berlin, but his lectures drew minuscule audiences. In Berlin he was sued for personal injury by a middle-aged seamstress, Caroline Marquet, whom he had physically thrown out of the anteroom of his apartment because she had repeatedly irritated him by sewing there. She won the case, and he was forced to pay damages for the rest of her life. After the incident, he left again for Italy. His misogyny was becoming more apparent as he made love to many women, regarding them all with contempt. For him the sexual impulse was "a demon that strives to pervert, confine, and overthrow everything," and he held women accountable for the resulting havoc. His philosophy explained love as a deceit played by Nature to suit her only purpose: procreation. "It is only the man whose intellect is clouded by his sexual impulse that could give the name of the fair sex to the undersized, narrow-shouldered, broad-hipped, and short-legged race." Despising and pitying women, he saw them as possessing only one virtue: the allure of youth, soon to fade after the pretty face and full breasts had enticed a man into marriage. He could be charming, though, to the younger and prettier ladies, with his mastery of languages and literature and occasional magic tricks.

After one happy year he retreated to Munich, deathly ill with syphilis. Bedridden for many months, Schopenhauer feared the disease would destroy what he valued most: his mind. Recovered, he wrote an article in which he presented his theory of tetragamy. The theory advocated that two men share a woman as a wife until she was past childbearing age. At that point they should marry a second young woman, while continuing to care for their first wife. Later, his essay "On Women" (published in book form as *Parerga* in 1851) established for all time his reputation as a woman hater.

Yet, he never banished women from his life. In his journal he wrote of a "Fraulein Medon," an actress of great charm. He courted and won her and again thought of marriage. In his careful analysis, she was "quite satisfactory" either as a lover or as a wife. But once again his caution and cynicism emerged. He was in love, but he was also a philosopher. His pessimism won and the notion of marriage was dropped. For Schopenhauer, absolute confidence in the immortality of his work was more meaningful than any children he could have left behind. He died alone, at 72, of a lung hemorrhage.

HIS THOUGHTS: "The relation of the sexes is the invisible central point of all action and conduct. It is the cause of war and the end of peace." Even though Schopenhauer resented his desires, he never denied them. "The more I see of men the less I like them; if I could but say so of women too, all would be well."

—*C.L.W. and L.S.*

XVI

Play For Pay

The Epicurean Delight

NINON DE LENCLOS (May, 1620–Oct. 17, 1705)

HER FAME: Ninon was the most celebrated French courtesan of her day. She lived according to the philosophy of Epicurus, placing more importance on the quality of life's pleasures than on the quantity. Still, in a span of 20 years she managed to fill her carnal dance card with the names of 4,959 men.

HER PERSON: Ninon's father was a musician and a pimp who educated his daughter in all things worldly. By age 12 she could dance, play the harpsichord, and appreciate good literature. In addition to the social graces, Ninon studied the complexities of human relationships, both sexual and platonic, and resolved early on to resist the traditional female role. "I soon saw that women were put off with the most frivolous and unreal privileges, while every solid advantage was retained by the stronger sex. From that moment I determined on abandoning my sex and assuming that of the men." Her parents died before she turned 20; fortunately, she was more than prepared to face the cold, cruel world alone.

Financed by admirers, Ninon established a salon in Paris, where she entertained the most prominent literary and political figures of 17th-century France. In addition, she founded a "school of gallantry" for aristocratic boys, whom she taught basic Epicureanism and the art of pleasing a woman. "Men lose more hearts by awkwardness than virtue preserves," she told her young pupils.

Her looks were striking—a perfect oval face topped by reddish-blond ringlets; thick black eyebrows and dark eyes; and a body that inspired poets and painters. According to legend, she was visited on her 18th birthday by a mysterious old man, who offered her a choice from among three gifts—the highest rank, immeasurable riches, or eternal beauty. Supposedly, Ninon chose the last and lived her 85 years like an unfading rose. In truth, she aged gracefully, but she aged nonetheless. When she died, she punctuated her long career as a progressive thinker with one last gesture—willing money for books to young Voltaire.

SEX LIFE: Ninon loved eroticism but shunned outright debauchery. To her, love-making was an art, not to be sullied by low behavior. Her salon was not a hotbed of free love. On the contrary, it was quite respectable to be a member of Ninon's inner circle, where art and philosophy were the principal topics of discussion.

She did not sleep with all her admirers. The playwright Molière and the philosopher Saint-Évremond, for instance, maintained only a platonic relationship with Ninon. The rest of her male friends fell into three groups—payers, martyrs, and favorites. The payers supported her in exchange for visiting rights, but their visits were rare because Ninon did not favor these men. When she eventually achieved financial independence, she dismissed her payers. The martyrs haunted her salon and awaited her caprice, while the favorites shared her bed for as long as she willed. Ninon routinely broke off her affairs at their peak. This way, both she and her lover retained nothing but pleasant memories of the relationship.

Ninon's disregard for religion prompted King Louis XIV's mother, Anne of Austria, to have her confined in a monastery. Ninon's friends quickly obtained her release, but there is no evidence that she was in a hurry to leave. Of her nearly 5,000 recorded lovers, 439 were monks.

It was rumored that Ninon maintained a very active love life until her death. Actually, she retired as a courtesan at about age 50, thereafter amusing herself with occasional sexual adventures.

SEX PARTNERS: When Ninon was a tender 15 years old, she succumbed to the persuasive powers of a man named Saint-Étienne, a notorious seducer of virgins. However, once Ninon lost her virginity, Saint-Étienne was no longer interested in her. She next became infatuated with the handsome Chevalier de Raré, who charmed her with his soulful eyes. They vented their passion when and where they could, pausing once in a doorway to kiss and grope one another while a beggar looked on. Ninon broke off the affair when her mother's health began to worsen and there was little time left for romance.

After her mother's death, Ninon began to accept money from her first "payer," Coulon, a drunkard whom she found disagreeable. At about this time, she met her first real love, Gaspard de Coligny. To her great disappointment, she found Coligny completely inadequate as a lover, lacking both stamina and technique. She later learned that Coligny was more enthusiastic in bed with his own sex. He eventually left her to return to his "pretty boys."

Determined to place in her favor the odds of finding a virile lover, Ninon simultaneously carried on affairs with the Abbé Dessiat and the Maréchal d'Estrées. However, when Ninon became pregnant, the question of paternity had to be settled by a toss of the dice. Thus, the Maréchal d'Estrées was named as father of Ninon's first child. She was said to have also given birth to a child by the Chevalier de Méré, who was over 70 years old when he courted her. Advanced age was seldom a barrier to Ninon, who reportedly had the power to resurrect even a long-dead libido.

As a rule, Ninon retained a "favorite" for a few months at the most. The Marquis de Villarceaux was an exception; she lived at his country estate for three years and once spent eight days in bed with him, allegedly to speed his recovery from a long illness. After she had broken off the affair, she recommended Villarceaux to a friend, Madame Scarron (later Madame de Maintenon, wife and mistress to Louis XIV), who was greatly in need of sexual fulfillment. The woman's marriage to writer

Paul Scarron, another friend of Ninon's, was clouded by her overpowering inhibitions and her husband's progressive paralysis. Ninon came to the woman's rescue with the right man at the right time. It was not the first time she had set up a female friend with an ex-lover. She routinely advised Madame de la Suze on the sexual expertise of various men, and Ninon's evaluations were always highly accurate.

Two men who ranked low on Ninon's list of competent lovers were soldiers, the Comte de Navailles and the Duc d'Enghien. Navailles fell asleep while she was preparing for bed, so she donned his uniform and crawled under the covers with him. Navailles awakened with a start, and what followed is not known. What is certain, however, is the fact that Ninon never again took a blond man as a lover. Enghien managed to stay awake, but in spite of his reputation as a formidable warrior, he failed her on the bedroom battlefield. Afterwards, she quoted to him a classical maxim: "A hairy man is either passionate or strong." Then she added, "You must be very strong."

The Comte de Sévigné likewise rated poorly in Ninon's estimation. She deliberately seduced him in order to aggravate his lover, an actress of whom Ninon was jealous. But the attraction was purely political, for she found the count to be "a man impossible to define … a soul of boiled beef, a body of damp paper, with a heart like a pumpkin fricasseed in snow." Her victory won, she quickly dumped him.

A persistent but probably apocryphal story has it that a tragic incident occurred to Ninon when she was in her 60s, after she had retired from the courtesan life. She still received a few young men, the sons of close friends, and educated them in gentlemanly virtues. One of them, the son of Monsieur de Gersay, fell in love with Ninon. She had the best of reasons for discouraging his attentions; he was in fact her son. The boy was unaware of his true parentage, because Ninon had insisted that De Gersay keep it a secret. She tried to thwart the young man's attentions by pleading advanced age. She called his passion for her "ridiculous" and sent him away. But she soon called him back, having decided to reveal the true nature of their relationship. Before she could speak, though, he began again to profess his love. Ninon angrily protested, "This dreadful love cannot go on. Do you realize who you are and who I am?" She then told him. Taken aback, he repeated the word *mother*, went out into Ninon's garden, and fell on his sword, killing himself.

—*M.J.T.*

"The Beautiful Little Thing"

VIRGINIA OLDOINI, COUNTESS DI CASTIGLIONE
(Mar. 22, 1837–Nov. 28, 1899)

HER FAME: Regarded in the courts of Turin and Paris, and in London society, as the most beautiful woman of her time, the countess was a secret agent in France representing those who fought for the unification of Italy.

HER PERSON: Born in Florence, Italy, "Nicchia" Oldoini was the product of a noble but disinterested father and an ailing mother. She was raised amid wealth and luxury in a Florentine palace by her grandfather, a renowned jurist and scholar named Lamporecchi. As Nicchia matured, it became evident to all eyes that she had the looks of a goddess. At 18 she was chosen by her cousin, Premier Camillo Benso di Cavour, and King Victor Emmanuel II, of Sardinia, to represent their cause in France. Their cause was to bring together the small states of Italy into one nation. But they could not do it alone. Austria controlled northern Italy. King Victor Emmanuel II and Cavour needed the help of France. And to obtain this help they sent the Countess di Castiglione to seduce Napoleon III, the emperor of France.

The countess fulfilled her mission. Her dazzling beauty made her the sensation of Paris. She was partially responsible for encouraging Napoleon's army to go to war against the Austrians in Italy. By 1861, with the help of Giuseppe Garibaldi, Italy was one nation and Victor Emmanuel II was its king.

SEX LIFE: The young Countess di Castiglione was clever and witty, but basically she was cold, arrogant, egocentric, selfish, and spoiled. Despite her endless sexual activity, she did not enjoy sex as a carnal delight. She enjoyed sex as a means of humbling men, using them.

Few men could resist her breathtaking beauty. She had rich brown hair, slanted blue eyes, parted lips ("like an opening crimson flower"), a dimpled chin, a perfect body ("faultless in its symmetry"). Attending balls at the Empress Eugénie's prim crinoline court and elsewhere, the countess used her state of undress as a lure. At a ball given by the Count Walewski, France's new foreign minister, Nicchia entered attired as the Queen of Hearts, a strip of gauze across her breasts with two hearts sewed on to hide her nipples, and a transparent skirt with a heart sewn on to cover her vaginal mound. But her pubic hair could clearly be seen, provoking Empress Eugénie to remark acidly, "Countess, your heart seems a little low."

SEX PARTNERS: Nicchia got off to a fast start when she was 16. Her first lover was an Italian naval officer, Marquis Ambrogio Doria. Shortly after, she took his brothers, Andrea and Marcello, to bed. About this time she started a diary, with her sexual activities kept carefully in code: "B—a kiss; BX—beyond a kiss; F—everything!" Her family was worried about *F* and decided to get her married. Just then an eligible young nobleman, searching for a bride and advised to have a look at Nicchia, showed up. He was Conte Francesco Verasis di Castiglione, an aide to King Victor Emmanuel II. Her family forced her to marry the count in January, 1854. She found him to be a weakling, and told everyone, "I am married to an imbecile." She slept with him until they had a child, a son named George, and then she refused to share his bed again. Bored, she frittered away the count's fortune; in fact, she put him 2 million francs in debt. By now, Premier Cavour had discovered that his cousin, the new countess, could be most useful if she were put to seducing Napoleon III. He outlined his scheme to King Victor Emmanuel II. The king had to be convinced of Nicchia's wonders firsthand. He tried her out in bed and pronounced her satisfactory. Leaving behind her bankrupt husband and infant child, the countess was off to Paris in November, 1855. (She did not see her husband again until 12 years later, when she returned to Italy for the wedding of the king's son. At the wedding her husband, riding his horse alongside the bridal coach, tumbled off his mount and was crushed to death by the wheels of the carriage.)

Upon her first arrival in Paris, the countess was 18 years old. Invited to a fancy-dress ball at the Tuileries, she made a memorable entrance. Attired in a low-cut tight gown, she was the center of all attention. The guards, ushers, and servants all fell back to make way for her. Some male guests clambered atop tables for a sight of her. Johann Strauss, conducting a waltz, stopped the music. Emperor Napoleon III, deep in conversation with the British ambassador, abruptly excused himself and asked her for the next dance.

After that, Louis Napoleon began to woo the countess. He presented her with a house in the Rue de la Pompe. He gave her a 100,000-franc emerald and a 442,000-franc pearl necklace. He visited her house almost nightly. The countess was flirtatious but played hard to get. After months of wooing, Louis Napoleon invited her to Compiègne, his château outside Paris. During a theatrical presentation, one evening, she excused herself to the emperor and empress, pleading a headache. Shortly after, the solicitous emperor visited her room and found her in bed wearing her most fashionable gray batiste and lace nightgown. He undressed and slipped into bed with her. Not long before, the emperor had complained to his physician that sexual intercourse no longer "contributed to his sound sleep." But that night he slept soundly.

They made love regularly for over a year. She became known as "the woman with the cunt of imperial gold." In court circles it was generally believed that she had presented Louis Napoleon with a son, who grew up to be the well-known Paris dentist Dr. Hugenschmidt. Gradually, as the affair progressed, the emperor's ardor cooled. He told one friend, "She talks about herself too much. She has bandied about our relationship. She allows herself to be seen in bed by all and sundry wearing monogrammed underwear that I had sent her." One night in 1859, an Italian tried to assassinate Louis Napoleon in her bedroom. A bodyguard saved the emperor. Days later, the Countess di Castiglione was deported from France.

Back in Italy, the countess wrote King Victor Emmanuel II, "If you want me, call me." The king replied, "I want you." He set her up as his mistress in the Pitti Palace in Florence and gave her a pension of 12,000 francs a year. After two years, and the intercession of French friends, Louis Napoleon allowed her to return to Paris. While no longer his official mistress, she became what he called one of his "little diversions." This was not enough for her. She began to entertain many men in her bed. The only qualifications required: a noble birth or wealth. She slept with the French foreign minister, Prince Henri de la Tour d'Auvergne, for four years. But other lovers overlapped. A senior member of the richest family in the world, 70-year-old Baron James de Rothschild, fell in love with her. A lady friend advised her, "Try to keep alive the passion of the old baron, maybe you will profit richly by it. Make available 'the beautiful little thing.'" The countess finally had sex with the old baron, and then also made herself available to his three sons. Her most incredible coupling was with the eccentric British millionaire, the fourth Marquis of Hertford. He wrote her: "Give me one night of love, without excluding any erotic refinements, in exchange for a million francs." The price for a single night of her favors amused the countess. She accepted. She did not know that Hertford was a stallion. Once in her bed, he made love to her nonstop the entire night. After he left, she was a wreck, unable to leave her bed for three days.

In a letter, Nicchia's husband had once warned her, "The day will come when your fatal beauty will have disappeared and the flatterers will be rarer." The countess dreaded that day. At the age of 40 she took a ground-floor apartment in the Place Vendôme, shuttered the windows, covered all mirrors. She admitted no friends, no relatives, dabbled in spiritualism, and taught her pet dogs, Kasino and Sandouga, to waltz. She never went out in daylight, took her dogs walking only at night. She sat alone in her unkempt dark rooms with her memories, deluding herself into believing she was ill and impoverished. She was neither. One night she was discovered dead of cerebral apoplexy, with rats gnawing at her body. At her instructions, she was buried wearing the gray batiste and lace nightgown she had worn at Compiègne the night she gave herself to the emperor, with her two pet dogs stuffed and placed at her feet in the coffin.

—I.W.

Royal Favorite

LA BELLE OTERO (Nov. 4, 1868–Apr. 10, 1965)

HER FAME: Often called the last of the great courtesans, La Belle Otero (or Caroline Otero) was the professional name of Augustina Otero Iglesias, from Valga, a hamlet in Galician Spain. Officially she was a dancer, singer, and actress in the world's music halls, but in reality she was mistress to some of the most famous men in the world. During her lifetime she made and lost approximately $25 million.

HER PERSON: The illiterate daughter of the town prostitute, Otero grew up in poverty without a father. At the age of 11 she was brutally raped by the village shoemaker, who had become excited by watching her dance. The rape left her with a broken pelvis, permanently unable to bear children. She departed Valga the next year and wandered to Barcelona, realizing, like so many young girls before her, that prostitution was the only way to survive.

When she was 14, she met a Catalan named Paco Colli, who had been a dancer all his life. He taught Otero the ways of the stage—dancing, singing, acting—and performed as her pimp, since she had to continue sleeping with men in order to support Paco and herself. Paco also took her to the French Riviera, where in 1889 he decided to marry her. She declined his proposal and instead became a music hall star and courtesan until she retired more than 25 years later.

During her heyday Otero was as famous as any star Hollywood would later produce. Of her American debut on Oct. 1, 1890, the New York *Tribune* headline declared: OTERO CONQUERS NEW YORK. A reviewer for *The New York Times* marveled, "She appears to dance all over. Every muscle, from her dainty toes to the crown of her head, is brought into play, and the consequent contortions are wonderful and, at times, startling." Acton Davies, writing for the New York *Sun*, dissented, saying, "We have seen Otero sing, we have heard her dance."

She was a compulsive gambler and occasionally mixed business with pleasure. An employee at the casino in Monte Carlo maintained that Otero, running low on funds, went to bed at a nearby hotel with 11 men in a 24-hour period. He added that she never spent more than a half hour away from the gaming tables during this marathon. In her lifetime, she lost an estimated $20 million at the casino. Asked what she would have done with that money if she hadn't been a gambler, Otero replied, "I might have endowed a university for prostitutes. Think of the variety of courses we could have offered."

SEX LIFE: People said that she was a nymphomaniac, or that she sought to punish men in retaliation for her childhood rape. In any case, Otero was a strikingly beautiful woman, around 5 ft. 10 in. tall, with measurements of 38-21-36. Her face was symmetrically oval, her hair black and silky, her teeth pearly white. Her friend, French writer Colette, said that Otero's breasts "were of curious shape, reminding one of elongated lemons, firm and upturned at the tips." An anonymous source added that Otero's breasts "preceded her by a quarter of an hour." The touch of foul language in her speech titillated her patrons, and she believed in always making a man feel like a king in the bedroom, whether he was royalty or not. During her prime, Otero charged $10,000, or the equivalent in jewelry, for a night of her services.

SEX PARTNERS: According to Otero's autobiography, on Nov. 4, 1898, a group of men with whom Otero had been having profitable affairs for several years gathered to give her a birthday party. The guest list was impressive, including King Leopold II of Belgium, Prince Nicholas I of Montenegro, Prince Albert of Monaco, the Grand Duke Nicholas of Russia, and Albert, Prince of Wales, who would become King Edward VII of the United Kingdom.

Otero made love with Baron Lepic in a hot-air balloon floating 200 ft. over the Aube River near Provins, France. On June 15, 1902, the New York *World* reported that "the gondola remained high above the earth for more than an hour." Sixty years later, Otero purred, "It was an experience *every* woman should enjoy."

Otero did not limit herself to royalty. William K. Vanderbilt, of the famous (and rich) American family, offered Otero a yacht and showered her with $250,000 worth of jewels, including a pearl necklace Napoleon III had given the Empress Eugénie.

Her five-year affair with the Muzaffar-ed-Din, shah of Persia, netted Otero a stream of jewels. "He was a dirty, smelly old man, and very strange in his desires," she recalled. "He visited me every afternoon at two o'clock and left at five. Ten minutes later one of his servants would be at the door to hand my maid a gold, inlaid cassette, lined with velvet. It contained a single jewel but a very magnificent stone—diamond, ruby, pearl, jade, or emerald, some worth as much as 25,000 francs. I would remove the jewel and return the box."

For her part, Otero later wrote that she did not always enjoy sex with her men, but she was unfailingly hospitable. In the 1890s, Prince Albert of Monaco earned low marks because he had trouble getting an erection. After a night of conversation, he finally did, and Otero exaggerated the truth to tell him he was "formidable"—whereupon he "strutted around the room." The grateful Albert set her up in a choice apartment and gave her more than $300,000 worth of gems. "He was not a very virile man and I don't think he got his money's worth," Otero concluded. "But as long as he didn't care, neither did I, and he seemed to enjoy taking me where we could be seen together publicly."

In 1894 Prince Nicholas of Montenegro (who would become his country's first and last king) moved into the apartment Albert had given Otero. The tall, slender prince was in his early 50s, and their relationship lasted for several years. After presenting Otero with "a simply gorgeous diamond bracelet and at least five ... beautiful watches," he persuaded her to visit his palace in 1897. Otero later complained, "I saw practically nothing the whole trip ... all the prince wanted to do was to make love to me so I obliged."

Sixty-year-old King Leopold II of Belgium "was not very generous at the start but I taught him how to give. He was an apt student." They met in 1894 and were part-time lovers for three or four years. Leopold, said Otero, "gave me my own small villa by the sea" at Ostend, in west Flanders, then an exclusive summer resort.

One of the richest men in the world, Nicholas II, czar of Russia, had a bad complexion and rarely bathed. "He really stank," said Otero, and was still shaken from an assassination attempt that had occurred six years earlier. "There were always a half-dozen huge, black-bearded armed guards at our bedroom door, some more at every window, and if there was a rear exit, he'd have half a regiment posted there. It almost felt like I was undressing in an army barracks or a bullfighting arena. If I happened to move a chair suddenly or drop a perfume bottle, Nick would jump out of bed screaming with fright." But Otero "grew quite fond of him" even though "he had the strangest views about sex."

When she returned to Paris in September of 1897, the Prince of Wales was waiting for her. "He was surprisingly virile and generous," but he had to stand her up one night in London when his official mistress, Lillie Langtry, arrived unexpectedly.

The Khedive of Cairo saw her perform and, after three torrid days in his palace, gave her a 10-carat diamond ring with a setting of 12 pearls worth half a million francs at the time.

On a visit to Monte Carlo in 1905, Otero "deflowered" 19-year-old King Alfonso XIII of Spain. "He was rather aloof at first," she remembered, "but I taught him how to relax." In 1913, at the age of 27, he set the 44-year-old Otero up in Madrid in the last apartment she would ever occupy courtesy of a royal client.

Otero's 40th birthday had found her with a new lover, Aristide Briand, who would become one of France's greatest statesmen and win the 1926 Nobel Peace Prize. Otero must have sensed his coming greatness, because his appearance did not foretell such a future: "He was … hideously ugly. He was fat. He dressed like a slob—often there'd be remains of an omelet on his vest, his nails were black, but there was a fascination to him I never found in any other man." He could only afford "an occasional cheap jewel and flowers," Otero recalled. "Once … he made love to me eight times before morning. And he was 50 years old at the time." Their affair lasted 10 years.

When La Belle Otero retired in 1914, she had amassed a fortune, and for a while the money kept coming, occasionally from secret benefactors. In 1935, at age 66, she was still beautiful, but age eventually crept up on her, and her money disappeared in the casinos. She was alone when she died of a heart attack at age 96 in Nice, France, but she never had any regrets about her life.

HER THOUGHTS: "I have been a slave to my passions, but never to a man."
—A.L.G. and L.S.

Uncultured Pearl

CORA PEARL (1835–July 8, 1886)

HER FAME: Despite her poor manners, incomprehensible French, and penchant for cruel practical jokes, Cora Pearl enjoyed a long reign as the most popular courtesan in the Paris of Napoleon III.

HER PERSON: Cora was born Emma Elizabeth Crouch to a family of 16 children in Devonshire, England. Her father was a musical director and the composer of "Kathleen Mavourneen," a popular ballad of the time, which he sold for £20 to a publisher who earned £15,000 from it. Cora, however, did not sell her wares so cheaply, and the time came when a single night with her cost 10,000 francs.

The age at which Cora began her mercenary career is uncertain, but she was apparently young enough to be lured into a low-class pub by promises of sweets. There, a merchant gave the naive girl her first taste of gin. When she woke up in his bed the following morning, he compensated her with a £5 note. Thus, she had inadvertently begun her career. That same day she left home and soon began an apprenticeship in a London brothel. From there she moved to Paris, where she worked independently. Among her customers were the wealthiest and most powerful men of her day, whom she collectively called her "Golden Chain" of lovers. Later in life, Cora wrote her memoirs and sent excerpts to former clients, offering to delete certain parts in exchange for money. The extortion scheme was apparently a success, for the published version made dull reading.

Cora was fond of practical jokes. She once lured a prominent Parisian into a compromising position in her bedroom, only to throw open the closet doors and reveal a contingent of his friends. Another time Cora hosted a dinner party at which she was brought out naked on a silver platter in order to win a bet. She had wagered that she could serve "a meat nobody could cut."

Her face was plain, but she had beautiful skin and hair and her body was one of the most perfect in France. With it she earned a vast fortune. Ironically, when Cora died of cancer at the age of 51, she was penniless and alone.

SEX LIFE: Cora arrived in Paris in 1858 with the proprietor of the Argyle Rooms, a seedy London brothel where she had perfected her bedroom skills. The trip was for pleasure rather than business, but duty eventually called and Cora's patron returned to England without her. She took up with a sailor for a while, and when he shipped out she was fortunate enough to meet a mysterious man known as "Roubisse," who procured for her the first in her golden chain of clients.

For six years she was the mistress of Victor Massena, third Duc de Rivoli. The staid aristocrat indulged her every whim, yet Cora later described Massena as "the man who received the least in return." Throughout their relationship, which ended in 1869 when Massena drifted out of her life, she had many other lovers. One of these was 17-year-old Prince Achille Murat, a grandnephew of Napoleon I. While the young man was not rich, Cora helped him run through what money he did have. He fought (and won) a duel over Cora's bills once, and got so badly into debt that Emperor Napoleon III sent him to Africa.

Once Cora herself fought a duel, with Marthe de Vère, a fellow courtesan, over a good-looking Serbian prince. Riding whips were used as weapons. Both Cora and Marthe remained in seclusion for a week to let the wounds on their faces heal. The prince, in the meantime, disappeared.

After Murat, the next link in Cora's golden chain was William, Prince of Orange, heir to the throne of the Netherlands. The Prince of Orange had little to his credit besides money, and Cora found him tiresome. However, a woman who would bathe nude in a champagne-filled silver tub in front of her dinner guests might easily find many men tiresome.

Cora was ice-skating one day when she was picked up by the Duc de Morny, the second most powerful man in France, the emperor's half brother. "Cora on the ice?" he said to her. "What an antithesis!" She replied, "Well, since the ice is broken, take me for a drink." De Morny was a stepping-stone to Prince Napoleon, "Plon-Plon" to his friends, who fell madly in love with Cora. The prince installed her in a grand house and gave her a monthly allowance of 12,000 francs. But her barnyard manners and cockney-accented French annoyed the prince at times, as did her habit of entertaining hordes of men. During one party, when Cora was the only woman at a table full of male admirers, she coyly remarked, "There is only one of you with whom I am still a virgin."

Although there is no conclusive evidence that Plon-Plon's cousin, Napoleon III, was among Cora's lovers, it is reasonable to assume that he was. It was a rare man indeed who did not sample Cora's perfect body. She was a sexual common denominator, a conversation piece when men talked among themselves, and it is unlikely that the emperor overlooked her.

For a time all Paris was buzzing with the tragic story of one of Cora's lovers, Alexandre Duval, a gentleman with a fortune of 10 million francs. Duval showered Cora with gifts of carriages, horses, jewelry, furnishings, and other expensive items. He once gave her a book, which she contemptuously tossed aside, not realizing that its 100 pages consisted of 1,000-franc bank notes. Despite the lavish presents, Cora treated Duval with disdain. And when he eventually shot himself in her house, Cora coldly remarked, "The dirty pig. He fucked up my beautiful rug!" Duval recovered at length from both the bullet wound and his near fatal devotion to Cora.

Cora's spurned lovers might have been gratified to see her in her later years— hungry, homeless, hustling cheap tricks in the slums. An English journalist, Julian B. Arnold, stumbled upon Cora in Monte Carlo, where she sat weeping on a curbstone. Taking pity on her, Arnold took her home to his villa until he could arrange for her transportation to Paris. That night as Arnold sat reading in his study, Cora entered in a dressing gown. She let the gown fall to the floor and stood naked before him. "A woman's vanity," she said, "should be my sufficient excuse. I found it difficult to rest until I had shown you that, if Cora Pearl has lost all else, she still retains that which made her famous—a form of loveliness."

HER THOUGHTS: "I may say I have never had a preferred lover.... A handsome, young, and amiable man who has loyally offered me his arms, his love, and his money has every right to think and call himself my favorite lover, my lover for an hour, my escort for a month, and my friend forever. That is how I understand the business."

—M.S.

XVII

Everybody's Doing It

Philosopher Of Love

NATALIE BARNEY (Oct. 31, 1876–Feb. 12, 1972)

HER FAME: The leading lesbian of her time, Barney was a writer of epigrams, memoirs, and poetry, but she was most widely known for her affairs and intrigues with beautiful, brilliant, and famous women, and for her salon, which was a meeting place for an international cultural elite for more than 60 years.

HER PERSON: Known as *"l'Amazone"* ("the Amazon") because of Remy de Gourmont's immortalization of her in his *Lettres à l'Amazone*, Natalie was raised in Cincinnati, O. She had an early predilection for all things French and could speak

Barney (r) and friend

the language perfectly while still a child. Born into the "fabulous Barney fortune" (her grandparents on both sides were industrial magnates), Natalie was able to make trips abroad at an early age. At 11 she was placed in a French boarding school, where she realized she was a lesbian: "My only books / Were women's looks." Back in America, she was whisked around high-society circles in Washington, D.C., until she had made her debut and was free to settle in Paris. At 32 she bought the townhouse at 20 rue Jacob (the street on which courtesan Ninon de Lenclos had lived two centuries earlier) which was to become the most famous literary salon of her time. Known for its cucumber sandwiches and chocolate cakes, it boasted such regulars as Anatole France, Paul Valéry, André Gide, Gertrude Stein, and Ezra Pound. Once Mata Hari arrived, completely naked, on a bejeweled white horse. Though some of Natalie's writing was favorably received, she was much like her friend Oscar Wilde, who said, "I've put my genius into my life; I've put only my talent into my works." Radclyffe Hall's *The Well of Loneliness*, Liane de Pougy's *Idylle Saphique* ("Sapphic Idyll"), and most of Renée Vivien's poetry were but a few of the literary works Natalie inspired.

SEX LIFE: Composed, willful, and independent, Natalie Barney saw her life as a series of love affairs. Having learned to masturbate in the bathtub, she was a sensualist at an early age. As she put it: "Yes, at 12 I knew exactly what I liked and I firmly decided not to let myself be diverted from my tastes." Though not conventionally beautiful, she was bewitching, with a head of long, untamed blond hair, small breasts, and piercing blue eyes. She wore long flowing gowns, which were usually white. Many men courted her assiduously, but Barney remained a "friend of men, lover of women." She enjoyed feminine women, once remarking, "Why try to resemble our enemies?" She would have sex at any time, and often in unusual places or circumstances; in fields and streams, in theater boxes, or with two women at a time, and she had an unquenchable thirst for conquest. Sometimes when lovers became disgusted with Natalie's unfaithfulness, they would try to resist her, but they rarely succeeded. As one ex-lover, who had sworn off lesbianism and married, said after seeing Natalie: "[For a few minutes] I committed the delicious sin of abandoning myself to her caresses." The Amazon was notoriously good at what she did.

SEX PARTNERS: Barney's liaisons numbered over 40, not including countless casual affairs. She had her first physical relationship when she was 16, and had several others before her first famous affair at 22, when she courted and won the fabulously beautiful Liane de Pougy. Liane was the most famous courtesan of the period, and the two women carried on a passionate affair in between Liane's trips with princes and various nobility who required her services. Years after, when Liane had married a prince, she allowed Natalie to caress her only above the waist. Later Natalie was to say that Liane had been her "greatest sensual pleasure," whereas Liane, turning pious, called Natalie her "greatest sin." During one of Liane's absences, Natalie met and fell in love with Renée Vivien, a brilliant poet who was morbidly obsessed with the idea of death. Renée could not tolerate Natalie's promiscuity and eventually refused to see her anymore, whereupon Natalie resorted to such pranks as dressing in white and having herself delivered to Renée's door in a white satin coffin. Renée came to be unaffected by such dramatics and died a few years later of what Colette termed "voluntary consumption" (she weighed 65 lb.), but by then Natalie had gained her reputation as a *femme fatale*.

After Renée Vivien, Natalie took a host of other lovers, who sometimes stayed simultaneously at 20 rue Jacob. Her greatest problem was keeping peace within the harem. Dolly Wilde, who in both looks and wit resembled her uncle Oscar, would shut herself up in her room with drugs and alcohol when Natalie betrayed her; once she slit her wrists and was nursed by Natalie's maid. When in better spirits, Dolly enlivened Natalie's salons with her witty remarks. Dolly was ousted, however, when Romaine Brooks, an American painter living in Paris, jealously ordered Natalie to get rid of Dolly. When Romaine spoke, Natalie obeyed.

Romaine was Natalie's longest and most serious relationship. They met as both neared their 40s, and remained together—living sometimes apart, sometimes in adjoining houses—for over 50 years. But even as an octogenarian, Natalie had a wandering eye. At 82 she met and seduced a 58-year-old woman who was formerly the heterosexual wife of a retired ambassador. Romaine put up with this liaison for 11 years, and then the embittered woman of 94 refused ever to see Natalie again. That broke Natalie's heart. Romaine died two years later, and in another two years Natalie followed suit. Her funeral, like all her salons, was on a Friday.

HER ADVICE: Natalie felt that sleeping in the same bed with a lover was a dangerous practice, leading to "the beginning of an end." She wrote: "And how many lovers, even the most infatuated and tender ones, leave a stiffened arm under the other's neck. One wakes up worrying about having snored. This *forgetfulness of the other* in sleep—whether by night or day—seems to me to be the greatest of discourtesies and dangers."

HER THOUGHTS: "What did you love the most?"
"Love.
"And if you had to make several choices?"
"I would choose love several times." (From *Éparpillements* ["Scatterings"].)
—*J.H.*

Uncle Miltie

MILTON BERLE (July 12, 1908-March 27, 2002)

HIS FAME: A comedian and actor, Berle is perhaps best known for his major role in popularizing television during its infancy. His Tuesday night comedy and variety show, originally called *Texaco Star Theater*—which ran on NBC from 1948 until 1956—earned its star a 30-year contract with the network and the nickname "Mr. Television."

HIS PERSON: Milton Berle, whose real name was Berlinger, was born in New York City. A precocious child, he began entering "Charlie Chaplin contests" at the age of six and usually won. He would sell the prizes, normally $2 loving cups, for 25¢. Not until his mother, Sarah, started managing his career did young Milton reap any worthwhile return for his efforts. Milton and Mom hit the vaudeville circuit, where she would sit in the audience and prompt laughter and applause. By literally growing up onstage, Berle honed his skills as a comedian, a film and stage actor, and a master of ceremonies, building a repertoire of comedy material that is today unparalleled. In the belief that all jokes are in the public domain, he has unabashedly collected material from other comedians, thus earning himself the sobriquet "the Thief of Badgags." Berle's own unique brand of no-holds-barred humor has continually won him new audiences. In

1980, 60 years after his Broadway debut in *Florodora*, Berle was back onstage in *Guys and Dolls*. At the age of 72 he finished a movie called *Off Your Rocker*. This endless activity has prompted his wife, Ruth, to comment, "I can't wait until Milton gets old."

SEX LIFE: Because Berle sometimes appeared in drag in comedy sketches, an insecure segment of the public has questioned his masculinity. In reply to those who suspected him of being a homosexual or transvestite, Berle wrote, "To the best of my knowledge, Milton isn't. And so what? To me gay is just another way of life, not better, not worse. Just different." On one occasion, he did dress in women's clothing to achieve sexual gratification indirectly; he put on a dress so he could accompany a girl to her room at the Barbizon for Women, a hotel where men were not allowed above the lobby floor. Mostly, however, he dressed in drag merely as a form of "low comedy." His sex life, on the other hand, he has always taken quite seriously.

In November, 1920, Berle made his first Broadway appearance in *Florodora*, a show which marked another first in his life. One Saturday afternoon, after a matinee, he was ascending a staircase to his dressing room when he paused to ogle a scantily clad Florodora girl. Spotting the wide-eyed boy, the girl lured him into her dressing room; when he emerged, he was a man. The metamorphosis took only a few seconds: "One second her hand was undoing my buttons, the next she had me inside her—and from what I know now, there was room in there for the entire [Florodora] Sextet." His second sexual encounter was with a member of the Mollie Williams Beef Trust burlesque show. He fondly recalled the episode as being "like a green pea going into the Holland Tunnel." He had wisely shrouded his pea in a prophylactic, which a friend had given him, and he afterwards invested in his own tin of condoms. While prepared for any future tryst, he was not prepared for his mother's reaction when the tin accidentally fell out of his pocket in front of her. After an uncomfortable moment, she responded with a tact rare in mothers of any generation. "Every time you go out," she said, "make sure you use them."

Thanks to Mom, he did not always have to go out. On several occasions, sexual opportunity knocked on his dressing-room door when his mother brought girls from the audience backstage to meet her talented son. Mom would introduce them and then discreetly slip out of the room, leaving the two young people to the mercy of their hormones. Not a panderer, but a pragmatist, Berle's mother explained to him, "Who can say what can go wrong if the body doesn't get what it wants?"

When Berle went hunting on his own, his taste in women proved to be eclectic. He had a brief affair with Louise Cook, a black belly dancer, and several clandestine encounters with Aimee Semple McPherson, the famous evangelist. He cut a wide swath through show-biz womanhood, dallying with Betty Hutton, Dorothy Kilgallen, Wendy Barrie, and Marilyn Monroe, whom he took to trendy Hollywood hot spots because "it was like taking a hungry kid into a bakery." Serious romance eluded him until he met an actress he calls

"Linda Smith." To be sure, Berle and Linda had their differences. He was a life-long teetotaler; she drank heavily ("When I think about Linda today, I see her as a woman with one hand with fingers on it and the other arm ending in a wrist attached to a highball glass.") Despite their star-crossed relationship, Linda became pregnant with Berle's baby and he asked her to marry him. She refused, choosing to wed an older man, a producer who could help advance her career. Although the producer was impotent most of the time, Linda successfully convinced him that the baby was indeed his. A boy was born and grew up never knowing that Milton Berle was his real father.

When Berle finally did marry a show girl named Joyce Matthews in 1941, the solid, happy relationship he had longed for still eluded him. His work dominated their life together, and their marriage was further strained by their fruitless efforts to have a child. They finally adopted a baby girl, Victoria, but their spell of happiness was brief, and they were divorced in 1947. Joyce subsequently attempted to commit suicide with an overdose of sleeping pills. In 1949 they decided to give their union a second chance and renewed their marriage vows. However, it was an ill-fated reconciliation; once again Joyce attempted suicide, and once again they were divorced. Later Joyce was twice wed to showman Billy Rose.

In 1951 Berle met Ruth Cosgrove, who worked in Sam Goldwyn's publicity department. Ruth was "a cute brunette with short curly hair and a good figure," who impressed Berle with her unabashed criticism of his work. They were married in December, 1953. Eight years later they adopted a son, Billy. After years of one-night stands, unrequited loves, and tragic entanglements, Berle had found in Ruth "love to last a lifetime."

MEDICAL REPORT: According to Hollywood legend, Milton Berle is the John Dillinger of show business. He tells of an incident that occurred in the Luxor Baths in New York, when a stranger said to him, "Hey, Berle, I hear you got a big one," and offered to bet $100 that his own organ was larger than the comedian's. Berle refused the bet, but was goaded by a friend to "just take out enough to win."

—*M.J.T.*

The Dancing Revolutionary

ISADORA DUNCAN (May 27, 1878–Sept. 14, 1927)

HER FAME: Rejecting the rigid disciplines of ballet and other formal dance techniques, Isadora Duncan created her own stage routines. Her graceful, free-flowing movements and imaginative pantomimes, performed to great classical music, helped modern dance gain formal recognition as a new creative art.

HER PERSON: Isadora's unique style was inspired by Greek and Italian art and based loosely upon the calisthenics system of François Delsarte, which advocated coordination of voice with body gestures. In April, 1898, after her entire wardrobe was lost in New York City's disastrous Hotel Windsor fire, Isadora introduced an innovative twist at her next appearance—an improvised costume that left little to the imagination. One newspaper critic described it sarcastically as "a species of surgical bandage of gauze and satin."

Undaunted, Isadora sailed for Europe where—in a see-through diaphanous tunic of Liberty silk, adorned with colorful streamers of varying lengths—she became the barefoot dancing darling of the continent. Touring first with the Loie Fuller troupe, she was soon taken on by impresario Alexander Gross and booked for solo appearances in Budapest, Berlin, Vienna, and other major capitals. A shocked but titillated audience arrived en masse to see the nearly nude nymph glide, pose, and leap about the carpeted stage, accompanied by such well-known compositions as Strauss' "Blue Danube" and Chopin's "Funeral March."

A firm believer in free love, Isadora subsequently jolted her U.S. fans by touring while obviously pregnant with her second child, although she had not bothered to marry the child's father. She remained the "Pet of Society" for over two decades; however, her personal life dissolved in tragedy in 1913. In a freak accident, her car—momentarily driverless—rolled backward down a slope, drowning her two children and their nurse in the muddy Seine. Professionally, as well as emotionally, Isadora never fully recovered.

In 1922 her outspoken views on atheism and the Bolshevik Revolution brought further woes. Coming to the U.S. from Moscow with her Russian husband, she infuriated Boston theatergoers by waving a red scarf at them from the stage. In Chicago the tour earned the animosity of evangelist Billy Sunday. Playing upon the "Red Menace" theme, he labeled her "that Bolshevik hussy who doesn't wear enough clothes to pad a crutch." In Indianapolis, Ind., the mayor bluntly called Isadora a nude dancer whose appearance might well earn her a trip to jail by paddy wagon.

Broke and disillusioned, Isadora returned to Europe. She eked out a twilight existence, shuttling between Paris and the Riviera, until a second freak automobile accident occurred in 1927. Getting into a Bugatti, she tossed her trademark scarf about her throat, cheerily calling out, "Farewell, my friends, I am going to glory!" The dangling scarf caught in the spokes of a rear wheel as the car started up, and her neck was instantly snapped.

SEX LIFE: Isadora kept her virginity until age 25, but quickly made up for lost time. Her favors were dispensed initially to Oscar Beregi, a handsome Hungarian actor then appearing on the Budapest stage as Shakespeare's Romeo. Mutually smitten at first sight, they galloped off to the downy privacy of a peasant four-poster bed in the Danube countryside. The dark-eyed Magyar's offstage, all-day marathon left the dancer so exhausted that she admittedly limped around during her Urania Theater recital that night. But the delighted Isadora rapidly booked Beregi again, especially after he promised that she "finally would know what heaven was on earth."

In December, 1904, Isadora began a torrid liaison with theatrical designer Gordon Craig, the son of English actress Ellen Terry. For two wild weeks the lovers copulated repeatedly on some old blankets spread over artificial rose petals strewn on the black, waxed floor of Craig's high-rise studio in Berlin. The non-stop orgy paused only for an occasional meal, ordered "on credit" and delivered while "Topsy"—Craig's pet name for Isadora—shivered outside on the narrow balcony. Her frantic manager had to cancel her shows while he searched police-station blotters, fearing abduction or worse. Eventually he gave up and published a discreet newspaper notice that "Fräulein Duncan has regrettably been taken seriously ill with tonsillitis." Nine months later, the "tonsillitis" was named Deirdre, Isadora's own contribution to the brood of six such free-love productions sired by Craig in his lifetime.

In 1906 Isadora became the mistress of Paris Singer, one of the 23 children of sewing-machine magnate Isaac Singer. The playboy millionaire gave her seven years of lavish living, along with the chromosomes for her second love child, Patrick. The idyllic affair ended in 1913, when both children died tragically and Isadora fled, first to Italy, then France, where a willing sculptor fathered a third baby. The boy lived only an hour. At the close of WWI, Isadora took on a new lover, pianist-composer Walter Rummel, her "archangel." He showed great talent, but an aging and jealous Isadora called it quits in Greece when she suspected that his "shining wings" were also being folded about a young dryad in her dance troupe.

In 1922, when she was 44, Isadora set aside her aversion to marriage long enough to become the wife of the Russian Revolution's poet laureate, Sergei Esenin, 17 years her junior. The brief marriage was a disaster. Esenin, half-mad and alcoholic, left a trail of broken liquor bottles and furniture on both sides of the Atlantic. His inebriated scampering in the nude down hotel corridors and distribution of her money and clothes to friends and relatives proved too much for even the liberated Isadora to handle. She coaxed him back to Moscow the next year and quietly went her own way.

BAREFOOT QUOTATIONS: "Any intelligent woman who reads the marriage contract, and then goes into it, deserves all the consequences."

"Toe walking deforms the feet; corsets deform the body; and nothing is left to be deformed but the brain and there is not much of this in the women who dance modern dances."

"*Vot Bog!*" Translation: "This is God!" (Isadora's reply in Russian, as she pointed to a nearby bed, when Esenin joked about her personal beliefs on religion.)
—*W.K.*

The Most Dangerous Woman In The World

EMMA GOLDMAN (June 27, 1869–May 14, 1940)

HER FAME: Emma Goldman was an American anarchist agitator, editor, and lecturer who devoted her life to the support of social and political causes. She spoke out in favor of feminism, birth control, freedom of speech, workers' rights, and free love, and against war, conscription, economic exploitation, and government in general. Although few of her views are considered unusual today, in her time she was beaten, jailed, deported from the U.S., and dubbed "the most dangerous woman in the world."

HER PERSON: Born to struggling Jewish parents in Kovno, Lithuania, Emma developed an early rebellious nature in response to the authoritarianism of her father and her teachers. When her father, Abraham, tried to marry her off at the age of 15, Emma pleaded with him to let her continue her studies instead. He threw one of her books into the fire and told her, "Girls do not have to learn much! All a Jewish daughter needs to know is how to prepare gefilte fish, cut noodles fine, and give the man plenty of children." The following year Emma convinced her father to allow her to go to America with her older half sister, Helena. But he only consented after Emma, who had been forced to quit school and go to work in a corset factory, made a serious threat to jump into the Neva River.

Helena and Emma joined their sister, Lena, in Rochester, N.Y. Expecting to find the U.S. a land of freedom and equality, Emma was disappointed by the horrible living and working conditions that were the lot of her fellow Jewish immigrants. While working in sweatshops, she began to attend German Socialist meetings and soon she was reading about anarchism, the theory which advocates abolishing government and replacing it with voluntary cooperatives and federations.

In 1889 Emma moved to New York City in order to join the anarchist movement. With the encouragement of the fiery editor and agitator Johann Most, she became an effective orator. In 1893 she was jailed for nine months on a charge of inciting to riot after she told a New York crowd of unemployed workers to steal bread if they had no money to buy it.

Continuing her speeches in America and Europe, Emma also studied nursing and midwifery, which provided her with an occupation and exposed her to the desperate needs of the impoverished women who pleaded with her for abortions and an end to childbearing. She also learned about modern European theater, and her lectures on the subject played a major part in introducing Americans to the work of Ibsen, Shaw, and Strindberg. In 1906 she founded *Mother Earth*, an anarchist journal which she edited until its suppression in 1917.

In 1916 Emma spent 15 days in jail in New York City after giving a public speech in favor of birth control. When WWI began, Emma and her lover and lifelong friend, Alexander Berkman, opposed American involvement and organized an anticonscription campaign. Arrested for conspiracy to obstruct the operation of the selective service law, they were sentenced to two years in prison. When Goldman completed her sentence, she was stripped of her U.S. citizenship and she and Berkman and 247 other "subversives" were put on a boat to Russia. Arriving in January of 1920, Emma and Berkman quickly found themselves at odds with the new Bolshevik government. When Lenin started rounding up anarchists, Goldman and Berkman fled the country. In 1923 Emma published *My Disillusionment with Russia*, a libertarian criticism of the Communist regime. In 1931, with Berkman's help, she finished her two-volume autobiography, *Living My Life*. While working in Toronto on behalf of the Spanish anarchists then fighting Franco, Emma suffered a paralytic stroke and died in 1940 at the age of 70.

SEX PARTNERS: When Emma was 15, a 20-year-old hotel clerk in St. Petersburg attempted to force himself on her sexually, but Emma saved herself by screaming. In February, 1887, feeling lonely and depressed in Rochester, Emma consented to marry Jacob Kershner, who worked beside her in a sweatshop. Unfortunately, Kershner was impotent, and within a year she demanded a divorce. After working at a corset factory in New Haven, Conn., she returned to Rochester and agreed to remarry Kershner after he threatened to commit suicide. But his impotence continued and they grew apart intellectually as well. At 20 Emma left her husband and moved to New York City.

There she met Alexander Berkman, a stern Jewish anarchist from Russia. Called Sasha, he was extremely concerned with revolutionary ethics. His friend Fedya was an artist who, although an anarchist, was more committed to beauty than to politics. When Fedya bought bouquets of flowers for Emma, Sasha ranted that it was a waste of money which would be better spent on the Cause. Emma felt love for both of them, but especially Sasha, with whom she lost her virginity. She called him "my boy" although he was only one and a half years younger than she. Emma lived together with Sasha, Fedya, and another woman, but she also spent time with the infamous Johann Most. Most was the model for the mad-bomber anarchist stereotype. Poor medical treatment resulting from a jaw infection had left him disfigured and ugly. He saw Emma as a protégée, and she saw him as an idol. "I yielded to Most's trembling embrace," she wrote of the night before her first speaking tour, "his kisses covering my mouth as of one famished with thirst. I let him drink."

During this period Emma learned that she had an inverted womb and would have to undergo an operation if she ever wanted to bear children. She refused the operation, vowing to find an outlet for her mother need "in the love of *all* children."

In May of 1892 news came that striking workers of the Homestead, Pa., mills of the Carnegie Steel Company had been shot and killed by Pinkerton thugs hired by company chairman Henry Clay Frick. Sasha was so outraged that he decided to assassinate Frick. However, he didn't own a gun and didn't have enough money to buy one. Emma, ever resourceful, decided to raise the money by selling her body. On a Saturday evening she paraded up and down 14th Street in an attempt to attract customers, but hurried away nervously whenever one approached. Finally, a tall, well-dressed 61-year-old man picked her up and went with her to a saloon. Recognizing her amateur status, he told her: "You haven't got it, that's all there is to it." He gave her a $10 bill and said, "Take this and go home." Astounded, she accepted the money and sent it to Sasha, who was waiting in Pittsburgh. Alexander Berkman did shoot Frick on July 23, 1892. He stabbed him, too, but he failed to kill him. Frick, although badly injured, was back to work in a week. Berkman was sentenced to 20 years in prison.

When Johann Most wrote an article critical of Berkman's act, Emma was furious at his betrayal of her Sasha. Most had gone to jail in England for advocating tyrannicide, and he constantly spoke out in favor of acts of violence, yet he had no praise for the attack on Frick. Goldman attended Most's next lecture and sat in the front row. As Most prepared to begin his speech, Emma rose up and demanded that he defend his statements against Alexander Berkman. Most mumbled that she was a "hysterical woman" but said nothing more. Pulling a horsewhip out of her cloak, Goldman flailed Most across the face and neck, broke the whip over her knee, and threw the pieces at him. An enraged crowd surrounded her, but she was rescued by Fedya and other friends.

In December of 1892 Emma met tall, blond 40-year-old Edward Brady, who had just arrived in America after spending 10 years in an Austrian prison for publishing anarchist literature. With Brady she experienced her first orgasm. "In the arms of Ed I learned for the first time the meaning of the great life-giving force. I understood its full beauty, and I eagerly drank its intoxicating joy and bliss. It was an ecstatic song, profoundly soothing by its music and perfume. My little flat … became a temple of love."

Emma and Ed began living together, but he became jealous of the time she devoted to her lectures, meetings, and political activities. To please Brady, she turned down speaking engagements and spent more time at home. But Emma was bending herself unnaturally. Finally, after an argument in which Ed criticized the books she read, Emma gave him a tongue-lashing. "Under the pretext of a great love," she cried, "you have done your utmost to chain me to you, to rob me of all that is more precious to me than life. You are not content with binding my body, you want also to bind my spirit! First the movement and my friends—now it's the books I love…. You are not going to clip my wings, you shan't stop my flight. I'll free myself even if it means tearing you out of my heart!" Her "ecstatic song" had become "a cracked bell." Reconciliations followed, but after Ed faked a suicide attempt "just to scare you a little and cure your mania for meetings," Emma left him for good, seven years after they first met.

On May 18, 1906, Alexander Berkman was released from prison after 14 years of incarceration. Emma greeted him with motherly affection, which he resented. He suffered deep depression and didn't fill up with life again until he fell in love with a 15-year-old girl and also agreed to take over editorship of *Mother Earth*. In 1908

Emma began a 10-year involvement with 30-year-old Dr. Ben L. Reitman, known in Chicago as the "King of Hoboes" because he had a following of transients. He called her his "blue-eyed mommy" and she treated him like an overgrown child—which he was. Goldman later described their first night together. "I was caught in the torrent of an elemental passion I had never dreamed any man could rouse in me. I responded shamelessly to its primitive call, its naked beauty, its ecstatic joy."

Emma's friends were shocked by her closeness with the frivolous and some-what roguish Reitman, who became her manager. He had little, if any, ideological commitment. He was a dedicated fund raiser, although it later came out that he had pocketed some of the proceeds from Goldman's lectures and sent the money to his mother. Once he had the bad taste to precede Emma's lecture "The Failure of Christianity" with a plea to the atheistic crowd to join him in a prayer to God "to help the poor working people." When Ben brought his mother to live with Emma and him, the relationship became particularly strained. Eventually Emma threw a chair at Ben and ordered him and his mother to leave the house. Reitman gained some respect in the movement in 1912 when a vigilante group kidnapped him in San Diego, tortured him, burned "IWW" on his buttocks with a cigar, covered him with tar and sagebrush (no feathers were available), and forced him to kiss the flag and sing "The Star-Spangled Banner." In New York, Emma, citing the right to freedom of speech, convinced her anarchist comrades to allow Ben to teach Sunday school classes in the office of *Mother Earth*. Ironically, their final separation came when Ben, who wanted children, fell in love with and married one of his Sunday school students.

After her flight from Russia, the 53-year-old Goldman took on a new lover, 29-year-old Arthur Swenson, but their age difference took its toll after a few months. In 1926 Emma married James Colton, a Welsh miner, which allowed her to have a British passport. He did it as a favor. In her 993-page autobiog-raphy, Emma devoted one sentence to her marriage to Colton.

There remains one last incident in Emma Goldman's sex life. In 1934 a 36-year-old blind comrade, Dr. Frank G. Heiner of Chicago, proposed that they share sexual intimacy. She turned down his "offer of sweet love," but when Mrs. Heiner wrote a letter of support for the idea, Emma allowed him to visit her in Toronto. For two weeks they enjoyed a "world of beauty." Years later Heiner recalled that the 65-year-old Goldman had "stimulated me as much mentally as physically."

HER THOUGHTS: "How can such an all-compelling force [as love] be syn-onymous with that poor little State- and Church-begotten weed, marriage?"

—*D. W.*

Private Eyes

J. EDGAR HOOVER (Jan. 1, 1895–May 2, 1972)

HIS FAME: As director of the U.S. Federal Bureau of Investigation from 1924 until his death 48 years later, John Edgar Hoover organized the FBI into a scientific law-enforcement agency which mercilessly prosecuted small-time gangsters and political dissidents and maintained files on thousands of Americans from all walks of life. Hoover dominated federal law enforcement for so long that in 1971 Martha Mitchell was able to remark accurately, "If you've seen one FBI director, you've seen them all."

SEX LIFE: "I was in love once when I was young," Hoover remarked, "but then I became attached to the Bureau." In fact, there is no evidence that Hoover ever made love. He did date in high school, but never "went steady." He became captain of the school cadets and his friends teased him that he was "going steady with Company A." He was a champion debater, particularly when arguing against woman's suffrage. His father died when he was 26 years old, and Hoover, a devoted son, chose to live alone with his mother for the remainder of her life, which was 17 years. He never married, expressing the belief that women are a hindrance to the development of a man's career.

Hoover's only intimate friend for the last 44 years of his life was Clyde Tolson, a tall native of Missouri, who served as confidential secretary to three U.S. secretaries of war before joining the FBI in 1928. Hoover and Tolson lunched together every day, and on Saturdays they went to the races. Tolson called Hoover "Eddie" and never seemed to take his eyes off him in public. People who knew them said they were so alike in their thinking that they became known as the "unipersonality."

Periodically, rumors spread that J. Edgar Hoover and Clyde Tolson were homosexual lovers. Hoover took these charges very seriously, claiming that they were made by "public rats," "guttersnipes," and "degenerate pseudo [which he pronounced "swaydo"] intellectuals." When Hoover died, Tolson received most of his $551,500 estate, as well as the flag that had draped his coffin.

Although Hoover and Tolson were definitely a tight couple, it is true that two men can remain close friends for decades without engaging in sex together. And Hoover was not without certain traditional attitudes of male sexuality.

For example, he displayed a gallery of famous nudes in his home, including Marilyn Monroe's celebrated calendar photo. He enjoyed cracking jokes about sex, and it was rumored that he kept pornographic magazines in his desk. If J. Edgar Hoover did enjoy sexy stories and pictures of naked women, he did not have to seek out commercial publications. He had his own private collection. The "OC" files (official and confidential) were kept in Hoover's office under special lock and key. These files contained potentially embarrassing information, sexual and otherwise, about government officials and various public figures.

Sometimes when his agents turned up a particularly juicy item, Hoover would pass it on to the current president and to members of the Cabinet. However, the OC files were also said to contain stories about the extramarital affairs of Franklin D. Roosevelt and his wife Eleanor, as well as incidents from the lives of Richard Nixon and John F. Kennedy.

Once, FBI agents raided the apartment of black radical Angela Davis and found some photographs taken while she and her boyfriend were making love. When Hoover learned of the existence of these photos, he was outraged that they hadn't been brought to him immediately, and the agent who had held them back was denied his next promotion.

HIS OBSESSION: The FBI began tapping the phone of the Rev. Martin Luther King, Jr., in 1957, but it wasn't until 1964 that Hoover became truly obsessed with ruining King's reputation. To this end, he ordered his agents to spy on the black leader day and night, authorizing wiretaps in 15 different hotels while King was staying in them. Eventually Hoover obtained tapes that proved King had engaged in extramarital sexual activities, and Hoover made copies of these tapes available to members of the press, to the Congress, and to President Lyndon Johnson. Prior to King's audience with the pope in August, 1964, Hoover had sent the pontiff derogatory information about King, but the pope ignored Hoover and went ahead with the meeting as scheduled.

While King was preparing to go to Stockholm to receive the Nobel Peace Prize, Hoover's attacks on his character reached a peak. During one session with reporters, Hoover called King "the most notorious liar in the country." Three days later Hoover and Tolson had excerpts of the hotel tapes sent to King's wife, Coretta. Enclosed in the package was an unsigned note addressed to Dr. King which threatened release of the tapes and said, "Your end is approaching ... you are finished ... you are done. There is but one way out for you. You better take it before your filthy, abnormal fraudulent self is bared to the nation."

HIS THOUGHTS: "I regret to say that we of the FBI are powerless to act in cases of oral-genital intimacy, unless it has in some way obstructed interstate commerce."

—*D. W.*

The Modern Bluebeard

HENRI DÉSIRÉ LANDRU (Apr. 12, 1869–Feb. 25, 1922)

HIS FAME: In France, between 1914 and 1919, 10 women and a boy mysteriously vanished. Though their bodies were never found, Henri Landru was arrested, tried, and convicted of their murder. In addition to being adjudged guilty of mass murder, Landru was accused of having had relations with— and then swindling—at least 283 women of modest means, mostly middle-aged.

HIS PERSON: Paris-born Henri Landru was short, frail, bespectacled, red-bearded, and bald and had large, luminous, hypnotic, black eyes—an unlikely-looking

Landru and Fernande Segret, who survived

sort to have seduced as many women in five years as Don Juan did in a lifetime. Landru's father was a stoker in a foundry, his mother a part-time seamstress. He attended Catholic school and sang in the church choir. In his early years he worked as an architect's draftsman, and later served in the French army. In 1900, while working unsuccessfully as a dealer in secondhand items, he forsook the straight and narrow and embarked upon a life of petty thievery and fraud. His first recorded crime was an attempt at defrauding a widow with a promise of marriage, and between 1900 and 1914 he did several prison terms for fraud. In 1914 he was sentenced *in absentia* to four years on Devil's Island, and he thereafter eluded police by using various aliases. In 1919 he was captured by the police, who were looking into the disappearance of two women. An incriminating diary was produced, and 295 bone fragments believed to belong to two or three different corpses were found in his kitchen stove. He was charged with 11 murders, and following a widely publicized trial during which he calmly and coolly stonewalled all attempts to break him down ("the women went where their destiny called them"), he was sentenced to the guillotine. "Ah, well," he said as he was led to his death. "It is not the first time an innocent man has been condemned.... I will be brave. I will be brave."

SEX LIFE: Landru's first recorded affair was with his young cousin, Marie Remy. He was 22, she 16. She became pregnant and subsequently they married and had four children. He remained a loving husband and father, although he did not live with his family in later years.

Landru met his victims in various ways. He placed lonely-hearts ads in Paris newspapers. He answered similar ads placed by single women. He dabbled in

Landru's victims

"matrimonial agencies." He made casual pickups on the street. His victims, mostly plainlooking, ranged from a former prostitute to a 19-year-old servant girl (probably just an idle affair, for she had little money). When apprehended he was living with his young, attractive mistress, Fernande Segret, a self-described "lyric artist." Her recollection of how they met is representative of his technique. Segret and a girl friend had just descended from a tram. "Scarcely had we gone a few yards ... when a man accosted us, saluted us very respectfully, and addressing himself to me, asked if we would allow him to accompany us for a few minutes.... We refused ... and quickened our pace to get away from him. But our follower would not be shaken.... He suggested that young girls in Paris go out all too often alone with the risk of being accosted by bad characters, and all sorts of annoyances from men. Such a statement made us laugh loudly; our follower took advantage of it to stay." A few days later, at dinner with her family, she said, "He talked on abundantly with a most lively wit, and every subject he touched he seemed to be at home in. His courteous and agreeable manners impressed me. Without ever forgetting that he was in the presence of ladies he poured out jokes, witty retorts, and even juggled for us with the napkin rings ... all the time garnishing his talk with the most wonderful puns."

According to his records Landru enjoyed about 50 women a year, and sometimes met with as many as seven a day. At his trial, Segret, the only woman to live with Landru during that period and remain alive—in fact, she had four children by him—testified that she found him an extremely passionate but normal lover. "I have not a single reproach against him. I loved him very deeply. I was very, very happy with him." Many of the women he seduced and abandoned were questioned, but not one testified against him. Some even called him kindly, considerate, and affectionate. His wife maintained, "My misfortune has been to love my husband too well."

QUIRKS: Landru was a meticulous, parsimonious, abstemious, vain man who compulsively kept a diary of all his expenses, conquests, and daily movements. Next to his victims' names he made copious notes like "Madame Jaume: 39, looks younger…. Very strong Catholic. Afraid of divorce." And then there were the ominous notations: "1 single and 1 return ticket." Other entries included the purchase of 7 saw blades, 7 dozen hacksaws, ax blades, and circular saws. For what possible use? In searching his villa police found a variety of women's clothing, women's false hair, dental plates, and trinkets as well as some male costumes of the 18th century. Landru's courtroom behavior was eccentric, belying the seriousness of the charges. He was a master of deadpan humor. One day he informed the judge that he wished to make a statement. Landru bowed to the court and said that he had to confess to having committed adultery with hundreds of women and that in so doing he'd grievously wronged his wife. When asked, before the guillotining, why he'd trimmed his beard, he replied simply that he wanted to please the ladies.

The final irony was that Landru worked so hard for so little. His crimes netted him in all about $8,000.

AFTERMATH: In 1968, almost a half century after Landru had gone to his Maker, a French newspaper announced that this modern Bluebeard's confession had been found. Scribbled in Landru's hand on the back of a framed sketch he had presented to one of his lawyers before going to the guillotine was the following: "I did it. I burned their bodies in my kitchen oven." And what had happened to Landru's mistress, Fernande Segret? She was thought long dead when a French film, *Landru*, written by Françoise Sagan, was exhibited in movie theaters worldwide. Suddenly Segret reappeared, a governess working in Lebanon, quite alive. She sued the French filmmakers for 200,000 francs and settled for 10,000. With this tidy sum she retired comfortably to a senior citizens' home in Normandy. But she was notorious again, and recognized. To rid herself of Landru forever she finally committed suicide by drowning.

—*C.H.S.*

A Woman Ahead Of Her Time

MARIA MONTESSORI (Aug. 31, 1870–May 6, 1952)

HER FAME: Maria Montessori pioneered preschool education, first by teaching the mentally retarded, later by devising methods still used in Montessori schools worldwide today. Her pedagogical revolution occurred so rapidly that she was known as an "educational wonder-worker" in the U.S. before WWI. The first Montessori-trained students included Douglas Fairbanks, Jr., and the grandchildren of Alexander Graham Bell.

HER PERSON: Maria Montessori believed in action, not rhetoric, and pointed to her achievements as evidence of what women could accomplish through work. She started early, winning her astonished father's permission to study engineering at the age of 13. She conquered the opposition of the medical authorities in Rome (by appealing to Pope Leo XIII for support), entered medical school, and finished with double honors and a standing ovation from her colleagues. A reporter sent to interview Italy's first female doctor arrived expecting a stern, bony woman in men's clothing. He was delighted to find Maria attractive and gracious, and noted the flowers, needlework, and musical scores scattered among the chemistry experiments and medical books in her apartment. "The delicacy of a talented young woman combined with the strength of a man—an ideal one doesn't meet with every day," was the reporter's enthusiastic pronouncement. Maria soon became resentful of this sort of publicity and vowed, "My face will not appear in the newspapers anymore and no one will dare to sing of my so-called charms again. I shall do serious work!"

She brought a clinician's eye to her specialty, children's nervous disorders, and realized that retarded children were bright enough to invent games to overcome their boredom. Maria became one of the first to teach the retarded, and went on to open Casa dei Bambini ("Children's House") for neglected Roman slum children in 1907. The success of her methods was so spectacular (some of her retarded students were getting normal-level test scores) that she finally gave up medicine to devote her full time to training teachers and writing and lecturing about her program. Called by the *Times* of London "the best type of woman a country could hope to produce," Montessori continued working until her death at 81 of a cerebral hemorrhage.

SEX LIFE: In 1896, when she was 26, Maria was working in the psychiatric clinic of the University of Rome as a researcher. There she met Giuseppe Montesano, an assistant doctor. A year later Maria joined the clinic staff as an assistant doctor and subsequently worked alongside Dr. Montesano. In this period, Maria's friendship with Montesano ripened, and the two became lovers. Soon Maria was pregnant. On Mar. 31, 1898, she gave birth to a child out of wedlock, a son she and Montesano named Mario.

Convinced by her mother that a scandal could destroy her career, Maria turned her son over to a wet nurse. Eventually a family in the country took the boy and raised him, keeping details of his birth a secret. Meanwhile Maria and Montesano had agreed not to marry each other and had pledged not to marry anyone else. But Maria's lover broke his word and did marry another. By then Maria and Montesano were codirectors of the State Orthophrenic School of Rome (an institution for the mentally retarded). Dismayed by her partner's action, Maria resigned as head of the school and broke off all ties with Montesano. Her one experience with love had been tragic, and Maria Montessori never again opened her heart to a man.

Meanwhile Maria's seven-year-old son, Mario, was attending a boarding school near Florence. From time to time the boy was visited by a "beautiful lady." Mario began to believe that this lady was his mother. Yet Maria did not publicly acknowledge Mario until 54 years after his birth, when her will revealed him as "*il mio figlio*" ("my son"). A year after Maria's mother died, Mario, now 15, confronted Maria and said, "I know you are my mother." When he asked to leave his boarding school to live with her, she did not object, but she insisted that he start using her surname. So Maria kept her agreement to protect her former lover and, in a way, denied his existence at the same time. Mario followed his mother into the field of preschool education and became her constant companion, even after he married and had four children of his own. For the rest of his mother's life Mario was identified as her adopted son, nephew, or secretary.

Maria was too brilliant and independent to be the unwitting victim of a casual affair. She championed a "new woman" who would "marry and have children out of choice, not because matrimony and maternity are imposed on her." The moral revivals of the future, she believed, would revolve around "the struggle against the sexual sins" of a society in which women were the slaves, the men the "lords, in a barbaric sense, of sexual life."

In spite of her progressive beliefs, Maria Montessori was still a woman of her time. She would say, "Excuse me if I show you this," when she used an anatomical drawing to illustrate a lecture. She could be excessively modest; for example, she insisted that her students precede her up stairways so that they wouldn't catch a glimpse of her legs under the long skirts she always wore.

HER ADVICE: "I wish that I could make all women fall in love with scientific reasoning. It doesn't suffocate the voice of the heart but augments it and supports it."

—*D.M.L.*

Lady With A Hatchet

CARRY NATION (Nov. 25, 1846–June 9, 1911)

HER FAME: Among the most famous of all temperance reformers, Carry Nation was a crusader whose enthusiasm in the war against vice has scarcely been rivaled anywhere. She raged against alcohol, tobacco, sex, politics, government, the Masonic Lodge, lawyers, foreign foods, and Theodore Roosevelt, to name only a few of her pet peeves. She was and is best known for her "hatchetations"— during which she destroyed bars and other dens of iniquity single-handedly with a hatchet.

HER PERSON: Born Carry Moore in Garrard County, Ky., she had a father who was a prosperous slaveowning stock dealer and a mother who suffered from the fixed delusion that she was Queen Victoria, complete with royal carriage and scepter. There were a great number of eccentrics in Carry's family, most notably one aunt who, at the time of the full moon, made repeated attempts to climb onto the roof and transform herself into a weather vane. Carry's odd relatives and her own early religious visions probably served to influence her development toward fanaticism.

Although erratically educated, Carry was certified to be a teacher. She became interested in temperance in 1890. At that time she was a resident of Kansas, which was a dry state. When a new U.S. Supreme Court ruling permitted wet states to export liquor in "original packages" to dry states, Carry felt that the law of Kansas was being undermined and she began her crusade. With a handful of female followers she marched on saloons. While her followers sang hymns outside, Carry stormed into the saloons and wielded her hatchet. She was in and out of jails more than 30 times, paying her fines by lecturing and selling souvenir hatchets. In her heyday she was a forbidding figure; nearly 6 ft. tall and weighing 176 lb., she wore stark black-and-white clothing, with a hatchet brooch pinned to her expansive bosom. She died at age 64 in Leavenworth, Kans. Her legacy was the 1919 Prohibition Amendment to the U.S. Constitution.

LOVE LIFE: Carry's mother and numerous aunts trained her to look upon every man as a potential seducer. Therefore, when she received gentlemen callers, there was no hand holding or hay riding. Instead, they discussed literature or the Bible. She said of herself: "Oh, I was a great lover," and in her autobiography she wrote: "There are pages in my life that have had much to do with bringing me in sympathy with the fallen tempted natures. These I cannot write, but let no erring, sinful man or woman think that Carry Nation would not understand, for Carry Nation is a sinner saved by grace." However, her concept of sin was so exaggerated that she was probably referring to her fantasies.

In 1865 Charles Gloyd, a handsome young doctor from Ohio, became a boarder at the Moore household. Although Mrs. Moore forbade the two young people to be alone in the same room together, Gloyd managed to woo Carry nonetheless. One day he caught her in his arms and kissed her on the mouth. She covered her face with her hands and cried, "I'm ruined! I'm ruined!" Their courtship lasted two years. Things took a turn for the worse on their wedding day, when Gloyd showed up drunk for the ceremony. Carry wrote of the days that followed: "I did not find Dr. Gloyd the lover I expected. He was kind but he seemed to want to be away from me; used to sit and read, when I was hungry for his caresses and love." After a few months she left him, at her parents' urging, when she was pregnant and on the edge of a nervous breakdown. Six months later Gloyd died as a result of his heavy drinking.

Several years later, living with her daughter and mother-in-law, Carry was in financial difficulty. She turned to the Lord, saying, "Lord, you see the situation. I cannot take care of Mother and Charlien. I want you to help me. If it is best for me to marry, I will do so. I have no one picked out, but I want you to select the one you think best." Within six months she was married to David Nation, an extremely ugly widower 19 years her senior, who was a minister and a lawyer. Their marriage was rocky, and Carry was bitter that she had not found true love. Her new husband resented her overzealous Christianity and religious visions, and although she wept at his lack of affection, she found sex repugnant.

After 24 miserable years together, Nation divorced Carry on grounds of desertion. In her final analysis, men were "nicotine-soaked, beer-besmeared, whiskey-greased, red-eyed devils" and "two-legged animated whiskey flasks." In addition to fighting her war on fermented grains, Carry was something of a feminist; she preached against corsets and advocated a matriarchal society.

QUIRKS: The product of a deeply repressed sexuality, Carry's hatred of all things sexual and her battle tactics in fighting them became increasingly warped. She began her career of interference by attacking necking couples and lecturing them on the evils of buggy riding and "spooning," all the while brandishing a ferocious-looking umbrella with a sharpened tip. (She had not yet picked up the hatchet.) She also stopped women on the street to alert them against seduction, describing it in graphic anatomical detail. She established a "Home for the Wives of Drunkards" and started a newspaper called *The Hatchet*. In it she ran a column entitled "Private Talks to Boys and Girls." Its main theme was the evils of self-abuse, and its language was so explicit that one reader called it "a blueprint for masturbation."

Claiming that God had told her to use a hatchet, she began to wreak real havoc. To protect themselves, bar owners went so far as to hire bodyguards, equip their bars with trapdoors, or keep cages of rats to let loose on unwelcome visitors. One saloon keeper even designed a portable bar with the strength of a tank, which he planned to take on tour through the dry states in open defiance of Carry and her hatcheteers. One of her most celebrated smashings occurred in Wichita, Kans., at the beautifully ornate bar of the Hotel Carey. Famed for its lovely interior decoration, the bar proudly sported a life-size painting of a nude Cleopatra bathing, along with scantily clothed attendants. When Carry saw it, she hit the ceiling. The place deserved "hatchetation." She proceeded to completely destroy the bar single-handedly, throwing rocks and axing away wildly. She caused thousands of dollars' worth of damage. She told the bartender, "It's disgraceful! You're insulting your mother by having her form stripped naked and hung up in a place where it is not decent for a woman to be when she has her clothes on!" Not wishing to risk similar treatment, a hotel owner in New York City abjectly draped with cheesecloth the naked statue of Diana decorating his lobby. Mrs. Nation had told him, "Look here, my man, you cover up that nasty thing or there'll be a little hatchetation around here!"

—*A. W.*

The Rites Of Spring

WASLAW NIJINSKY (Mar. 12, 1890–Apr. 8, 1950)

HIS FAME: During his brief but glorious career as the premier danseur of the Imperial Russian Ballet at St. Petersburg's Maryinsky Theater and of Sergei Diaghilev's Ballets Russes, Nijinsky performed the leading male roles in such works as *Le Spectre de la Rose* ("The Specter of the Rose"), *Petrouchka*, and his masterpiece, *Le Sacre du Printemps* ("The Rite of Spring"). Rejecting the conventional forms of classical ballet, he perfected leaps in which he appeared to hang in midair. His daringly original choreography and dramatic acting spurred the art of ballet to great heights and earned him a reputation as a genius.

HIS PERSON: The son of two professional dancers, Nijinsky was born in Kiev in the Ukraine. "A delicate child, awkward, temperamentally backward and slow-thinking," he began dancing early, and by the age of three was touring with his parents' troupe. As a student he demonstrated unparalleled ability and once performed 10 entrechats—crossing and uncrossing the legs—in a single jump.

When Nijinsky was nine, his father deserted the family in favor of a pregnant mistress. His mother urged him all the harder to excel in dance, since a ballet career would insure money and prestige. He graduated from St. Petersburg's Imperial School of Ballet in the spring of 1907 and joined the Imperial Russian Ballet as a soloist.

In 1909 he met dance impresario Sergei Diaghilev and began collaborating with him as a dancer and later as a choreographer. When he danced in Paris with the Ballets Russes, he created a sensation. In 1911 Nijinsky was dismissed from the Imperial Ballet for appearing onstage without his full costume. He was promptly offered a place in the Ballets Russes. There he choreographed and danced his most legendary roles. *L'Après-midi d'un Faune* ("The Afternoon of a Faun") created a minor scandal in 1912; in the final scene Nijinsky simulated masturbation. The police warned him to rewrite the scene or risk having the show closed. He refused to change the passage, but no performances were actually raided.

In 1913 Nijinsky married Countess Romola de Pulszky. The marriage offended Diaghilev so much that he dismissed his star performer. Nijinsky then formed his own dance troupe, which toured for about a year, appearing in London and in the U.S. But his talents did not extend to running the business aspects of a dance company, and it failed.

During WWI Nijinsky was imprisoned in Austria-Hungary on charges of spying for Russia. He was not permitted to perform, and not until he was freed in 1916 was he able to return to his career. He again toured, but in 1919, at 29, he suffered a nervous breakdown. He stopped dancing, was plagued by insomnia, headaches, persecution mania, schizophrenia, and depression. Until his death from kidney disease in 1950, he lived most of his last 30 years in a Swiss insane asylum.

LOVE LIFE: Nijinsky's tumultuous love life contributed significantly to his insanity. He had a passive nature in love, perhaps because he reserved his full vitality for performing on stage. A naive and beautiful young man, Nijinsky began an intimate relationship with 30-year-old Prince Pavel Dmitrievich Lvov in 1908. Tall, blue-eyed, and handsome, Lvov was instantly attracted to the muscular Nijinsky. The prince initiated his friend into the intoxicating delights of nightclub life and provided him with his first homosexual experience. However, Lvov was disappointed with the dancer's small penis; as one biographer described him, "Nijinsky was small in a part where size is usually admired." The prince was not possessive; he even arranged Nijinsky's first sexual experience with a woman—a prostitute. Nijinsky was frightened and repelled by the encounter.

Lvov, who was generous with gifts, won the heart of his lover. But after a few months the prince withdrew, having grown bored with the dancer he considered just "another of his toys." Before they parted, however, Lvov introduced Nijinsky to Sergei Diaghilev, the cultivated ballet producer who had founded the Ballets Russes. Twenty years older than Nijinsky, Diaghilev was an unabashed homosexual. His first—and last—experience with a woman (his 18-year-old cousin) had been marred by a subsequent venereal infection. The two men became lovers. Nijinsky had grown accustomed to being passed around, but his initial lovemaking with Diaghilev disturbed him. "I trembled like a leaf," wrote Nijinsky. "I hated him, but pretended."

"Chinchilla," as Diaghilev was called because of the white streak in his dyed black hair, stripped his lover of independence. He scrutinized Nijinsky's personal and professional life and warned him against ever sleeping with women, telling him such acts would impair his dancing. So persuasive and insistent was Diaghilev that Nijinsky once turned down a sexual offer from Isadora Duncan, whom the two men met in Venice in 1909. She had suggested to Nijinsky that he father her next baby, but he refused.

Diaghilev repeatedly encouraged his lover to consent to a *ménage à trois* with a young boy, but Nijinsky was already finding the act of love extremely difficult with just one person. By 23 he felt he was growing too old to be Diaghilev's "boy." In September of 1913, while the entire Ballets Russes was en route to South America aboard the S.S. *Avon*, Nijinsky became engaged to coquettish Romola de Pulszky. She was 23 and the daughter of Hungarian actress Emilia Markus. Romola had been pursuing Nijinsky for months, had even taken up ballet in order to be near him. According to Hungarian tradition, the exchange of engagement rings authorized freedom to indulge in premarital intercourse. But whether it was Nijinsky's shyness, the couple's language barrier, or his emphatic desire for a proper Catholic wedding, they did not consummate their romance until after their wedding on Sept. 10, 1913.

Diaghilev was surprised and insulted by this wedding and retaliated by firing Nijinsky. He refused to answer his former lover's letters. Soon after the marriage, Nijinsky gained another ardent admirer. The Duchess of Durcal, a beautiful redhead, fell so desperately in love with him that she offered herself as his mistress. Romola had no objections, and Nijinsky had sex with the duchess at least once. He regretted it later, saying, "I am sorry for what I did. It was unfair to her, as I am not in love."

As Nijinsky's mental health began to deteriorate, he and Romola took separate bedrooms. Sometimes he would slip out at night and walk the streets, searching for prostitutes—just to talk. He would return home, sexually aroused by these women, and masturbate in his bedroom "in order to protect myself from catching a venereal disease."

Romola gave birth to the first of their two daughters in 1914—the second was born in 1920—and a few years later Diaghilev reentered Nijinsky's life. Romola objected to Diaghilev's peacemaking attempts and even brought a 500,000-franc lawsuit against him, as compensation for her husband's past performances in the Ballets Russes. She won the suit, but Diaghilev never paid. Instead he made an overt move to win back Romola's husband. She pulled one way, Diaghilev pulled the other way, and Nijinsky, no longer dancing and with no outlet for his frustrations, lapsed into a catatonic world.

—*A.K. and K.P.*

The First Free-Lover

JOHN HUMPHREY NOYES (Sept. 3, 1811–Apr. 13, 1886)

HIS FAME: John Humphrey Noyes, social visionary and originator of the term "free love," gained notoriety in the mid-19th century for preaching a form of promiscuity and birth control to his followers, who were called Perfectionists. He argued that since the Second Coming had already occurred (in 70 A.D.) a sinless existence—perfection— was possible on earth by simply accepting Christ into one's soul. These beliefs found expression in his creation of the most successful of American utopias, the Oneida Community in New York State, which thrived for over a quarter of a century and at its peak had 300 members.

HIS PERSON: Noyes was raised by a strong and devout mother, who prayed that her firstborn son would become a minister. Business deals and a political career often kept his father away from their home in Brattleboro, Vt. When Noyes was 20, he experienced a religious awakening. According to one of his biographers, "light gleamed upon his soul," and by nightfall he had decided to devote himself to God. Another turning point in his life occurred three years later when he was a student at Yale Theological Seminary in New Haven. In a revelation that shocked the ecclesiastical world, Noyes made his "confession of salvation from sin." Expelled from school and stripped of his preacher's license, Noyes vowed to continue spreading his Perfectionist beliefs. This he did, eventually establishing the first of the self-sufficient communities of love among the saved in Putney, Vt. The unorthodox sex practices of these communities were probably influenced by still another event in his life. When he was 23 and a virgin, he experienced a traumatic rejection from his first love and first convert to the new religion. Thirty-one-year-old Abigail Merwin, his pretty "angel," was very attracted to the fiery prophet, but she married a schoolteacher after her family persuaded her that Noyes was crazy. For several years Noyes pursued her, going so far as to follow her to her new home in Ithaca, N.Y., in the belief that they were joined in "immortal marriage" and before long she would realize her mistake. When that didn't happen, he rejected conventional marriage. "When the will of God is done on earth there will be no marriage," he wrote in a letter to a close

The Utopian Oneida community. John Humphrey Noyes standing in forefront

friend. As God's representative, he resolved to create the perfect society, where "marriage" is "free to every guest" but devoid of all "exclusiveness, jealousy, and quarreling." That vision of a social arrangement which would protect him from emotional involvement and rejection was realized in the Oneida Community.

SEX LIFE: "The Honorable John," as Noyes was called by his many grandchildren, was not always filled with honorable intentions. As Father of the Community, he used his position to get whatever he wanted and whomever he wanted.

In an imperfect world, reasoned Noyes, one had to be practical. That was the justification he gave for marrying homely Harriet Holton, a wealthy heiress who had been sending him regular contributions. Though he felt "no particular love of the sentimental kind" for her, and despite the fact that just a year before their marriage he had spoken out against monogamy, he married her in order to stifle rumors of his promiscuity. The marriage was a disappointment. Harriet gave birth to four stillborn babies and only one live child during their first six years of matrimony. Unable to tolerate imperfection, Noyes found a solution in self-control during sex, *coitus reservatus*, or as he called it, "male continence." It was essentially sexual intercourse without ejaculation. Noyes claimed that male continence was easy and that his wife's experience was "very satisfactory, as it had never been before." Apparently Harriet was able to have orgasms with this method. About this time Noyes felt an "increase of brotherly love" for a female disciple named Mary Cragin. At the same time, Harriet fell in love with Mary's husband, George. When

Noyes realized this, armed as he was with his "greatest discovery" of male continence, he decided it was time to begin his ideal society. Thus, in 1846, "complex marriage" was born. A year later, charged with adultery, Noyes fled from Vermont to New York, where he established the Oneida Community.

By 1850 complex marriage was in full swing at Oneida. "Abound," Noyes told members in 1869 (before that members tried not to have children). The female orgasm was a desired consequence of every sexual encounter, because the more love one gave, the closer to God one became. In theory, each woman was free to refuse any man's advances—including those of her husband. But in actuality, women submitted to prominent members of the community out of fear of being criticized as selfish. Emotional attachments, even of a mother to her child, were considered selfish and sinful. After all, those personal feelings would undermine communal spirit. Once Noyes told a man who was devoted to a particular lady, "You do not love her, you love happiness."

Promiscuity was rigorously enforced; violators were banished from the community or demoted in their work. To prevent unwanted pregnancies, young men were taught the art of self-control by older women, who were usually past menopause. Noyes appointed himself responsible for initiating women into the sexual experience.

SEX PARTNERS: Practicing what he preached, Noyes took hundreds of lovers during his lifetime. His strong sex drive lasted well into his 60s, when he sired at least 9 of the 58 children born under the community's selective breeding experiment. All the women, perhaps attracted more by his power than his looks, were eager to sleep with their spiritual leader. However, Noyes took particular delight in acting as "first husband" to the virgins—some as young as 10 years old, who had not even begun to menstruate. This practice got him into trouble in 1877 when jealous males, angry over his attempted monopoly on young girls, threatened to bring charges of statutory rape against him. With religious leaders also demanding action against the "ethics of the barnyard," Noyes fled to Canada. Resettling at Niagara Falls, he died there at the age of 74, surrounded by his faithful wife, sisters, and a small group of followers.

HIS THOUGHTS: "There is no more reason why sexual intercourse should be restrained by law, than why eating or drinking should be—and there is as little occasion for shame in the one case as in the other."

"It is as foolish and cruel to expend one's seed on a wife merely for the sake of getting rid of it, as it would be to fire a gun at one's best friend merely for the sake of unloading it."

—*S.L.W.*

Arctic Explorer

ROBERT PEARY (May 6, 1856–Feb. 20, 1920)

HIS FAME: The expedition officially credited with being the first to reach the North Pole—on Apr. 6, 1909—was led by explorer Robert Edwin Peary. Peary was also the first to offer conclusive evidence that Greenland was an island.

HIS PERSON: Born in Cresson, Pa., Robert was not quite three years old when his father died. Mary Wiley Peary moved her only child to a small town near Portland, Me. Peary's pampered childhood was less than pleasant—his mother dressed him in girlish clothes, including a bonnet to protect his fair skin—and few boys his age would play with what they called "a sissy."

When Peary entered Bowdoin College, he was a tall and athletic man who was accepted by his peers, yet he lacked pleasing character traits. Later he was considered ruthless and driven, and he was often jealous of rival explorers. His dedication to his work was obsessive. Over the years, he uncomplainingly lost eight toes to frostbite. He was motivated by his own proclamation: "I don't want to live and die without accomplishing anything or without being known beyond a narrow circle of friends."

In 1886 he conducted his first exploration of the Far North and decided to make Arctic research his lifework. Teaming up with a black assistant named Matthew Henson—and often accompanied by his wife, Josephine—Peary spent the next 23 years traveling through the polar region and at times living among the Eskimos.

Peary's disposition made him hard to live with. Matthew Henson particularly felt the brunt of Peary's personality and prejudices. Although Henson was intensely loyal, Peary called him "my colored boy" and a "dark-skinned, kinky-haired child of the Equator" and doubted that a Negro could survive in the cold climates of the North. Nevertheless, it was Henson who was alongside Peary on Apr. 6, 1909, when, despite the unbearable cold and hunger, the two men, four Eskimos, and their dogs reached latitude 90°—the North Pole.

Or did they reach it? No sooner had Peary returned to civilization than he discovered that a former associate, Dr. Frederick Cook, claimed he himself had reached the pole a year earlier. A bitter public fight ensued, during which Peary's

Peary's Eskimo mistress, Allakasingwah

character and his ability as a geographer were both questioned. However, by 1911 Peary, who had been financed by the National Geographic Society and the U.S. Congress, had secured his place in history as the first man to reach the coveted goal.

LOVE LIFE: On the surface, Peary had a rather conventional love life. Overprotected by his mother, he gravitated toward motherly, traditional women.

His first sweetheart was Mary "May" Kilby, a fellow student at Portland High School. When he graduated from college in 1877, he became a surveyor in Fryeburg, Me., where May visited him. Subsequently they became engaged. But Peary would not control his wanderlust, and toward the end of 1879 he asked May to "release" him. She broke the engagement, and he wrote in his diary, "The past is dead. *Vive la future!*"

On Aug. 11, 1888, he married Josephine Diebitsch of Washington, D.C., who announced that she planned to accompany her new husband on his trips to Greenland. Others may have raised eyebrows, but Peary was delighted; he had a strong sense of home and hearth and liked the fact that wherever he was to go, Josephine would be there to make a home for him. She became the first white woman to winter with an Arctic expedition. In 1893 their daughter, Marie Ahnighito, was born in Greenland, farther north than any white child had been born up to that time.

Mrs. Peary wrote in her diary about the horrors of Eskimo life, stating that Eskimos weren't clean and—even more upsetting—that they practiced wife swapping, of which she would have no part.

However, Peary adapted quite readily to the native customs, calling the Eskimos "my dusky children of the Pole." In 1894, while Josephine was away, he began an affair with a 14-year-old Etah Eskimo girl named Allakasingwah, or familiarly to him, "Ally." Out of their passionate lovemaking they had at least one child, a son named Kahdi. Peary photographed his Eskimo mistress topless for his "scientific" memoirs, called her his "café-au-lait hostess," and said that the "buxom and oleaginous" Ally belonged to "a race of naive children of nature, who are hampered by no feelings of false modesty or bashfulness in expressing their tender feelings."

While living with the Eskimos, Peary no doubt took advantage of the native custom which allowed a visiting adult male to sleep with the wife of his host.

Josephine knew of his philandering but swallowed her pride in a letter to her husband. "Come home," she wrote, "and let Marie and I love you and nurse you. Don't let your pride keep you back. Who will ever remember it [his infidelity] 10 years from now? ... Oh, Bert, Bert. I want you too much."

When he returned to the U.S., Peary's mistress and son were left behind, their whereabouts unknown. Cook used the affair with Ally against Peary. During the media battle between the two explorers, Cook produced the topless photograph of Ally holding a child and added a caption: "Polar Tragedy—a Deserted Child of the Sultan of the North and Its Mother."

Peary, Josephine, and their children—Marie and Robert, Jr.—moved to Washington, D.C., where Peary retired from the navy with the rank of rear admiral. In his last days he was a strict father and devoted husband. Peary died of pernicious anemia in February, 1920.

—A.L.G.

The Adulterous Diarist

SAMUEL PEPYS (Feb. 23, 1633–May 26, 1703)

HIS FAME: As England's first secretary of the Admiralty, Pepys doubled the size of the English navy and greatly increased its efficiency, establishing a tradition of order and discipline that allowed Britannia to rule the waves in the century that followed. However, what immortalized Samuel Pepys was the 1,250,000-word diary he kept from 1660 to 1669. In it he described in vivid detail the coming and going of the plague and the great fire of London.

Pepys at 33

HIS PERSON: Despite his humble origins, Pepys' intelligence and diligence allowed him to move up in society until, under King James II, he was one of the most powerful men in England. At the time of his marriage to Elizabeth Marchant de Saint-Michel, a poor and beautiful 15-year-old, Pepys was employed as a factotum, or general servant, for his cousin Adm. Edward Montagu (later the Earl of Sandwich). After serving as a clerk and secretary, Pepys began his rise in the naval bureaucracy, later becoming a trusted confidant of King Charles II and King James II. By 1678 Pepys' attacks on corruption had made him many enemies, some of whom were powerful enough to have him thrown into the Tower of London, charged with treason and popery. However, he survived these attacks, and during the reign of King James II, Pepys controlled a larger budget than that of any other department of state. He lived out a peaceful retirement, enjoying friendships with John Dryden, Sir Christopher Wren, and Sir Isaac Newton.

Pepys' diary, kept between the ages of 26 and 36, is extraordinary not only for its descriptions of great historical events, but for its revelation of a very human human. The reader suffers along with Pepys in his bouts with constipation and jealousy, feels his pride at acquiring a new pocket watch or periwig, and empathizes with his struggles with his barely controllable sex drive. He kept the diary under lock and key and protected himself further by writing in shorthand. Certain passages, particularly those dealing with his erotic affairs, were further disguised by the scattered use of words from Spanish, French, Dutch, Greek, Italian, and Latin. For example, on June 3, 1666, Pepys noted: "… and so to Mrs. Martin and there did what *je voudrais avec* her, both *devante* and backward, which is also *muy bon plazer*." On Nov. 28 of the same year: "… and Pegg with me in my closet a good while, and did suffer me *a la besar mucho et tocar ses cosas* upon her breast—wherein I had great pleasure."

The diary was first published in 1825, but even the 10-volume Wheatley edition of 1893-1899 left out 90 passages that dealt too explicitly with sex and defecation. It was not until the 1970s that these sections were finally made public, over 300 years after they were written.

SEX LIFE: Samuel Pepys had been married four years when he began his diary. The young Mrs. Pepys, petty and annoying as she might sometimes appear, endured quite a lot of pettiness herself. On Dec. 19, 1661, Pepys called her a "whore" because her ribbons didn't match. On Jan. 9, 1663, he tore up all the letters he had written to her. On Apr. 5, 1664, he became so angry with her that he pulled her nose, and on Dec. 19, 1665, he punched her in the eye. On July 12, 1667, he pulled her nose again. Nonetheless, he always felt guilty after these outbursts. On Oct. 23, 1662, after sporting together in bed, Pepys described Elizabeth and himself as "a very happy couple."

However, 1663 was to change their relationship. Elizabeth persistently complained because her husband made her stay at home and deprived her of the pleasures of London. Finally Pepys broke down and allowed her to take dancing lessons from a married instructor named Pembleton. It wasn't long before Pepys was outrageously jealous. On May 15 he checked to make sure his wife was wearing drawers. On May 24 he noticed Pembleton leering at her during church services. Two days later he hurried home during the afternoon. Finding his wife and Pembleton alone, he sneaked upstairs to see if any of the beds had been used. (They hadn't.) Meanwhile, Elizabeth was becoming jealous of Samuel's growing closeness with her maid, Ashwell. Pepys solved the problem in mid-June by sending his wife and Ashwell to the country for two months.

Previously Pepys had engaged in minor extramarital flirtations, but nothing serious. For example, on Feb. 6, 1660, he had "a very high bout" with Mistress Ann. "I rattled her up." And on Aug. 12 of that year, he wrote of shopgirl Betty Lane, "I was exceeding free in dallying with her and she not unfree to take it."

But in 1663, with his wife out of town, he met again with Betty Lane and their affair shifted gears. July 18: "I had my full liberty of towzing her and doing what I would. Of which I am heartily ashamed, but I do resolve never to do so more." However, on Sept. 24, with his wife back in London, he returned to Betty Lane and "did what I would with her, but only the main thing." Again he felt guilty and resolved "never to do the like again."

On Jan. 16, 1664, he "did what I would" with Betty Lane once again and wrote, "I hope it will be the last occasion of my life." It wasn't. While his wife was in the country again, Pepys learned that Betty Lane had married and was now Mrs. Martin. His reaction? "I must have a bout with her very shortly to see how she finds marriage." Three days later, being in "an idle and wanton humor," he had his bout and scored twice in an hour.

By this time Pepys was ready to branch out. Attracted to "Bagwell's Wife," he seduced her in small steps for a year until, on Nov. 15, 1664, he was able to boast to his diary, "after many protestings by degrees I did arrive at what I would, with great pleasure." And a month later (the day after he punched his wife in the eye): "I tried to do what I would and against her will I did enough for my contentment." Eventually he broke down Mrs. Bagwell's resistance completely, but not before he had injured his left forefinger in a struggle with her on Feb. 20, 1665.

For the next three years Pepys kissed and played with the breasts of many women, most, but not all of them, of the lower classes. However, he "did what he would" with only a handful, one of whom was Doll Lane, Betty's sister, with whom he first became involved in 1666 while Betty was pregnant. On Oct. 21, he did what he would with her "and might have done anything else."

All this time Elizabeth Pepys was unaware of her husband's infidelities, although she was jealous of his friendships with certain women and angry at the rumors that he partied and made merry in her absence. But in October of 1668, Pepys' extramarital bubble burst, and all because of his involvement with a girl he never even did what he would with. Deborah Willet came to work for the Pepyses on Sept. 30, 1667. She was a pretty young virgin whose breasts were just beginning to grow. By Dec. 22 Pepys had kissed her for the first time, and by the following August he was touching her "with great pleasure." Then came Oct. 25, 1668: "… and after supper, to have my head combed by Deb, which occasioned the greatest sorrow to me that ever I knew in this world; for my wife, coming up suddenly, did find me imbracing the girl *con* my hand *sub su* coats; and endeed, I was with my *main* in her cunny. I was at a wonderful loss upon it, and the girl also." Not knowing how much his wife had seen, Pepys admitted nothing, but that night Elizabeth became so upset that she admitted for the first time that she was a Roman Catholic.

The Pepys household continued in a state of extreme tension for two weeks, with Elizabeth watching her husband's every move and making sure that she didn't so much as smile at Deborah Willet. On Nov. 9 he managed to fling a note to Deborah telling her that he had denied ever having kissed her and advising her to do the same. However, the next day, when he returned home from the office for lunch, Pepys found his wife "mightily troubled again, more than ever, and she tells me that it is from her examining the girl and getting a confession now from her of all, even to the very *tocando su* thing with my hand—."

Understandably outraged by her husband's infidelity and lying, Elizabeth forced Pepys to fire Deborah Willet. But the night before she left, he confessed to his diary, "The truth is, I have a great mind for to have the maidenhead of this girl, which I should no doubt to have if *yo* could get time *para* be *con* her—but she will be gone and I know not whither." However, he also noted the next day that he had made love to his wife "more times since this falling-out than in I believe 12 months before—and with more pleasure to her than I think in all the time of our marriage before."

Within the week, Pepys had tracked down Deborah Willet, kissed her, and given her fatherly advice. But Elizabeth found out immediately and demanded that Pepys write a letter to Deborah in which he called her a "whore" and said he hated her. This he did, but only after Will Hewer, Pepys' lifelong friend, agreed to deliver the letter and, with a wink, assured him that Deborah would never see the offensive portions.

Eventually life calmed down for Samuel and Elizabeth. However, on Apr. 9, 1669, Pepys was back with Mrs. Martin, doing what he would, and also with her sister, who was now Mrs. Powell. On Apr. 15 he even met with Deborah in an alehouse and kissed her and touched her breasts. Six weeks later, the threat of losing his eyesight forced Pepys to give up his diary. On Nov. 10 Elizabeth, after suffering a high fever, died at the age of 29. Shortly after his wife's death Pepys became passionately close to a witty young lady named Mary Skinner. Twenty years later she moved in with him, without scandal, and she nursed and consoled him in his old age. Not surprisingly, Pepys never remarried, preferring, no doubt, to do what he would for the rest of his life.

HIS THOUGHTS: Dec. 25, 1665: "To church in the morning, and there saw a wedding ... and the young people so merry one with another, and strange to see what delight we married people have to see these poor fools decoyed into our position, every man and woman gazing and smiling at them."

—D. W.

The Celebrity Collector

ALMA MAHLER WERFEL (1879–Dec. 11, 1964)

HER FAME: A classical composer who received scant recognition, Alma Mahler Werfel gained prominence through her association with famous men. Described by her admirers as the "most beautiful *femme fatale* of turn-of-the-century Vienna," Alma was married in succession to the composer Gustav Mahler, the noted architect Walter Gropius, and the Austrian writer Franz Werfel. A complete list of her lovers would read like a history of the intelligentsia of eastern Europe.

HER PERSON: "What I really loved in a man was his achievement," Alma Werfel wrote in her autobiography, *And the Bridge Is Love*. "The greater the achievement, the more I must love him." Alma lived up to her words, with the help of some of the greatest musicians, painters, and writers of her day.

Born in Vienna to the landscape painter Emil J. Schindler, Alma had wit and intelligence honed by the scores of intellectuals and artists who flocked to her family's home. She received a formal education in music and composition from many of Vienna's finest musicians and composers. When she became a teenager and blossomed into a classical beauty with high cheekbones, sensual eyes, and a full figure, her teachers avidly courted her. At 17 she was aggressively pursued by 37-year-old artist Gustav Klimt. But Alma held her admirers at bay because she "believed in a virginal purity in need of preservation." She changed her mind at the age of 21 and began chasing after men of artistic achievement, involving herself in three marriages and innumerable affairs. Initially attracted to brilliant father figures, she married Gustav Mahler when he was 41 and she was 23. Later she reversed roles and married the poet and novelist Franz Werfel, who was 12 years her junior.

SEX LIFE: A "small, repugnant, chinless, toothless, and unwashed gnome" was Alma's description of her teacher, Alexander von Zemlinsky. The Viennese musician and composer attracted her anyway. "I long so madly for his embraces. I shall never be able to forget how his touch stirred me to the depths of my soul ... such a feeling of ecstasy filled my being.... I want to kneel down in front of him and kiss his open thighs—kiss everything, everything! Amen!"

During her affair with Zemlinsky, Alma met Gustav Mahler at a party. He was a handsome but austere man, prone to attacks of nervous tension. His fame as a composer was based on his romantic symphonies, particularly the Eighth Symphony, known as the *Symphony of a Thousand*. Alma was in awe of Mahler's musical genius but had doubts about accepting his marriage proposal. "Do I really love him?" she wrote in her diary. "I've no idea.... So many things about him annoy me: his smell—the way he sings—something in the way he speaks!" She finally agreed to marry him because "I am filled to the brim with my mission of smoothing the path of this genius."

Mahler confessed to Alma that he was a virgin, and said he was worried about his ability to consummate their marriage. She agreed to participate in a premarital rehearsal. After engaging in several sessions of lovemaking, she wrote, "Joy, beyond all joy," in her diary, and soon she was suffering the "dreadful torment" of pregnancy. But on their wedding night a few months later, Mahler was impotent. When this problem continued, a frustrated Alma suggested that he consult their friend Sigmund Freud. The great analyst recommended that Mahler, who adored his mother, call his wife by his mother's name, Marie. This seemed to work, and the couple had another child together, a daughter who became a sculptress.

However, their marriage still wasn't satisfactory to Alma. Mahler had insisted that she give up her musical career when they married, saying, "You … have only *one* profession from now on: *to make me happy*!" She hated being a traditional wife and mother. "I often feel as though my wings had been clipped. Gustav, why did you tie me to yourself—me, a soaring, glittering bird—when you'd be so much better off with a gray, lumbering one?"

During their marriage Alma flirted with Mahler's rival, composer Hans Pfitzner. "I do not fight the sensuous excitement caused by his touch," she confessed, "an excitement I have not felt for so long."

After Mahler's death in 1911, Alma was courted by her late husband's physician, Dr. Joseph Fraenkel. In turning down Fraenkel's marriage proposal, she wrote: "My watchword is: *Amo—ergo sum* [I love, therefore I am!]. Yours: *Cogito—ergo sum* [I think, therefore I am!]".

Next, Alma became involved with Austrian painter and playwright Oskar Kokoschka, whom she described as a "handsome figure but disturbingly coarse." Beginning his career as a portrait painter, Kokoschka became famous for the daring use of color and form in his landscapes. When he asked to paint Alma's portrait, she wrote in her diary, "We hardly spoke—and yet he seemed unable to draw. We got up. Suddenly, tempestuously, he swept me into his arms. To me it was a strange, almost shocking kind of embrace." She enjoyed that embrace for three years, which she called "one fierce battle of love. Never before had I tasted so much tension, so much hell, so much paradise." Kokoschka wanted to marry her, but when she had an abortion in 1913, it spelled the end of their affair.

In 1915 Alma married the renowned architect Walter Gropius, whose advances she had spurned when married to Mahler. Their marriage lasted four years and produced one child. While wed to Gropius, Alma became enchanted with the poetry of Franz Werfel, whose first prose piece, *Not the Murderer* (1920), marked the beginning of the expressionist movement in German literature. A stocky man with burning eyes and elegant features, Werfel achieved his greatest popularity as a result of his book *The Song of Bernadette*, which was later made into a highly successful film. In 1917 Alma and Werfel began an affair. "It was inevitable ... that our lips would find each other.... I am out of my mind. And so is Werfel," Alma wrote. The poet agreed. "We made love," he said of their first sexual encounter. "I did not spare her. At dawn I went back to my room.... There is something suicidal in her climactic surrender." Alma became pregnant with Werfel's child while still married to Gropius. The child, a boy, was born in 1918 and died less than a year later. After the birth of Alma's son, Gropius agreed to a divorce. Alma moved in with Werfel, and they were eventually married in 1929, when she was 50 years old. She remained passionate throughout their 16-year marriage.

An admirer, the German dramatist Gerhart Hauptmann, once said to Alma, "In another life, we two must be lovers. I make my reservation now." His wife overheard this request and quickly replied, "I'm sure Alma will be booked up for there, too."

—*R.S.F.*

Designing Lover

FRANK LLOYD WRIGHT (June 8, 1867–Apr. 9, 1959)

HIS FAME: Regarded as the greatest American architect of the 20th century, his creative, trend-setting designs for nearly 800 buildings earned him a reputation as one of the giants of modern architecture. Among his most famous projects are the Edgar J. Kaufmann house, known as "Falling Water," near Pittsburgh, Pa.; the administration buildings of the Johnson Wax Company in Racine, Wis.; and the Guggenheim Museum in New York City, which was opened in 1959, following Wright's death.

HIS PERSON: Wright was the product of a broken home. His minister father,

Wright, 28, took this photo himself.

William C. Wright, divorced his wife, Anna, because she refused him "intercourse as between husband and wife." The elder Wright moved out of their Madison, Wis., home in 1885, and Frank, who continued to live with or near his mother until she died in 1923, never again saw his father.

Trained as an engineer, Wright worked for six years in the architectural firm of Louis Sullivan and Dankmar Adler before establishing his own office in Chicago in 1893. By the turn of the century the 33-year-old, predominantly self-taught designer had a lucrative business and was known for his revolutionary "prairie school" of architecture—a style widely recognized for its radical approach to building modern homes.

But despite his architectural achievements, Wright's love life was marred by a series of scandalous romances.

LOVE LIFE: Guided by conflicting sexual morals, Wright fluctuated between puritanism and liberalism. He denounced marriage, claiming no person should "own" another, and scorned fatherhood, saying the idea of having a child deeply disturbed him. However, he married three times, fathered seven children, and engaged in a number of adulterous affairs. These he justified by proclaiming that it was more honorable to live openly with a mistress than to carry on secret affairs.

He considered himself a lady-killer in his later years, but when at 21 he married 18-year-old Catherine Tobin, he was a beginner in the art of lovemaking. A handsome man with auburn hair, his classic features couldn't mask his shyness; the very sight of a young girl could make him run like "a scared young stag, scampering back into his woods."

In his autobiography Wright wrote that his and Catherine's marriage on a rainy day in June resembled a funeral more than a wedding. As the years passed, Catherine's affection for him turned to "an almost bitter love." She shouldered the burdens of raising their six children with little help from him, and turned her head when he began seeing other women.

Many of his female clients were infatuated with him, but it was Mamah Borthwick Cheney—wife of one of his friends—who stole his heart. Impulsively, in September, 1909, he eloped to Europe with Mrs. Cheney, who was known in social circles as a capricious, temperamental lady. Although Catherine refused to give him a divorce, the lovers returned to the U.S. in 1910. Wright designed a home called Taliesin in Spring Green, Wis., in which he and Mamah lived. On Aug. 4, 1914, their romance ended tragically when an insane servant set fire to the house and then chopped Cheney, her two children, and four neighbors to death with an ax as they tried to escape the inferno.

On the verge of a nervous breakdown, Wright rebuilt Taliesin as a memorial to Mamah. In 1915 he installed another mistress, Miriam Noel, an unstable sculptor who had fallen in love with his picture. He was finally able to secure a divorce from Catherine in November, 1922, 13 years after their initial separation. One year later Miriam, distinguished-looking with her reddish-brown hair and monocle, married Wright. But Wright often felt lonely despite Miriam's companionship, and instead of strengthening their "luckless love affair," their marriage destroyed it. Growing increasingly neurotic and unbalanced, Miriam left him in April, 1924, five months after they were wed.

The 57-year-old architect almost immediately became involved with the beautiful 26-year-old Olga Milanoff Hinzenberg. The press called her "the Montenegrin dancer," thus giving rise to rumors that she was an immoral, flighty chorus girl. Jealous of Wright's newfound love, Miriam harassed him with an outpouring of legal actions and appalling statements aimed at aborting his affair with Olga (known as Olgivanna). At one point Miriam even tried to move back into Taliesin by force. Wright's loyal employees were able to rebuff her, but she did succeed in forcing Olgivanna into temporary hiding.

Nevertheless, divorcée Olgivanna solidly occupied Wright's heart and home, and they both ignored the fact that he was legally married to another. By the end of 1925 she had given birth to Wright's daughter, whom they named Iovanna. Wright finally secured a divorce, and he and Olgivanna exchanged wedding vows in August, 1928. During the last 30 years of his life they remained devoted to each other, and after his death Olgivanna took over as director of Taliesin West, Wright's school for apprentice architects.

—A.K.

Sexual Characteristics

HANGING ON: LATE VIRGINITY LOSERS

Catherine II
Isadora Duncan
Havelock Ellis
Johann Wolfgang
von Goethe

Victor Hugo
D. H. Lawrence
Bertrand Russell
Marie Stopes
Mao Tse-tung

Mark Twain
H. G. Wells
Mary Wollstonecraft
Virginia Woolf

EARLY TO BED: PRECOCIOUS SEX AND LOSS OF VIRGINITY

Pope Alexander VI
Gabriele D'Annunzio
Josephine Baker
Natalie Barney
John Barrymore
Lord Byron
Cleopatra
Kurt Cobain

Mahatma Gandhi
Jean Harlow
Jimi Hendrix
Ninon de Lenclos
Louis XIV
Amedeo Modigliani
Marilyn Monroe
Aristotle Onassis

La Belle Otero
Cora Pearl
Eva Perón
Édith Piaf
Rainer Maria Rilke
Jean Jacques Rousseau
Thomas Wolfe

MEN WHO ENJOYED GIRLS 16 YEARS OR YOUNGER

John Barrymore
Lewis Carroll (platonic)
Casanova
Charlie Chaplin
Kurt Cobain

Errol Flynn
Paul Gauguin
Johann Wolfgang
von Goethe
Howard Hughes

Samuel Pepys
Elvis Presley
Marquis de Sade
Mark Twain (platonic)

OUTSIZE ORGANS

Milton Berle
Wilt Chamberlain
Charlie Chaplin
Charles I

Gary Cooper
Jimi Hendrix
Guy de Maupassant
Aristotle Onassis

Grigori Rasputin
Henri de Toulouse-Lautrec

MINUTE MEMBERS

Napoleon Bonaparte
Frédéric Chopin
Edward VIII

Farouk I
F. Scott Fitzgerald
Ernest Hemingway

Waslaw Nijinsky
Rainer Maria Rilke

WEIRD QUIRKS AND FETISHES

Natalie Barney (men's clothes)
James Boswell (arborophilia)
Carlos Castaneda (said that sperm was poisonous)
Colette (men's clothes)
Aleister Crowley (hunchbacks, dwarves)
Havelock Ellis (urination voyeur)
Clark Gable (cleanliness)
Mahatma Gandhi (sleeping naked)
André Gide (deformity fetish)

Jean Harlow (dyed pubic hair)
Adolf Hitler (coprophilia)
Howard Hughes (cleanliness, body hair)
Victor Hugo (feet)
Michael Hutchence (auto-erotic asphyxiation)
James Joyce (graphomania, underwear)
Martin Luther (coprophilia)
Yukio Mishima (white gloves, armpit hair, sweat)

Marilyn Monroe (dyed pubic hair)
Adelina Patti (liked a midget)
Jean Jacques Rousseau (exhibitionist, inanimate objects)
Algernon Swinburne (babies, corporal punishment)
Henri de Toulouse-Lautrec (unexpected erogenous zones)

TROILISM AND MÉNAGES À TROIS

Honoré de Balzac
Natalie Barney
Casanova
Aleister Crowley
Paul Gauguin
George Gershwin

Jack Johnson
Janis Joplin
John F. Kennedy
Guy de Maupassant
Edna St. Vincent Millay
Elvis Presley

Grigori Rasputin
Jean Jacques Rousseau
Bertrand Russell
Marquis de Sade
Mary Wollstonecraft
Brigham Young

BIGAMISTS, POLYGAMISTS

Honoré de Balzac
James Boswell
Sir Richard Burton
Claude Debussy
Aleister Crowley
Alexandre Dumas *père*
Farouk I
William Faulkner
W. C. Fields
W. Scott Fitzgerald

Errol Flynn
Paul Gauguin
Henry VIII
Victor Hugo
Lillie Langtry
Jack London
W. Somerset Maugham
King Mongkut
Benito Mussolini
Pablo Picasso

Ezra Pound
Bertrand Russell
Lillian Russell
Leopold Stokowski
Rudolph Valentino
H. G. Wells
Alma Mahler Werfel
Brigham Young
Émile Zola

OPEN MARRIAGES

Colette
Aleister Crowley
Havelock Ellis
William Faulkner
Errol Flynn
Victor Hugo

Carl Gustav Jung
Lillie Langtry
Charles Laughton
Edna St. Vincent Millay
Pablo Picasso
Ezra Pound

Grigori Rasputin
Bertrand Russell
Jean-Paul Sartre
Anna Nicole Smith
Marie Stopes
H. G. Wells

ORGIASTS

Pope Alexander VI
Gabriele D'Annunzio
Honoré de Balzac
Natalie Barney
John Barrymore
Sarah Bernhardt
James Boswell
Clara Bow
Sir Richard Burton
Lord Byron
Casanova
Catherine II
Charlie Chaplin

Cleopatra
Gary Cooper
Joan Crawford
Aleister Crowley
Fëdor Dostoevski
Alexandre Dumas *père*
Isadora Duncan
Farouk I
Errol Flynn
Clark Gable
Paul Gauguin
Johann Wolfgang
    von Goethe

Jimi Hendrix
Victor Hugo
Janis Joplin
John F. Kennedy
Lillie Langtry
Guy de Maupassant
Amedeo Modigliani
Elvis Presley
Grigori Rasputin
Babe Ruth
Marquis de Sade
Stendhal
Leo Tolstoi

HOMOSEXUALS

André Gide
Christopher Isherwood
Charles Laughton
T. E. Lawrence

W. Somerset Maugham
Waslaw Nijinsky
Pëtr Ilich Tchaikovsky
William Tilden Jr.

Paul Verlaine
Oscar Wilde

LESBIANS

Natalie Barney

Emily Dickinson

Gertrude Stein

BISEXUALS

Aleister Crowley
Gabriele D'Annunzio
Napoleon Bonaparte
Sir Richard Burton
Lord Byron
Casanova
Colette
James Dean
Frederick II
Sigmund Freud

André Gide
Billie Holiday
Janis Joplin
D. H. Lawrence
W. Somerset Maugham
Edna St. Vincent Millay
Yukio Mishima
Waslaw Nijinsky
Marquis de Sade
George Sand

Anna Nicole Smith
Bessie Smith
Algernon Swinburne
Vincent Van Gogh
Malcolm X
Paul Verlaine
Oscar Wilde
Mary Wollstonecraft
Virginia Woolf
Voltaire

MOTHER-FIXATED

Honoré de Balzac
J. M. Barrie
Johannes Brahms
James Dean
Sigmund Freud

J. Edgar Hoover
D. H. Lawrence
Yukio Mishima
Jim Morrison
Sir Isaac Newton

Stendhal
August Strindberg
Pëtr Ilich Tchaikovsky
Paul Verlaine
William Tilden

INTERFERED WITH WHEN YOUNG

John Barrymore
Lord Byron
Billie Holiday
Carl Gustav Jung

D. H. Lawrence
La Belle Otero
Anna Nicole Smith
Leo Tolstoi

Virginia Woolf
Émile Zola

SEX TRIALS AND FAMOUS SCANDALS

Alexander II
Gabrielle D'Annunzio
J. M. Barrie
John Barrymore
Clara Bow
Lord Byron
Enrico Caruso
Charlie Chaplin
Joan Crawford
Aleister Crowley
Father Divine
Alexandre Dumas *père*
Edward VII
Edward VIII

Errol Flynn
André Gide
Maxim Gorki
Jean Harlow
Howard Hughes
Lillie Langtry
D. H. Lawrence
Jack London
Louis XIV
General Douglas
    MacArthur
Mata Hari
W. Somerset Maugham
Aimee Semple McPherson

Lola Montez
Lillian Russell
Babe Ruth
Marquis de Sade
George Sand
Marie Stopes
William Tilden Jr.
Paul Verlaine
H. G. Wells
Oscar Wilde
Brigham Young
Émile Zola

VENEREAL DISEASE

Cesare Borgia
James Boswell
Lord Byron
Casanova
Frédéric Chopin
Alexandre Dumas *père*
Paul Gauguin
Francisco de Goya

Henry VIII
James Joyce
Edmund Kean
W. Somerset Maugham
Guy de Maupassant
Lola Montez
Benito Mussolini
Marquis de Sade

Arthur Schopenhauer
Stendhal
Mao Tse-Tung
Henri de Toulouse-Lautrec
Vincent Van Gogh
Paul Verlaine
Oscar Wilde

PRODIGIOUS PROGENITORS

Pope Alexander VI
James Boswell
Charlie Chaplin
Charles II
Charles Dickens
Alexandre Dumas *père*
Sigmund Freud
Mahatma Gandhi
Paul Gauguin
Francsico de Goya

Victor Hugo
Carl Gustav Jung
Louis XIV
Louis XV
Martin Luther
Maria Luisa
Karl Marx
King Mongkut
Wolfgang Amadeus
    Mozart

Napoleon III
Franklin D. Roosevelt
Jean Jacques Rousseau
August Strindberg
Leo Tolstoi
Mao Tse-tung
Queen Victoria
Brigham Young

GREAT LOVERS AND SATYRS

Pope Alexander VI
Gabriele D'Annunzio
Honoré de Balzac
Natalie Barney
John Barrymore
Sarah Bernhardt
Napoleon Bonaparte
James Boswell
Clara Bow
Lord Byron
Casanova
Catherine II
Wilt Chamberlain
Charlie Chaplin
Charles II
Aleister Crowley
Alexandre Dumas *père*
Edward VII
Duke Ellington

Errol Flynn
Paul Gauguin
George Gershwin
Jimi Hendrix
Howard Hughes
Victor Hugo
Janis Joplin
John F. Kennedy
Aly Kahn
Lillie Langtry
Ninon de Lenclos
Franz Liszt
Jack London
Louis XIV
Louis XV
Guy de Maupassant
Edna St. Vincent Millay
Amedeo Modigliani
King Mongkut

Marilyn Monroe
Napoleon III
Aristotle Onassis
La Belle Otero
Cora Pearl
Edith Piaf
Pablo Picasso
Elvis Presley
Ayn Rand
Grigori Rasputin
Bertrand Russell
Babe Ruth
Marquis de Sade
Leopold Stokowski
Henri de Toulouse-Lautrec
H. G. Wells
Alma Mahler Werfel
Thomas Wolfe

SEX WITH PARTNERS 20 YEARS (OR MORE) OLDER

Honoré de Balzac
Clara Bow
Maria Callas
Casanova
Edward VII
Jean Harlow

Henry VIII
Ninon de Lenclos
Mata Hari
Marilyn Monroe
Waslaw Nijinsky
La Belle Otero

Eva Perón
Marquis de Sade
Anna Nicole Smith
Thomas Wolfe

SEX WITH PARTNERS 20 YEARS (OR MORE) YOUNGER

Alexander II
Honoré de Balzac
Natalie Barney
John Barrymore
Sarah Bernhardt
Enrico Caruso
Casanova
Carlos Castaneda
Catherine II
Wilt Chamberlain
Charlie Chaplin
Colette
Aleister Crowley
Charles Dickens
Fëdor Dostoevski
Alexander Dumas *père*
Edward VII
William Faulkner

W. C. Fields
Henry Ford
Paul Gauguin
André Gide
Johann Wolfgang
    von Goethe
Francisco de Goya
Henry VIII
Adolf Hitler
Howard Hughes
Victor Hugo
Christopher Isherwood
T. E. Lawrence
Franz Liszt
Mata Hari
W. Somerset Maugham
Yukio Mishima
Aristotle Onassis

Adelina Patti
Edith Piaf
Pablo Picasso
Elvis Presley
Ayn Rand
Bertrand Russell
Marquis de Sade
George Sand
Jean-Paul Sartre
Leopold Stokowski
August Strindberg
Richard Wagner
Duke of Wellington
H. G. Wells
Oscar Wilde
Brigham Young
Émile Zola

SEX WITH PARTNERS TWENTY YEARS (OR MORE) OLDER

Gabrielle D'Annunzio
Natalie Barney
Sarah Bernhardt
Charlie Chaplin
Colette
Havelock Ellis
Benjamin Franklin

Johann Wolfgang
    von Goethe
Victor Hugo
Ninon de Lenclos
Franz Liszt
Louis XIV
W. Somerset Maugham

Pablo Picasso
Bertrand Russell
Leopold Stokowski
Leo Tolstoi
H. G. Wells
Alma Mahler Werfel
Brigham Young

VOYEURS

Pope Alexander VI
Lord Byron
Casanova
Charlie Chaplin
Farouk I

Errol Flynn
William Gladstone
Victor Hugo
Martin Luther
Elvis Presley

Marquis de Sade
Bessie Smith
Stendhal

FANS OF FLAGELLATION; MASOCHISTS OR SADISTS

Sir Richard Burton
Aleister Crowley
Fëdor Dostoevsky
Adolf Hitler
Michael Hutchence
James Joyce

D. H. Lawrence
T. E. Lawrence
Yukio Mishima
Amedeo Modigliani
Benito Mussolini
Grigori Rasputin

Jean Jacques Rousseau
Marquis de Sade
Algernon Swinburne
Paul Verlaine

INCEST

Pope Alexander VI
John Barrymore
James Boswell
Lord Byron

Casanova
Cleopatra
Colette
Benito Mussolini

Marquis de Sade
H. G. Wells

Index

Athman, 159, 160
Atlas Shrugged, 483, 484, 486
atropine, 179
Atwill, Lionel, 79
Auber, Daniel, 267
Auden, W. H., 168, 169, 170, 233
Aunet, Léonie d', 167
Austen, Sarah, 368
Austin, Mary (Mrs. Jack Johnson), 425
Autobiography of Alice B. Toklas, The, 114
Averill Women's Club, 179
Avon, S.S. (ocean liner), 537
Axinya, 203
Aznavour, Charles, 270

Baca, Maria Amalia, 398
Bachardy, Don, 168, 170
Bagwell, Mrs., 545
Bailey, Ruth, 470
Baird, George Alexander, 80
Baird, Helen, 154
Baker, Josephine, 15–17
Bakrow, Beatrice, 173, 175
Balabanoff, Angelica, 379
Balcombe, Florrie, 211
"Ball and Chain," 292
Ballet de Paris, 412
Ballets Russes, 98, 535, 536, 537
Balzac, Honoré de, 91, 125–127, 472
"Bambino, the," 426, 427
Bankhead, Tallulah, 52, 58, 183, 430
barbiturates, 448
Bardac, Emma, 254
Barnacle, Nora, 170, 171
Barney, Natalie, 110, 515–517
Barras, Paul, 308
Barrie, Elaine, 53
Barrie, James M., 127–130
Barrie, Wendy, 518
Barry, Griffin, 492
Barry, Joan, 56
Barrymore, Diana, 52
Barrymore, Ethel, 51
Barrymore, John, 51–53, 57, 425
Barrymore, Lionel, 51
Barrymore, Maurice, 51
Barton, Catherine, 480
Barucci, Giulia, 323

Bathe, Hugo de, 80
Bay of Pigs fiasco, 362
Bayeu, Francisco, 92
Bayeu, Josefa, 92, 93, 94
Beadnell, Maria, 145, 146
Bean, Roy, Judge, 79
Beauharnais, Joséphine de, 308
Beaulieu, Priscilla, 300
Beauvoir, Roger de, 151
Beauvoir, Simone de, 494, 495
Beauvoisin, Mlle., 191
Begbie, Alison, 224
Begemann, Margot, 91
Behrs, Sofya Andreevna, 201, 203
Bekyeshova, Dunia, 451
Belboeuf, "Missy" de, 110
Belgiojoso, Christine, 263
Bell, Alexander Graham, 531
Bell, Quentin, 117
Bell, Rex, 20
Belle of Amherst, The, 226
Bello, Marino, 28
Belmonte, Juan, 419–420
Belmonte, Juan, Jr., 420
Beloff, Angelina, 101
Benjamin, Dorothy, 252
Beregi, Oscar, 520, 521
Béreyter, Angéline, 198
Bergman, Ingrid, 58
Berkman, Alexander, 523, 524, 525
Berle, Milton, 38, 448, 517–519
Berlin novels, 168
Bern, Paul, 29, 30
Bernays, Martha, 465
Bernays, Minna, 465
Bernhardt, Sarah, 74–76, 143, 167, 212, 323
Bernis, François de, 26
Bernstein, Aline, 216
Berny, Laure de, 126
Bezzi-Scali, Christina, 479
Big Brother and the Holding Company, 292
Bigelow, Lucy, 456
Birkhead, Larry, 44
Bishop, John, 229, 230
Black, Dora, 492
Blaine, James G., 355, 356
Blanchard, Maria, 101
Blangini, Felix, 312